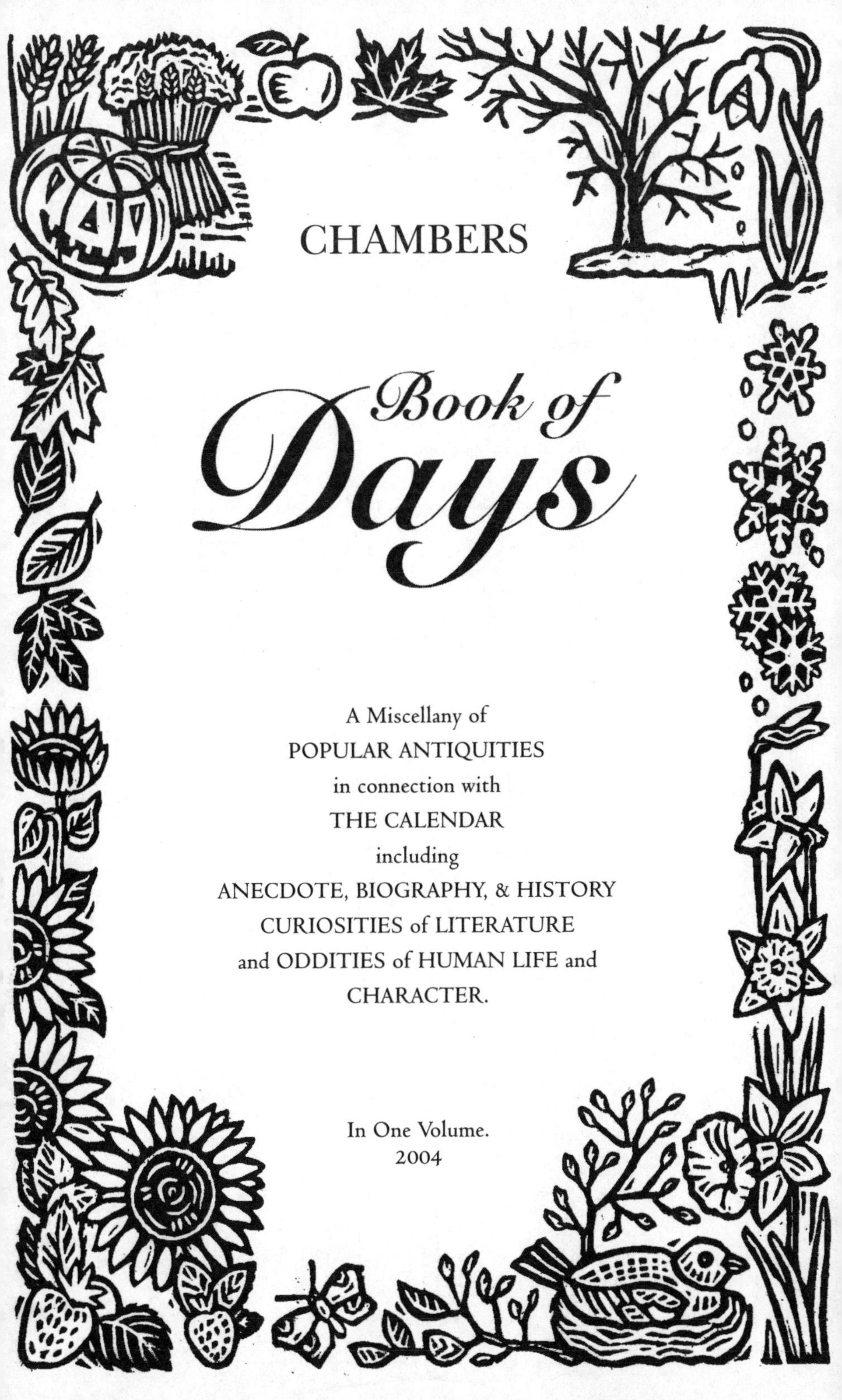

CHAMBERS

Book of Days

A Miscellany of
POPULAR ANTIQUITIES
in connection with
THE CALENDAR
including
ANECDOTE, BIOGRAPHY, & HISTORY
CURIOSITIES of LITERATURE
and ODDITIES of HUMAN LIFE and
CHARACTER.

In One Volume.
2004

CHAMBERS
An imprint of Chambers Harrap Publishers Ltd
7 Hopetoun Crescent, Edinburgh, EH7 4AY

First published by Chambers Harrap Publishers Ltd 2004

A CIP catalogue record for this book is available from the British Library.

ISBN 0550 10083 0

Designed and typeset by Chambers Harrap Publishers Ltd, Edinburgh
Printed in Great Britain by Bath Press Ltd

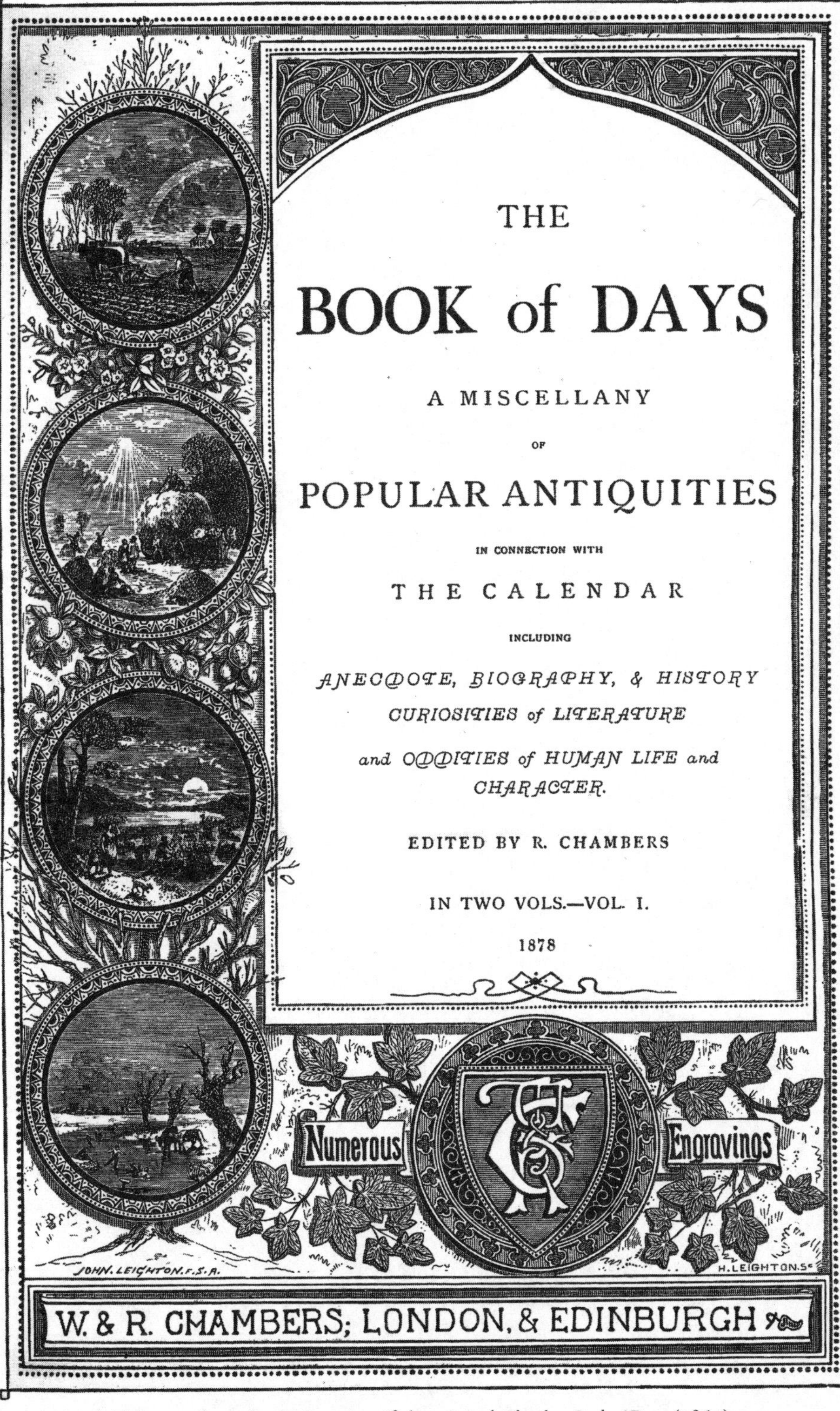
THE
BOOK of DAYS
A MISCELLANY
OF
POPULAR ANTIQUITIES
IN CONNECTION WITH
THE CALENDAR
INCLUDING
ANECDOTE, BIOGRAPHY, & HISTORY
CURIOSITIES of LITERATURE
and ODDITIES of HUMAN LIFE and
CHARACTER.
EDITED BY R. CHAMBERS
IN TWO VOLS.—VOL. I.
1878
Numerous
Engravings
JOHN. LEIGHTON. F.S.A.
H. LEIGHTON. Sc
W. & R. CHAMBERS; LONDON, & EDINBURGH
Title page from the1878 reprint of the original *Chambers Book of Days* (1864).

Contents

Contributors

Author

Rosalind Fergusson

Managing Editor

Una McGovern

On this Day Material

Angus Mcfadzean
Hazel Norris
Elaine O'Donoghue
Camilla Rockwood
Bernard Tennant

Publishing Manager

Patrick White

Original Artwork

Owain Kirby

Prepress Manager

Sharon McTeir

Prepress Controller

Vienna Leigh

Preface

The first *Chambers Book of Days* was published in 1864 in two hefty volumes and described itself as 'A Miscellany of Popular Antiquities in Connection with the Calendar, including Anecdote, Biography, and History, Curiosities of Literature, and Oddities of Human Life and Character'. Whilst this new *Book of Days*, coming one hundred and forty years later, does not claim to be as all-encompassing as its ancestor, it has been our intention to preserve its structure and tenor. Thus, 'on this day' information, including birth and death days, is given for each day of the year, alongside longer descriptions of the features and associations of certain days and of the seasons, all interspersed with excerpts from the original edition written in true Victorian style, and literary and other quotations.

In a departure from the original edition, however, articles on the days of the week have also been given, summarizing their origins, characteristics and associations.

The sentiments expressed in the conclusion to the original preface by the editor Robert Chambers are shared by the individuals who have contributed to this modern edition:

> *'It is given to few to feel assured that every particular of a favourite object has been duly accomplished, and the individual who has superintended the birth of these pages is certainly not of that happy minority. He would say, nevertheless, that he has done his best, with the means and opportunities at his disposal, to produce a work answering to his plan, and calculated to improve, while it entertains, and mingling the agreeable with the instructive.'*

The Calendar

The word 'calendar' has its origins in the Latin word *calendae* (or *kalendae*), meaning the first day of the month. On this day in Ancient Rome a herald would proclaim (*calare*) the days that would follow, announcing forthcoming festivals and days on which business could and could not be transacted. Hence a *calendarium* meant a book in which accounts (typically settled monthly) were kept. From this comes the Old French word *calendier*, meaning 'a list or register', which emerges in English in the twelfth century as *kalender*, with its present meaning of 'a system of divisions of the year'.

The current system used in the West for dividing up the year into months and days is based on that introduced by Julius Caesar in 46 BC, and known as the 'Julian calendar'. The Roman calendar originally recognized ten months and began with March. (This accounts for the fact that the months from September to December, which are now the ninth to twelfth months, are named after the Latin words for 'seven', 'eight', 'nine' and 'ten' respectively.) At an early period, however, two additional months were added at the start of the year – tradition ascribes this act to the reign of King Numa (715–673 BC) – to give the twelve-month sequence from January to December that is in use today. The main drawback of this arrangement was that the twelve months contained only 355 days between them, and additional 'intercalary' months had to be added periodically to ensure that the calendar kept pace with the seasons.

The Julian calendar aimed to remedy this unsatisfactory arrangement. It added additional days to give the months their present number of days. This produced a system whereby three years of 365 days were followed by a leap year of 366 days. This system was a vast improvement on the one that preceded it, but the average length of the calendar year was still approximately eleven minutes longer than the actual time that it takes for the earth to rotate around the sun. This meant that the equinoxes occurred progressively earlier and earlier in the calendar year. In order to rectify this discrepancy, Pope Gregory XIII introduced a new system in 1582. Under the new 'Gregorian calendar', leap years occur in every year that is divisible by four, except for years ending in 00, which are leap years only when divisible by 400 (thus 2000 was a leap year, but not 1900). The Gregorian calendar was adopted in Britain in 1752. To readjust the calendar year to the solar cycle, eleven days were omitted from that year's calendar, so that 2 September was followed by 14 September.

The Gregorian calendar is now in use in most of the world, but there are various other calendars in use, many of which are based around the 29-day lunar cycle rather than the solar cycle. The Jewish calendar is based on twelve lunar months with an additional month included in some years to keep in step with the solar cycle. The Islamic calendar is also based on twelve lunar months, but without the possibility of additional 'leap months', so that the calendar year has 354 or 355 days and is shorter than the solar year.

But the calendar is not the sole preserve of astronomers and accountants. For almost the entire span of human history, the cycles of nature and the stars have been an inspiration to poets. Hesiod, writing in the 8th century BC, composed a poem called *Works and Days* in which he recorded the times when farmers should perform various tasks. This tradition was taken up in Roman times by Ovid, who composed the *Fasti*, a poetical treatment of the calendar, combining stories about the constellations with celebrations of religious festivals and episodes from Roman history. The calendar has also been the inspiration for some of the finest poetry in English literature, including Edmund Spenser's *The Shepheards Calender* (1579), James Thomson's *The Seasons* (1730) and John Clare's *The Shepherd's Calendar* (1827).

The Days of the Week

Sunday

The child that is born on the Sabbath day,
Is bonny and blithe and good and gay.

Traditional rhyme.

And God said, Let there be light: and there was light. And God saw the light, that it was good: and God divided the light from the darkness. And God called the light Day, and the darkness he called Night. And the evening and the morning were the first day.

Genesis 1.3–5.

The feeling of Sunday is the same everywhere, heavy, melancholy, standing still. Like when they say 'As it was in the beginning, is now, and ever shall be, world without end.'

Jean Rhys, *Voyage in the Dark* (1934).

Every day is like Sunday
Every day is silent and grey

Morrissey, 'Every Day is Like Sunday' (1988).

Origins

Sunday is named after the sun. The Anglo-Saxons called it *Sunnandaeg*, a direct translation of the Latin *dies solis* ('day of the sun'), and the modern German name is *Sonntag*. The French *dimanche*, Italian *domenica* and Spanish and Portuguese *domingo*, on the other hand, are derived from the Latin *dies dominica* ('day of the Lord'). This is a relic of the Christian system of naming the days (a modified version of the Jewish nomenclature, in which Sunday was called 'first day', Monday 'second day', and so on).

Superstitions

If you sneeze or cut your nails on a Sunday, according to proverbial rhymes, the Devil will be with you throughout the coming week. It was formerly said that a similar fate awaited those who engaged in various other activities, such as gathering hazelnuts or participating in ball games, on this day: superstition merged with religion to ban both work and play on the Christian Sabbath.

Sunday is a bad day for courtship ('Sunday's wooing draws to ruin') but a good day for marriage or travel. In the Roman classification of days as good, bad or neutral, Sunday was one of the neutral days, considered appropriate for launching a ship or setting out on a voyage.

> *I always love to begin a journey on Sundays, because I shall have the prayers of the church, to preserve all that travel by land, or by water.*
>
> Jonathan Swift, *Polite Conversation* (1738).

Characteristics

Sunday is the **Christian Sabbath**, or day of rest and worship, commemorating Christ's resurrection from the dead on this day (Easter Sunday). Although Christ had condemned the restrictions placed on human activity on the Jewish Sabbath – 'The sabbath was made for man, and not man for the sabbath' (Mark 2.27) – the fact that Sunday was a feast day in the Christian Church made it inappropriate for work. It was not until the 16th century, however, that the name Sabbath was applied to Sunday, by the British Protestants, and it was the Puritans among them who insisted on its strict observance, prohibiting everything from household chores to recreational exercise.

Playing cards or gambling on a Sunday were long frowned upon, as was falling asleep in church. One story from Dartmoor combines elements of both these beliefs. In Widecombe, a local ne'er-do-well card player called Jan Reynolds made a pact with the devil that the devil could take his soul if he found Jan sleeping in church. Jan was soon found doing so, playing cards in hand, and the devil took him up and carried him away on his black horse. In mid-flight, the cards fell from the Jan's hand, and the stone outlines of a large diamond, a spade, a club and a heart can today be seen on the moor, as a reminder of the wickedness of sleeping in church and Sabbath card playing.

In the past, some of the restrictions placed on the activities allowed on a Sunday were enshrined in law, whereas others were simply a matter of social or religious convention. At the 1924 Olympics in Paris, Scottish athlete and missionary Eric Liddell (1902–45) would have been favourite to win the 100 metres had he not refused to take part on religious grounds because the heats were to be run on a Sunday. Instead he won the bronze medal in the 200 metres, and then caused a sensation by winning the gold medal in the 400 metres (at which he was comparatively inexperienced).

Over the course of time many Sunday restrictions were gradually relaxed in much of the UK ...

> *A decision of the courts decided that the game of golf may be played on a Sunday, not being a game within the view of the law, but being a form of moral effort.*
>
> Stephen Leacock, *Over the Footlights*, 'Why I Refuse to Play Golf' (1923).

... although some areas still follow religious observances which forbid certain activities, such as drinking.

The legislation relating to **Sunday trading**, some of which predated the Reformation, was finally amended in the late 20th century, despite the protests of the 'Keep Sunday Special' campaign. The change came about after widespread flouting of the law by large stores, whose profits were only slightly dented by the fines thus incurred.

For many people the modern Sunday remains a day of rest and recreation, apart from light, undemanding tasks such as washing the car or weeding the garden. Practising Christians attend at least one church service, usually in the morning, and the afternoon is traditionally given over to leisure pursuits and family activities.

> *Down the road someone is practising scales,*
> *The notes like little fishes vanish with a wink of tails,*
> *Man's heart expands to tinker with his car*
> *For this is Sunday morning, Fate's great bazaar.*
>
> Louis MacNeice, *Poems*, 'Sunday Morning' (1935).

Sunday meals

In most British households in modern times, the main meal of the day during the working week is usually eaten in the evening, but many families – whether churchgoing or not – have kept up the tradition of having a roast dinner in the middle of the day on Sundays. The archetypal **Sunday lunch** is roast beef with Yorkshire pudding, though lamb, pork or poultry are equally acceptable, and in its native county Yorkshire pudding was originally served before the meat course, to curb the appetite. A lighter Sunday tea is often taken in the late afternoon or early evening.

Things were somewhat different in 19th-century Scotland:

> *The Sunday-tea ... is enjoyed with all the more relish that the previous dinner has been generally rather meagre, to avoid as much as possible the necessity of cooking on the Sabbath, and also somewhat hurried, being partaken of 'between sermons,' as the very short interval between the morning and afternoon services is termed in Scotland. Whatever may be said of the rigour of Sunday observance in the north, our recollections of the evening of that day are of the most pleasant description, and will doubtless be corroborated by the memories of many of our Scottish readers.*
>
> *Chambers Book of Days* (1864).

Bloody Sunday

On 30 January 1972, in the early years of the 'Troubles' between Catholics and Protestants in Northern Ireland, a peaceful civil rights protest in the Bogside district of Londonderry turned violent and 13 civilians lost their lives (another died later from his injuries). The day is now known as **Bloody Sunday**. In defiance of a ban on marches and parades, a crowd of several thousand had taken to the streets to protest against the policy of internment without trial. When they reached an army barricade, some of the more unruly demonstrators began throwing bottles and stones at the British troops, who eventually responded with gunfire. An initial inquiry ruled that the first shots in the battle had come not from the soldiers themselves, but from armed demonstrators or snipers. The evidence was insubstantial and flawed, however, and after a lengthy campaign a second inquiry was launched in 1998.

Sunday's children

Famous people born on Sunday include the actor, director and screenwriter Woody Allen, the actress Ingrid Bergman, the couturier Coco Chanel, the naturalist Charles Darwin, the aviator Amelia Earhart, the ballerina Margot Fonteyn, the mountaineer Edmund Hillary, the filmmaker Alfred Hitchcock, the poet Ted Hughes, the statesman Abraham Lincoln, the soprano Nellie Melba, the actor Robert Redford, the novelist George Sand, the poet Alfred, Lord Tennyson, the painter J M W Turner and the composer Giuseppe Verdi.

Monday

> *Monday's child is fair of face.*
>
> Traditional rhyme.

> *And God said, Let there be a firmament in the midst of the waters, and let it divide the waters from the waters. And God made the firmament, and divided the waters which were under the firmament from the waters which were above the firmament: and it was so. And God called the firmament Heaven. And the evening and the morning were the second day.*
>
> Genesis 1.6–8.

> *On Monday, when the sun is hot*
> *I wonder to myself a lot:*
> *'Now is it true, or is it not,*
> *That what is which and which is what?'*
>
> A A Milne, *Winnie-the-Pooh* (1926).

> *Monday, Monday, can't trust that day*
> *Monday, Monday, sometimes it just turns out that way*
>
> The Mamas and the Papas, 'Monday Monday', (1966).

Origins

Monday is named after the moon. The Anglo-Saxons called it *Mōnandaeg*, a direct translation of the Latin *lunae dies* ('day of the moon'), from which the modern French *lundi*, Italian *lunedì*, Spanish *lunes* and Welsh *dydd Llun* are derived. The German name is *Montag*.

Superstitions

According to proverbial rhymes, Monday is a good day to get married

('Monday for wealth'), but a bad day to sneeze ('Sneeze on Monday, sneeze for danger'). Cutting hair or nails on this day is variously said to bring health or news. Other superstitions warn against moving house or giving money away on Monday. Regional beliefs inevitably contradict one another: it is a lucky day in Ireland, but an unlucky day in Wales, for embarking on a new enterprise.

In the Roman classification of days as good, bad or neutral, Monday was one of the neutral days, considered appropriate for such tasks as manuring land and making wells. According to other sources, however, Monday was not to be trusted, and three Mondays of the year (usually the first in April, the first in August, and the last in December) were deemed particularly inauspicious.

Characteristics

> *Monday is the day that everything starts all over again,*
> *...*
> *It is the day when life becomes grotesque again,*
> *Because it is the day when you have to face your desk*
> *again.*
>
> Ogden Nash (1902–71), 'Every Day is Monday'.

In most offices, factories and schools, Monday is the beginning of the working week. For every person who greets the day with eager anticipation and enthusiasm, there are many more who experience a **Monday morning feeling** ranging from general listlessness or depression to acute anxiety and dread. 'I don't like Mondays' was the reason given by a 16-year-old US schoolgirl, Brenda Ann Spencer, for opening fire with a rifle on a group of children arriving at school in San Diego on 29 January 1979. Eight of the children were injured, and two men who came to their rescue were killed. The horrific event was immortalized in a number one hit released later that year:

> *Tell me why*
> *I don't like Mondays*
> *I want to shoot*
> *The whole day down.*
>
> Boomtown Rats, 'I Don't Like Mondays' (1979).

A few times a year, the beginning of the working week is postponed and the weekend is extended with a welcome extra day of rest and recreation. Most of the UK enjoys three **Bank Holiday Mondays**, two in May and one in August, as well as Easter Monday. If any of the other statutory public holidays (such as Christmas Day, Boxing Day or New Year's Day) falls on a Saturday or Sunday, the following Monday is usually given in lieu. Other Mondays celebrated with particular traditions and festivities, especially in former times, include Handsel Monday (after New Year, see January), Plough Monday (after Epiphany, see January) and Collop Monday (before Lent, see February). In some countries there is a tendency to move public holidays (eg Washington's birthday in the USA) from a specific date to the nearest Monday, to give workers a long weekend and avoid breaking up the working week; this process is sometimes called 'Mondayization' (especially in New Zealand).

St Monday

In certain crafts and trades, notably shoemaking, Monday was often marked by absenteeism or lack of productivity, as workers recovered from the excesses of the day before. The unofficial holiday that ensued was facetiously known as **St Monday**, as if it were a saint's feast day. Although this practice is sometimes held up as an example of 'working-class idleness', it must be remembered that in the past the working week was long and hard, and Sunday was the only official day off. The custom gradually fell into disuse as the weekend was extended to include at least part of Saturday, although absenteeism on Mondays is still a problem today.

Washday

'Twas on a Monday morning
When I beheld my darling,
She looked so neat and charming
In ev'ry high degree.
She looked so neat and nimble, O,
A-washing of her linen, O,
Dashing away with the smoothing iron,
Dashing away with the smoothing iron,
Dashing away with the smoothing iron,
She stole my heart away.

Traditional song.

In former times, when doing the weekly household laundry was a major, labour-intensive chore, Monday was washday for housewives and servants everywhere. Even if the washing was done at home, rather than in a public washhouse, it had to be hung out in the open air to dry, so nobody could get away with postponing the arduous task without incurring the disapproval of the neighbours:

> *They that wash on Monday, have all the week to dry*
> *They that wash on Tuesday, are not so much awry*
> *They that wash on Wednesday, are not so much to blame*
> *They that wash on Thursday, wash for shame*
> *They that wash on Friday, wash in need*
> *They that wash on Saturday: Oh, they're sluts indeed!*
>
> Traditional rhyme.

Black Monday

The name **Black Monday** has been applied to various dates in history, the most famous being the day in mid-April 1360 when the army of King Edward III, besieging Paris, was struck by such severe weather that thousands of men and horses were killed. The date has been variously identified as 13 or 14 April and fell in the week after Easter, although it is popularly associated with Easter Monday, which was also known as Black Monday (or **Bloody Monday**) by children returning to school on this day.

Another Black Monday occurred on 19 October 1987, when one of the most spectacular stock-market crashes in recorded history caused share-price indexes to plummet all around the world. It was not immediately apparent what triggered the crash, or where it originated, but economists' fears that it would precipitate a global recession proved unfounded.

Monday's children

'Monday's child is fair of face': the actress Greta Garbo, renowned for her beauty, was born on this day. Other famous Monday's children include the mathematician Charles Babbage, the inventor John Logie Baird, the politician Aneurin Bevan, the nurse Edith Cavell, the novelist George Eliot, the philosopher Georg Hegel, the psychiatrist Carl Jung, the tennis player Billie Jean King, the singer Cliff Richard, the philanthropist John D Rockefeller, the statesman Franklin D Roosevelt, the conductor Malcolm Sargent, Queen Victoria and the writer Oscar Wilde.

Tuesday

> *Tuesday's child is full of grace.*
>
> Traditional rhyme.

> *And God said, Let the waters under the heaven be gathered together unto one place, and let the dry land appear: and it was so… And God said, Let the earth bring forth grass, the herb yielding seed, and the fruit tree yielding fruit after his kind, whose seed is in itself, upon the earth: and it was so… And the evening and the morning were the third day.*
>
> Genesis 1.9–13.

Origins

Tuesday is named after the Germanic god Tiw (or Tiu), a warlike deity; the Anglo-Saxons called it *Tīwesdaeg*, from which the German *Dienstag* is derived. Tiw was associated with Mars, the Roman god of war; the Latin name of the day was *Martis dies* ('day of Mars'), from which the modern French *mardi*, Italian *martedì*, Spanish *martes* and Welsh *dydd Mawrth* are derived. (Note that the Latin names of Tuesday, Wednesday, Thursday, Friday and Saturday refer to the planets, not the gods – they are based on the astrological theory, of ancient Egyptian origin, that each day is governed by one of the seven planets Mars, Mercury, Jupiter, Venus, Saturn, Sun and Moon.)

Superstitions

According to proverbial rhymes, Tuesday is a good day for getting married ('Tuesday for health'), while sneezing on this day augurs an encounter ('Sneeze on Tuesday, kiss a stranger'). Cutting hair or nails on Tuesday is variously said to bring wealth or a new pair of shoes. Other regional superstitions state that it is lucky to sow seed on this day but unlucky to meet a left-handed person.

In the Roman classification of days as good, bad or neutral, Tuesday was one of the bad days. However, being the day of the god of war, it was considered appropriate for enlisting in the army or buying weapons. Tuesday is also considered unlucky in modern Greece, being the day on which Constantinople fell to the Ottoman Turks (Tuesday 29 May 1453).

Budget day

In the latter half of the 20th century, Tuesday was traditionally **Budget day** – the day on which the Chancellor of the Exchequer announces to Parliament and the British electorate the good news and bad news regarding changes in taxation, the government's spending plans for the future, and other fiscal policies. The choice of Tuesday seems to be arbitrary, although it has been suggested that it allowed MPs from distant constituencies plenty of time to travel to London after the weekend. In recent years Wednesday has been the preferred day, but in the early 20th century the Budget speech was often delivered on a Monday or Thursday.

Black Tuesday

The Great Depression of the 1930s is generally considered to have begun on 29 October 1929, known as **Black Tuesday**. This was the date of the Wall Street Crash, the day on which the US stock market suffered huge losses, compounding those already experienced in the preceding days. The effects reverberated throughout the industrialized world and led to a massive economic slump, with widespread bankruptcy and unemployment and severe disruption to international trade.

Super Tuesday

Super Tuesday is the name given to one of the most important days of the process to determine candidates for the US presidential election. It was created in 1988, when a number of southern states decided to hold their primaries on the same day in March. This was an attempt to redress a perceived imbalance in the influence that the southern states felt the northern states, such as the relatively small New Hampshire, had on the presidential race by voting early. The huge numbers of votes cast on Super Tuesday means that the day is seen as make-or-break for would-be presidential candidates.

Tuesday's children

Famous people born on Tuesday include the explorer Roald Amundsen, the astronaut Neil Armstrong, the poet John Betjeman, the composer Johannes Brahms, the entrepreneur Richard Branson, the actor Charlie Chaplin, the psychiatrist Sigmund Freud, the writer Thomas Hardy, the statesman John F Kennedy, the economist John Maynard Keynes, the civil rights leader Martin Luther King Jnr, the aviator Charles Lindbergh, the political theorist Karl Marx, the actress Marilyn Monroe, the racing driver Stirling Moss, the composer Wolfgang Amadeus Mozart, the painter Pablo Picasso, the singer Elvis Presley, the cricketer Garry Sobers and the engineer Thomas Telford.

Wednesday

> *Wednesday's child is full of woe.*
>
> Traditional rhyme.

> *And God made two great lights; the greater light to rule the day, and the lesser light to rule the night: he made the stars also. And God set them in the firmament of the heaven to give light upon the earth, and to rule over the day and over the night, and to divide the light from the darkness: and God saw that it was good. And the evening and the morning were the fourth day.*
>
> Genesis I.16–19.

Origins

Wednesday is named after the Germanic god Woden (or Odin), all-wise and all-seeing; the Anglo-Saxons called it *Wōdnesdaeg*. Woden was associated with the Roman god Mercury, perhaps because both had the power to travel at speed, Woden with his eight-legged horse and Mercury with his winged sandals. The Latin name of the day was *Mercurii dies* ('day of Mercury'), from which the modern French *mercredi*, Italian *mercoledì*, Spanish *miércoles*, and Welsh *dydd Mercher* are derived. The German name *Mittwoch*, on the other hand, simply means 'midweek'.

Superstitions

Wednesday is the optimum day for marriage ('Wednesday best day of all'), while a sneeze on this day ('Sneeze on Wednesday, get a letter') may be a good or bad omen, depending on the contents of the missive. Cutting hair or nails on Wednesday is also said to bring news, according to one version of the proverbial rhyme; the other has 'cut them for health'. Like Monday, this is an unlucky day in Wales for embarking on a new enterprise. In the Roman classification of days as good, bad or neutral, Wednesday was one of the neutral days, considered appropriate for such tasks as installing bailiffs and agents.

Early closing

At the beginning of the 20th century, many shops were open all day from Monday to Saturday and did not close until late in the evening. A campaign was launched to restrict the working hours of shop assistants by introducing **early closing** (which initially meant closing at 5pm rather than 10pm) on one day of the week. The campaign was supported by notable figures such as the writer H G Wells, who had had first-hand experience of shop work as a draper's apprentice in what he described as 'the most miserable years of my life'. As the century progressed, and trade-union activity increased, legislation was introduced to reduce shop opening hours and it became customary for many shops to close at lunchtime on Wednesday or Thursday. Some small shops, especially in rural areas of the UK, still have **half-day closing** on one of these days (usually Wednesday), but most have abandoned the practice in the modern, competitive retail world.

Red Wednesday

The Persian New Year begins with the spring equinox, and the last Wednesday of the old year is known as **Red Wednesday**. It takes its name from the flames of bonfires lit on the eve of this day, which is also celebrated by Iranian Zoroastrians with traditions similar to those of Hallowe'en in the Western world and with rituals intended to remove any remaining bad fortune or ill health.

Wednesday's children

'Wednesday's child is full of woe': the writer Virginia Woolf and the painter Vincent Van Gogh, both of whom committed suicide, were born on this day. Other famous people born on Wednesday include the jazz musician and singer Louis Armstrong, the inventor Alexander Graham Bell, the footballer George Best, the engineer Isambard Kingdom Brunel, the writer T S Eliot, Queen Elizabeth II, the soldier and writer T E Lawrence (Lawrence of Arabia), the singer and songwriter John Lennon, the actor Laurence Olivier, the suffragette Emmeline Pankhurst, the physicist Ernest Rutherford and the Anglican prelate Desmond Tutu.

Thursday

> *Thursday's child has far to go.*
>
> Traditional rhyme.

> *And God created great whales, and every living creature that moveth, which the waters brought forth abundantly, after their kind, and every winged fowl after his kind: and God saw that it was good. And God blessed them, saying, Be fruitful, and multiply, and fill the waters in the seas, and let fowl multiply in the earth. And the evening and the morning were the fifth day.*
>
> Genesis 1.21–3.

> *Thursday come, and the week is gone.*
>
> Traditional saying.

Origins

Thursday is named after Thor (or Thunor), the Germanic god of thunder; the Anglo-Saxons called it *Thunresdaeg*. Thor was associated with the Roman god Jupiter (or Jove), a supreme deity armed with a thunderbolt; the Latin name of the day was *Jovis dies* ('day of Jupiter'), from which the modern French *jeudi*, Italian *giovedì*, Spanish *jueves*, and Welsh *dydd Iau* are derived. The German name is *Donnerstag* ('day of thunder').

Superstitions

According to proverbial rhymes, Thursday is a bad day to get married ('Thursday for crosses') but a good day to sneeze ('Sneeze on Thursday, something better'). Cutting hair or nails on this day is variously said to bring a new pair of shoes or wealth. Other regional superstitions state that Thursday is a good day for baptism but a bad day for moving house. It is one of only two days in the week (the other being Tuesday) when thunder may be welcomed by farmers, auguring 'plenty of sheep and corn'. In the Roman classification of days as good, bad or neutral, Thursday was one of the good days, considered auspicious for seeking favours from those in positions of power.

Polling day

In the UK, both general elections and local elections are traditionally held on Thursdays. This is enshrined in custom, but not in the constitution – British prime ministers have the right to 'go to the country' on any day they choose. However, only one general election since the mid-1920s has been held on a different day (Tuesday 27 October 1931).

There has been some speculation as to the reason for this tradition. According to popular opinion, Thursday is considered the most convenient day of the week: the results are announced on Friday, giving the winners and losers two free days to celebrate or drown their sorrows (and move into or out of 10 Downing Street) before the return to work on Monday. It has also been suggested that, in former times, a higher turnout of the electorate might have been expected on Thursday, which was market day in many towns. Perhaps the most creative theory holds that the minds of the voters were most likely to be swayed in the public houses on Friday and Saturday (as they drank their wages away) and in church on Sunday, so the choice of Thursday would have put the maximum distance between these influences and the ballot box.

Black Thursday

The name Black Thursday is applied to 6 February 1851 in Australia, when bushfires in Victoria spread through the tinder-dry vegetation over a quarter of the state. Approximately one million sheep and many thousands of cattle were killed in the blaze, which also claimed the lives of at least twelve people, and temperatures in excess of 47°C (117°F) were recorded in Melbourne on that day.

Holy Thursday

In ancient times, Thursday was a holiday in honour of the supreme deity Jupiter. This custom persisted in some countries after the advent of Christianity and was condemned by religious figures of the 6th and 7th centuries. There are, however, a number of Christian feast days that fall on Thursday, notably Ascension Day (after Rogation Sunday), Maundy Thursday (before Good Friday), and Corpus Christi (after Trinity Sunday). Ascension Day and Maundy Thursday are sometimes known as Holy Thursday.

Thursday's children

'Thursday's child has far to go': the explorers Henry Morton Stanley and Fridtjof Nansen were born on this day. Other well-known Thursday's children include the poet Robert Burns, the physicist Marie Curie, the film producer Walt Disney, the inventor Thomas Alva Edison, the actor John Gielgud, the revolutionary Che Guevara, the dramatist Henrik Ibsen, the surgeon Joseph Lister, the actress Sophia Loren, the statesman Nelson Mandela, the singer and songwriter Paul McCartney, the sculptor Auguste Rodin and the novelist Émile Zola.

Friday

> *Friday's child is loving and giving.*
>
> Traditional rhyme.

> *And God made the beast of the earth after his kind, and cattle after their kind, and every thing that creepeth upon the earth after his kind: and God saw that it was good. And God ... created man in his own image, in the image of God created he him; male and female created he them. And God blessed them, and God said unto them, Be fruitful, and multiply, and replenish the earth, and subdue it .... And God saw every thing that he had made, and, behold, it was very good. And the evening and the morning were the sixth day.*
>
> Genesis 1.25–31.

> *Friday and the week is seldom alike.*
>
> Traditional saying.

Origins

Friday is named after the Germanic goddess Frigga (or Frija), the wife of Woden; the Anglo-Saxons called it *Frīgedaeg* and the modern German name is *Freitag*. Frigga was associated with Venus, the Roman goddess of love; the Latin name of the day was *Veneris dies* ('day of Venus'), from which the French *vendredi*, Italian *venerdì*, Spanish *viernes*, and Welsh *dydd Gwener* are derived.

Superstitions

Friday is generally considered to be one of the unluckiest days of the week. According to proverbial rhymes, it is a bad day for everything: getting married ('Friday for losses'), sneezing ('Sneeze on Friday, sneeze for sorrow'), cutting hair ('Friday's hair and Saturday's horn, goes to the devil on Monday morn'), or cutting nails ('Cut your nails on a Friday, cut them for woe'). Other superstitions warn against moving house, setting out on a journey, or embarking on any new enterprise on a Friday.

Some cultures, however, hold the opposite viewpoint, and in the Roman classification of days as good, bad or neutral, Friday was one of the good days, considered auspicious for betrothals and sending children to school. The writer Charles Dickens also regarded it as a lucky day:

> *I was born on a Friday, and it is a most astonishing coincidence that I have never in my life – whatever projects I may have determined on, otherwise – never begun a book, or begun anything of interest to me, or done anything of importance to me, but it was on a Friday.*
>
> Charles Dickens, letter to Angela Burdett-Coutts (5 September 1857).

Friday the 13th

The notion that Friday is unlucky dates from the Middle Ages and is usually associated with the fact that Christ was crucified on this day; it is also said to be the day on which Adam and Eve ate the forbidden fruit and were expelled from the garden of Eden. The superstitious fear of Friday the 13th, however, is of relatively recent origin, dating from the late 19th or early 20th century. Before then, 13 was considered unlucky only as the number of diners around a table (as at Christ's Last Supper) – it was (and still is) popularly believed that if 13 people sit down to dine together, one will die within the year.

Traditions

In the early Christian Church, it was customary to fast (ie abstain from eating meat) on Wednesdays and Fridays, because Christ was betrayed and arrested on Wednesday and died on the cross on Friday. (The Gaelic names for Wednesday – Irish Gaelic *An Chéadaoin* and Scottish Gaelic *Di-ceudain* – Thursday – *An Déardaoin* and *Dior-daoin* – and Friday – *An Aoine* and *Di-h-aoine* – literally mean 'first fast', 'day between two fasts', and 'fast'). This custom was retained in the Eastern Orthodox Church, but Western Christians eventually abandoned the Wednesday observance. They continued for many years to fast on Fridays, however, hence the tradition of eating fish on this day.

In Islam, Friday is the day of assembly, when Muslims gather at the mosque in the middle of the day for **Friday Prayer**. The imam delivers a sermon, reminding the congregation of Islamic teachings and duties, before leading the prayer. All adult male Muslims are required to attend unless prevented by sickness, disability or other unavoidable circumstances. Although Muslims take part in prayer five times daily throughout the week, the Friday Prayer at noon is considered of special significance, and in countries where Islam is the dominant religion, Friday is a day of rest equivalent to the Christian or Jewish Sabbath.

Characteristics

For many people, Friday is the last day of the working week, greeted with such elation that it has spawned the catchphrase 'Thank God it's Friday', abbreviated to TGIF. (Those who receive weekly wages have further cause for celebration, as Friday is usually pay-day.) It is also known as **POETS day**, an acronym of 'push off early, tomorrow's Saturday', referring to a practice that has driven some companies to readjust the hours of the working week and allow employees to take part or all of Friday afternoon off in return for starting earlier or finishing later from Monday to Thursday. Other companies call it **dress-down Friday** and give those who are normally expected to follow a formal dress code the opportunity to wear more casual attire for one day a week. This relatively recent custom has had mixed results: some have found that the relaxed, informal atmosphere leads to greater productivity, whereas others report the opposite.

Red Friday

On 31 July 1925, a threatened strike by miners and other workers was called off when the government agreed to subsidize the coal industry and set up an inquiry to investigate the grievances that had triggered the threat – a proposed reduction in wages and an increase in working hours. This was hailed as a major victory and the day was dubbed Red Friday. The jubilation was short-lived, however: the inquiry approved the proposals and recommended that the subsidy be discontinued, precipitating the nine-day General Strike of May 1926.

Friday's children

'Friday's child is loving and giving': the nurse Florence Nightingale and the philanthropist William Wilberforce were born on this day. Other well-known Friday's children include the actress Brigitte Bardot, the cellist Pablo Casals, the statesman Benjamin Disraeli, the physicist Albert Einstein, the writer Victor Hugo, the pop singer Michael Jackson, the explorer David Livingstone, the bacteriologist Louis Pasteur, the children's writer Beatrix Potter, the racing driver Michael Schumacher, the composer Jean Sibelius and the novelist H G Wells.

Saturday

> *Saturday's child works hard for its living.*
>
> Traditional rhyme.

> *And on the seventh day God ended his work which he had made; and he rested on the seventh day from all his work which he had made. And God blessed the seventh day, and sanctified it: because that in it he had rested from all his work which God created and made.*
>
> Genesis 2.2–3.

> *There is never a Saturday without some sunshine.*
>
> Traditional saying.

Origins

Saturday is named after Saturn, the Roman god of agriculture, rather than a Germanic equivalent deity, as in the names of the four preceding days. The Anglo-Saxons called it *Saeternesdaeg*, directly translating the Latin *Saturni dies* ('day of Saturn'). The French *samedi* and German *Samstag*, on the other hand, are derived from the Latin *sabbati dies* ('Sabbath day'), like the Italian *sabato* and the Spanish and Portuguese *sábado*: these are relics of the Judaeo-Christian system of naming the days. The alternative German name, *Sonnabend*, means 'Sunday eve'.

Superstitions

In modern times, Saturday is the most popular day for weddings (being a non-working day for most people), but according to the proverbial rhyme, this is the worst day of the week to get married ('Saturday, no luck at all'). Sneezing and cutting hair or nails on Saturday may augur a pleasant encounter ('see your true love tomorrow'), although an alternative version of the rhyme predicts travel: 'Cut your nails on a Saturday, a journey to go.' Regional folklore warns against hiring servants on this day ('Saturday servants never stay, Sunday servants run away'), and those who move house will soon find themselves moving again: 'Saturday's flittings light sittings.' A new moon on Saturday night is not a good omen: 'A Saturday's moon, if it comes once in seven years, it comes too soon.'

In ancient times, Saturday was regarded as one of the unluckiest days of the week, being governed by the malevolent planet Saturn. In the Roman classification of days as good, bad or neutral, it was one of the bad days: babies born on Saturday were said to have little chance of survival, and anything undertaken on this day was likely to be problematic, unsuccessful or disastrous.

Characteristics

Before the 'invention' of the two-day **weekend**, Saturday was a normal working day for many people and Sunday was their only day of rest. The gradual introduction of the five-day working week, however, made Saturday a time for leisure, recreation, social gatherings and entertainment. It was particularly popular for activities that were forbidden – or at least discouraged – on Sundays, and it remains the favoured day for many sporting fixtures, such as football matches and horse races. The two-day weekend also gave a boost to the tourism industry: people had time to travel further afield in their non-working hours, and many seaside resorts developed and prospered as a result.

For much of the 20th century, children throughout the UK were kept out of mischief on Saturday mornings with special screenings of suitable films at the local cinema. **Saturday cinema** clubs were set up for the purpose, complete with all the paraphernalia of membership – badges, cards and songs – and some were lucky enough to receive a visit from one or more of their celluloid heroes.

The Jewish Sabbath

In Judaism, Saturday is the Sabbath (*Shabbat*), or day of rest, commemorating the seventh day on which God rested after the creation of the universe. (The word *sabbath* is ultimately derived from the Hebrew verb meaning 'to rest').

> *Remember the sabbath day, to keep it holy. Six days shalt thou labour, and do all thy work: But the seventh day is the sabbath of the Lord thy God: in it thou shalt not do any work, thou, nor thy son, nor thy daughter, thy manservant, nor thy maidservant, nor thy cattle, nor thy stranger that is within thy gates: For in six days the Lord made heaven and earth, the sea, and all that in them is, and rested the seventh day: wherefore the Lord blessed the sabbath day, and hallowed it.*
>
> Exodus 20.8–11.

Saturday

Orthodox Jews observe the Sabbath by refraining from work and other forbidden activities between sunset on Friday and sunset on Saturday. Others simply regard it as their day of worship, attending synagogue services and participating in traditional rituals and ceremonies in the home, such as lighting candles and enjoying festive meals with family and friends.

Black Saturday

On 4 August 1621, the Parliament of Scotland met to enact the legislation that forced episcopacy (Church government by bishops), among other things, on the people of that country. The opposition of the Scottish Protestants to these ordinances was reinforced by what seemed to be a heavenly sign of disapproval, and the day went down in history as Black Saturday.

> *On the day on which they were to be sanctioned, a heavy cloud had hung above Edinburgh since morning; that cloud waxed ever the darker as the hour approached when the articles were to be ratified, till at last it filled the Parliament Hall with the gloom of almost night. The moment the Marquis of Hamilton, the commissioner, rose and touched the Act with the royal sceptre, the cloud burst in a terrific storm right over the Parliament House. Three lurid gleams, darting in at the large window, flashed their vivid fires in the commissioner's face. Then came terrible peals of thunder, which were succeeded by torrents of rain and hail that inundated the streets, and made it difficult for the members to reach their homes. The day was long remembered in Scotland by the name of 'Black Saturday.'*
>
> James A Wylie, *The History of Protestantism* (1828).

Saturday's children

Famous people born on Saturday include the boxer Muhammad Ali, the novelist Jane Austen, the athlete Roger Bannister, Fidel Castro, the painter Paul Cézanne, the statesman Charles de Gaulle, the singer and songwriter Bob Dylan, the bacteriologist Alexander Fleming, Mahatma Gandhi, the sculptor Barbara Hepworth, Adolf Hitler, the pop singer Madonna, the composer Gustav Mahler, the physicist Guglielmo Marconi, the tenor Luciano Pavarotti, the philosopher Bertrand Russell, the explorer Robert Falcon Scott, the dramatist George Bernard Shaw, the poet William Wordsworth and the architect Frank Lloyd Wright.

The Year

January

Gemstone: Garnet
Flower: Carnation or snowdrop

> *Married in January's hoar and rime,*
> *Widowed you'll be before your time.*
>
> Traditional rhyme.

> *January is the open gate of the year, shut until the shortest day passed, but now open to let in the lengthening daylight, which will soon fall upon dim patches of pale green, that shew where spring is still sleeping. Sometimes between the hoary pillars – when the winter is mild – a few wan snowdrops will peep out and catch the faint sunlight which streams in coldly through the opening gateway, like timid messengers sent to see if spring has yet stirred from her long sleep.*
>
> *Chambers Book of Days* (1864).

Origins

January, the first month of the year, takes its name from the Roman god Janus, the guardian of doorways and bridges. Janus had two faces, looking in opposite directions – back towards the old year and forward to the new. The months of January and February are said to have been added to the Roman calendar (in which March was formerly the first of ten months) during the reign of Numa Pompilius (715–673 BC).

> *Hark, the cock crows, and yon bright star*
> *Tells us, the day himself's not far;*
> *And see where, breaking from the night,*
> *He gilds the western hills with light.*
> *With him old Janus doth appear,*
> *Peeping into the future year,*
> *With such a look as seems to say,*
> *The prospect is not good that way.*
>
> Charles Cotton (1630–87), 'The New Year'.

Characteristics

Although the shortest day is past and gone, January is a dark month in (northern) Europe: the nights are still long, and in dull weather it often feels as if there is very little daylight at all. Frost, ice and snow take their toll on non-hibernating wildlife, especially birds, as well as causing major problems for road-users (motorists and pedestrians alike). Once the New Year celebrations are over, it is time for all to return to work – gone are the days when the festive season lasted for the full twelve days of Christmas.

History

Old Celtic names for the month describe it as 'the dead month', 'the end of winter' (in a calendar where February was the first month of spring) or simply 'the beginning of the year'. The Anglo-Saxons called it *Wolfmonath*, perhaps because it was a time when these ravening beasts were most likely to take human prey.

Weather

It is said that 'as the day lengthens, the cold strengthens', and January is usually the coldest month of the year. For those who pay heed to weather lore, however, frost and snow are not unwelcome at this time – mild weather in any of the winter months, especially January, is an ill omen: 'Summer in winter, and a summer's flood, never boded England good'; 'If January's calends be summerly gay, 'twill be winterly weather till the calends of May'; 'A January spring is good for nothing'.

Ploughing

Ploughing the fields in preparation for sowing is the first task of the agricultural year. The first Monday after Epiphany (6 January) is known as **Plough Monday**: this was formerly the day on which farmhands returned to work after the Christmas holiday – not that they actually did much work on this day, which was marked by various customs and ceremonies and usually ended in general merrymaking. The plough would be blessed at the church and then paraded around the parish by labourers collecting money from householders, often with the threat of unauthorized use of the implement on their premises if they refused. In some places the labourers (variously known as **Plough Jags**, **Plough Bullocks**, **Plough Stots**, etc) performed a mumming play; in others, a traditional dance called a **molly dance**. In an ancient custom recently revived at Whittlesey, Cambridgeshire, the star attraction is a man or boy disguised as a **straw bear**, who formerly made his rounds on the Tuesday after Plough Monday and now appears on the following Saturday, towards the end of a five-day festival.

Yes, thus the Muses sing of happy swains,
Because the Muses never knew their pains:
They boast their peasants' pipes, but peasants now
Resign their pipes and plod behind the plough.

George Crabbe, *The Village* (1783).

Non-fixed notable dates

Non-fixed notable dates in January include:

Handsel Monday: The first Monday after New Year's Day, when gifts were traditionally given to servants and children in former times. Such gifts, often of money, were said to bestow good fortune on the recipient for the coming year. This was primarily a Scottish custom, and after the calendar reform of 1752 it was sometimes observed on the first Monday after 12 January instead.

Seijin no hi or **Coming of Age Day:** In Japan, the second Monday in January is a public holiday marked by a ceremony for all those who have just reached (or are about to reach) their 20th birthday, the Japanese age of majority. The ceremony, which formerly took place on 15 January each year, consists of speeches and presentations and is usually followed by parties and other festivities. The young people dress formally for the occasion, the women in long-sleeved kimonos and the men in business suits.

Martin Luther King Day: In the USA, the third Monday in January is a national holiday commemorating the life and achievements of Martin Luther King, Jnr (1929–68). Held in the month of King's birthday, this has been a national holiday since 1986. (See also 4 April, anniversary of King's death.)

Up-Helly-Aa: A fire festival that takes place in Lerwick in the Shetland Islands on the last Tuesday of January. It features a torchlit procession led by the Guiser Jarl and his squad of 'Vikings', appropriately dressed, who bear a longship through the streets of the town and finally set it ablaze with their flaming torches. This colourful and spectacular ceremony is of relatively recent origin in its current form – in the mid-19th century the participants carried burning tar barrels, and the Viking theme was not introduced until the 1880s.

1 January

> *It may safely be said that New-Year's Day has hitherto been observed in Scotland with a heartiness nowhere surpassed. It almost appears as if, by a sort of antagonism to the general gravity of the people, they were impelled to break out in a half-mad merriment on this day. Every face was bright with smiles; every hand ready with the grasp of friendship. All stiffness arising from age, profession, and rank, gave way.*
>
> *Chambers Book of Days* (1864).

For many people, especially in Scotland, the celebrations of New Year's Eve continue into **New Year's Day** without a break. According to tradition, the first person to enter a household on 1 January must have certain characteristics (eg dark hair and male gender) and bear certain gifts (eg coal and whisky) to bring luck for the coming year. Such visitors are made welcome with appropriate refreshments, and in Scotland people go from house to house for this purpose, a tradition known as **first-footing**. In the Isle of Man the first-footer is known as the **Quaaltagh** but, similarly, a man of dark hair and complexion is preferred.

In the past, over-indulgence in alcohol and lack of sleep on New Year's Eve inevitably led to widespread absenteeism or poor performance in the workplace on 1 January, and in 1974 it was finally declared a public holiday throughout the UK. In former times it was considered unlucky to do any work at all on this day, even household chores: those who washed clothes or linen, for example, ran the risk of washing away one of their nearest and dearest, according to superstitious belief. It was also considered unlucky to let your fire go out, or to remove or discard anything from the house without first bringing something in:

> *Take out, then take in*
> *Bad luck will begin.*
> *Take in, then take out*
> *Good luck comes about.*
>
> Traditional rhyme.

It was formerly customary for relatives and friends to exchange gifts on New Year's Day, rather than at Christmas. These ranged from simple, home-made items (such as an apple or orange stuck with cloves) to lavish, expensive presents given and received by royalty or members of the nobility. This custom dated from ancient Roman times, when it was accompanied by great revelry – eating, drinking, singing, dancing, etc. The Christian Church frowned on these pagan celebrations and declared the more appropriate date of the Annunciation, or Lady Day (25 March), as the 'official' start of the year. (In the Church calendar 1 January was the feast of the **Circumcision of Christ**, eight days after his birth, but this was not widely observed until the eleventh century.) However, most people continued to celebrate 1 January in the time-honoured fashion, and it was eventually re-adopted as New Year's Day throughout the Christian world.

New Year's Day is also associated with the making of **resolutions**. The changing of the year provides an ideal time for renewal, and many start the year with a list of good intentions. In the past, it was also common for people to make certain that all their debts were cleared so that they could start the New Year with a 'clean slate'.

Of the various folk traditions associated with New Year's Day in the UK, one of the most unusual is the **Mari Lwyd**, a decorated horse's skull (or wooden replica) carried on a pole, which is still seen in some Welsh towns and villages. Its bearers call at pubs or houses where they must stand at the door and engage in a series of exchanges in rhyme or song with those inside before being admitted. (This battle of wits, or *pwnco*, intended to keep the Mari Lwyd party out for as long as possible, has been abandoned in some modern versions of the custom.) The Mari Lwyd has its origins in pagan celebrations associated with the winter solstice and the cycle of death and rebirth in nature.

In Orkney, the residents of Kirkwall play a mass football game on New Year's Day. Known as **the Ba'**, the game is also played on Christmas Day, and involves two teams of indeterminate size playing with a cork-filled leather ball (the ba' itself). (See February for further mass football games.)

On this day:

Born: Swiss reformer Ulrich Zwingli (1484); American patriot Paul Revere (1735); English novelist and critic E M Forster (1879); US law enforcement official J Edgar Hoover (1895); US novelist and short-story writer J D Salinger (1919)

Died: English dramatist William Wycherley (1716); German physicist Heinrich Rudolph Hertz (1894); English architect Sir Edwin Landseer Lutyens (1944); French actor and entertainer Maurice

Chevalier (1972); US tennis player Helen Wills Moody (1998)

1651 Charles II (1630-85) was crowned King of Scotland in Scone.

1660 English diarist and Admiralty official Samuel Pepys (1633–1703) began his famous diary.

1752 With the British Calendar Act of 1751, 1 January officially became New Year's Day in England and Wales; previously, 25 March had been the official start of the New Year.

1781 The first all-iron bridge in the world, across the River Severn in Shropshire, opened to traffic and charged its first tolls.

1801 The Act of Union came into force, uniting Britain and Ireland and creating the United Kingdom.

1801 Italian astronomer Giuseppe Piazzi (1746–1826) discovered the very first minor planet (or asteroid), which he named Ceres.

1833 The first 'fire brigade', the London Fire Engine Establishment, was formed from ten insurance company fire services.

1856 Van Diemen's Land was officially renamed Tasmania.

1863 The Emancipation Proclamation issued by US President Abraham Lincoln (1809–65) came into effect.

1877 British Queen Victoria (1819–1901) was proclaimed Empress of India.

1892 Ellis Island, the US immigration station, opened.

1894 The first ships sailed the full length of the Manchester Ship Canal.

1901 A federal Commonwealth of Australia was established by agreement between the six colonies (New South Wales, Tasmania, Victoria, South Australia, Queensland and Western Australia).

1927 The British Broadcasting Corporation (BBC) was established by Royal Charter; John Reith (1889–1971) became the first Director-General.

1942 World War II – the Declaration of the United Nations was signed by the USA, the UK, the USSR and China.

1947 The British coal industry was nationalized and became the National Coal Board.

1948 British railways were nationalized.

1951 *The Archers* was first broadcast on BBC radio.

1958 The Treaty of Rome came into force, establishing the European Economic Community and the European Atomic Energy Commission;

the original members were France, West Germany, Italy, Belgium, the Netherlands and Luxembourg.

1959 Cuban dictator General Fulgencio Batista (1901–73) was overthrown by Fidel Castro (born 1927).

1961 The farthing ceased to be legal tender in the UK.

1964 The BBC television programme *Top of the Pops* was first broadcast, presented by Jimmy Savile (born 1926); the first show featured the Rolling Stones, Dusty Springfield, the Dave Clark Five and the Hollies, amongst others.

1969 In the Queen's New Year Honours list, West Indian cricketer and politician Learie Constantine (1901–71) became the first black person to be awarded a peerage.

1970 The voting age was lowered from 21 years to 18 years in the UK.

1970 The half-crown ceased to be legal tender in the UK.

1973 The UK, Ireland and Denmark became members of the European Economic Community.

1974 Self-government was reinstated in Northern Ireland, following a period of British direct rule.

1978 South African journalist and campaigner Donald Woods (1933–2001) arrived in the UK after being forced into exile from South Africa.

1981 Greece became the tenth member of the European Community.

1984 Brunei became an independent state after 95 years as a British Protectorate.

1986 Spain and Portugal became the eleventh and twelfth members of the European Community.

1992 Boutros Boutros-Ghali (born 1922) became the sixth Secretary-General of the United Nations.

1993 Czechoslovakia separated into two separate nations, the Czech Republic and the Republic of Slovakia.

1994 In Mexico the *Ejército Zapatista de Liberación Nacional*, 'Zapatista National Liberation Army', launched a rebellion in the southern state of Chiapas.

1995 The World Trade Organization was formally established.

1995 English builder Fred West (born 1942) was found hanged in his cell at Winson Green Prison, Birmingham; he was awaiting trial for the murders of twelve women.

1999 The Euro was introduced as the currency of participating nations of the European Union.

2 January

Since 1973, 2 January has been a public holiday in Scotland, giving those north of the border an extra day to recover from Hogmanay excesses (although the Act that allowed for its creation was passed in 1971).

On this day:

Born: English general James Wolfe (1727); German physicist Rudolf Clausius (1822); English composer Sir Michael Tippett (1905); US novelist, critic and popular scientist Isaac Asimov (1920); English photographer David Bailey (1938)

Died: English astronomer and geophysicist Sir George Airy (1892); US singing cowboy Tex Ritter (1974); US jazz pianist Errol Garner (1977); English writer and broadcaster Frank Muir (1998)

1492 Spain conquered Granada, ending Muslim rule.

1788 Georgia became the fourth state to ratify the Constitution of the USA.

1896 The 'Jameson Raid' in the Transvaal in support of British settlers against the Boers ended in disaster for the British troops.

1903 US President Theodore Roosevelt (1858–1919) closed down a Mississippi post office for attempting to force the resignation of black postmistress Minnie Geddings Cox (1869–1933).

1905 The Russians surrendered Port Arthur in Manchuria to the Japanese.

1946 King Zog I of Albania (1895–1961) was deposed whilst out of the country; a republic was declared nine days later.

1959 The USSR launched Luna 1, the first man-made object to escape Earth's gravity.

1971 Sixty-six people were killed at the Ibrox football ground in Glasgow when a barrier collapsed; the resultant report stated that any stadium with a capacity of over 10,000 must be licensed by a local authority.

1980 The UK's first steel industry strike since 1926 began; it lasted for three months.

1996 US peacekeepers were deployed in Bosnia.

1999 Darren Gough (born 1970) became the first England bowler since 1899 to take an Ashes hat-trick.

3 January

Feast day of **St Geneviève**, patron saint of Paris, whose prayers are said to have averted an attack on that city by Attila the Hun in AD 451.

On this day:

Born: US abolitionist and feminist Lucretia Mott (1793); English statesman Clement Attlee, 1st Earl Attlee (1883); South African-born British writer and philologist J R R Tolkien (1892); US astronomer William Morgan (1906); English conductor David Atherton (1944)

Died: English potter Josiah Wedgwood (1795); French publisher, lexicographer and encyclopedist Pierre Larousse (1875); Czechoslovakian novelist and short-story writer Jaroslav Hasek (1923); Irish-born British traitor William Joyce, known as 'Lord Haw-Haw' (1946); US hotelier Conrad Hilton (1979)

1521 German religious reformer and founder of the Reformation Martin Luther (1483–1546) was excommunicated by Pope Leo X (1475–1571).

1777 At the Battle of Princeton, George Washington (1732–99) defeated the British under Charles Cornwallis (1738–1805).

1840 The first successful deep-sea sounding – at a depth of 2,425 fathoms – was taken by James Clark Ross (1800–62) on board HMS *Erebus* in the South Atlantic Ocean.

1868 The Tokugawa Shogunate was abolished in Japan with the restoration of the Meiji dynasty.

1888 The first paper drinking straws were patented in the USA.

1938 The first foreign-language broadcast by the BBC was made with the inauguration of the Arabic Service.

1947 The opening session of the US Congress was televised for the first time to viewers in Washington, Philadelphia and New York City.

1959 Alaska became the 49th state of the USA.

1962 Cuban prime minister Fidel Castro (born 1927) was excommunicated by Pope John XXIII (1881–1963).

1971 Open University programmes were first broadcast on radio and television in the UK.

1991 Eight diplomats from the Iraqi embassy in London were expelled from the UK by the Foreign Office as tensions increased in the build-up to the Gulf War.

4 January

> *He always said that Coniston would get him some time, and that the lake used to wink at him … and say, 'I'll get you one day', and of course she did.*
>
> Gina Campbell, interview on BBC radio *Woman's Hour* (7 November 2002).

On this day in 1967, the British engineer and racer Donald Campbell was killed in an attempt to break his own water-speed record on Coniston Water in the Lake District. Travelling at a speed of more than 300mph, his jet-powered hydroplane, *Bluebird*, flipped into the air and disintegrated on landing. Campbell's body and the remains of the boat were not located and recovered from the depths of the lake until 2001.

Born in 1921, Donald Campbell was the son of Sir Malcolm Campbell (1885–1949), who had broken speed records on land and water in the 1930s. Donald followed his father's example, setting a land-speed record of 403.1mph and a water-speed record of 276.33mph in Australia in 1964. His daughter Gina, who was just 17 years old when he died, continued the family tradition by breaking the women's water-speed record in New Zealand in 1990.

On this day:

Born: Italian composer Giovanni Battista Pergolesi (1710); French educationalist Louis Braille (1809); English educationalist and inventor of a shorthand system Sir Isaac Pitman (1813); US heavyweight boxer Floyd Patterson (1935); Welsh physicist and Nobel Prize winner Brian Josephson (1940)

Died: English botanist and chemist Stephen Hales (1761); French writer and Nobel Prize winner Albert Camus (1960); US-born British poet, critic and dramatist and Nobel Prize winner T S Eliot (1965); Austrian-born British naturalist and writer Joy Adamson (1980)

1642 King Charles I (1600–49) marched to Westminster to arrest five Members of Parliament on a charge of treason; his attempt failed when they took refuge in the Guildhall.

1884 The Fabian Society was founded in London (although the Fabians had been meeting during the previous year as the Fellowship of the New Life).

1885 The first appendectomy in the USA was performed in Davenport, Iowa by one Dr William Grant.

1896 Utah became the 45th state of the USA.

1932 India's National Congress was declared illegal by the British government and its leader, Mahatma Gandhi (1869–1948), was arrested in Bombay (now Mumbai).

1936 In the USA, the first popular music chart appeared in *Billboard* magazine.

1948 Burma (now Myanmar) became an independent republic outside the Commonwealth.

1951 North Korean and Communist Chinese forces captured the South Korean capital city of Seoul.

1958 The USSR's Sputnik I satellite fell from orbit after completing 1,367 circuits of the earth and travelling approximately 35 million miles.

1958 Edmund Hillary (born 1919) arrived at the South Pole as part of the British Commonwealth Trans-Antarctic Expedition.

2000 Israel and Palestine agreed to implement proposals to transfer a portion of West Bank land to Palestine.

2000 Catherine Hartley and Fiona Thornewill became the first British women to walk across Antarctica to the South Pole when they arrived after a journey of more than two months.

5 January

On 5 January 1753, a crowd of people gathered around the **Holy Thorn at Glastonbury** – the bush that was said to have grown from Joseph of Arimathea's staff – to see if it would blossom on that day. The bush traditionally blossomed on Christmas Day each year, but the changeover from the 'Old Style' Julian calendar to the 'New Style' Gregorian calendar in September 1752 had caused 25 December to fall eleven days early and the branches had remained bare. It was generally decided that if the thorn blossomed on 5 January instead, this would be a sign that the reformed calendar was not to be trusted in such matters. Sure enough, the blossom appeared on cue, and thereafter many activities that took place on particular holy days were transferred to the appropriate equivalent 'New Style' date. For example, although Lammas remained on 1 August, a number of the fairs and other events associated with it moved to 12 August, sometimes known as 'Old Lammas Day'. Similarly, the start of the oyster season, which formerly fell on St James's Day (25 July), was changed to 5 August ('Old St James's Day').

On this day:

Born: Scottish writer Thomas Pringle (1789); French mathematician Camille Jordan (1838); US inventor of the safety razor King Camp Gillette (1855); Spanish king Juan Carlos (1938); Italian pianist Maurizio Pollini (1942)

Died: English king and saint Edward the Confessor (1066); 30th President of the USA Calvin Coolidge (1933); US botanist and scientist George Washington Carver (1943); Welsh politician and biographer Roy Jenkins, Lord Jenkins of Hillhead (2003)

1665 The world's first scholarly journal, the *Journal des Scavans*, devoted to science, the arts and law, was published in Paris.

1809 The Treaty of the Dardanelles was drawn up between the UK and the Ottoman Empire.

1818 The first ocean liner, the Black Ball Line's *James Monroe*, sailed from New York City, USA, on her maiden voyage to Liverpool, England, arriving 28 days later on 2 February.

1896 The discovery by German physicist Wilhelm Röntgen (1845–1923) of

the electromagnetic rays that later became known as X-rays was reported in the Austrian press.

1925 Nellie Tayloe Ross (1876–1977) became the first female governor in the USA when she succeeded her husband as governor of Wyoming.

1940 FM radio, which used frequency modulation to remove static from sound broadcasts, was demonstrated for the first time by Edwin Howard Armstrong (1890–1954) in the USA.

1941 World War II – English pioneering female aviator Amy Johnson (1903–41), who had joined the Air Transport Auxiliary as a pilot, disappeared after baling out over the Thames Estuary.

1964 Pope Paul VI (1897–1978) became the first pope in over 150 years to leave Italy when he visited Israel. When he met the Ecumenical Patriarch of Constantinople, Athenagoras I (1886–1972), in Jerusalem it was the first time in 500 years that leaders of the Roman Catholic and Russian Orthodox Churches had met.

1968 *Gardeners' World* was first shown on the BBC.

1971 The first one-day international cricket match took place between Australia and England in Melbourne.

1981 Peter Sutcliffe (born 1946), the 'Yorkshire Ripper', was arrested in connection with the murders of 13 women in northern England and the Midlands.

1993 The *MV Braer* oil tanker ran aground in strong winds off the south of the Shetland Islands, Scotland, leaking 84,700 tonnes of crude oil into the North Sea.

6 January

We three kings of Orient are;
Bearing gifts we traverse afar,
Field and fountain, moor and mountain,
Following yonder star.

John H Hopkins, Jnr, 'We Three Kings' (1857).

This is the Christian festival of **Epiphany**, commemorating the manifestation of the young Christ to the Magi – the three wise men who had travelled from the East, following a star and bearing gifts of gold, frankincense and myrrh. In the Orthodox Church it marks the baptism of Christ by John the Baptist some 30 years later. Also known as **Twelfth Day** or **Twelfth Night** (although the latter name sometimes refers to its eve), 6 January is the last of the twelve days of Christmas and is the date by which Christmas decorations must be taken down to avoid bad luck.

> *In its character as a popular festival, Twelfth-Day stands only inferior to Christmas. The leading object held in view is to do honour to the three wise men, or, as they are more generally denominated, the three kings. It is a Christian custom, ancient past memory, and probably suggested by a pagan custom, to indulge in a pleasantry called the Election of Kings by Beans. In England, in later times, a large cake was formed, with a bean inserted, and this was called Twelfth-Cake. The family and friends being assembled, the cake was divided by lot, and whoever got the piece containing the bean was accepted as king of the day, and called King of the Bean.*
>
> *Chambers Book of Days* (1864).

The **Twelfth Cake** ceremony described above is no longer observed in the UK, but a relic of the tradition survives in the British custom of baking a coin into the Christmas cake, which is made to a similar recipe. In France, however, it remains a popular occasion, with family and friends invited to share the *galette des rois*: a large round pastry with an almond-paste filling, now usually supplied by the local *pâtisserie* with a gold cardboard crown for the lucky finder of the *fève* (the 'bean', or a china substitute). On Twelfth Night at London's Drury Lane Theatre, the cast of the current show enjoy a glass of wine and a piece of **Baddeley cake**, served by attendants in powdered wigs and 18th-century livery, courtesy of the actor and former chef Robert Baddeley, who died in 1794 and left a sum of money in his will to fund this annual treat.

> *On the twelfth day of Christmas, my true love gave to me:*
> *Twelve drummers drumming, eleven pipers piping,*
> *Ten lords a-leaping, nine ladies dancing,*
> *Eight maids a-milking, seven swans a-swimming,*
> *Six geese a-laying, five gold rings,*
> *Four calling birds, three French hens, two turtle doves,*
> *And a partridge in a pear tree.*
>
> Traditional song.

Another surviving Twelfth Day tradition is the **Haxey Hood Game**, played in the Lincolnshire village of that name on 6 January each year (or 5 January if

Twelfth Day falls on a Sunday). The 'hood' is a leather tube encasing a length of heavy rope and the object of the game is to convey it, by means of a 'sway' (the movement of a scrum of local men and boys), into one of two pubs in Haxey or nearby Westwoodside. The game is refereed by a number of **Boggans** dressed in red; other characters include the Fool, who introduces the action and is 'smoked' with burning straw for his pains, and the Lord, who wears a top hat and carries a 'magic' willow wand. The game is of uncertain origin, but legend has it that a certain Lady Mowbray once lost her hood in the wind and was so amused by the spectacle of 13 local labourers trying to recover it that she inaugurated an annual re-enactment of the event.

Unusually, while many see 6 January as the official end of Christmas, the island community on Foula, in the Shetland Islands, begin their Yule celebrations on this day. Following the feast days of the old Julian calendar, the islanders then celebrate their New Year's Day on 13 January.

On this day:

Born: English king Richard II (1367); French aeronautical inventor Jacques Étienne Montgolfier (1745); German archaeologist Heinrich Schliemann (1822); Australian philosopher Samuel Alexander (1859); English actor, writer and comic Rowan Atkinson (1955)

Died: English critic and playwright John Dennis (1734); English novelist and diarist Fanny Burney (1840); Austrian botanist and pioneer of biological heredity Gregor Mendel (1884); 26th President of the USA Theodore Roosevelt (1919); US jazz trumpeter, composer and bandleader Dizzy Gillespie (1993)

871 King Ethelred of Wessex (died 871) and his younger brother Alfred (849–99), later Alfred the Great, defeated the Danes at the Battle of Ashdown.

1066 King Harold II (c.1022–1066), England's last Anglo-Saxon king, was crowned.

1540 England's King Henry VIII (1491–1547) married his fourth wife, Anne of Cleves (1515–57).

1841 The first registered letters were introduced in the UK at a charge of one shilling per letter, and the 'Penny Red' stamp replaced the 'Penny Black'.

1896 Cecil Rhodes (1853–1902) resigned as Premier of South Africa's Cape Colony in the aftermath of the Jameson Raid.

1912 New Mexico became the 47th state of the USA.

1924 The first radio transmission of a church service was broadcast by the BBC from St Martin-in-the-Fields, London.

1926 The German airline Lufthansa was established as Deutsche Luft Hansa Aktiengesellschaft; it was formed by a merger between the companies Junkers Luftverkehr and Deutsche Aero Lloyd, and was renamed Lufthansa in 1933.

1931 The refurbished Sadler's Wells Theatre opened in London with a performance of Shakespeare's *Twelfth Night*.

1939 The discovery of nuclear fission was published in *Naturwissenschaften* by Otto Hahn (1879–1968) and Lise Meitner (1878–1968) of the Kaiser Wilhelm Institute for Chemistry in Berlin.

1977 EMI ended its contract with controversial punk rock group the Sex Pistols.

2001 Congress confirmed the result of the disputed US presidential election, and declared George W Bush (born 1946) to be the 43rd President of the USA.

7 January

Partly work and partly play
Ye must on St Distaff's Day:
From the plough soon free your team;
Then come home and fodder them.
If the maids a-spinning go,
Burn the flax and fire the tow:
Scorch their plackets, but beware
That ye singe no maiden-hair.
Bring in pails of water then,
Let the maids bewash the men.
Give St Distaff all the right:
Then bid Christmas sport good-night
And next morrow, every one
To his own vocation.

Robert Herrick, *Hesperides*, 'St Distaff's Day; or, the Morrow after Twelfth-day' (1648).

In former times, 7 January was jocularly known as **St Distaff's Day**. It was the female equivalent of Plough Monday (described in the introduction to this month): nominally the day on which work resumed after the Christmas festivities, but effectively a day of transition between the two. The stereotypical tool of the trade for women was the distaff, used for the spinning of flax.

> *To spin – how essentially was the idea at one time associated with the female sex! even to that extent, that in England spinster was a recognised legal term for an unmarried woman – the spear side and the distaff side were legal terms to distinguish the inheritance of male from that of female children – and the distaff became a synonym for woman herself ... Now, through the change wrought by the organised industries of Manchester and Glasgow, the princess of the fairy tale who was destined to die by a spindle piercing her hand, might wander from the Land's End to John o' Groat's House, and never encounter an article of the kind, unless in an archaeological museum.*
>
> *Chambers Book of Days* (1864).

On this day:

Born: 13th President of the USA Millard Fillmore (1800); Hungarian-born US film executive Adolph Zukor (1873); English writer and naturalist Gerald Durrell (1925); US actor Nicolas Cage (1964)

Died: English queen Catherine of Aragon (1536); English court goldsmith and miniaturist Nicholas Hilliard (1619); English physician and women's medical education pioneer Sophia Jex-Blake (1912); Croatian-born US physicist and electrical engineer Nikola Tesla (1943); US poet, biographer, novelist and academic John Berryman (1972)

1451 Glasgow University was founded.

1610 Italian astronomer and mathematician Galileo Galilei (1564–1642) first observed Jupiter's four satellites with his newly-invented telescope; he named them Callisto, Europa, Ganymede and Io.

1785 The first aerial crossing of the English Channel was made by Frenchman Jean-Pierre Blanchard (1753–1809) and American John Jeffries (1744–1819) in a hot-air hydrogen balloon.

1789 The USA held its first national presidential election.

1927 The first transatlantic telephone service between London and New York City began with a three-minute call costing £15.

1928 London's Tate Gallery was flooded and many paintings were damaged when the River Thames burst its banks.

1979 In Cambodia, the regime of Pol Pot (1925–98) was overthrown by Vietnamese troops.

1986 US President Ronald Reagan (1911–2004) severed economic links with Libya.

1990 The Leaning Tower of Pisa was closed to the public when its accelerated 'leaning' became a danger to tourists.

1993 The first solo expedition on foot to the South Pole ended when Norwegian Erling Kagge (born 1963) reached the Pole, having dragged his sled 870 miles in 50 days.

1999 The impeachment trial of US President Bill Clinton (born 1946) began in the US Senate.

8 January

Elvis Presley, the undisputed 'King of Rock-and-roll', was born in Tupelo, Mississippi on this day in 1935. He began singing in the local Pentecostal church choir, taught himself to play the guitar, and released his first hit single, 'That's All Right Mama', in 1954. Within a few years his fame had spread worldwide, with classic songs such as 'Heartbreak Hotel' (1956), 'Blue Suede Shoes' (1956), 'All Shook Up' (1957), 'Jailhouse Rock' (1958) and 'King Creole' (1958). Presley's unique style was a combination of white country-and-western and black rhythm-and-blues, performed on stage with overtly sexual gyrations that earned him the nickname 'Elvis the Pelvis'. He went on to become a popular icon, appearing on the silver screen throughout the 1960s and making a successful return to the nightclub circuit in the 1970s.

After Presley's sudden death in 1977, his Memphis home, Graceland, became a shrine for his fans, who gather there on 8 January each year to celebrate his birthday. Some maintain that he is still alive, their conviction fuelled by numerous alleged sightings of him all over the world.

On this day:

Born: German writer on jurisprudence Samuel Freiherr von Puffendorf (1632); English novelist Wilkie Collins (1824); English astronomer Sir Frank Dyson (1868); English theoretical physicist Stephen Hawking (1942)

Died: Venetian merchant, traveller and writer Marco Polo (1324); Italian painter and architect Giotto (1337); French poet Paul Verlaine (1896); English soldier and founder of the Boy Scouts Lord Baden-Powell (1941); French statesman François Mitterrand (1996)

1297 François Grimaldi, disguised as a monk, entered the Genoese-controlled fortress, let in his own soldiers, and established the Grimaldi dynasty in Monaco.

1815 The British were defeated by US forces in the Battle of New Orleans, which took place two weeks after the War of 1812 had ended in a peace treaty.

1889 The first 'tabulating machine' or data-processing computer was patented by Dr Herman Hollerith (1860–1929) of New York City; this was the beginning of the IBM company.

1904 Pope Pius X (1835–1914) banned Catholic women from wearing low-cut dresses in the presence of church officials.

1918 World War I – US President Woodrow Wilson (1856–1924) put forward his 'Fourteen Points' for world peace in his address to the US Congress.

1923 The first outside broadcast took place; the BBC transmitted the first act of Mozart's *The Magic Flute* from the Royal Opera House, Covent Garden, London.

1926 Ibn Saud (1880–1953) changed his tile from Sultan to King of the Hejaz; on the same date in 1932 he renamed his country Saudi Arabia.

1933 An anarchist uprising took place in Barcelona, Spain.

1940 World War II – food rationing (initially bacon, butter and sugar) was introduced in the UK.

1959 General Charles de Gaulle (1890–1970) became president of the Fifth French Republic.

1989 A British Midland Boeing 737 aircraft crashed on the M1 motorway, killing 46 people.

9 January

On this day:

Born: English critic and Poet Laureate Thomas Warton (1728); German chemist Richard Abegg (1869); English variety artist and singer Dame Gracie Fields (1898); US folk singer and civil rights campaigner Joan Baez (1941)

Died: Italian mathematician and scholar Maria Gaetana Agnesi (1799); German-born British astronomer Caroline Herschel (1848); New Zealand short-story writer Katherine Mansfield (1923); English comedian and actor Peter Cook (1995)

1522 Adrian of Utrecht, Regent of Spain, was elected Pope Adrian VI (1459–1523).

1788 Connecticut became the fifth state to ratify the Constitution of the USA.

1799 Income tax was introduced into the UK, at a rate of 10% (two shillings in the pound), supposedly as a temporary measure to fund the Napoleonic wars.

1806 Lord Nelson (1758–1805), English admiral and hero of the Battle of Trafalgar, was buried in St Paul's Cathedral, London.

1894 *Edison Kinetoscopic Recording of a Sneeze*, a short film showing Fred Ott sneezing, became the first copyrighted motion picture; Ott was the assistant of Thomas Edison (1847–1931).

1905 In Russia a group of workers went to the Winter Palace in St Petersburg to present a petition to Nicholas II (1868–1918), where they were joined by a large but peaceful crowd; troops opened fire, killing over 100 people and wounding several hundred more, marking the beginning of the Russian Revolution of 1905.

1923 The first successful flight in an autogiro, a forerunner of the helicopter, was made by Spanish aeronautical engineer Juan de la Cierva (1895–1936) in Spain.

1957 Anthony Eden (1897–1977) resigned as the UK's prime minister.

1960 Work began on the building of the Aswan High Dam in Egypt.

1972 The UK's National Union of Mineworkers went on strike for the first time since 1926, bringing blackouts, candles and power cuts across the country.

1972 The first *Queen Elizabeth* liner was burnt out in Hong Kong harbour.

1986 British Defence Secretary Michael Heseltine (born 1933) resigned from office over a political disagreement that became known as the Westland Affair.

1997 Tony Bullimore, a participant in the Vendée Globe single-handed non-stop round-the-world yacht race, was rescued after five days in the hull of his capsized boat in the Southern Ocean.

10 January

On 10 January 1979, returning to London from a four-nation summit in Guadeloupe, Prime Minister James Callaghan (born 1912) was met at the airport by reporters who questioned him about the industrial unrest that was causing increasing disruption to British lives and businesses. His reply, 'I don't think other people in the world would share the view [that] there is mounting chaos', was immortalized as 'Crisis? What crisis?' in the headline of *The Sun* newspaper the following day.

The situation rapidly deteriorated into what became known as the Winter of Discontent, with widespread strikes affecting key services, and the days of the Labour government were numbered. On 28 March 1979, Callaghan lost a vote of no confidence brought by Margaret Thatcher (born 1925); five weeks later, the Conservatives came to power.

On this day:

Born: German astronomer Simon Marius (1570); Danish physician, naturalist and theologian Nicolaus Steno (1638); Scottish jurist Thomas Erskine (1750); English sculptor Dame Barbara Hepworth (1903); US astrophysicist and Nobel Prize winner Robert Woodrow Wilson (1936)

Died: Swedish naturalist and physician Carolus Linnaeus (1778); English novelist and dramatist Mary Russell Mitford (1855);

US firearms manufacturer Samuel Colt (1862); US crime writer Dashiell Hammett (1961); French couturier Coco Chanel (1971)

1645 Archbishop of Canterbury William Laud (1573–1645) was beheaded for treason.

1863 The first section of the London Underground, between Paddington and Farringdon, was opened to passengers.

1906 The first two-way transatlantic radio telegraphy transmission took place between the National Electric Signalling Company stations at Brant Rock, Massachusetts, USA, and Machrihanish in Scotland.

1920 The League of Nations came into being through the Treaty of Versailles.

1929 The comic-strip character Tintin first appeared in the children's supplement of the newspaper *Le Vingtième Siècle*; Tintin was created by Belgian cartoonist Hergé (1907–83).

1957 Harold Macmillan (1894–1986) began his first term as the UK's prime minister.

1968 John Gorton (1911–2002) became the Australian prime minister.

1984 For the first time in over 100 years, the USA and the Vatican established full diplomatic relations.

1990 China's premier Li Peng (born 1928) lifted martial law, which had been imposed in May 1989.

2003 North Korea withdrew from a global treaty barring it from manufacturing nuclear weapons.

11 January

Since the loss of eleven days in the calendar reform of 1752, 11 January has been celebrated as 'Old New Year's Eve' in the Scottish village of Burghead on the Moray Firth with a ceremony known as the **Burning of the Clavie**, a fire festival that is thought to be of ancient pagan origin. The 'clavie' is a blazing tar barrel carried on a pole through the streets of the village by the Clavie King and his assistants, who present smouldering faggots as tokens of

good fortune to selected householders along the way. The procession ends at the top of Doorie Hill, where the clavie is set down on a stone pillar, its flames fuelled by extra tar or creosote, and eventually collapses. The onlookers stay to watch it burn out, scramble for the lucky embers scattered over the hillside, then disperse to continue their celebrations in the traditional manner.

On this day:

Born: Italian painter of the Lombard school Parmigianino (1503); Scottish-born Canadian statesman Sir John Macdonald (1815); US-born British department store founder Harry Gordon Selfridge (1858); South African writer and educator Alan Paton (1903); English trade union leader Arthur Scargill (1938)

Died: Italian painter Domenico Ghirlandaio (1494); German physiologist Theodor Schwann (1882); English novelist, poet and dramatist Thomas Hardy (1928); Irish poet and playwright Pádraic Colum (1972); English actor Michael Williams (2001)

1569 The prize draw for Britain's first national lottery was held at St Paul's Cathedral, London, with all proceeds going to fund public works.

1866 The Australian steamer *London*, en route to Melbourne, sank in the Bay of Biscay with the loss of 220 lives.

1922 In Canada, insulin was successfully used to treat a diabetic patient – 14-year-old Leonard Thompson – for the first time.

1935 US aviator Amelia Earhart (1897–1937) began the trip from Hawaii to California that would make her the first woman to fly solo across the Pacific Ocean.

1946 In the absence of King Zog I (1895–1961), Albania was declared a republic by General Enver Hoxha (1908–85).

1954 At 7:55pm, 32-year-old George Cowling of the Meteorological Office became the first weatherman to appear on BBC television.

1962 An estimated 4,000 people were killed when a huge avalanche in the Andes, Peru, buried the village of Ranrahirca and eight other settlements.

1963 The first discotheque, the Whisky-A-Go-Go, opened in Los Angeles, California, USA.

1973 The first graduates of the Open University were awarded their degrees.

1974 The world's first surviving sextuplets were born to the Rosenkowitz family in Cape Town, South Africa.

1981 A British team led by Ranulph Fiennes (born 1944) completed the longest and fastest crossing of Antarctica to date.

1996 Ryutaro Hashimoto (born 1937) was elected as Japan's new prime minister, following the resignation of previous premier Murayama Tomiichi (born 1924).

2000 The *Solway Harvester* dredger sank in a storm off the Isle of Man, drowning its crew of seven fishermen.

2003 Two days before leaving office, Illinois governor George Ryan (born 1934) commuted or overturned the sentences of all 167 inmates on death row in his state.

12 January

The American revolutionary and political leader John Hancock was born in Massachusetts on this day in 1739. After graduating from Harvard he worked for a Boston mercantile house owned by his uncle and inherited the business, together with a large fortune, on his uncle's death in 1764. He became involved with the revolutionary movement in the early 1770s and served as president of the Continental Congress from 1775 to 1777.

Hancock was the first person to sign the Declaration of Independence; writing his name in large, bold letters, he allegedly remarked, 'There, I guess King George will be able to read that.' (The phrase *John Hancock* subsequently became a US colloquial term for a signature.) He was elected governor of Massachusetts in 1780 and died during his ninth term of office in 1793.

On this day:

Born: English colonialist and Governor of Massachusetts John Winthrop (1588); French inventor and engineer Jean Joseph Étienne Lenoir (1822); US writer Jack London (1876); US businessman Jeff Bezos (1964)

Died: Holy Roman Emperor Maximilian I (1519); French mathematician Pierre de Fermat (1665); English novelist Nevil

Shute (1960); US lawyer and politician Cyrus Vance (2002); English pop singer with the Bee Gees Maurice Gibb (2003)

1866 The Royal Aeronautical Society was inaugurated as the Aeronautical Society of Great Britain.

1879 The Zulu War, between the British forces of the Cape Colony and the people of Zululand, began.

1895 The National Trust (originally conceived as the 'National Trust for Places of Historic Interest or Natural Beauty') was founded.

1906 The British Liberal Party, led by Henry Campbell-Bannerman (1836–1908) swept to power in its biggest election landslide ever, and ushered in a period of great social and progressive legislation.

1915 A proposal to give women the right to vote was rejected by the US Senate.

1932 Hattie W Caraway (1878–1950), an Arkansas Democrat, became the first woman elected to the US Senate.

1954 Queen Elizabeth II (born 1926) opened the New Zealand parliament, the first time a reigning monarch had done so in the country's history.

1957 Elvis Presley (1935–77) recorded 'All Shook Up' in a studio in California, USA.

1964 The Sultan of Zanzibar was banished in a rebellion, and the country became a republic.

1970 The Boeing 747 'jumbo' jet aircraft landed at London's Heathrow airport, completing its first transatlantic flight from New York City, USA.

1971 Anarchist group The Angry Brigade were responsible for the explosion of two bombs outside the Hertfordshire home of Employment Secretary Robert Carr.

1982 Mark Thatcher (born 1953), son of the British prime minister Margaret Thatcher (born 1925), lost his way and was missing for two days in the Sahara desert whilst competing in the Paris–Dakar Car Rally.

1991 The US Congress authorized President George Bush (born 1924) to use military power to expel Iraqi troops from Kuwait, precipitating the start of the Gulf War.

13 January

Feast day of **St Hilary**, Bishop of Poitiers in the mid-fourth century AD, after whom the Hilary term in some universities and lawcourts is named.

On this day:

Born: German physicist and Nobel Prize winner Wilhelm Wien (1864); US singer and vaudeville entertainer Sophie Tucker (1884); English children's author Michael Bond (1926); English actor Orlando Bloom (1977)

Died: English poet Edmund Spenser (1599); English religious leader and founder of the Society of Friends George Fox (1691); Irish writer and poet James Joyce (1941); English GP and mass murderer Dr Harold Shipman (2004)

1873 The UK's first dynamite factory began production at Ardeer in Scotland.

1893 The Independent Labour Party was formed at Bradford, Yorkshire, and led by Keir Hardie (1856–1915).

1898 Émile Zola's (1840–1902) defence of Captain Alfred Dreyfus (c.1859–1935), entitled 'J'accuse', was published in Paris.

1910 The first live radio broadcast of an opera was from New York City's Metropolitan Opera, with Italian tenor Enrico Caruso (1873–1921) singing *Cavalleria Rusticana* and *Pagliacci*.

1964 Breakthrough Beatles record 'I Want to Hold Your Hand' topped the charts in the USA.

1972 An army commander seized control of Ghana in a bloodless coup while the Ghanaian prime minister, Dr Kofi Busia (1913–78), was receiving medical treatment in London.

1982 A Boeing 737 aircraft crashed into a bridge over the Potomac River in Washington, DC, killing 78 people.

1990 Democrat Douglas Wilder (born 1931) of Virginia became the USA's first elected black governor.

1993 Former East German leader Erich Honecker (1912–94), who was awaiting trial on charges of manslaughter, was released from his Berlin prison on grounds of ill health and fled to Chile.

1993 US, British and French aircraft carried out bombing raids on Iraqi missile sites and radar installations in response to Iraqi incursions along the border with Kuwait.

2001 An earthquake in El Salvador, measuring 7.6 on the Richter scale, killed more than 800 people.

14 January

The 14th of January is celebrated in All Souls College, Oxford, by a great merrymaking, in commemoration of the finding of an overgrown mallard in a drain, when they were digging a foundation for the college buildings, anno 1437 … We obtain no particulars of the merrymaking beyond a quaint song said to have been long sung on the occasion:

THE MERRY OLD SONG OF THE ALL SOULS' MALLARD.

Griffin, bustard, turkey, capon,
Let other hungry mortals gape on;
And on the bones their stomach fall hard,
But let All Souls' men have their mallard.
Oh! by the blood of King Edward,
Oh! by the blood of King Edward,
It was a wopping, wopping mallard.

…

Therefore let us sing and dance a galliard,
To the remembrance of the mallard:
And as the mallard dives in pool,
Let us dabble, dive, and duck in bowl.
Oh! by the blood of King Edward,
Oh! by the blood of King Edward,
It was a wopping, wopping mallard.

Chambers Book of Days (1864).

14 January

The boisterous torchlit duck-hunt that formerly took place annually on **Mallard Day** is now restricted to the first year of every century. In other years the occasion is celebrated in a more subdued manner with the traditional song, the words of which have undergone some amendment over the centuries. It is thought that the original 'mallard' may simply have been the seal of a certain clerk named William Mallard, found by medieval workmen at the site.

On this day:

Born: Italian jurist and writer Alberico Gentili (1552); Alsatian medical missionary, theologian, musician, philosopher and Nobel Prize winner Albert Schweitzer (1875); English stage director Trevor Nunn (1940); US actress Faye Dunaway (1941)

Died: English astronomer and mathematician Edmond Halley (1742); English children's writer and mathematician Lewis Carroll (1898); US film actor Humphrey Bogart (1957); French-born US writer Anaïs Nin (1977); English educationalist and consumer protection pioneer Lord Young (2002)

1604 The Hampton Court Conference, intended to settle differences between leading Anglicans and Puritans, opened at Richmond-upon-Thames, London; it eventually led to the preparation of the King James Bible.

1797 Napoleon I (1769–1821) defeated the Austrian army at the Battle of Rivoli.

1858 Italian patriot and revolutionary Felice Orsini (1819–58) and three fellow conspirators threw bombs in an attempt to assassinate Napoleon III (1808–73); they failed, although 156 bystanders were injured by the blasts.

1878 At Osborne House on the Isle of Wight, Queen Victoria (1819–1901) witnessed a demonstration of the newly-invented telephone.

1896 The first public screening of a motion picture was given by the Royal Photographic Society in London.

1900 The opera *Tosca*, by Giacomo Puccini (1858–1924), had its première at the Teatro Constanzi in Rome, Italy, the setting for the drama.

1907 An earthquake in Kingston, the capital of Jamaica, destroyed the city and killed over 1,000 people.

1943 World War II – the Casablanca Conference on strategy took place between British Prime Minister Winston Churchill (1874–1965) and US President Franklin D Roosevelt (1882–1945).

1953 Josip Broz Tito (1892–1980) was elected president of the new Yugoslav Republic by the country's parliament.

1954 Baseball player Joe DiMaggio (1914–99) married film star Marilyn Monroe (1926–62) in San Francisco, California, USA.

1969 Solo space mission Soyuz 4 was launched by the USSR.

1975 Seventeen-year-old Lesley Whittle was abducted from her home by Donald Neilson (born 1936).

1994 The Duchess of Kent (born 1933) became the first member of the Royal Family to convert to Catholicism in over 300 years.

15 January

On this day:

Born: French journalist and political theorist Pierre Joseph Proudhon (1809); Hungarian-born US physicist Edward Teller (1908); US actor Lloyd Bridges (1913); Egyptian statesman Gamel Abd al-Nasser (1918); US clergyman, civil rights leader and Nobel Prize winner Martin Luther King, Jnr (1929)

Died: English mistress of Lord Nelson, Emma, Lady Hamilton (1815); German Communist leader Rosa Luxemburg (1919); Lesotho king Moshoeshoe II (1996)

AD 69 Roman emperor Servius Sulpicius Galba (born 3 BC) was assassinated by the praetorian guard in the Roman Forum.

1535 Under the Act of Supremacy, King Henry VIII (1491–1547) became Supreme Head of the Church of England.

1559 The coronation of Queen Elizabeth I (1533–1601) took place in Westminster Abbey, London.

1759 The British Museum in London opened to the public.

1880 The first British telephone directory was published with over 255 names covering three London exchanges.

1927 The BBC broadcast a rugby match between England and Wales from Twickenham, the first running commentary on a sporting event.

1934 Radio Luxembourg began broadcasting, the first commercial radio station available in the UK.

1943 The Pentagon, the USA's defence headquarters building, was completed.

1967 In the USA the first Super Bowl final was won by the Green Bay Packers.

1973 Following peace talks in Paris, President Richard Nixon (1913–94) ordered a halt to the US bombing of North Vietnam.

16 January

On this day:

Born: French tyre manufacturer André Michelin (1853); US actress and singer Ethel Merman (1909); US zoologist Dian Fossey (1932); US writer and critic Susan Sontag (1933)

Died: English historian Edward Gibbon (1794); Italian composer Amilcare Ponchielli (1886); US actress Carole Lombard (1942); English journalist and novelist Auberon Waugh (2001); Congolese politician Laurent Kabila (2001)

1547 Ivan the Terrible (1530–84) assumed power, becoming the first ruler of Russia to adopt the title of 'tsar'.

1661 King Charles II (1630–85) appointed Henry Bishop as the first Postmaster General; Bishop used postmarks for the first time.

1780 British admiral George Rodney (1718–92) relieved Gibraltar when he defeated a Spanish squadron off Cape St Vincent.

1883 In the USA, the Pendleton Civil Service Reform Act provided for the open selection of government employees and guaranteed the right of

citizens to compete for federal appointment without regard to politics, religion, race or national origin.

1909 The Antarctic expedition led by British explorer Ernest Shackleton (1874–1922) successfully reached the South Pole.

1920 The 18th (or Prohibition) Amendment came into force in the USA, making the sale of alcohol illegal.

1929 *The Listener* was first published in the UK.

1943 World War II – the Royal Air Force carried out the first air raid on Berlin.

1944 World War II – US general Dwight D Eisenhower (1890–1969) was appointed Supreme Commander of the Allied Forces in Europe.

1957 The Cavern Club, later famous for its association with the Beatles, opened in Liverpool, England.

1969 Philosophy student Jan Palach (1948–69) set fire to himself in Wenceslas Square in Prague, in protest at the Soviet invasion of Czechoslovakia; he died five days later, and was mourned by thousands.

1979 The Shah of Iran (1919–80) and his family fled their country for exile in Egypt.

1981 Irish political activist and MP Bernadette McAliskey (born 1947) and her husband were shot in their home in an assassination attempt.

2001 The oil tanker *Jessica* ran aground off the island of San Cristobal in the Galapagos Islands; it went on to leak thousands of gallons of oil.

17 January

This is **St Antony's Day**, the feast day of St Antony (or Anthony) of Egypt, remembered for the temptations he suffered during his 20 years of solitude in the desert, which were vividly depicted by the 15th-century Dutch painter Hieronymus Bosch and the 19th-century French writer Gustave Flaubert, among others. He is regarded as the father of monasticism, having founded various communities of hermits in the latter part of his very long life (c.251–356 AD). In 1089, several centuries after his death, he was credited with preventing a serious epidemic of erysipelas by curing sufferers who visited his shrine; this inflammatory skin disease subsequently became known as 'St Antony's fire'.

17 January

The patron saint of domestic animals, especially pigs, St Antony has a pig and a bell as his emblems – the smallest pig (ie the runt) of a litter is sometimes called a 'tantony pig' and the smallest bell in a church tower a 'tantony bell'. In 1998, a famous pair of runaway pigs had particular cause to celebrate on St Antony's Day. Dubbed the Tamworth Two (because of their breed) and nicknamed Butch and Sundance (because of their behaviour), they had escaped from the abattoir more than a week earlier and managed to evade capture for several days. Pursued by the media, the fugitives soon became national heroes and the *Daily Mail* bought exclusive rights to their story. Butch was cornered on 15 January and Sundance the following afternoon, but their courage and popularity had won them a reprieve: their death sentence was commuted to life imprisonment in comfortable surroundings at the Rare Breeds Centre in Kent.

On this day:

Born: German botanist after whom the fuchsia was named Leonhard Fuchs (1501); Spanish dramatist Pedro Calderón de la Barca (1600); English poet and novelist Anne Brontë (1820); Welsh statesman David Lloyd George, 1st Earl Lloyd-George of Dwyfor (1863); US boxer Muhammad Ali (1942)

Died: Thai conjoined twins Eng and Chang Bunker (1874); 19th President of the USA Rutherford B Hayes (1893); English philanthropist Quintin Hogg (1903); US Beat poet Gregory Corso (2001); Spanish novelist and Nobel Prize winner Camilo José Cela (2002)

1377 The Papal See returned from Avignon, France, to Rome, Italy.

1746 The Jacobites defeated the English government troops at the Battle of Falkirk.

1773 Captain James Cook (1728–79) became the first person to cross the Antarctic Circle in his ship *Resolution*.

1852 The Sand River Convention brought agreement between the British and the Boers, giving the latter the right to manage their own affairs in the Transvaal; in effect, it established the South African Republic.

1893 A revolution took place in Hawaii as a group of sugar planters and businessmen forced Queen Liliuokalani (1838–1917) to abdicate.

1916 The Professional Golfers Association (PGA) was founded in the USA.

1929 The character of Popeye first appeared in the comic strip 'Thimble Theatre' by Elzie Segar (1894–1938).

1977 Murderer Gary Gilmore (1940–77) became the first person to be executed in the USA after the reinstatement of the death penalty in 1976.

1983 The BBC transmitted the UK's first breakfast television programme, fronted by Frank Bough (born 1933) and Selina Scott (born 1951).

1991 Operation Desert Storm began as Gulf War allies mounted a missile attack on Iraq in order to liberate Kuwait.

1994 A State of Emergency was declared in Los Angeles, California, following an earthquake which measured 6.6 on the Richter scale.

1995 A massive earthquake measuring 7.2 on the Richter scale hit the city of Kobe, Japan.

1997 Israel handed over its military headquarters in Hebron to the Palestinians and withdrew from the West Bank city, bringing its 30-year occupation to a close.

18 January

When I was One,
I had just begun.

When I was Two,
I was nearly new.

When I was Three,
I was hardly Me.

When I was Four,
I was not much more.

When I was Five,
I was just alive.

But now I am Six, I'm as clever as clever.
So I think I'll be six now for ever and ever.

A A Milne, *Now We Are Six*, 'The End' (1927).

18 January

Alan Alexander Milne (who died in 1956) was born in London on this day in 1882. After graduating from Cambridge University he worked as assistant editor of *Punch* magazine and wrote a number of successful light comedies, such as *Mr Pim Passes By* (1919) and *The Dover Road* (1922). In the 1920s he began writing poems and stories for his young son, Christopher Robin, creating characters (based on the boy's soft toys) that were to win the hearts and minds of generations of children worldwide. Winnie-the-Pooh and his friends (Eeyore the donkey, Piglet, Kanga, Roo, Rabbit, Owl, Tigger, etc) went on to star in a number of Disney films, but for many people the 'real' characters are those depicted in E H Shephard's 'decorations' for A A Milne's four original books: *When We Were Very Young* (1924), *Winnie-the-Pooh* (1926), *Now We Are Six* (1927) and *The House at Pooh Corner* (1928).

On 18 January each year, some fans celebrate A A Milne's birthday as **Pooh Day**, with appropriate songs and games – notably Poohsticks, which involves dropping sticks from the upstream side of a bridge then running to the downstream side to see which one appears first:

> *So the next time he dropped one big one and one little one, and the big one came out first, which was what he had said it would do, and the little one came out last, which was what he had said it would do, so he had won twice … And that was the beginning of the game called Poohsticks, which Pooh invented, and which he and his friends used to play on the edge of the Forest.*
>
> A A Milne, *The House at Pooh Corner* (1928).

On this day:

Born: English physician, scholar and thesaurus creator Peter Mark Roget (1779); Australian statesman and first prime minister Sir Edmund Barton (1849); British-born US actor Cary Grant (1904); Australian politician Paul Keating (1944)

Died: Tenth President of the USA John Tyler (1862); English writer and Nobel Prize winner Rudyard Kipling (1936); English politician Hugh Gaitskell (1963); English photographer and designer Sir Cecil Beaton (1980)

1486 First Tudor King of England Henry VII (1457–1509) married Elizabeth of York, the eldest daughter of Edward IV (1442–83).

1778 English navigator Captain James Cook (1728–79) discovered the Hawaiian islands.

1788 English naval commander Arthur Phillip (1738–1814) landed at Botany Bay in Australia, and went on to establish the country's first penal colony at Port Jackson.

1879 The first edition of *The Boy's Own Paper* was published in the UK.

1912 English explorer Captain Scott (1868–1912) and four other members of his expedition reached the South Pole one month after Norwegian Roald Amundsen (1872–1928).

1919 The Paris Peace Conference opened – a meeting of 32 'allied and associated powers' to draw up a peace settlement after World War I.

1943 World War II – the breaking of the long Nazi siege of Leningrad was announced by the Soviets.

1967 Jeremy Thorpe (born 1929) was elected leader of the British Liberal Party.

1993 For the first time, all 50 states of the USA observed the Martin Luther King, Jnr holiday.

19 January

On this day:

Born: Scottish engineer and inventor James Watt (1736); US Confederate general Robert E Lee (1807); French painter Paul Cézanne (1839); English novelist Nina Bawden (1925); English conductor Sir Simon Rattle (1955)

Died: German poet and dramatist Hans Sachs (1576); Austrian-born US actress Hedy Lamarr (2000); Italian politician Bettino Craxi (2000); French journalist, feminist, broadcaster and politician Françoise Giroud (2003)

1809 Scottish soldier John Moore (1761–1809) led his army to triumph over French forces in a desperate battle at La Coruña, but was mortally wounded at the moment of victory.

1853 The opera *Il Trovatore*, by Giuseppe Verdi (1813–1901), had its première at the Teatro Apollo, Rome, Italy.

1915 Neon-tube lighting for signs and advertisements was patented by the French chemist and physicist Georges Claude (1870–1960).

1937 US millionaire businessman, film producer, director and aviator Howard Hughes (1905–76) set a transcontinental air record with a monoplane flight from Los Angeles, California to Newark, New Jersey.

1958 English explorer and scientist Vivian Fuchs (1908–99) reached the South Pole.

1966 Indira Gandhi (1917–84) became prime minister of India, following in the footsteps of her father Jawaharlal Nehru (1889–1964).

1987 Disabled author Christopher Nolan (born 1965) won the Whitbread Book Award for *Under the Eye of the Clock*.

1997 Palestinian resistance leader Yasser Arafat (born 1929) returned to the city of Hebron for the first time in over 30 years.

2001 US President Bill Clinton (born 1946), on his last day in office, publicly admitted that he had lied under oath about his affair with White House intern Monica Lewinsky (born 1973).

20 January

St. Agnes' Eve – Ah, bitter chill it was!
The owl, for all his feathers, was a-cold;
The hare limped trembling through the frozen grass,
And silent was the flock in woolly fold.
. . .
They told her how, upon St. Agnes' Eve,
Young virgins might have visions of delight

And soft adorings from their loves receive
Upon the honey'd middle of the night,
If ceremonies due they did aright;

> *As, supperless to bed they must retire,*
> *And couch supine their beauties, lily white;*
> *Nor look behind, nor sideways, but require*
> *Of Heaven with upward eyes for all that they desire.*
>
> John Keats, *Lamia, Isabella, The Eve of St. Agnes and Other Poems*, 'The Eve of St. Agnes' (1820).

This is **St Agnes's Eve**, probably more famous than the saint's feast day itself thanks to Keats's poem. It was a day on which girls and unmarried women who wished to dream of their future husbands would perform certain rituals before retiring for the night. These included transferring pins one by one from a pincushion to their sleeve while reciting the Lord's Prayer, or abstaining from food and drink all day, walking backwards up the stairs to bed, and eating a portion of **dumb cake** (previously prepared with a group of friends in total silence, and often containing an unpleasantly large proportion of salt) before lying down to sleep.

St Agnes, patron saint of virgins, was martyred in the early fourth century AD at the tender age of 12 or 13, apparently for refusing to consider marriage (unlike the superstitious females mentioned above) and consecrating her maidenhood to God. Her emblem is a lamb, perhaps because of the similarity of its Latin name, *agnus*, to her own.

On this day:

Born: American Revolutionary leader Richard Henry Lee (1732); Danish novelist, essayist, poet and Nobel Prize winner Johannes Jensen (1873); US comedian George Burns (1896); Italian film director Federico Fellini (1920); US astronaut 'Buzz' Aldrin (1930)

Died: English architect Sir John Soane (1837); French painter Jean François Millet (1875); British king George V (1936); Romanian-born US swimmer and actor Johnny Weissmuller (1984); Scottish footballer and football manager Sir Matt Busby (1994)

1265 Britain's first parliament assembled at Westminster Hall, London, convened by Simon de Montfort (c.1208–1265).

1649 King Charles I (1600–49) was charged with high treason.

1778 English navigator Captain James Cook (1728–79) became the first known European to land on islands he named the Sandwich Islands, in honour of the Earl of Sandwich (1718–92).

1840 A uniform penny postage rate was introduced in the UK; postage rates were now calculated on the weight of the letter rather than the distance it was being sent, with a minimum charge of one penny.

1936 King Edward VIII (1894–1972) succeeded his father on the British throne; he abdicated on 11 December.

1937 Franklin D Roosevelt (1882–1945) began his record fourth term as president of the USA.

1961 John F Kennedy (1917–63) was sworn in as the first Roman Catholic president of the USA.

1972 Unemployment in the UK rose to 1,023,583, crossing the one million mark for the first time in almost 40 years.

1981 The Iran Hostage Crisis ended as Ronald Reagan (1911–2004) was inaugurated as US President; Iran released the US hostages who had been held since 4 November 1979 when the US embassy in Tehran was seized by a mob. They had been in captivity for 444 days.

1987 English religious adviser Terry Waite (born 1939), special envoy of the Archbishop of Canterbury, disappeared in Beirut, Lebanon; Waite was held hostage by an Islamic militia group for almost five years.

21 January

> *While the State exists, there can be no freedom. When there is freedom there will be no State.*
>
> Lenin, *State and Revolution* (1919).

Lenin, the first head of government of the USSR, died on this day in 1924. His body was embalmed and displayed for public veneration in Moscow's Red Square and on 24 January 1924 the city of St Petersburg was renamed Leningrad in his honour until the fall of the USSR in the 1990s.

Born Vladimir Ilyich Ulyanov in 1870, he was a student of Karl Marx's theory of scientific socialism, from which he developed his own version,

subsequently known as Leninism. Arrested for his revolutionary opinions and activities, he spent several years in exile, returning to Russia at the time of the unsuccessful uprising of 1905. After a further period in exile, he led the Bolsheviks to power in the Russian Revolution of October 1917, which overthrew the provisional government set up earlier that year and paved the way for the establishment of the USSR in 1922.

On this day:

Born: French couturier Christian Dior (1905); English actor Paul Scofield (1922); US golfer Jack Nicklaus (1940); Spanish tenor Placido Domingo (1941)

Died: US inventor Elisha Gray (1901); English biographer Lytton Strachey (1932); English novelist and essayist George Orwell (1950); US singer-songwriter and actress Peggy Lee (2002)

1793 King Louis XVI (1754–93) was guillotined in Paris, ending 1,025 years of monarchy in France.

1911 The first Monte Carlo Car Rally was held in the south of France.

1954 The first nuclear-powered submarine, the *Nautilus*, was launched in the USA.

1976 The first commercial Concorde flights were made when the British Airways plane flew from London, UK, to Bahrain, and the Air France plane from Paris, France, to Rio de Janeiro, Brazil.

1976 Western newspapers went on sale in the USSR for the first time.

1977 US President Jimmy Carter (born 1924) issued pardons to the majority of those who had evaded the Vietnam War draft.

1998 Pope John Paul II (born 1920) visited Cuba for the first time.

22 January

> *Remember on St Vincent's Day,*
> *If the sun his beams display,*
> *Be sure to mark the transient beam,*
> *Which through the casement sheds a gleam,*
> *For 'tis a token bright and clear*
> *Of prosperous weather all the year.*
>
> Traditional rhyme.

This is the feast day of St Vincent of Saragossa, the first Spanish martyr, who died in the early fourth century AD (after enduring a variety of tortures without complaint, according to legend). The weather on **St Vincent's Day** is used in amateur forecasting and divination: wind and sun on 22 January are favourable omens for the coming year's crops of grain and grape.

On this day:

Born: French mathematician and physicist André Marie Ampère (1775); English–Scottish poet Lord Byron (1788); Swedish dramatist and novelist August Strindberg (1849); English actor John Hurt (1940)

Died: British queen Victoria (1901); 36th President of the USA Lyndon B Johnson (1973); US food critic and cookery writer Craig Claiborne (2000); English sculptor Kenneth Armitage (2002)

1840 The first British colonists reached Port Nicholson in New Zealand.

1879 The Battle of Rorke's Drift began in southern Africa between British troops and local Zulu soldiers.

1924 Ramsay MacDonald (1866–1937) became the UK's first Labour prime minister.

1944 Word War II – Allied forces landed at Anzio on Italy's western coast.

1973 The US Supreme Court legalized abortion in its historic but controversial *Roe* vs *Wade* decision.

1980 Soviet physicist, dissident and Nobel Prize winner Andrei Sakharov (1921–89) was sent into internal exile in the 'closed city' of Gorky (now Nizhny Novgorod); he was eventually released in 1986 under the personal orders of President Mikhail Gorbachev (born 1931).

1998 On the first day of his trial, the so-called 'Unabomber' Theodore Kaczynski (born 1942) pleaded guilty, thus escaping a possible death sentence but agreeing that he would be jailed for life without parole.

23 January

William Pitt (the Younger) died on this day in 1806, apparently with the words, 'Oh, my country! how I leave my country!', although the first edition of the source from which this line was taken had 'love' in place of 'leave', while popular tradition maintains that the great statesman's last utterance was far more prosaic: 'I think I could eat one of Bellamy's veal pies'.

Pitt was born in 1759, the son of William Pitt, 1st Earl of Chatham, known as Pitt the Elder (1708–78). He entered Parliament in 1781, was appointed Chancellor of the Exchequer the following year, and became prime minister at the age of 24, the youngest person to hold this office in British history. Notable achievements of his first premiership included a reduction in the national debt, the passing of a series of acts reforming the administration of India (1784, 1786, 1793), and the union of Britain and Ireland in 1800. He resigned in 1801 but returned three years later in the face of the increasing threat posed by Napoleon I (1769–1821); the greatest triumph of his second term of office was the British victory at the Battle of Trafalgar on 21 October 1805, just three months before his death.

On this day:

Born: French painter Édouard Manet (1832); German physicist Ernst Abbe (1840); Belgian guitarist Django Reinhardt (1910); French actress and director Jeanne Moreau (1928); Dutch actor Rutger Hauer (1944)

Died: English navigator William Baffin (1622); Italian historical philosopher Giambattista Vico (1744); English writer Charles

Kingsley (1875); Russian ballerina Anna Pavlova (1931); German-born Australian photographer Helmut Newton (2004)

1668 A Triple Alliance was agreed between the Dutch Republic, England and Sweden against France.

1849 Elizabeth Blackwell (1821–1910) became the first woman doctor in the USA.

1933 The 20th Amendment to the US Constitution was ratified – moving the date of the presidential inauguration to 20 January.

1964 The 24th Amendment to the US Constitution was ratified – eliminating tax as a prerequisite for voting.

1973 A ceasefire agreement was signed in Paris, bringing the Vietnam War to an end; the ceasefire took effect at midnight on 27 January.

1980 US President Jimmy Carter (born 1924) announced the Carter Doctrine, a statement that the oil reserves in the Persian Gulf were of vital interest to the USA and that any attempt by an outside nation to take the region would be met by US military intervention.

1983 The Soviet satellite Cosmos 1402 re-entered the Earth's atmosphere, crashing into the Indian Ocean.

1997 US diplomat Madeleine Albright (born 1937) was sworn in as Secretary of State; she was the first woman to hold that office, making her the highest-ranking woman in the history of the US government.

24 January

On this day:

Born: English dramatist and poet William Congreve (1670); Prussian king Frederick II, known as Frederick the Great (1712); US novelist and short-story writer Edith Wharton (1862); US actor Ernest Borgnine (1917); English ethnologist and writer Desmond Morris (1928)

Died: English politician Lord Randolph Churchill (1895); Italian painter and sculptor Amedeo Modigliani (1920); English statesman and Nobel Prize winner Sir Winston Churchill (1965); US film director George D Cukor (1983)

AD 41 Roman emperor Caligula (AD 12–41) was assassinated.

661 Caliph Ali, son-in-law of the prophet Muhammad, was murdered in the mosque in Kufa, Iraq.

1679 King Charles II (1630–85) dissolved the Cavalier Parliament.

1848 Gold was discovered by James W Marshall (1810–85) at Sutter's Mill near Coloma, California, USA, precipitating the Gold Rush of 1849.

1908 English soldier Robert Baden-Powell (1857–1941) organized England's first Boy Scout troop.

1946 A United Nations resolution establishing the Atomic Energy Commission was passed.

1989 US serial killer Ted Bundy (1946–89) was executed in Florida, USA.

2003 In the USA, the new Department of Homeland Security officially came into being as Tom Ridge (born 1945) was sworn in as its first Secretary; its creation was described as the 'most significant transformation of the US government since 1947'.

25 January

Robert Burns, the Scottish poet, first saw the light on the 25th January 1759 in a small cottage by the wayside near the Bridge of Doon, two miles from Ayr. A wonderful destiny was that of the peasant's babe born that day – a life of toil, imprudence, poverty, closed in early death, but to be followed by an afflatus of popular admiration and sympathy such as never before nor since attended a literary name in any country. The strains of Burns touch all hearts. He has put words together, as scarcely any writer ever did before him. His name has become a stenograph for a whole system of national feelings and predilections.

Chambers Book of Days (1864).

25 January

The birthday of Robert Burns (1759–96) on 25 January is celebrated by people of Scottish descent all over the world. The central attraction of the **Burns Night** festivities is a traditional **Burns Supper** of haggis (a dish made of the heart, lungs and liver of a sheep or calf, chopped up with suet, onions and oatmeal and traditionally boiled in a sheep's stomach-bag) served with tatties and neeps (potatoes and mashed swede). The meal begins with the 'Selkirk Grace', a short rhyme of unknown authorship: 'Some hae meat and canna eat / And some wad eat that want it; / But we hae meat and we can eat, / And sae the Lord be thankit.' The company then stand to 'receive the haggis', as it is ceremoniously piped into the room and set down in front of the chief guest, who recites Burns's poem 'To a Haggis'.

> *Fair fa' your honest, sonsie face,*
> *Great Chieftain o' the Puddin-race!*
> *Aboon them a' ye tak your place,*
> *Painch, tripe, or thairm:*
> *Weel are ye wordy of a grace*
> *As lang's my arm.*
>
> Robert Burns, 'To a Haggis' (1786).

When the speaker reaches the line, 'an cut you up wi' ready slight' the haggis is slit open from end to end. After toasting the haggis with a dram of whisky, the diners tuck in. Further toasts and speeches follow the meal, and the merrymaking continues with poems and songs, notably 'Auld Lang Syne'.

On this day:

Born: Irish physicist and chemist Robert Boyle (1627); French mathematician Joseph Louis Lagrange (1736); English novelist, critic and essayist Virginia Woolf (1882); Philippine politician Cory Aquino (1933)

Died: US gangster Al Capone (1947); Soviet politician Mikhail Suslov (1982); US film actress Ava Gardner (1990); Dutch athlete Fanny Blankers-Koen (2004)

1533 Anne Boleyn (1501–36) was secretly married to King Henry VIII (1491–1547).

1817 The première of the comic opera *La Cenerentola*, by Gioacchino Rossini (1792–1868), was held in Rome, Italy.

1919 As part of the Treaty of Versailles, the League of Nations (the

forerunner of the United Nations) was established, with the UK, France, Italy and Japan as its four permanent members.

1924 The first Winter Olympics were opened at Chamonix, France, with 16 competing nations.

1949 In the USA, the first Emmy Awards were presented.

1959 Pope John XXIII (1881–1963) forecast the first Ecumenical Council since 1870, known as Vatican II.

1971 General Idi Amin (1925–2003) deposed Milton Obote (born 1924) as president of Uganda in a military coup.

1981 The 'Gang of Four' – ex-Labour cabinet ministers Roy Jenkins (1920–2003), Shirley Williams (born 1930), David Owen (born 1938) and William Rodgers (born 1928) – unveiled the Limehouse Declaration, which paved the way for the formation of the Social Democratic Party.

1999 An earthquake measuring 6 on the Richter scale struck Colombia, leaving 1,000 people dead and thousands more injured.

26 January

This is **Australia Day**, a public holiday throughout that country, commemorating the foundation of the first colony of European settlers at Port Jackson (now Sydney, capital of New South Wales) on 26 January 1788. The immigrants, mainly convicts, had travelled from England in a fleet of eleven ships under the command of Captain Arthur Phillip, who subsequently became the founder and first governor of New South Wales.

Australia Day is celebrated with various festivities, including the presentation of community awards, ceremonies at which new citizens are formally welcomed to the country, and a wide range of local events. Formerly known as Foundation Day, in the early 19th century it was chiefly marked by sporting activities, such as horse-racing and boating: the Australia Day Regatta in Sydney Harbour has been held every year since its inception (as the Anniversary Regatta) in 1836.

On this day:

Born: English golfer Sir Henry Cotton (1907); French jazz violinist

Stephane Grappelli (1908); US actor Paul Newman (1925); English cellist Jacqueline du Pré (1945); Canadian ice hockey player Wayne Gretzky (1961)

Died: English physician and pioneer of vaccination Edward Jenner (1823); US actor Edward G Robinson (1973); US tennis player Don Budge (2000); English historian Hugh Trevor-Roper, Baron Dacre (2003); Scottish painter Wilhelmina Barns-Graham (2004)

1837 Michigan became the 50th state of the USA.

1841 Hong Kong became a British sovereign territory.

1915 In the USA, the Rocky Mountain National Park was established by Congress.

1926 The first public demonstration of a television image was given by Scottish electrical engineer John Logie Baird (1888–1946).

1950 India became a democratic republic.

1982 Unemployment in the UK topped three million for the first time since the 1930s.

1998 US President Bill Clinton (born 1946) made his famous denial of an affair with White House intern Monica Lewinsky (born 1973), announcing on television from the White House that 'I did not have sexual relations with that woman.'

27 January

On 27 January 1945, towards the end of World War II, the Nazi concentration camp at Auschwitz was liberated by the Allies. The anniversary of that event, already observed as a day of solemn reflection in Germany and other countries, was first observed as **Holocaust Memorial Day** in the UK in 2001. Hosted by a different city each year, its main objective is to ensure that the atrocities perpetrated at Auschwitz and similar camps are neither forgotten nor repeated. It also serves to draw attention to victims of genocide and other crimes against humanity elsewhere in the modern world and, more

generally, to fight bigotry and promote such ideals as tolerance, justice, freedom and equality through education and example.

On this day:

Born: Austrian composer Wolfgang Amadeus Mozart (1756); Prussian king and German emperor Wilhelm II (1859); US composer Jerome Kern (1885); English actor and manager Brian Rix (1924); Northern Irish peace activist and Nobel Prize winner Mairead Corrigan-Maguire (1944)

Died: Italian composer Giuseppe Verdi (1901); US gospel singer Mahalia Jackson (1962); English aircraft designer and sportsman Thomas Sopwith (1989); US television presenter Jack Paar (2004)

1880 US inventor and physicist Thomas Edison (1847–1931) received a patent for his electric incandescent lamp.

1945 World War II – Soviet soldiers liberated the Nazi concentration camps at Auschwitz and Birkenau, Poland.

1967 The Outer Space Treaty, prohibiting the placement of nuclear weapons in orbit around the Earth, was opened for signature by the United Nations.

1967 The command module of the USA's Apollo 1 space mission caught fire at Cape Kennedy, Florida, during a launch pad test, killing its crew of three astronauts.

1973 The Vietnam War ceasefire came into effect.

1995 French footballer Eric Cantona (born 1966) was fined £20,000 and banned from playing football for nine months after aiming a kung-fu style kick at a fan.

28 January

On 28 January 1986, onlookers watched in horror and disbelief as the US space shuttle *Challenger* exploded just 73 seconds after lift-off from the launch pad at Cape Canaveral, Florida. All seven astronauts on board (including Christa McAuliffe, a schoolteacher who would have been the first civilian in space) were killed, doubling at a single stroke the total number of people killed in 25 years of space exploration.

On this day:

Born: English king Henry VII (1457); English printer John Baskerville (1706); British–US explorer and journalist Sir Henry Morton Stanley (1841); Polish-born US pianist Artur Rubinstein (1887); English saxophonist Ronnie Scott (1927)

Died: English navigator Sir Francis Drake (1596); English scholar and diplomat Sir Thomas Bodley (1613); Irish poet and Nobel Prize winner W B Yeats (1937); Swedish children's novelist Astrid Lindgren (2002); New Zealand novelist and short-story writer Janet Frame (2004)

1754 In a letter to a friend, Horace Walpole (1717–97) coined the word 'serendipity', from the title of the fairy tale 'The Three Princes of Serendip'; its heroes 'were always making discoveries, by accidents and sagacity, of things they were not in quest of'.

1871 The Siege of Paris by the Prussian Army ended when the Government of National Defence asked for an armistice.

1896 Walter Arnold of Kent became the first British motorist to be fined for speeding at eight miles an hour in a two-mile-an-hour area.

1953 Despite a series of appeals to the British government and to the Queen, all of which received vigorous public support, Derek Bentley (c.1933–1953) was hanged for his involvement in the murder of a policeman the year before; his conviction was overturned in 1998.

1974 The Israeli army ended its siege of Suez.

The BBC radio programme 'Desert Island Discs' was broadcast for the first time on 29 January 1942. One of the longest running shows in radio history,

it was devised by Roy Plomley and presented by him until his death in 1985, when Michael Parkinson took over for a short time before being replaced by Sue Lawley in 1988.

The 'castaway' on the first 'Desert Island Discs' was the actor and comedian Vic Oliver. Guests from outside the world of entertainment have included writers (Margaret Drabble, Kingsley Amis), politicians (Margaret Thatcher, Tony Blair), sportspeople (Chris Bonington, Henry Cooper) and scientists (Richard Doll, Jane Goodall).

On this day:

Born: English radical political writer Thomas Paine (1737); British composer Frederick Delius (1862); Spanish novelist Vicente Blasco Ibáñez (1867); US actor Victor Mature (1916); Australian feminist and author Germaine Greer (1939)

Died: British and Hanoverian king George III (1820); English artist, humorist and traveller Edward Lear (1888); French Impressionist painter and etcher Alfred Sisley (1899); US lyric poet Robert Frost (1963); US comedian Jimmy Durante (1980)

1616 Dutch mariner Willem Schouten (c.1580–1625) was the first to round Cape Horn.

1635 The name and role of the Académie française were established.

1856 The Victoria Cross, the UK's highest military award for valour, was instituted by Royal Warrant.

1861 Kansas became the 29th state of the USA.

1886 German engineer Karl Benz (1844–1929) patented the first petrol-driven car.

1916 World War I – tanks were first demonstrated by the British military.

1929 The first US guide dog school, 'The Seeing Eye', was established.

2003 In a landmark case, 38-year-old solicitor Sally Clark was cleared of killing her two baby sons by the Court of Appeal; she had been jailed in 1999.

30 January

> *Though the anniversary of the execution of Charles I is very justly no longer celebrated with religious ceremonies in England, one can scarcely on any occasion allow the day to pass without a feeling of pathetic interest in the subject. The meek behaviour of the King in his latter days, his tender interviews with his little children when parting with them for ever, the insults he bore so well, his calmness at the last on the scaffold, combine to make us think leniently of his arbitrary rule, his high-handed proceedings with Nonconformists, and even his falseness towards the various opposing parties he had to deal with. When we further take into account the piety of his meditations ... we can scarcely wonder that a very large proportion of the people of England of his own generation, regarded him as a kind of martyr, and cherished his memory with the most affectionate regard.*
>
> *Chambers Book of Days* (1864).

King Charles I (born 1600) was beheaded on this day in 1649. His long-running dispute with parliament had culminated in the English Civil War, which began in 1642 and continued after his death. The monarchy was replaced by a Protectorate led by Oliver Cromwell, then by his son Richard, until 1660, when Charles II was restored to the throne. For 200 years after the Restoration, 30 January was observed as a holy day with fasting and solemn church services in honour of the 'murdered' king.

On this day:

Born: English writer Walter Savage Landor (1775); US actor Gene Hackman (1931); English actress Vanessa Redgrave (1937); US golfer Curtis Strange (1955)

Died: Indian leader Mahatma Gandhi (1948); US aviation pioneer Orville Wright (1948); French composer Francis Poulenc (1963); English actor Stanley Holloway (1982); US physicist and double Nobel Prize winner John Bardeen (1991)

1790 The first lifeboat, *The Original*, was launched at South Shields, England.

1858 The Hallé Orchestra held its first concert, at the Free Trade Hall in Manchester, England.

1933 Adolf Hitler (1889–1945) was appointed Chancellor of Germany.

1965 Winston Churchill (1874–1965) was buried with a full state funeral.

1968 The Tet Offensive began when the Viet Cong launched an attack against US bases and more than 100 South Vietnamese towns; the offensive proved to be a turning point in the Vietnam War.

1969 The Beatles performed together in public for the last time, on the roof of Apple Studios in London.

1972 The British Army opened fire during a Catholic civil rights protest march in Londonderry, Northern Ireland, killing 14, mainly young, demonstrators; the incident became known as 'Bloody Sunday'.

1976 Muriel Naughton became the first woman jockey to ride under National Hunt rules as an amateur at Ayr racecourse, Scotland.

1980 *Newsnight* was first shown on the BBC.

2003 Richard Reid (born 1973), the so-called 'Shoe Bomber' who had attempted to blow up a transatlantic flight with explosives hidden in his shoes, was sentenced to life imprisonment by a US court.

31 January

On this day:

Born: Austrian composer Franz Schubert (1797); US novelist Zane Grey (1872); US novelist and journalist Norman Mailer (1923); US composer Philip Glass (1937); English actress Minnie Driver (1971)

Died: British claimant to the throne Bonnie Prince Charlie (1788); Russian ballerina Anna Pavlova (1931); English novelist, playwright, and Nobel Prize winner John Galsworthy (1933); Polish-born US film producer Samuel Goldwyn (1974); US dramatist, director, producer and actor George Abbott (1995)

31 January

1606 English conspirator Guy Fawkes (born 1570) was executed.

1858 The steam-driven ship *Great Eastern*, designed by English engineer and inventor Isambard Kingdom Brunel (1806–59), was launched.

1865 The 13th Amendment to the US Constitution was passed by Congress, decreeing that 'neither slavery nor involuntary servitude … shall exist within the United States, or any place subject to their jurisdiction'.

1867 Nelson's Column was unveiled in Trafalgar Square, London.

1949 The first edition of *Book At Bedtime* was broadcast on BBC radio.

1953 Severe storms and floods caused huge damage along the east coast of the UK, drowning some 280 people and making thousands homeless.

1958 Explorer I, the first successful US satellite, was launched from Cape Canaveral, Florida.

1961 The first 'chimponaut', a chimpanzee called Ham, entered space as part of the US Mercury programme. He survived. Previously monkeys, pigs, bears and mice had been used.

1968 The Republic of Nauru in the Pacific Ocean gained independence.

1983 The wearing of car seatbelts by drivers and passengers in the front seats of cars became compulsory in the UK.

1990 The McDonald's Corporation opened its first fast-food restaurant in Russia in Moscow.

2000 GP Dr Harold Shipman (1946–2004) was sentenced to life imprisonment for murdering 15 of his patients; officials estimated that he had killed more than 200 others.

February

Gemstone: Amethyst
Flower: Primrose or violet

Married in February's sleepy weather,
Life you'll tread in time together.

Traditional rhyme.

February comes in like a sturdy country maiden, with a tinge of the red, hard winter apple on her healthy cheek, and as she strives against the wind, wraps her russet-coloured cloak well about her, while with bent head, she keeps throwing back the long hair that blows about her face, and though at times half blinded by the sleet and snow, still continues her course courageously ... the mellow-voiced blackbird and the speckle-breasted thrush make music among the opening blossoms of the blackthorn, to gladden her way; and she sees faint flushings of early buds here and there, which tell her the long miles of hedgerows will soon be green.

Chambers Book of Days (1864).

Origins

February, the second month of the year, takes its name from the Latin *februa*, a feast of expiation and purification held at this time in ancient Rome.

Characteristics

February is the shortest month of the year – perhaps mercifully so, in view of its weather and the lack of any distinctive or redeeming features. It does, however, give some tantalizing glimpses of the approach of spring, with the gradual lengthening of the hours of daylight and first signs of new growth on plants and trees.

History

The Anglo-Saxons called it *Solmonath* ('cake month'), because cakes and other offerings were presented to the gods at this time. Some Celtic names allude to its being cut short, as in the modern Scottish-Gaelic *Gearran*, which literally means 'gelding'. February has always been a month of variable length, gaining an extra day in leap years (or, from the opposite viewpoint, losing a day in three out of every four years).

Thirty days hath September,
April, June, and November;
All the rest have thirty-one,
Excepting February alone,
Which hath but twenty-eight days clear
And twenty-nine in each leap year.

Traditional rhyme.

Weather

February is renowned for having the most unpleasant weather of the year. Rain and snow are welcomed by farmers, however, to prepare the ground for the sowing and germination of seed: 'February fill dyke, be it black or be it white, but if it be white, it's the better to like'; 'If in February there be no rain, 'tis neither good for hay nor grain'; 'Much February snow a fine summer doth show'. Unseasonably fine and warm weather is not a good omen of things to come – 'All the months of the year curse a fair Februeer'.

Shrovetide and Lent

In the Christian Church, the 40 days (excluding Sundays) before Easter Day are known as **Lent**, a period of fasting symbolic of that spent by Christ in the wilderness (Matthew 4.2). Although many of the rules concerning what should and should not be eaten during this period have been relaxed, many people try to give up something pleasurable, such as chocolate or alcohol, for the duration. The days immediately preceding Lent are known as **Shrovetide**, a time for the *shriving* (ie confession and absolution) of sins.

Ash Wednesday, the first day of Lent, can fall on any date between 4 February and 10 March. It takes its name from the custom of marking a cross of ashes on the forehead of churchgoers on this day, a reminder that 'dust thou art, and unto dust shalt thou return' (Genesis 3:19).

Shrove Tuesday, the day before Ash Wednesday, was (and still is, in some cultures) marked by boisterous celebrations, being the last opportunity for

revelry before Easter. It was also a time for using up foodstuffs forbidden during Lent, notably eggs and milk, hence the tradition of making and eating pancakes on this day – in modern times it is probably better known as **Pancake Day**.

> *When Shrove Tuesday dawned, the bells were set a ringing, and everybody abandoned himself to amusement and good humour. All through the day, there was a preparing and devouring of pancakes, as if some profoundly important religious principle were involved in it. The pancake and Shrove Tuesday are inextricably associated in the popular mind and in old literature. Before being eaten, there was always a great deal of contention among the eaters, to see which could most adroitly toss them in the pan.*
>
> *Chambers Book of Days* (1864).

A number of Shrove Tuesday customs involving pancakes survive in various parts of the UK. At Olney in Buckinghamshire, for example, there is a **Pancake Race** for female contestants who must wear an apron and toss a pancake in their frying pan at least three times before they reach the finish. Tradition claims that the race dates back to an incident in 1445 when a housewife ran towards the church on hearing the bells whilst still carrying her frying pan. The race continues to be run from the Market Place to half-way down Church Lane, but the exact date of the first race is difficult to establish. The Olney Race is twinned with a similar event in the town of Liberal, Kansas, in the USA.

In the **Pancake Greaze** at Westminster School in London, the cook tosses a huge pancake over an iron bar in the school hall and delegated students scramble for it; whoever grabs the largest piece wins a prize. The first recorded Pancake Greaze took place in 1753. The origin of the word Greaze is not certain, but one theory from Westminster School is that in the past all the boys were taught in forms in the main school hall. These 'forms' consisted of a long seat against the wall on which the boys sat. A favoured game when the master was not looking was for the boys at each end to push inwards and try to squeeze, or grease or 'greaze' the boys who sat on the middle of the form out. Greaze was then perhaps used for any form of boisterous game.

Other customs associated with this day include **Royal Shrovetide Football**, played at Ashbourne in Derbyshire between teams of Upp'ards and Down'ards (ie people born above or below Henmore Brook, the river that flows through the town). The game is very much a moving scrum or brawl. The two sets of goalposts, at two mills, are over two miles apart and the ball (hand painted and cork-filled) is carried, kicked or thrown by the players. Rather than a traditional kick-off, the ball is 'turned up'or thrown in the air (in 1928 the Prince of Wales 'turned up' the ball, hence the 'Royal' Shrovetide Football). Goals are not scored, but 'goaled' and the game is played on both Shrove Tuesday and Ash Wednesday. The event has its own anthem, 'The Shrovetide Song', which was written in 1891 and includes the chorus:

> *'Tis a glorious game, deny it who can*
> *That tries the pluck of an Englishman.*

An event with a long history, the first known mention of Shrovetide Football at Ashbourne comes from Charles Cotton's *Burlesque on the Great Frost* of 1683. Occasional attempts have been made to ban the game, but it has endured. Since 1891 it has only once been cancelled altogether – because of the foot-and-mouth outbreak in 2002. Other Shrove Tuesday football games are held in Atherstone in Warwickshire, at Alnwick in Northumberland, and at Corfe Castle in Dorset the Order of Purbeck Marblers and Stonecutters also play football through the village as part of their annual celebrations.

Played with a similar disregard for fixed rules is **Hurling the Silver Ball**. Once played throughout Cornwall, and an ancient custom, this game is now restricted to St Columb (on Shrove Tuesday and the second following Saturday) and St Ives (on the first Monday after 3 February). In St Columb a small ball made of apple wood coated with silver, and bearing the inscription, 'Town and County do your best, For in this parish I must rest', is 'cast up' in the market square and the game then proceeds in a similar fashion to Shrovetide Football, although the ball is not generally kicked. The competing teams are Town (those from the built-up area at the centre of the parish) and County (those from outlying areas). The game ends when a goal is scored or the ball is carried over the parish boundary. The St Ives game is a little more refined, with the silver ball passed hand to hand. The winner receives the 'crown money', ie 25p.

In Scarborough the local residents take part in a **Shrovetide Skipping** festival, on the foreshore road. Young and old alike skip, in groups or alone, from noon until dark. This custom can be traced back at least until 1903, and some believe its origins lay in the fishermen sorting their ropes at this time, and discarding those that were no longer sound.

In France and other countries with French immigrant heritage, Shrove Tuesday is known as **Mardi Gras** ('Fat Tuesday'). For the residents of New Orleans, this means **carnival**. This is a huge and spectacular event which has developed from the private masked balls of the French in New Orleans in the early 18th century. Since 1872 the carnival has had its own colours – purple,

green and gold – and a parade of 1892 gave these colours symbolic meanings – purple representing justice, green representing faith and gold representing power. Extravagant parades include the floats of various 'Krewes'. These are associations which owe their origins to the Mystick Krewe of Comus, a secret society formed in 1857 with the aim of preserving Mardi Gras celebrations by planning the first parade. Mardi Gras 'throws' are also an established tradition which goes alongside the parade. Trinkets were first thrown to the crowd in the early 1870s, and today coloured aluminium doubloons are thrown from the floats. They depict the parade theme on one side and the Krewe's emblem on the other.

The Australian city of Sydney also hosts a world famous Mardi Gras carnival. The **Sydney Gay and Lesbian Mardi Gras**, originally held as a gay rights protest in 1978, has now developed into a massive month-long festival.

The word 'carnival' is ultimately derived from the Latin *carnem levare*, to put away meat (with reference to the forthcoming fast), and pre-Lenten carnivals are also held elsewhere: in S Europe, Trinidad, and Rio de Janeiro, for example.

Collop Monday, the day before Shrove Tuesday, was a time for using up fresh or salted meat, traditionally eaten with eggs on this day. (A 'collop' is a slice of meat or bread.) The custom is rarely observed in modern times, bacon and eggs being less of a novelty than pancakes for most people.

Non-fixed notable dates

Other non-fixed notable dates in February include:

> **Presidents Day:** The third Monday in February is a public holiday in the USA in honour of all past presidents of the nation. Established in 1971, it is also a joint commemoration of the birthdays of Abraham Lincoln (12 February) and George Washington (22 February), formerly celebrated on those dates.

1 February

This was formerly the festival of **Imbolc** (or **Oimelc**), marking the beginning of spring in the Celtic calendar, with particular reference to lambing and the milking of ewes. It merged with the feast day of St Brigid (or Bridget), abbess of Kildare in the late fifth and early sixth centuries, whose identity is associated with that of a Celtic goddess. One of Ireland's best-loved saints, she is also revered in Scotland and England, where she is known as St Bride. A number of churches are dedicated to her, notably one in Fleet Street, London.

> *Adjoining to St Bride's Churchyard, Fleet-street, is an ancient well dedicated to the saint, and commonly called Bride's Well. A palace erected near by took the name of Bridewell. This being given by Edward VI to the city of London as a workhouse for the poor and a house of correction, the name became associated in the popular mind with houses having the same purpose in view. Hence it has arisen that the pure and innocent Bridget – the first of Irish nuns – is now inextricably connected in our ordinary national parlance with a class of beings of the most opposite description.*
>
> *Chambers Book of Days* (1864).

St Brigid's Day and its eve were formerly celebrated in Ireland with various traditions, which included the making of rush crosses and the eating of festive fare, butter and buttermilk being important ingredients in the latter (Brigid is the patron saint of dairymaids, among others, and her emblem is a cow).

On this day:

Born: Irish-born US composer Victor Herbert (1859); English footballer Sir Stanley Matthews (1915); Scottish novelist, short-story writer, biographer and poet Dame Muriel Spark (1918); US pop singer with the Everly Brothers Don Everly (1937)

Died: English writer Mary Shelley (1851); English caricaturist and illustrator George Cruikshank (1878); Portuguese king Carlos I and his son Crown Prince Luís Filipe (1908); US film comedian 'Buster' Keaton (1966)

1587 Queen Elizabeth I (1533–1603) signed the death warrant for the execution of Mary, Queen of Scots (1542–87).

1709 Scottish sailor Alexander Selkirk (1676–1721), marooned for four years and four months on the uninhabited island of Más a Tierra in the Juan Fernández chain, was rescued; he became the model for the novel *Robinson Crusoe* (1719) by the English writer Daniel Defoe (1660–1731).

1790 The first ever session of the US Supreme Court was due to be held in New York City under Chief Justice John Jay, but the assembly had to be postponed to the following day as a result of the late arrival of some of the judges.

1811 The Bell Rock Lighthouse, off the east coast of Scotland, was lit for the first time.

1880 The first issue of *The Stage* newspaper was published as *The Stage Directory – a London and Provincial Theatrical Advertiser.*

1884 The first volume of the *Oxford English Dictionary* was published; the first edition wouldn't be completed until 1928.

1865 US President Abraham Lincoln (1809–65) approved the 13th Amendment to the US Constitution, abolishing slavery; it was ratified on 6 December the same year.

1893 US inventor and physicist Thomas Edison (1847–1931) completed the construction of the first film studio, known as the Black Maria, in New Jersey, USA.

1896 The première of the opera *La Bohème*, by Giacomo Puccini (1858–1924), was held in Turin, Italy.

1898 The first individual car insurance policy in the USA was issued by the Travelers Insurance Company of Hartford, Connecticut, to a Dr Truman J Martin of Buffalo, New York; it covered him for accidents with horses.

1910 The first 62 Labour Exchanges opened in the UK.

1920 The Royal Northwest Mounted Police changed their name to the Royal Canadian Mounted Police.

1942 World War II – Vidkun Quisling (1887–1945) became Norwegian prime minister for the second time; his name became synonymous with 'traitor' as he headed a puppet government.

1952 Television detector vans, designed to catch people who had not paid their television licence fees, were demonstrated for the first time.

1960 Four black students staged a sit-in at a whites-only lunch counter at a Woolworth's store in Greensboro, North Carolina, focusing attention on civil rights across the southern USA.

1979 The Iranian religious and political leader Ayatollah Khomeini (1900–89) returned from exile in Paris to a rapturous reception in Iran.

1979 Trevor Francis (born 1954) became the first £1m footballer when he signed for the English team Nottingham Forest.

1984 British Chancellor Nigel Lawson (born 1932) announced that the halfpenny coin would be withdrawn from circulation in the UK.

1991 South African president F W de Klerk (born 1936) announced the repeal of all remaining apartheid laws.

2003 The US space shuttle *Columbia* disintegrated on re-entry into the Earth's atmosphere, killing its crew of seven astronauts.

2 February

This is **Candlemas**, a holy day also known as the **Purification of the Blessed Virgin** and the **Presentation of the Lord**. Forty days after the birth of Christ, in accordance with the law of the Jews, Mary went to the temple to be ritually cleansed (a custom later known as 'churching') and to present her male firstborn child to the Lord. While she was there, a man called Simeon recognized the baby as 'the Lord's Christ' and hailed him as 'A light to lighten the Gentiles, and the glory of thy people Israel' (Luke 2.25–32). In the Christian Church this event was commemorated with a special mass, preceded by a procession with candles, hence the name Candlemas. Churchgoers also brought household candles for a blessing that was supposed to ward off evil in the home, but this practice was banned after the Reformation.

In former times, the Christmas season did not 'officially' end until Candlemas, and decorative evergreen branches were left in place until the eve of that festival, when superstition insisted that every trace of them be removed:

> *Down with the holly, ivy, all*
> *Wherewith ye dress'd the Christmas hall;*
> *That so the superstitious find*
> *Not one least branch left there behind;*

> *For look, how many leaves there be*
> *Neglected there, maids, trust to me,*
> *So many goblins you shall see.*
>
> Robert Herrick, *Hesperides*, 'Ceremony upon Candlemas Eve' (1648).

There is much weather lore attached to Candlemas, and some of it is contradictory, but the majority opinion seems to favour bad weather as the better omen:

> *On Candlemas Day, if the sun shines clear, the shepherd had rather see his wife on the bier.*
>
> Traditional saying.

> *If Candlemas Day be dry and fair,*
> *The half o' winter's to come and mair;*
> *If Candlemas Day be wet and foul*
> *The half o' winter's gane at Yule.*
>
> Traditional rhyme.

In the USA, a weather-forecasting ritual based on a similar belief takes place on 2 February, known as **Groundhog Day**. The groundhog (woodchuck) is said to emerge from hibernation on this day to check out the weather: if it is dull or wet he stays up and about because winter will soon be over, but if he can see his shadow (ie if it is sunny and dry) he goes back to his burrow to sleep for another six weeks. This custom, derived from German proverbial wisdom (where it applies to the badger), was brought to the attention of the wider world through the comedy film *Groundhog Day* (1993), in which a cynical, selfish and generally obnoxious TV weatherman (played by Bill Murray) is sent to Punxsutawney, Philadelphia, to cover the story and finds himself trapped there in a personal time warp, condemned to relive the day over and over again until he proves that he is a reformed character.

On this day:

Born: English playwright and religious writer Hannah More (1745); French politician Charles Maurice de Talleyrand-Périgord (1754); English physician and writer Henry Havelock Ellis (1859); US jazz saxophonist Stan Getz (1927)

Died: Russian chemist and inventor of the periodic table Dmitri Ivanovich Mendeleyev (1907); US boxer John L Sullivan (1918); English philosopher, mathematician, writer and Nobel Prize winner Bertrand Russell (1970); English bassist with the Sex Pistols Sid Vicious (1979); US actor, dancer, choreographer and film director Gene Kelly (1996)

1461 The future King Edward IV (1442–83) defeated Lancastrian forces in a great battle at Mortimer's Cross in Herefordshire.

1536 Spanish explorer Pedro de Mendoza (1487–1537) founded a city that would later become the Argentinian capital, Buenos Aires.

1848 The Treaty of Guadalupe Hidalgo settled the Mexican War (1846–8) between Mexico and the USA; Mexico yielded all of Texas, Arizona, Nevada, California and Utah, and parts of New Mexico, Colorado and Wyoming, while the USA paid $15,000,000, and assumed $3,250,000 worth of Mexican debts.

1880 The first shipment of frozen meat from Australia arrived in London, reportedly in excellent condition; the ship, the *Strathleven*, had left Melbourne in December 1879.

1901 The body of Queen Victoria (1819–1901) was taken by train from London to Windsor, where her funeral was held at St George's Chapel within the castle.

1943 World War II – the Battle of Stalingrad, fought between Nazi German and Soviet troops in and around Stalingrad (now Volgograd) on the River Volga during the winter of 1942–3, came to an end; the German army surrendered, yielding 91,000 prisoners of war.

1972 A crowd of demonstrators burnt down the British embassy in Dublin in reprisal protests against 'Bloody Sunday'.

1977 The Pompidou Centre in Paris opened to the public for the first time.

1990 South African president F W de Klerk (born 1936) announced that the ban on anti-apartheid groups, including the ANC, would be lifted; he also committed himself to releasing Nelson Mandela (born 1918) from prison.

3 February

This is the feast day of St Blaise (or Blasius), patron saint of wool-combers, who is also said to have saved the life of a young boy by miraculously removing a fishbone that was stuck in his throat. For this reason, he is invoked against throat ailments in a church ceremony performed on **St Blaise's Day**: the priest blesses two candles, ties them together to form a cross, and holds them against the throat of anyone desirous of such protection or relief.

> *St Blasius is generally represented as bishop of Sebaste in Armenia, and as having suffered martyrdom in the persecution of Licinius in 316. The fact of iron combs having been used in tearing the flesh of the martyr appears the sole reason for his having been adopted by the woolcombers as their patron saint. The large flourishing communities engaged in this business in Bradford and other English towns, are accustomed to hold a septennial jubilee on the 3rd of February, in honour of Jason of the Golden Fleece and St Blaize; and, not many years ago, this fête was conducted with considerable state and ceremony.*
>
> *Chambers Book of Days* (1864).

On this day:

Born: English-born first woman US physician Elizabeth Blackwell (1821); English statesman and prime minister Robert Cecil (1830); US writer Gertrude Stein (1874); US illustrator Norman Rockwell (1894); Irish entertainer Val Doonican (1927)

Died: English prince John of Gaunt, Duke of Lancaster (1399); 28th President of the USA and Nobel Prize winner Woodrow Wilson (1924); US rock singer, songwriter and guitarist Buddy Holly (1959); English actor Boris Karloff (1969); US film-maker John Cassavetes (1989)

1823 The première of the opera *Semiramide*, by Gioacchino Rossini (1792–1868), was held in Venice, Italy.

1870 The 15th Amendment to the US Constitution was ratified, stating that 'the right of citizens of the United States to vote shall not be denied or abridged by the United States or by any State on account of race, color, or previous condition of servitude'.

1913 The 16th Amendment to the US Constitution was ratified, stating that 'Congress shall have power to lay and collect taxes on incomes ... '

1954 Queen Elizabeth II (born 1926) became the first reigning monarch to visit Australia.

1960 Prime Minister Harold Macmillan (1894–1986) made his 'Wind of Change' speech in the South African parliament.

1966 Russia's unmanned *Luna IX* spacecraft made the first controlled landing on the Moon.

1978 Egyptian president Anwar el-Sadat (1918–81) arrived in the USA to hold talks with President Jimmy Carter (born 1924) for peace in the Middle East.

1998 A NATO military jet aircraft cut through a gondola cable in the Dolomites near Trento, Italy, sending a cable car crashing to the ground; all 20 people inside were killed.

4 February

On this day:

Born: Polish-born American soldier and patriot Tadeusz Kosciuszko (1746); US aviator Charles Lindbergh (1902); US golfer Byron Nelson (1912); US civil rights activist Rosa Lee Parks (1913); US rock singer Alice Cooper (1948)

Died: Roman emperor Lucius Septimius Severus (AD 211); German archaeologist Robert Koldewey (1925); US entertainer Liberace (1987); French composer Iannis Xenakis (2001)

1893 Liverpool Overhead Railway, the world's first electrified elevated railway, opened.

1927 Sir Malcolm Campbell (1885–1949) reached 174.88mph in his car *Bluebird* on Pendine Sands in Wales.

1938 Chancellor Adolf Hitler (1889–1945) took personal command of the German Army and made Joachim von Ribbentrop (1893–1946) his Foreign Minister.

1945 World War II – the Yalta Conference in the Crimea took place between Allied leaders Sir Winston Churchill (1874–1965), Franklin D Roosevelt (1882–1945) and Joseph Stalin (1879–1953).

1948 Ceylon (later Sri Lanka) became an independent self-governing state within the Commonwealth.

1962 The *Sunday Times* published the *Sunday Times Colour Section*, the first newspaper colour supplement in the UK.

1974 An IRA bomb killed twelve soldiers and members of their families returning on a bus from Manchester to Catterick Camp in Yorkshire.

1974 US newspaper heiress Patty Hearst (born 1954) was kidnapped by a group calling itself the Symbionese Liberation Army; she caused a scandal by later joining the group.

1976 An earthquake in Guatemala killed over 23,000 people.

1976 Concorde received an initial licence – for a trial period of 16 months – to land in Washington, DC and New York City in the USA.

1987 The USA regained the America's Cup for yachting from Australia.

1997 In a civil suit charging him with unlawful death, brought by relatives of the victims, former American football player O J Simpson (born 1947) was found liable for the deaths of his former wife Nicole Brown Simpson (1959–94) and her friend Ronald Goldman (1968–94).

1998 An earthquake measuring 6.1 on the Richter scale struck northern Afghanistan, leaving 4,000 people dead.

On 5 February 1953, the rationing of sweets and chocolate was finally abolished, after more than ten years, and shops throughout the UK reported a brisk trade in everything from lollipops to liquorice. An earlier attempt to remove confectionery from the ration books, in 1949, had underestimated

the nation's hunger for these items and ended in failure when demand outstripped supply. During the latter half of World War II, the weekly ration of sweets and chocolate was a mere 2oz per person, although this was gradually increased to a more generous 6oz in the post-war years.

On this day:

Born: English statesman and prime minister Sir Robert Peel (1788); Scottish inventor John Boyd Dunlop (1840); US-born British inventor and engineer Sir Hiram Maxim (1840); US politician and lawyer Adlai Stevenson (1900); US baseball player Hank Aaron (1934)

Died: Scottish historian and essayist Thomas Carlyle (1881); English actor George Arliss (1946); US poet Marianne Moore (1972); US film-maker Joseph L Mankiewicz (1993)

1782 Spain captured Menorca from the United Kingdom.

1811 The Prince of Wales, the eldest son of King George III (1738–1820), was appointed Prince Regent during his father's mental illness; he was later to succeed as King George IV (1762–1830).

1887 The première of the opera *Otello*, by Giuseppe Verdi (1813–1901), was held at La Scala, Milan, Italy.

1920 The Royal Air Force College, the world's first Military Air Academy, was founded at Cranwell, Lincolnshire.

1924 The BBC's Greenwich time signal, the 'pips', was first broadcast.

1941 World War II – the Air Training Corps (ATC) was officially established.

1945 World War II – US troops under General Douglas MacArthur (1880–1964) entered Manila, capital of the Philippines.

1953 Disney's film *Peter Pan* was released.

1982 Laker Airways collapsed with debts of over £270m.

1983 Klaus Barbie (1913–91), a Nazi Gestapo officer in Lyons during World War II, was extradited from Bolivia to stand trial in France.

1990 The BBC transmitted the last time signal 'pips' from Greenwich, 66 years to the day after the first broadcast; henceforth it generated its own 'pips'.

6 February

In New Zealand this is **Waitangi Day**, a public holiday commemorating the signing of the Treaty of Waitangi on 6 February 1840. The treaty was an agreement between the British government and the Maoris, giving the latter authority over the lands they possessed. Infringement of this treaty led to hostilities in the latter half of the 19th century, and the rights of the Maori people have periodically been the subject of dispute and debate since then: the ceremonies of Waitangi Day have often been disrupted by protests. Celebrations include performances of the *haka* (a traditional Maori war dance), the launching of *waka* (traditional canoes) and the promotion of Maori art and culture, as well as multicultural events. First celebrated in 1935, Waitangi Day did not become an official national holiday until the mid-1970s.

On this day:

Born: English dramatist Christopher Marlowe (1564); US baseball player Babe Ruth (1895); 40th President of the USA and former film actor Ronald Reagan (1911); French film critic and director François Truffaut (1932); Jamaican singer and guitarist Bob Marley (1945)

Died: Norman founder of Fountains Abbey and Archbishop of York Thurstan (1140); British king Charles II (1685); English landscape gardener Lancelot 'Capability' Brown (1783); British king George VI (1952); Austrian-born British biochemist and Nobel Prize winner Max Perutz (2002)

1788 Massachusetts became the sixth state to ratify the Constitution of the USA.

1952 Princess Elizabeth (born 1926) became the new sovereign upon the death of her father, King George VI (1895–1952); she formally acceded to the throne two days later.

1958 An aeroplane carrying the Manchester United football team crashed on take-off in Germany killing 23 people, including eight footballers. The crash became known as the Munich air disaster.

1995 The US space shuttle *Discovery* and Russia's Mir space station rendezvoused in space.

1997 In a landmark decision, the Court of Appeal ruled that Diane Blood could use her late husband's sperm to have children, despite the fact that he had not given his consent before his death.

2000 Hillary Rodham Clinton (born 1947), wife of US President Bill Clinton (born 1946), officially declared her candidacy for the US Senate seat for New York, thereby becoming the first First Lady ever to run for public office.

7 February

On this day:

Born: English politician and scholar Sir Thomas More (1478); English writer Charles Dickens (1812); Austrian psychiatrist Alfred Adler (1870); US novelist and Nobel Prize winner Sinclair Lewis (1885); English actor Pete Postlethwaite (1945)

Died: English composer William Boyce (1779); South African politician and architect of apartheid Daniel F Malan (1959); Jordanian king Hussein (1999)

1301 Prince Edward (later Edward II, 1284–1327) was given the title 'Prince of Wales', the first heir to the throne to bear the title.

1649 The office of king was formally abolished in Britain.

1845 William Mulcahy, a drunken visitor to the British Museum, smashed the Portland Vase, a priceless ten-inch dark blue glass vessel.

1914 The première of the Keystone Studios short film *Kid Auto Races at Venice* was held; it featured Charlie Chaplin (1889–1977) in his 'Tramp' guise for the first time.

1940 Disney's film *Pinocchio* had its world première in New York City, USA.

1964 The Beatles made their first visit to the USA.

1965 Vietcong forces attacked the US base at Pleiku, killing eight US soldiers

and destroying ten planes; US President Lyndon B Johnson (1908–73) ordered retaliatory raids against North Vietnam.

1971 A referendum in Switzerland gave women the right to vote and stand for parliament.

1974 Just days after miners announced an all-out strike, Prime Minister Edward Heath (born 1916) called a General Election to be held on 23 February.

1976 Diane Thorne, riding Ben Ruler at Stratford, became the first woman jockey to win a National Hunt race.

1976 At Croydon, Surrey, Joan Bazely became the first woman to referee a football match between two men's teams.

1991 The IRA attacked the War Cabinet in 10 Downing Street, London, with mortar bombs fired from vehicles parked in Whitehall.

1992 Government ministers of European member states signed the Treaty on European Union and the Maastricht Final Act, bringing the new European Union into being.

2000 In the UK, a hijacked Ariana Afghan Airlines Boeing 727, carrying 187 people, landed at Stansted Airport, leading to days of negotiation; the passengers and crew were eventually released and 19 people arrested.

8 February

The prize stallion Shergar was kidnapped on 8 February 1983 from the Ballymany stud farm in County Kildare, Ireland. Winner of the 1981 Derby, and valued at £10m for his breeding potential, Shergar was owned by a syndicate whose members included the Aga Khan (born 1936). A ransom was demanded but not paid – for fear of encouraging copycat crimes – and the horse was never found.

On this day:

Born: US general William Tecumseh Sherman (1820); Malaysian statesman and prime minister Tunka Abdul Rahman Putra (1903); US film actress Lana Turner (1920); US composer of film music John Williams (1932); US author John Grisham (1955)

Died: Scottish queen Mary, Queen of Scots (1587); Russian tsar and emperor Peter I, the Great (1725); Scottish children's writer R M Ballantyne (1894); Irish novelist, playwright and philosopher Dame Iris Murdoch (1999); US economist and Nobel Prize winner Herbert Simon (2001)

1861 Secessionist states met in Alabama to form the Confederate States of America, eventually precipitating the American Civil War.

1904 The Russo-Japanese War began with a Japanese surprise attack on Port Arthur, Manchuria.

1910 The Boy Scouts of America were incorporated by William D Boyce (1858–1929).

1924 The 'gas chamber' as a form of execution was first used when prisoner Gee Jon was executed in Nevada State Prison, Nevada, USA.

1943 World War II – the Japanese evacuated their last remaining troops from Guadalcanal in the Solomon Islands, South Pacific.

1952 Princess Elizabeth (born 1926) proclaimed herself Queen Elizabeth II and officially acceded to the British throne.

1974 The US space station Skylab returned to Earth after a then record 84 days and 1 hour in space.

While I cannot take the time to name all the men in the State Department who have been named as members of the Communist Party and members of a spy ring, I have here in my hand a list of 205 that were known to the Secretary of State as being members of the Communist Party and who, nevertheless, are still working and shaping the policy of the State Department.

Joseph R McCarthy, speech at Wheeling, West Virginia (9 February 1950).

This speech made by the US Republican Senator Joseph R McCarthy (1909–57) on 9 February 1950 is generally regarded as the beginning of the

infamous anti-communist 'witch hunts' that became known as McCarthyism. As chairman of the Committee on Un-American Activities, McCarthy accused citizens from all walks of life of communist sympathies, often on the basis of little or no evidence, provoking mass hysteria and destroying the careers of many innocent people. His list of communist infiltrators in the State Department never materialized, and in 1954 he was formally censured for behaviour 'contrary to Senate traditions'. He died three years later, at the age of 48.

On this day:

Born: US Imagist poet Amy Lowell (1874); Austrian composer Alban Berg (1885); US composer and singer Carole King (1942); US writer Alice Walker (1944); Scottish golfer Sandy Lyle (1958)

Died: English astronomer Nevil Maskelyne (1811); Russian novelist Fyodor Dostoevsky (1881); Soviet aircraft designer Sergei Vladimirovich Ilyushin (1977); British princess Margaret (2002)

1649 King Charles I (1600–49) was buried at Windsor, rather than Westminster Abbey, to avoid civil unrest.

1721 The first British Parliamentary question was asked by Earl Cowper, and answered by the Earl of Sunderland.

1801 The Treaty of Luneville was signed between France and Austria.

1849 The Roman Republic was proclaimed by Rome's new Assembly.

1893 The première of the opera *Falstaff*, by Giuseppe Verdi (1813–1901), was held at La Scala, Milan, Italy.

1916 World War I – military conscription of unmarried men aged between 18 and 41 began in the UK.

1923 The airline Aeroflot was founded in the USSR.

1933 The Oxford Union debated and passed the famous motion 'that this House will in no circumstances fight for King and Country'.

1942 World War II – soap rationing, a monthly allowance of 4 ounces of household soap or 2 ounces of toilet soap, began in the UK.

1969 The largest commercial aircraft in the world, the Boeing 747, made its first flight.

1972 Prime Minister Edward Heath (born 1916) declared a state of emergency during the miners' strike.

1986 Halley's Comet made its closest passage to the Sun on its 76-year orbit.

1995 The first spacewalk by a British astronaut was made by Michael Foale (born 1957).

1996 The IRA ceasefire ended with a bomb explosion in the South Quay area of London Docklands, killing two people.

10 February

This is the feast day of St Scholastica, the lesser-known sister of St Benedict, who founded the Benedictine order of monks in the early sixth century. **St Scholastica's Day** is remembered in Oxford as the date of a dispute in 1355 that escalated into a three-day riot in which 63 students were killed. It was apparently sparked by a complaint about the quality of wine served to a group of students at the Swindlestock Tavern and fuelled by the tension between town and gown that already existed in the city.

> *On the 10th of February ... a dire conflict took place between the students of the University of Oxford and the citizens. The contest continued three days. On the second evening, the townsmen called into their assistance the country people; and thus reinforced, completely overpowered the scholars, of whom numbers were killed and wounded. The citizens, were, consequently, debarred the rites and consolations of the church; their privileges were greatly narrowed; they were heavily fined; and an annual penance for ever was enjoined that on each anniversary of St Scholastica, the mayor and sixty-two citizens attend at St Mary's Church, where the Litany should be read at the altar, and an oblation of one penny made by each man.*
>
> *Chambers Book of Days* (1864).

On this day:

Born: English social reformer Samuel Plimsoll (1824); English statesman and prime minister Harold Macmillan, 1st Earl of Stockton (1894); German playwright and poet Bertolt Brecht

(1898); US swimmer Mark Spitz (1950); Australian golfer Greg Norman (1955)

Died: Scottish nobleman and husband of Mary, Queen of Scots Henry Stewart, Lord Darnley (1567); Russian poet and writer Alexander Pushkin (1837); Scottish physicist and inventor of the kaleidoscope Sir David Brewster (1868); English surgeon and 'father of antiseptic surgery' Joseph Lister, 1st Baron Lister (1912); US novelist and biographer Alex Haley (1992)

1763 The Treaty of Paris, the peace settlement ending the Seven Years War (1756–63), was signed by Britain, France and Spain. Spain surrendered Florida to the British but received the Louisiana Territory and New Orleans from France, and Havana and Manila from Britain, while France ceded Canada, America east of the Mississippi, Cape Breton and the St Lawrence islands, Dominica, Tobago, the Grenadines and Senegal to Britain.

1806 Lord Grenville (1759–1834) formed the coalition government of 'All the Talents', which, before its dissolution in 1807, abolished the slave trade.

1840 Queen Victoria (1819–1901) married Prince Albert of Saxe-Coburg-Gotha (1819–61).

1897 The famous slogan 'All the News That's Fit to Print' appeared on the front page of *The New York Times* for the first time; it was first used the previous year on the editorial page.

1931 New Delhi was formally inaugurated as capital of India.

1962 The USSR freed Captain Francis Gary Powers (1929–77), pilot of a US spy plane that was shot down over Russia in May 1960, in exchange for the return of Soviet spy Colonel Rudolph Abel (1903–71).

1996 World chess champion Garry Kasparov (born 1963) was defeated by the IBM computer 'Deep Blue' in the first match of a tournament held in Philadelphia, Pennsylvania, USA; Kasparov did, however, eventually win the tournament.

11 February

In Japan, this is **National Foundation Day** (or **Kenkoku kinen-no-hi**), a national holiday that commemorates the legendary founding of the Japanese Empire in 660 BC, when the Emperor Jimmu is said to have come to power. Originally established as **Empire Day** (**Kigen-setsu**) in 1872, when Japan adopted the Gregorian calendar, it was discontinued during World War II but revived in 1966 with its current name.

On this day:

Born: US inventor and physicist Thomas Edison (1847); Egyptian king Farouk I (1920); English fashion designer Mary Quant (1934); US actor Burt Reynolds (1936)

Died: French philosopher and mathematician René Descartes (1650); French physicist Jean Foucault (1868); Scottish writer and statesman John Buchan (1940); Russian film director Sergei Eisenstein (1948); US poet Sylvia Plath (1963)

1531 King Henry VIII (1491–1547) was recognized by the English clergy as Supreme Head of the Church of England.

1826 London University (later University College London) was granted its charter.

1858 Bernadette Soubirous (1844–79), later St Bernadette, saw her first vision of a 'lady in white' at Lourdes, France.

1929 Under the Lateran Treaty, the Vatican became an independent Papal State within the city of Rome.

1945 World War II – the Yalta Conference of Allied leaders, which began on 4 February, ended in an agreement to set up the United Nations Organization.

1970 Japan became the fourth country (after the USSR, USA and France) to have sent a satellite into space with the launch of the Osumi satellite.

1975 Margaret Thatcher (born 1925) was elected to lead the Conservative Party, becoming the first woman leader of a political party in the UK.

1976 John Curry (1949–94) became the first Briton to win the gold medal for men's figure skating at the Winter Olympics.

1990 South African lawyer and civil rights activist Nelson Mandela (born 1918) was released from jail.

2000 The Northern Ireland Assembly and Executive were suspended at midnight; devolved government was not resumed until May.

12 February

Abraham Lincoln was born on this day in 1809, in a backwoods cabin in Kentucky, the son of a pioneer farmer. The family moved around for several years before settling in Indiana in 1816, where they remained until 1830, when they relocated to Illinois. Largely self-taught, Lincoln embarked on the study of law and began to practise in 1836; he married Mary Todd in 1842 and entered politics as a congressman five years later. His anti-slavery convictions drew him to the newly formed Republican Party and in 1861 he was elected 16th President of the USA.

Lincoln's presidency was dominated by the American Civil War, which broke out soon after his inauguration and ended with the surrender of the Confederates in the month of his death. In Washington on 14 April 1865, as he sat with his wife at the theatre, he was assassinated by John Wilkes Booth, an actor who supported the Confederate cause. A set of poems published by Walt Whitman soon afterwards summed up the feelings of a nation in mourning for one of the greatest statesmen in their history:

O Captain! my Captain! our fearful trip is done,
The ship has weather'd every rack, the prize we sought is won,
. . .
Exult O shores, and ring O bells!
But I with mournful tread
Walk the deck my Captain lies,
Fallen cold and dead.

Walt Whitman, *Leaves of Grass*, 'Memories of President Lincoln', 'O Captain! My Captain!' (1865).

12 February

Lincoln's birthday was formerly celebrated with a public holiday on 12 February throughout the USA; it is now jointly commemorated on Presidents Day (see February).

On this day:

Born: English physician, poet and composer Thomas Campion (1567); English naturalist Charles Darwin (1809); Italian stage, opera and film director Franco Zeffirelli (1923); US writer for teenagers Judy Blume (1938)

Died: English queen Lady Jane Grey (1554); German philosopher Immanuel Kant (1804); English actress and King Edward VII's mistress Lily Langtry (1929); French chef Auguste Escoffier (1935); US strip cartoonist Charles Schulz (2000)

1851 Edward Hargreaves (1816–91) discovered gold in Australia's Summerhill Creek in New South Wales, leading to the first Australian 'gold rush'.

1909 The National Association for the Advancement of Colored People (NAACP) was founded by Ida Wells-Barnett (1862–1931), W E B Du Bois (1868–1963) and others 'to renew the struggle for civil and political liberty'.

1981 The Reverend Ian Paisley MP (born 1926) was suspended from the House of Commons after calling Northern Ireland Secretary Humphrey Atkins (born 1922) a liar.

1993 The South African government and the African National Congress agreed plans for an elected interim government of both blacks and whites.

1993 Toddler James Bulger went missing from a shopping centre in Bootle, Merseyside; two ten-year-old boys were later convicted of his murder.

1999 US President Bill Clinton (born 1946) was acquitted by the Senate on impeachment charges of perjury and obstruction of justice following his affair with White House intern Monica Lewinsky (born 1973).

13 February

On this day:

Born: Scottish physiologist, surgeon and founder of scientific surgery John Hunter (1728); Belgian-born French novelist Georges Simenon (1903); US actress Kim Novak (1933); English actor Oliver Reed (1938); English rock singer and songwriter Peter Gabriel (1950)

Died: English queen Catherine Howard (1542); German composer Richard Wagner (1883); English suffragette Dame Christabel Pankhurst (1958); French-born US film director Jean Renoir (1979); US country music singer and songwriter Waylon Jennings (2002)

1692 Government forces, consisting, in part, of the Campbells, slaughtered members of the MacDonald clan at the 'Massacre of Glencoe'.

1741 The first edition of *The American Magazine*, the first magazine in America, was published.

1793 Britain, Prussia, Austria, Holland, Spain and Sardinia formed 'the First Coalition' against France.

1854 Cheltenham Ladies College, the first public school for girls in the UK, opened.

1866 The infamous James–Younger gang robbed their first bank in Liberty, Missouri, USA.

1945 World War II – the Royal Air Force began massive firebombing of Dresden, Germany.

1960 The first French atom bomb tests took place in the Sahara Desert.

1974 The novelist Alexander Solzhenitsyn (born 1918) was stripped of his citizenship and expelled from the USSR following the publication abroad of the first part of his trilogy *The Gulag Archipelago*.

1982 The tallest woman in history, 17-year-old Zeng Jinlian of Hunan Province, China, died; she was 8ft 1in (2.46m) tall.

1991 During the Gulf War US missiles destroyed an Iraqi bunker in Baghdad, killing more than 300 civilians, in what became known as the Amirya bombing.

1998 In Worcester, the warmest February day in the UK was recorded at 19.6°C.

St Valentine, set thy hopper by mine.

Traditional saying (a 'hopper' is a seed-basket, used when working in the fields).

This is the feast day of St Valentine, a third-century martyr about whom little is known for certain; he has been variously identified as a Roman priest and as Bishop of Terni, Italy. The association of **St Valentine's Day** with love and lovers, which has been traced back to the 14th century, probably derives from the date itself: 14 February is the eve of the **Lupercalia**, an ancient Roman festival of fertility, and is also the day on which birds are traditionally thought to choose their mates ('On St Valentine, all the birds of the air in couples do join', according to proverbial wisdom). In modern times it is probably the most widely celebrated saint's day in the calendar, although it is often simply called **Valentine's Day**, acknowledging its secular nature.

A **valentine** is a person chosen as a sweetheart, or a card or gift sent to that person on 14 February. The choosing of a valentine formerly took place on St Valentine's Eve, by means of divination rituals or the drawing of lots. The latter was a fairly light-hearted activity, which did not necessarily lead to a lasting relationship, and was apparently engaged in by single and married people alike. It was customary to show one's appreciation of being so chosen by giving a gift to the chooser – Samuel Pepys complains in a number of his diary entries of the expense thus incurred. Then as now, the choice of a valentine was also sometimes based on desire alone: the sending of a message or love-token on Valentine's Day was and still is a means of tentatively – and often anonymously – professing feelings that may or may not be requited.

Valentine's cards began to appear in the 19th century and ranged from the elaborate and romantic to the comic and rude. The predominance of the latter, often sent as a practical joke, caused the celebration of Valentine's Day to fall from favour for a time.

> *Valentine's Day is now almost everywhere a much degenerated festival, the only observance of any note consisting merely of the sending of jocular anonymous letters to parties whom one wishes to quiz [or poke fun at], and this confined very much to the humbler classes. The approach of the day is now heralded by the appearance in the print-sellers' shop windows of vast numbers of missives calculated for use on this occasion, each generally consisting of a single sheet of post paper, on the first page of which is seen some ridiculous coloured caricature of the male or female figure, with a few burlesque verses below. … Maid-servants and young fellows interchange such epistles with each other on the 14th of February, no doubt conceiving that the joke is amazingly good; and, generally, the newspapers do not fail to record that the London postmen delivered so many hundred thousand more letters on that day than they do in general. Such is nearly the whole extent of the observances now peculiar to St Valentine's Day.*
>
> *Chambers Book of Days* (1864).

The custom was subsequently revived and went from strength to strength – by the latter half of the 20th century, any adolescent schoolgirl who did not receive a single card on 14 February was judged to be a very unfortunate soul indeed. Some people (old enough to know better) now opt to go public, exchanging sentimental messages in the personal columns of newspapers and magazines. The worst of these, using pet names and language best confined to the love nest, can cause toe-curling embarrassment to the reader, a far cry from the romantic poetry of yesteryear.

> *Thy bright eyes govern better than the Sun,*
> *For with thy favour was my life begun,*
> *And still I reckon on from smiles to smiles,*
> *And not by summers, for I thrive on none*
> *But those thy cheerful countenance compiles;*
> *Oh! if it be to choose and call thee mine,*
> *Love, thou art every day my Valentine!*
>
> Thomas Hood (1799–1845), 'Sonnet: For the 14th of February'.

On this day:

Born: English economist and clergyman Thomas Robert Malthus (1766); US inventor of the typewriter Christopher Latham Sholes (1819); US comedian Jack Benny (1894); English film director Alan Parker (1944); English footballer and manager Kevin Keegan (1951)

Died: English navigator Captain James Cook (1779); English judge and jurist Sir William Blackstone (1780); English biologist and humanist Sir Julian Sorell Huxley (1975); English novelist Sir P G Wodehouse (1975)

1488 The Great Swabian League, an association of Swabian cities and provinces of southwestern Germany, was formed.

1849 The first photograph of a serving US President was taken when a daguerreotype of James K Polk (1795–1849) was made by Mathew B Brady (1823–96).

1852 The Great Ormond Street Hospital for Children in London admitted its first patient.

1859 Oregon became the 33rd state of the USA.

1895 The première of the play *The Importance of Being Earnest*, by Oscar Wilde (1854–1900), was held at the St James' Theatre in London.

1912 Arizona became the 48th state of the USA.

1929 The St Valentine's Day Massacre took place in Chicago, Illinois, USA, when members of a gang led by Al Capone (1899–1947) machine-gunned to death seven members of the gang led by his rival 'Bugs' Moran (1893–1957).

1946 The Bank of England was nationalized.

1946 The ENIAC (Electronic Numerical Integrator And Computer), the first electronic digital computer, was demonstrated at the University of Pennsylvania in the USA; the computer was formally dedicated in a ceremony the following day, and continued working until 1955.

1950 China and the USSR signed the 30-year Sino-Soviet Treaty of Friendship, Alliance and Mutual Assistance.

1963 Harold Wilson (1916–95) became leader of the Labour Party in the UK.

1989 In Iran, the Ayatollah Khomeini (1900–89) issued a *fatwa* ordering the execution of British author Salman Rushdie (born 1947) for blasphemy in his book *The Satanic Verses* (1988).

1993 Lithuania's first genuinely democratic presidential election was won by Algirdas Brazauskas (born 1932).

2003 Tobacco advertising was banned in the UK as the Tobacco Advertising and Promotions Act (2002) came into force.

15 February

In 1971, this was the date of the decimalization of British currency, an event that became known as D-day. No longer was the pound divided into 20 shillings of 12 pence each – the 'new penny' was worth one-hundredth of a pound, and the former shilling was worth 5p. Some of the new coins had been introduced two or three years earlier: 5p and 10p pieces were used interchangeably with the shilling and florin (two-shilling piece) from 1968, and the 50p coin, with its unique heptagonal shape, replaced the ten-shilling note in 1969.

The changeover to the new currency went relatively smoothly (although there were inevitably some claims of price inflation in the process of conversion) and even those who initially opposed it were eventually won over by the ease of performing basic calculations in decimal units. The remaining pre-decimal coins were gradually phased out (the old sixpence, worth 2.5p, was one of the last to go) but it was some time before people shook off the habit of mentally converting any price that seemed exorbitant: 'Eighty pence? That's sixteen shillings – what a rip-off!'

On this day:

Born: Italian astronomer, mathematician and natural philosopher Galileo Galilei (1564); French king Louis XV (1710); US goldsmith and jeweller Charles Lewis Tiffany (1812); Irish-born British explorer Sir Ernest Shackleton (1874); US animator and creator of *The Simpsons* Matt Groening (1954)

Died: Dutch naturalist Jan Swammerdam (1680); German writer Gotthold Ephraim Lessing (1781); English statesman and prime minister Herbert Henry Asquith (1928); Scottish Royal Air Force chief Lord Dowding (1970)

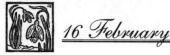

1898 During a goodwill visit, US battleship USS *Maine* was blown up after hitting a mine in Havana harbour, instigating the Spanish–American War.

1942 World War II – Singapore fell to the Japanese.

1944 World War II – the Second Battle of Monte Cassino began as the Allies bombed the ancient monastery outside Rome, Italy.

1952 The funeral of King George VI (1895–1952) was held at St George's Chapel within Windsor Castle; the funeral procession from Westminster Hall to Windsor was broadcast by the BBC.

1965 The red maple leaf on a white background between two red stripes officially became the new national flag of Canada, and was raised for the first time at a ceremony in Ottawa.

1978 Leon Spinks (born 1953) beat Muhammad Ali (born 1942) to become world heavyweight boxing champion.

16 February

On this day:

Born: English scientist Sir Francis Galton (1822); English historian G M Trevelyan (1876); Welsh baritone Sir Geraint Evans (1922); US tennis player John McEnroe (1959)

Died: English physician Dr Richard Mead (1754); English lifeboat pioneer Lionel Lukin (1834); Italian poet and Nobel Prize winner Giosuè Carducci (1907); English barrister and politician Lord Hore-Belisha (1957); US artist Keith Haring (1990)

1906 US inventors John Harvey Kellogg (1852–1943) and W K Kellogg (1860–1951) founded the Battle Creek Toasted Cornflake Company,

later to become the W K Kellogg Company, in Battle Creek, Michigan, USA.

1918 Lithuania became independent.

1937 Nylon was patented in the USA by Wallace H Carothers (1896–1937) and his team at the DuPont Company.

1940 World War II – HMS *Cossack* rescued 299 British prisoners from the German ship *Altmark* in Norwegian waters.

1959 Fidel Castro (born 1927) became prime minister of Cuba.

1999 Kurdish protestors demonstrated across Europe and occupied diplomatic embassies in several countries after Kurdish rebel leader Abdullah Ocalan (born 1948) was captured by the Turkish authorities.

17 February

The Swiss educationalist Johann Heinrich Pestalozzi died on this day in 1827, having devoted his life to poor, neglected and orphaned children. Born in Zurich in 1746, he was inspired by the writings of Jean-Jacques Rousseau to set up a residential farm school in 1774 with the aim of teaching underprivileged children the basic practical skills required for self-reliance. After the failure of this project he devoted himself to writing for many years, setting out his philosophy, his ideas on social and political reform, and his theory of education in such works as *Evening Hours of a Hermit* (1780) and *How Gertrude Educates her Children* (1801). The innovative Pestalozzian method was finally put into practice at his school in Yverdon, founded in 1805, which attracted visitors from all over Europe and the USA, many of whom returned to set up similar establishments in their own countries.

On this day:

Born: Italian composer Arcangelo Corelli (1653); French physician and inventor of the stethoscope René Laënnec (1781); French politician André Maginot (1877); Australian comedian and writer Barry Humphries (1934); US basketball player Michael Jordan (1963)

Died: Italian philosopher Giordano Bruno (1600); French playwright

Molière (1673); Apache leader Geronimo (1909); English actor–manager Sir Donald Wolfit (1968)

1863 A committee was formed in Geneva, Switzerland, to investigate the proposals of Jean Henri Dunant (1828–1910) for the foundation of what would later become the International Committee of the Red Cross.

1904 The première of the opera *Madama Butterfly*, by Giacomo Puccini (1858–1924), was held at La Scala, Milan, Italy.

1924 The chimes of Big Ben were first used as a time signal by the BBC.

1972 US President Richard Nixon (1913–94) left the USA for China, the first visit there by a US president.

1979 China invaded Vietnam.

1992 US serial killer Jeffrey Dahmer (1960–94) was convicted of 15 murders and sentenced to 15 life sentences after admitting to acts of dismemberment, necrophilia and cannibalism with 17 men and boys.

2003 London became the first city in the UK to introduce a congestion charge for vehicles entering central areas.

18 February

Among the old historic traditions of the Tower of London is the story that George Duke of Clarence, brother of Edward the Fourth, who met his death on February 18, 1478, was, by order of his other brother, Richard Duke of Gloucester, drowned in a butt of Malmsey wine in the above prison. It is said that, being condemned to die, the Duke's partiality for Malmsey led him to select this strange mode of quitting life. There is considerable confusion in the narratives: first, Sir Thomas More insinuates that Gloucester's efforts to save Clarence were feeble; next, Lord Bacon accuses him of contriving his brother's death; and Shak[e]speare characterizes him as the associate of the murderers; while Sandford makes him the actual murderer.

Chambers Book of Days (1864).

The circumstances of the death of the Duke of Clarence on this day in 1478, and the role of the Duke of Gloucester (1452–85), later King Richard III, in his murder or execution, have been the subject of much scholarly debate. Clarence had quarrelled both with his elder brother, King Edward IV (1442–83), who suspected him of plotting a rebellion and had him condemned to death for treason, and with his younger brother, Richard, who had married the sister of Clarence's wife and forced him to share the vast estate he had inherited from his father-in-law, the Earl of Warwick (1428–71). Whoever was to blame for his death, it was undoubtedly to Richard's advantage, conveniently removing one of the obstacles that stood between him and the throne.

On this day:

Born: English thriller writer Len Deighton (1929); US novelist and Nobel Prize winner Toni Morrison (1931); Czechoslovakian-born US film director Miloš Forman (1932); US actor John Travolta (1954)

Died: Italian painter Fra Angelico (1455); German religious reformer and founder of the Reformation Martin Luther (1546); New Zealand detective novelist and theatre director Ngaio Marsh (1982); French painter Balthus (2001)

1678 English writer and preacher John Bunyan (1628–88) published the first part of *The Pilgrim's Progress*.

1861 Jefferson Davis (1808–89) was inaugurated as President of the Confederate States in Montgomery, Alabama, USA.

1876 A direct telegraph link was established between the UK and New Zealand.

1930 The planet Pluto was discovered by US astronomer Clyde Tombaugh (1906–97).

1968 British Standard Time was introduced for a trial period of three years, putting the UK one hour ahead of Greenwich Mean Time for the entire year.

1979 The BBC television programme *Antiques Roadshow* was first broadcast.

19 February

The Women's Institute movement came into existence on 19 February 1897. Although it is often regarded as quintessentially British, the organization was founded in Canada, initially in affiliation with the Farmers' Institute, by Adelaide Hoodless (1857–1910), a campaigner for the education of rural women in domestic science and homecraft. In recent years, the WI has taken steps to shake off its 'jam and Jerusalem' image, notably by the publication in 2000 of a calendar featuring photographs of unclothed (but tastefully posed) members of a Yorkshire branch of the organization.

On this day:

Born: Polish astronomer Nicolaus Copernicus (1473); English actor, theatre manager and playwright Sir David Garrick (1717); Italian soprano Adelina Patti (1843); US pianist, composer and bandleader Stan Kenton (1912); British prince Andrew, Duke of York (1960)

Died: French novelist, writer, diarist and Nobel Prize winner André Gide (1951); English film director, scriptwriter and producer Michael Powell (1990); Chinese president Deng Xiaoping (1997)

1674 Britain and the Netherlands signed the Peace of Westminster, ending the third Anglo-Dutch War.

1800 Napoleon I (1769–1821) proclaimed himself First Consul becoming, in effect, the dictator of France.

1878 Thomas Edison (1847–1931) received a patent for the phonograph, the first device for recording sound.

1910 Manchester United Football Club played their first game on their ground at Old Trafford; they lost 4–3 to Liverpool.

1945 World War II – US troops landed on Iwo Jima, the most important and largest of the Japanese Volcano Islands, in the western Pacific Ocean, at the beginning of one of the major battles of the war.

1948 Irish statesman Éamon de Valera (1882–1975) stood down after 16 years as prime minister of Ireland.

1976 Iceland broke off diplomatic relations with UK over disputed fishing limits.

1992 North Korea and South Korea announced an end to hostilities between the two countries.

2001 The Terrorism Act (2000), replacing the Prevention of Terrorism Act (1973), came into force, banning 21 organizations on the grounds that their supporters in the UK promoted terrorism in the UK or abroad.

20 February

Relatively few people are unfortunate enough to die on their birthday, but the bacteriologist René Jules Dubos was one of them. Born in France on 20 February 1901, he died exactly 81 years later, on 20 February 1982. After studying in Paris and New Jersey, Dubos settled in the USA and became a US citizen in 1938. His research into soil micro-organisms led to the discovery of tyrothricin, the first antibiotic to be commercially produced.

On this day:

Born: Hungarian political leader and revolutionary Béla Kun (1886); Polish-born British ballet dancer and teacher Dame Marie Rambert (1888); Soviet politician Aleksei Nikolayevich Kosygin (1904); US film director Robert Altman (1925); US actor and director Sidney Poitier (1927)

Died: Scottish king James I (1437); Scottish radical politician Joseph Hume (1855); US abolitionist Frederick Douglass (1895); US naval commander and Arctic explorer Robert Peary (1920); Australian-born US composer and pianist Percy Grainger (1961)

1547 The nine-year-old King Edward VI (1537–53) was crowned in Westminster Abbey, London.

1816 The première of the opera *The Barber of Seville*, by Gioacchino Rossini (1792–1868), was held in Rome, Italy.

1938 Anthony Eden (1897–1977) resigned as Foreign Secretary in opposition to the appeasement policies towards Germany followed by Prime Minister Stanley Baldwin (1867–1947).

1947 Earl Mountbatten of Burma (1900–79) was appointed as India's last Viceroy to oversee the transfer of power leading to India's independence in 1948.

1962 John Glenn (born 1921) became the first US astronaut to orbit the Earth.

1985 The sale of contraceptives was made legal in the Irish Republic.

1986 The main module of Mir, the first space station designed for semi-permanent orbit, was launched by the USSR.

1993 Two ten-year-old boys, Jon Venables and Robert Thompson, were charged with the abduction and murder of toddler James Bulger.

21 February

> *They shall not pass.*
>
> Attributed to Marshal Pétain during the defence of Verdun (1916).

On 21 February 1916, one of the longest and hardest-fought campaigns of World War I began, with the German bombardment of the French at Verdun in NE France. In the ten months that followed, territory was successively captured and recaptured in a series of attacks and counter-attacks; the advance of the Germans was finally thwarted, but not without heavy losses on both sides.

On this day:

Born: French composer Léo Delibes (1836); English-born US poet and essayist W H Auden (1907); Zimbabwean president Robert Mugabe (1924); US film director Sam Peckinpah (1925); English writer Jilly Cooper (1937)

Died: Dutch philosopher and theologian Benedict de Spinoza (1677); English agriculturist Jethro Tull (1741); Canadian physiologist and Nobel Prize winner Sir Frederick Grant Banting (1941); Australian pathologist and developer of the antibiotic penicillin Howard Florey (1968); English actor John Thaw (2002)

1858 Edwin T Holmes of Boston, Massachusetts installed the world's first burglar alarm.

1885 The Washington Monument was dedicated in Washington, DC.

1925 *The New Yorker* magazine was first published.

1965 US black nationalist leader Malcolm X (1925–65) was assassinated as he began a speech to his followers at the Audubon Ballroom just outside the district of Harlem in New York City.

1975 Former Attorney-General John Mitchell (1913–88), Chief of White House Staff H R Haldeman (1926–93), and domestic affairs advisor John Erlichman (1925–1999) were sentenced to prison for their part in the 'Watergate Affair'.

1989 Leading Czech playwright Vaclav Havel (born 1936), who would later become the country's president, was jailed on political grounds.

1997 The 'Bridgewater Three', convicted for the murder of 13-year-old paper boy Carl Bridgewater, were freed from jail after 18 years when the Court of Appeal ruled that their convictions were unsafe.

2001 The European Commission banned all UK exports of live animals, meat and dairy products following the UK's foot-and-mouth outbreak, the first in the UK since 1967.

22 February

This is **Washington's birthday**, which was celebrated throughout the USA with a public holiday on 22 February until the establishment of Presidents Day on the third Monday of the month. George Washington was one of those people whose lifetime straddled the calendar reform of 1752 and whose date of birth therefore underwent a change: he was born on 11 February 1732 but did not celebrate his twenty-first birthday until 22 February 1753, having 'lost' eleven days in the changeover from the Julian calendar to the Gregorian calendar in September 1752. (To add to the confusion, he was born at a time when the year officially began in March, so the year of his birth is sometimes given as 1731/2.)

George Washington was born in Virginia into a family whose ancestral line has been traced back to Washington in NE England (although it was from Sulgrave Manor in Northamptonshire that his great-grandfather emigrated to the New World). Little is known of his childhood, and the famous story of the hatchet and the cherry tree is undoubtedly apocryphal:

> *'George,' said his father, 'do you know who killed that beautiful little cherry-tree yonder in the garden?' This was a tough question; and George staggered under it for a moment; but quickly recovered himself; and looking at his father, with the sweet face of youth brightened with the inexpressible charm of all-conquering truth, he bravely cried out, 'I can't tell a lie, Pa; you know I can't tell a lie. I did cut it with my hatchet.'*
>
> Mason Locke Weems, *The Life of George Washington* (1806).

In his early twenties Washington embarked on a military career, and by the time the American War of Independence broke out in 1775 he had established a national reputation that secured his appointment as commander-in-chief of the colonial army. After the war was won he turned his attention to politics, presiding over the Constitutional Convention of 1787 and becoming the first President of the USA in 1789. He was elected to a second term in 1793 but resigned in 1797 and died two years later.

On this day:

Born: US poet, essayist and diplomat James Lowell (1819); Spanish film director Luis Buñuel (1900); English actor Sir John Mills (1908); Austrian racing driver Niki Lauda (1949)

Died: French acrobat and tightrope walker Charles Blondin (1897); Austrian composer Hugo Wolf (1903); Anglo-Irish novelist and short-story writer Elizabeth Bowen (1973); English pianist Solomon Cutner (1988); Angolan soldier and nationalist Jonas Savimbi (2002)

1819 Spain and USA signed the Adams–Onís Treaty, by which Florida was formally ceded to the USA.

1879 Frank Winfield Woolworth (1852–1919) opened a store in Utica, New York, USA, for five-cent goods only.

1886 *The Times* became the first newspaper to run a 'Personal' column on its classified page.

1956 Portsmouth beat Newcastle United in the Football League's first floodlit football match.

1958 Egypt and Syria were officially united as the United Arab Republic.

1979 St Lucia gained its independence within the Commonwealth.

1991 In the Gulf War, US President George Bush (born 1924) issued an ultimatum to Iraq to withdraw from Kuwait or face full-scale land war.

2001 In a landmark ruling, the UN International Criminal Tribunal for the former Yugoslavia at the Hague convicted three former Bosnian Serbs of crimes against humanity and war crimes committed in 1992.

23 February

The Cato Street Conspiracy, led by the revolutionary fanatic Arthur Twistlewood, was a plot to overthrow the British government by murdering all the members of the Cabinet as they dined together on 23 February 1820 at Lord Harrowby's house in Grosvenor Square, London.

> *It was arranged that some of the conspirators should watch Lord Harrowby's house; one was to call and deliver a dispatch-box at the door; the others were then to rush in, and … assassinate the ministers as they sat at dinner; bringing away as special trophies, the heads of Lord Sidmouth and Lord Castlereagh, in two bags provided for the purpose! They were then to set fire to the cavalry barracks; and the Bank of England and the Tower of London were to be taken by the people, who, it was hoped, would rise upon the spread of the news. It can scarcely be believed that such a scheme should have been seriously planned in the metropolis only forty years since; yet such was the fact.*
>
> *Chambers Book of Days* (1864).

The authorities learnt of the plot, and a number of the conspirators were arrested that evening at their meeting place in Cato Street. Thistlewood escaped but was captured the next day; he and four of his associates were subsequently charged with high treason and executed.

On this day:

Born: English portrait painter Sir Joshua Reynolds (1792); English painter Sir George Watts (1817); German writer Erich Kästner (1899); US actor Peter Fonda (1939)

Died: Australian operatic soprano Dame Nellie Melba (1931); English painter L S Lowry (1976); US pop artist and film-maker Andy Warhol (1987); English footballer Sir Stanley Matthews (2000)

1836 The Siege of the Alamo began at San Antonio, Texas, USA, when 180 Texans defended the Alamo for twelve days against several thousand Mexicans until the last survivors were overwhelmed.

1874 Major Walter Wingfield patented the game of lawn tennis under the name *sphairistike*.

1893 German engineer Rudolf Diesel (1858–1913) was granted Patent Number 67207 by the German Imperial Patent Office for the diesel engine.

1898 French novelist Émile Zola (1840–1902) was imprisoned in Paris following the publication of his letter 'J'accuse', which accused the French government of anti-Semitism in the case of Captain Alfred Dreyfus (c.1859–1935).

1917 Russia's 'February Revolution' began.

1919 Benito Mussolini (1883–1945) founded the Italian Fascist Party.

1920 The Marconi Company began the first regular public radio broadcasting service from Chelmsford, UK; it ran 30-minute programmes of readings from newspapers and gramophone records until 6 March.

1942 World War II – 'Lend–Lease', the arrangement by which the USA lent or leased war supplies and arms to the UK and other Allies, began.

1942 World War II – a Japanese submarine shelled an oil refinery near Santa Barbara, California, USA, the first attack by Japan on the US mainland.

1950 The BBC first televised the results of a British general election.

1959 The first session of the European Court of Human Rights took place at Strasbourg, France.

1970 Guyana was proclaimed a republic.

1997 Researchers at the Roslin Institute near Edinburgh, Scotland, announced the birth of 'Dolly' – the world's first cloned sheep, who had been born the previous July.

24 February

This is one of the feast days of St Matthias, the apostle who was chosen to replace Judas Iscariot after the death of Christ. (In 1969, his feast day was moved to 14 May in the Roman Catholic Church.) According to various weather proverbs, a frost on **St Matthias's Day** will last for anything from a week to two months.

On this day:

Born: German folklorist Wilhelm Grimm (1786); Scottish footballer Denis Law (1940); French racing driver Alain Prost (1955); US computer inventor and entrepreneur Steve Jobs (1955)

Died: English natural philosopher and chemist Henry Cavendish (1810); US engineer Robert Fulton (1815); English doctor and man of letters Thomas Bowdler (1825); Egyptian prime minister Ahmed Pasha (1945); US publisher Malcolm Forbes (1990)

1582 Pope Gregory XIII (1502–85) announced that the Roman Catholic world would use the new Gregorian calendar.

1868 President Andrew Johnson (1808–75) was impeached by the US House of Representatives; the Senate later acquitted him of the charges by a single vote.

1887 The first telephone link between capital cities was established between Paris, France, and Brussels, Belgium.

1920 Nancy Astor (1879–1964), the first woman MP to sit in the House of Commons, made her maiden speech, becoming the first woman to speak in Parliament.

1932 Sir Malcolm Campbell (1885–1949) beat his earlier land speed record with a speed of 253.968mph in his car *Bluebird* at Daytona Beach, Florida, USA.

1938 The first nylon product, a toothbrush, was produced in New Jersey, USA.

1946 Juan Perón (1895–1974) was elected president of Argentina for the first time.

1966 Kwame Nkrumah (1909–72), first president of Ghana, was exiled as a result of an army coup.

1991 In the Gulf War, the ground campaign for the liberation of Kuwait began.

1999 The Lawrence Report was published, criticizing London's Metropolitan Police in its handling of the investigation into the murder of black teenager Stephen Lawrence (1974–93).

25 February

On this day:

Born: French Impressionist artist Pierre Auguste Renoir (1841); English novelist, critic and composer Anthony Burgess (1917); English actor Sir Tom Courtenay (1937); English film-maker Lord Puttnam (1941)

Died: English soldier and courtier Robert Devereux, Earl of Essex (1601); German-born British journalist Paul Julius Reuter (1899); English cartoonist and illustrator Sir John Tenniel (1914); Australian cricketer Sir Don Bradman (2001)

1308 Edward II (1284–1327) was crowned King of England.

1570 Pope Pius V (1504–72) excommunicated Queen Elizabeth I (1533–1603) and declared her to be a usurper to the throne.

1862 US Congress authorized the issue of banknotes, known as 'greenbacks', during the American Civil War.

1899 The first driver to die in a car accident was one F R Sewell, who was test-driving a Daimler car down Grove Hill in Harrow when the rear wheels collapsed.

1956 Nikita Khrushchev (1894–1971) denounced Joseph Stalin (1894–1971) in a speech to the Congress of the Communist Party in Moscow, USSR.

1964 Cassius Clay (born 1942), later to change his name to Muhammad Ali, knocked out Sonny Liston (1932–70) to win the world heavyweight boxing title for the first time.

1994 Militant Jewish settler Baruch Goldstein shot 29 Muslims praying in a mosque in Hebron, Israel; many more people were injured as they tried to escape the massacre.

2001 A new outbreak of foot-and-mouth disease, which had previously been thought to be contained, was confirmed in the UK in north Devon.

26 February

The Grand National, the most famous steeplechase of the racing calendar, was first run on this day in 1839, at Aintree Racecourse on the outskirts of Liverpool. On that occasion the winner was a horse called 'Lottery', and a certain Captain Becher (1797–1864) was thrown from his mount at a jump now known as Becher's Brook. In modern times the race is usually run in early April; it is no stranger to controversy, although some of the 30 obstacles on the 4.5 mile course have recently been modified to reduce the likelihood of injury to the four-legged participants. One of the most famous horses in the history of the Grand National is Red Rum, who came home first for a record-breaking third time in 1977, having previously won the race in 1973 and 1974. After his death in 1995 he was buried near the winning post of the course, and a statue was erected in front of the grandstand.

On this day:

Born: French poet and writer Victor Hugo (1802); US clothing manufacturer and creator of jeans Levi Strauss (1829); US showman William F 'Buffalo Bill' Cody (1846); English actress

Margaret Leighton (1922); US rhythm and blues pianist and singer Fats Domino (1928)

Died: French political philosopher and diplomat Joseph de Maistre (1821); US inventor Richard Gatling (1903); Scottish comic singer Sir Harry Lauder (1950); Moroccan king Mohammed V (1961)

1797 The first Bank of England one-pound notes were issued.

1815 Napoleon I (1769–1821) escaped from the island of Elba and returned to France.

1848 Friedrich Engels (1820–95) and Karl Marx (1818–83) published the *Communist Manifesto*.

1852 The British troopship HMS *Birkenhead* sank off the coast of Africa with the loss of more than 450 lives.

1919 The Grand Canyon was officially designated as a National Park in the USA.

1935 RADAR – *ra*dio *d*etection *a*nd *r*anging – was first demonstrated by its inventor Sir Robert Watson-Watt (1892–1973).

1952 Prime Minister Winston Churchill (1874–1965) announced that the UK had produced an atomic bomb.

1982 A hijacked Air Tanzania airliner landed at Stansted Airport in the UK: the hijackers gave themselves up two days later and all passengers were released.

1993 A bomb exploded underneath the World Trade Center in New York City, killing six people and injuring more than 1,000 others.

1995 The 233-year-old Barings merchant bank collapsed as a result of fraudulent dealings by trader Nick Leeson (born 1967).

2004 The first British citizenship ceremony was held in Brent, London; 19 immigrants swore an 'oath of allegiance to the Queen' and 'pledged to uphold British democratic values'.

27 February

The US poet Henry Wadsworth Longfellow was born in Portland, Maine, on 27 February 1807. He set his sights on a literary career at an early age and ultimately became Professor of Modern Languages and Literature at Harvard University (1836–54). His early poems were published in various magazines, and in 1839 his first verse collection, *Voices of the Night*, appeared. This was followed in 1841 by *Ballads and Other Poems*, containing 'The Village Blacksmith' and 'The Wreck of the Hesperus'. Longfellow's gift for storytelling made him one of the most popular poets of his era throughout the English-speaking world. His longer narrative poems include *Evangeline* (1849), *The Song of Hiawatha* (1858) and *The Courtship of Miles Standish* (1858). In 1863 he published *Tales of a Wayside Inn*, inspired by Chaucer's *Canterbury Tales* and containing the famous poem 'Paul Revere's Ride' (quoted at 18 April). He died in 1882.

> *Life is real, life is earnest!*
> *And the grave is not its goal;*
> *Dust thou art, to dust returnest,*
> *Was not spoken of the soul.*
> ...
> *Lives of great men all remind us*
> *We can make our lives sublime,*
> *And departing, leave behind us*
> *Footprints on the sands of time.*
>
> Henry Wadsworth Longfellow, *Voices of the Night*, 'A Psalm of Life' (1839).

On this day:

Born: English actress Dame Ellen Terry (1848); Austrian social philosopher and founder of anthroposophy Rudolf Steiner (1861); Italian tenor Enrico Caruso (1873); US contralto Marian Anderson (1897); US actress Dame Elizabeth Taylor (1932)

Died: English diarist and writer John Evelyn (1706); Scottish physician and writer John Arbuthnot (1735); Russian composer and scientist Aleksandr Borodin (1887); Irish humorist Spike Milligan (2002)

1844 The Dominican Republic declared its independence.

1868 English statesman and novelist Benjamin Disraeli (1804–81) became prime minister for the first time.

1879 Ira Remsen (1846–1927) and his assistant Constantin Fahlberg of John Hopkins University, Baltimore, USA, announced the discovery of saccharin.

1900 The Labour Party was founded in the UK by combining the Independent Labour Party, the Fabian Society and the Trade Union movement, with Ramsay MacDonald (1866–1937) as its first Secretary.

1933 The Reichstag, the German parliament building, burned down; the new Nazi government insisted that the act was evidence of a wider communist conspiracy and used the event to suppress the German Communist Party.

1951 The 22nd Amendment to the US Constitution was ratified, precluding any future president from serving more than two terms of four years in office.

1991 Kuwaiti forces re-entered Kuwait City and US President George Bush (born 1924) announced conditions for a ceasefire in the Gulf War.

28 February

This is the feast day of **St Oswald**, Bishop of Worcester and Archbishop of York. St Oswald died on 29 February 992, and until 1968 his feast day was celebrated on 29 February in leap years.

> *Oswald was an Anglo-Saxon prelate who was rewarded with the honour of canonization for the zeal with which he had assisted Dunstan and Odo in revolutionizing the Anglo-Saxon church, and substituting*

the strict monachism of the Benedictines for the old genial married clergy; or, in other words, reducing the Church of England to a complete subjection to Rome. … Oswald died on the day before the kalends of March, that is, on the last day of the previous month; and he is the only saint who takes his place in the calendar for that day.

Chambers Book of Days (1864).

On this day:

Born: US chemist and Nobel Prize winner Linus Pauling (1901); English poet and critic Sir Stephen Spender (1909); US film director Vincente Minelli (1910); Italian-born US racing driver Mario Andretti (1940)

Died: French poet, politician and historian Alphonse Lamartine (1869); US novelist Henry James (1916); Indian statesman and first president of the Republic of India Rajendra Prasad (1963); Swedish politician Olof Palme (1986); English athlete and founder of the London Marathon Chris Brasher (2003)

1784 English evangelist John Wesley (1703–91) issued the Deed of Declaration, which provided the rules and regulations of Methodism.

1900 British troops in the town of Ladysmith were relieved by General Sir Redvers Buller (1839–1908) after 118 days during the Boer War in southern Africa.

1931 Oswald Mosley (1896–1980) founded his 'New Party', which later evolved into the British Union of Fascists.

1975 An underground train crash at London's Moorgate Tube Station killed at least 30 people and seriously injured more than 50.

1991 The Gulf War ended as Iraq accepted the resolutions made by the United Nations.

2001 Ten people died in a railway accident near Selby, North Yorkshire, when a motor vehicle slid down an embankment onto the track and caused a passenger express and a freight train to collide.

29 February

This is **Leap Year Day** (or **Leap Day**), which occurs only once every four years, when the year number is divisible by four but does not end in 00. (An exception is made in years divisible by 400, such as 2000, which was a **leap year**). This complicated rule is necessary to keep the calendar year in line with the solar year of 365.2422 days. Leap Year Day is known as an **intercalary day**, ie one inserted between others, and a formal synonym for 'leap year' is **bissextile year**, from the Latin *annus bissextilis*. In the calendar devised by Julius Caesar, the intercalary day was added after 24 February, which was effectively counted twice: 24 February was *sextus Kalendas Martias* (sixth day before the calends of March) and the following day was *bis sextus Kalendas Martias* (twice sixth day before the calends of March). The latter was commonly shortened to *bissextus*, hence *annus bissextilis* and 'bissextile year'.

People born on 29 February are obliged to celebrate their birthday on 28 February or 1 March in non-leap years. The usual choice is 28 February, and this is the date on which such people legally come of age. The popular notion that Job was born on this day is based on the biblical text 'Let the day perish wherein I was born' (Job 3.3) – 29 February is sometimes known as **Job's Birthday**.

Various superstitions and customs have attached themselves to Leap Year Day, or to leap years in general. On 29 February, women who are tired of waiting for their loved ones to 'pop the question' are entitled to take the initiative and propose marriage (compare Sadie Hawkins Day in November, when girls and women in the USA are encouraged to take the initiative). Often referred to as 'The Ladies' Privilege', it was believed that a man proposed to on 29 February could not refuse, or if he did his refusal had to be accompanied by a compensatory gift such as a silk gown or gloves. One story for the origins of 'The Ladies Privilege' goes back to fifth-century Ireland. St Bridget complained to St Patrick that women never had the chance to propose. St Patrick initially suggested that women be allowed to propose on one day in every seven years, but St Bridget was adamant it should be more often, so a compromise of every four years was reached.

Some people consider it unlucky to embark on any major enterprise (including marriage) in a leap year, or to sow seeds and plant crops on the intercalary day.

On this day:

Born: American mystic and religious leader Ann Lee (1736); Italian operatic composer Gioacchino Rossini (1792); US inventor John Philip Holland (1840); Indian politician and prime minister Ranchhodji Morarji Desai (1896)

Died: English prelate and Archbishop of Canterbury John Whitgift (1604); English actor Roland Culver (1984)

1528 Scottish Lutheran theologian and martyr Patrick Hamilton (1503–28) was burned to death before St Salvator's College, St Andrews.

1692 Arrest warrants were issued for three women – Sarah God, Sarah Osborne and Tituba – in the Salem witch hysteria in Massachusetts, America.

1960 The Moroccan seaport of Agadir was almost entirely destroyed by an earthquake, killing more than half its population.

1968 Dr Jocelyn Bell Burnell (born 1943), a graduate student at Cambridge University, announced the discovery of the pulsar.

1984 Canadian prime minister Pierre Trudeau (1919–2000) announced his retirement from office.

1992 Voting began in the Bosnia-Herzegovina referendum; it resulted in a vote for sovereignty and independence from Yugoslavia.

2004 Haitian president Jean-Bertrand Aristide (born 1953) went into exile following increasing civil unrest and violence in his country.

2004 *Lord of the Rings: The Return of the King* won eleven Oscars® at the 76th Annual Academy Awards ceremony, equalling the record held by *Ben Hur* (1959) and *Titanic* (1997).

Spring

The year's at the spring,
And days at the morn;
Morning's at seven;
The hill-side's dew-pearled;
The lark's on the wing;
The snail's on the thorn;
God's in His heaven –
All's right with the world.

Robert Browning, *Pippa Passes* (1841).

In the Spring a fuller crimson comes upon the robin's breast;
In the Spring the wanton lapwing gets himself another crest;
In the Spring a livelier iris changes on the burnished dove;
In the Spring a young man's fancy lightly turns to
thoughts of love.

Alfred, Lord Tennyson, *Poems*, 'Locksley Hall' (1841).

> *It is not spring until you can plant your foot on twelve daisies.*
>
> Traditional saying.

Origins

The word *spring* is of Old English origin and has many other meanings; it was probably chosen as the name of the season because this is the time when plants spring up and grow. The Latin name for the season was *ver*, a word that is found in the adjective *vernal*, meaning 'of the spring'.

> *In those vernal seasons of the year, when the air is calm and pleasant, it were an injury and sullenness against nature not to go out, and see her riches, and partake in her rejoicing with heaven and earth.*
>
> John Milton, *Of Education* (1644).

Season

Astronomically taken to be the period from the vernal equinox to the summer solstice (occurring around 21 March and 21 June respectively in the northern hemisphere), spring is the time of new birth and new growth in the natural world.

Characteristics

A time of new beginnings, spring is regarded as the first season of the year – indeed, 25 March was once celebrated as New Year's Day. It is the time when life returns to the countryside after the barren months of winter. The monochrome landscape is repainted with the fresh greens of new leaves, the delicate pinks of fruit-tree blossom, and the bright colours of spring flowers. In the animal kingdom this is the breeding season, and the reproductive urge in humans is also popularly believed to be at its strongest: some of the traditional May Day festivities are said to have their origins in fertility rituals.

For those who make their living from the land, spring is a busy time of year – at least in the early part of the season. As the weather becomes warmer and the days grow longer, town and city folk feel more inclined to activity (both indoors and outdoors), especially those with a house and garden to maintain: the sound of the first lawnmower in the suburbs has been facetiously equated to the sound of the first cuckoo in the countryside.

Easter

Springtime and Eastertide are inextricably linked: many of the secular customs associated with Easter have their roots in pagan spring festivals. The name *Easter* may be derived from *Eostre*, the name of an Anglo-Saxon goddess associated with the spring, or it may simply be related to *east*, the direction of dawn, the rebirth of the day, symbolic of new beginnings. The Anglo-Saxon name for April, the month in which Easter most frequently falls, was *Eastermonath*. Easter Day can fall on any date from 22 March to 25 April (it is the Sunday following the first full moon on or after 21 March, the vernal equinox), and many other moveable feasts of the Christian calendar are dependent on this date, from Shrovetide in February or March to Whitsuntide in May or June.

Palm Sunday, the Sunday before Easter, marks the beginning of **Holy Week**. It is so named because it commemorates the triumphal entry of Christ into Jerusalem, his path strewn with palm branches. Since the Middle Ages, churchgoers have had 'palm' crosses (made from any suitable plant, such as willow or yew) blessed by their priest on this day.

> *After the Reformation, 1536, Henry VII declared the carrying of palms on this day to be one of those ceremonies not to be contemned or dropped. The custom was kept up by the clergy till the reign of Edward VI, when it was left to the voluntary observance of the people. ... It has continued down to a recent period, if not to the present day, to be customary in many parts of England to go a-palming on the Saturday before Palm Sunday; that is, young persons go to the woods for slips of willow, which seems to be the tree chiefly employed in England as a substitute for the palm, on which account it often receives the latter name. They return with slips in their hats or button-holes, or a sprig in their mouths, bearing the branches in their hands.*
>
> *Chambers Book of Days* (1864).

In some English churches small buns called **pax cakes** (symbolic of peace and goodwill) are given to the congregation as they leave after the Palm Sunday service. Elsewhere, the day was formerly known as **Fig Sunday**, from a reference to this fruit in Mark 11.12: 'And seeing a fig tree afar off having leaves, he came, if haply he might find any thing thereon'.

Maundy Thursday, the day before Good Friday, was formerly marked by a ceremony in which the monarch washed the feet of a selected number of poor people, in commemoration of Christ's washing his disciples' feet before the Last Supper. This has been replaced by the giving of alms, in the form of specially minted coins (**maundy money**), to one man and one woman for each year of the sovereign's age. In 2003 the foot-washing ceremony was revived by the Archbishops of Canterbury and Westminster, who performed this service for 12 members of their congregations. The word *Maundy* comes from *Mandatum novum do vobis* ('A new commandment I give unto you'), the opening words of John 13.34.

Good Friday, commemorating Christ's crucifixion, is a public holiday in much of the UK. There are a number of superstitions relating to this day, notably that it is a good day for planting potatoes and sowing parsley. Hot-cross buns are traditionally eaten on Good Friday; any that are left over are supposed to remain fresh for ever, because they are marked with the holy cross, and their crumbs can be used as a remedy for digestive upsets. Now available in supermarkets for several weeks before Easter, they were formerly sold by street vendors on Good Friday morning:

> *Hot cross buns! Hot cross buns!*
> *One a penny, two a penny, hot cross buns!*
> *Give them to your daughters, give them to your sons.*
> *One a penny, two a penny, hot cross buns!*
>
> Traditional street vendors' cry.

At the London pub, The Widow's Son, a **Hot Cross Bun Ceremony** takes place each Good Friday. In the early 19th century, a widow who lived on the site was expecting her sailor son back home for Easter, and placed a hot cross bun ready for him on Good Friday. The son never returned, but undaunted the widow left the bun waiting for him and added a new bun each year. Successive landlords have kept the tradition going after the pub was opened.

Easter Saturday is marked in the small Pennine town of Bacup with the **Bacup Nutters Dance**. Each year a team of folk-dancers with blackened faces dance through the town from boundary to boundary. A form of morris dancing, the blackened faces may either reflect a need for the dancers to disguise their faces from evil spirits, or have a mining connection. The tradition of the dance is thought to date back to 1857.

Easter Sunday, or **Easter Day**, is the principal festival of the Christian calendar, celebrating Christ's Resurrection. It was once believed that the sun danced for joy as it rose on this day, and people would flock to high places to observe this phenomenon. For centuries, **Easter eggs** have been given to friends and family. Formerly, decorated hardboiled eggs were given. These could be dyed by boiling the egg with a variety of natural products (onion skins make the egg shells yellow, grass makes the shells green), and then decorated by scratching a design through the dye. Chocolate eggs are now the most common form of Easter gift. The egg is symbolic of new life; it was also a forbidden food during Lent, making a welcome return to the menu on

Easter Day. Easter eggs are sometimes known as **pace eggs**, a name that is ultimately derived from *Pesach* (Passover) and survives chiefly in such traditions as the **Midgley Pace Egg Play**, a mumming play performed in and around the Yorkshire village of Midgley on Good Friday.

A variety of games have developed alongside Easter eggs (many of which take place on Easter Monday, see below) including **Easter egg hunts**. Parents hide Easter eggs in the garden for children to discover. In recent years such games have been linked to the **Easter Bunny**, which only arrived in Britain relatively recently. German references to an **Easter Hare** laying eggs date back to at least the late 1500s, and it may be that settlers of German descent brought the tradition to America, where the hare developed into a bunny. Another egg game is **egg tapping**, which in some ways resembles conkers. Two eggs are tapped together end to end until one of the eggs cracks. The cracked egg is then handed over to the winner whose egg is still unscathed.

One of the most famous **egg rolling** events takes place at the White House on Easter Monday. First held on 2 April 1877 and reintroduced by President Eisenhower in 1953, this is the White House's largest public celebration. All manner of egg-related organized games are played, as well as the famous egg-rolling race. According to legend, public egg rolling in Washington, DC, (originally on the grounds of the Capitol) can be traced back to the early 1800s. There are a number of possible variations to the game – egg races vary from those traditionally held in Scotland and England, where children must roll their eggs downhill and the last child with an unbroken egg wins, to **egg and spoon** races and competitions where an egg must be pushed along the length of the course using only your nose.

Easter Monday, another public holiday in much of the UK, has little religious significance but is the occasion for numerous secular customs. At Biddenden in Kent, the **Biddenden Dole**, in the form of bread, cheese, tea (formerly beer) and cakes, is distributed. The cakes bear an image of two women said to be the founders of this charity, a pair of Siamese twins who were born in 1100 and died within hours of each other at the age of 34. At Hallaton in Leicestershire, the **Hare Pie Scramble and Bottle Kicking** begins with the blessing of a pie (usually made with beef rather than hare), which is subsequently broken up and thrown to the assembled crowd. This is followed by an unruly football game between the villages of Hallaton and Medbourne. Small wooden barrels filled with ale are used like rugby balls in the no-holds barred contest, the object of which is to get each of three casks to a touchline in either village. Perhaps the most bizarre tradition, however, was that of **lifting**, which took place on Easter Monday and Easter Tuesday in the 18th and 19th centuries:

> *In Lancashire, and in Cheshire, Staffordshire and Warwickshire, and perhaps in other counties, the ridiculous custom of 'lifting' or 'heaving' is practised. On Easter Monday the men lift the women, and on Easter Tuesday the women lift or heave the men. The process is performed by two lusty men or women joining their hands across each other's wrists; then, making the person to be heaved sit down on their arms, they lift him up aloft two or three times, and often carry him several yards along a street.*
>
> *Chambers Book of Days* (1864).

Other religious festivals

Pesach (or **Passover**) is a Jewish festival that takes place in the month of Nisan (March–April): Christ's Last Supper with his disciples was the Passover feast. It is from the word *Pesach* that *paschal*, an adjective relating both to Passover and the Christian festival of Easter, is derived. Pesach commemorates the exodus of the Israelites from Egypt, specifically God's passing over their houses when he killed the first-born children of the Egyptians. It is marked by the eating of unleavened bread (all traces of leaven must be removed from the house before the festival) and by a special ceremonial family meal (**Seder**) accompanied by various rituals, such as blessings, prayers, songs and the retelling of the story of the exodus.

Shabuoth (or **Shavuot**) is the Jewish **Feast of Weeks**, falling in the month of Sivan (May–June), 50 days after Passover. It commemorates God's giving of the Ten Commandments to Moses on Mount Sinai and also celebrates the harvest of the first fruits. Traditions associated with this festival include eating dairy products (probably because the Israelites became bound by kosher dietary laws on receiving the Torah from God but did not immediately have any kosher meat to eat), decorating homes and synagogues with flowers and greenery, and reading the book of Ruth. Like the Christian festival of Whitsun, Shabuoth is also called **Pentecost**.

Whit Sunday (or **Pentecost**) is a Christian festival that falls between 10 May and 13 June, on the seventh Sunday after Easter Day. It commemorates the descent of the Holy Ghost on Christ's apostles, who 'began to speak with other tongues, as the Spirit gave them utterance' (Acts 2.4). Named after the white robes worn by people converted or baptized at this time, Whit Sunday was formerly followed by a public holiday, **Whit Monday**, and the extended weekend was known as **Whitsun**

or **Whitsuntide.** When the public holiday was changed to the last Monday in May (now officially known as the Spring Bank Holiday), many of its associated customs and festivities moved with it. One of the surviving traditions of Whitsuntide takes place on the evening of Whit Sunday at St Briavels in Gloucestershire, when bread and cheese are thrown from the top of a high wall to the crowd below, who scramble for their share. Observance of this custom is supposed to preserve the right of local people to cut timber in a nearby wood.

March

Gemstone: Aquamarine
Flower: Violet or daffodil

> *Married when March winds shrill and roar,*
> *Your home will be on a distant shore.*
>
> Traditional rhyme.

> *March is the first month of Spring. He is Nature's Old Forester, going through the woods and dotting the trees with green, to mark out the spots where the future leaves are to be hung. The sun throws a golden glory over the eastern hills, as the village-clock from the ivy-covered tower tolls six, gilding the hands and the figures that were scarcely visible two hours later a few weeks ago. The streams now hurry along with a rapid motion, as if they … were eager to rush along the green meadow-lands, to tell the flowers it is time to awaken.*
>
> *Chambers Book of Days* (1864).

Origins

March, the third month of the year, takes its name from Mars (Latin *Martius*), the god of war – this is the month when military campaigns generally began, after the end of winter. In the early Roman calendar it was the first month of the year.

> *I Martius am! Once first, and now the third!*
> *To lead the Year was my appointed place;*
> *A mortal dispossessed me by a word,*
> *And set there Janus with the double face.*
> *Hence I make war on all the human race;*

March

I shake the cities with my hurricanes;
I flood the rivers and their banks efface,
And drown the farms and hamlets with my rains.

Henry Wadsworth Longfellow, *In the Harbor*, 'The Poet's Calendar' (1882).

Characteristics

March is often regarded as the first month of spring, but astronomically it straddles the seasons, the first 20 days belonging to winter. In some respects it is a month of preparation and anticipation: for farmers it is the sowing season, and in the Christian Church it is largely dominated by the Lenten fast and the approach of Easter. In March the countryside begins its transition from brown to green and the earliest spring flowers, such the primrose and the crocus, appear in fields and gardens. For many birds and animals March is also the beginning of the breeding season, and the behaviour of one particular animal at this time has given rise to the saying 'mad as a March hare'.

History

Lide, an early name for March, is derived from the Old English *Hlyda*, which probably referred to the loudness of the wind in this month. The word survived in a country proverb that recommended the eating of 'leeks in Lide and ramsins [garlic] in May'. The Anglo-Saxons named it *Lenetmonath* ('length month'), which refers to the lengthening of the days during this month; it is also related to the words *Lenten* and *Lent*.

Weather

Windy and dry weather in March is generally considered to be a good thing: 'March winds and April showers bring forth May flowers', 'A bushel of March dust is worth a king's ransom', and 'A dry and cold March never begs for bread'. However, there is some contradiction in the weather lore: the saying 'March comes in like a lion and goes out like a lamb' gives the lie to a popular rhyme about the **borrowing days** (either the last three days of March or the first three days of April).

March borrowed from April
Three days and they were ill

The first was snow and sleet
The next was cold and wet
The third was such a freeze
The bird's nests stuck to trees.

Traditional rhyme.

All in all, March is often not a pleasant month, as the Canadian writer and broadcaster Garrison Keillor remarked:

March is the month that God designed to show those who don't drink what a hangover is like.

Garrison Keillor, National Public Radio broadcast (1 December 1991).

Non-fixed notable dates

Non-fixed notable dates in March include:

Mothering Sunday: The fourth Sunday in Lent (Mid-Lent Sunday), falling between 1 March and 4 April, depending on the date of Easter Day. Mothering Sunday was originally marked by processions to the mother church of the diocese. When these were discontinued it became a day on which young people working away from home, notably those in domestic service, would return to visit their mothers, traditionally bearing a gift of **Simnel cake**. This is a rich fruit cake filled and decorated with marzipan: twelve balls of marzipan placed on the top represent the months of the year (or, if the cake is baked for Easter instead, eleven balls represent the apostles minus Judas Iscariot).

The harshness and general painfulness of life in old times must have been much relieved by certain simple and affectionate customs which modern people have learned to dispense with. Amongst these was a practice of going to see parents, and especially the female one, on the mid Sunday of Lent, taking for them some little present, such as a cake or a trinket … One can readily imagine how, after a stripling or maiden had gone to service, or launched in independent housekeeping, the old bonds of filial love would be brightened by this pleasant annual visit.

Chambers Book of Days (1864).

In the UK in modern times, Mothering Sunday is more often known as **Mother's Day**, a name imported from the USA (where it falls in May) during World War II. Mothers receive cards and gifts from their daughters and sons, and some of those whose children are still at home are treated to a day of rest.

Commonwealth Day: On the second Monday in March the links between the nations of the Commonwealth are reinforced and celebrated. The Head of the Commonwealth (the British monarch) issues a message to all the citizens of the Commonwealth, and the day is marked with various special events, such as sports tournaments, concerts or tree-planting ceremonies. In 1958, Commonwealth Day replaced **Empire Day**, which had been celebrated since Queen Victoria's reign. On that day schoolchildren would deck themselves in red, white and blue, the colours of the Union Jack, or take prams and bicycles to school festooned with ribbons or rosettes in these colours.

Kiplingcotes Derby: Said to be the oldest flat race in England, the Kiplingcotes Derby is held in Yorkshire on the third Thursday in March and has been run since 1519, with rules drawn up in 1618 and a permanent endowment given in 1669. The race often has fewer than a dozen entrants, invites horses of all ages and distinctions and takes entrants on the morning of the race. The course is uphill, along lanes and farm tracks and riders must weigh more than 10st or wear weights. In the past it was possible for the second prize to be more valuable than the first, since the runner-up received the sum of the entrance fees, rather than the fixed amount of the first prize. The race has been held every year, and even during the restrictions of the foot-and-mouth outbreak of 2001 a single entrant walked his horse around the course to preserve the unbroken record.

British Summer Time: On the last Sunday in March, clocks throughout the United Kingdom (and other countries of the European Community) are put forward by one hour to take maximum advantage of the longer daylight hours. The change officially occurs at 1am Greenwich Mean Time (GMT), which becomes 2am British Summer Time (BST).

1 March

> *St David's Day, put oats and barley in the clay.*
>
> Traditional saying.

St David (or Dewi) is the patron saint of Wales. Little is known for certain about his life: he is said to have been the son of a prince or chieftain of Cardigan and to have founded several Welsh monasteries, notably one at Menevia (now St David's in Pembrokeshire), of which he was abbot-bishop. The date of his death is variously given as 544, 589 or 601.

> *St David has been invested by his legendary biographers with extravagant decoration. According to their accounts, he had not merely the power of working miracles from the moment of his birth, but the same preternatural faculty is ascribed to him while he was yet unborn! An angel is said to have been his constant attendant on his first appearance on earth, to minister to his wants, and contribute to his edification and relaxation; ... he healed complaints and re-animated the dead; whenever he preached, a snow-white dove sat upon his shoulder!*
>
> *Chambers Book of Days* (1864).

Customs associated with **St David's Day** include the wearing of one of the national symbols of Wales, either a leek (in the hatband) or a daffodil (in the buttonhole). The daffodil, traditionally said to bloom for the first time on 1 March, is the modern preference, for obvious reasons. (The similarity of the word *daffodil* to *Dafydd*, a Welsh form of *David*, is probably coincidental, as the saint is called *Dewi* in Wales and the flower name was *affodil*, a variant of *asphodel*, until the 16th century.)

The significance of the leek has been the subject of much debate. St David is popularly thought to have instructed his men to wear leeks in battle so that they could be easily distinguished from the enemy. (In Shakespeare's play *Henry V*, the Welsh soldier Fluellen makes reference to this story.) An alternative explanation is simply that leeks, like daffodils, are readily available at this time of year. It was formerly customary on 1 March for villagers to help out any neighbours who had failed to finish their ploughing before the end of February; each would bring a contribution, often in the form of a leek, to the communal meal that was served at the end of the day.

1 March

St David's Day is now marked by Welsh people all over the world. Male voice choirs give concerts, traditional Welsh dishes such as cawl (broth and meat) and bara brith ('speckled bread') are eaten, and Welsh song, dance and poetry are celebrated.

The less well-known tradition of **Whuppity Scoorie** also takes place on 1 March each year. In the Royal Burgh of Lanark, Scotland, children race around the church of St Nicholas, making lots of noise and armed with paper balls tied to pieces of string with which they try to hit each other. The children then scramble for pennies from the Common Good Fund. The origins of the tradition are obscure, but it could relate to the lengthening of the days at this time of year, or be a method of chasing away evil spirits. One further suggestion is that it relates to the 'scooring' or cleansing of local ne'er-do-wells, by whipping them and dunking them in the local river.

On this day:

Born: English biographer Lytton Strachey (1880); US trombonist and bandleader Glenn Miller (1904); English actor David Niven (1910); Israeli soldier, statesman and Nobel Prize winner Yitzhak Rabin (1922); English vocalist with The Who Roger Daltrey (1944)

Died: Italian composer Girolamo Frescobaldi (1643); Italian writer, adventurer and political leader Gabriele d'Annunzio (1938); English footballer Dixie Dean (1980); US comedian of the Three Stooges trio Joe Besser (1988)

1493 Europeans first heard news of the New World when Martín Alonso Pinzón (c.1441–1493), a member of the expedition led by Christopher Columbus (1451–1506), returned to Spain in the *Pinta*; Columbus himself arrived back two weeks later.

1498 Vasco da Gama (c.1469–1525) discovered Mozambique.

1546 Scottish reformer George Wishart (c.1513–1546) was burned to death at St Andrews.

1562 The massacre of the Protestant Huguenots at Vassay began the French Wars of Religion.

1692 In Massachusetts a female slave named Tituba who had been accused of practising witchcraft confessed, leading to further accusations and the outbreak of mass hysteria known as the Salem Witch Trials.

1711 The first issue of *The Spectator* was published.

1781 The Articles of Confederation, the constitution of the USA from 1781 to 1788, was formally ratified; it established a single-house Congress, with one vote for each state and with no executive, courts or independent revenue.

1803 Ohio became the 17th state of the USA.

1815 Napoleon I (1769–1821) escaped from Elba and landed on the French coast on his way to Paris.

1864 The Raid on Richmond took place in the American Civil War.

1867 Nebraska became the 37th state of the USA.

1872 Over two million acres of Idaho, Montana and Wyoming were designated as the USA's first national park, Yellowstone.

1896 The Battle of Adowa, or Adwa, began between Ethiopian and Italian forces; the Italians were decisively defeated, ensuring Ethiopian independence for another 40 years.

1912 Suffragettes organized a hammer attack on shop windows in Oxford Street and Regent Street, London.

1936 The Cheltenham Gold Cup was won for the fifth consecutive year by Golden Miller.

1946 The Bank of England was nationalized into public ownership.

1949 US boxer Joe Louis (1914–81) retired as undefeated heavyweight boxing champion of the world.

1954 The USA exploded hydrogen bombs at Bikini Atoll in the Pacific Ocean.

1966 The USSR's robotic spacecraft *Venera 3* made the first landing on Venus.

1966 Chancellor of the Exchequer James Callaghan (born 1912) announced to the House of Commons that the UK would change to a decimal system of currency in 1971.

1992 Bosnia and Herzegovina declared independence from Yugoslavia.

1999 The Landmines Act (1998) came into force as part of a worldwide ban initiated by the United Nations.

2 March

Feast day of **St Chad** (or Ceadda), bishop of Mercia at Lichfield and patron saint of mineral springs (such as St Chad's Well in Lichfield, in which he is reputed to have stood naked to pray).

On this day:

Born: German-born US composer Kurt Weill (1900); US children's author and illustrator Dr Seuss (1904); Russian statesman and Nobel Prize winner Mikhail Gorbachev (1931); US vocalist with the Carpenters Karen Carpenter (1950)

Died: English evangelist and founder of Methodism John Wesley (1791); Russian tsar Nicholas I (1855); English novelist, poet and essayist D H Lawrence (1930); English pop singer Dusty Springfield (1999)

1331 The Conquest of Nicaea took place, in which the Byzantine town of Nicaea fell to the Ottomans under Orhan (1288–1359).

1836 The independent Republic of Texas was created by the signing of the Texas Declaration of Independence by 58 citizens of Mexico.

1836 The first point-to-point meeting was organized by the Worcester Hunt.

1882 An assassination attempt was made by Roderick Maclean on Queen Victoria (1819–1901) as she travelled through Windsor.

1946 North Vietnamese leader Ho Chi Minh (1892–1969) was formally elected president of the Democratic Republic of Vietnam.

1949 A US Air Force B50 aeroplane, *Lucky Lady II*, commanded by Captain James Gallagher, landed in Texas at 9:22am having completed the first non-stop round-the-world flight; it had taken off from the same air force base four days earlier, and refuelled four times in mid-air.

1958 The English explorer and scientist Vivian Fuchs (1908–99) reached Scott Base, Victoria Land, having led the first expedition to cross Antarctica; the expedition had travelled 2,200 miles in 99 days, having set out from Shackleton Base, Weddell Sea, on 24 November the previous year.

1969 The maiden flight of the first French Concorde took place.

1970 Rhodesia was proclaimed a republic by its leader Ian Smith (born 1919).

2000 Former Chilean dictator General Augusto Pinochet Ugarte (born 1915) left the UK to return to Chile after Home Secretary Jack Straw (born 1946) announced his decision to drop extradition proceedings by Spain on the grounds of Pinochet's ill health.

3 March

Feast day of **St Winwaloe** (or Winnold), founder of a Breton monastery and mentioned in an English proverb forecasting stormy weather on this day: 'First comes David, next comes Chad, then comes Winnold, roaring like mad.'

On this day:

Born: English poet and politician Edmund Waller (1606); Scottish-born US inventor of the telephone Alexander Graham Bell (1847); English conductor Sir Henry Wood (1869); US actress Jean Harlow (1911); English actress Miranda Richardson (1958)

Died: English experimental philosopher and architect Robert Hooke (1703); Scottish architect Robert Adam (1792); Hungarian-born British writer and journalist Arthur Koestler (1983); US stage, radio and film actor Danny Kaye (1987)

1585 The first purpose-built covered theatre opened at Vicenza, Italy.

1802 Beethoven's (1770–1827) Piano Sonata no14 in C sharp minor, 'Moonlight', was published.

1820 The Missouri Compromise was agreed; it was decided to admit Missouri, with slavery, and Maine (formerly part of Massachusetts), without it, to statehood simultaneously, in order to preserve a sectional balance in the US Senate.

1845 Florida became the 27th state of the USA.

1875 The première of the opera *Carmen*, by Georges Bizet (1838–75), was held in Paris.

1878 The Treaty of San Stefano ended the Russo-Turkish War.

1918 World War I – the Treaty of Brest-Litovsk was signed between the Central Powers (Germany and Austria-Hungary) and the new Soviet state of Russia, by which Russia withdrew from the war.

1923 The first edition of *Time* magazine was published in the USA.

1931 *The Star-Spangled Banner* was adopted as the US national anthem. It had been written in 1814 by Francis Scott Key (1780–1843) as the poem 'The Defence of Fort McHenry', and later set to a tune, 'To Anacreon in Heaven', by the English composer, John Stafford Smith (1750–1836).

1972 The USA's *Pioneer 10* spacecraft was launched; it later made a Jupiter fly-by, crossed Pluto's orbit and became the first man-made object to escape the solar system.

1974 A Turkish Airlines DC10 aeroplane crashed soon after take-off from Paris, killing 346 people.

1985 The National Union of Mineworkers voted to end its yearlong strike.

4 March

On this day:

Born: Italian violinist and composer Antonio Vivaldi (1678); Scottish portrait painter Sir Henry Raeburn (1756); English astronomer, author and broadcaster Sir Patrick Moore (1923); Scottish footballer and manager Kenny Dalglish (1951)

Died: Egyptian and Syrian Sultan during the Crusades Saladin (1193); French Egyptologist who deciphered the Rosetta Stone Jean François Champollion (1832); Russian novelist and dramatist Nikolai Gogol (1852); English builder who

originated 'daylight saving' William Willett (1915); Chinese feminist writer and Communist Party activist Ding Ling (1986)

1461 Edward of York (1442–83) succeeded the deposed King Henry VI (1421–71), assuming the English throne as King Edward IV.

1675 The first Astronomer Royal, John Flamsteed (1646–1719), was appointed by King Charles II (1630–85).

1681 English Quaker leader William Penn (1644–1718) received a grant of land in North America from King Charles II (1630–85); he named it Pennsylvania in honour of his father.

1789 The Constitution of the USA came into force as the first meeting of Congress took place in New York City, also beginning the term of office of President George Washington (1732–99), although Washington did not take the oath of office until April. All subsequent US presidents were inaugurated on this day until 1933, when the 20th amendment to the Constitution decreed that noon on 20 January would be the new changeover date.

1791 Vermont became the 14th state of the USA.

1824 The Royal National Lifeboat Institution was founded by Sir William Hillary (1771–1847).

1877 The première of the ballet *Swan Lake*, by Pyotr Ilyich Tchaikovsky (1840–93), was held at the Bolshoi Theatre, Moscow.

1890 The Forth Rail Bridge on the Firth of Forth near Edinburgh, Scotland, was officially opened by Edward, Prince of Wales (1841–1910).

1893 Grover Cleveland (1837–1908) was inaugurated as 24th President of the USA; he had also previously served as the 22nd President between 1885 and 1889.

1975 English film actor and director Charlie Chaplin (1889–1977) was knighted.

1980 Robert Mugabe (born 1924) won elections in Zimbabwe to become the new prime minister.

1986 The *Today* newspaper was launched, the UK's first national colour newspaper.

5 March

On this day in 1512 the Flemish geographer and cartographer Gerardus Mercator was born. He is remembered for Mercator's projection, a method of map-drawing commonly used for nautical charts, in which the lines of latitude and longitude are represented as parallel straight lines intersecting at right angles. A development of this projection is used for land maps such as the British Ordnance Survey series. Mercator is also credited with the introduction of the term *atlas* to denote a book of maps, having published such a book in 1585 with a cover illustration of Atlas holding a globe on his shoulders. (In Greek mythology, Atlas was a Titan who was forced as a punishment to hold the heavens on his shoulders.) Mercator died in 1594.

On this day:

Born: English king Henry II (1133); English actor Sir Rex Harrison (1908); English actress and singer Elaine Paige (1951)

Died: Italian painter Correggio (1534); Italian physicist and inventor of the electric battery Alessandro Volta (1827); Soviet revolutionary and leader Joseph Stalin (1953); Russian composer Sergei Prokofiev (1953); US actor John Belushi (1982); English couturier and royal dressmaker Sir Hardy Amies (2003)

1770 The 'Boston Massacre' took place in Massachusetts, America, when British troops opened fire on an unruly crowd and killed five people; this was the first bloodshed of the American Revolution.

1856 The original Covent Garden Theatre was destroyed by fire.

1933 The Nazi Party won almost 44% of the vote in German parliamentary elections.

1936 The Spitfire, the wartime fighter aircraft designed by Reginald Mitchell (1895–1937), made its maiden flight from Eastleigh airport in Hampshire.

1946 Winston Churchill (1874–1965) made his 'Iron Curtain' speech about the threat from the USSR at Fulton, Missouri, USA, saying that 'an Iron Curtain has descended across Europe'.

1960 US popular singer Elvis Presley (1935–77) was discharged from the army with the rank of sergeant after service in Germany.

1966 A BOAC Boeing 707 aeroplane crashed into Mt Fuji, Japan, killing 124 people.

1993 Canadian track athlete Ben Johnson (born 1961) was banned for life by the IAAF after he failed a drugs test.

1998 Water, in the form of ice, was discovered at the north and south poles of the Moon by a NASA *Lunar Prospector* spacecraft.

6 March

On this day:

Born: Italian sculptor, painter and poet Michelangelo (1475); French writer and dramatist Cyrano de Bergerac (1619); English poet Elizabeth Barrett Browning (1806); New Zealand soprano Dame Kiri Te Kanawa (1944)

Died: US writer Louisa M Alcott (1888); German engineer and inventor of the motorcycle Gottlieb Daimler (1900); Welsh actor, composer, songwriter and dramatist Ivor Novello (1951); US novelist and Nobel Prize winner Pearl S Buck (1973); US painter Georgia O'Keeffe (1986)

1714 Emperor Charles VI (1685–1740) signed the Treaty of Rastatt, ending hostilities which had lingered after the Peace of Utrecht (1713) which ended the War of the Spanish Succession (1702–13).

1836 'The Siege of the Alamo' ended, with the deaths of US adventurer Jim Bowie (1790–1836) and frontiersman Davy Crockett (1786–1836).

1853 The première of the opera *La Traviata*, by Giuseppe Verdi (1813–1901), was held in Venice, Italy.

1856 The Supreme Court ruled against US slave Dred Scott (c.1795–1858) in a celebrated case which had made legal and constitutional history as

Scott sought to obtain his freedom on the grounds that he lived in the free state of Illinois.

1899 Commercial Aspirin® was patented in Berlin by German chemist Dr Felix Hoffmann (1868–1946).

1930 US businessman and inventor Clarence Birdseye (1886–1956) first put frozen foods on sale in Massachusetts, USA.

1957 Ghana became the first British colony in Africa to achieve independence.

1964 Constantine II (born 1940) succeeded Paul I (1901–64) as King of Greece.

1987 The ferry *Herald of Free Enterprise* sank off Zeebrugge, Belgium, after setting sail with her bow doors open; almost 200 passengers drowned.

1988 Three members of the IRA were shot dead in Gibraltar.

On this day:

Born: English astronomer Sir John Herschel (1792); Dutch artist Piet Mondrian (1872); French composer Maurice Ravel (1875); Antiguan cricketer Sir Viv Richards (1952)

Died: Italian scholastic philosopher and theologian St Thomas Aquinas (1274); French prime minister and Nobel Prize winner Aristide Briand (1932); English novelist, painter and critic Wyndham Lewis (1957); US screenwriter, film producer and director Stanley Kubrick (1999)

1804 The Royal Horticultural Society was founded as the Horticultural Society of London by Sir Joseph Banks (1744–1820) and John Wedgwood (1766–1844).

1821 The Battle of Rieti saw the defeat of Italian patriot and general Guglielmo Pepe (1783–1855) by Austrian troops sent to restore the full powers of Ferdinand I (1751–1825).

1876 Alexander Graham Bell (1847–1922) was issued with US patent number 174,465 for the first telephone.

1945 World War II – Allied troops crossed the River Rhine at Remagen in their final advance on Berlin.

1968 The first colour news programme, *Newsroom*, was broadcast.

1969 London Underground's Victoria Line, from Walthamstow Central to Victoria, was officially opened by Queen Elizabeth II (born 1926).

1987 Indian cricketer Sunil Gavaskar (born 1949) became the first player to score more than 10,000 Test runs.

8 March

International Women's Day was established at the International Socialist Women's Conference in Copenhagen in 1910. In the early years, the main aims of International Women's Day were the promotion of women's rights (especially at work and in politics) and the achievement of universal women's suffrage. As time passed and battles were won, it became a day for celebrating the progress that had been made by women's groups around the world and for focusing attention on specific issues, such as the plight of women living in developing countries or under oppressive regimes. Since 1975 the United Nations have celebrated International Women's Day on 8 March, promoting a particular theme each year since 1996.

On this day:

Born: US Supreme Court judge Oliver Wendell Holmes (1841); Scottish children's writer Kenneth Grahame (1859); US dancer Cyd Charisse (1921); English actress Lynn Redgrave (1943)

Died: English iron-master Abraham Darby (1717); French composer Hector Berlioz (1869); German army officer and airship pioneer Count Ferdinand von Zeppelin (1917); Irish ballerina Dame Ninette de Valois (2001)

1481 English printer William Caxton (c.1422–c.1491) completed a translation of a French work, *The Mirror of the World*, into English.

1702 Anne (1665–1714), daughter of King James VII and II (1633–1701), became Queen of Great Britain and Ireland when the childless King William III (1650–1702) died after falling off his horse.

1862 A sea battle between the USS *Monitor* and CSS *Merrimack* took place off Hampton Roads, Virginia, during the American Civil War; it was the first battle between ironclad, steam-powered warships and it changed the nature of naval combat.

1961 The first US nuclear-powered submarine arrived at Holy Loch, Scotland.

1963 The Revolutionary Command Council took power in Syria.

1974 The third Paris airport, Charles de Gaulle, opened.

2001 The jet-powered speedboat *Bluebird* was raised from Coniston Water in the Lake District, where it had crashed killing Donald Campbell (1921–67) 34 years earlier.

9 March

Forty Martyrs' Day, celebrated on 9 March in some Orthodox Christian Churches, commemorates the death of 40 Christian soldiers in the Roman army. Executed in the early fourth century in Armenia for openly confessing their Christianity, the soldiers were made to stand naked on an icy pond throughout a winter's night, and died of exposure. Some accounts suggest that one of the forty turned his back on Christianity in order to live, but that another soldier who was watching over the Christians was so inspired by them that he became a Christian himself and joined them in death. Their sacrifice is marked by the preparation of dishes containing 40 different herbs, for example, or cakes with 40 layers of pastry.

On this day:

Born: Spanish explorer after whom the continent of America was named Amerigo Vespucci (1451); English politician Ernest Bevin (1881); English poet and novelist Vita Sackville-West (1892); US chess player Bobby Fischer (1943)

Died: Italian courtier, musician and favourite of Mary, Queen of Scots David Rizzio (1566); French cleric, diplomat and politician Cardinal Jules Mazarin (1661); Prussian king and first German emperor Wilhelm I (1888); English politician Lord Butler (1982)

1562 Naples brought in the death penalty for anyone caught kissing in public.

1796 Napoleon I (1769–1821) married widow Vicountess Joséphine de Beauharnais (1763–1814).

1831 King Louis Philippe (1773–1850) founded *La légion étrangère*, the French Foreign Legion.

1849 The première of the opera *The Merry Wives of Windsor*, by Otto Nicolai (1810–49), was held in Berlin, Germany.

1930 The BBC's first regional radio programmes were broadcast.

1932 Éamon de Valera (1882–1975) was elected prime minister of Ireland.

1959 The Barbie® doll went on sale for the first time.

1967 The daughter of Soviet revolutionary leader Joseph Stalin (1879–1953), Svetlana Alliluyeva (born 1926), defected to the West.

1973 A referendum in Northern Ireland, boycotted by many Catholics, resulted in a 57% vote in favour of remaining part of the United Kingdom.

1994 The IRA launched a mortar attack on Heathrow Airport.

10 March

On 10 March 1876, a complete sentence of intelligible speech was transmitted by telephone for the first time, when the inventor Alexander Graham Bell (1847–1922) summoned his assistant Thomas Watson (1854–1934) with the words: 'Mr Watson, come here; I want you'. Various speech sounds had been transmitted by telephone several months earlier, in

June 1875, but this message is generally regarded as the first telephone conversation.

On this day:

Born: English painter William Etty (1787); French composer Arthur Honegger (1892); US jazz cornettist Bix Beiderbecke (1903); British prince Edward, Earl of Wessex (1964)

Died: Italian patriot and political leader Giuseppe Mazzini (1872); US abolitionist Harriet Tubman (1913); Czechoslovakian diplomat and politician Jan Masaryk (1948); English motorcycle racer Barry Sheene (2003)

1862 The first US banknotes were issued.

1880 The Salvation Army's pioneer party, aiming to spread the organization in the USA, landed in New York City.

1906 London Underground's Bakerloo Line was officially opened.

1914 Velázquez's (1599–1660) *Venus and Cupid* (c.1658), known as the 'Rokeby Venus', was slashed in a political protest by suffragette Mary Richardson (1889–1961) in London's National Gallery.

1923 Spanish anarcho-syndicalist Salvador Seguí (1887–1923) was assassinated in Barcelona.

1956 Peter Twiss (born 1921) set a new world airspeed record when he flew a Fairey Delta 2 aircraft at 1,822kph.

1969 James Earl Ray (1928–98) was sentenced to 99 years in jail for the murder of Martin Luther King, Jnr (1929–68).

1987 Charles Haughey (born 1925) was elected prime minister of Ireland for the third time.

2000 Fifty-five Oscar® statuettes for the annual Academy Awards ceremony were stolen.

11 March

> *March 11th, 1811, is a black-letter day in the annals of Nottinghamshire. It witnessed the commencement of a series of riots which, extending over a period of five years, have, perhaps, no parallel in the history of a civilized country for the skill and secrecy with which they were managed, and the amount of wanton mischief they inflicted.*
>
> *Chambers Book of Days* (1864).

The Luddites were a group of framework-knitters who regarded the new machinery that had been introduced into the hosiery trade as a threat to their livelihoods. Apparently led by one Ned Ludd, they formed themselves into groups bent on destruction; during the night of 11 March 1811, they smashed a number of stocking frames at Arnold, a village near Nottingham. Similar acts were perpetrated in the following weeks, and it was a full year before the situation was brought under some semblance of control.

On this day:

Born: English sugar magnate, art patron and philanthopist Sir Henry Tate (1819); English car and speedboat racer Sir Malcolm Campbell (1885); English politician Harold Wilson, Baron Wilson of Rievaulx (1916); Australian-born US newspaper publisher Rupert Murdoch (1931)

Died: Scottish explorer and fur-trader Sir Alexander Mackenzie (1820); British-born Australian novelist Rolf Boldrewood (1915); Scottish bacteriologist and discoverer of penicillin Sir Alexander Fleming (1955); US Arctic and Antarctic explorer and aviator Richard Evelyn Byrd (1957); English double-agent Donald Maclean (1983)

1702 The first English daily newspaper, the *Daily Courant*, was published.

1851 The première of the opera *Rigoletto*, by Giuseppe Verdi (1813–1901), was held in Venice, Italy.

1917 World War I – Baghdad was captured by the British.

1926 Éamon de Valera (1882–1975) resigned as leader of the Irish political group Sinn Fein.

1941 World War II – the 'Lease-Lend' Bill was signed by President Franklin D Roosevelt (1882–1945), by which the USA lent or leased war supplies and arms to the UK and other Allies.

1985 Mikhail Gorbachev (born 1931) became General Secretary of the Communist Party of the USSR.

1990 Lithuania proclaimed its independence from the USSR.

1996 John Howard (born 1939) was sworn in as prime minister of Australia.

2004 In Madrid, Spain, a series of bomb explosions on commuter trains killed at least 200 people and injured 1,000 in one of Europe's worst ever terrorist attacks.

12 March

Pope Gregory I (known as St Gregory the Great) died on this day in 604. Born into a patrician family in Rome, Gregory held public office before founding and entering a monastery. Among many other noteworthy achievements, he was indirectly responsible for the conversion of the Angles and Saxons to Christianity, a mission that he initially attempted to undertake himself, but ultimately had to delegate to St Augustine. This mission was apparently inspired by the beauty of a group of fair-haired English slave boys he encountered in Rome: on ascertaining their nationality, he punned that they were 'not Angles, but angels', and resolved that their race should be saved from hell.

In the Roman Catholic Church, **St Gregory's Day** is now observed on 3 September, the day of his consecration as pope in 590.

On this day:

Born: English composer of 'Rule, Britannia' Thomas Arne (1710); Turkish general and president Mustapha Kemal Atatürk (1881); Russian dancer and choreographer Vaslav Nijinsky (1890); US 'Beat' novelist Jack Kerouac (1922); US singer and actress Liza Minnelli (1946)

Died: Italian soldier Cesare Borgia (1507); Chinese revolutionary politician Sun Yat-Sen (1925); US jazz saxophonist, bandleader and composer Charlie 'Bird' Parker (1955); US-born British violinist Yehudi Menuhin, Lord Menuhin (1999)

1609 Britain colonized Bermuda when a fleet of settlers, commanded by English colonist George Somers (1554–1610), was shipwrecked and claimed the islands for the British Crown.

1829 Cambridge University challenged Oxford University to a rowing race; the resulting Boat Race was held on 10 June.

1857 The première of the opera *Simon Boccanegra*, by Giuseppe Verdi (1813–1901), was held in Venice, Italy.

1912 The first Girl Scout meeting in the USA was held in Savannah, Georgia.

1913 Australia's new federal capital was formally named Canberra.

1930 Mahatma Gandhi (1869–1948) began his campaign of civil disobedience in India by leading a 320-kilometre march to the sea to collect salt in symbolic defiance of a government monopoly.

1932 The first broadcast was made from the BBC's new Broadcasting House.

1938 Germany occupied Austria.

1968 Mauritius became an independent state within the Commonwealth; it became a republic on the same date in 1992.

1979 A coup in Grenada ousted the prime minister, Eric Gairy (1922–97).

1984 The yearlong British miners' strike began.

1994 The first women were ordained by the Church of England in a ceremony at Bristol Cathedral.

1999 The Czech Republic, Hungary and Poland joined NATO.

2000 Pope John Paul II (born 1920) publicly issued a *mea culpa* asking God's pardon for the past sins of the Roman Catholic Church.

13 March

On 13 March 1781, the planet Uranus was discovered by the German-born British astronomer Sir William Herschel (1738–1822).

> *It was on the evening of the 13th of March, 1781, that the patient German, while examining some small stars in the constellation Gemini, marked one that was new to him; he applied different telescopes to it in turn, and found the results different from those observable with fixed stars. Was it a comet? He watched it night after night, with a view of solving this question; and he soon found that the body was moving among the stars … The attention of astronomers both at home and abroad was excited; and calculations were made to determine the orbit of the supposed comet. None of these calculations, however, accorded with the observed motion; and there arose a further question, 'Is it a planet?'*
>
> *Chambers Book of Days* (1864).

It was subsequently established that this was indeed a new planet, the furthest known planet from the sun at that time (Neptune had not yet been discovered). It was given the name of a Greek mythological figure, in accordance with the other planets, although *Herschel* (as a tribute to the discoverer) and *Georgium Sidus* (as a tribute to the king) had also been suggested.

On this day:

Born: English clergyman and chemist Reverend Joseph Priestley (1733); US astronomer Percival Lowell (1855); New Zealand-born English novelist Sir Hugh Walpole (1884); US vocalist, pianist and songwriter Neil Sedaka (1939)

Died: English actor Richard Burbage (1619); Russian tsar Alexander II (1881); 23rd President of the USA Benjamin Harrison (1901); US civil liberties lawyer Clarence Darrow (1938); Polish film director Krzysztof Kieslowski (1996)

1759 Halley's Comet passed its perihelion; Edmond Halley (1656–1742) had predicted its return more than 70 years earlier.

1873 The Scottish Football Association was founded.

1930 The discovery of the planet Pluto was confirmed by US astronomer Clyde Tombaugh (1906–97); the planet's existence had been predicted years earlier by fellow astronomer Percival Lowell (1855–1916).

1935 Driving tests were introduced in the UK on a voluntary basis, becoming compulsory in June.

1938 The union of Austria and Germany (the 'Anschluss') was formally proclaimed.

1954 The Vietnamese assault on French-occupied Dien Bien Phu in north-west Vietnam began; the battle ended in May in a humiliating defeat for the French, bringing to an end the French colonial presence in Vietnam.

1986 Robotic probe Giotto, launched by the European Space Agency, had a close-up rendezvous with Halley's Comet.

1996 Thomas Hamilton (1952–96) killed 16 primary school children and their teacher in a massacre in Dunblane, Scotland.

14 March

Admiral John Byng (born 1704), the son of the British naval commander George Byng, 1st Viscount Torrington, was executed in Portsmouth on this day in 1757. Byng had been sent to relieve the British base at Menorca, blockaded by the French, but after a short engagement with the enemy fleet he decided that his forces were inadequate and retreated to Gibraltar. At a court martial in Portsmouth he was charged with neglect of duty, which carried a mandatory death sentence. His case was taken up by the French writer Voltaire, who corresponded with Richelieu on the matter; both were of the opinion that the charge was unjust. Nonetheless, Byng was found guilty and shot. With biting satire, Voltaire introduced the episode into his story *Candide*:

> *'What is all this?' asked Candide, 'and what devil reigns here?' He asked who was this large man who had just been killed with such ceremony. 'An admiral,' he was told. 'And why kill the admiral?'*

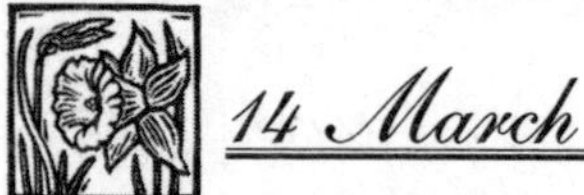

14 March

> *'Because he did not kill enough people; he had to give battle to a French admiral, and it was found that he did not go close enough to him.' 'But surely the French admiral was as far from the English admiral as he was from the other?' 'That is undeniably true. But in this country it is considered a good thing to kill an admiral from time to time, to encourage the others.'*
>
> Voltaire, *Candide* (1759).

The closing words of the passage are often used allusively in other contexts, sometimes in the original French: *pour encourager les autres.*

On this day:

Born: Austrian violinist, conductor and composer Johann Strauss, the Elder (1804); German–Swiss–US mathematical physicist and Nobel Prize winner Albert Einstein (1879); English film actor Sir Michael Caine (1933); English javelin thrower Tessa Sanderson (1957)

Died: German social, political and economic theorist Karl Marx (1883); US inventor of the roll film and the Kodak camera George Eastman (1932); US film actress Susan Hayward (1975); US choreographer and director Busby Berkeley (1976); Austrian film director Fred Zinnemann (1997)

1885 The première of the comic opera *The Mikado*, by Arthur Sullivan (1842–1900) and W S Gilbert (1836–1911), was held at the Savoy Theatre, London.

1915 World War I – the German cruiser *Dresden* was sunk.

1918 Moscow was reinstated as the capital city of Russia.

1936 The first direct London–Hong Kong airmail postal service was inaugurated by Imperial Airways.

1950 The Federal Bureau of Investigation (FBI) published the first of its 'Ten Most Wanted' lists of fugitives.

1951 Seoul was recaptured by United Nations troops in the Korean War.

1953 Nikita Khrushchev (1894–1971) became General Secretary of the Communist Party of the USSR.

1991 The 'Birmingham Six', six men found guilty of the IRA bombing of

pubs in Birmingham in 1974, were set free after 16 years of wrongful imprisonment.

2002 Five new cities – Lisburn, Newport, Newry, Preston and Stirling – were created to mark the Golden Jubilee of Queen Elizabeth II (born 1926), bringing the total number of cities in the UK to 66.

15 March

> *Beware the ides of March.*
>
> William Shakespeare, *Julius Caesar* (1599).

In the ancient Roman calendar, the *Ides* denoted the 15th day of March, May, July and October, and the 13th day of other months. It is the **Ides of March**, however, that are best-known, as the day in 44 BC on which Julius Caesar met his death at the hands of a group of conspirators led by Marcus Junius Brutus and Gaius Cassius Longinus, who stabbed him in the Senate House, Rome. Shakespeare famously gives Caesar's dying words as '*Et tu, Brute*' (You too, Brutus). The assassination was motivated by a desire to restore republican freedom to a country that was increasingly dominated by its dictator. The bloody act failed to achieve its aims, however, and led instead to further civil war.

On this day:

Born: Seventh President of the USA Andrew 'Old Hickory' Jackson (1767); English prime minister William Lamb, Viscount Melbourne (1779); Liberian president J J Roberts (1809); US rock singer and bandleader Sly Stone (1944)

Died: Italian painter and poet Salvator Rosa (1673); English metallurgist and inventor Sir Henry Bessemer (1898); Argentinian–Greek ship-owner Aristotle Onassis (1975); US paediatrician Dr Benjamin Spock (1998); English actress Dame Thora Hird (2003)

1493 Having reached the New World, the explorer Christopher Columbus (1451–1506) arrived back in Spain, where he was received with the highest honours.

1820 Maine became the 23rd state of the USA.

1869 The first professional baseball team, the Cincinnati Red Stockings, played their first game.

1877 The first cricket Test Match began in Melbourne between England and Australia; it was won by Australia by 45 runs.

1909 US-born British merchant Harry Gordon Selfridge (1858–1947) opened his department store on Oxford Street in London.

1917 Nicholas II (1868–1918), the last Tsar of Russia, abdicated.

1919 The American Legion was founded in Paris.

1937 The first 'blood bank' was set up by Dr Bernard Fantus (1874–1940) in Cook County Hospital, Chicago, USA.

1956 The première of the musical *My Fair Lady*, by Frederick Loewe (1904–88) and Alan Jay Lerner (1918–86), was held on Broadway, New York City.

1964 Elizabeth Taylor (born 1932) married Richard Burton (1925–84) in Montreal, Canada.

1990 British-based journalist for *The Observer* Farzad Bazoft (1958–90) was executed in Iraq.

16 March

This day is celebrated by Finnish inhabitants of Minnesota and elsewhere as **St Urho's Day**. The fictitious figure of St Urho is said to have been invented in 1956 as a rival for St Patrick, whose feast day is widely celebrated in the USA, by an American of Finnish descent. (Like the stories of other saints of greater antiquity, there are already conflicting accounts of the circumstances of St Urho's creation.) The choice of the name, Finnish for 'hero', may have been inspired by Urho Kekkonen, then president of Finland. The legend attached to St Urho claims that he banished grasshoppers (or, in the original version, frogs) from Finland and saved the grape crop from destruction, a parody of the tale about St Patrick's banishing snakes from Ireland. A statue of St Urho holding a pitchfork with a giant grasshopper impaled on the tines stands in Menahga, Minnesota.

St Urho's Day is now celebrated throughout the USA with a variety of events, most of which feature Finnish food and involve dressing up as grasshoppers, or in the saint's colours of purple and green. St Urho's fame has spread as far afield as his 'native' Finland, where a bar in Helsinki bears his name.

On this day:

Born: Fourth President of the USA James Madison (1751); English explorer of Australia Matthew Flinders (1774); German physicist Georg Ohm (1787); French poet and Nobel Prize winner Sully-Prudhomme (1839); Italian film director Bernardo Bertolucci (1941)

Died: English illustrator Aubrey Beardsley (1898); Romanian sculptor Constantin Brancusi (1957); Scottish economist, administrator and social reformer William Henry Beveridge (1963); US blues musician T-Bone Walker (1975)

1190 The Jewish massacre took place at York Castle, England, when the entire Jewish community was driven to suicide or murdered by Christian townsfolk.

1660 The English 'Long Parliament', which had sat intermittently since November 1640, was finally dissolved.

1802 The United States Military Academy was established at West Point, New York.

1827 The first black-owned and run newspaper, *Freedom's Journal*, was founded in New York City.

1872 The first English Football Association Cup Final took place at the Kennington Oval in London; the Wanderers beat the Royal Engineers 1–0.

1926 US physicist, rocket engineer and inventor Dr Robert H Goddard (1882–1945) fired the first liquid-fuel rocket at Auburn, Massachusetts, USA; the event has been described by NASA as 'a feat as epochal in history as that of the Wright brothers at Kitty Hawk'.

1935 Adolf Hitler (1889–1945) reintroduced military conscription in Germany, in defiance of the Treaty of Versailles (1919).

1968 The My Lai massacre took place in Vietnam, when several hundred unarmed villagers were murdered by US troops.

1973 Queen Elizabeth II (born 1926) opened the new London Bridge; the old bridge had been sold and rebuilt in Arizona, USA.

1976 Harold Wilson (1916–95) resigned as prime minister of the UK.

1978 Aldo Moro (1916–78), a former Italian prime minister, was kidnapped by the Red Brigade; he was later found murdered.

1978 The oil tanker *Amoco Cadiz* ran aground off Brittany, France; over the following days it disgorged some 200,000 tons of oil.

2000 In the US, Independent Counsel Robert Ray declared that he had found 'no substantial and credible evidence' that First Lady Hillary Rodham Clinton (born 1947) was involved in the case of missing FBI files on senior Republicans in the so-called 'Filegate' affair.

17 March

In the late fourth century or early fifth century the possibly Welsh-born patron saint of Ireland, St Patrick, was captured by pirates and sold into slavery in Ireland. Six years later, he escaped and made his way to France, where he became a monk, and subsequently a bishop, before returning as a missionary to Ireland around 432. The country already had a bishop, Palladius, but Patrick proved to be a more forceful advocate of Christianity and succeeded in suppressing the power and influence of the Druids. There are numerous legends associated with him: he is said to have used the three leaves of the **shamrock** (variously identified as the lesser yellow trefoil, clover, wood sorrel or watercress) to illustrate the doctrine of the Trinity, and he is also said to have banished snakes from Ireland (and there are still no snakes there):

> *The greatest of St Patrick's miracles was that of driving the venomous reptiles out of Ireland, and rendering the Irish soil, for ever after, so obnoxious to the serpent race, that they instantaneously die on touching it. Colgan seriously relates that St Patrick accomplished this feat by beating a drum, which he struck with such fervour that he knocked a*

> *hole in it, thereby endangering the success of the miracle. But an angel appearing mended the drum; and the patched instrument was long exhibited as a holy relic.*
>
> *Chambers Book of Days* (1864).

St Patrick's Day is a public holiday in Ireland and is observed worldwide by people of Irish descent. The original celebrations in Ireland were very different from the modern-day festivities. Whatever the date of Easter, St Patrick's Day always fell in the period of Lent, but the Lenten restrictions on eating and drinking were lifted for the duration and it was a time for great merrymaking in the community. Children proudly wore the crosses that they had prepared in the days before. A boy's cross was made from a circle drawn on white paper, with elliptical lines to make different areas which were then filled with different colours. The girl's version was a cross wrapped in ribbons with a green rosette in the centre. Neither resembled the red diagonal cross on a white background that is now associated with St Patrick.

As time went by, and the wearing of the shamrock became more popular than the wearing of the cross, the saint's feast day began to be celebrated with more pomp and ceremony outside his native Ireland: among the most prominent parades in the world are those in the USA. In New York a massive street parade along Fifth Avenue forms the centrepiece of the celebrations, a tradition which dates back to 1766. In recent years up to 300,000 marchers and two million spectators have brought New York to a halt. Boston's Charitable Irish Society was first formed in 1737 and Boston also holds a spectacular parade with floats, marching bands, live music and the now ubiquitous dyed green beer. The river in Chicago was first dyed green for the day in 1962 (although it actually stayed green for a week), and they too hold a parade. Even in Russia St Patrick's Day has a parade, held in Moscow since 1992.

Prompted by the enduring popularity of these and similar celebrations in other countries, the Irish authorities inaugurated the St Patrick's Day Festival in Dublin – as recently as 1995 – featuring a variety of cultural activities (including traditional Irish song and dance), fireworks, and a spectacular procession through the streets of the city.

On this day:

Born: English actor Edmund Kean (1789); English artist and book illustrator Kate Greenaway (1846); US singer and pianist Nat 'King' Cole (1919); Russian ballet dancer Rudolf Nureyev (1938)

Died: German mathematician and astronomer Friedrich Wilhelm Bessel (1846); Austrian physicist Christian Doppler (1853); English polar explorer Lawrence Oates (1912); Italian stage and film director Luchino Visconti (1976); English murderer and gang leader Ronnie Kray (1995)

1337 The Duchy of Cornwall was created by King Edward III (1312–77) for his son Edward (1330–76), the 'Black Prince'.

1776 British troops withdrew from the American town of Boston.

1845 Stephen Perry of London patented the rubber band.

1861 Victor Emmanuel II (1820–78) was declared to be the first King of Italy.

1897 Boxer Bob Fitzsimmons (1863–1917) became the World Heavyweight Champion when he defeated 'Gentleman' Jim Corbett (1866–1933) in Carson City, Nevada, USA.

1921 Dr Marie Stopes (1880–1958) opened her first family planning clinic at 61 Marlborough Road, Holloway, London.

1968 Anti-Vietnam War demonstrators attacked the US embassy in Grosvenor Square, London.

1969 Golda Meir (1898–1978) became Israel's first woman prime minister.

1991 A referendum was held by President Mikhail Gorbachev (born 1931) on the future of the USSR.

1992 In a referendum held by President F W de Klerk (born 1936), South Africa voted in favour of reforms to end apartheid.

18 March

On this day:

Born: Russian composer Nikolai Rimsky-Korsakov (1844); German engineer and inventor of the compression-ignition engine

Rudolf Diesel (1858); English prime minister Neville Chamberlain (1869); Irish jockey Pat Eddery (1952)

Died: Anglo-Saxon king Edward the Martyr (978); Italian painter Fra Angelico (1455); English politician and first prime minister of Great Britain Sir Robert Walpole (1745); US novelist Bernard Malamud (1986); US singer and songwriter with the Mamas and The Papas John Phillips (2001)

1662 The world's first scheduled bus service began in Paris.

1766 The Stamp Act (1765), a British Act which levied a direct tax on all papers required in discharging official business in the American colonies, was repealed by the British.

1834 The Tolpuddle Martyrs – six agricultural labourers from Tolpuddle, Dorset, who had been organized the previous year into a trade union – were convicted of taking illegal oaths and sentenced to transportation to Australia.

1850 The American Express Company was founded in Buffalo, New York, USA.

1871 The Paris Commune uprising began following France's humiliating defeat in the Franco-Prussian War.

1931 The Schick Company of Connecticut, USA, manufactured the first electric razors.

1958 Debutantes were presented to the Queen for the last time in the UK.

1965 Soviet astronaut Aleksei Leonov (born 1934) became the first man to walk in space from the spacecraft *Voskhod 2* in orbit round the Earth.

1967 The oil tanker *Torrey Canyon* ran aground between the Isles of Scilly and Land's End and began leaking her cargo of 120,000 tons of oil.

1977 President Marien Ngouabi (1938–77) of the Republic of Congo was assassinated in a military coup.

19 March

Feast day of **St Joseph**, husband of the Virgin Mary and patron saint of carpenters, working men, fathers and pastrycooks.

On this day:

Born: Scottish missionary and traveller David Livingstone (1813); English explorer, linguist and diplomat Sir Richard Burton (1821); US lawman and gunfighter Wyatt Earp (1848); US novelist Philip Roth (1933)

Died: US popular author and creator of Tarzan Edgar Rice Burroughs (1950); French physicist and Nobel Prize winner Louis-Victor Broglie (1987); Dutch-born US painter Willem de Kooning (1997)

721 BC The first recorded eclipse was seen in Ancient Babylon.

1859 The première of the opera *Faust*, by Charles Gounod (1818–93), was held in Paris.

1920 The US Senate voted against joining the League of Nations.

1932 Sydney Harbour Bridge was officially opened; construction had begun in December 1926.

1958 Madame Tussauds opened the UK's first Planetarium in London.

1964 The Great St-Bernard Tunnel between Switzerland and Italy, the first transalpine tunnel, was officially opened.

1970 West German chancellor Willy Brandt (1913–92) and East German prime minister Willi Stoph (1914–99) met in Erfurt; it was the first meeting of German leaders since partition.

1976 Princess Margaret (1930–2002) and Antony Armstrong-Jones, Lord Snowdon (born 1930), announced their separation.

1986 Prince Andrew, Duke of York (born 1960), became engaged to Sarah Ferguson (born 1959); the couple separated on this day in 1992.

1988 Two British soldiers were murdered by a mob in the vicinity of a Republican funeral in Northern Ireland.

20 March

Sir Isaac Newton died on 20 March 1727. Born in Lincolnshire in 1642, he studied at Trinity College, Cambridge, and was appointed Lucasian Professor of Mathematics there in 1669. Newton's most famous contribution to science is the law of gravity, inspired by the fall of an apple in his garden. He also formulated three laws of motion, the third of which states that 'to every action there is always opposed an equal reaction', and did important work on the nature of light and the construction of telescopes. However, he seems to have remained modest about his achievements:

> *I know not what I may appear to the world, but to myself I seem to have been only like a boy playing on the sea shore, and diverting myself in now and then finding a smoother pebble or a prettier shell than ordinary, whilst the great ocean of truth lay all undiscovered before me.*
>
> Sir Isaac Newton, quoted in D Brewster (ed) *Memoirs of Newton* (1855).

On this day:

Born: Roman poet Ovid (43 BC); Norwegian dramatist Henrik Ibsen (1828); English singer Dame Vera Lynn (1917); US film-maker Spike Lee (1957)

Died: English king Henry IV (1413); French army marshal and World War I commander Ferdinand Foch (1929); Irish author Brendan Behan (1964)

1602 The Dutch East India Company was founded.

1806 The foundation stone of Dartmoor Prison was laid; the prison, originally intended for French prisoners of war, was completed in May 1809.

1815 Napoleon I (1769–1821) entered Paris at the start of the 'Hundred Days', an interlude between his escape from Elba and his defeat at the

Battle of Waterloo, during which he tried to reconstitute the First Empire.

1852 The novel *Uncle Tom's Cabin*, by US novelist Harriet Beecher Stowe (1811–96), was published.

1854 Anti-slavery activists met in Ripon, Wisconsin, USA, to discuss the formation of a new political party – sowing the seeds for the US Republican Party.

1933 The Dachau concentration camp was founded in Germany on Himmler's orders to accommodate political detainees under brutal conditions; it was later expanded during World War II to hold detainees from throughout Europe.

1940 World War II – Édouard Daladier (1884–1970) resigned as prime minister of France.

1956 Tunisia became an independent sovereign state.

1966 The football World Cup's Jules Rimet trophy was stolen from Central Hall, Westminster, London.

1969 Beatle John Lennon (1940–80) married Yoko Ono (born 1933).

1974 Ian Ball (born 1947) fired six shots in an attempt to kidnap Princess Anne (born 1950) while she was being driven down Pall Mall, London.

1986 Jacques Chirac (born 1932) was elected prime minister of France for the second time.

1993 IRA bombs in the town centre of Warrington killed two children and injured almost 60 people.

1995 Members of the Japanese cult Aum Shinrikyo released the deadly nerve gas sarin in a crowded Tokyo subway, killing twelve people and injuring thousands.

1996 The British government admitted that bovine spongiform encephalopathy (BSE) and the human equivalent, Creutzfeldt-Jakob disease (CJD), were likely to be connected.

2000 Pope John Paul II (born 1920) began a historic tour of Jordan, Israel and the Palestinian territories.

21 March

This is the anniversary of the Sharpeville Massacre in 1960, when the police fired on a crowd of Black Africans engaged in a peaceful demonstration against apartheid in the town of Sharpeville, South Africa, killing 69 and wounding 180. In recognition of this event, after the abolition of apartheid in the early 1990s, the South African Human Rights Commission was launched on 21 March 1996 and the day is now observed as a public holiday, **Human Rights Day**, in South Africa.

On this day:

Born: German composer Johann Sebastian Bach (1685); Mexican national hero and president Benito Juárez (1806); US theatre manager Florenz Ziegfeld (1869); English theatre and film director Sir Peter Brook (1925)

Died: English Archbishop of Canterbury Thomas Cranmer (1556); Native American princess Pocahontas (1617); English poet and writer Robert Southey (1843); English stage and film actor Sir Michael Redgrave (1985)

1801 The British army routed Napoleon I's troops at the Battle of Alexandria in Egypt.

1829 A famous duel took place at Battersea Fields, London, between Arthur Wellesley, Duke of Wellington (1769–1852) and the Earl of Winchilsea; both took great care to avoid shooting each other.

1925 Governor Austin Peay (1876–1927) of the State of Tennessee approved the 'Butler Bill' banning the teaching of Charles Darwin's (1809–82) theory of evolution in the state.

1938 The first television news bulletin in the UK was broadcast by the BBC; it was a television recording of a radio news programme.

1990 Namibia declared independence from South Africa.

1999 The first non-stop round-the-world balloon flight was completed by Bertrand Piccard (born 1958) and Brian Jones (born 1947).

22 March

The German writer Johann Wolfgang von Goethe died on this day in 1832, his last words allegedly being 'More light!'

> *Johann Wolfgang Goethe was born in 1749, in the busy old-fashioned town of Frankfort-on-the-Maine; a child so precocious that we find it recorded that he could write German, French, Italian, Latin, and Greek, before he was eight. His age fulfilled the promise of youth: he grew up a genuine man, remarkable for endless activity of body and mind, a sage minister, a noble friend, and a voluminous writer.*
>
> *Chambers Book of Days* (1864).

Goethe's literary output included poems, the early autobiographical novel *Die Leiden des jungen Werthers* (1774, 'The Sorrows of Young Werther'), and dramas such as his masterpiece *Faust*, which he began in 1775 and completed shortly before his death. He also had an interest in science, especially the life sciences, and carried out significant research in anatomy – he discovered the intermaxillary bone in man (1784), and formulated a vertebral theory of the skull.

On this day:

Born: Flemish painter Sir Anthony Van Dyck (1599); French mime artist Marcel Marceau (1923); Bahamanian prime minister Sir Lynden Pindling (1930); English popular composer Lord Lloyd-Webber (1948)

Died: English reformer and novelist Thomas Hughes (1896); US showman Mike Todd (1958); US animated cartoonist William Hanna (2001)

1312 Pope Clément V (c.1260–1314) abolished the Knights Templar.

1765 The Stamp Act was passed; it levied a direct tax on all papers required in discharging official business in the American colonies, and was the first direct tax levied without the consent of the colonial assemblies. It

caused much discontent and provoked the colonists' famous slogan, 'No taxation without representation'.

1888 The English Football League was founded at a meeting at Anderton's Hotel, Fleet Street, London.

1895 The first public showing of a celluloid cinematograph film, showing employees leaving a factory in Lyons, was held by brothers Auguste (1862–1954) and Louis Lumière (1865–1948) at the Société d'Encouragement à l'Industrie Nationale in Paris.

1942 World War II – Morse code news broadcasts began on the BBC for the members of the French Resistance.

1945 The League of Arab States was founded in Cairo, Egypt; the Arab League Charter was signed the following day, but the anniversary is commemorated on this day.

1956 Martin Luther King, Jnr (1929–68) was convicted of organizing a boycott of buses (1955–6) in Montgomery, Alabama, USA, after the arrest of Rosa Parks (born 1913).

1960 The laser was patented by Arthur L Schawlow (1921–99) and Charles H Townes (born 1915).

1995 Having spent a record 438 consecutive days in space aboard the Mir space station, Russian cosmonaut Valery Polyakov (born 1942) returned to Earth.

2000 Cormac Murphy-O'Connor (born 1932) was installed as the tenth Archbishop of Westminster.

23 March

This day is **World Meteorological Day**, celebrating the foundation of the World Meteorological Organization on 23 March 1950. A ceremony takes place at the World Meteorological Organization's headquarters in Geneva, and each year a different theme is chosen, focusing on a particular issue of meteorology or hydrology and its significance to humanity.

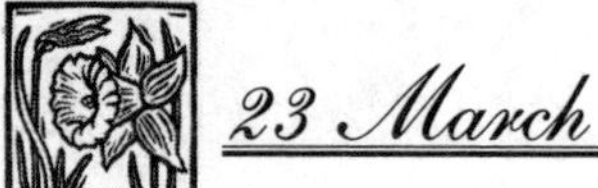

23 March

On this day:

Born: Spanish painter Juan Gris (1887); US film actress Joan Crawford (1906); English car and speedboat racer Donald Campbell (1921); English athlete and first person to run the four-minute mile Sir Roger Bannister (1929); English oarsman Sir Steve Redgrave (1962)

Died: French novelist Stendhal (1842); Hungarian-born US actor Peter Lorre (1964); English motorcycle racer Mike Hailwood (1981)

1839 The word 'ok' first appeared in print in the newspaper the *Boston Morning Post*.

1849 The Battle of Novara saw the defeat by the Austrian general Count Joseph Radetzky von Radetz (1766–1858) of the Piedmontese forces, leading to the abdication of King Charles Albert (1798–1849).

1861 London's first trams began operating.

1900 English archaeologist Arthur Evans (1851–1941) began his excavations that would discover the ancient city of Knossos, Crete.

1918 World War I – the German massive long-range gun 'Big Bertha' was fired at Paris for the first time from woods near Laon; 16 people were killed.

1919 Benito Mussolini (1883–1945) founded the Italian Fascist Party (*Partito Nazionale Fascista*, PNF) at a meeting in Milan.

1956 Pakistan became an independent Islamic republic.

1956 Queen Elizabeth II (born 1926) laid the foundation stone for the new Coventry Cathedral.

1998 Russian president Boris Yeltsin (born 1931) sacked his prime minister and the entire Cabinet.

1998 The film *Titanic* (1997) won eleven Oscars® at the 70th Annual Academy Awards ceremony, including those for Best Picture and Directing.

2001 Veteran Russian space station Mir was brought down into the Pacific Ocean without mishap after 15 years in orbit.

24 March

In 1877 the annual Oxford and Cambridge University Boat Race took place on this date and ended in a dead heat. This had never happened before and has not happened since, although the finish in the 2003 race was very close, with Oxford winning by just one foot. The Boat Race, first held in 1829, takes place on a stretch of the River Thames between Putney Bridge and Chiswick Bridge. The boats are rowed by a crew of 8 (plus a cox), who undergo rigorous training before the event.

To date, Cambridge has won the race more often than Oxford, and also holds the record for winning by the greatest margin (20 lengths, in 1900). Apart from the 1877 dead heat, other dramatic events have included various sinkings. In 1912 both the Oxford and Cambridge boats sank necessitating a rerun of the race the following day (when Oxford won). Other such sinkings include 1859 (Cambridge), 1925 (Oxford), 1951 (Oxford) and 1978 (Cambridge). In 1898 the Cambridge boat was described as being 'waterlogged', but the crew still managed to finish the race.

On this day:

Born: English craftsman, poet and socialist William Morris (1834); Hungarian-born US magician and escape artist Harry Houdini (1874); English comedian and actor Tommy Trinder (1909); US poet and publisher Lawrence Ferlinghetti (1919); US actor Steve McQueen (1930)

Died: English queen Elizabeth I (1603); US poet Henry Wadsworth Longfellow (1882); French novelist and pioneer of science fiction Jules Verne (1905); English queen Mary (1953); Swiss physicist and deep-sea explorer Auguste Piccard (1962)

1603 King James VI of Scotland (1566–1625) succeeded Queen Elizabeth I (1533–1603) of England, becoming King James VI and I of England and Scotland.

1944 World War II – 76 prisoners of war, held by the Germans at Stalag Luft III prison camp in modern-day Poland, broke out through a long tunnel; the event was later immortalized in the 1963 film *The Great Escape*.

1946 The weekly radio programme *Letter from America* with Alistair Cooke (1908–2004) was first broadcast on the BBC.

1958 Popular singer Elvis Presley (1935–77) joined the US Army.

1970 One of the world's rarest stamps, the 'one cent British Guiana', was sold at auction to a US syndicate for $240,000.

1976 Isabel Perón (born 1931) was ousted as president of Argentina by a military coup.

1989 The oil tanker *Exxon Valdez* ran aground on Bligh Reef off Alaska, USA, at 12:04am; the tanker went on to spill approximately eleven million gallons of oil.

1999 Italian politician Romani Prodi (born 1939) was nominated as the new president of the European Union Commission; his presidency was confirmed by a vote in September.

25 March

> *And the angel said unto her, Fear not, Mary: for thou has found favour with God. And, behold, thou shalt conceive in thy womb, and bring forth a son, and shalt call his name JESUS.*
>
> Luke 1.30–31.

This is the day of the **Annunciation**, also known as **Lady Day**: the day on which the angel Gabriel appeared to the Virgin Mary, nine months before the birth of Christ. A holy day in the Church calendar, it was adopted as New Year's Day by a number of Christian countries (including many European countries), who disapproved of the pagan festivities associated with 1 January. In England, 25 March was regarded as the first day of the year for official purposes until the mid-18th century; it is the first of the **Quarter Days**, when legal contracts (such as those between landlords and tenants) traditionally begin and end. The other Quarter Days fall on 24 June, 29 September and 25 December.

It is considered unlucky for Easter Day to fall on 25 March: 'When Our Lord falls in Our Lady's lap, then let England beware a rap'. However, prophecies that the world would end at the next conjunction of the Annunciation with Easter Sunday (or Good Friday) have repeatedly been proved wrong, and

unfortunate events that have occurred on such dates can be dismissed as mere coincidence.

On Lady Day, inhabitants of Tichborne and nearby villages in Hampshire are given a quantity of flour made from locally grown wheat, distributed at the local church after a short service. This is the **Tichborne Dole**, a custom dating from the twelfth century. The dole originally took the form of a loaf of bread: 1,400 loaves were baked for the occasion, and if demand exceeded supply, the remaining applicants received a small sum of money instead.

> *The legend tells that, at some remote period, a Lady Mabella, on her death-bed, besought her lord, the Tichborne of those days, to supply her with the means for bequeathing a gift or dole of bread to any one who should apply for it annually on the Feast of the Annunciation of the Blessed Virgin. Sir Roger promised her the proceeds of as much land as she could go over while a brand or billet of a certain size was burning: she was nearly bedridden, and nearly dying; and her avaricious lord believed that he had imposed conditions which would place within very narrow limits the area of land to be alienated. But he was mistaken. A miraculous degree of strength was given to her. She was carried by her attendants into a field, where she crawled round many goodly acres. A field of twenty-three acres, at Tichborne, to this day, bears the name of the Crawl.*
>
> *Chambers Book of Days* (1864).

Lady Mabella also prophesied that a curse would befall the family if the dole was stopped. Her warnings included the collapse of the family home, the birth of seven daughters and no sons and the dying out of the family name. The custom was temporarily discontinued at the end of the 18th century (having begun to attract too many undesirable characters in search of a free loaf and whatever else could be stolen from the neighbourhood) and part of the family mansion did fall down, the next heir to the baronetcy had seven daughters and no sons and the family name changed to Doughty. The dole is now given out in the form of a gallon of flour for adults and half a gallon for children. The field which Lady Mabella struggled around is still called 'The Crawls'.

On this day:

Born: Italian conductor Arturo Toscanini (1867); Hungarian composer Béla Bartók (1881); English film director Sir David Lean (1908); English pop singer, songwriter and pianist Sir Elton John (1947)

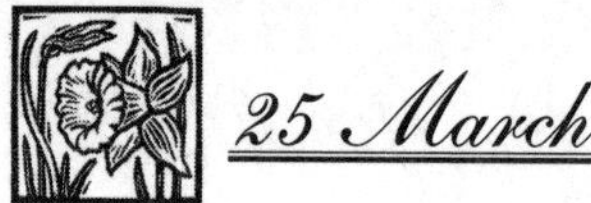

25 March

Died: French composer Claude Debussy (1918); Saudi Arabian king Faisal (1975); Australian pianist Eileen Joyce (1991); English football commentator Kenneth Wolstenholme (2002)

1306 Robert the Bruce (1274–1329) was crowned King of Scotland; he reigned as Robert I until June 1329.

1802 The Treaty of Amiens was signed, marking the end of the first stage of the wars between the UK and revolutionary France.

1807 The Abolition of the Slave Trade Act became law in the UK.

1843 The Rotherhithe Tunnel under the River Thames from Rotherhithe to Wapping, designed by French engineer Marc Isambard Brunel (1769–1849), was officially opened.

1876 Scotland won the first Scotland versus Wales football match 4–0.

1920 The 'Black and Tans', additional members of the Royal Irish Constabulary recruited by the British government to cope with Irish nationalist unrest, arrived in Ireland.

1949 *Hamlet* (1948) became the first British film to win an Oscar® for Best Picture at the 21st Annual Academy Awards ceremony; Laurence Olivier (1907–89) also won the Oscar® for Best Actor for his performance in the title role.

1957 The Treaty establishing the European Economic Community, or 'Common Market', was signed in Rome.

1969 Beatle John Lennon (1940–80) and his new wife Yoko Ono (born 1933) began their 'bed-in' in room 902 of the Hilton Hotel, Amsterdam, the Netherlands; the couple stayed in bed until 31 March to promote world peace.

1980 Robert Runcie (1921–2000) was enthroned as the Archbishop of Canterbury.

1999 NATO airstrikes on Serbia and Kosovo began.

26 March

Feast day of **St William of Norwich**, a young boy who went missing in Holy Week 1144 and was found dead on Easter Saturday, allegedly the victim of a ritual murder by Jews.

On this day:

Born: US poet Robert Frost (1874); US playwright Tennessee Williams (1911); French conductor and composer Pierre Boulez (1925); US pop singer and film actress Diana Ross (1944)

Died: English playwright and Baroque architect Sir John Vanbrugh (1726); German composer Ludwig van Beethoven (1827); US poet Walt Whitman (1892); French actress Sarah Bernhardt (1923); English actor, playwright and composer Sir Noël Coward (1973)

1839 The annual Henley-on-Thames Rowing Regatta was established at a meeting in Henley Town Hall; the races became known as Henley Royal Regatta in 1851.

1885 The first cremation in the UK, of a Mrs Pickersgill, was held at a new crematorium in Woking, Surrey.

1923 The BBC's first daily weather broadcast was made.

1924 The première of the play *Saint Joan*, by George Bernard Shaw (1856–1950), was held in London.

1953 The Lari Massacre took place during the Mau Mau emergency in Kenya, in which over 100 Kikuyu of the loyal chief Luka were killed by insurgents.

1960 The Grand National horse race was televised for the first time.

1971 Bangladesh declared its independence from Pakistan; war followed, but the country achieved full independence on 16 December 1971.

1973 The British Stock Exchange admitted women for the first time.

1979 Prime Minister Menachem Begin (1913–92) of Israel and President Anwar el-Sadat (1918–81) of Egypt signed a peace accord brokered by President Jimmy Carter (born 1924) at the White House, Washington, DC.

1981 The Social Democratic Party (SDP) was formed in the UK by the so-called 'Gang of Four', comprising David Owen (born 1938), Shirley Williams (born 1930), Roy Jenkins (1920–2003) and Bill Rodgers (born 1928).

1989 The first general elections to elect members of the new Congress of People's Deputies were held in the USSR.

1992 Cosmonaut Sergei Krikalev (born 1958) returned to Earth after spending 313 days aboard the Mir space station; he had left as a citizen of the USSR in May, but returned to the new state of Russia, within the new Commonwealth of Independent States, the USSR having broken up in the intervening months.

2000 Russia's acting president Vladimir Putin (born 1952) won more than 50 per cent of the vote in Russian presidential elections; the result was officially announced the following day.

2001 The Postal Services Act came into effect in the UK, changing the Post Office from a statutory authority into a government-owned public limited company.

27 March

On 27 March 1790 the shoelace is said to have been invented, providing an alternative to buckles as a means of fastening footwear.

On this day:

Born: French financier and town-planner Baron Georges Eugène Haussmann (1809); German physicist, discoverer of X-rays and Nobel Prize winner Wilhelm Konrad von Röntgen (1845); English politician and prime minister James Callaghan, Lord Callaghan of Cardiff (1912); US jazz singer and pianist Sarah Vaughan (1924)

Died: Scottish and English king James VI and I (1625); Italian decorative painter Giovanni Battista Tiepolo (1770); Scottish

chemist and physicist Sir James Dewar (1923); Scottish economist and educationalist Sir Kenneth Alexander (2001); US film-maker Billy Wilder (2002)

1625 King Charles I (1600–49) succeeded his father as King of Great Britain and Ireland.

1794 The US Navy was established when Congress authorized the construction of six ships.

1871 Scotland defeated England by one try in the first ever international rugby match.

1914 The first successful blood transfusion using the citrate method – previously collected and stored blood treated with sodium citrate as an anticoagulant – was carried out by the Belgian Albert Hustin (1882–1967).

1958 Nikita Khrushchev (1894–1971) became Chairman of the Council of Ministers (prime minister) of the USSR.

1964 An earthquake of magnitude 8.4 on the Richter scale hit Alaska; it was the strongest ever recorded in North America.

1977 Two aircraft – a Pan Am 747 and a KLM 747 – collided in fog on a runway at Tenerife Airport in the Canary Islands; 583 people were killed.

1980 The accommodation platform of the *Alexander Keilland* oil rig overturned in the North Sea, with the loss of 123 lives.

1993 Jiang Zemin (born 1926) was elected president of China.

28 March

No woman in my time will be Prime Minister or Chancellor of the Exchequer or Foreign Secretary – not the top jobs. Anyway, I would not want to be Prime Minister; you have to give yourself 100 per cent.

Margaret Thatcher, in the *Sunday Telegraph* (26 October 1969).

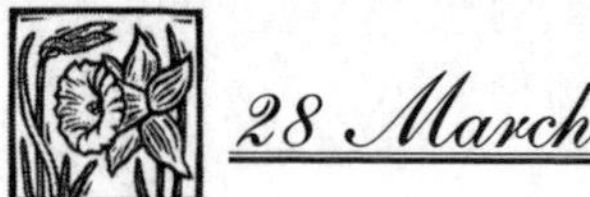

28 March

On 28 March 1979, Margaret Thatcher (born 1925), leader of the Conservative opposition in the House of Commons, brought a vote of no confidence in the Labour government led by Sir James Callaghan and thus took an important step towards becoming the first woman prime minister of the UK. Callaghan lost the vote by a minority of one and Thatcher came to power at the general election five weeks later. She remained in office until November 1990, becoming the longest-serving British prime minister of the 20th century.

On this day:

Born: Italian painter Raphael (1483); Spanish mystic and writer St Teresa of Ávila (1515); Russian novelist Maxim Gorky (1868); English television presenter Michael Parkinson (1935)

Died: English novelist, critic and essayist Virginia Woolf (1941); Russian composer and pianist Sergei Rachmaninov (1943); 34th President of the USA Dwight Eisenhower (1969); Russian-born French painter Marc Chagall (1985); British actor and playwright Sir Peter Ustinov (2004)

AD 193 Marcus Didius Julianus (c.135–193 AD) became Roman emperor by bribing the Praetorian Guard in a famous auction of the Empire held after the death of Publius Helvius Pertinax (AD 126–93).

1854 The UK and France declared war on Russia, starting the Crimean War.

1881 US showman P T Barnum (1810–91) joined with his rival James A Bailey (1847–1906) to found the famous Barnum and Bailey Circus, promoted as 'The Greatest Show on Earth'.

1896 The première of the opera *Andrea Chénier*, by Umberto Giordano (1867–1948), was held at La Scala, Milan, Italy.

1910 The first seaplane, built by Henri Fabre (1882–1984), had its maiden flight from Martigues, near Marseilles, France.

1913 The first Morris Oxford car came off the Cowley production line in Oxfordshire.

1917 World War I – the Women's Army Auxiliary Corps (WAAC) was founded.

1939 The Spanish Civil War ended as General Franco (1892–1975) and the Nationalists entered Madrid.

1942 World War II – British forces attacked the German-occupied French

port of St Nazaire, ramming HMS *Campbeltown* against the dock gates and then detonating the cargo of explosives she held; this put Normandie Dock out of action for the rest of World War II and prevented its use in repairing the German battleship the *Tirpitz*.

1964 The UK's first pirate radio station, Radio Caroline, started transmissions from a ship moored offshore.

1967 Bombs were used to destroy the wrecked oil tanker *Torrey Canyon* off Land's End; the bombing lasted three days before the tanker finally sank.

1968 The Broadway première of the controversial hippie musical *Hair* was held at the Biltmore Theatre, New York City, USA.

1979 A series of mechanical problems, human errors and poor decisions led to a partial meltdown of the reactor core and the release of dangerous radioactive gases from the Three Mile Island nuclear power plant near Harrisburg, Pennsylvania, USA.

29 March

The first London Marathon was run on 29 March 1981, instigated by middle-distance runner Chris Brasher (1928–2003). Some 6,700 participants – less than one third of those who had applied to take part – set off in drizzle to run the 26-mile route from Greenwich Park to Buckingham Palace, and more than 5,300 managed to reach the finish line. The fastest time recorded on that day was 2 hours, 11 minutes, and 48 seconds; the slowest was around 7 hours. Since then, the London Marathon has gone from strength to strength, with an average of 30,000 people taking part each year (many in fancy dress), and huge sums of money have been raised for charity through the sponsorship of individual competitors.

On this day:

Born: Tenth President of the USA John Tyler (1790); English architect Sir Edwin Landseer Lutyens (1869); US singer Pearl Bailey (1918); English politician and prime minister John Major (1943)

Died: Swedish mystic, theologian and scientist Emanuel Swedenborg

(1772); English hymnwriter, evangelist and founder of Methodism Charles Wesley (1788); English writer, feminist and pacifist Vera Brittain (1970); English actor Bill Travers (1994)

1461 One of England's bloodiest battles took place at Towton in Yorkshire when, in heavy snow, the Yorkists decisively defeated the Lancastrians despite heavy casualties on both sides.

1629 The Edict of Restitution was proclaimed by Emperor Ferdinand II (1578–1637) during the Thirty Years War; it decreed that all ecclesiastical property confiscated since 1552 should be restored to its original owners, so Ferdinand hoped to recover the lands which had been lost to Protestantism in the intervening years.

1677 The Test Act to curb Catholic influence at court received the Royal Assent of Charles II (1630–85); every office holder had to take Oaths of Supremacy and Allegiance, and to take communion according to the rites of the Church of England.

1867 The British North America Act was passed by Parliament in the UK; it sanctioned the confederation of Nova Scotia, New Brunswick, Quebec and Ontario, thus giving rise to the dominion of Canada.

1871 Queen Victoria (1819–1901) officially opened the Royal Albert Hall in memory of her husband, Prince Albert (1819–61).

1879 The première of the opera *Eugene Onegin*, by Pyotr Ilyich Tchaikovsky (1840–93), was held in Moscow.

1912 Captain Robert Scott (1868–1912) wrote his last diary entry before dying on his return voyage from the South Pole: 'We shall stick it out to the end, but we are getting weaker, of course, and the end cannot be far. It seems a pity, but I do not think I can write more'.

1920 William Robertson (1860–1933) attained the rank of field marshal – the first British soldier ever to rise from private, the rank in which he enlisted in 1877.

1920 Danish prime minister Carl Theodore Zahle (1866–1946) was dismissed by the Danish King Kristian X (1870–1947), causing the so-called Easter Crisis.

1951 The première of the musical *The King and I*, by Richard Rodgers (1902–79) and Oscar Hammerstein (1895–1960), was held at the St James Theatre on Broadway, New York City.

1971 US Army Lieutenant William Calley (born 1943) was convicted for his part in the My Lai massacre in South Vietnam on 16 March 1968.

1971 US hippie cult leader and murderer Charles Manson (born 1934) was found guilty of nine murders and sentenced to death; the following year the death penalty was abolished in California and his sentence was commuted to life imprisonment.

1973 The last US troops left Vietnam after the end of US involvement in the war.

1974 The US spaceship *Mariner 10* took close-up photographs of the planet Mercury as it flew past at an altitude of 756 kilometres.

1979 In the USA, the House Select Committee on Assassinations issued its final report on the murders of President John F Kennedy (1917–63), Martin Luther King, Jnr (1929–68) and Robert F Kennedy (1925–68).

1993 Édouard Balladur (born 1929) became prime minister of France.

30 March

The Flemish painter Vincent Van Gogh was born on this day in 1853. The son of a Lutheran pastor, he spent the early years of his adult life as an evangelistic preacher before embarking on the study of art. With the help of his brother Theo, an art dealer, he settled in Paris and made the acquaintance of Paul Gauguin, Henri Toulouse-Lautrec and Georges Seurat. It was at Arles in Provence, however, that he produced some of his finest paintings, notably *Sunflowers* and *The Chair and the Pipe* (both 1888), and it was there that he cut off part of his ear (as an act of remorse after threatening Gauguin with a razor during a quarrel). He was subsequently admitted to an asylum and released under supervision in 1890. Later that year he shot himself, at the scene of his last painting, *Cornfields with Flight of Birds*.

Like many other artists before and since, Van Gogh made little money from his work while he was alive (some say that he only sold one painting during his lifetime, although he did trade others for equipment, which would then have been sold on).

> *I cannot help it that my paintings do not sell. The time will come when people will see that they are worth more than the price of the paint.*
>
> Vincent Van Gogh, letter to his brother Theo (24 October 1888).

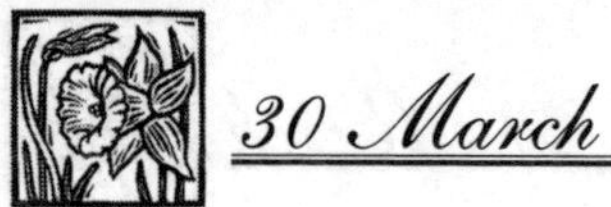

30 March

On 30 March 1987, the anniversary of his birth, Van Gogh's painting *Sunflowers* was sold in London to a Japanese buyer for just under $40m (about £24,750,000).

On this day:

Born: Spanish artist Francisco de Goya (1746); US film actor, director and producer Warren Beatty (1937); English rock and blues guitarist Eric Clapton (1945)

Died: Scottish anatomist and obstetrician William Hunter (1783); French statesman and prime minister Léon Blum (1950); US film actor James Cagney (1986); British queen Elizabeth, the Queen Mother (2002)

1282 The 'Sicilian Vespers', a wholesale massacre of the French in Sicily, began; it was so called because the first killings occurred during a riot in a church outside Palermo at vespers (evensong) on Easter Monday.

1842 The world's first operation under anaesthetic was performed in Georgia, USA, by Dr Crawford Williamson Long (1815–78), using ether inhaled from a flannel.

1856 The Treaty of Paris ended the Crimean War.

1858 Hyman Lipman of Philadelphia, Pennsylvania, USA, patented the first pencil with an eraser attached to the end.

1867 The USA purchased Alaska from Russia for $7.2m – two cents an acre.

1912 The Treaty of Fez was signed, establishing Spanish Morocco with the capital Tétouan and French Morocco with the capital Rabat.

1979 Shadow Northern Ireland Secretary Airey Neave (1916–79) was killed by a car bomb outside the House of Commons.

1981 John Hinckley (born 1955) attempted to assassinate US President Ronald Reagan (1911–2004) outside the Washington Hilton Hotel.

1997 Channel Five television station went on air in the UK at 6pm; it was launched by pop group The Spice Girls.

31 March

In ancient Rome, this was the eve of the festival of Venus Verticordia ('changer of hearts'), celebrated in a poem of unknown date and authorship, *Pervigilium Veneris*. The poem has the refrain *Cras amet qui numquam amavit quique amavit cras amet* (Tomorrow let him love, he who has never loved, and he who has loved, tomorrow let him love).

It is perhaps fitting, therefore, that two famous English poets should have entered and left the world on this day: Andrew Marvell was born on 31 March 1621 and John Donne died exactly ten years later, on 31 March 1631. Both penned famous verses on the theme of seduction:

> *Had we but world enough, and time,*
> *This coyness Lady were no crime.*
> *We would sit down, and think which way*
> *To walk, and pass our long love's day.*
>
> Andrew Marvell, 'To His Coy Mistress' (c.1650).

> *License my roving hands, and let them go*
> *Before, behind, between, above, below.*
> *O my America! my new-found-land,*
> *My kingdom, safeliest when with one man manned.*
>
> John Donne, *Elegies*, 'To His Mistress Going to Bed' (c.1595).

On this day:

Born: French philosopher and mathematician René Descartes (1596); Austrian composer Joseph Haydn (1732); German chemist, physicist and inventor of the Bunsen burner Robert Bunsen (1811); Scottish actor Ewan McGregor (1971)

Died: English landscape painter John Constable (1837); English novelist Charlotte Brontë (1855); US athlete Jesse Owens (1980)

1492 The Expulsion of the Jews decree was issued by Spanish monarchs Ferdinand, the Catholic (1452–1516) and Isabella I of Castile (1451–1504); Jewish people were given four months to accept baptism or leave Spain.

1836 The first instalment of the monthly serial the *Pickwick Papers* by Charles Dickens (1812–70) was published.

1889 Construction of the Eiffel Tower in Paris was completed; it stood 312 metres high, including the flagpole at the top.

1936 The decisive battle of the Italian invasion of Abyssinia, the Battle of Maichew or Mai Ceu, took place; Emperor Haile Selassie (1891–1975) was defeated and the Italians prepared for the final advance on Addis Ababa.

1943 The première of the musical *Oklahoma!*, by Richard Rodgers (1902–79) and Oscar Hammerstein (1895–1960), was held on Broadway, New York City.

1959 The Dalai Lama, originally Tenzin Gyatso (born 1935), arrived in India to seek refuge from Chinese Communists in Tibet; he had fled from Lhasa on 17 March.

1968 US President Lyndon B Johnson (1908–73) announced an end to escalation of the Vietnam War and a new readiness to negotiate.

1973 Red Rum won the Grand National for the first time in the then record time of 9 minutes and 1.9 seconds.

1979 The British military presence in Malta came to an end.

1986 The Greater London Council and six other metropolitan councils across the UK were abolished.

1990 Poll tax demonstrations in London resulted in several hundred people being injured or arrested.

1992 United Nations Resolution 748 placed an arms embargo on Libya.

Gemstone: Diamond
Flower: Daisy or sweet pea

Married beneath April's changing skies,
A chequered path before you lies.

Traditional rhyme.

April presents no prettier picture than that of green fields, with rustic stiles between the openings of the hedges, where old footpaths go in and out, winding along, until lost in the distance; with children scattered here and there, singly or in groups, just as the daisies are, all playing or gathering flowers ... All day long the bees are busy among the bloom, making an unceasing murmur, for April is beautiful to look upon; and if she hides her sweet face for a few hours behind the rain-clouds, it is only that she may appear again peeping out through the next burst of sunshine in a veil of fresher green, through which we see the red and white of her bloom.

Chambers Book of Days (1864).

Origins

April, the fourth month of the year, was associated by the Romans with the goddess Venus, and the word *April* may be related to her Greek name, Aphrodite. Both this and the traditional etymology, from the Latin *aperire*, to open (with reference to the opening of buds), are rejected by some scholars in favour of an ancient derivation from a word meaning 'other' (dating from a time when March was the first month of the year).

Characteristics

April is the month when spring begins to make its presence felt. Deciduous trees produce new leaves and blossom; wild flowers such as daisies, cowslips and bluebells appear in the fields and woodland; and birds build their nests and fill the air with song – it is in April that the first call of the cuckoo is traditionally heard (see below).

History

April was the first month of the ancient Alban calendar and the second month of the early Roman calendar. Its association with the goddess of love – 1 April was celebrated in ancient Rome as the day of Venus Verticordia ('changer of hearts') and her companion Fortuna Virilis ('bold fortune') – undoubtedly has much to do with the reproductive activity in the animal kingdom at this time of the year. The Anglo-Saxons called it *Eastermonath*, *Ostermonath* or *Eosturmonath*, names that have obvious connections with *Easter* and may be derived from *east* (the direction of the sunrise, or of the cold winds that can prevail at this time of year) or from *Eostre*, thought to be the name of a pagan goddess of the spring.

Weather

April is known for the unpredictability and changeability of its weather: 'April weather, rain and sunshine both together.' The proverbial April showers are welcomed by farmers and gardeners alike, but the month is also notorious for sharp frosts that can literally nip young plants in the bud. The blossoming of the blackthorn towards the end of the month is often accompanied by a period of unseasonably cold weather – a **blackthorn winter**. Thunder in April is traditionally regarded as a favourable omen: 'When April blows his horn, it's good for hay and corn.'

Attitudes to April are as mixed as the weather itself. The poet Robert Browning (1812–89) sang its praises:

Oh, to be in England
Now that April's there,
And whoever wakes in England
Sees, some morning, unaware,
That the lowest boughs and the brushwood sheaf
Round the elm-tree bole are in tiny leaf,
While the chaffinch sings on the orchard bough
In England – now!

Robert Browning, *Dramatic Romances and Lyrics*,
'Home-Thoughts, from Abroad' (1845).

The poet and dramatist T S Eliot (1888–1965) took a less sanguine view:

> *April is the cruellest month, breeding*
> *Lilacs out of the dead land, mixing*
> *Memory and desire, stirring*
> *Dull roots with spring rain.*
>
> T S Eliot, *The Waste Land* (1922).

The cuckoo

Traditional sayings fail to agree on which day of April the cuckoo should arrive, but the month itself is not disputed: 'The cuckoo comes in April, and stays the month of May; sings a song at midsummer, and then goes away'. There are numerous superstitions relating to the bird – girls may ask it when they will marry, or old men when they will die, and the calls that follow indicated the number of years each must wait. On hearing the first cuckoo, for prosperity you should turn or jingle any money in your pocket, and to avoid a year of idleness or illness you should get up and run. If the call comes from your right you will have good luck, but if you are standing on bare earth you will be dead within twelve months. It is possible to see cuckoos throughout the UK, although they are more prevalent in central and southern England. Unfortunately their numbers have declined in recent years.

Non-fixed notable dates

Non-fixed notable dates in April include:

Arbor Day: Observed throughout the USA, Arbor Day is marked by the planting of trees by the general public for practical and aesthetic purposes. The tradition originated in Nebraska on 10 April 1872, when more than one million trees were planted to provide shade, shelter, fuel, fruit and beauty for residents of the prairie state. It was inspired by the newspaper editor Julius Sterling Morton, a former governor of Nebraska, and in 1885 the date of the celebration was moved closer to his birthday on 22 April. National Arbor Day takes place on the last Friday in April, but individual states observe Arbor Day on different dates, in tune with the best local conditions for tree planting.

Hocktide: The Sunday after Easter Day is called **Low Sunday**, and the

Monday and Tuesday that follow are known as Hocktide. These two days usually fall in April, although the Monday can be as early as 30 March and the Tuesday as late as 4 May. Hocktide was formerly marked by various customs, notably the capturing and ransoming of men by women on one day and of women by men on the other. Of the surviving Hocktide festivities, that of Hungerford in Berkshire is probably the best known. Dating from the 14th century, it takes place on the Tuesday and is connected with the preservation of grazing and fishing rights on certain properties of the town. Residents of these properties are called to a meeting of the Court where various officials are elected, including the **Tutti Men** (Tithingmen). The Tutti Men march around the town bearing decorated wooden poles with an orange fixed to the top and accompanied by an **Orange Man** carrying a bag of oranges. Their duty is to exact payment of a penny from each man and a kiss (in exchange for an orange) from each woman. Later in the day the remaining oranges are thrown to the assembled children of the town, while newcomers or visitors are subjected to the ordeal of **shoeing the colt**, a mock ceremony in which a 'blacksmith' pretends to hammer nails into the unfortunate person's shoe until he or she offers to buy a round of drinks.

Baisakhi (or **Vaisakhi**): A Sikh festival usually celebrated on 13 or 14 April, the anniversary of the day in 1699 on which the new **Khalsa** order of Sikhism was founded by Guru Gobind Singh at Anandpur in the Punjab. The Khalsa purified the Sikh religion and imposed a new code of discipline, including the wearing of the turban and the adoption of the name *Singh* or *Kaur* by men and women respectively. The festival of Baisakhi is celebrated with worship, processions and other special events, and many Sikhs mark the day by making a pilgrimage to Anandpur.

April

> *On the first of April you may send a fool whither you will.*
>
> Thomas Fuller, *Gnomologia* (1732).

> *The first of April is the day we remember what we are the other 364 days of the year.*
>
> Attributed to Mark Twain (1835–1910).

The first day of April, known as **April Fool's Day** or **All Fools' Day**, is marked by the playing of practical jokes on all and sundry. The origin of this tradition is unknown, but it is generally thought to derive from the French *poisson d'avril* (literally, 'April fish'). The French term was used in the late 15th century for a go-between in an amorous liaison, and it may subsequently have been extended to anyone sent on a fool's errand. The ***poisson d'avril*** custom also involved pinning a paper fish to the back of someone's clothing – without his or her knowledge, of course – to make that person a butt of ridicule.

All Fools' Day has been observed in England and elsewhere since the mid-17th century, when the practical jokes generally took the form of sending gullible victims in search of something such as elbow grease or pigeon's milk, or simply sending them from one person to another with a supposedly important message. This developed into more general hoaxing, such as setting all the clocks of the household one hour ahead or telling a neighbour about a new bylaw that all the front doors in the street must be painted a particular colour. Traditionally, the joking must end at midday, and anyone 'fooled' after this time is entitled to retort, 'April Fool's Day's past and gone, you're the fool and I am none' or 'April Fool is gone and past, you're the biggest fool at last'. In Scotland the day is traditionally known as **Huntigowk Day**, with 'hunt-the-gowk' meaning the making of a fool, or a fool's errand, and in England it was often referred to as **April Noddy Day**, with 'noddy' meaning fool. Such is the Scottish taste for japery, in some parts the pranks continue into 2 April with **Tailie Day** or **Preen-tail Day**. Similar to the French *poisson d'avril*, this day is dedicated to attaching paper tails to unsuspecting victims.

In modern times, the mass media have become increasingly involved in the trickery. Examples from the latter part of the 20th century include hoax news reports such as the famous 1957 spaghetti harvest prank, when the Panorama news show on British television showed a Swiss family picking the pasta from the trees. In 1974 a prankster in Alaska set fire to a heap of used tyres in the crater of a dormant volcano terrifying local residents into believing that the volcano had become active again. In 1976 respected English astronomer Sir Patrick Moore (born 1923) announced on national radio that a temporary decrease in gravity due to planetary alignment would occur at 9.47am; some of the more suggestible listeners claimed to have experienced a floating sensation at that given moment. The *Guardian* newspaper of 1 April 1977 included an article on the nonexistent republic of San Serriffe (which comprised the islands of Upper Caisse and Lower Caisse). An Australian millionaire businessman towed what was alleged to be an iceberg from the Antarctic into Sydney Harbour in 1978 amid great publicity. More recently, in 1998, a fast-food chain published a full-page advertisement for a left-handed burger (with the contents rotated through 180°) and the 'New Mexicans for Science and Reason' newsletter featured an item which claimed that the Alabama state legislature had voted to change the value of pi to 3.

> *Sometimes the opportunity is taken by ultra-jocular persons to carry out some extensive hoax upon society. For example, in March 1860, a vast multitude of people received through the post a card having the following inscription ... 'Tower of London. Admit the Bearer and Friend to view the Annual Ceremony of Washing the White Lions, on Sunday, April 1st, 1860. Admitted only at the White Gate. It is particularly requested that no gratuities be give to the Wardens or their Assistants.' The trick is said to have been highly successful. Cabs were rattling about Tower Hill all that Sunday morning, vainly endeavouring to discover the White Gate.*
>
> *Chambers Book of Days* (1864).

On this day:

Born: English physician and discoverer of the circulation of the blood William Harvey (1578); Russian composer Sergei Rachmaninov (1873); US actress Debbie Reynolds (1932); English cricketer David Gower (1957)

Died: French and English queen Eleanor of Aquitaine (1204); US pianist and composer Scott Joplin (1917); Polish-born US businesswoman Helena Rubinstein (1965); US dancer, teacher,

choreographer and pioneer of modern dance Martha Graham (1991)

1789 Enough representatives arrived at the US Congress for it to achieve its first quorum.

1875 The first daily newspaper weather chart began to appear in *The Times.*

1918 World War I – the Royal Air Force was established in the UK.

1945 World War II – the Battle of Okinawa between US and Japanese forces in the Pacific began.

1954 The US Air Force Academy was founded in Colorado.

1970 In the USA, television and radio advertisements for cigarettes were banned under legislation signed by President Richard Nixon (1913–94). The ban came into effect on 1 January 1971.

1976 The Lomé Convention, a series of agreements between the European Communities and a number of developing nations in Africa, the Caribbean and the Pacific, came into force.

1999 In Canada, the creation of the autonomous territory of Nunavut for the Inuit people was implemented.

1999 A legally binding minimum wage was introduced in the UK.

2001 Former Yugoslav president Slobodan Milosevic (born 1941) was finally arrested after a 36-hour armed siege at his Belgrade home.

2 April

On this day in 1513, the Spanish explorer Juan Ponce de León (1460–1521) discovered Florida. He had been sent to find the fabled island of Bimini, which was said to contain a fountain whose waters would bestow perpetual youth on those who bathed in them. Having explored much of the coastline of the peninsula, he assumed it to be an island and named it after the Easter Festival of Flowers, *Pascua Florida*, which was taking place in his native Spain around that time. Ponce de León was subsequently appointed governor of the new territory, but failed in his mission of colonization. In modern Florida, 2 April is celebrated as **Pascua Florida Day**.

On this day:

Born: Frankish king and Christian Emperor of the West Charlemagne (742); Danish writer Hans Christian Andersen (1805); German painter and sculptor Max Ernst (1891); English athlete Linford Christie (1960)

Died: German botanist and botanical artist Johann Dillenius (1747); English economist and politician Richard Cobden (1865); US artist and inventor Samuel Morse (1872); British writer C S Forester (1966); French statesman Georges Pompidou (1974)

1559 The Treaty of Cateau-Cambrésis was negotiated between the French and Spanish crowns; it brought an end to the wars waged by Charles V (1500–58) in Europe.

1744 The first golf tournament, held at Leith Links near Edinburgh, in Scotland, was won by local surgeon John Rattray.

1792 The US Congress passed the Coinage Act, which created the first US mint in Philadelphia, Pennsylvania.

1801 English admiral Lord Nelson (1758–1805), having disregarded orders to withdraw, went on to win the Battle of Copenhagen against the Danish fleet.

1877 The first annual White House Easter Egg Roll was held in Washington, DC.

1905 The Simplon rail tunnel under the Alps opened, linking Switzerland and Italy.

1917 World War I – US President Woodrow Wilson (1856–1924) outlined the case for the USA to declare war on Germany.

1977 In the UK, Red Rum won the Grand National for a record third time; the race also included its first woman jockey, Charlotte Brew, riding Barony Fort.

1978 Glamorous soap opera *Dallas* had its première on US television.

1983 Argentina began a full-scale invasion of the Falkland Islands at 4am; the first soldiers landed at 6am and by lunchtime the Argentinian flag was flying above Government House in the capital, Stanley.

1998 French politician Maurice Papon (born 1910) was jailed for deporting thousands of Jews to concentration camps during World War II, when he was a member of the collaborationist Vichy government in France.

3 April

Feast day of **St Richard of Chichester**, formerly celebrated in Droitwich, Worcestershire (his birthplace) with a well-dressing on this day.

On this day:

Born: US author Washington Irving (1783); South African statesman J B M Hertzog (1866); English actor Leslie Howard (1893); US actor Marlon Brando (1924); English primatologist and conservationist Jane Goodall (1934)

Died: Spanish painter Bartolomé Murillo (1682); US Wild West outlaw Jesse James (1882); German composer Johannes Brahms (1897); English impresario and manager Richard D'Oyly Carte (1901); English writer Graham Greene (1991)

1721 The Whig politician Robert Walpole (1676–1745) became Great Britain's first prime minister.

1860 In the USA, the Pony Express service began work, delivering letters through a network of riders and 190 way stations.

1913 English suffragette Emmeline Pankhurst (1857–1928) was sentenced to prison for inciting supporters to place explosives outside the home of Welsh Liberal statesman David Lloyd George (1863–1945).

1922 Soviet revolutionary and leader Joseph Stalin (1879–1953) was appointed General Secretary of the Communist Party in Russia.

1930 Prince Ras Tafari Makonnen (1891–1975) was proclaimed Emperor of Ethiopia as Haile Selassie I.

1933 Two British planes made aviation history by being the first to fly over the peak of Mt Everest in the Himalayas.

1948 The Marshall Plan (or European Recovery Programme) was signed by US President Harry S Truman (1884–1972).

1954 The 100th Boat Race between Oxford University and Cambridge University rowing clubs was won by Oxford.

1968 The première of the film *2001: A Space Odyssey*, directed by Stanley Kubrick (1928–99), was held.

1987 Jewellery that belonged to Wallis Simpson (1896–1986), the Duchess of Windsor, was sold at auction for £31m.

1996 Theodore Kaczynski (born 1942), the notorious 'Unabomber', was arrested in Montana, USA.

4 April

> *I have a dream. I have a dream that my four little children will one day live in a nation where they will not be judged by the colour of their skin but by the content of their character.*
>
> Martin Luther King, Jnr, speech at Washington civil rights rally (15 June 1963).

The US Black civil rights leader Martin Luther King, Jnr was assassinated on 4 April 1968 in Memphis, Tennessee, where he was to have led a sanitation workers' protest. He was shot in the neck on a hotel balcony by a white man, James Earl Ray, who was sentenced to life imprisonment. Ray initially confessed to the murder, then tried to claim that he had been part of a government-led conspiracy, but no evidence has ever emerged to support the conspiracy theory. The assassination sparked race riots throughout the USA.

King was born in 1929 in Atlanta, Georgia, the son of an African-American Baptist minister. After completing his doctorate at Boston University in 1955 he followed his father into the ministry; around the same time, he became involved in the Black civil rights movement. His charismatic personality and eloquent oratory made him a natural leader, and his admiration for the philosophy and achievements of Mahatma Gandhi led him to advocate a similar policy of non-violence and passive resistance to White-on-Black harassment and oppression. In 1964 he was awarded the Nobel Peace Prize. In the USA, Martin Luther King Day is commemorated on the third Monday in January (see January).

On this day:

Born: French painter Pierre Paul Prud'hon (1758); German-born British electrical engineer Sir William Siemens (1823); Japanese naval officer Isoroku Yamamoto (1884); US playwright and author Robert E Sherwood (1896); US writer Maya Angelou (1928)

Died: Scottish mathematician John Napier (1617); Irish playwright, novelist and poet Oliver Goldsmith (1774); German engineer and car manufacturer Karl Benz (1929); US actress Gloria Swanson (1983)

1581 After his return from circumnavigating the globe, English navigator Francis Drake (c.1540–1596) was knighted on board his ship *The Golden Hind* by Queen Elizabeth I (1533–1603).

1818 The first official US flag was approved by Congress.

1841 US President William Henry Harrison (1773–1841) died after only one month in office; he had caught pneumonia during his inauguration ceremony.

1887 Susanna Salter (1860–1961) of Argonia, Kansas, became the first woman in the USA to be elected mayor.

1924 The first schools' broadcast was made by the BBC.

1932 Vitamin C was first isolated.

1939 King Faisal II (1935–58) acceded to the throne of Iraq.

1949 The North Atlantic Treaty Organization (NATO) was established.

1970 The main women's peace camp at Greenham Common was cleared of protestors by police and bailiffs; the protestors returned to the site's other camps to continue their demonstrations.

1979 The deposed Pakistani prime minister Zulfikar Ali Bhutto (1928–79) was executed by the new regime led by General Mohammed Zia ul-Haq (1924–88).

1981 Oxford University's first woman cox, 23-year-old Susan Brown, steered her crew to victory over Cambridge University in the annual Boat Race.

5 April

On this day in 1955, the following statement was issued from Buckingham Palace:

> *The Right Honourable Sir Winston Churchill had an audience with the Queen this evening and tendered his resignation as Prime Minister and First Lord of the Treasury, which Her Majesty was graciously pleased to accept.*

Sir Winston Leonard Spencer Churchill (1874–1965), who was then 81 and in failing health, was subsequently replaced as prime minister by Sir Anthony Eden (1897–1977). This had been Churchill's second premiership of the UK, beginning in 1951; his first had spanned the war years from 1940 to 1945.

Born in 1874, Churchill entered politics in 1900 as a Conservative MP. He joined the Liberal Party in 1906 and held various ministerial posts until the early 1920s, when he fell from favour for a time. After returning to power as prime minister in 1940, with a memorable speech in which he claimed to 'have nothing to offer but blood, toil, tears and sweat', he remained in power through World War II. Looking back at this time on the occasion of his 80th birthday, Churchill was modest about his achievements:

> *I have never accepted what many people have kindly said – that I inspired the nation. It was the nation and the race living around the globe that had the lion heart. I had the luck to be called upon to give the roar.*
>
> Sir Winston Churchill, speech to both Houses of Parliament in Westminster Hall (November 1954).

On this day:

Born: English political philosopher Thomas Hobbes (1588); American-born English merchant and benefactor of Yale University Elihu Yale (1649); US educationalist Booker T

Washington (1856); US actor Gregory Peck (1916); US soldier and politician Colin Powell (1937)

Died: French Revolutionary leader Georges Danton (1794); English cricketer and publisher John Wisden (1884); US soldier Douglas MacArthur (1964); Chinese general and politician Chiang Kai-shek (1975); US poet Allen Ginsberg (1997)

1355 King Charles IV (1316–78) was crowned in Rome as Holy Roman Emperor.

1614 Native American princess Pocahontas (1595–1617), daughter of King Powahatan, married English settler John Rolfe (1585–1622) in Jamestown, Virginia.

1768 The first American Chamber of Commerce was founded in New York City.

1818 Bernardo O'Higgins (1778–1842) led his revolutionaries to the victory that gave his country, Chile, its independence from Spain; he eventually became the first leader of the new Chilean state.

1895 Irish writer and wit Oscar Wilde (1854–1900) lost his criminal libel action against the Marquis of Queensberry (1844–1900), and was himself arrested on charges of gross indecency.

1902 A section of terracing collapsed at Glasgow's Ibrox Park football ground, killing 20 people and injuring over 500.

1951 US Communist spies Julius (1918–53) and Ethel Rosenberg (1915–53) were sentenced to death in the USA for passing atomic secrets through an intermediary to the Soviet vice-consul.

1976 English Labour politician James Callaghan (born 1912) became prime minister of the UK on the resignation of Harold Wilson (1916–95).

1997 BBC correspondent Martin Bell (born 1938) announced he would stand for election on an anti-corruption ticket against Neil Hamilton (born 1949), the sitting Conservative MP, at Tatton in Cheshire.

6 April

> *In this world nothing can be said to be certain, except death and taxes.*
>
> Benjamin Franklin, letter to Jean Baptiste Le Roy (13 November 1789).

In the UK, the tax year (or fiscal year) begins on 6 April. The reason for this apparently arbitrary choice of date goes back to the mid-18th century, predating income tax itself (which was introduced as a temporary measure in 1799 to fund the Napoleonic wars). The **Julian calendar**, originally devised by Julius Caesar in 45 BC, was used in Great Britain and her colonies until 1751, although other countries had adopted the **Gregorian calendar** of Pope Gregory XIII in 1582. Each century in the Julian calendar was longer by about a day than a century based on astronomical calculations, hence the introduction of the Gregorian calendar, which put matters right. The basic difference between the two is that the Julian calendar has a leap year every four years, whereas the Gregorian calendar does not have a leap year if the year number ends in 00 and is not divisible by 400 (thus 2000 was a leap year but 1900 was not).

The adjustment to the Gregorian calendar was made by 'losing' the appropriate number of days from the year in which it was adopted; in Great Britain, this resulted in the omission of eleven days from September 1752. As the financial year was deemed to begin on Lady Day (25 March) at that time, the corresponding date in 1753 had to be eleven days later (5 April) to make the financial year 1752–3 a full twelve months long. It was considered necessary to make a further adjustment in 1800 (because this would have been a leap year in the Julian calendar) and for fiscal purposes the year has begun on 6 April ever since. For other purposes, the discrepancy between **Old Style** (Julian calendar) and **New Style** (Gregorian calendar) dates is usually eleven days.

On this day:

Born: Scottish philosopher, historian and economist James Mill (1773); French painter and teacher Gustave Moreau (1826); Polish-born US trade unionist, labour leader and social reformer Rose Schneiderman (1882); Dutch-born US aircraft

engineer Anthony Fokker (1890); US scientist and Nobel Prize winner James Watson (1928)

Died: English king Richard I, the Lionheart (1199); Italian painter Raphael (1520); German painter and engraver Albrecht Dürer (1528); Russian-born US composer Igor Stravinsky (1971); Tunisian statesman and president Habib Bourguiba (2000)

1320 The Declaration of Arbroath asserted the separate nationhood of Scotland, in response to a demand from Pope John XXII (c.1245–1334) that the Scots make peace with England.

1789 The first US Congress began regular sessions in New York City.

1896 The first modern Olympic Games opened in Athens, Greece.

1909 US naval commander and explorer Robert E Peary (1856–1920) became the first person to reach the North Pole.

1917 World War I – the USA officially declared war on Germany.

1938 Teflon was invented by US chemist Roy J Plunkett (1911–94).

1941 World War II – Germany invaded Greece.

1960 The film *Ben Hur* won a record-breaking eleven Oscars®.

1989 The British government abolished legislation guaranteeing 'jobs for life' to dock workers.

1994 President Juvénal Habyarimana (1937–94) of Rwanda and President Cyprien Ntaryamira (1955–94) of Burundi were killed when the plane in which they were travelling was shot down, leading to increased ethnic violence in both countries.

2000 In Zimbabwe, the Land Acquisition Act was passed by parliament, enabling the government to take over white-owned farms without compensation and to redistribute them to poor black people.

On this day:

Born: Spanish Jesuit missionary St Francis Xavier (1506); English poet William Wordsworth (1770); Chilean poet, diplomat, teacher and Nobel Prize winner Gabriela Mistral (1889); US jazz singer Billie Holiday (1915); US film director Francis Ford Coppola (1939)

Died: Spanish painter El Greco (1614); US showman P T Barnum (1891); US car engineer and manufacturer Henry Ford (1947); Scottish racing driver Jim Clark (1968)

1712 Nine white people were killed in the New York Slave Revolt; following the incident, 21 black people were killed for their participation in the rebellion.

1795 The metric system was adopted in France.

1827 The first matches were sold by English inventor and chemist John Walker (c.1781–1859) from his shop in Stockton-on-Tees to a local solicitor, who paid him one shilling for 100.

1862 During the American Civil War, the Battle of Shiloh ended in victory for Federal troops led by General Ulysses S Grant (1822–85).

1906 Mt Vesuvius erupted, devastating the nearby city of Naples and killing over 100 people.

1939 World War II – Italian troops began their invasion of Albania.

1943 Swiss chemist Albert Hofmann (born 1906) first produced the drug lysergic acid diethylamide (LSD).

1948 The World Health Organization constitution came into force.

1956 Spain relinquished its Moroccan protectorate.

1976 Deng Xiaoping (1904–97), deputy prime minister of China, was deposed by the country's leadership.

1986 English electronic engineer and inventor Clive Sinclair (born 1940) sold his computing business to rival company Amstrad.

2001 NASA launched its Mars Odyssey space mission.

8 April

This day is observed by many Buddhists as **Buddha's birthday**, although the exact date of that event is uncertain. The founder of Buddhism was born Gautama Siddhartha, the son of a tribal leader in what is now Nepal, probably around 563 BC. He is said to have attained enlightenment while sitting under a banyan tree at Buddh Gaya in Bihar, India.

Buddha's birthday is celebrated in Japan on 8 April as the flower festival of **Hana Matsuri**. At Buddhist temples, a flower-strewn shrine containing a statue of the infant Buddha is sprinkled with sweet tea in commemoration of his legendary baptism with pure water from the heavens.

On this day:

Born: Dutch still-life painter Cornelis de Heem (1631); English conductor Sir Adrian Boult (1889); US actress Mary Pickford (1893); Rhodesian politician Ian Smith (1919); Ghanaian civil servant, diplomat and Nobel Prize winner Kofi Annan (1938)

Died: Florentine ruler Lorenzo de' Medici (1492); US inventor of the elevator Elisha Graves Otis (1861); Russian dancer and choreographer Vaslav Nijinsky (1950); Spanish painter Pablo Picasso (1973); Guyanese-born British politician Bernie Grant (2000)

1838 The steamship *Great Western*, designed by Isambard Kingdom Brunel (1806–59), set off from Bristol, England, on its maiden voyage to New York City, USA; it was the first steamship to go into regular transatlantic passenger service.

1904 The UK and France signed the Entente Cordiale, which settled long-standing disputes between the two countries over such places as Morocco, Egypt and Newfoundland.

1913 China's first Parliament was opened in Beijing.

1953 On the outbreak of the Mau Mau uprising and the subsequent emergency, Kenyan nationalist and political leader Jomo Kenyatta (c.1889–1978) was tried, found guilty on what later proved to be perjured evidence, and detained until 1961.

1985 Australian-born US publisher Rupert Murdoch (born 1931) bought 50 per cent of the Twentieth Century Fox Film Corporation.

1986 Film actor Clint Eastwood (born 1930) was elected Mayor of Carmel, California, USA.

1990 English golfer Nick Faldo (born 1957) won his second successive US Masters trophy after a play-off.

1995 In Atlanta, Georgia, USA, 31-year-old prisoner Nicholas Ingram became the first Briton to die in the electric chair.

9
April

On this day:

Born: English engineer and inventor Isambard Kingdom Brunel (1806); French Symbolist poet Charles Baudelaire (1821); US singer and actor Paul Robeson (1898); Spanish golfer Severiano Ballesteros (1957)

Died: English king Edward IV (1483); French monk, physician and satirist François Rabelais (1553); English philosopher and statesman Francis Bacon, Baron Verulam of Verulam and Viscount St Albans (1626); English poet, painter and translator Dante Gabriel Rossetti (1882); US architect Frank Lloyd Wright (1959)

1865 The American Civil War ended when Confederate General Robert E Lee (1807–70) surrendered to General Ulysses S Grant (1822–85) at Appomattox Court House, Virginia.

1866 The US Civil Rights Bill of 1866 was passed, allowing black people the rights and privileges of US citizenship.

1869 The Hudson's Bay Company ceded its territorial rights to Canada.

1940 World War II – Germany began its invasions of Norway and Denmark.

1947 The first edition of *How Does Your Garden Grow?* was broadcast on BBC radio; it was later renamed *Gardeners' Question Time.*

1969 The maiden flight of the first British Concorde took place.

1969 Wolverhampton's Transport Committee overturned its ban on the wearing of turbans and beards by its Sikh employees after a long campaign.

1970 Paul McCartney (born 1942) sought a writ in the High Court to dissolve the Beatles' business partnership.

1980 Two Soviet cosmonauts were launched into space with the Soyuz 35 mission, going on to set a new space endurance record of 185 days (they returned to Earth on 11 October 1980).

1992 A general election in the UK resulted in a record-breaking fourth term of office for the Conservative Party.

1995 The nationalist ZANU (PF) party, led by Robert Mugabe (born 1924), won the Zimbabwean general election.

1999 The president of Niger, Ibrahim Baré Maïnassara (1949–99), was assassinated.

10 April

On this day in 1633 the herbalist Thomas Johnson put a bunch of bananas in his shop window in Snow Hill, London. This was the first time that the fruit had been so displayed in England, and it was not until the late 19th century that bananas were regularly imported into the UK. However, a banana skin dating from around 1500 has been found by archaeologists near Southwark, on the south bank of the River Thames, suggesting that at least one specimen of the fruit had found its way into the country in Tudor times.

On this day:

Born: Scottish king James V (1512); Dutch jurist, politician, diplomat, poet and theologian Hugo Grotius (1583); English founder of the Salvation Army William Booth (1829); US newspaper proprietor Joseph Pulitzer (1847); US novelist and travel writer Paul Theroux (1941)

Died: Italian pope Gregory XIII (1585); Mexican revolutionary Emiliano Zapata (1919); French pioneer of motion photography Auguste Lumière (1954); English writer Evelyn Waugh (1966); Japanese astronomer and comet discoverer Yuji Hyakutake (2002)

1710 The 1709 Copyright Act, known as the Statute of Anne, came into force, allowing authors to hold exclusive rights to their works for a fixed period after death.

1790 The first patent act was signed in the USA, laying the foundation of the country's modern patent system.

1849 US mechanic Walter Hunt (1796–1859) patented the safety pin in the USA; English inventor Charles Rowley also patented a safety pin on 12 October the same year, unaware of Hunt's invention.

1858 Big Ben, the Great Bell of Westminster, was cast in the Whitechapel Bell Foundry.

1864 Austrian Archduke Maximilian (1832–67) was crowned emperor of Mexico.

1868 The première of the *German Requiem*, by Johannes Brahms (1833–97), was held at Bremen Cathedral, Germany.

1916 The first Professional Golf Association (PGA) Championship was held at Siwanoy golf course, New York, USA.

1924 The first book of crossword puzzles was published in New York City by the newly established firm of Simon & Schuster.

1968 The ferry TEV *Wahine* capsized in the harbour at Wellington, New Zealand, killing 51 people.

1981 Irish revolutionary and hunger striker Bobby Sands (1954–81), in prison for terrorism, won a seat in the British parliament in the Fermanagh and South Tyrone by-election.

1998 The Good Friday Agreement was reached in Northern Ireland.

2001 In the Netherlands, mercy killing in cases of unbearable terminal illness was legalized.

11 April

Feast day of **St Guthlac**, a hermit who lived in the Fens, in whose honour Crowland Abbey was built by King Ethelbald.

On this day:

Born: English physician James Parkinson (1755); German-born British pianist and conductor Sir Charles Hallé (1819); US politician and lawyer Dean Acheson (1893); US widow of politician Robert F Kennedy Ethel Kennedy (1928)

Died: Welsh prince of Gwynedd Llywelyn Ap Iorwerth (1240); Italian High Renaissance architect Donato Bramante (1514); Scottish novelist and pioneer in Canada John Galt (1839); US detective-story writer S S Van Dine (1939); Italian writer and chemist Primo Levi (1987)

1689 King William III (1650–1702) and his wife Queen Mary II (1662–94) were crowned joint sovereigns of England and Scotland.

1713 The Treaty of Utrecht ended hostilities in the War of the Spanish Succession and left Gibraltar and parts of Canada ceded to Great Britain.

1814 Napoleon I (1769–1821) abdicated as emperor of France and was exiled to the Island of Elba.

1899 The treaty that ended the Spanish–American War came into effect.

1945 World War II – Allied soldiers liberated Buchenwald concentration camp near Weimar, Germany.

1957 The UK agreed to self-government for Singapore.

1961 The trial of Austrian Nazi war criminal Adolf Eichmann (1906–62) began in Jerusalem, Israel, ending with a guilty verdict on 15 December; he was later hanged.

1968 In the USA, the Civil Rights Act of 1968 was signed into law.

1979 In Uganda, the military dictatorship of Idi Amin (1925–2003) was overthrown.

1981 Riots broke out in Brixton, London, sparked by perceived racial discrimination in the area by the Metropolitan police.

1990 Customs and Excise officers in Middlesbrough detained a shipment of steel cylinders, alleged to be the barrel of an illegal 'supergun', bound from the UK for Iraq.

12 April

> *I could have gone on flying through space forever.*
>
> Yuri Gagarin, in the *New York Times* (14 April 1961).

The race between the USA and the USSR to send the first human being into space was won on 12 April 1961, when the Soviet cosmonaut Yuri Gagarin (1934–68) orbited the earth for 108 minutes in the spacecraft *Vostok*. Gagarin, a major in the Soviet air force who had trained for two years for this historic flight, subsequently became a national hero and an international spokesman on space activities. He died in 1968, aged 34, when his aeroplane crashed in training. In Russia this day is celebrated each year as **Cosmonauts Day**, in honour of Gagarin's achievement and all cosmonauts.

The first US manned space flight took place on 5 May 1961, when Alan Shepard (1923–98) was launched on a 15-minute mission in the spacecraft *Freedom 7*.

On this day:

Born: US politician Henry Clay (1777); Spanish opera singer Montserrat Caballé (1933); English footballer Bobby Moore (1941); US author Tom Clancy (1947)

Died: English architect and landscape designer William Kent (1748); Russian bass opera singer Feodor Chaliapin (1938); 32nd President of the USA Franklin D Roosevelt (1945); US boxer Joe Louis (1981)

1606 The Union Jack was adopted by King James VI and I (1566–1625) as the official flag of the United Kingdom.

1709 The first issue of *The Tatler* magazine was published.

1861 The American Civil War began with the bombardment of Fort Sumter in South Carolina.

1864 A Civil War massacre took place at Fort Pillow, Tennessee.

1914 The première of the play *Pygmalion*, by George Bernard Shaw (1856–1950), was held in London.

1954 US rock and roll pioneer Bill Haley (1925–81) and his band The Comets recorded the song 'Rock Around the Clock'.

1955 The polio vaccine developed by US virologist Jonas E Salk (1914–95) was confirmed as safe and effective.

1975 The USA completely pulled out of its involvement in Cambodia's civil war.

1981 The USA launched the space shuttle *Columbia* for the first time.

2000 Queen Elizabeth II (born 1926) presented the George Cross medal to the Royal Ulster Constabulary (RUC), the police force of Northern Ireland.

2004 West Indian cricketer Brian Lara (born 1969) beat the record for the highest individual test match innings with a score of 400 not out against England in Antigua.

13 April

On Tuesday last Mr Handel's Sacred Grand Oratorio, the MESSIAH, was performed at the New Musick Hall in Fishamble Street; the best Judges allowed it to be the most finished piece of Musick. Words are wanting to express the exquisite Delight it afforded to the admiring crowded audience. The Sublime, the Grand, and the Tender, adopted to the most elevated, majestick and moving Words, conspired to transport and charm the ravished heart and ear. It is but Justice to Mr

13 April

> *Handel, that the World should hear he generously gave the money arising from this Grand Performance, to be equally shared by the Society for relieving Prisoners, the Charitable Infirmary, and Mercer's Hospital, for which they will ever gratefully remember his Name.*
>
> *Dublin Journal* (17 April 1742).

George Frideric Handel's (1685–1759) oratorio *Messiah* had its first performance on 13 April 1742 in Dublin, Ireland. Probably Handel's best-known and best-loved work, at its Dublin première it was performed by a chorus of 14 men and 26 boys, a small string orchestra, a chamber organ, and a harpsichord (played by the composer himself). Since then it has frequently been performed by much larger groups, often to the detriment of the piece. Perhaps the worst example of such excess was an 1882 performance by a choir of 4,000 accompanied by an orchestra of 500.

The climax of the oratorio is the Hallelujah Chorus, of which Handel once remarked, 'Whether I was in my body or out of my body as I wrote it I know not. God knows'. The composer Joseph Haydn (1732–1809), hearing it in Westminster Abbey, is said to have wept with emotion and declared, 'He is the master of us all'. It is traditional for the audience to stand during this chorus, a custom that originated in 1743 at a London performance in the presence of George II (1683–1760). The King rose to his feet at this point and the audience dutifully did likewise. It is generally thought that the King's action was a spontaneous response to the awe-inspiring grandeur of the chorus; however, it has also been suggested that he mistakenly thought the words 'And he shall reign for ever' referred to himself or, more mischievously, that he had dozed off just before the chorus and leapt up in fright or anger when awakened by the opening 'Hallelujah'.

Another famous story relating to *Messiah* tells of a rehearsal at which the conductor Sir Thomas Beecham (1879–1961) asked the choir, 'When we sing "All we, like sheep, have gone astray", might we please have a little more regret and a little less satisfaction?' A similar story is told of Sir Malcolm Sargent (1895–1967) – who is said to have asked the female members of the choir to sing 'For unto us a child is born' with 'just a little more reverence, please, and not so much astonishment' – suggesting that one or both of these anecdotes may be apocryphal.

On this day:

Born: French queen and regent Catherine de Médicis (1519); Third President of the USA Thomas Jefferson (1743); English engineer and inventor Richard Trevithick (1771); Northern

Irish poet, critic and Nobel Prize winner Seamus Heaney (1939); Russian chess player Garry Kasparov (1963)

Died: French poet Jean de La Fontaine (1695); English biologist and academic W F B Weldon (1906); Scottish poet, novelist and short-story writer George Mackay Brown (1996); Italian novelist and poet Giorgio Bassani (2000)

1598 King Henry IV of France (1553–1610) signed the Edict of Nantes, granting rights to the Protestant Huguenot minority.

1829 The Catholic Emancipation Act became law in the UK.

1848 Sicily, the largest island in the Mediterranean, gained its independence from Naples.

1919 The Amritsar Massacre took place as British troops shot into a crowd who were agitating for Indian self-rule, leaving 379 people dead and 1,200 wounded.

1935 The first London to Australia commercial air service was inaugurated by Imperial Airways and Qantas.

1936 A record ten goals in one football match were scored by Joe Payne of Luton Town in a match against Bristol Rovers.

1951 Scotland's Stone of Destiny, which had been stolen on the previous Christmas Day by Scottish Nationalists, was returned to Westminster Abbey, London.

1964 Ian Smith (born 1919) replaced Winston Field as prime minister of Southern Rhodesia.

1964 US actor Sidney Poitier (born 1924) became the first black person to win the Best Actor Oscar® for his role in *Lilies of the Field* (1963).

1992 Neil Kinnock (born 1942) resigned as Leader of the Labour Party in the UK following a general election defeat.

At 11.40pm on 14 April 1912, the liner *Titanic*, on her maiden voyage, struck an iceberg that ripped a huge hole in her side. The ship had been built with 16 watertight compartments in the hull that rendered her practically unsinkable, but five of these were ruptured in the collision. Two and a half hours later the *Titanic* went down, with the loss of more than 1,500 lives.

The main reason for the huge death toll was the shortage of lifeboat spaces: there were actually only enough lifeboats on board to accommodate 1178 of the 2224 passengers and crew. Some of these were not loaded to full capacity, and only just over 700 people survived. The liner *California* was in the vicinity at the time of the tragedy but the crew were unaware of what was going on, as their radio operator was off duty, and it was the liner *Carpathia* that finally came to the rescue.

The sinking of the *Titanic* has been the subject of numerous books and films, some based on survivors' accounts, some on rumour and speculation. For many people, the definitive fictionalized version is Roy Baker's 1958 film *A Night to Remember*, based on Walter Lord's book of the same name, and considered to be a more realistic representation of what actually happened on that fateful night than the blockbusting 1997 film *Titanic* by James Cameron, despite the far superior special effects that the latter had at its disposal.

On this day:

Born: Flemish cartographer Abraham Ortelius (1527); Dutch physicist Christiaan Huygens (1629); English actor Sir John Gielgud (1904); Haitian politician François 'Papa Doc' Duvalier (1907); Scottish actor Robert Carlyle (1961)

Died: English soldier and statesman Richard Neville, Earl of Warwick, 'the Kingmaker' (1471); German-born English composer George Frideric Handel (1759); English politician Ernest Bevin (1951); French socialist, feminist and writer Simone de Beauvoir (1986)

1828 Noah Webster (1758–1843) published *Webster's American Dictionary of the English Language*, the first dictionary of US English.

1865 US President Abraham Lincoln (1809–65) was shot by assassin John Wilkes Booth (1839–65) while attending Ford's Theatre in Washington, DC; he died the following day.

1900 The French president Emile Loubet (1838–1929) opened the Paris International Exhibition.

1929 The first Monaco Grand Prix motor race was held.

1931 The UK's *Highway Code* was first published.

1931 The Second Republic, Spain's first democratic regime in nearly 60 years, was established.

1939 *The Grapes of Wrath*, by US author and Nobel Prize winner John Steinbeck (1902–68), was first published.

1970 An explosion on the USA's Apollo 13 space mission in the early hours of the morning greatly endangered the mission; all three astronauts on board later returned safely to Earth.

1979 Yusuf Lule (1912–85) was sworn in as president of Uganda after eight years of military dictatorship by Idi Amin (1925–2003).

1981 The first US space shuttle, *Columbia*, landed safely in California, USA, after its first test flight.

2002 Venezuelan president Hugo Chavez (born 1954) resumed his office only two days after being deposed by a military coup.

15 April

> *To devise is the work of the master, to execute the act of the servant.*
>
> Leonardo da Vinci, *Treatise on Painting* (1651).

The Italian artist and scientist Leonardo da Vinci was born on this day in 1452, the illegitimate son of a Florentine notary and a peasant woman. He studied art in Florence before settling in Milan, where he painted one of his most famous works, the *Last Supper* (1498), on the wall of a convent refectory. His best-known painting is undoubtedly the *Mona Lisa*, completed around 1504, which now hangs in the Louvre, Paris.

Leonardo was the outstanding all-round genius of the Renaissance. He had a wide knowledge and understanding far beyond his times of most of the sciences, including biology, anatomy, physiology, hydrodynamics, mechanics and aeronautics, and his notebooks, written in mirror writing, contain original remarks on all of these. He died in 1519.

On this day:

Born: Indian founder of Sikhism Guru Nanak (1469); Scottish Arctic and Antarctic explorer Sir James Clark Ross (1800); US athlete Evelyn Ashford (1957); English actress Emma Thompson (1959)

Died: French courtier Madame de Pompadour (1764); English poet and critic Matthew Arnold (1888); French existentialist philosopher, dramatist and novelist Jean-Paul Sartre (1980); Swedish-born US film actress Greta Garbo (1990); Cambodian politician Pol Pot (1998)

1755 English writer, critic, lexicographer and conversationalist Dr Samuel Johnson (1709–84) published his *Dictionary* in two volumes.

1912 The world's largest and most luxurious liner, the *Titanic*, sank within three hours of striking an iceberg (see 14 April).

1923 The first commercial screening of a sound-on-film production took place at New York City's Rialto Theater.

1942 World War II – King George VI (1895–1952) conferred the George Cross for civilian gallantry on the island of Malta, in recognition of its bravery in the face of Italian and German attacks.

1986 US warplanes bombed targets in Benghazi and Tripoli, Libya, in retaliation for a Libyan terrorist attack.

1989 Sheffield's Hillsborough football ground was the scene of the UK's worst sporting disaster, in which 96 people were killed and over 200 injured when an influx of supporters caused Liverpool fans to be crushed against a metal fence.

1991 European Community foreign ministers reached an agreement to lift most of the remaining sanctions against South Africa.

1999 UK Home Secretary Jack Straw (born 1946) authorized extradition of the former Chilean dictator Augusto Pinochet (born 1915) to Argentina.

16 April

This is the feast day of **St Bernadette of Lourdes**, and also the date of her death in 1879. Bernadette Soubirous, born in 1844, was a young peasant girl who claimed to have had 18 visions of the Virgin Mary at a grotto near Lourdes, the site of a spring with miraculous curative powers, which has since become a place of international pilgrimage. She attended a local school run by the Sisters of Charity of Nevers, became a nun in 1866, was beatified in 1925 and was canonized in 1933.

On this day:

Born: Irish-born British physician and naturalist Sir Hans Sloane (1660); US aviation pioneer Wilbur Wright (1867); Irish dramatist J M Synge (1871); English film actor and director Sir Charlie Chaplin (1889); English novelist and poet Sir Kingsley Amis (1922)

Died: Italian architect, goldsmith and sculptor Filippo Brunelleschi (1664); Spanish artist Francisco de Goya (1828); Scottish writer and social reformer Samuel Smiles (1904); English film director Sir David Lean (1991); US novelist Ralph Waldo Ellison (1994)

1746 The Battle of Culloden took place near Inverness; it was the last major battle on British soil, and marked the end of the Forty-Five Rebellion when the English defeated the Scots.

1862 In the USA, slavery was abolished in the District of Columbia.

1883 Paul Kruger (1825–1904) was elected president of the South African Republic.

1912 US aviator and journalist Harriet Quimby (1882–1912) became the first woman to fly across the English Channel.

1948 The Organization for European Economic Co-operation (OEEC) was established in Paris.

1951 Seventy-five lives were lost when the British submarine *Affray* sank in the English Channel.

1953 The Royal Yacht *Britannia* was launched by Queen Elizabeth II (born 1926) and Prince Philip (born 1921) in Glasgow.

1964 The twelve-strong gang of 'Great Train Robbers' were sentenced to a total of 307 years in jail.

1996 Prince Andrew, Duke of York (born 1960), and Sarah, Duchess of York (born 1959), announced their plans to divorce.

17 April

On this day:

Born: US banker, financier and art collector J Pierpont Morgan (1837); Soviet politician Nikita Khrushchev (1894); US writer and playwright Thornton Wilder (1897); English yachtswoman and writer Clare Francis (1946)

Died: US statesman, diplomat, printer, publisher, inventor and scientist Benjamin Franklin (1790); English literary forger William Henry Ireland (1835); English poet Basil Bunting (1985); US-born British photographer, businesswoman and campaigner Linda McCartney (1998)

1421 A dyke burst at Dort in Holland, drowning some 100,000 people.

1492 Genoese explorer Christopher Columbus (1451–1506) was granted a commission to explore the 'western ocean' by Ferdinand and Isabella of Castile, the King and Queen of Spain.

1521 Martin Luther (1483–1546) was cross-examined on his faith at the Diet of Worms.

1961 Cuban exiles opposed to President Fidel Castro (born 1927) and sponsored by the USA landed at Bahía de Cochinos ('Bay of Pigs') on the southern coast of Cuba; the invasion soon failed.

1969 At the age of 21, Irish political activist Bernadette Devlin (born 1947) became the UK's youngest ever woman MP.

1975 Five years of war in Cambodia ended with the capture of Phnom Penh by Communist insurgents.

1984 Twenty-five-year-old WPC Yvonne Fletcher was killed by gunshots during a demonstration outside the Libyan embassy in London, leading to a 15-year breakdown in diplomatic relations between the UK and Libya.

1986 English journalist John McCarthy (born 1957) was abducted in Lebanon and held hostage until 8 August 1991.

1989 The Polish trade union movement Solidarity was granted legal status.

1999 A nail bomb planted by right-wing extremist David Copeland (born 1976) exploded near a market in Brixton, London, injuring 50 people.

18 April

On the night of 18 April 1775, the American patriot Paul Revere (1735–1818) rode from Charleston to Lexington and Lincoln, rousing the Minutemen (militiamen who were prepared to take up arms at very short notice) as he went, warning the people of Massachusetts that British troops were on their way. This was the eve of the Battle of Lexington and Concord, which marked the beginning of the American Revolution, otherwise known as the American War of Independence. The event was memorialized in a poem by Longfellow:

So through the night rode Paul Revere;
And so through the night went his cry of alarm
To every Middlesex village and farm,
A cry of defiance, and not of fear,
A voice in the darkness, a knock at the door,
And a word that shall echo for evermore!
For, borne on the night-wind of the Past,
Through all our history, to the last,
In the hour of darkness and peril and need,
The people will waken and listen to hear
The hurrying hoof-beats of that steed,
And the midnight message of Paul Revere

Henry Wadsworth Longfellow, *Tales of a Wayside Inn*,
'The Landlord's Tale: Paul Revere's Ride' (1863).

On this day:

Born: Italian noblewoman Lucrezia Borgia (1480); English financier Sir Francis Baring (1740); US civil liberties lawyer Clarence Darrow (1857); British-born US conductor Leopold Stokowski (1882); English actress Hayley Mills (1946)

Died: Italian painter Filippino Lippo (1504); English physician and poet Erasmus Darwin (1802); German–Swiss–US mathematical physicist and Nobel Prize winner Albert Einstein (1955); English sculptor Dame Elisabeth Frink (1993); Norwegian anthropologist Thor Heyerdahl (2002)

1906 The city of San Francisco, California, USA, was struck by an earthquake.

1909 The Vatican beatified the French patriot and martyr Joan of Arc (c.1412–1431).

1949 The Republic of Ireland Act came into force; Ireland left the British Commonwealth and proclaimed itself the Republic of Eire.

1951 The European Steel and Coal Community, a forerunner of the Common Market and the European Economic Community (EEC), was founded.

1954 General Gamal Abd-al Nasser (1918–70) became prime minister and military governor of Egypt; he later became president.

1956 Prince Rainier III of Monaco (born 1923) married US actress Grace Kelly (1929–82).

1978 The US Senate voted to return control of the Panama Canal Zone, 8 kilometres of land flanking the canal on either side, to the Republic of Panama.

1980 The name of Zimbabwe's capital city was changed from Salisbury to Harare.

1996 The Israeli bombing of a UN peacekeepers' base in southern Lebanon killed 101 refugees who were sheltering there.

19 April

In the late 19th century, 19 April was celebrated as **Primrose Day** in memory of Benjamin Disraeli, 1st Earl of Beaconsfield, who died on this day in 1881 (he was born in 1804). People were encouraged to pay tribute to the statesman, twice prime minister of the UK (1868; 1874–80), by wearing primroses on this day. It was said that Disraeli was particularly fond of primroses, but his writings suggest the opposite. The myth seems to have its origin in a simple misunderstanding: when Queen Victoria sent a wreath of primroses to Disraeli's funeral with a note stating that they were 'his favourite flower', people assumed that the word 'his' referred to Disraeli, but in fact it referred to Victoria's late husband, Prince Albert.

On this day:

Born: English political economist David Ricardo (1772); US special agent Eliot Ness (1903); English actor Dudley Moore (1935); French conductor Yan Pascal Tortelier (1947)

Died: English poet Lord Byron (1824); English naturalist Charles Darwin (1882); French physicist and Nobel Prize winner Pierre Curie (1906); English novelist and short-story writer Dame Daphne du Maurier (1989)

1587 Francis Drake (c.1540–1596) sacked Cadiz, Spain, and sank the Spanish fleet, describing his action as 'the singeing of the King of Spain's beard'.

1775 The Battles of Lexington and Concord, the first battles of the American Revolution, were fought in Massachusetts.

1850 The Clayton–Bulwer Treaty, a US–British agreement on the terms for building a canal across Central America, was signed.

1928 The final volume of the first edition of the *Oxford English Dictionary* was published; the first volume had been published in 1884.

1951 The first 'Miss World' contest was held in London's Lyceum Ballroom and won by Miss Sweden, Kerstin 'Kiki' Haakonson.

1971 Russia launched Salyut 1, the world's first space station.

1990 A Civil War truce was called in Nicaragua.

1993 More than 70 members of the Branch Davidian sect led by David Koresh (1959–93) died when a siege of their heavily armed compound near Waco, Texas, USA, by US authorities ended in a severe fire.

1995 A truck bomb exploded outside a government building in Oklahoma City, Oklahoma, USA, killing 168 people and injuring 500 others.

On this day:

Born: French president and emperor Napoleon III (1808); Austrian-born German dictator Adolf Hitler (1889); Spanish artist Joán Miró (1893); US actress Jessica Lange (1949)

Died: French pope Clement V (1314); German composer Karl Gottfried Loewe (1869); Irish writer Bram Stoker (1912); English Anglican missionary Trevor Huddleston (1998); German-born British biophysicist and Nobel Prize winner Sir Bernard Katz (2003)

1653 Oliver Cromwell (1599–1658) dismissed 'The Rump', the 60 remaining members of the 'Long Parliament' who had continued sitting without facing re-election.

1657 The English navy under Admiral Robert Blake (1599–1657) sank the Spanish fleet at Santa Cruz, off Tenerife in the Canary Islands.

1770 Captain James Cook (1728–79) first sighted New South Wales, Australia.

1949 The first Badminton Horse Trials were held at the estate of the Duke of Beaufort in Gloucestershire.

1968 Pierre Trudeau (1919–2000) became prime minister of Canada.

1968 Conservative right-winger Enoch Powell (1912–98) made his infamous 'rivers of blood' speech.

1981 Steve Davis (born 1957) defeated Doug Mountjoy (born 1942) at The Crucible Theatre, Sheffield, to win the first of his six World Snooker Championships.

1999 Two US high-school students, Eric Harris (1981–99) and Dylan Klebold (1981–99), went on a shooting spree at Columbine High School, Denver, Colorado, killing 13 people as well as themselves.

21 April

This is the birthday of Queen Elizabeth II, born on this day in 1926. Her 'official' birthday is celebrated on a Saturday in June, in accordance with a tradition dating back to the reign of her father, King George VI (1895–1952).

On this day:

Born: German educationalist and founder of the kindergarten system Friedrich Froebel (1782); English poet and novelist Charlotte Brontë (1816); Scottish-born US naturalist John Muir (1838); English dramatist, novelist and barrister Sir John Mortimer (1923)

Died: Italian theologian and philosopher St Anselm (1109); French philosopher and scholar Peter Abelard (1142); French dramatist and poet Jean Racine (1699); US writer and journalist Mark Twain (1910); US singer, pianist and composer Nina Simone (2003)

753 BC According to the Roman historian Varro (116–27 BC), Rome was founded by Romulus.

1916 Roger Casement (1864–1916), Irish patriot and British consular official, landed at Banna Strand, Kerry, Ireland, in a German submarine to take part in the Easter Rising; he was later arrested, tried for treason and hanged.

1918 World War I – German airman Baron Manfred von Richthofen

(1882–1918), known as the 'Red Baron', was shot down and killed.

1945 World War II – the Soviet Army reached the outskirts of Berlin, Germany.

1955 In the UK, Fleet Street newspapers were published for the first time in nearly a month following the end of strike action.

1960 Brasília was inaugurated as the capital of Brazil.

1964 BBC2 began transmitting television programmes with *Play School*.

1967 A military junta took over the running of Greece.

1975 South Vietnamese president Nguyen Van Thieu (1923–2001) resigned; the Vietnam War ended days later in victory for the North Vietnamese.

1987 A car bomb exploded in the Sri Lankan capital, Colombo, killing more than 100 people.

1989 Tiananmen Square in Beijing was filled with many thousands of students and workers demonstrating against the severity of the Chinese government's regime.

1996 The general election in Italy was won by the Olive Tree Alliance; its leader Romano Prodi (born 1939) was appointed prime minister in May.

22 April

This day is widely celebrated as **Earth Day**, on which communities around the world organize and participate in events intended to raise awareness of environmental issues, such as tree-planting or having a 'car-free day'. The celebration of Earth Day on 22 April is somewhat controversial, as many people maintain that 21 March (the date of the vernal equinox) is the true Earth Day and celebrate it accordingly. The first Earth Day was instigated in the USA as a nationwide environmental protest, by Senator Gaylord Nelson in 1970. In 1990, people in 141 countries took part in Earth Day, and the number of participants grows each year.

On this day:

Born: English novelist Henry Fielding (1707); German philosopher Immanuel Kant (1724); Russian revolutionary Vladimir Ilyich

Lenin (1870); US nuclear physicist Robert J Oppenheimer (1904); US actor Jack Nicholson (1937)

Died: English inventor of the spinning jenny James Hargreaves (1778); English landscape painter John Crome (1821); English engineer Sir Henry Royce (1933); US photographer Ansel Adams (1984); 37th President of the USA Richard Nixon (1994)

1500 Brazil was 'discovered' and claimed for Portugal by Pedro Alvarez Cabral (c.1467–c.1520). On 26 January the same year Spanish explorer Vicente Yáñez Pinzón (c.1460–c.1524) had discovered the country, but he failed to claim it for Spain.

1838 The British steamship *Sirius* became the first vessel to cross the Atlantic using steam power only.

1860 John McDouall Stuart (1815–66), Scottish-born Australian explorer, became the first European to reach the geographical centre of Australia.

1884 The most destructive earthquake recorded in the UK occurred in Essex and East Anglia.

1915 World War I – during the Battle of Ypres, Germany became the first nation to use poison gas.

1964 Greville Wynn, sentenced in Moscow, USSR, for spying for the UK, was exchanged for Soviet spy Gordon Lonsdale.

1969 British yachtsman Robin Knox-Johnston (born 1939) in his ketch *Suhaili* completed the first solo non-stop circumnavigation of the Earth; it had taken 312 days.

2000 Six-year-old Cuban boy Elián Gonzalez was seized from his relatives' house in Miami by US government agents and reunited with his father. The child had been at the centre of a custody battle between his father and relatives in Florida since his mother drowned while attempting to emigrate illegally to the USA.

23 April

> *Whatever the real character of St George might have been, he was held in great honour in England from a very early period. While in the calendars of the Greek and Latin churches he shared the twenty-third of April with other saints, a Saxon Martyrology declares the day dedicated to him alone; and after the Conquest his festival was celebrated after the approved fashion of Englishmen … In the first year of the reign of Henry V, a council held at London decreed, at the instance of the king himself, that henceforth the feast of St George should be observed by a double service; and for many years the festival was kept with great splendour at Windsor and other towns.*
>
> *Chambers Book of Days* (1864).

Few facts are known about St George, other than that he died a martyr's death, probably in 303. He is thought to have been a soldier, and visions of him during the First Crusade were reported as omens of victory, leading to his adoption as the patron saint of arms and chivalry. In the mid-14th century he was chosen as patron of the Order of the Garter (also known as the Order of St George), and by the early 15th century he was accepted as patron saint of England. He is also the patron saint of archers, the Greek army, members of the Scout Association, and people with syphilis, among others.

The legend of **St George and the Dragon**, in which the hero fights and kills a dragon to save the life of a princess (and to secure the conversion to Christianity of her father's subjects) dates from the twelfth century. Like other dragon legends before and since, it is an allegory of the triumph of good over evil, of light over darkness, or, in a more pagan interpretation, of spring over winter. A re-enactment of the slaying of the dragon formed a colourful and dramatic part of **St George's Day** festivities throughout the Middle Ages; by the time of the Reformation, St George's Day processions had become one of the highlights of the calendar. Although such worshipping of saints was banned by Henry VIII, the festivities continued in a more secular form for many years, and St George's fight with the dragon eventually became part of the May Day and Midsummer celebrations.

In modern times, St George's Day is marked by few festivities in England, despite various campaigns to have the day declared a public holiday or to

encourage people to fly St George's flag (a red cross on a white background) or wear a red rose in their buttonhole.

In Bermuda, 23 April is **Peppercorn Day**, on which the Masonic Lodge that occupies the Old State House on St George's Island must pay its annual rent of one peppercorn to the Governor. The 'rent' is collected with much pomp and circumstance in a traditional civic and military ceremony dating from 1816.

On this day:

Born: English painter J M W Turner (1775); 15th President of the USA James Buchanan (1791); German theoretical physicist and Nobel Prize winner Max Planck (1858); US singer and songwriter Roy Orbison (1936)

Died: English playwright, poet and actor William Shakespeare (1616); Welsh religious poet Henry Vaughan (1695); French chemist Auguste Laurent (1853); English poet Rupert Brooke (1915); Austrian-born US film director and producer Otto Preminger (1986)

1348 King Edward III (1312–77) created the Order of the Garter.

1661 Charles II (1630–85) was crowned King of England.

1702 Queen Anne (1665–1714) was crowned in Westminster Abbey; she suffered a crippling attack of gout and had to be carried into the abbey on an open chair by Yeomen of the Guard.

1924 King George V (1865–1936) and Queen Mary (1867–1953) opened the British Empire Exhibition in Wembley, London; the event was broadcast on BBC radio, the first such broadcast by a British monarch.

1968 In the UK, 5p and 10p decimal coins were introduced in readiness for the official changeover to decimal currency in February 1971.

1979 Teacher and activist Blair Peach (1946–79) was killed in a clash with police officers during an anti-racism demonstration in Southall.

1984 The discovery of HIV, the virus responsible for AIDS, was announced in Washington, DC.

1994 Scientists discovered the 'top quark'; they announced their discovery on 2 March the following year.

24 April

> *'Tis now, replied the village belle,*
> *St Mark's mysterious eve,*
> *And all that old traditions tell*
> *I tremblingly believe;*
> *How, when the midnight signal tolls,*
> *Along the churchyard green,*
> *A mournful train of sentenced souls*
> *In winding-sheets are seen.*
> *The ghosts of all whom death shall doom*
> *Within the coming year,*
> *In pale procession walk the gloom,*
> *Amid the silence drear.*
>
> James Montgomery, 'St Mark's Eve', reproduced in *Chambers Book of Days* (1864).

It was formerly believed that the wraiths of those who were to die in the following year would appear in the churchyard around midnight on **St Mark's Eve**, and people often maintained a vigil in the church porch on 24 April to see which of their neighbours – or their own family – were so doomed. The wraiths were said to enter the church in the order in which they would die, often with some indication of the manner of their death, such as a rope around the neck. Those who would merely suffer serious illness were believed to look through the door without crossing the threshold.

There were other, less macabre customs associated with this night: young girls would engage in various rituals to ascertain the identity of their future husband, one of which involved hanging up their smocks and waiting for an apparition:

> *On St Mark's Eve, at twelve o'clock,*
> *The fair maid she will watch her smock,*
> *To find her husband in the dark,*
> *By praying unto good St Mark.*
>
> *Poor Robin's Almanack* (1770).

On this day:

Born: English novelist Anthony Trollope (1815); English statesman, economist, chemist and patent-lawyer Sir Stafford Cripps (1889); US novelist and poet Robert Penn Warren (1905); English writer, broadcaster and caterer Sir Clement Freud (1924); US singer, actress, composer and director Barbra Streisand (1942)

Died: English writer and adventurer Daniel Defoe (1731); US comedian Bud Abbot (1974); US socialite and wife of Edward, Duke of Windsor, Wallis Simpson (1986); South African politician Oliver Tambo (1993); English sculptor Lynn Chadwick (2003)

1800 US President John Adams (1735–1826) allocated funds for the development of the Library of Congress, which later grew into one of the world's most influential national libraries.

1895 Captain Joshua Slocum (1844–c.1910), in the sloop *Spray*, set sail from Boston, Massachusetts, USA, to sail around the world single-handed; he completed the 75,000-kilometre journey on 27 June 1898.

1898 After refusing to withdraw from Cuba, Spain declared war on the USA.

1916 The Easter Rising, a rebellion of Irish nationalists, began in Dublin, Ireland.

1957 *The Sky at Night*, presented by astronomer and broadcaster Sir Patrick Moore (born 1923), was first broadcast by the BBC.

1967 Cosmonaut Vladimir Komarov (1927–67) became the first known casualty of space flight when he crashed to Earth on the Soyuz 1 mission.

1970 China launched its first space satellite.

1970 The Gambia, a British colony since 1843, was proclaimed a republic within the Commonwealth.

1975 The Baader–Meinhof gang blew up the West German embassy in Stockholm, Sweden, killing several hostages.

1982 The first British soldier died in the Falklands War when his Sea King helicopter crashed.

1990 The Hubble Space Telescope, the first optical space-based telescope, was launched.

1993 An IRA bomb exploded in the City of London, killing one person and injuring 40 others.

25
April

In Australia and New Zealand, this is **ANZAC Day**, which commemorates the landing of troops from those nations (the *A*ustralia and *N*ew *Z*ealand *A*rmy *C*orps) at Gallipoli in Turkey on 25 April 1915, early in World War I. The Gallipoli campaign, launched by Allied forces in response to Turkey's attack on Russia, was the first major operation on the Eastern Front but ended in failure, with many thousands of casualties, including more than 10,000 ANZAC deaths.

On ANZAC Day, also known as the One Day of the Year, servicemen and servicewomen who died in both World Wars, and in other more recent conflicts, are remembered with solemn ceremonies and parades in towns and cities across Australia and New Zealand.

On this day:

Born: English soldier and statesman Oliver Cromwell (1599); English Anglican churchman and poet John Keble (1792); Italian physicist, inventor and Nobel Prize winner Guglielmo Marconi (1874); US jazz and popular singer Ella Fitzgerald (1918); US actor Al Pacino (1940)

Died: Swedish astronomer Anders Celsius (1744); English poet William Cowper (1800); English novelist Anna Sewell (1878); English film director Sir Carol Reed (1976); English actress Dame Celia Johnson (1982)

1707 In the Battle of Almansa, a crucial episode in the War of the Spanish Succession, the Franco-Spanish army won a decisive victory.

1792 Nicolas-Jacques Pelletier, a convicted highwayman, became the first person in France to be executed by the guillotine.

1859 Construction of the Suez Canal began in Egypt.

1926 The première of *Turandot*, by Giacomo Puccini (1858–1924), was held at La Scala, Milan, Italy.

1945 World War II – the Battle of Berlin began when advancing Soviet troops surrounded the German city.

1953 US biologist James D Watson (born 1928) and English molecular biologist Francis Crick (born 1916), both subsequent Nobel Prize winners, were the first to describe the structure of DNA in an article in *Nature* magazine.

1980 An attempted helicopter rescue operation using US Marines, aimed at ending the Iran hostage crisis, failed, causing President Jimmy Carter (born 1924) and his administration great political embarrassment.

1982 In the Falklands War, British troops retook the island of South Georgia.

1990 The Sandinista National Liberation Front lost power in Nicaragua after more than a decade; the opposition's Violetta Chamorro (born 1919) was elected president.

26 April

At about 1.20am on 26 April 1986, the chain reaction inside one of the four reactors at the Chernobyl nuclear power plant went out of control, resulting in massive explosions that blew the 1,000-ton cover off the reactor. Thirty people were killed instantly, and many more died as a result of the radioactivity that was discharged. In the following weeks more than 130,000 people were evacuated from the area around the Chernobyl plant, which was located north of Kiev in Ukraine (then part of the USSR). The Soviet authorities were slow to report the accident – the worst civil nuclear catastrophe of all time – and it was not until 28 April that the official news agency, Tass, released its first report. The abnormally high levels of radioactivity in the atmosphere had already been detected by monitoring stations in Scandinavia, and the contamination subsequently spread to other countries in Europe, including parts of the UK.

On this day:

Born: Roman emperor and philosopher Marcus Aurelius (AD 121); French painter Eugène Delacroix (1798); Irish newspaper magnate Harold S Harmsworth (1868); Australian novelist and playwright Morris West (1916); US comedienne and dramatic actress Carol Burnett (1933)

Died: English Anglican historian, clergyman and opponent of the theatre Jeremy Collier (1726); US assassin John Wilkes Booth (1865); US burlesque dancer and actress Gypsy Rose Lee (1970); US jazz pianist, organist and bandleader Count Basie (1984)

1478 In the Cathedral of Santa Maria del Fiore, Florence, Giuliano (1453–78) and Lorenzo de' Medici (1449–92) were stabbed during a High Mass as part of the Pazzi Conspiracy.

1564 William Shakespeare (1564–1616) was baptized at Holy Trinity Church, Stratford-upon-Avon, England.

1923 The Duke of York, later King George VI (1895–1952), married Lady Elizabeth Bowes-Lyon (1900–2002) in Westminster Abbey, London.

1937 On the orders of the Spanish High Command, the Basque town of Guernica was bombed by the Luftwaffe during the Spanish Civil War.

1945 World War II – Marshal Philippe Pétain (1856–1951), who led France's Vichy collaborationist regime during the Occupation, was arrested.

1962 The first US rocket, Ranger IV, landed on the Moon, but was unable to transmit pictures because of a technical problem.

1964 The country now known as Tanzania was formed from the union of Tanganyika, Zanzibar and Pemba.

1993 Chancellor Norman Lamont (born 1942) and Prime Minister John Major (born 1943) announced that the UK's two-year economic recession was officially over.

1994 The new South African constitution came into force and free democratic elections were held.

2001 In the UK, the first 15 'people's peers', chosen by a seven-member commission, were appointed to sit in the House of Lords.

27
April

Feast day of **St Zita**, patron saint of housewives, servants and bakers, and sometimes invoked by people who cannot find their keys.

On this day:

Born: Anglo-Irish feminist and writer Mary Wollstonecraft (1759); 18th President of the USA Ulysses S Grant (1822); English mountaineer Edward Whymper (1840); Irish poet and critic Cecil Day-Lewis (1904); French actress Anouk Aimée (1932)

Died: Portuguese navigator Ferdinand Magellan (1521); US poet and essayist Ralph Waldo Emerson (1882); Russian composer and pianist Aleksandr Scriabin (1915); Ghanaian politician and president Kwame Nkrumah (1972)

1296 The Scottish defeat by the English at the Battle of Dunbar left Scotland without a king until Robert Bruce (1274–1329) was crowned in 1306.

1613 King James VI and I (1566–1625) granted Belfast its Charter of Incorporation as a city.

1867 The première of the opera *Roméo et Juliette*, by Charles Gounod (1818–93), was held at the Théâtre Lyrique, Paris.

1909 The 'Young Turks' revolutionary group deposed the Sultan of Turkey, Abd-ul-Hamid II (1842–1918), who was then exiled.

1956 US boxer Rocky Marciano (1923–69) retired as the undefeated heavyweight champion of the world.

1956 The first television broadcast by a British prime minister was made by Anthony Eden (1897–1977).

1961 Sierra Leone became an independent republic within the Commonwealth.

1984 The siege of the Libyan embassy in London ended after eleven days.

1992 The Federal Republic of Yugoslavia was proclaimed in Belgrade.

1992 English Labour politician Betty Boothroyd (born 1929) was elected the first woman Speaker of the House of Commons.

28 April

On the 28th April 1772, there died at Mile End a goat that had twice circumnavigated the globe; first, in the discovery ship Dolphin, under Captain Wallis; and secondly, in the renowned Endeavour, under Captain Cook. The lords of the Admiralty had, just previous to her death, signed a warrant, admitting her to the privileges of an in-pensioner of Greenwich Hospital, a boon she did not live to enjoy.

Chambers Book of Days (1864).

On this day:

Born: Fifth President of the USA James Monroe (1758); English factory reformer and philanthropist Lord Shaftesbury (1801); Zambian politician Kenneth Kaunda (1924); English cricketer Mike Brearley (1942)

Died: Scottish anatomist, surgeon and neurophysiological pioneer Sir Charles Bell (1842); English novelist Richard Hughes (1976); English footballer and manager Sir Alf Ramsey (1999); Russian soldier and politician Alexander Lebed (2002)

1603 The funeral of Queen Elizabeth I (1533–1603) took place in London; tens of thousands of people lined the streets to watch the procession.

1788 Maryland became the seventh state to ratify the Constitution of the USA.

1789 Fletcher Christian (c.1764–c.1794) led the mutiny on the *Bounty*.

1945 World War II – Benito Mussolini (1883–1945) was captured by partisans and shot while trying to flee Italy.

1947 Thor Heyerdahl (1914–2002) and his crew of five set out on the

Kon-Tiki expedition to travel 6,900 kilometres from South America to Polynesia on a rope and balsa craft.

1967 Boxer Muhammad Ali (born 1942) refused induction into the US Army, citing religious grounds.

1969 General Charles de Gaulle (1890–1970) resigned as president of France after being defeated on a referendum.

1986 The Soviet authorities admitted for the first time that there had been an accident at the Chernobyl nuclear power plant.

1989 Hyper-inflation resulted in Argentina running out of money, leaving thousands of people with no access to cash.

1996 Gunman Martin Bryant (born 1967) killed 35 people on a shooting spree in Port Arthur, Tasmania, Australia.

2001 The first space tourist, US businessman Dennis Tito (born 1940), lifted off on his visit to the International Space Station.

29 April

In Japan, this is **Greenery Day** (or **Midori no hi**), the beginning of a succession of national holidays known as Golden Week. It formerly marked the birthday of Emperor Hirohito (1901–89), and is now set aside for the appreciation and preservation of Japan's natural environment.

On this day:

Born: US newspaper publisher William Randolph Hearst (1863); English conductor and impresario Sir Thomas Beecham (1879); US jazz pianist, composer and bandleader Duke Ellington (1899); Indian-born US conductor Zubin Mehta (1936)

Died: Italian mystic St Catherine of Sienna (1380); Burundian king Ntare V (1972); English film-maker Sir Alfred Hitchcock (1980); US tenor James McCracken (1988)

1429 Joan of Arc (c.1412–1431) entered the besieged city of Orleans with an advance guard, leading to a victory over the English a week later.

1913 Swedish-born engineer Gideon Sundback patented the modern version of the zip or 'separable fastener'.

1916 The Easter Rising in Dublin collapsed when Irish rebels surrendered to the British authorities.

1933 In the English FA Cup Final between Everton and Manchester City, numbers were used on football players' shirts for the first time.

1945 World War II – US troops liberated the Dachau concentration camp on the outskirts of Munich, Germany.

1945 World War II – the German army in Italy surrendered to the Allies.

1978 A group of rebel military officers claimed to have successfully seized power from the old regime in Afghanistan.

1986 The funeral of Wallis Simpson (1896–1986), Duchess of Windsor, was held at St George's Chapel within Windsor Castle.

1990 Twenty-one-year-old Scottish player Stephen Hendry (born 1969) became the youngest ever winner of the World Snooker Championship.

1992 Fierce race riots erupted in Los Angeles, California, USA, after the acquittal of four white police officers who had been videotaped beating black motorist Rodney King (born 1965).

30 April

The eve of May Day is a time when witches are believed to fly abroad. In Germany it is known as **Walpurgisnacht**, a night that bears the name of an English nun, St Walburga (or Walpurgis), who became abbess of Heidenheim in the eighth century. The connection with her is coincidental: 30 April happens to be the eve of the day in 870 when her remains were transferred to Eichstätt, to a new church built in her honour. There may also be some confusion with Waldborg, a pagan fertility goddess.

On Walpurgisnacht, witches are said to gather at the Brocken, the highest peak in the Harz Mountains of Germany. There they carouse with the Devil

until midnight, when the Queen of May appears. (In other parts of the country, other high places are said to be the scene of the revelries.) The night is marked by fancy-dress celebrations, with costumes similar to those of Hallowe'en, and by singing and dancing around bonfires.

In Ireland and Scotland in former times, bonfires were lit on this night (the eve of the festival of Beltane) and cattle driven between the flames to protect them from witchcraft and other undesirable influences. Other protective measures included putting primroses, marsh marigolds, and other spring flowers in cattle sheds, or around the house, to keep witches and malevolent fairies at bay.

On this day:

Born: US actress and singer Eve Arden (1908); Dutch queen Juliana (1909); US country singer and songwriter Willie Nelson (1933); New Zealand film director Jane Campion (1954)

Died: French painter Édouard Manet (1883); English scholar and poet A E Housman (1936); Russian-born US choreographer George Balanchine (1983); US blues singer, composer and guitarist Muddy Waters (1983)

1789 George Washington (1732–99) was inaugurated as the first President of the USA.

1803 The USA almost doubled in size when President Thomas Jefferson (1743–1826) purchased the Louisiana Territory from France for $15m.

1812 Louisiana became the 18th state of the USA.

1900 Casey Jones (1863–1900), an engineer with the Illinois Central Railroad, died in a famous train crash in Vaughan, Mississippi; he had forfeited his chance to jump in order to stay at the controls.

1902 The première of the opera *Pelléas et Mélisande*, by Claude Debussy (1862–1916), was held at the Opéra-Comique, Paris.

1938 The BBC televised the FA Cup Final, between Preston North End and Huddersfield Town, for the first time.

1973 US President Richard Nixon (1913–94) admitted responsibility for the Watergate scandal, but denied any personal involvement.

1975 The Vietnam War ended when North Vietnam's victory was completed with the capture of Saigon (renamed Ho Chi Minh City).

1980 Princess Beatrix of the Netherlands (born 1938) became queen after the abdication of her mother, Queen Juliana (1909–2004).

Gemstone: Emerald
Flower: Lily of the valley or hawthorn

> *Married when bees over May blossom flit,*
> *Strangers around your board will sit.*
>
> Traditional rhyme.

> *May brings with her the beauty and fragrance of hawthorn blossoms and the song of the nightingale. Our old poets delighted in describing her as a beautiful maiden, clothed in sunshine, and scattering flowers on the earth, while she danced to the music of birds and brooks. She has given a rich greenness to the young corn, and the grass is now tall enough for the flowers to play at hide-and-seek among, as they are chased by the wind. The grass also gives a softness to the dazzling white of the daisies and the glittering gold of the buttercups.*
>
> *Chambers Book of Days* (1864).

Origins

May, the fifth month of the year, probably takes its name from Maia, a Roman goddess of growth (but a different deity from the mother of Hermes, who bore the same name). According to an alternative explanation, the word *May* is derived from *Maiores*, which referred to the senate in the original constitution of ancient Rome (as opposed to the *Iuniores* – the lower level of the legislature – from which the word *June* is derived).

May

Characteristics

May is the month when nature makes its greatest display of fertility.

> *The month of May was come, when every lusty heart beginneth to blossom, and to bring forth fruit. For, like as herbs and trees bring forth fruit and flourish in May, in like wise every lusty heart that is any manner a lover, springeth, burgeoneth, buddeth, and flourisheth in lusty deeds. For it giveth unto all lovers courage, that lusty month of May.*
>
> Sir Thomas Malory, *Morte d'Arthur* (c.1470).

In the agricultural world it is a relatively quiet period, between sowing and reaping – hence the profusion of customs associated with the month that make pleasurable use of this leisure time, from the activities of May Day (1 May) to those of Oak Apple Day (29 May).

History

The Irish-Gaelic name for the month is *Bealtaine*, which also denotes the festival (Beltane) that takes place on 1 May. In Scottish Gaelic it is *Cèitean*, which means 'beginning': this was the first month of summer in the Celtic calendar. The Anglo-Saxons named it *Tri-Milchi*, because cattle feeding on the lush green pastures could be milked three times a day.

Weather

Prolonged spells of warm weather in May are a welcome foretaste of summer, but it is dangerous to assume that winter is altogether past and gone. The proverb 'Ne'er cast a clout till May be out' warns against discarding winter clothes before the end of the month (not, as some people believe, before the may blossom appears on the hawthorn). Another warns against taking an early dip: 'He who bathes in May, will soon be laid in clay'. Similar observations about May weather are to be found in literature:

> *Rough winds do shake the darling buds of May.*
>
> William Shakespeare, *Sonnets*, sonnet 18 (1609).

> *Let no man boast himself that he has got through the perils of winter till at least the seventh of May.*
>
> Anthony Trollope, *Doctor Thorne* (1858).

> *May is a pious fraud of the almanac.*
> *A ghastly parody of real Spring*
> *Shaped out of snow and breathed with eastern wind.*
>
> James Russell Lowell, *Under the Willows* (1869).

Superstitions

Although May is traditionally a time for merrymaking, there are some rather gloomy superstitions attached to the month. It is a bad time to marry ('Marry in May, rue for aye') or to give birth ('May chickens come cheeping', meaning that children born this month are sickly). Ill health in May, however, can be a good thing: 'Whoever is ill in the month of May, for the rest of the year is healthy and gay'. In Cornwall it was formerly considered unlucky to buy a broom in May, perhaps because the purchaser would be suspected of being a witch. In contrast to these ill-tidings, **May dew** was thought to have particularly beneficial properties for the complexion. The most potent May dew was that collected on the morning of 1 May and women who washed their faces in this would be restored to beauty.

Non-fixed notable dates

Non-fixed notable dates in May include:

Rogation Days: The fifth Sunday after Easter Day is called **Rogation Sunday**, and the Monday, Tuesday and Wednesday that follow are known as the Rogation Days. These three days usually fall in May, although the Monday can be as early as 27 April and the Wednesday as late as 2 June. They were formerly marked by the ceremony of **beating the bounds**, in which the residents of a parish would walk around its perimeter, led by members of the clergy, with the dual aim of memorizing the position of the boundaries and praying for a successful harvest along the way. The 'beating' was originally suffered by young boys in the procession, who received a thrashing or other punishment at key points, to help them remember; in later revivals of the custom it was the 'bounds' themselves (hedges, boundary stones, etc) that were beaten, with long rods carried for this purpose.

In the Dartmoor village of Belstone, the ceremony of beating the bounds takes place every seven years. There, tradition dictates that the beating is given by the oldest man to the youngest child, who is upended, hit with a Union Jack and has their head banged against a chosen boundary stone before they receive their monetary reward. Part of the Belstone parish boundary is formed by a river, and there is a long-running dispute between Belstone and the neighbouring parish of South Tawton as to on which side of the river the boundary stone should be positioned. In the past this has led to the two parishes throwing their rival's stone into a deep pool in the river each time they beat the bounds.

Similar to beating the bounds, **riding the marches** or **common riding** still takes place in the Scottish Borders, although different towns celebrate this tradition at different times of the year. Local dignitaries will ride out on horseback along the town's marches (or boundaries) and in modern times the common riding is often associated with a town fair or other festivity.

Ascension Day: The Thursday after Rogation Sunday is Ascension Day, commemorating Christ's ascension to heaven, watched by his apostles.

> *And when he had spoken these things, while they beheld, he was taken up; and a cloud received him out of their sight.*
>
> Acts 1.9.

It falls between 30 April and 3 June, 40 days after Easter Sunday. According to superstition, water that falls as rain or is taken from a holy well on Ascension Day can be used for medicinal purposes, especially as a cure for sore eyes. Various traditions are associated with this day, notably the ceremony of **well-dressing**, in which a town or village well is decorated with flowers, ribbons and often elaborate pictures made by pressing petals, stones or shells into clay.

Bank Holidays: The first and last Mondays in May are public holidays in most of the UK. The first is in lieu of Labour Day (1 May), and is unofficially known as the **May Day Bank Holiday**; the second is a replacement for the former public holiday on Whit Monday, and is officially known as the **Spring Bank Holiday**. Many of the traditions formerly associated with May Day itself now take place over the first

Bank Holiday weekend. The second, which usually enjoys better weather, has acquired customs and festivals that formerly took place at Whitsuntide or on Ascension Day. One of these is **Hunting the Earl of Rone**, which takes place at Combe Martin in Devon: over the course of the weekend the 'Earl' is pursued through woodland by a troop of 'Grenadiers', caught and made to sit backwards on a donkey, paraded down to the beach, accompanied by a 'Fool' and a 'Hobby Horse', then thrown into the sea. In Gloucestershire the spectacular annual **cheese-rolling** event is thought to have originally taken place at midsummer, but was later moved to Whit Monday and now takes place on Spring Bank Holiday. Each year a large Double Gloucester cheese is released at the top of a precipitous slope at Cooper's Hill, and competitors chase after it. Many injuries are suffered, and few people remain upright, but the fastest down the hill wins the cheese and this possibly ancient tradition remains very popular.

Another tradition which has been associated with both Whit Monday and the Spring Bank Holiday is the **Corby Pole Fair**. Held every 20 years in Corby, Northamptonshire, the fair is said to have been founded by a Charter granted to the village in 1585 by Queen Elizabeth I (1533–1603). Some say that the Charter was granted by the Queen in gratitude to the villagers who rescued her when she was lost in a bog following a hunting accident. One of the features of the fair is that Corby is barricaded off and anyone who wishes to enter has to pay a toll. Anyone who refuses to pay is carried through the fair – on a pole for man, and a chair for women – and placed in the stocks.

1 May

> *Then while time serves, and we are but decaying;*
> *Come, my Corinna, come, let's go a-Maying.*
>
> Robert Herrick, 'Corinna's Going a-Maying' (1648).

May Day has been marked by festivities of various kinds since ancient times. In Scotland and Ireland it was **Beltane**, a pagan festival marked by the lighting of bonfires and the performance of rituals associated with the future wellbeing of livestock: this was the first day of summer in the Celtic calendar, when cattle were led up into the hills to graze. In other parts of the UK, however, the age-old May Day traditions had more to do with trees and plants than animals, especially the custom of **bringing in the May** or **going a-Maying**.

> *In the sixteenth century it was still customary for the middle and humbler classes to go forth at an early hour of the morning, in order to gather flowers and hawthorn branches, which they brought home about sunrise, with accompaniments of horn and tabor, and all possible signs of joy and merriment. With these spoils they would decorate every door and window in the village. By a natural transition of ideas, they gave to the hawthorn bloom the name of the May; they called this ceremony 'the bringing home the May;' they spoke of the expedition to the woods as 'going a-Maying.'*
>
> *Chambers Book of Days* (1864).

This custom dates from the 13th century or earlier in England. It was followed by the crowning of the **Queen of the May**, or **May Queen**: supposedly the prettiest girl in the village, and perhaps a representation of the Roman goddess Flora, who was worshipped in the five-day festival of **Floralia** that took place around this time in ancient Rome. The focal point of the May Day festivities was the **maypole** – a tall tree trunk decorated with flowers, branches, garlands and flags, and often painted with brightly coloured stripes – around which the people of the village would dance in a circle. (The maypole has been interpreted as a phallic symbol, although there is no evidence that it was ever intended as such.) In some villages the maypole remained in place throughout the month of May – even all year round – and

was used for other traditional celebrations of late spring, such as those associated with Whitsuntide.

Needless to say, the activities of 1 May also involved much amorous and riotous behaviour among both young and old: the gathering of flowers and branches was not the only thing that went on in the woods that day, and the thirsty work of dancing led to the quaffing of much ale, cider and other locally brewed beverages. The merrymaking sometimes got out of hand, leading to condemnation of the whole May Day tradition in certain quarters. In the mid-17th century the Puritans uprooted and destroyed the maypoles and banned all associated festivities, but the celebrations were revived after the Restoration in 1660 and have continued in various forms to this day (although some of the traditional activities now take place over the Bank Holiday weekend at the beginning of May, rather than on May Day itself).

There are numerous other customs associated with May Day past and present. In some rural areas it was celebrated as **Robin Hood's Day**, with mumming plays and games based on the exploits of the legendary hero. In some urban areas it was a holiday for **chimney-sweeps**, who would parade around the town or city in colourful attire, dancing or begging for money, accompanied by a figure called **Jack in the Green** (a man dressed as a bush). A modern revival of the **Sweeps Festival** is held in Rochester in Kent and since 1983 Hastings has held an annual Jack in the Green festival. Other modern revivals often include other activities associated with 'Merrie England', such as **morris dancing**. The village of Padstow, in Cornwall, has a May Day festival that centres on a **hobby horse** (the **'Obby 'Oss**), which dances through the streets accompanied by a band of singers and musicians. According to local superstition, any woman momentarily whisked under the skirt that hangs from the framework of the 'Obby 'Oss will either be married or fall pregnant within a year. A hobby horse also makes an appearance in Minehead in Somerset on May Day. A somewhat more sober tradition is observed in Oxford, where visitors gather on Magdalen Bridge in the early hours of the morning to hear the **choir of Magdalen College** sing a Latin hymn at the top of the college tower at 6am.

Since 1973 the town of Tetbury in Gloucestershire has held a May Day **woolsack race**. With its origins in the 16th century (and the town's importance as a centre of wool production in medieval times) competitors carry a sack of wool up a steep hill and a prize is awarded for the fastest time.

In modern times, 1 May is also celebrated as **Labour Day** by trade unions, socialist movements and others. It is marked by rallies and marches, and sometimes by protests and riots, in countries throughout the world. The Labour Day celebration originated in the USA in 1867, when the working day was reduced from ten hours to eight hours with effect from this date, first in Illinois and subsequently elsewhere. In other countries, trade unionists and socialists began to demand a day's holiday on 1 May; this is the origin of the public holiday on the first Monday of May in the UK, instituted in 1978.

On this day:

Born: English essayist and politician Joseph Addison (1672); Irish-born English soldier, statesman and prime minister Arthur Wellesley, Duke of Wellington (1769); Irish-born US labour agitator Mary Harris Jones (1830); English actress Joanna Lumley (1946)

Died: Italian pope Marcellus II (1555); Czech composer Antonín Dvorák (1904); English town-planner and reformer Sir Ebenezer Howard (1928); English diplomat, writer and critic Sir Harold Nicholson (1968); Brazilian racing driver Ayrton Senna (1994)

1707 The Act of Union united Scotland and England.

1786 The première of the opera *Le nozze di Figaro* (*The Marriage of Figaro*), by Wolfgang Amadeus Mozart (1756–91), was held in Vienna, Austria.

1851 Queen Victoria (1819–1901) opened the Great Exhibition at the Crystal Palace in Hyde Park, London.

1884 Construction work began on the world's first skyscraper – the Home Insurance Company building in Chicago, USA.

1925 Cyprus became a British colony.

1931 In the USA, New York City's Empire State Building was officially opened.

1932 The BBC's Broadcasting House in Portland Place, London, was officially opened.

1941 The première of the film *Citizen Kane*, by Orson Welles (1915–85), was held at the RKO Palace Theater in New York City.

1942 World War II – Japanese troops captured Mandalay, Burma (now Myanmar).

1945 World War II – German Nazi politician Joseph Goebbels (1897–1945) committed suicide in a bunker in Berlin, Germany.

1945 World War II – the capture of the capital, Rangoon, marked the final defeat of the Japanese in Burma (now Myanmar).

1960 A US U-2 spy plane was brought down over Sverdlovsk in the USSR, leading to the cancellation of a summit meeting between US President Dwight D Eisenhower (1890–1969) and Soviet Premier Nikita Khrushchev (1894–1971).

1961 Betting shops became legal in the UK.

1961 Fidel Castro (born 1927) abolished elections in Cuba.

1988 The IRA killed three British servicemen in the Netherlands.

1997 The Labour Party, under Tony Blair (born 1953), won a landslide victory in the UK's general election, taking 419 seats; the Conservatives won 165 seats and the Liberal Democrats 46.

2 May

On this day in 1982, during the Falklands War between the UK and Argentina, the British nuclear submarine HMS *Conqueror* sank the Argentinian cruiser *General Belgrano*, with more than 300 fatalities, the first major loss of life in the conflict. The event was famously reported in the *Sun* newspaper with the headline GOTCHA!, but this was changed on grounds of sensitivity in later editions, when it was feared that the entire crew might have perished.

Although the Argentinians retaliated on 4 May by sinking HMS *Sheffield*, there were far fewer casualties on that occasion, and the attack on the *Belgrano* (which was subsequently declared to have been sailing away from the Falkland Islands, outside the exclusion zone, at the time) remained the most controversial incident of the war. Prime Minister Margaret Thatcher (born 1925), who had authorized the action, was grilled on the subject both in Parliament and on national television.

Eighteen years later, relatives of the Argentinian sailors who died when the *Belgrano* went down attempted to take legal action against the British government, but their case was rejected by the European Court of Human Rights.

On this day:

Born: Russian empress Catherine II, the Great (1729); English humorous writer, novelist and playwright Jerome K Jerome

(1859); German airman Baron Manfred von Richthofen, known as the Red Baron (1882); US lyricist Lorenz Hart (1895); English footballer David Beckham (1975)

Died: Italian painter, sculptor, architect and engineer Leonardo da Vinci (1519); French poet and dramatist Alfred de Musset (1857); US politician Joseph McCarthy (1957); Australian neurophysiologist and Nobel Prize winner Sir John Carew Eccles (1997)

1497 Italian-born English navigator and explorer John Cabot (c.1450–c.1499) left Bristol in search of a route to Asia; he sighted land on 24 June (probably Cape Breton Island, Nova Scotia), and claimed North America for England.

1670 The Hudson Bay Company was founded.

1935 The première of the musical *Glamorous Night*, by Ivor Novello (1893–1951), was held at the Drury Lane Theatre, London.

1936 Emperor Haile Selassie (1892–1975) and his family were exiled from Addis Ababa, the capital of Abyssinia (now Ethiopia).

1952 The world's first jet airliner, the De Havilland Comet 1, set off on its maiden flight from London, UK, to Johannesburg, South Africa.

1955 Public broadcasting on very high frequencies (VHF) began in the UK.

1959 Scotland's first nuclear power station officially opened at Chapelcross, near Annan in Dumfriesshire.

1969 The liner *Queen Elizabeth II* began her maiden voyage.

1997 Tony Blair (born 1953) became the youngest British prime minister since 1812 following Labour's landslide general election victory the previous day.

3 May

This is **Rood Day**, or the **Invention of the Cross**. The word 'rood' is of Old English origin, and means gallows or cross, with **holy-rood** meaning Christ's

Cross. This day commemorates the supposed discovery in AD 326 by St Helena (mother of Constantine the Great) of the cross on which Christ was crucified.

> *The statement usually given is that Helena went to Jerusalem, and there compelled the Jews to bring from their concealment and give up to her this and other crosses, and that its identity was established by a miracle: the body of a dead man was placed on each of the crosses, and when it touched the true one, the dead man immediately came to life.*
>
> *Chambers Book of Days* (1864).

This was followed by a further, more lucrative 'miracle': fragments cut from the cross were sold to pilgrims, but the wood of the original was apparently able to reproduce itself, so that the supply of these relics was never exhausted. The theologian and reformer John Calvin (1509–64) subsequently calculated that if all the pieces of the 'true cross' displayed in churches around the Christian world were put back together, it would have taken at least 300 men to support its weight.

The discovery of Christ's cross is also celebrated in the more ancient festival of Holy Cross Day or Holy Rood Day (14 September).

On this day:

Born: Italian statesman, writer and political philosopher Niccolo Machiavelli (1469); English explorer John Hanning Speke (1827); Israeli politician Golda Meir (1898); US singer and film actor Bing Crosby (1903); US boxer Sugar Ray Robinson (1921)

Died: English Gunpowder Plot conspirator Henry Garnett (1606); English poet and satirist Thomas Hood (1845); Danish politician Thorvald Stauning (1942); English politician Baroness Castle (2002)

1512 The Fifth Lateran Council began.

1788 Britain's first daily evening newspaper, the *Star and Evening Advertiser*, was launched.

1810 Lord Byron (1788–1824) swam the Hellespont, the Turkish strait separating Europe from Asia.

1903 The first electric train ran through the Mersey Tunnel.

1947 The Japanese Peace Constitution came into effect, replacing the authoritarian Meiji Constitution.

1951 King George VI (1895–1952) opened the Festival of Britain on London's South Bank.

1986 Twenty-one people died when a terrorist bomb exploded on an airliner at Colombo airport in Sri Lanka.

1999 The frozen body of English mountaineer George Mallory (1886–1924), missing since 1924, was discovered near the summit of Mt Everest.

4 May

In China this is **Youth Day**, an official national holiday, commemorating the anti-imperialist student demonstrations that took place in Tiananmen Square, Beijing, on 4 May 1919. These protests, specifically against the Chinese government's foreign policy and the pro-Japanese stance of some of its ministers, were the climax of what subsequently became known as the **May Fourth Movement**, a nationwide political and cultural campaign among China's young intellectuals. Students and others again protested at Tiananmen Square on 4 June 1989, when hundreds of pro-democracy demonstrators were shot dead by the Chinese army.

On this day:

Born: Italian harpsichord-maker and inventor of the pianoforte Bartolommeo Cristofori (1655); English biologist T H Huxley (1825); Egyptian statesman and president Hosni Mubarak (1928); Belgian-born British actress Audrey Hepburn (1929)

Died: English mathematician and divine Isaac Barrow (1677); English writer Sir Osbert Sitwell (1969); Yugoslav leader and president Josip Broz Tito (1980); English actress Diana Dors (1984)

1471 King Edward IV (1442–83) defeated the Lancastrian forces in a decisive battle during the Wars of the Roses.

1494 Christopher Columbus (1451–1506) visited Jamaica on his second voyage to the New World.

1780 The first Derby horse race was run on Epsom Downs; it was won by a horse named Diomed.

1896 The *Daily Mail* newspaper was launched in the UK.

1904 Charles Rolls (1877–1910) and Henry Royce (1863–1933) signed an agreement in Manchester to set up the Rolls-Royce Motor Company.

1926 The UK's first General Strike began; it lasted nine days.

1953 Prince Philip, Duke of Edinburgh (born 1921), received his pilot's wings.

1970 At Kent State University, Ohio, USA, four students were shot dead by the National Guard while protesting against the Vietnam War.

1979 Conservative Party leader Margaret Thatcher (born 1925) became the UK's first woman prime minister.

1982 The British destroyer HMS *Sheffield* was hit by an Argentinian Exocet missile during the Falklands War.

2000 Ken Livingstone (born 1945) became London's first elected mayor.

5 May

Napoleon I (born 1769) died on this day in 1821, at the age of 51. The last years of the former emperor of France were spent on the island of St Helena, where he had been banished by the British government in 1815, after his second abdication. (The first, in 1814, had been followed by a year's exile on the island of Elba and a brief return to action that culminated in his defeat at the Battle of Waterloo on 18 June 1815.)

On St Helena Napoleon's health deteriorated, perhaps as a result of the unaccustomed inactivity of his new lifestyle, and towards the end of 1817 he began to show signs of stomach illness, possibly cancer or an ulcer. In April 1821, bedridden, he dictated his last will, which contained a bitter accusation: 'I die before my time, killed by the English oligarchy and its hired assassins'. Conspiracy theorists later claimed that he had been poisoned with arsenic, traces of the substance having been found in his hair, but there is no firm evidence that this was the case.

5 May

Napoleon's body was returned to France and reached its final resting place, a magnificent tomb at the Hôtel des Invalides, Paris, in 1861.

On this day:

Born: Danish philosopher and theologian Søren Kierkegaard (1813); German social, political and economic theorist Karl Marx (1818); US chef James Beard (1903); English actor and writer Michael Palin (1943); English actor Richard E Grant (1957)

Died: German economist and politician Ludwig Erhard (1977); Northern Irish hunger striker Bobby Sands (1981); Soviet chess player Mikhail Botvinnik (1995); South African nationalist Walter Sisulu (2003)

1646 King Charles I (1600–49) surrendered to the Scots at Newark.

1760 English aristocrat Laurence Shirley, 4th Earl of Ferrers (1720–60), became the last nobleman in England to be hanged as a felon when he was executed at Tyburn, London.

1865 The first train robbery in the USA took place at North Bend, Ohio.

1930 English aviator Amy Johnson (1903–41) began her historic 19-day solo flight to Australia in her Gypsy Moth aircraft, *Jason*.

1949 The Council of Europe was founded.

1961 Commander Alan Shepard (1923–98) became the first US astronaut in space with a 15-minute flight in the spacecraft *Freedom 7*.

1967 The first all-British satellite, Ariel III, was launched from California, USA.

1980 The SAS stormed the Iranian embassy in London, ending a five-day terrorist siege.

6 May

On this day in 1954, Roger Bannister (born 1929) became the first person to run a mile in under four minutes. He broke the previous record by just over half of a second, achieving a time of 3 minutes 59.4 seconds. The historic event took place at an athletics meeting at Iffley Road, Oxford, in weather that was far from ideal, with strong crosswinds on the track. Bannister, a 25-year-old medical student, was running for the Amateur Athletic Association against Oxford University, where he had begun his studies.

Later in 1954, Bannister won a gold medal at the Commonwealth Games in Vancouver, competing against the Australian athlete John Landy (born 1930), who had already bettered his record; both completed the race in less than four minutes. At the end of the year Bannister retired from competitive athletics to complete his medical studies at St Mary's Hospital, London. He subsequently became a consultant neurologist. Knighted in 1975, he was appointed Master of Pembroke College, Oxford, in 1985. His lifetime of service to sport was recognized in 2002 with an honorary doctorate awarded by the universities of Manchester and Salford.

On this day:

Born: French Revolutionary politician Maximilien Robespierre (1758); Austrian neurologist and founder of psychoanalysis Sigmund Freud (1856); Italian-born US film actor Rudolf Valentino (1895); English politician and prime minister Tony Blair (1953); US actor George Clooney (1961)

Died: Dutch Roman Catholic theologian and founder of Jansenism Cornelius Jansen (1638); Scottish obstetrician and pioneer of anaesthesia Sir James Young Simpson (1870); US writer L Frank Baum (1919); English engineer Sir Donald Bailey (1985)

1527 The Sack of Rome by warring German and French troops began; thousands were killed or forced to flee, and churches, shrines and monuments were looted or destroyed, heralding the end of the Renaissance.

1536 King Henry VIII (1491–1547) ordered that a copy of the Bible be placed in every English church.

1626 Dutchman Peter Minuit (c.1580–1638) bought America's Manhattan Island from the Indians for a few trinkets of knives, beads and cloth worth 60 guilders ($24).

1642 The Canadian city of Montreal was founded as Ville Marie.

1840 The world's first postage stamp, the 'Penny Black', became valid for use in the UK.

1851 US inventor and manufacturer Linus Yale (1821–68) patented his door lock.

1882 Frederick Cavendish (1836–82) and Thomas Henry Burke (1829–82) were assassinated by the Irish Invincibles group in Dublin; their deaths became known as the Phoenix Park Murders.

1910 King George V (1865–1936) acceded to the British throne on the death of King Edward VII (1841–1910).

1915 US baseball player Babe Ruth (1895–1948) hit his first major league home run while playing for the Boston Red Sox against the New York Yankees.

1937 An explosion and fire on the *Hindenburg* airship killed 36 people.

1960 Princess Margaret (1930–2002) married photographer Anthony Armstrong-Jones (born 1930), later Lord Snowdon.

1966 The so-called Moors Murderers, Ian Brady (born 1938) and Myra Hindley (1942–2002), were found guilty of murdering two children and burying them on Saddleworth Moor near Oldham in Lancashire.

1994 The Channel Tunnel between the UK and France was officially opened.

On this day:

Born: English poet Robert Browning (1812); Russian composer Pyotr Ilyich Tchaikovsky (1840); Indian poet, philosopher and Nobel Prize winner Sir Rabindranath Tagore (1861); US actor

Gary Cooper (1901); Argentinian popular leader and social reformer Eva Perón (1919)

Died: British queen Mary of Modena (1718); Scottish engineer James Nasmyth (1890); English soapmaker and philanthropist William Lever, Viscount Leverhulme (1925); English politician George Lansbury (1940); US film actor Sir Douglas Fairbanks, Jnr (2000)

1663 The first Drury Lane Theatre opened in London.

1824 The première of the Ninth Symphony by Ludwig van Beethoven (1770–1827) was held in Vienna, Austria.

1832 Greece was proclaimed an independent kingdom under Otto I (1815–67).

1915 World War I – a German U-boat torpedoed the Cunard liner *Lusitania* off the coast of Ireland, resulting in 1,198 deaths.

1927 The UK's first motorcycle speedway racing event took place at Camberley Heath in Surrey.

1945 World War II – the war in Europe ended as General Alfred Jodl (1890–1946) signed the unconditional surrender in Rheims, France.

1960 Leonid Brezhnev (1906–82) was elected president of the USSR.

1965 Rhodesian prime minister Ian Smith (born 1919) swept to victory in the country's elections.

1976 An earthquake in northern Italy, measuring 6.5 on the Richter scale, killed more than 550 people.

8 May

One of the oldest surviving customs of the UK, the **Helston Furry Dance**, takes place in the Cornish town of that name on this day each year (unless 8 May falls on a Sunday or Monday, in which case it is moved to the preceding Saturday). It is thought to have its origins in a pagan festival celebrating the coming of spring. The word *furry* is possibly derived from a

Cornish word meaning 'fair' or 'festival'. The choice of date may be associated with the cult of St Michael the Archangel, patron saint of Helston, whose main feast day is 29 September, but who is celebrated as Protector of Cornwall on 8 May.

The programme for the day (known as **Furry Day**, **Floral Day** or **Flora Day**) features a number of dances along the narrow streets of the town, sometimes passing through private houses and gardens, performed to a traditional tune played by the local band. The first, at 7am, is for people who will be working later in the day. In mid-morning the children dance, dressed in white, and at noon the principal dance begins. The men wear top hats and morning coats, with a lily-of-the-valley buttonhole; the women wear long dresses in bright summer colours and large fancy hats. The town is decorated for the occasion with flowers and greenery brought in from the local countryside.

Another customary feature of the day is the **Hal-an-Tow**, performed during the morning by the youths of the town, who sing a traditional song about Robin Hood, St George, St Michael and others, wearing appropriate costumes and waving branches. The riotous behaviour formerly associated with the Hal-an-Tow caused it to be banned in the 19th century, but it was revived in amended form in 1930.

The Helston Furry Dance was lovingly described in a song by the musician and composer Katie Moss, written in 1911:

As I walked home on a summer night
When stars in heav'n were shining bright
Far away from the footlight's glare
Into the sweet and scented air
Of a quaint old Cornish town

Borne from afar on the gentle breeze
Joining the murmur of the summer seas
Distant tones of an old world dance
Played by the village band perchance
On the calm air came floating down

I thought I could hear the curious tone
Of the cornet, clarinet and big trombone
Fiddle, cello, big bass drum
Bassoon, flute and euphonium
Far away, as in a trance
I heard the sound of the Floral Dance

> *And soon I heard such a bustling and prancing*
> *And then I saw the whole village was dancing*
> *In and out of the houses they came*
> *Old folk, young folk, all the same*
> *In that quaint old Cornish town.*
>
> Katie Moss, 'The Floral Dance' (1911).

In 1977 this was brought to the attention of a wider public, when a recording of the tune by the Brighouse and Rastrick Brass Band reached number two in the British pop charts. Playing the record on his morning radio show, the DJ Terry Wogan (born 1938) began singing along to parts of the tune, which irritated some listeners but amused others. For the benefit of the latter he eventually released a vocal version of the full song, which made it to number 21 in January 1978.

On this day:

Born: Swiss philanthropist and Nobel Prize winner Jean Henri Dunant (1828); 33rd President of the USA Harry S Truman (1884); English naturalist and broadcaster Sir David Attenborough (1926); US novelist Thomas Pynchon (1937)

Died: French chemist Antoine Lavoisier (1794); English philosopher and social reformer John Stuart Mill (1873); US-born British merchant Harry Gordon Selfridge (1947); English actor and novelist Sir Dirk Bogarde (1999)

1559 Queen Elizabeth I (1533–1603) signed the Act of Uniformity.

1701 Captain William Kidd (c.1645–1701) was brought to trial at the Old Bailey in London for piracy.

1864 The Battle of Spotsylvania Courthouse began during the American Civil War.

1902 The Mt Pelée volcano on Martinique erupted, with the loss of more than 29,000 lives.

1945 World War II – Victory in Europe Day (VE Day) marked the unconditional surrender of German armed forces.

1956 *Look Back in Anger* by John Osborne (1929–94) opened at the Royal Court Theatre in London, starting a run of plays and films about 'angry young men'.

1962 London's last trolleybus ran.

1984 The USSR announced that its athletes would not attend the Los Angeles Olympic Games in the USA, blaming commercialization and a lack of security.

1984 The Thames Barrier in London was officially opened.

9 May

On this day in 1671, the Irish adventurer Thomas Blood (c.1618–1680), known as Colonel Blood, stole the crown of England. The ingeniously contrived plot involved first striking up an acquaintance with the keeper of the royal regalia, Talbot Edwards. Having gained his trust and esteem over a period of time, Blood was able to arrange a special visit to the jewel house on the morning of 9 May for a private viewing of the regalia with two 'friends'. Once inside, they bound and gagged Edwards, who nonetheless tried to raise the alarm:

> *Yet Edwards persisted in attempting to make all the noise he could, upon which they knocked him down by a blow on the head with a wooden mallet, and, as he still remained obstinate, they beat him on the head with the mallet until he became insensible; but recovering a little, and hearing them say they believed him to be dead, he thought it most prudent to remain quiet. The three men now went deliberately to work; Blood placing the crown for concealment under his cloak, while one of his companions, named Parrot, put the orb in his breeches, and the other proceeding to file the sceptre in two, for the convenience of putting it in a bag.*
>
> *Chambers Book of Days* (1864).

At this point the robbers were interrupted by Edwards's son and his brother-in-law, Captain Beckham; they made their escape with the crown and orb (Mr Parrot's breeches must have been ample) but were pursued and caught by Beckham. At his trial before King Charles II (1630–85), Blood succeeded with eloquent trickery in securing not only a pardon, but also a grant of land in Ireland and other favours.

On this day:

Born: US abolitionist John Brown (1800); Scottish novelist and dramatist J M Barrie (1860); English Egyptologist Howard Carter (1873); English dramatist, actor and director Alan Bennett (1934)

Died: American colonist, religious leader and Pilgrim Father William Bradford (1657); Danish organist and composer Diderik Buxtehude (1707); French chemist and physicist Joseph Louis Gay-Lussac (1850); Italian bass singer Ezio Pinza (1957); Nepalese mountaineer Tenzing Norgay (1986)

1785 English inventor Joseph Bramah (1748–1814) patented the beer pump for public houses.

1901 Australia's Commonwealth Parliament met for the first time in Melbourne.

1927 Australia's Parliament House opened in the new capital, Canberra.

1936 Italy invaded Abyssinia (now Ethiopia).

1949 Prince Rainier III (born 1923) succeeded his grandfather as Head of State in Monaco.

1950 The Schuman Plan, forerunner of the European Community, was announced in Paris.

1955 West Germany formally joined NATO.

1972 At least 20 anti-government protestors were killed and many others injured on the steps of the Metropolitan cathedral in San Salvador, the capital of El Salvador, when police opened fire.

1978 Aldo Moro (1916–78), former prime minister of Italy, was found murdered eight weeks after being kidnapped by the left-wing Red Brigade.

10 May

> *I have dedicated my life to this struggle of the African people. ... I have cherished the ideals of a democratic and free society in which all persons live together in harmony with equal opportunities. It is an ideal which I hope to live for, and to see realized.*
>
> Nelson Mandela, speech in court facing the death penalty (20 April 1964).

On 10 May 1994, Nelson Mandela (born 1918) became the first black president of South Africa. Born in 1918, Mandela studied law and set up a legal practice in Johannesburg. He became an active member of the ANC (African National Congress), campaigning vigorously against apartheid, and in 1964 he was sentenced to life imprisonment for various offences, including sabotage and treason. There followed a worldwide campaign for his release, which was eventually granted in 1990 by President F W de Klerk (born 1936), who had already begun to dismantle the apartheid system. In 1993 Mandela and de Klerk shared the Nobel Peace Prize for their reforms.

The 1994 election, in which the ANC won 252 of the 400 seats, was the first democratic election in the country's history. Addressing the crowds after his inauguration ceremony in Pretoria, President Mandela vowed that 'never again will this beautiful land experience the oppression of one by another'. He retired from the presidency in 1999 but remained active in international affairs.

On this day:

Born: Spanish novelist Benito Pérez Galdós (1843); German politician and Nobel Prize winner Gustav Stresemann (1878); US actor, dancer and singer Fred Astaire (1899); Irish singer and campaigner Bono (1960)

Died: English navigator and explorer George Vancouver (1798); US Confederate soldier 'Stonewall' Jackson (1863); US inventor John Wesley Hyatt (1920); US film actress Joan Crawford (1977)

1857 The Indian Uprising, a serious rebellion against British rule, began with the uprising at Meerut; the rebellion soon spread throughout northern India.

1869 The Central Pacific and Union Pacific railways met at Promontory, Utah, to complete the US transcontinental railway.

1940 World War II – Winston Churchill (1883–1967) became the British prime minister as German troops invaded Belgium and the Netherlands.

1941 World War II – deputy Nazi leader Rudolf Hess (1894–1987) parachuted alone into Scotland, apparently to negotiate a peace deal.

1990 *The European*, the first pan-European newspaper, was launched by publisher Robert Maxwell (1923–91).

1998 Sinn Fein voted to back the Good Friday peace agreement in Northern Ireland.

11 May

Spencer Perceval (born 1762), Conservative prime minister of the UK, was shot dead in the lobby of the House of Commons on this day in 1812. His assassin was John Bellingham, a merchant and broker who bore a grudge against the British government for failing to help him when was in severe legal and financial difficulties abroad. Perceval is the only British prime minister to have been killed while in office.

On this day:

Born: Russian-born US composer Irving Berlin (1888); English painter and official war artist Paul Nash (1889); US dancer, teacher, choreographer and pioneer of modern dance Martha Graham (1894); Spanish artist Salvador Dalí (1904); English actress Natasha Richardson (1963)

Died: English statesman and orator William Pitt, the Elder (1778); Finnish architect and designer Alvar Aalto (1976); Jamaican reggae singer and guitarist Bob Marley (1981); English novelist and scriptwriter Douglas Adams (2001)

868 A Chinese translation of the Buddhist Diamond Sutra was signed and dated by one Wang Jie; found in a walled-up cave in 1907, it is the earliest surviving dated printed book.

1745 The Battle of Fontenoy, in which French forces under Louis XV (1710–74) defeated an Anglo-Dutch-Austrian army, ensured the French conquest of Flanders in the War of the Austrian Succession.

1812 The waltz was introduced into British ballrooms; it was immediately condemned as immoral.

1858 Minnesota became the 32nd state of the USA.

1922 The UK's first radio station, 2LO, was established at Marconi House in London.

1949 An official proclamation in Siam changed the country's name to Thailand.

1964 The first Habitat store was opened in London by English designer and businessman Terence Conran (born 1931).

1971 The UK's oldest tabloid, the *Daily Sketch*, was published for the final time after 62 years.

1981 The première of the musical *Cats*, by Andrew Lloyd Webber (born 1948), was held in London.

1985 A fire at Bradford City's football stadium killed 55 and injured 150 fans.

2000 The Tate Modern gallery was officially opened in London.

May

Feast day of **St Pancras**, probably best known for the London railway station that bears his name and invoked by those seeking protection or relief from cramps.

On this day:

Born: English nurse and hospital reformer Florence Nightingale (1820); French composer Jules Massenet (1842); English composer Sir Lennox Berkeley (1903); US crime-story writer

Leslie Charteris (1907); US composer Burt Bacharach (1929)

Died: English architect Sir Charles Barry (1860); Czech composer Bedrich Smetana (1884); Austrian film director and actor Erich von Stroheim (1957); English Poet Laureate and novelist John Masefield (1967); Scottish politician John Smith (1994); US singer Perry Como (2001)

1588 Henri III (1551–89) was forced to flee Paris on the so-called Day of the Barricades in the French Wars of Religion.

1832 The première of the opera *L'elisir d'amore* (*The Elixir of Love*), by Donizetti (1797–1848), was held in London.

1870 The Manitoba Act was passed by the Canadian parliament, creating Canada's fifth province and the first western province; the day is now celebrated as Manitoba Day.

1937 The coronation of King George VI (1895–1952) took place at Westminster Abbey; the procession was televised by the BBC, the first coronation to be broadcast on television.

1949 The Berlin Blockade by Soviet forces was finally lifted after eleven months; 277,264 flights had had to be made to fly in food and essential supplies, costing the Allies £200 million.

1989 British World War II veteran Jackie Mann (1914–95) was kidnapped in Beirut, Lebanon.

2000 After more than 70 years of car production at Dagenham, Essex, Ford confirmed that it was to close its car plant.

13 May

This is **Abbotsbury Garland Day**, which has been celebrated in the Dorset village of that name for many years. The custom was originally associated with Abbotsbury's fishing fleet: garlands of flowers made by the fishermen's children were blessed at the village church in a special service, then hung on the boats and taken out to sea. In modern times the garlands are still made by local children, one with wild flowers and one with garden flowers, but the garlands are hung on poles, carried from house to house, and laid on the local war memorial at the end of the day. The children receive coins from admiring residents as a reward for their efforts, a practice that was allegedly condemned as begging by an officious village policeman in 1954. He confiscated the money, the children's parents protested to the Chief Constable, and the policeman found himself transferred to another locality.

On this day:

Born: English composer Sir Arthur Sullivan (1842); British physician, Nobel Prize winner and discoverer of the malaria parasite Sir Ronald Ross (1857); US boxer Joe Louis (1914); US actor Harvey Keitel (1941); US soul and pop singer Stevie Wonder (1950)

Died: French anatomist Georges Cuvier (1832); English architect John Nash (1835); US inventor and industrialist Cyrus Hall McCormick (1884); Norwegian explorer, biologist, oceanographer and Nobel Prize winner Fridtjof Nansen (1930); English poet and writer Laurie Lee (1997)

1846 The US Congress officially declared war on Mexico.

1940 World War II – Queen Wilhelmina (1880–1962) fled to London with members of her family and the Dutch government after the German invasion of the Netherlands.

1949 The UK's first jet bomber, the *Canberra*, made its maiden flight in Lancashire.

1954 The Saint Lawrence Seaway Act was signed by US President Dwight D Eisenhower (1890–1969), authorizing the construction of a series of canals that would allow ocean-going vessels to reach the Great Lakes from the Atlantic Ocean.

1958 In France, the Fourth Republic was brought down by the Algerian crisis.

1981 Pope John Paul II (born 1920) survived an assassination attempt in St Peter's Square, Rome.

1995 English mountaineer Alison Hargreaves (1962–95) became the first woman to climb Mt Everest alone and without oxygen.

14 May

> *On the 14th of May 1796, the immortal Edward Jenner conclusively established the important principles of vaccination; proving that it was possible to propagate the vaccine affection by artificial inoculation from one human being to another, and thereby at will communicate security to all who were liable to small-pox.*
>
> *Chambers Book of Days* (1864).

Edward Jenner's (1749–1823) experiment involved inoculating a boy with matter from a pustule on the hand of a woman with cowpox (the words *vaccine* and *vaccination* are derived from the Latin *vacca*, cow); the boy was subsequently inoculated with smallpox and found to be immune. This momentous discovery did not meet with universal acclaim when it was put into practice. Opponents of the procedure claimed that vaccinated children had all but changed into cattle; however, a significant number of influential physicians and surgeons were convinced of the value of vaccination and signed a declaration to that effect. During the following years, vaccination gradually replaced the former practice of inoculation with the smallpox virus itself – a procedure introduced from Turkey in the early 18th century at the instigation of the British writer and society hostess Lady Mary Wortley Montagu (1689–1762) – which was eventually outlawed.

On this day:

Born: Welsh social and educational reformer Robert Owen (1771); German conductor Otto Klemperer (1885); US film-maker George Lucas (1944); Australian actress Cate Blanchett (1969)

Died: Swedish dramatist and novelist August Strindberg (1912); US food manufacturer H J Heinz (1919); English novelist Sir H Rider Haggard (1925); English field marshal Viscount Allenby (1936); US film actress and dancer Rita Hayworth (1987); English actress Dame Wendy Hiller (2003)

1264 The Battle of Lewes took place in Sussex, England, between the troops of King Henry III (1207–72) and those of nobelman Simon de Montfort (c.1208–1265).

1607 The first permanent English settlement in America was established at Jamestown, Virginia.

1643 Louis XIV (1638–1715), the so-called Sun King, became King of France when he was only five years old; he went on to rule for 72 years.

1804 The Lewis and Clark expedition, led by US explorers William Clark (1770–1838) and Meriwether Lewis (1774–1809), set off from St Louis; it was the first overland journey across North America to the Pacific coast.

1842 The *Illustrated London News*, the first fully illustrated weekly, was launched.

1940 World War II – the Local Defence Volunteers (LDV), the home defence militia later known as the Home Guard or 'Dad's Army', was founded.

1942 World War II – the bill authorizing the Women's Army Auxiliary Corps was enacted by the US Congress.

1948 Statesman David Ben-Gurion (1886–1973) announced the creation of the independent State of Israel.

1955 The Warsaw Pact, the East European Mutual Assistance Treaty, was signed by Albania, Bulgaria, Czechoslovakia, East Germany, Hungary, Poland, Romania and the USSR.

1965 The John F Kennedy Memorial, on ground overlooking the site of the signing of the Magna Carta at Runnymede that previously belonged to the Crown and which now became the property of the USA, was unveiled by Queen Elizabeth II (born 1926) in the presence of the president's widow and children.

1973 The USA's first Skylab space station was launched.

1987 A State of Emergency was declared in Fiji after a military-led coup d'état.

1991 South African civil rights activist Winnie Mandela (born 1934) was found guilty of taking part in the kidnap of four youths.

15 May

Feast day of **St Dympna**, patron saint of the mentally ill, an Irish princess who is said to have been killed at Gheel in Belgium by her father after fleeing from his incestuous advances.

On this day:

Born: Austrian dramatist and novelist Arthur Schnitzler (1862); US actor Joseph Cotton (1905); English actor James Mason (1909); English dramatists Peter and Anthony Shaffer (1926); US painter, sculptor and printmaker Jasper Johns (1930)

Died: French abbess Héloïse (1164); English actor Edmund Kean (1833); US poet Emily Dickinson (1886); US painter Edward Hopper (1967); US country singer June Carter Cash (2003)

1536 Anne Boleyn (1501–36) and her brother were tried and found guilty of treason, adultery and incest.

1567 Scottish nobleman James Hepburn (c.1535–1578), 4th Earl of Bothwell, married Mary, Queen of Scots (1542–87) at the Palace of Holyroodhouse, Edinburgh.

1800 King George III (1738–1820) survived an assassination attempt by James Hadfield at the Drury Lane Theatre, London.

1918 The first regular airmail service was inaugurated between New York City and Washington, DC, by the US post office using army aircraft.

1930 Nurse Ellen Church became the world's first air stewardess on a flight from Oakland, California, to Chicago, Illinois, with Boeing Air Transport, later United Airlines.

1940 Nylon stockings were launched in the USA.

1941 The maiden flight of the UK's first jet aircraft, the Gloster E28/39, designed by English aeronautical engineer Sir Frank Whittle (1907–96), took place.

1957 The UK exploded its first hydrogen bomb over Christmas Island in the South Pacific.

1960 Russia launched Sputnik IV.

1963 Tottenham Hotspur became the first British football club to win a European trophy; they beat Atlético Madrid 5–1 in Rotterdam to win the European Cup Winners' Cup.

1972 US politician George Wallace (1919–98) was crippled by an assassination attempt while campaigning for the Democratic presidential nomination.

1993 In Paris, a two-day hostage crisis at a nursery school ended when police rescued six children and their teacher.

16 May

On this day:

Born: US reformer, abolitionist and educator Elizabeth Peabody (1804); Austrian-born British tenor Richard Tauber (1892); US actor Henry Fonda (1905); Irish actor Pierce Brosnan (1953); Belarusian gymnast Olga Korbut (1956)

Died: English poet Felicia Dorothea Hemans (1835); Australian statesman and prime minister Sir Robert Menzies (1978); US novelist and playwright Irwin Shaw (1984); US puppeteer and fantasy film-maker Jim Henson (1990)

1763 Dr Samuel Johnson (1709–84) and James Boswell (1740–95) met for the first time at Tom Davies's bookshop in Russell Street, London.

1770 The Dauphin of France, later Louis XVI (1754–93), married Marie Antoinette (1755–93).

1811 British, Portuguese and Spanish armies fought the Battle of Albuera, Spain, against the French in the Peninsular War.

1888 German-born US inventor Émile Berliner (1851–1929) first demonstrated the flat disc gramophone record; its performance was superior to the original cylinders produced by Thomas Edison (1847–1931).

1929 The first Academy Awards, or Oscars®, were presented in Hollywood, Los Angeles, California, USA.

1938 World War II – the Women's Voluntary Service for Air Raid Precautions was founded.

1943 World War II – the RAF's 617 squadron made their bouncing bomb raid on the Ruhr valley, Germany; they became known as the Dambusters.

1968 The tower block Ronan Point in London collapsed, killing three people.

1975 Japanese mountaineer Junko Tabei (born 1939) became the first woman to climb Mt Everest.

1977 The right-of-centre nationalist Likud Front, led by Menachem Begin (1913–92), ousted the Israeli Labour Party after 29 years of rule.

17 May

In Norway this is **National Independence Day**, or **Constitution Day**, commemorating the introduction of constitutional government on 17 May 1814. The country had been transferred from Danish to Swedish control in January 1814, but Norway did not achieve full independence from Sweden until October 1905.

On this day:

Born: English physician and pioneer of vaccination Edward Jenner (1749); English astronomer Sir Norman Lockyer (1836); Irish nationalist leader Timothy Michael Healy (1855); Swedish soprano Birgit Nilsson (1918); English dramatist Dennis Potter (1935)

Died: Florentine painter Sandro Botticelli (1510); English prelate Matthew Parker (1575); English philosopher and theologian Samuel Clarke (1729); US architect Cass Gilbert (1934); English novelist Nigel Balchin (1970); English prelate and Archbishop of Canterbury Donald Coggan (2000)

17 May

1792 The first organized New York City stock market was established.

1875 The first Kentucky Derby horse race took place in Louisville, Kentucky, USA.

1890 The première of the opera *Cavalleria rusticana*, by Pietro Mascagni (1863–1945), was held in Rome, Italy.

1890 The UK's first comic paper, *Comic Cuts*, was launched.

1900 English general Robert Baden-Powell (1857–1941) led the Relief of Mafeking after an eight-month siege by the Boers in South Africa.

1920 The Dutch airline KLM operated its first scheduled flight from London to Amsterdam, becoming the first commercial airline.

1954 In the landmark case of Brown versus the Board of Education of Topeka, Kansas, the US Supreme Court unanimously declared that 'separate educational facilities are inherently unequal', thus denying the legal basis for segregated classrooms and for ever changing race relations in the USA.

1961 Guildford Cathedral – one of only two Anglican cathedrals to be built in the UK on entirely new sites since medieval times – was consecrated.

1973 The Watergate hearings began in the US Senate.

1977 Queen Elizabeth II (born 1926) began her Silver Jubilee tour of the UK in Glasgow.

1978 The body of Charlie Chaplin (1889–1977) was found buried in a field, eleven weeks after it had been stolen from his grave.

1995 Jacques Chirac (born 1932) succeeded François Mitterand (1916–96) as president of France.

1997 Laurent Kabila (1939–2001) installed himself as president of Zaire, and renamed the country the Democratic Republic of the Congo.

2000 Two Royal Marine Commandos, Alan Chambers and Charlie Paton, became the first Britons to reach the North Pole unaided.

18 May

On this day:

Born: English philosopher, mathematician, writer and Nobel Prize winner Bertrand Russell, 3rd Earl Russell (1872); Italian-born US film director Frank Capra (1897); English ballerina Dame Margot Fonteyn (1919); Polish pope John Paul II (1920); Chinese actor Chow Yun-Fat (1955)

Died: French playwright Pierre Beaumarchais (1799); English novelist George Meredith (1909); Austrian composer Gustav Mahler (1911); US feminist, pacifist and first woman to serve in US Congress Jeannette Rankin (1973); US playwright and novelist William Saroyan (1981)

1804 Napoleon I (1769–1821) was proclaimed emperor of France.

1843 The Free Church of Scotland was founded.

1944 World War II – Allied Forces in Italy captured the hilltop monastery Monte Cassino, transformed into a fortress by the Germans.

1950 NATO was established as a permanent defence organization.

1951 The UK's first four-engined jet bomber, the Vickers Valiant, made its maiden flight from Wisley, Surrey.

1969 Graham Hill (1929–75), the UK's champion motor racing driver, won a record-breaking fifth Monaco Grand Prix.

1969 The US spacecraft Apollo 10 was launched as a precursor to the Moon landings.

1972 Bomb-disposal experts were parachuted from an RAF Hercules in response to a bomb threat on the *Queen Elizabeth II* in the Atlantic Ocean.

1991 Helen Sharman (born 1963) became the first British person in space as part of the Soyuz TM12 mission.

19 May

This is **St Dunstan's Day**, celebrated by some of the churches and other institutions that bear his name. Born in Somerset in the early tenth century, Dunstan studied at Glastonbury Abbey and became abbot there in 945. Later, as Archbishop of Canterbury, he instituted a number of major reforms, some of which were unpopular, such as the revival of monasticism in England and the obligatory payment of tithes by landowners. Patron saint of goldsmiths, his emblem is a pair of metalworker's tongs.

> *St Dunstan was one of those men who stamp their own character on the age they live in. He was in every way a remarkable man. And, like most remarkable men, he has been unduly extolled on one hand, and vilified on the other. Monkish writers have embellished his life with a multitude of ridiculous, or worse than ridiculous miracles; and their opponents have represented him as ambitious, bigoted, and utterly unscrupulous as to means, so that he only gained his end.*
>
> *Chambers Book of Days* (1864).

According to a Devonshire legend, St Dunstan was a keen brewer of beer who made a pact with the Devil to ensure the destruction of the apple crop on which his rivals, the cider makers, depended. In exchange for St Dunstan's soul, the Devil agreed to blight the apple trees with frost on 17, 18 and 19 May, at the height of their blossom. (A similar tale is told of St Frankan (or Frankin), an otherwise unknown figure, whose association with the Devil is blamed for severely cold weather on 19, 20 and 21 May.)

On this day:

Born: German philosopher Johann Gottlieb Fichte (1762); US-born British politician and first woman MP to sit in the House of Commons Nancy Astor (1879); US black nationalist leader Malcolm X (1925); British psychologist and writer Edward de Bono (1933); English rock musician and writer Pete Townshend (1945)

Died: English queen Anne Boleyn (1536); English statesman William Gladstone (1898); Anglo-Irish soldier and writer

T E Lawrence, known as Lawrence of Arabia (1935); US writer of light verse Ogden Nash (1971); Australian politician and prime minister Sir John Gorton (2002)

1536 English queen Anne Boleyn (1501–36) was beheaded.

1554 The then Princess Elizabeth (1533–1603), later Queen Elizabeth I, was released from the Tower of London and placed under house arrest in Woodstock, Oxfordshire.

1649 Oliver Cromwell (1599–1658) declared England to be a Commonwealth.

1802 The prestigious Légion d'honneur, France's highest decoration, was created by Napoleon I (1769–1821) for distinction in civil life or military service.

1849 William Hamilton fired blank shots at Queen Victoria (1819–1901) as she travelled in an open carriage.

1900 Tonga became a British protectorate.

1906 The Simplon Tunnel opened between Switzerland and Italy.

1936 The Pulitzer Prize-winning novel *Gone With the Wind*, by US author Margaret Mitchell (1900–49), was published.

1940 Winston Churchill (1874–1965) made his first broadcast on the BBC as prime minister.

1974 Valéry Giscard d'Estaing (born 1926) defeated François Mitterrand (1916–96) to become president of France.

1980 Mt St Helens volcano in Washington State erupted, killing 57 people.

1994 The first shuttles for heavy goods vehicles passed through the Channel Tunnel.

1997 The Health Secretary, Frank Dobson (born 1940), announced that tobacco sponsorship of British sporting events was to be banned.

20 May

On this day in 1927 Charles Lindbergh (1902–74) set off from New York on the first non-stop solo flight across the Atlantic, in the monoplane *Spirit of St Louis*. He arrived in Paris the next day, after a 33½-hour crossing. Exactly five years later, on 20 May 1932, Amelia Earhart (1897–1937) set off from Newfoundland on the first solo transatlantic flight by a woman. Her journey was shorter in time and distance: she landed in Ireland after less than 15 hours in the air.

Lindbergh received a prize of $25,000 and the Congressional Medal of Honor. Earhart also received a number of awards, including Outstanding Woman of the Year. The media coverage of her achievements included the question 'Can she bake a cake?', to which Earhart replied, 'I accept these awards on behalf of the cake bakers and all of those other women who can do some things quite as important, if not more important, than flying, as well as in the name of women flying today'.

On this day:

Born: French novelist Honoré de Balzac (1799); German-born US inventor Émile Berliner (1851); English detective-story writer Margery Allingham (1904); US film actor James Stewart (1908); US singer and actress Cher (1946)

Died: Genoese explorer Christopher Columbus (1506); French soldier and revolutionary the Marquis de Lafayette (1834); English writer and caricaturist Sir Max Beerbohm (1956); US palaeontologist Stephen Jay Gould (2002)

1347 Cola di Rienzo (c.1313–1354) took the title of Tribune of Rome and proclaimed the restoration of the Republic of Rome, inciting the people to rise up against senators and nobles.

1685 Titus Oates (1649–1705), English conspirator and concocter of the so-called Popish Plot, was flogged from Aldgate to Newgate Prison in London.

1795 The so-called White Terror began in the south of France when the

Jacobins were pursued by those they had persecuted in the revolutionary Reign of Terror of 1793–4.

1867 The foundation stone of London's Royal Albert Hall was laid by Queen Victoria (1819–1901).

1875 The Convention of the Metre was signed in Paris by 17 nations; it led to the creation of the International Bureau of Weights and Measures.

1913 The first RHS Chelsea Flower Show to be held in the grounds of the Royal Hospital at Chelsea was opened.

1939 Pan American Airways completed a New York City – Lisbon – Marseille route that inaugurated a transatlantic airmail service.

1941 World War II – German airborne troops invaded Crete.

1962 English footballer Bobby Moore (1941–93) played the first of his 108 international matches in a game against Peru; 90 of these matches were played as captain.

1964 The first few cases of an outbreak of nearly 500 were diagnosed as typhoid at the City Hospital in Aberdeen, Scotland.

1977 The last Direct Orient Express left Paris for Istanbul, Turkey.

2002 East Timor became fully independent from Indonesia.

21 May

> *21st May – a glorious day for beauty. I wish you could see how lovely our country is at this fine season.*
>
> William Wordsworth, Letter to William Boxall (21 May 1846).

The British weather on this day is not always so idyllic. On 21 May 1950 a tornado swept through southern England, from Buckinghamshire to Cambridgeshire, wrecking houses and other buildings, uprooting trees and lifting cars and livestock into the air. The tornado was accompanied by violent thunderstorms, which claimed at least three lives.

21 May

On this day:

Born: German painter and engraver Albrecht Dürer (1471); English Quaker prison reformer Elizabeth Fry (1780); US jazz pianist, composer and entertainer Fats Waller (1904); Soviet physicist, dissident and Nobel Prize winner Andrei Sakharov (1921)

Died: Swedish chemist Carl Wilhelm Scheele (1786); English aircraft designer Geoffrey De Havilland (1965); English popular romantic novelist Dame Barbara Cartland (2000); English actor Sir John Gielgud (2000)

1471 King Henry VI (1421–71) was murdered as he knelt in prayer in the Tower of London.

1502 The island of St Helena in the South Atlantic was first visited by the Portuguese explorer João da Nova (died 1509).

1553 Lady Jane Grey (1537–54) married Lord Guildford Dudley (died 1554) against her will.

1840 Captain William Hobson (1793–1842) claimed British sovereignty over the whole of New Zealand, although negotiations had not been completed.

1894 The Manchester Ship Canal was formally opened by Queen Victoria (1819–1901).

1904 FIFA, the International Football Federation, was founded in Paris.

1916 World War I – daylight saving was introduced in the UK to allow for greater production in factories and munitions works.

1927 US aviator Charles Lindbergh (1902–74) arrived in Paris after becoming the first man to fly solo across the Atlantic Ocean.

1932 US aviator Amelia Earhart (1897–1937) became the first woman to fly solo across the Atlantic Ocean.

1945 US film star Humphrey Bogart (1899–1957) married fellow star Lauren Bacall (born 1924).

1956 The USA performed the first airborne explosion of a hydrogen bomb over the Bikini Atoll in the Pacific.

1966 US boxer Cassius Clay (born 1942), later to change his name to Muhammad Ali, beat the UK's Henry Cooper (born 1934) to retain the world heavyweight boxing title.

1979 Elton John (born 1947) played the first of a series of concerts in

Leningrad and Moscow, becoming the first Western rock star to play in the USSR.

1981 François Mitterand (1916–96) was elected president of France.

1991 Rajiv Gandhi (1944–91), the former prime minister of India, was assassinated.

22 May

Whereas on May 22, 1819, the steamship The Savannah set sail from Savannah, Georgia, on the first successful transoceanic voyage under steam propulsion, thus making a material contribution to the advancement of ocean transportation: Therefore be it resolved by the Senate and House of Representatives of the United States of America in Congress assembled, that May 22 of each year shall hereafter be designated and known as National Maritime Day, and the president is authorized and requested annually to issue a proclamation calling upon the people of the United States to observe such National Maritime Day by displaying the flag at their homes or other suitable places and Government officials to display the flag on all Government buildings on May 22 of each year.

Joint resolution of Congress (20 May 1933).

The historic journey of the *Savannah*, in the days when such crossings were usually made under sail, caused some consternation as the steamship approached the coast of Ireland. Seen from a distance with smoke pouring from her funnel, she was assumed to be on fire, and the revenue vessel *Kite* was dispatched to her rescue.

Since 1933 a presidential proclamation has been made for **National Maritime Day**, encouraging Americans to fly the flag.

On this day:

Born: German composer Richard Wagner (1813); Scottish writer Sir Arthur Conan Doyle (1859); Belgian cartoonist Hergé (1907);

Northern Irish footballer George Best (1946); English supermodel Naomi Campbell (1970)

Died: Roman emperor Constantine I (AD 337); French poet and writer Victor Hugo (1885); US poet, fiction writer and dramatist Langston Hughes (1967); English theatre and film actress Dame Margaret Rutherford (1972); US middleweight boxing champion Rocky Graziano (1990)

1455 In the first battle of the Wars of the Roses the Lancastrians took St Albans from the Yorkists.

1897 London's Blackwall Tunnel under the Thames was opened by the Prince of Wales (later King Edward VII, 1841–1910); it was then the longest underwater tunnel in the world.

1906 US aviation pioneers Orville (1871–1948) and Wilbur Wright (1867–1912) were granted a patent for their flying machine.

1915 World War I – a troop train collided with a passenger train at Gretna Green, killing 227 people in the UK's worst train crash.

1923 English politician Stanley Baldwin (1867–1947) became prime minister when ill health forced Bonar Law (1858–1923) to resign.

1947 The Truman Doctrine was approved by the US Congress; a post-war foreign policy under which the USA promised military and economic aid to countries threatened by communism.

1960 Southern Chile was struck by one of the largest earthquakes of the 20th century – it measured 9.5 on the Richter scale and created a tsunami which spread to Japan, Hawaii and the Philippines.

1967 The Straits of Tiran, which control entry to the Red Sea from the Gulf of Aqaba, were closed by the Egyptian president Gamal Abd al-Nasser (1918–70).

1970 Following increasing pressure, the South African Cricket Council announced that the South African cricket team would not tour England that summer.

1972 Ceylon adopted a new constitution as the Republic of Sri Lanka within the Commonwealth.

1981 Peter Sutcliffe (born 1946), known as the Yorkshire Ripper, was sentenced to life imprisonment on 13 counts of murder and seven counts of attempted murder between 1976 and 1981.

23 May

In ancient Rome, this day was a festival in honour of Vulcan, god of fire and metalworking. It was marked by a ceremony called the **Tubilustrium**, which involved cleaning and purifying the *tubae*, the straight trumpets used during funerals, sacrifices, public games and military operations.

On this day:

Born: Swedish naturalist and physician Carolus Linnaeus (1707); US film actor Douglas Fairbanks, Snr (1883); English jazz trumpeter, bandleader and broadcaster Humphrey Lyttelton (1921); Russian chess player Anatoli Karpov (1951)

Died: Italian religious and political reformer Girolamo Savonarola (1498); Scottish merchant and privateer William Kidd, known as Captain Kidd (1701); Norwegian dramatist Henrik Ibsen (1906); US oil magnate and philanthropist John D Rockefeller (1937); US golfer Sam Snead (2002)

1430 French patriot Joan of Arc (c.1412–1431) was captured and sold to the English.

1533 The marriage of King Henry VIII (1491–1547) to Catherine of Aragon (1485–1536) was declared null and void, freeing him to marry Anne Boleyn (1501–36).

1618 The so-called Defenestration of Prague took place, when Bohemian nobles threw two Imperial governors out of a window, sparking the Thirty Years War.

1788 South Carolina became the eighth state to ratify the Constitution of the USA.

1797 The Bank of England was first caricatured as 'the Old Lady of Threadneedle Street' in a political cartoon by James Gillray (1757–1815).

1873 The North West Mounted Police, later to become the Royal Canadian Mounted Police, was established by Act of Parliament in Canada.

1931 Whipsnade Wild Animal Park in Bedfordshire first opened to the public.

1934 US thieves and murderers Bonnie Parker (1911–34) and Clyde Barrow (1909–34) were shot dead at a police roadblock in Louisiana, USA.

1960 Adolf Eichmann (1906–62), a Nazi leader wanted for humanitarian atrocities during World War II, was found and captured in Argentina by Israeli security forces.

1960 Twenty-five-year-old Nepalese climber Pemba Dorjie Sherpa reached the summit of Mt Everest in 12 hours 45 minutes, setting a new record for the ascent with oxygen; the record was broken three days later.

24 May

On this day:

Born: German instrument-maker and physicist Daniel Fahrenheit (1686); British queen Victoria (1819); French tennis player Suzanne Lenglen (1899); New Zealand-born Australian soprano Dame Joan Hammond (1912); US singer and songwriter Bob Dylan (1941)

Died: Polish astronomer Nicolaus Copernicus (1543); US journalist and antislavery campaigner William Lloyd Garrison (1879); US politician John Foster Dulles (1959); US jazz pianist, composer and bandleader Duke Ellington (1974); English politician Harold Wilson, Baron Wilson of Rievaulx (1995)

1683 Britain's first public museum, the Ashmolean in Oxford, opened its doors for the first time.

1738 John Wesley (1703–91), the founder of Methodism, 'felt his heart strangely warmed' while reading the preface by Martin Luther (1483–1546) to the Epistle to the Romans, and decided to devote his life to sharing his discovery with the world.

1809 Dartmoor Prison opened in Devon; it was originally built to house French and US prisoners of war.

1830 The first passenger railway in the USA was opened; it ran between Baltimore and Elliott's Mills, Maryland.

1844 Samuel Morse (1791–1872) transmitted the first official telegraph from Washington, DC, to Baltimore, Maryland, with the words 'What hath God wrought?'

1862 London's current Westminster Bridge was opened, replacing an earlier structure.

1883 In New York City, the Brooklyn Bridge was opened to the public.

1909 Bristol University was granted a Royal Charter by King Edward VII (1841–1910).

1930 English aviator Amy Johnson (1903–41) completed her solo flight from London to Australia in 19½ days when she landed her aircraft *Gypsy Moth* in Darwin.

1941 World War II – the German battleship *Bismarck* sank the British ship HMS *Hood*.

1956 The first Eurovision Song Contest was held in Lugano, Switzerland; the contest was won by the host country with the song *Refrain*, sung by Lys Assia.

1972 Glasgow Rangers football team defeated Dynamo Moscow in Barcelona to become the first Scottish side to win the UEFA Cup Winners' Cup.

1976 British and French Concordes made simultaneous flights from London and Paris respectively, to Washington Dulles International Airport in the USA.

1976 English Benedictine monk Basil Hume (1923–99) became the Archbishop of Westminster.

1993 Eritrea gained independence from Ethiopia after a 30-year war.

25 May

> *I know not whether Laws be right,*
> *Or whether Laws be wrong;*
> *All that we know who lie in gaol*
> *Is that the wall is strong;*
> *And that each day is like a year,*
> *A year whose days are long.*
>
> Oscar Wilde, *The Ballad of Reading Gaol* (1898).

On 25 May 1895, the Irish poet and dramatist Oscar Wilde (1854–1900) was found guilty of homosexual offences and sentenced to two years' hard labour in Reading jail. Wilde had been arrested the previous month, after an unsuccessful attempt to sue the Marquess of Queensberry (1844–1900) for libel. (Queensberry, the father of Wilde's lover Lord Alfred 'Bosie' Douglas (1870–1945), had left a card at Wilde's club accusing him of sodomy.) The libel trial had collapsed when evidence of Wilde's association with rent boys was revealed, hence the charge for which he was convicted.

While in jail, Wilde wrote a long letter of bitter reproach to Lord Alfred, which was later published as *De Profundis*. After his release in 1897, he turned his back on England and spent the remaining three years of his life in France and Italy, dying in Paris with the famous last words 'either that wallpaper goes or I do'.

On this day:

Born: Russian-born US aeronautical engineer Igor Sikorsky (1889); English broadcaster Richard Dimbleby (1913); US jazz trumpeter and bandleader Miles Davis (1926); English actor and director Sir Ian McKellen (1939); Canadian comedian and actor Mike Myers (1963)

Died: Spanish dramatist Pedro Calderón de la Barca (1681); English composer Gustav Holst (1934); English astronomer Sir Frank Dyson (1939); Cuban photographer Alberto Korda (2001)

1660 King Charles II (1630–85) landed at Dover, UK, ending nine years of exile following the Civil War.

1787 In the USA, delegates from seven states opened the Constitutional Convention.

1850 The hippopotamus Obaysch arrived at London's Regent's Park Zoo; he was the first live hippopotamus to be seen in Europe since Roman times and became a local celebrity.

1925 In Dayton, Tennessee, a grand jury indicted high-school biology teacher, John Scopes (1900–70), for violating the Butler Law, which outlawed the teaching of 'any theory that denies the divine creation of man and teaches instead that man has descended from a lower order of animals'.

1935 US athlete Jesse Owens (1913–80) set three world records (including one for the long jump which lasted for 25 years) and equalled another in the space of 45 minutes at a meeting in Michigan, USA.

1946 Jordan became independent from the UK.

1951 UK Foreign Office officials Guy Burgess (1910–63) and Donald Maclean (1913–83) disappeared; it was eventually discovered that they had spied for the USSR.

1953 The world's first atomic artillery shell was fired by the US Army in the Nevada Desert, USA.

1962 The new Coventry Cathedral, designed by Sir Basil Spence (1907–76), was consecrated.

1965 Muhammad Ali (born 1942) defeated Sonny Liston (c.1917–1970) to retain his heavyweight boxing title.

1967 Celtic football team defeated Inter Milan in Lisbon to become the first British club to win the European Cup.

1977 The first *Star Wars* film, directed by George Lucas (born 1944), was released.

1982 During the Falklands War, HMS *Coventry* and the container ship *Atlantic Conveyor* were hit by Argentinian missiles.

26 May

Early in World War II, between 26 May and 4 June 1940, more than 300,000 Allied troops were rescued from the beaches of Dunkirk in northern France by a fleet of ships and boats of all shapes and sizes, some of them private vessels manned by their owners. The evacuation, prompted by the relentless advance of the Germans through Belgium into France, ensured the survival of sufficient forces ultimately to win the war, as predicted by the writer J B Priestley (1894–1984) in a radio broadcast on 5 June 1940:

> *This little steamer, like all her brave and battered sisters, is immortal. She'll go sailing proudly down the years in the epic of Dunkirk. And our great-great-grandchildren, when they learn how we began this war by snatching glory out of defeat, and then swept on to victory, may also learn how the little holiday steamers made an excursion to hell and came back glorious.*
>
> J B Priestley, quoted in *The Listener* (13 June 1940).

On this day:

Born: Lithuanian-born US actor and singer Al Jolson (1886); US actor John Wayne (1907); English actor Peter Cushing (1913); US astronaut and first US woman in space Sally Ride (1951); English actress Helena Bonham Carter (1966)

Died: Anglo-Saxon scholar, theologian and historian St Bede, known as the Venerable Bede (735); English diarist and Admiralty official Samuel Pepys (1703); US explorer Lincoln Ellsworth (1951); German philosopher Martin Heidegger (1976)

1733 The flying shuttle, one of the most important inventions in the history of textile machinery, was patented by English inventor John Kay (1704–c.1780).

1805 Napoleon I (1769–1821) was crowned King of Italy.

1828 German foundling Kaspar Hauser was discovered, having wandered into Nuremberg's marketplace; though apparently 16 years old, his behaviour

was that of a small child. The 'Wild Boy' later gave an account of himself as having lived in a hole, looked after by a man who had brought him to Nuremberg; he died in December 1833 after a mysterious attack.

1868 The UK's last public execution took place outside Newgate Prison in London, when Michael Barrett was hanged for a Fenian bomb attack at Clerkenwell.

1906 Vauxhall Bridge, spanning the River Thames in London, was formally opened.

1908 William Knox D'Arcy made the first commercial discovery of oil in the Middle East at Masjid-I-Suleiman, south-west Persia (now Iran); in April the following year the Anglo-Persian Oil Company was founded, later to become British Petroleum (BP).

1913 The UK's first woman magistrate, Emily Duncan, was appointed at West Ham, London.

1923 The first Le Mans 24-hour motor race was held in France.

1948 In the South African elections, the Nationalist Party standing on the apartheid ticket swept to power; Daniel F Malan (1874–1959), became prime minister and immediately began implementing apartheid policies.

1950 Petrol rationing ended in the UK; it had been introduced during World War II.

1966 British Guiana became an independent Commonwealth state and was renamed Guyana.

1972 The state-owned travel firm Thomas Cook was sold to a group of private businesses.

2003 A new record for the ascent of Mt Everest with oxygen was set by 36-year-old Lakpa Gelu Sherpa from Nepal, who reached the summit in 10 hours 56 minutes.

27 May

The US feminist Amelia Jenks Bloomer was born on this day in 1818 (she died in 1894). A champion of women's rights and the temperance movement, she is chiefly remembered for her contribution to the vocabulary of underwear, her married surname being the origin of the word *bloomers*, which came to denote baggy long-legged women's knickers. The original garment favoured by Amelia Bloomer (but not designed by her) was a pair of loose-fitting trousers gathered at the ankle, which she wore as a gesture of equality with men, to escape the physical restrictions of feminine fashions such as the crinoline (or hooped petticoat).

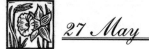

On this day:

Born: US frontier marshal Wild Bill Hickok (1837); English novelist, playwright and critic Arnold Bennett (1867); English actor Christopher Lee (1922); German-born US political scientist, diplomat and Nobel Prize winner Henry Kissinger (1923); Australian tennis player Pat Cash (1965)

Died: French theologian John Calvin (1564); Italian violinist Niccolò Paganini (1840); German physician, pioneer bacteriologist and Nobel Prize winner Robert Koch (1910); Indian statesman and first prime minister of independent India Jawaharlal Nehru (1964); Italian composer Luciano Berio (2003)

1199 King John (1167–1216) was crowned at Westminster, London.

1679 The Habeas Corpus Act became law in Britain, ensuring that prisoners must be brought before a court and not unlawfully detained.

1703 St Petersburg was founded as the capital of Russia.

1863 Broadmoor Asylum for the Criminally Insane opened in Berkshire.

1930 Richard Drew received a patent for cellophane adhesive tape.

1931 Swiss physicist Auguste Piccard (1884–1962) and his assistant Paul Kipfer made the first flight into the stratosphere, suspended in a metal cabin below a helium-filled balloon.

1936 The Cunard liner *Queen Mary* set out on her maiden voyage from Southampton, UK, to New York City, USA.

1937 The Golden Gate Bridge was officially opened in San Francisco, USA.

1941 World War II – the German battleship *Bismarck* was sunk by British forces.

1963 Jomo Kenyatta (c.1889–1978) was elected to be the first prime minister of Kenya.

1974 Jacques Chirac (born 1932) was elected Premier of France for the first time.

1994 After 20 years in exile, Russian writer and Nobel Prize winner Aleksandr Solzhenitsyn (born 1918) returned to Russia.

Feast day of **St Bernard of Menthon**, patron saint of mountaineers, after whom the St Bernard dog and two Alpine passes are named.

On this day:

Born: French doctor and revolutionary Joseph Guillotin (1738); English statesman and youngest British prime minister William Pitt, the Younger (1759); English novelist Ian Fleming (1908); US lawyer and politician Rudy Giuliani (1944); US soul singer Gladys Knight (1944)

Died: US lexicographer Noah Webster (1843); English poet and novelist Anne Brontë (1849); English musicologist, biblical scholar and civil engineer Sir George Grove (1900); British king and Duke of Windsor Edward VIII (1972); Belgian theoretical chemist and Nobel Prize winner Ilya Prigogine (2003)

1742 The first indoor swimming pool opened in Lemon Street, London.

1907 The first TT (Tourist Trophy) motorcycle race took place on the Isle of Man.

1934 The Dionne quintuplets, Annette, Cécile, Émilie, Marie and Yvonne, the first quintuplets to survive infancy, were born at Callander in Ontario, Canada.

1937 Neville Chamberlain (1869–1940) became prime minister of the UK.

1939 The Pact of Steel was signed, an offensive alliance between Fascist Italy and Nazi Germany.

1951 The BBC broadcast the first *Goon Show*, then called *Crazy People*, featuring Spike Milligan (1918–2002), Peter Sellers (1925–80) and Harry Secombe (1921–2001).

1967 Francis Chichester (1901–72) arrived in Plymouth after sailing single-handed around the world in his boat *Gypsy Moth IV*.

1974 British direct rule was reinstated in Northern Ireland.

1982 Pope John Paul II (born 1920) made the first papal visit to the UK since 1531.

1987 West German pilot Mathias Rust landed in Red Square, Moscow, USSR, having passed unchallenged through Soviet airspace.

1990 An all-woman crew skippered by Tracy Edwards (born 1962) sailed into Southampton having completed the Whitbread round-the-world yacht race in their yacht *Maiden*.

1998 Following nuclear tests in India, Pakistan exploded five underground nuclear devices.

29 May

This is **Oak Apple Day**, or **Royal Oak Day**, commemorating the restoration of King Charles II (1630–85) to the British throne on 29 May 1660, his 30th birthday.

> *The restoration of the king, after a twelve years' interregnum from the death of his father, naturally brought into public view some of the remarkable events of his intermediate life. None took a more prominent place than what had happened in September 1651, immediately after his Scottish army had been overthrown by Cromwell at Worcester. It was heretofore obscurely, but now became clearly known, that the royal person had for a day been concealed in a bushy oak in a Shropshire forest, while the Commonwealth's troopers were ranging about in search of the fugitives from the late battle. The incident was romantic and striking in itself, and, in proportion to the joy in having the king once more in his legal place, was the interest felt in the tree by which he had been to all appearance providentially preserved.*
>
> *Chambers Book of Days* (1864).

The oak was in the grounds of Boscobel, a mansion whose name was derived from the Italian *bosco bello*, beautiful wood. After the Restoration, the famous tree was stripped of its lower branches by souvenir hunters and had to be fenced in for protection.

For many years the anniversary of the Restoration was celebrated by the wearing of oak leaves or oak apples, and those who did not display such a symbol were often pinched or kicked in punishment. Oak Apple Day is still marked in some towns by the carrying of oak branches in procession or the placing of an oak wreath on a statue of Charles II. Gradually other customs attached themselves to the day, some of which were originally associated with May Day or Whitsuntide. These include **Castleton Garland Day**, which takes place in the Derbyshire village of that name and features a parade led by a king and queen dressed in the costume of the Restoration era, followed by their attendants, a number of schoolchildren and the village band. The garland itself is an elaborate structure covered with flowers, which is eventually hoisted to the top of the church tower.

At Great Wishford in Wiltshire, villagers exercise their ancient right to take wood from a nearby forest, Grovely Wood.

> *On 29 May each year – this year was no exception – the villagers of Great Wishford celebrate Oak Apple day. It was during the Whit recess this year, so fortunately I was able to enjoy it. I did not get up at dawn to exercise the right with the villagers to go into the forest to gather wood. In a very ancient ceremony probably going back to the 14th century, the boughs of oak that have been gathered are taken into Salisbury cathedral, a dance is performed in front of the altar, and the villagers shout, 'Grovely, Grovely, Grovely and all Grovely', and go back for a jolly good feast. That is history and reality and, for the souls of Great Wishford, a treasured part of their heritage.*
>
> Robert Key, in a parliamentary debate about rights of common (13 June 2000).

On this day:

Born: Spanish composer and pianist Isaac Albéniz (1860); English critic, novelist and poet G K Chesterton (1874); 35th President of the USA John F Kennedy (1917); English actor Rupert Everett (1959)

Died: Portuguese navigator and explorer Bartolomeu Diaz (1500); English chemist and inventor of the safety lamp Sir Humphry

Davy (1829); US actor John Barrymore (1942); Canadian-born US actress Mary Pickford (1979)

1453 Constantinople fell to the Turks.

1790 Rhode Island became the 13th state to ratify the Constitution of the USA.

1848 Wisconsin became the 38th state of the USA.

1871 The UK's first Bank Holiday was observed.

1942 Bing Crosby (1904–77) recorded Irving Berlin's (1888–1989) song *White Christmas.*

1953 New Zealand mountaineer Edmund Hillary (born 1919) and Nepalese mountaineer Tenzing Norgay (1914–86) reached the summit of Mt Everest.

1961 Prince Philip, Duke of Edinburgh (born 1921) was interviewed on *Panorama*, the first television interview with a member of the Royal Family.

1985 Thirty-nine people were killed when a wall collapsed at Heysel Stadium in Brussels as a result of rioting at the Liverpool versus Juventus European Cup final.

1990 Boris Yeltsin (born 1931) was elected president of the Russian Federation.

30 May

Feast day of French patriot and martyr **St Joan of Arc** (born c.1412), who was burnt at the stake in the marketplace of Rouen on this day in 1431, having been found guilty of heresy and sorcery.

On this day:

Born: US film director Howard Hawks (1896); US film executive Irving G Thalberg (1899); US clarinettist and bandleader

Benny Goodman (1909); Russian cosmonaut Aleksei Leonov (1934)

Died: English dramatist Christopher Marlowe (1593); Flemish painter Peter Paul Rubens (1640); English poet Alexander Pope (1744); French writer and historian Voltaire (1778); Russian lyric poet, novelist and translator Boris Pasternak (1960)

1498 Christopher Columbus (1451–1506) set sail on his third voyage, which would take him to South America.

1536 Henry VIII (1491–1547) married his third wife, Jane Seymour (c.1509–1537).

1814 The Treaty of Paris was signed by France and the victorious coalition of the UK, Austria, Prussia, Russia, Sweden and Portugal; it restored the Bourbon monarchy to France in place of the Napoleonic Empire.

1922 The Lincoln Memorial was dedicated in Washington, DC.

1959 New Zealand's Auckland Harbour Bridge was opened.

1966 The US spacecraft Surveyor 1 made a soft landing on the Moon.

1990 France banned imports of British beef following the BSE crisis.

1996 Prince Andrew, Duke of York (born 1960), and Sarah, Duchess of York (born 1959), were officially divorced.

31 May

Samuel Pepys (1633–1703) wrote the final entry in his *Diary* on this day in 1669.

> *And so I betake myself to that course, which is almost as much as to see myself go into my grave – for which, and all the discomforts that will accompany my being blind, the good God prepare me!*
>
> Samuel Pepys, *Diary*, closing words (31 May 1669).

31 May

Pepys's *Diary*, begun in 1660, is a unique record of the events of the decade it covered, including the Restoration, the great plague and the great fire of London. Written in a form of shorthand that was not deciphered until 1825, it also contains a wealth of detail about everyday life at the time, as well as amusing personal observations, such as his comment on the harpsichord-playing of a friend's daughter on 1 May 1663: 'Lord! it was enough to make any man sick to hear her; yet was I forced to commend her highly'.

On this day:

Born: US poet Walt Whitman (1819); British explorer Sir Francis Younghusband (1863); English actor Denholm Elliott (1922); US actor and director Clint Eastwood (1930); English religious adviser Terry Waite (1939)

Died: Italian painter Tintoretto (1594); Austrian composer Joseph Haydn (1809); English comic actor, singer and acrobat Joseph Grimaldi (1837); US boxer Jack Dempsey (1983)

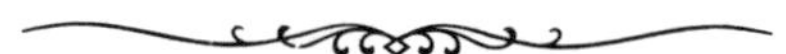

1787 The first match, Essex versus Middlesex, was played at Lord's cricket ground in London.

1859 Big Ben, the famous bell in the clock tower of the House of Commons, rang for the first time.

1902 The treaty that ended the Boer War, the Peace of Vereeniging, was signed at Pretoria in southern Africa.

1910 Transvaal, Natal, the Orange Free State and Cape Province were united to form the Union of South Africa, a dominion of the British Empire.

1911 The hull of the ill-fated liner *Titanic* was launched at its Belfast shipyard.

1915 World War I – London suffered its first air-raid.

1916 World War I – the Battle of Jutland, the first major challenge to British naval supremacy since the Battle of Trafalgar in 1805, began; Admiral Jellicoe (1859–1935) led the British Grand Fleet from Scapa Flow and intercepted the German High Seas Fleet of the west coast off Jutland, Denmark.

1961 South Africa became an independent republic and left the Commonwealth.

1996 Binyamin Netanyahu (born 1949) became prime minister of Israel.

Summer

Sumer is icumen in,
Lhude sing cuccu!
Groweth sed, and bloweth med,
And springth the wude nu.

Anonymous, 'Sumer is icumen in' (c.1250).

A something in a summer's day
As slow her flambeaux burn away
Which solemnizes me.

A something in a summer's noon –
An azure depth, a wordless tune,
Transcending ecstasy.

Emily Dickinson, *Poems*, 'Psalm of the Day' (1890).

Summer afternoon – summer afternoon; to me those have always been the two most beautiful words in the English language.

Henry James, quoted in Edith Wharton, *A Backward Glance* (1934).

Origins

The word *summer* is of Old English origin. The suggestion that it literally means 'more sun' is etymologically unsound. The Latin name for the season was *aestas*, from which the English words *aestival* ('of the summer') and *aestivate* ('to pass the summer') are derived, and also the French word *été* ('summer').

Season

Astronomically taken to be the period from the summer solstice to the autumnal equinox (occurring around 21 June and 23 September respectively in the northern hemisphere), summer is the time of hot weather, ripening fruit and grain, and holidays.

Weather

The British summer has always been renowned for the unreliability of its weather:

> *An English summer: three fine days and a thunderstorm.*
>
> Traditional saying.

> *Shall I compare thee to a summer's day?*
> *Thou art more lovely and more temperate.*
>
> William Shakespeare, *Sonnets*, sonnet 18 (1609).

> *The way to ensure summer in England is to have it framed and glazed in a comfortable room.*
>
> Horace Walpole, Letter to William Cole (28 May 1774).

> *The English winter – ending in July,*
> *To recommence in August.*
>
> Lord Byron, *Don Juan* (1819–24).

Nonetheless, it is invariably the time of year when temperatures are at their highest. The hottest days of the year are the **dog days**, a period of uncertain definition, but generally reckoned to last from 3 July to 11 August. Associated with the rising of the Dog Star (Sirius or Canicula), they are sometimes called the **canicular days**. According to ancient superstition, disease and disaster were rife at this time and dogs were at their most susceptible to rabies: in some towns and cities all dogs had to wear muzzles in public places for the duration.

Characteristics

The face of the countryside gradually changes from the fresh greens and bright colours of June, through the gold and brown of ripening crops and scorched grass in July and August, to the early signs of the approach of autumn in September. Those who make their living from the land are busy with haymaking, fruit-picking, sheep-shearing and preparing for harvest, but for those with leisure hours to fill it is a time for picnics and barbecues, swimming and sailing, or simply relaxing in the sun. There is no excuse for anything but healthy eating at this time of year, with a steady succession of locally grown fresh produce coming into season: asparagus, cherries, strawberries, blackcurrants, new potatoes, tomatoes, plums and corn on the cob.

Summer holidays

> *One of the symptoms of approaching nervous breakdown is the belief that one's work is terribly important, and that to take a holiday would bring all kinds of disaster. If I were a medical man, I should prescribe a holiday to any patient who considered his work important.*
>
> Bertrand Russell, *Conquest of Happiness* (1930).

The annual summer holiday for the masses – a week or fortnight spent at the seaside or some other desirable location, at home or abroad – is a relatively recent invention. In the late 18th and early 19th centuries, seaside towns were chiefly patronized by royalty: Lyme Regis in Dorset gained its Latin epithet from its association with King George III (1738–1820), and Brighton in Sussex became a fashionable resort in the regency period of his son, the future King George IV (1762–1830), who commissioned the oriental-style Royal Pavilion. It was the development of the railways in the Victorian era that gave the middle and lower classes access to the restorative benefits of sea bathing and salt air, and resorts began to spring up around the coast, from

Blackpool in the west to Scarborough in the east, enjoying their heyday in the first half of the 20th century.

In the industrial towns and cities of northern England and elsewhere, **wakes week** was an annual shutdown that served a dual purpose, enabling factory owners to carry out regular maintenance and giving their employees a well-earned break. It takes its name from local saint's day celebrations, otherwise known as 'wakes', when an overnight vigil in the church was followed by feasting and merrymaking. In other parts of the UK, some people enjoyed a working holiday – picking hops or fruit in the fresh country air of a Kent farm, for example, was a welcome change from life on the grimy streets of London.

Foreign travel, formerly restricted to the idle rich, did not become widely accessible to lesser mortals until the latter half of the 20th century, with the advent of package holidays to places where summer sunshine was more or less guaranteed. The countries of S Europe remain the most popular destinations, but cheap air travel has opened up a world of possibilities.

> *Holidays are the greatest learning experience unknown to man.*
>
> Frank Ogden, *Ogdenisms: The Frank Ogden Quote Book* (1994).

Customs

The pleasant weather and long daylight hours of the summer months encourage outdoor activities; many fairs and festivals, both ancient and modern, are traditionally held at this time of year. Country fairs were originally used for trading purposes, before the advent of shops and livestock markets, and were often associated with religious festivals such as Lammas (1 August) or saints' days. Some festivities have pagan roots, notably those associated with the summer solstice (21 June) and Midsummer (23–4 June).

Other summer customs include **rushbearing**, which now takes place in just a few localities, notably Ambleside and Grasmere in Cumbria. It derives from the time when rushes were laid on the bare earth or cold stone of the church floor to protect the feet of the congregation. These were annually renewed, usually as part of the celebrations associated with the feast day of the church's patron saint (especially if this occurred during the summer months), and various traditions became associated with the occasion. The **Ambleside rushbearing** takes place in July, the **Grasmere rushbearing** in August, and the ceremonies are similar in their modern form. The people of the community parade to the church carrying single rushes, rushes decorated with flowers, or elaborate shapes made of rushes; after a special service, these are left behind

to decorate the church, and the children who carried them in the procession receive a piece of gingerbread.

Doggett's Coat and Badge Race, a rowing match on the River Thames for members of the Company of Watermen and Lightermen, was founded in 1715 by the actor–manager Thomas Doggett (c.1660–1721) and is the oldest annual event of the British sporting calendar.

> *The competitors are six young watermen, whose apprenticeship ends in the same year – the prize, a waterman's coat and silver badge. The distance rowed extends from the Old Swan at London Bridge, to the White Swan at Chelsea, against an adverse tide; so none but men of great strength, skill, and endurance need attempt the arduous struggle. ... Dogget[t] was an ardent politician, and an enthusiastic advocate of the Hanoverian succession. It was in honour of this event that he gave a waterman's coat and badge to be rowed for on the first anniversary of the accession of the First George to the British throne. And at his death he bequeathed a sum of money, the interest of which was to be appropriated annually, for ever, to the purchase of a like coat and badge, to be rowed for on the 1st of August, in honour of the day. And with the minute attention to matters of dress which distinguished him as an actor, and in accordance with his political principles, he directed that the coat should be of an orange colour, and the badge should represent the white horse of Hanover.*
>
> *Chambers Book of Days* (1864).

In modern times, the race is dependent on the state of the tide and usually takes place in July. The competitors have an easier time of it, not only because the boats are lighter, but because they now row with, rather than against, the tide.

Religious festivals

Two important Hindu festivals occur during the summer season:

> **Raksha Bandhan** falls on the day of the full moon in the Hindu month of Sravana (July–August). The central feature of the festival is a traditional ceremony in which a sister ties a decorative coloured thread (rakhi) to her brother's wrist as a symbol of love and affection, cementing their relationship and binding him to protect her. Sometimes the threads are tied by other family members, by friends, or by priests, but it is usually girls or women who do the tying – they may even go to prisons, orphanages or similar institutions to tie rakhi on the inmates.

Other events of the day include religious rituals, the preparation and consumption of traditional foodstuffs, and the exchanging of gifts.

Janamashtami, in the Hindu month of Bhadrapada (August–September), commemorates the birth of Krishna, the eighth incarnation of the deity Vishnu, who killed the evil Kansa, King of Mathura. After a day of fasting, devotees flock to Krishna temples, specially decorated for the occasion, to pray and sing. At midnight the temple bells ring, announcing the moment at which Krishna is said to have been born, and there is great rejoicing. Other features of the festival, which is chiefly celebrated in N India (especially Mathura), include the depiction of events from the early life of Krishna in dramas and tableaux.

June

Gemstone: Pearl or moonstone
Flower: Rose or honeysuckle

Married in the month of roses – June,
Life will be one long honeymoon.

Traditional rhyme.

June has now come, bending beneath her weight of roses, to ornament the halls and bowers which summer has hung with green. For this is the Month of Roses, and their beauty and fragrance conjure up again many in poetical creation which Memory had buried ... This is the season to wander into the fields and woods, with a volume of sterling poetry for companionship, and compare the descriptive passages with the objects that lie around. We never enjoy reading portions of Spenser's Faery Queen so much as when among the great green trees in summer.

Chambers Book of Days (1864).

Origins

June, the sixth month of the year, probably takes its name from the Roman goddess Juno. According to an alternative explanation, the word *June* is derived from *Iuniores*, which referred to the lower level of the legislature in the original constitution of ancient Rome (as opposed to the *Maiores* – the senate – from which the word *May* is derived).

Characteristics

June is generally regarded as the first month of summer, although the first 20 days belong to spring, astronomically speaking. The hours of daylight are at their longest: in northernmost parts of Europe there is very little darkness in the latter half of the month, around the time of the summer solstice (21 June). In the countryside, and in parks and gardens in urban areas, a brilliant array of colour is displayed by ripening crops, flowers, shrubs and grass that has not yet been scorched by the hot sun.

History

Celtic names for June contain words for 'mid' or 'middle', as this month was regarded by the Celts as the height of summer. In Welsh it is *Mehefin*, in Irish-Gaelic *Meitheamh*, and a former Scottish-Gaelic name is *Meadhan-Samhraidh*.

Weather

Weather lore tells us that 'a calm June puts the farmer in tune'. Warm dry weather in June is welcomed by farmers, for tasks such as haymaking. However, their crops need rain for growth, as well as sun for ripening: 'June damp and warm does the farmer no harm'. Too much rain and no sun, on the other hand, is a disaster: 'A cold and wet June spoils the rest of the year'. In the UK, any of these combinations is possible, but typical June weather is generally perceived as being pleasant, with the sun at its hottest around the time of the solstice.

And what is so rare as a day in June?
Then, if ever, come perfect days.

James Russell Lowell, 'The Vision of Sir Launfal' (1848).

Yes; I remember Adlestrop –
The name, because one afternoon
Of heat the express-train drew up there
Unwontedly. It was late June.

Edward Thomas, 'Adlestrop' (1915).

The rose

The rose is at its most prolific and beautiful in June. The red rose is the symbol of love, of England and St George, of Lancashire and of the British Labour Party. For the first of these reasons it is much in demand out of season, especially on St Valentine's Day (14 February), when large numbers are imported from Colombia and elsewhere.

> *O my love's like a red, red rose*
> *That's newly sprung in June:*
> *O my love's like the melodie*
> *That's sweetly play'd in tune.*
>
> Robert Burns, 'A Red, Red Rose' (1794).

In some parts of the UK, notably Devon and Cornwall, it was formerly believed that a rose plucked by a young woman at midnight on Midsummer Eve (23 June) and wrapped in paper would remain fresh until Christmas Day. If she then wore it on her dress, it would be snatched away by the young man who was destined to become her husband.

A relatively recent June tradition involving roses takes place on the Sunday nearest the feast day of **St Alban** (22 June) in the Hertfordshire city of that name. At a special children's service in the cathedral, every child in the congregation places a rose on the shrine of the martyr.

Non-fixed notable dates

Non-fixed notable dates in June include:

Official birthday of the British sovereign: Countries of the Commonwealth celebrate the official birthday of the British sovereign during the month of June. In the UK it is the second or third Saturday; in Ireland and New Zealand it is the first Monday; in Australia, Bermuda, Fiji and elsewhere it is the second Monday. The choice of this month is purely pragmatic: the weather is considered to be somewhat more reliable at this time of year for the various festivities that take place. (June was chosen by King George VI, whose actual birthday fell in December.) The day is marked in London by the ceremony of **Trooping the Colour**, which takes place in the presence of the monarch – and crowds of onlookers of all nationalities – on Horse Guards Parade, Whitehall. This colourful military show has its origin in the custom of carrying the flag of the battalion down the ranks of soldiers so that all would recognize it in battle. Its value as a tourist attraction was recognized by King George V, who introduced many of the features of the modern spectacular in the early 20th century.

Father's Day: Observed on the third Sunday of June, this is a celebration of relatively recent US origin. Consequently, it has no traditional activities associated with it in the UK (unlike its counterpart Mothering Sunday, or Mother's Day, in March) and is usually simply marked by the giving of cards and gifts.

The Derby: A major event of the racing calendar, the Derby was formerly run on the first Wednesday in June and now takes place on the Saturday following this date. It is a flat race for three-year-old horses at Epsom, Surrey. The event is named after the 12th Earl of Derby, who inaugurated it in 1780, in which year it was won by a horse called Diomed. The 1913 Derby was famously marred by a tragic incident: the British suffragette Emily Davison tried to stage a protest by seizing the reins of King George V's horse but was trampled underfoot and died later in hospital.

Bawming the Thorn: Bawming the Thorn takes place every June in the Cheshire village of Appleton. The thorn tree in the centre of the village is adorned with garlands and ribbons, and the local children form a procession and dance and sing around the thorn. The original hawthorn tree in Appleton was said to have grown from a cutting from the Holy Thorn at Glastonbury (see 5 January) although the current tree is a 1960s replacement.

1 June

The first major naval battle between British and French fleets in the French Revolutionary Wars took place on this day in 1794, known as the Glorious First of June. The French fleet, commanded by Admiral Villaret-Joyeuse (1750–1812), had been sent to escort a convoy of grain ships from the USA bearing vital supplies for France. The task of the British fleet, commanded by Lord Howe (1726–99), was to prevent them. The encounter was a victory for Howe, in that Villaret-Joyeuse lost more men and ships and the French fleet was forced to withdraw, but the British failed to prevent the cargo of grain from reaching safe harbour at Brest. Nonetheless, news of the outcome was greeted with great enthusiasm in Great Britain.

> *We should need to bring back the horrors of the first French Revolution to enable us to understand the wild delight with which Lord Howe's victory, in 1794, was regarded in England. A king, a queen, and a princess guillotined in France, a reign of terror prevailing in that country, and a war threatening half the monarchs in Europe, had impressed the English with an intense desire to thwart the republicans. ... The English valued this victory quite as much for the moral effect it wrought in Europe generally, as for the immediate material injury it inflicted on the French.*
>
> *Chambers Book of Days* (1864).

On this day:

Born: US Mormon leader Brigham Young (1801); US film actress Marilyn Monroe (1926); English cartoonist, caricaturist and animator Gerald Scarfe (1936); US actor Morgan Freeman (1937)

Died: Scottish painter Sir David Wilkie (1841); English actor Leslie Howard (1943); US writer Helen Keller (1968); English radio engineer and inventor of the hovercraft Sir Christopher Cockerell (1999); South African cricketer Hanse Cronje (2002)

1792 Kentucky became the 15th state of the USA.

1796 Tennessee became the 16th state of the USA.

1913 Georges Carpentier (1897–1975) of France defeated Bombardier Billy Wells (1889–1967) of the UK to win the European heavyweight boxing championship.

1938 Superman, created by US students Joseph Shuster (1914–92) and Jerry Siegel (1914–96), made his first appearance in *Action Comics #1*.

1953 Gordon Richards (1904–86) became the first British jockey to receive a knighthood.

1958 General Charles de Gaulle (1890–1970) became the head of an emergency government in France.

1967 The Beatles' album *Sergeant Pepper's Lonely Hearts Club Band* was released.

1979 Rhodesia formally declared an end to white rule, and changed its name to Zimbabwe.

1985 The so-called Battle of the Beanfield took place when police clashed with a convoy of travellers heading for a midsummer festival at Stonehenge in Wiltshire.

1990 US President George Bush (born 1924) and Soviet president Mikhail Gorbachev (born 1931) signed an agreement on the reduction of chemical weapons.

1993 A football match in Bosnia was shelled by Serb artillery forces, killing eleven people.

2001 The Nepalese monarchy was thrown into crisis when Crown Prince Dipendra murdered King Birendra and most of the royal family before killing himself.

The Coronation of Elizabeth II (born 1926) as Queen of Great Britain and Northern Ireland and Head of the Commonwealth took place on this day in 1953. The ceremony was performed in Westminster Abbey, London, by the Archbishop of Canterbury, Geoffrey Fisher (1887–1972), in the presence of heads of state and other dignitaries from all over the Commonwealth. The

events of the day were witnessed by 8,000 guests in the Abbey, 3 million onlookers who lined the streets to watch the procession to and from the ceremony, and more than 20 million television viewers worldwide who tuned in to the BBC's live coverage, which was broadcast in 44 languages. Some people bought their first television set expressly for this purpose, and invited neighbours around to share the historic occasion.

Elizabeth II came to the throne after the death of her father King George VI (born 1895) in February 1952. In June 1977 her Silver Jubilee was celebrated with street parties and other festivities throughout the country, and in June 2002 her Golden Jubilee was marked in similar style, together with a grand Jubilee tour of the UK and Commonwealth.

On this day:

Born: French writer the Marquis de Sade (1740); English novelist, poet and dramatist Thomas Hardy (1840); English composer Sir Edward Elgar (1857); US actress and gossip columnist Hedda Hopper (1885); Greek king Constantine II (1940)

Died: Italian revolutionary, soldier and politician Giuseppe Garibaldi (1882); English poet and novelist Vita Sackville-West (1962); New Zealand racing driver Bruce McLaren (1970); Spanish guitarist Andrés Segovia (1987)

1420 King Henry V of England (1387–1422) married the King of France's daughter, Catherine de Valois (1401–37).

1692 Bridget Bishop was the first woman to be tried and convicted of witchcraft at the Salem Witch Trials in the village of Salem, Massachusetts.

1896 Guglielmo Marconi (1874–1937) was granted the first patent for a system of wireless broadcasting.

1909 The première of the ballet *Les Sylphides*, with music by Frédéric Chopin (1810–49) and choreography by Michel Fokine (1880–1942), was danced by Vaslav Nijinsky (1890–1950) and Anna Pavlova (1881–1931) at the Théâtre du Chatelet in Paris.

1924 The US government granted citizenship to all Native Americans.

1938 As sons of the US ambassador to the UK, Robert and Edward Kennedy opened the Regent's Park Children's Zoo in London.

1979 Pope John Paul II (born 1920) visited Poland, the country of his birth, becoming the first pope to visit a Communist country.

1985 Hooliganism by English football fans led to English clubs being banned from playing in European competitions.

2002 British explorers Caroline Hamilton and Ann Daniels became the first all-female expedition to walk all the way to both Poles.

2003 Beagle 2, the UK's first Mars probe, was launched as part of the European Space Agency's Mars Express programme.

3 June

Edward, Duke of Windsor (1894–1972), married Mrs Wallis Simpson (1896–1986) on this day in 1937. Formerly King Edward VIII of Great Britain and Northern Ireland, he had abdicated in December 1936, after less than eleven months on the throne, because of his desire to marry the twice-divorced US socialite, who was considered unacceptable as a British queen consort.

> *I have found it impossible to carry the heavy burden of responsibility, and to discharge my duties as King as I would wish, without the help and support of the woman I love.*
>
> King Edward VIII, radio broadcast to the nation (11 December 1936).

The wedding ceremony was performed by an Anglican clergyman in France, at the Château de Candé in the Loire Valley. After their marriage, the Duke and Duchess of Windsor lived mainly in France, moving to the Bahamas (where Edward had been appointed governor) during World War II. They were largely shunned by the British royal family until 1967, when they were invited to attend the unveiling of a plaque dedicated to Edward's mother, Queen Mary (1867–1953). Edward died in 1972 and was buried in the royal burial ground at Frogmore, near Windsor Castle. His widow died 14 years later and was buried at his side.

On this day:

Born: Scottish geologist James Hutton (1726); US philosophical

theologian Henry James (1811); British king George V (1865); US actor and painter Tony Curtis (1925)

Died: French composer George Bizet (1875); Czech-born Austrian novelist Franz Kafka (1924); English journalist and children's writer Arthur Ransome (1967); English actor Robert Morley (1992); Mexican-born US actor Anthony Quinn (2001)

1083 St Peter's Cathedral in Rome was captured when King Henry IV of Germany (1050–1106) stormed the city.

1098 The First Crusade took Antioch after a siege lasting five months.

1621 The Dutch West India Company was granted a charter to trade.

1950 The peak of Annapurna in the Himalayas, Nepal, was reached for the first time by an expedition of French climbers.

1965 US astronaut Edward White (1930–67) became the first man to 'walk' in space when he spent 20 minutes outside the Gemini 4 spacecraft.

1968 US pop artist and film-maker Andy Warhol (1928–87) was shot and wounded by Valerie Solanas (1936–88).

1981 The racehorse Shergar, owned by the Aga Khan (born 1937), won the Epsom Derby by a record ten lengths.

1982 Israeli ambassador Shlomo Argov (1929–2003) was shot on a London street.

4 June

On this day in 1783, the Montgolfier brothers, Joseph Michel (1740–1810) and Jacques Étienne (1745–99), gave the first public demonstration of their latest invention, the hot-air balloon, at Annonay, near Lyons, in France. A small fire beneath the opening of the balloon (a large bag made from paper and linen) caused it to fill with smoke and heated air and rise more than 1,000ft into the sky, where it remained for ten minutes. In September 1783, the experiment was repeated, in the presence of King Louis XVI (1754–93) and Marie Antoinette (1755–93), with three 'passengers' – a sheep, a duck, and a rooster – suspended in a basket below the balloon. Two months later, the first human air travellers flew 5½ miles in a Montgolfier balloon over Paris.

On this day:

Born: French physician and economist François Quesnay (1694); British and Hanoverian king George III (1738); Russian-born US actress Alla Nazimova (1879); Austrian politician and chancellor Viktor Klima (1947); US actress Angelina Jolie (1975)

Died: Italian adventurer Giacomo Girolamo Casanova (1798); German emperor and Prussian king Kaiser Wilhelm II (1941); US silent actress Dorothy Gish (1968); New Zealand politician Sir Walter Nash (1968); Peruvian statesman and president Fernando Belaúnde Terry (2002)

1647 The English army seized King Charles I (1600–49) as a hostage.

1831 Prince Leopold of Saxe-Coburg (1790–1865) was proclaimed the first monarch of Belgium.

1913 English suffragette Emily Davison (1872–1913) was trampled by the King's horse at the Derby; she died of her injuries a few days later.

1940 World War II – the evacuation of Allied troops from Dunkirk was completed successfully.

1944 World War II – Allied troops liberated Rome.

1946 Argentinian soldier and statesman Juan Perón (1895–1974) became president of Argentina.

1970 The British protectorate of Tonga became an independent member of the Commonwealth.

1989 Soldiers and tanks fired on students and workers demonstrating in Tiananmen Square, Beijing, China, killing hundreds of people; the actual death toll is not known.

2002 Thousands of people thronged the streets of London to watch the Golden Jubilee celebrations of Queen Elizabeth II (born 1926).

5 June

This is **World Environment Day**, devoted to raising public awareness of environmental issues and encouraging political action to protect the environment. It was established by the United Nations General Assembly in 1972. The day is celebrated in many ways – from green concerts to tree planting and bicycle parades. Each year the United Nations Environment Programme also announces a theme and a host nation for the main celebrations.

On this day:

Born: Scottish economist and philosopher Adam Smith (1723); English economist John Maynard Keynes, 1st Baron Keynes of Tilton (1883); Spanish poet and playwright Federico García Lorca (1898); English novelist Margaret Drabble (1939); English dramatist, director and film-maker Sir David Hare (1947)

Died: German composer and pianist Carl von Weber (1826); US short-story writer O Henry (1910); British soldier and statesman Lord Kitchener (1916); US punk musician Dee Dee Ramone (2002)

1249 King Louis IX (1214–70) of France landed in Egypt with the Seventh Crusade.

1940 World War II – the Battle of France began.

1963 John Profumo (born 1915), the UK's Secretary of State for War, resigned after admitting he had lied to the House of Commons about his affair with Christine Keeler (born 1942).

1967 The Six-Day War between Israel and the Arab States began.

1968 US Senator Robert F Kennedy (1925–68) was shot by Sirhan Sirhan (born c.1943) immediately after his victory in the California presidential primary. He died the next day.

1975 The Suez Canal, closed for eight years, was reopened by Egypt to all but Israeli shipping.

1988 Kay Cottee (born 1954) sailed into Sydney Harbour, Australia, becoming the first woman to have made a non-stop, solo circumnavigation of the world.

1989 The victory of Poland's Solidarity party over the Communists, in the country's first free elections since World War II, was confirmed.

1991 In Oslo, Norway, Soviet president Mikhail Gorbachev (born 1931) was forced by two anti-Soviet protestors to interrupt his Nobel Peace Prize speech.

6 June

> *We shall go on to the end. We shall fight in France … We shall fight on the beaches … We shall never surrender.*
>
> Winston Churchill, speech in the House of Commons (4 June 1940).

On 6 June 1944, four years after this rousing and prophetic speech by Sir Winston Churchill (1874–1965), more than 150,000 British, US and Canadian troops landed on the beaches of Normandy in northern France in Operation Overlord, better known as D-Day. This was the beginning of the Allied invasion of Europe that would ultimately lead to victory in World War II. It was an amphibious operation, under the supreme command of General Dwight D Eisenhower (1890–1969), with troops landing by air and sea. They met with heavy resistance from German coastal batteries, but the number of casualties was relatively small and did not prevent the inland advance from proceeding almost exactly as planned.

The D of D-Day, popularly thought to be short for 'Debarkation' or 'Disembarkation', simply stands for 'Day': this is the military method of referring to the unnamed date of a secretly planned offensive. In France it is called *Jour-J*, for the same reason.

On this day:

Born: French dramatist Pierre Corneille (1606); Russian poet and writer Alexander Pushkin (1799); German novelist and Nobel Prize winner Thomas Mann (1875); Latvian-born British philosopher and historian of ideas Sir Isaiah Berlin (1909); Swedish tennis player Björn Borg (1956)

Died: English philosopher, writer on jurisprudence and social reformer Jeremy Bentham (1832); Swiss-born US car designer and racing driver Louis Chevrolet (1941); Swiss psychologist and psychiatrist Carl Jung (1961); US oil executive, billionaire and art collector Jean Paul Getty (1976)

1520 The ceremonial Field of the Cloth of Gold meeting, between Henry VIII of England (1491–1547) and Francis I of France (1494–1547), took place in Picardy, France.

1727 James Figg beat Ned Sutton in the first boxing title fight for the Championship of England, which also involved competing with swords and cudgels.

1844 The Young Men's Christian Association (YMCA) was founded in London by English social reformer George Williams (1821–1905).

1933 The first drive-in cinema was opened in Camden, New Jersey, USA, with room for 400 cars.

1949 The novel *Nineteen Eighty-Four* by George Orwell (1903–50) was published.

1953 British champion jockey Gordon Richards (1904–86) won the Epsom Derby for the first time on his 28th attempt.

1984 The holiest shrine of Sikhism, the Golden Temple at Amritsar, was stormed by Indian troops, resulting in an estimated 1,000 deaths.

1994 A group of asylum seekers staged a rooftop protest against conditions at Campsfield immigration centre in Oxford; the centre was eventually closed down.

1996 Former US Senator George Mitchell (born 1933) was named by the UK and Ireland as the chair of the Northern Ireland peace talks.

7 June

King Robert I of Scotland, better known as Robert the Bruce, died on this day in 1329. At his request, his heart was removed from his body before burial and taken on a pilgrimage to the Holy Land. Unfortunately, the knight bearing it was killed before he reached his destination, and the embalmed organ was returned to Scotland and buried in Melrose Abbey.

Born in 1274, Robert the Bruce joined the Scottish revolt led by William Wallace (c.1274–1305) in 1297. After stabbing his rival John Comyn in a Dumfries church on 10 February 1306, he claimed the throne of Scotland and was crowned several weeks later at Scone. In the years that followed he led the Scots against the English in their battle for independence, securing a significant victory at Bannockburn on 24 June 1314.

The well-known legend of Robert the Bruce and the persevering spider probably dates from 1306 or 1307, when he was forced into exile during a setback in his fortunes. As he lay on his bed in despair, he watched a spider swinging from the roof, trying to attach the end of its thread to spin a web. On the seventh attempt it was successful, and Robert took this as a sign that he should return to Scotland for a further battle with the English, having already suffered six defeats. According to Sir Walter Scott (1771–1832), people with the name of Bruce thereafter took great care not to kill any spider, in recognition of the service this creature had performed.

On this day:

Born: Scottish civil engineer John Rennie (1761); French Post-Impressionist painter Paul Gauguin (1848); Welsh pop singer Tom Jones (1940); US pop singer Prince (1958)

Died: Scottish king Robert the Bruce (1329); US wit, short-story writer and journalist Dorothy Parker (1967); English novelist and critic E M Forster (1970); US writer Henry Miller (1980)

1654 Louis XIV (1638–1715), the 'Sun King', was crowned in Rheims, France.

1906 The ill-fated Cunard liner *Lusitania*, which would be sunk by a German U-boat in 1915, was launched.

1929 With the ratification of the Lateran Treaty, the Papal State, which had been dissolved in 1870, was revived as the State of Vatican City.

1942 World War II – the US Pacific Fleet defeated the Japanese in the Battle of Midway.

1945 The première of the opera *Peter Grimes*, by Benjamin Britten (1913–76), was held at Sadler's Wells in London.

1946 BBC Television resumed normal transmissions after World War II with the same Mickey Mouse cartoon that had been showing when the service was shut down in September 1939.

1948 Czechoslovakian president Eduard Beneš (1884–1948) resigned from office after the Communist takeover of the country.

1977 In London, over a million people lined the streets to watch the Queen's Silver Jubilee procession.

1981 Israel conducted a bombing raid on an Iraqi nuclear plant near the city of Baghdad.

1996 The government of Myanmar (formerly Burma) introduced a strict new law designed to further restrict the free flow of information within the country.

2000 UK prime minister Tony Blair (born 1953) was heckled by the Women's Institute during a speech he gave at their conference.

8 June

The day on which two inventions that would ease the burden of housewives and domestic servants were patented: the washing machine in 1824 and the vacuum cleaner in 1869.

On this day:

Born: German composer Robert Schumann (1810); English painter Sir John Millais (1829); US architect Frank Lloyd Wright (1867); English molecular biologist and Nobel Prize winner

Francis Crick (1916); English computer scientist Tim Berners-Lee (1955)

Died: Arab prophet and founder of Islam Muhammad (632); English-born American radical political writer Thomas Paine (1809); French novelist George Sand (1876); English poet Gerard Manley Hopkins (1889); Nigerian soldier, politician and president Sani Abacha (1998)

1333 King Edward III (1312–77) seized control of the Isle of Man from the Scots.

1861 The state of Tennessee became the last of eleven southern states to secede from the Union.

1925 The première of the play *Hay Fever*, by Noël Coward (1899–1973), was held at the Ambassador's Theatre in London.

1953 The première of the opera *Gloriana*, by Benjamin Britten (1913–76), was held at the Royal Opera House, Covent Garden, London.

1968 James Earl Ray (1928–98) was arrested in London for the murder of US clergyman, civil rights leader and Nobel Prize winner Martin Luther King, Jnr (1929–68).

1978 New Zealand-born British yachtswoman Naomi James (born 1949) completed a solo circumnavigation of the world in record time, beating the previous record by two days.

1986 Kurt Waldheim (born 1918) was elected president of Austria.

1990 Czechoslovakia held a free election for the first time in over 40 years.

1999 Former Conservative cabinet minister Jonathan Aitken (born 1942) was sentenced to 18 months in jail after admitting that he had lied in court during a failed libel action.

June

This is the feast day of **St Columba** (also known as Colm Cille, meaning 'Colm of the Churches') the 6th-century Irish missionary who founded a

monastery on the Scottish island of Iona. According to a Gaelic rhyme recorded in the late 19th century by Alexander Carmichael and published in his collection *Carmina Gadelica*, St Columba's Day is particularly lucky if it falls on a Thursday:

Thursday of Columba benign
Day to send sheep on prosperity,
Day to send cow on calf,
Day to put the web in the warp.

Day to put coracle on the brine,
Day to place the staff to the flag,
Day to bear, day to die,
Day to hunt the heights.

Day to put horses in harness,
Day to send herds to pasture,
Day to make prayer efficacious,
Day of my beloved, the Thursday,
Day of my beloved, the Thursday.

The saint is credited with numerous miracles, such as driving away a monster that lurked in the waters of Loch Ness by making the sign of the cross, thereby securing the conversion of the Picts. He is also said to have carried St John's wort under his armpit, a practice subsequently believed to ward off evil.

On this day:

Born: Roman emperor Nero (AD 68); English railway engineer George Stephenson (1781); US composer Cole Porter (1891); English gynaecologist and pioneer of in vitro fertilization Patrick Steptoe (1913); US actor Johnny Depp (1963)

Died: English writer Charles Dickens (1870); Chiricahua Apache chief Cochise (1874); Canadian-born British newspaper magnate and politician Lord Beaverbrook (1964); English actress Dame Sybil Thorndike (1976); Chilean pianist Claudio Arrau (1991)

1549 The first *Book of Common Prayer*, compiled by Thomas Cranmer (1489–1556), was adopted by the Church of England.

1898 The UK signed an agreement to lease Hong Kong from China for 99 years.

1904 The London Symphony Orchestra gave its first concert.

1908 Tsar Nicholas II (1868–1918) came on board the British Royal Yacht in the Baltic Sea to meet King Edward VII (1841–1910), the first meeting between a Russian Tsar and a British monarch.

1938 The BBC televised the Trooping the Colour ceremony for the first time.

1958 Gatwick Airport was reopened by the Queen after a major programme of redevelopment and expansion.

1959 The first US Polaris submarine, the USS *George Washington*, was launched.

1975 Proceedings from the House of Commons were broadcast on live radio for the first time.

1991 In the Philippines, the Mt Pinatubo volcano erupted after lying dormant for over 500 years.

10 June

On this day in 1935, the US surgeon Robert Holbrook Smith, known as 'Dr Bob', had his last alcoholic drink, marking the foundation of the organization Alcoholics Anonymous. Both he and his co-founder William Griffith Wilson (known as 'Bill W') were alcoholics; they had met for the first time earlier that year and pledged to help each other give up the bottle for good. During the following years they set up a number of self-help groups for alcoholics and published the textbook of the programme, *Alcoholics Anonymous*. This, together with media publicity, caused the organization to mushroom: by the end of 1941 there were 8,000 members in the USA, and by the mid-1970s there were over a million members worldwide.

On this day:

Born: British claimant to the throne James Stuart, the Old Pretender (1688); US writer and Nobel Prize winner Saul Bellow (1915); US actress and singer Judy Garland (1922); US illustrator and children's author Maurice Sendak (1928)

Died: French mathematician and physicist André Marie Ampère (1836); British composer Frederick Delius (1934); US film actor Spencer Tracy (1967); English author and traveller Hammond Innes (1998); US politician Donald Regan (2003)

1190 During the Third Crusade, Emperor Frederick I, Barbarossa (born c.1123) was drowned at Cilicia.

1793 The first public zoo, the Jardin des Plantes, opened in Paris.

1809 Napoleon I (1769–1821) was excommunicated by Pope Pius VII (1742–1823).

1829 The first Oxford versus Cambridge University Boat Race took place at Henley-on-Thames.

1854 In London, the Crystal Palace was reopened, having been moved from Hyde Park to a new location at Sydenham.

1865 The première of the opera *Tristan und Isolde*, by Richard Wagner (1813–83), was held in Munich, Germany.

1909 The Cunard liner *Slavonia* became the first to use the SOS distress signal after it was wrecked off the Azores.

1940 World War II – Italy declared war on the UK and France, and Canada declared war on Italy.

1967 Israel agreed to the UN call for a ceasefire, ending the Six-Day War.

1981 English athlete Sebastian Coe (born 1956) broke his own world 800m record in Florence, Italy.

2000 London's new Millennium Bridge swayed so much under the weight of huge opening-day crowds that it had to be closed for safety checks.

11 June

Barnaby bright, Barnaby bright, the longest day and the shortest night.

Traditional saying.

11 June

St Barnabas's Day, which now falls on 11 June, was formerly the date of the summer solstice, before the adjustment made in the changeover from the 'Old Style' Julian calendar to the 'New Style' Gregorian calendar in 1752. Barnabas, described in the Bible as 'a good man, and full of the Holy Ghost and of faith' (Acts 11.24), was a cousin of Christ's apostle Mark who worked with Paul and accompanied him on his early missionary journeys. In the agricultural calendar, St Barnabas's Day traditionally marked the start of haymaking, and the saint is sometimes depicted with a hay rake in his hands.

> *It appears to have been customary on St Barnaby's day for the priests and clerks in English churches to wear garlands of the rose and the woodroff. A miraculous walnut-tree in the abbey churchyard of Glastonbury was supposed to bud invariably on St Barnaby's day.*
>
> *Chambers Book of Days* (1864).

On this day:

Born: English suffragette and educational reformer Dame Millicent Fawcett (1847); German composer Richard Strauss (1864); US actor Gene Wilder (1935); Scottish racing driver Sir Jackie Stewart (1939)

Died: English explorer Sir John Franklin (1847); British artist Sir Frank Brangwyn (1956); US actor John Wayne (1979); English popular novelist Catherine Cookson (1998)

1509 King Henry VIII (1491–1547) married his first wife, Catherine of Aragon (1485–1536).

1727 King George II (1683–1760) succeeded his father on to the British throne.

1903 King Alexander and Queen Draga of Serbia were assassinated in a coup.

1952 English cricketer Denis Compton (1918–97) hit his 100th first-class century.

1960 The première of the opera *A Midsummer Night's Dream*, by Benjamin Britten (1913–76), was held at the Jubilee Hall, Aldeburgh.

1963 In Saigon, a Buddhist monk named Quang Duc immolated himself as a public protest against the South Vietnamese government of President Ngo Dinh Diem (1901–63).

1977 Dutch marines attempted to rescue 55 hostages who had been held on a Dutch train for 20 days by South Moluccan terrorists.

1987 Conservative prime minister Margaret Thatcher (born 1925) won a third successive victory with a large majority in the UK's general election.

1997 Vittorio Emanuele (born 1937), the son of Italy's last king, was allowed to return home after 50 years of exile.

12 June

> *It's a wonder I haven't abandoned all my ideals, they seem so absurd and impractical. Yet I cling to them because I still believe, in spite of everything, that people are truly good at heart. It's utterly impossible for me to build my life on a foundation of chaos, suffering and death. I see the world being slowly transformed into a wilderness, I hear the approaching thunder that, one day, will destroy us too, I feel the suffering of millions. And yet, when I look up at the sky, I somehow feel that everything will change for the better, that this cruelty too shall end, that peace and tranquillity will return once more.*
>
> Anne Frank, diary entry for 15 July 1944, in *The Diary of a Young Girl: The Definitive Edition* (1995).

Anne Frank was born on this day in 1929 in Frankfurt am Main, the daughter of a Jewish industrialist. The family moved to Amsterdam in 1933. On her 13th birthday, 12 June 1942, Anne received the diary that was to make the remainder of her tragically short life so well known. She wrote her first entry in the diary that day: 'I hope I shall be able to confide in you completely, as I have never been able to do in anyone before, and I hope that you will be a great support and comfort to me'.

During the following two years, Anne recorded in her diary not only the thoughts and feelings of an adolescent girl, but also the harrowing events of that time. Anne and her family went into hiding, along with four others, in a set of rooms above the offices of her father's company.

The final entry in the diary is dated 1 August 1944, three days before Anne and her family were betrayed, arrested and deported. Anne and her sister

12 June

Margot died in the Bergen-Belsen concentration camp in March 1945. Their mother Edith had died two months earlier, in the women's camp at Auschwitz-Birkenau. Their father Otto Frank survived and edited the diary for publication in 1947. Since then, it has been published in more than 50 languages and read by millions worldwide.

On this day:

Born: English statesman and prime minister Sir Anthony Eden (1897); German-born US actress Uta Hagen (1919); 41st President of the USA George Bush (1924); US jazz pianist, bandleader and composer Chick Corea (1941)

Died: US civil rights activist Medgar Evers (1963); South African-born British holiday camp promoter Billy Butlin (1980); Polish-born British ballet dancer and teacher Dame Marie Rambert (1982); US film actor Gregory Peck (2003)

1458 Magdalen College, Oxford, was officially founded.

1667 The first successful blood transfusion, from a sheep to a 15-year-old boy, was carried out in Paris by Professor Jean-Baptiste Denys.

1837 The first practical electric telegraph was patented by English inventors William Cooke (1806–79) and Charles Wheatstone (1802–75).

1897 In Switzerland, the forerunner of the Swiss Army Knife was patented by cutlery maker Carl Elsener.

1898 A revolutionary movement in the Philippines declared the country's independence from Spain.

1930 Max Schmeling, German heavyweight boxing champion, won the world title on a disqualification against US boxer Jack Sharkey.

1964 South African lawyer and anti-apartheid leader Nelson Mandela (born 1918) was sentenced to life imprisonment for sabotage.

1967 The US Supreme Court struck down state laws that prohibited interracial marriage.

1975 Indian prime minister Indira Gandhi (1917–84) was found guilty of electoral corruption and barred from office for six years.

1979 US racing cyclist Bryan Allen, in his *Gossamer Albatross* pedalo, became the first man to 'pedal' across the English Channel.

2000 Yemen signed a 'final and permanent' border agreement with Saudi Arabia, ending over 65 years of territorial dispute.

13 June

Feast day of **St Anthony of Padua**, patron saint of Portugal and Brazil (as well as the town of Padua in Italy), who is invoked for help in finding lost property.

On this day:

Born: English novelist and diarist Fanny Burney (1752); Irish poet and Nobel Prize winner W B Yeats (1865); English detective-story writer Dorothy L Sayers (1893); English jockey Peter Scudamore (1958)

Died: Macedonian king Alexander the Great (323 BC); Austrian theologian, philosopher and novelist Martin Buber (1965); Saudi Arabian king Khalid (1982); US actress Geraldine Page (1987)

1381 English rebel Wat Tyler (died 1381) led the Peasants' Revolt against serfdom and poor labour conditions.

1842 Queen Victoria (1819–1901) made her first railway journey from Slough to Paddington; the Great Western railway engineer Isambard Kingdom Brunel (1806–59) acted as deputy engine-driver.

1855 The première of the opera *The Sicilian Vespers*, by Giuseppe Verdi (1813–1901), was held in Paris.

1886 King Ludwig II of Bavaria (1845–86) drowned in mysterious circumstances, shortly after having been declared insane.

1900 The Boxer Rebellion, intended to rid the country of foreign influence, began in China.

1944 World War II – the first German V-1 Flying Bomb struck Southampton, UK.

1956 The last remaining British troops finally pulled out of the Suez Canal Zone in Egypt.

1974 Charles, Prince of Wales (born 1948), made his maiden speech in the House of Lords during a debate on sport and leisure.

1981 A 17-year-old man fired six blank cartridges at Queen Elizabeth II (born 1926) during the annual Trooping the Colour ceremony in London.

2000 Mehmet Ali Agca, the Turkish gunman who attempted to assassinate Pope John Paul II (born 1920) in 1981, was pardoned by the Italian government.

14 June

O say, can you see, by the dawn's early light,
What so proudly we hailed at the twilight's last gleaming?
Whose broad stripes and bright stars, through the perilous fight,
O'er the ramparts we watched were so gallantly streaming!
...
Now it catches the gleam of the morning's first beam,
In full glory reflected, now shines on the stream:
'Tis the star-spangled banner; O long may it wave
O'er the land of the free, and the home of the brave!

Francis Scott Key, 'The Star-Spangled Banner' (1814).

In the USA this is **Flag Day**, commemorating the adoption of the Stars and Stripes as the national flag on this day in 1777. Flag Day was officially established in 1916, although some groups had already celebrated the flag's birthday on this day. In 1949, President Truman (1884–1972) signed an Act of Congress which designated 14 June as National Flag Day.

The original flag had one stripe and one star for each of the 13 states that constituted the country at that time. The 13 stars and stripes were increased to 15 when Vermont and Kentucky joined the Union, but as others followed, it became impossible to incorporate sufficient stripes for all. In 1818, therefore, it was decreed that the number of stripes would be reduced to 13, symbolizing the 13 original colonies, and that the total number of states would be represented by the stars alone.

Flag Day provides an opportunity for Americans to pledge allegiance to their nation and to 'Old Glory' or the 'Star-Spangled Banner' as the flag is variously known.

On this day:

Born: US novelist Harriet Beecher Stowe (1811); US photojournalist Margaret Bourke-White (1906); Argentinian Communist revolutionary leader Che Guevara (1928); German tennis player Steffi Graf (1969)

Died: US general and turncoat Benedict Arnold (1801); English suffragette Emmeline Pankhurst (1928); Scottish electrical engineer and television pioneer John Logie Baird (1946); US librettist, lyricist and playwright Alan Jay Lerner (1986)

1645 Oliver Cromwell (1599–1658) led his army to a decisive victory over the Royalists at the Battle of Naseby.

1800 Napoleon I (1769–1821) defeated the Austrians at the Battle of Marengo in Northern Italy.

1841 The first Canadian parliament was opened in Kingston, Ontario.

1940 World War II – the French capital Paris fell to the Germans.

1940 World War II – a Nazi concentration camp was opened at Auschwitz in Poland.

1970 Bobby Charlton (born 1937) played his 106th and final football international for England in the World Cup quarter-final at Estadio Guanajuato in León, Mexico.

1982 A ceasefire was agreed between Argentinian forces and British troops in the Falklands War.

15 June

> *Given by our hand in the meadow that is called Runnymede, between Windsor and Staines, on the fifteenth day of June in the seventeenth year of our reign.*
>
> *Magna Carta* (1215).

On this day in 1215, King John (1167–1216) set his seal on Magna Carta, the 'Great Charter' drawn up by the barons of England, who had risen in rebellion against his oppressive and arbitrary rule, their anger exacerbated by the extortionate taxes levied as a result of his disastrous foreign policy. The charter confirmed the freedom of the Church, defined the feudal rights and obligations of various sections of the community, and set out the principles of justice and law. Of lasting significance is the fact that it placed restrictions on the power of the king himself, thereby sowing the seeds of constitutional democracy. The barons had authority to 'claim immediate redress' if the king should 'transgress any of the articles of the peace or of this security'; if redress was not made, they could 'distrain upon and assail us [the king] in every way possible, ... by seizing our castles, lands, possessions, or anything else saving only our own person and those of the queen and our children'.

Magna Carta failed in its attempt to prevent civil war, which broke out between King John and his barons months later. Rebel extremists had refused to honour their part of the agreement, and the king had the charter annulled by Pope Innocent III (1160–1216) in August 1215. A number of revised versions were issued after the death of King John, by the governing council of his young son King Henry III (1207–72) in 1216 and 1217, and by Henry himself in 1225.

Four copies of the original Magna Carta of 1215 have survived to this day: two are in the British Library, one is at Lincoln Cathedral, and the other is at Salisbury Cathedral.

On this day:

Born: Norwegian composer Edvard Grieg (1843); Japanese naval officer and planner of the Pearl Harbor attack Nagano Osami (1880); US singer and songwriter Harry Nilsson (1941); English actor, director and writer Simon Callow (1949)

Died: Burgundian duke Philip, the Good (1467); Eleventh President of the USA James K Polk (1849); Irish writer and reformer Caroline Sheridan Norton (1877); US jazz and popular singer Ella Fitzgerald (1996)

1381 Wat Tyler (died 1381), English rebel and leader of the Peasants' Revolt, was beheaded at Smithfield in London.

1752 By using a kite in a storm, the US statesman, diplomat, printer, publisher, inventor and scientist Benjamin Franklin (1706–90) proved that lightning was electricity.

1836 Arkansas became the 25th state of the USA.

1844 US inventor Charles Goodyear (1800–60) patented his vulcanized rubber process.

1846 A treaty was signed between the USA and the UK to settle the boundary dispute between the USA and Canada.

1887 British cooper Carlisle D Graham went over Niagara Falls in a barrel for the third time.

1915 The first meeting of the Women's Institute (WI) in the UK took place in North Wales.

1919 British aviators John Alcock (1892–1919) and Arthur Whitten Brown (1886–1948) completed the first non-stop transatlantic flight, from Newfoundland to Ireland in a Vickers-Vimy biplane, in just over 16 hours.

1969 Georges Pompidou (1911–74) was elected president of France.

1977 Spain held its first free parliamentary election since the beginning of the Spanish Civil War in 1936.

1996 An IRA bomb caused extensive damage and injuries to 200 people in a central Manchester shopping centre.

16
June

yes and how he kissed me under the Moorish wall and I thought well as well him as another and then I asked him with my eyes to ask again yes and then he asked me would I yes to say yes my mountain flower and first I put my arms around him yes and drew him down to me so he could feel my breasts all perfume yes and his heart was going like mad and yes I said yes I will Yes.

James Joyce, *Ulysses*, closing words (1922).

On 16 June 1904, the Irish writer James Joyce (1882–1941) and his future wife, Nora Barnacle (1884–1951), 'walked out' together for the first time. Ten years later, Joyce commemorated this event by setting his novel *Ulysses*, which recounts the events of a single day in the lives of Leopold Bloom and Stephen Dedalus as they wander through Dublin, on 16 June 1904. *Ulysses* was inspired by Homer's *Odyssey*, an epic poem about the adventures of the Greek hero Odysseus (Latin name, Ulysses), represented by Bloom in Joyce's novel. Odysseus's faithful wife, Penelope, is represented by Molly Bloom (Leopold's wife), whose unpunctuated monologue forms the final chapter of the book.

Joyce's longest and most ambitious work, *Ulysses* was serialized in the US magazine *The Little Review* from 1918 and published in Paris in 1922, but was initially deemed too obscene for publication in the UK. This ban was lifted in the 1930s, and the novel was highly acclaimed by those who were not too daunted by the content and structure to read it to the end. Since the mid-1950s, Joyceans all over the world have celebrated 16 June as **Bloomsday**. In Dublin, the festivities involve readings from *Ulysses* and re-enactments of key scenes at various locations, as well as more general merrymaking in the pubs and restaurants of the city. Similarly, in other parts of the world, the celebrations centre on acting out sections of the novel in public, and encouraging an ever wider audience to read the works of Joyce.

On this day:

Born: Apache leader Geronimo (1829); English-born US comic actor Stan Laurel (1890); English politician Enoch Powell (1912); US writer Joyce Carol Oates (1938)

Died: English soldier John Churchill, 1st Duke of Marlborough (1722); Hungarian politician and prime minister Imre Nagy (1958); US rocket pioneer Wernher von Braun (1977); Japanese empress Nagako (2000)

1487 The Battle of Stoke, the last battle in the Wars of the Roses, took place.

1880 The ladies of General Booth's (1829–1912) Salvation Army first displayed their distinctive black bonnets during a march from Hackney to Whitechapel.

1903 Pepsi-Cola was officially registered as a trademark with the US Patent Office.

1903 US car engineer and manufacturer Henry Ford (1863–1947) founded his motor manufacturing company.

1935 The New Deal programme began; it was designed by US President Franklin D Roosevelt (1882–1945) to help the country recover from the Great Depression.

1961 Russian ballet dancer Rudolf Nureyev (1938–93) defected to the West while appearing in Paris with the Kirov Ballet.

1963 Valentina Tereshkova (born 1937) became the first woman in space as part of the USSR's Vostok 6 mission.

1976 In Soweto, near Johannesburg, South African security forces fired on a crowd of protestors opposing the compulsory use of the Afrikaans language in black schools; over 300 people were killed.

17 June

On this day in 1972, five burglars were arrested in Washington, DC. They had broken into the Democratic National Committee headquarters at an office and hotel complex called Watergate, a name that was to become synonymous with political scandal. Photographic equipment and electronic bugging devices were found at the scene of the crime, and a number of links were subsequently discovered between the burglary and Republican President Richard Nixon's (1913–94) campaign for re-election.

Vigorous denials of any White House involvement enabled Nixon to return to power after the November 1972 election, but his days as president were numbered. The media had already begun to uncover other tales of political corruption and espionage, and the Watergate investigation revealed a cover-up, despite Nixon's famous promise in April 1973 that there would be 'no whitewash at the White House'. A number of presidential aides and advisers resigned, and Nixon's reluctance to hand over unabridged tape recordings of incriminating conversations with his staff ultimately led to a call for his impeachment. In August 1974 he became the first US president to resign from office, but an unconditional pardon granted by his successor, Gerald Ford (born 1913), ensured that he escaped any further punishment.

On this day:

Born: English evangelist and founder of Methodism John Wesley (1703); French composer Charles Gounod (1818); English comedienne and actress Beryl Reid (1920); English politician Ken Livingstone (1945); US singer Barry Manilow (1946)

Died: English essayist and politician Joseph Addison (1719); English Benedictine monk and cardinal Basil Hume (1999); Scottish churchman and cardinal Thomas Winning (2001); US chemist and Nobel Prize winner Donald Cram (2001)

1775 British troops won the Battle of Bunker Hill during the American War of Independence.

1789 In France, the Third Estate proclaimed itself the French National Assembly.

1867 The first operation under antiseptic conditions was performed at Glasgow Infirmary on Isabella Lister by her brother, surgeon Joseph Lister (1827–1912).

1940 World War II – over 2,500 lives were lost when the troop ship *Lancastria* was sunk by German aircraft off the coast of France.

1944 Iceland became an independent republic.

1959 US entertainer Liberace (1919–87) was awarded libel damages of £8,000 after the *Daily Mirror* implied he was a homosexual.

1967 China exploded its first hydrogen bomb.

1974 An IRA bomb attack injured eleven people at the Houses of Parliament in London.

1991 The South African parliament voted to end the race classification on which apartheid policies were based.

> *So great a soldier taught us there*
> *What long-enduring hearts could do*
> *In that world-earthquake, Waterloo!*
>
> Alfred, Lord Tennyson, 'Ode on the Death of the Duke of Wellington' (1852).

The Battle of Waterloo was fought on this day in 1815. Earlier that year the French emperor Napoleon I (1769–1821), previously defeated by the allied forces of Europe, had returned from exile on the island of Elba, raised a new army, and marched into Belgium. Just before midday on 18 June he launched an attack on the Duke of Wellington's (1769–1852) army of British, Dutch, Belgian and German soldiers stationed near the village of Waterloo, south of Brussels. After five hours of fighting, Wellington's forces were reinforced by the Prussian troops of Field Marshal von Blücher (1742–1819), who played a crucial (and sometimes forgotten) role in the subsequent victory. The Prussians had been defeated – but not destroyed – by the French two days earlier, at Ligny, and Napoleon's delay in commencing battle at Waterloo, due to the sodden state of the ground, gave them time to regroup and return to the fray.

Napoleon's defeat at Waterloo brought his brief return to power to an end. Four days later he abdicated, for the second time, and the following month he was banished to St Helena, where he died on 5 May 1821.

On this day:

Born: French politician Édouard Daladier (1884); Russian duchess Anastasia Romanov (1901); US novelist Jerzy Kosinski (1933); English songwriter, vocalist and musician with the Beatles Sir Paul McCartney (1942)

Died: English writer and champion of the poor William Cobbett (1835); Russian novelist Maxim Gorky (1936); US actress

Ethel Barrymore (1959); US radical journalist I F Stone (1989)

1155 Frederick I, Barbarossa (1123–1190) was crowned Holy Roman Emperor.

1812 The US Congress declared war on the UK over trade restrictions.

1953 Egypt was declared a republic, with General Mohammed Neguib (1901–84) as its first president.

1958 The première of the opera *Noye's Fludde*, by Benjamin Britten (1913–76), was held at the Aldeburgh Festival.

1975 The UK's first North Sea oil came ashore.

1979 US President Jimmy Carter (born 1924) and Soviet president Leonid Brezhnev (1906–82) signed the Strategic Arms Limitation Talks (SALT) Treaty II in Vienna, Austria.

1983 The USA's first female astronaut, Sally Ride (born 1951), went into space on board the space shuttle *Challenger*.

1998 The British government announced the introduction of a National Minimum Wage from 1 April 1999.

1999 Violent anti-capitalist demonstrations in London resulted in over 50 people injured and 16 arrests; the protests were timed to coincide with the opening of the G8 summit in Germany.

2000 At Dover, the bodies of 58 illegal immigrants from China were found in a Dutch-registered container lorry which had just arrived from the Belgian port of Zeebrugge.

19 June

On this day in 1885, the Statue of Liberty arrived in the harbour of New York City, in the form of 350 pieces of copper packed in more than 200 crates. A gift from France, designed by the French sculptor Frédéric Auguste Bartholdi (1834–1904), it was reassembled at its destination and dedicated by President Grover Cleveland (1837–1908) in October 1886. The 300ft statue was originally called 'Liberty Enlightening the World'. On its pedestal are engraved the following lines:

> *Give me your tired, your poor,*
> *Your huddled masses yearning to breathe free,*
> *The wretched refuse of your teeming shore.*
> *Send these, the homeless, tempest-tossed to me.*
> *I lift my lamp beside the golden door.*
>
> Emma Lazarus, 'The New Colossus' (1883).

On this day:

Born: French mathematician, physicist, theologian and man of letters Blaise Pascal (1623); Scottish field marshal Earl Haig (1861); German-born British biochemist and Nobel Prize winner Sir Ernst Chain (1906); Burmese political leader Aung San Suu Kyi (1945); Indian-born British novelist Salman Rushdie (1947)

Died: Scottish novelist and dramatist J M Barrie (1937); US actress Jean Arthur (1991); English novelist and Nobel Prize winner Sir William Golding (1993); Japanese statesman and prime minister Noboru Takeshita (2000)

1464 The first mail service was set up by decree of Louis XI of France (1423–83), although it only operated for the king and the royal court.

1846 The first competitive baseball game was played between the New York Nine and the Knickerbockers at the Elysian Fields, Hoboken, New Jersey, USA.

1862 Slavery became illegal in US territories.

1961 Kuwait gained full independence from the UK.

1975 An inquest jury in London decided that the missing Lord Lucan (born 1934) was guilty of the murder of his children's nanny, Sandra Rivett.

1978 English cricketer Ian Botham (born 1955) became the first player in the game's history to score a century and take eight wickets in a single Test match innings.

1997 The fast-food chain McDonald's was awarded a partial victory, and £60,000 libel damages, in the so-called McLibel case against two environmental campaigners.

1997 William Hague (born 1961) defeated former chancellor Kenneth Clarke (born 1940) to become the youngest Conservative party leader since 1783.

On the 20th of June 1649 there died, in his own house at Rosemary Lane, Richard Brandon, the official executioner for the City of London, and the man who, as is generally supposed, decapitated Charles the First. A rare tract, published at the time, entitled The Confession of the Hangman, states that Brandon acknowledged he had £30 for his pains, all paid him in half-crowns, within an hour after the blow was given.

Chambers Book of Days (1864).

On this day:

Born: German-born French composer Jacques Offenbach (1819); US playwright Lillian Hellman (1907); US film actor Errol Flynn (1909); British television presenter and broadcaster Johnny Morris (1916); US pop and rock musician with the Beach Boys Brian Wilson (1942)

Died: Dutch navigator Willem Barents (1597); Mexican revolutionary Pancho Villa (1923); US gangster Bugsy Siegel (1947); US biochemist Erwin Chargaff (2002)

1756 The infamous Black Hole of Calcutta incident took place, in which an unconfirmed number of British prisoners died.

1789 In France, representatives of the Third Estate met and took the so-called Tennis Court Oath at the Palace of Versailles.

1819 The first steamship to cross the Atlantic, the *Savannah*, reached Liverpool after a voyage lasting more than 27 days.

1837 Queen Victoria (1819–1901) acceded to the British throne on the death of her uncle King William IV (1765–1837).

1863 West Virginia became the 35th state of the USA.

1895 The Kiel Canal, connecting the North Sea with the Baltic, was officially opened by Kaiser Wilhelm II (1859–1941).

1947 The première of the opera *Albert Herring*, by Benjamin Britten (1913–76), was held at Glyndebourne.

1949 US tennis player Gertrude 'Gorgeous Gussie' Moran shocked Wimbledon audiences by wearing lace-trimmed knickers under her short skirt for her appearance on Centre Court.

1960 The BBC's Nan Winton became the first female television newsreader.

1963 The USA and the USSR agreed to set up a 'hot line' to maintain contact in the event of international tension.

1987 The first Rugby World Cup was won by New Zealand on home soil.

1999 The NATO bombing campaign against Yugoslavia came to an end.

21 June

This is the **summer solstice**, the longest day of the year, marking the end of spring and the beginning of summer in the astronomical division of the seasons. In Norway, 'Land of the Midnight Sun', part of the sun's disc is visible above the horizon throughout the night around this time of year, and in the northernmost parts of the UK there is little full darkness:

> *At Edinburgh, the longest day is about 17½ hours. At that season, in Scotland, there is a glow equal to dawn, in the north, through the whole of the brief night. The present writer was able at Edinburgh to read the title-page of a book, by the light of the northern sky, at midnight of the 14th of June 1849. In Shetland, the light at midnight is like a good twilight, and the text of any ordinary book may then be easily read.*
>
> *Chambers Book of Days* (1864).

People often gather at Stonehenge in SW England to watch the sun come up on the morning of the summer solstice. On this day it rises almost directly over a stone known as the Heel Stone (or Hele Stone, perhaps from the

Greek *helios*, sun) and shines through the opening of the horseshoe-shaped arrangement of stones at the centre of the structure. It has been suggested that the stones were aligned in this way for the purposes of sun worship or astronomical calculation, but neither theory has been supported with any conclusive evidence. In relatively recent times, members of modern Druidic and other pagan cults have held ceremonies at Stonehenge at the summer solstice. By the mid-1980s these gatherings were attracting so many people and vehicles that they were controversially banned for several years; in the late 1990s a compromise was reached, granting access to the monument for 12 hours around the time of sunrise on 21 June.

On this day:

Born: American theologian Increase Mather (1639); French philosopher, dramatist, novelist and Nobel Prize winner Jean-Paul Sartre (1905); US actress Jane Russell (1921); French novelist Françoise Sagan (1935); Pakistani politician Benazir Bhutto (1953)

Died: Italian statesman, writer and political philosopher Niccolò Machiavelli (1527); English architect and stage designer Inigo Jones (1652); Russian composer Nikolai Rimsky-Korsakov (1908); US blues singer and guitarist John Lee Hooker (2001); US writer Leon Uris (2003)

1675 The foundation stone of the new St Paul's Cathedral was laid in London, the old one having been destroyed by the Great Fire of 1666.

1788 New Hampshire became the ninth state to ratify the Constitution of the USA, with the effect that the US Constitution came into force.

1868 The première of the opera *Die Meistersinger von Nürnberg*, by Richard Wagner (1813–83), was held in Munich, Germany.

1937 The BBC televised the Wimbledon tennis championships for the first time.

1948 Columbia Records introduced long-playing records with microgrooves, as developed by Dr Peter Goldmark (1906–77).

1963 Cardinal Giovanni Battista Montini (1897–1978) became Pope Paul VI.

1970 English golfer Tony Jacklin (born 1944) became the first Englishman in 50 years to win the US Open Golf Championship.

1977 Menachem Begin (1913–92) became prime minister of Israel; the following year, he won the Nobel Peace Prize.

22 June

The Royal Greenwich Observatory was founded by King Charles II (1630–85) on this day in 1675. Its first Astronomer Royal, John Flamsteed (1646–1719), was instructed to 'apply himself with the most exact care and diligence to the rectifying the tables of the motions of the heavens, and the places of the fixed stars, so as to find out the so much desired longitude of places for the perfecting the art of navigation'. The Observatory was housed in a building designed by Sir Christopher Wren (1632–1723) at Greenwich (on the south bank of the River Thames), which became the source of the prime meridian, longitude 0°. In the 19th and 20th centuries one of its principal tasks was the annual compilation of the *Nautical Almanac*, giving the precise positions of the sun, moon and planets for the benefit of mariners using sextants.

After World War II the institution moved to Herstmonceux Castle in Sussex, then to Cambridge, where it remained until its controversial closure on 31 October 1998. The original building at Greenwich has become a centre for astronomy, part of the National Maritime Museum.

On this day:

Born: German-born US novelist Erich Maria Remarque (1898); English mountaineer and social reformer Sir John Hunt (1910); English cleric and campaigner for nuclear disarmament Bruce Kent (1929); US actress Meryl Streep (1949)

Died: English poet and novelist Walter de la Mare (1956); US film producer David O Selznick (1965); US actress and singer Judy Garland (1969); US actor, dancer and singer Fred Astaire (1987)

1377 At the age of ten, King Richard II (1367–1400) acceded to the English throne.

1535 English prelate and humanist St John Fisher (born 1469) was beheaded for refusing to recognize King Henry VIII (1491–1547) as head of the Church of England.

1611 English navigator Henry Hudson (1550–1611), his son and seven others were cast adrift in arctic conditions in what is now Hudson's Bay, and never seen again.

1679 At the Battle of Bothwell, the Covenanters were defeated by the Duke of Monmouth's (1649–85) troops.

1817 Windham Sadler became the first aeronaut to cross the Irish Sea by balloon.

1911 The coronation of King George V (1865–1936) took place at Westminster Abbey, London.

1911 Liverpool's Royal Liver Clock, known as 'Great George', was started at the precise moment of the king's coronation, with the help of a telephone link.

1941 World War II – Germany invaded the USSR in Operation Barbarossa.

1948 The SS *Empire Windrush* arrived in Tilbury, bringing the first Caribbean migrants to the UK following the end of World War II.

1979 Former Liberal Party leader Jeremy Thorpe (born 1929) was acquitted at the Old Bailey on charges of conspiracy to murder Norman Scott.

1981 In New York City, Mark Chapman (born c.1955) pleaded guilty to the murder of former Beatle John Lennon (1940–80).

23 June

> *If we shadows have offended,*
> *Think but this, and all is mended:*
> *That you have but slumbered here,*
> *While these visions did appear.*
>
> William Shakespeare, *A Midsummer Night's Dream* (1595).

This is **Midsummer Eve** or **Midsummer Night**, also known as **St John's Eve**, although most of the activities associated with it are probably of pagan origin. These include dancing around – or jumping through – bonfires, gathering branches and flowers to decorate the home and ward off evil spirits, and performing divination rituals to ascertain the identity of one's future lover or spouse. The bonfires were traditionally lit on the hilltops, so that they could be seen for many miles, and people danced or walked around them in a clockwise direction, representing the apparent daily motion of the sun. Sometimes blazing torches lit from the bonfire were carried through the surrounding fields and villages. Torchlit processions were also a feature of the Midsummer Eve vigil in larger towns and cities:

> *It was customary in towns to keep a watch walking about during the Midsummer Night, although no such practice might prevail at the place from motives of precaution ... In London, during the middle ages, this watch, consisting of not less than two thousand men, paraded both on this night and on the eves of St Paul's and St Peter's days. The watchmen were provided with cressets, or torches, carried in barred pots on the tops of long poles, which, added to the bonfires on the streets, must have given the town a striking appearance in an age when there was no regular street-lighting. The great came to give their countenance to this marching watch, and made it quite a pageant.*
>
> *Chambers Book of Days* (1864).

Among the plants thought to have particular supernatural power on Midsummer Eve were St John's wort, plantain, orpine, mugwort and hemp. Pieces of orpine (a purple-flowered, broad-leaved plant) were used to make 'Midsummer Men': two stalks of the plant (typically representing a girl and her boyfriend) were left standing side by side overnight; if they were found to be leaning towards each other in the morning, the relationship would be a lasting one. It was also believed that the seed of certain fern plants was visible only on Midsummer Eve, and that those who managed to catch the seed as it fell to the ground would be invisible while they carried it.

On this day:

Born: US sexologist and zoologist Alfred Kinsey (1894); English mathematician Alan Turing (1912); English cricketer Sir Leonard Hutton (1916); US pianist and conductor James Levine (1943)

Died: Spanish explorer Pedro de Mendoza (1537); English traveller Lady Hester Stanhope (1839); US virologist Jonas Salk (1995); Greek politician and prime minister Andreas Papandreou (1996)

1314 The Battle of Bannockburn began in Scotland.

1372 At the Battle of La Rochelle, an English fleet was destroyed by Henry of Castile (1333–79).

1586 The Star Chamber suppressed all provincial printing offices.

1757 Britain's empire in India began with the defeat by English general Robert Clive (1725–74) of Indian forces at the Battle of Plassey in Bengal.

1868 US engineer Christopher Latham Sholes (1819–90) received a patent for the typewriter.

1956 Gamal Abd al-Nasser (1918–70) was elected president of Egypt.

1972 UK Chancellor Anthony Barber (born 1920) announced the intended temporary flotation of the pound.

1985 An Air India aircraft, flying from Toronto, Canada, to London, UK, was blown up off the coast of Ireland, killing all 329 people on board; the bomb was suspected to have been planted by Sikh extremists.

1992 New York Mafia boss John Gotti (1940–2002), known as the Teflon Don, was sentenced to life imprisonment.

1994 South Africa reclaimed its seat at the United Nations General Assembly.

24 June

Although astronomically the summer solstice occurs on 21 June, tradition throughout Europe has taken 24 June to be **Midsummer Day** and the principal feast day of St John the Baptist, who was born six months before Christ. (The date of his death, 29 August, is also a feast day in the Christian Church.) John the Baptist's parents were the priest Zacharias and Elisabeth, who 'both were well stricken in years' (Luke 1.7). Elisabeth was thought to be barren, and on learning from the angel Gabriel that his wife would conceive, Zacharias lost the power of speech until the baby was born and named John. Later, as an itinerant preacher, John baptized people in preparation for the coming of Christ, whom he greeted with the words 'Behold the Lamb of God, which taketh away the sin of the world' (John 1.29). He was imprisoned by Herod Antipas, whom he had condemned for marrying his brother's wife, Herodias; Herod reluctantly had John beheaded at the request of his stepdaughter Salome: 'she, being before instructed of her mother, said, Give me here John Baptist's head in a charger' (Matthew 14.8). On **St John's Day** (or the nearest Sunday) a special sermon is preached from a stone pulpit in St John's Quadrangle at Magdalen College, Oxford. At Penzance in Cornwall, a festival called **Golowan** (literally, 'Feast of John') is held around 24 June. Of ancient origin, the festival was banned in the late 19th century, because of the boisterous nature of some of the activities, but was revived in the early 1990s. Its traditional features include fireworks, a Serpent Dance through the streets of the town, and a Quay Fair at the harbour.

One further Midsummer Day tradition takes place annually in London. The **Knollys Rose Ceremony** dates back to 1381 when a fine was imposed on Sir Robert Knollys (and all his heirs) for building a covered bridge between his two properties on Seething Lane without permission. Each year the fine is paid when a red rose is taken from Seething Lane Gardens and taken by the churchwardens of All Hallows by the Tower to be presented to the Lord Mayor.

On this day:

Born: Austrian-born US physicist and Nobel Prize winner Victor Hess (1883); US boxer Jack Dempsey (1895); Argentinian racing driver Juan Fangio (1911); French film director Claude Chabrol (1930)

Died: Roman emperor Vespasian (AD 79); Italian noblewoman Lucrezia Borgia (1519); 22nd and 24th President of the USA Grover Cleveland (1908); US television actor and comedian Jackie Gleason (1987)

1314 At the Battle of Bannockburn, the Scots, under Robert the Bruce (1274–1329), defeated the much larger English army led by King Edward II (1284–1327).

1497 Italian-born English navigator and explorer John Cabot (c.1450–c.1499) sighted Cape Breton Island and claimed the mainland of North America for England.

1509 The Coronation of King Henry VIII (1491–1547) took place.

1812 Napoleon I (1769–1821) began his invasion of Russia.

1859 The Battle of Solferino took place in Northern Italy, witnessed by Swiss businessman Henri Dunant (1828–1910), whose experience of the event inspired him to found the International Red Cross.

1916 World War I – the First Battle of the Somme began.

1940 World War II – France signed an armistice with Italy.

1963 Zanzibar became internally self-governing, shortly before achieving independence.

1967 The encyclical *Sacerdotalis Caelibatus*, concerning the celibacy of priests, was issued by Pope Paul VI (1897–1978).

1973 The world's oldest statesman, Irish president Éamon de Valera (1882–1975), announced his retirement from politics at the age of 90.

1974 The UK government admitted that it had recently exploded a nuclear device as a test in the USA.

1981 The UK's Humber Bridge opened to traffic.

25 June

This is the date of Custer's Last Stand, the infamous day in 1876 when the US cavalry officer George Armstrong Custer (born 1839) led a column of

some 650 soldiers into battle against thousands of Native American warriors in the valley of the Little Big Horn River. Custer had been ordered to wait for reinforcements before launching the attack, and his decision to 'go it alone' – variously seen as an act of great courage or great folly – resulted in the death of 267 officers and men, including Custer himself.

On this day:

Born: Russian tsar Nicholas I (1796); Anglo-Irish writer and nationalist Erskine Childers (1870); English naval commander and statesman Earl Mountbatten (1900); US film director Sydney Lumet (1924)

Died: English comedian Tony Hancock (1968); Scottish biologist and Nobel Prize winner John Boyd Orr (1971); US composer and lyricist Johnny Mercer (1976); French naval officer and underwater explorer Jacques Cousteau (1997)

1788 Virginia became the tenth state to ratify the Constitution of the USA.

1867 A patent for barbed wire was granted to one Lucien B Smith.

1932 The first England-India Test cricket match began at Lord's cricket ground in London.

1950 The Korean War began when forces from North Korea invaded the South.

1953 English murderer John Reginald Christie (1898–1953) was sentenced to death for the murder of four women.

1967 The first worldwide live satellite programme, *Our World*, was broadcast.

1975 Mozambique achieved independence from Portugal.

1991 The former Yugoslav republics of Slovenia and Croatia declared their independence.

1997 An accident occurred in space when an unmanned cargo ship collided with Russian space station Mir, causing considerable damage.

On this day in 1284, 130 children were allegedly led out of the town of Hamelin in N Germany by the Pied Piper, a handsome young man wearing colourful attire and playing a pipe. According to an embellished form of the legend that dates from the mid-16th century, the Pied Piper had rid the town of rats and had not been paid his agreed fee, so he lured the children away as an act of revenge. The children disappeared into a nearby hill and were never seen by their parents again.

On this day:

Born: Scottish physicist and mathematician William Thomson, Lord Kelvin (1824); German aviation designer and engineer Wilhelm Messerschmitt (1898); Hungarian-born US actor Peter Lorre (1904); Italian conductor Claudio Abbado (1933)

Died: Roman emperor Julian, the Apostate (AD 363); Spanish soldier and conqueror of Peru Francisco Pizarro (1541); English inventor of the spinning mule Samuel Crompton (1827); US public opinion pollster George Gallup (1984); US politician Strom Thurmond (2003)

1483 Richard, Duke of Gloucester, began to rule as King Richard III (1452–85).

1843 Hong Kong was declared a British crown colony.

1846 The Corn Laws were passed in the UK, in an unsuccessful attempt to stabilize wheat prices.

1906 The first Grand Prix motor race took place at Le Mans, France.

1909 The Victoria and Albert Museum was reopened in London by King Edward VII (1841–1910).

1917 World War I – US troops first arrived in France.

1945 The United Nations Charter was signed by representatives of 50 countries at a conference in San Francisco, USA.

1959 Sweden's Ingemar Johansson (born 1932) knocked out the USA's

Floyd Patterson (born 1935) to become world heavyweight boxing champion.

1959 Queen Elizabeth II (born 1926) and US President Dwight D Eisenhower (1890–1969) took part in an opening ceremony for the St Lawrence Seaway, linking the Great Lakes to the Atlantic Ocean.

1960 Madagascar, as the Malagasy Republic, became independent from France.

1963 US President John F Kennedy (1917–63) made a speech in West Berlin, offering US solidarity to the citizens of West Germany and declaring 'Ich bin ein Berliner'.

2000 The publicly funded international Human Genome Project and a US private company, Celera Genomics, jointly announced the completion of a working draft of the human genetic blueprint – the 'Book of Life'.

27 June

> *Science may have found a cure for most evils; but it has found no remedy for the worst of them all – the apathy of human beings.*
>
> Helen Keller, *My Religion* (1927).

Helen Adams Keller was born on this day in 1880 in Alabama. A severe illness in infancy deprived her of sight and hearing, but intensive tuition from Anne Sullivan (1866–1936), using methods based on the sense of touch, gave her the gift of language. She became an accomplished student, graduating from Radcliffe College in 1904, and pursued a successful career as a lecturer, writer and campaigner for the disabled. She died in 1968.

On this day:

Born: French king Louis XII (1462); US poet Paul Laurence Dunbar (1872); Portuguese cellist Guilhermina Suggia (1888); French actress Isabelle Adjani (1955)

Died: Italian artist and art historian Giorgio Vasari (1574); English naval commander Samuel Hood (1816); US religious leader and founder of the Mormons Joseph Smith (1844); US film and stage actor Jack Lemmon (2001)

1693 The first women's magazine, *The Ladies' Mercury*, was published in London; it included a page of questions and answers which became known as a 'problem page'.

1743 King George II (1683–1760), the last British monarch personally to lead his troops into battle, defeated the French at the Battle of Dettingen.

1893 A major stock market crash began in New York City, leading to a severe economic depression.

1905 A mutiny took place on board the Russian battleship *Potemkin*, in Odessa harbour on the Black Sea.

1944 World War II – the Allies recaptured the port of Cherbourg from the Germans.

1950 US President Harry S Truman (1884–1972) ordered US air and sea forces to support South Korea in battle against North Korea.

1954 In the USSR, the world's first atomic power station went into production near Moscow.

1961 English prelate Arthur Michael Ramsey (1904–88) was enthroned as the 100th Archbishop of Canterbury.

1991 Yugoslav tanks, troops and aircraft invaded the newly independent republic of Slovenia.

28 June

This is **St Peter's Eve**, which was formerly marked by festivities and rituals similar to those of Midsummer Eve (23 June). Fairies and witches were said to fly abroad throughout the period between these two dates. In parts of Lincolnshire, girls believed that they would dream of their future husband if they went to bed on 28 June with a bunch of keys (St Peter's symbol) tied with a lock of their hair.

On this day:

Born: Flemish painter Peter Paul Rubens (1577); French political philosopher, educationalist and author Jean Jacques Rousseau (1712); Italian dramatist, novelist, short-story writer and Nobel Prize winner Luigi Pirandello (1867); French-born US experimental surgeon and Nobel Prize winner Alexis Carrel (1873); US film actor and director Mel Brooks (1926)

Died: Fourth President of the USA James Madison (1836); English field marshal Lord Raglan (1855); Irish explorer Robert Burke (1861); Spanish pianist and conductor José Iturbi (1980); English music critic and impresario Sir William Glock (2000)

1645 Royalist troops lost the city of Carlisle during the English Civil War.

1746 Flora MacDonald (1722–90) rescued Bonnie Prince Charlie (1720–88) after his defeat at Culloden by dressing him as a woman and escaping by boat to Portree on the island of Skye.

1838 Queen Victoria (1819–1901) was crowned in Westminster Abbey, a year after having ascended the throne.

1914 In Sarajevo, a Serbian nationalist assassinated Archduke Franz Ferdinand (1863–1914), the heir to the Austro-Hungarian throne, setting in motion the events that led to World War I.

1919 World War I – the Treaty of Versailles between Germany and the Allies was signed, fixing reparation settlements and marking the end of the war.

1935 US President Franklin D Roosevelt (1882–1945) ordered the construction of a national gold vault at Fort Knox in Kentucky, USA.

1939 The first transatlantic passenger airline service, from New York City, USA, to Southampton, UK, in a Boeing 314 flying boat, began.

1950 The city of Seoul in South Korea was captured by North Korean forces.

1976 The Seychelles became an independent republic within the British Commonwealth.

1991 Former British prime minister Margaret Thatcher (born 1925) announced her intention to give up her seat in the House of Commons.

2001 Former Yugoslav president Slobodan Milosevic (born 1941) was handed over to the international criminal tribunal for the former Yugoslavia, based in the Hague, where he would face indictment for crimes against humanity and for violation of the Geneva Convention.

Feast day of **St Peter and St Paul**, apostles of Christ who were martyred at Rome during Emperor Nero's (AD 37–68) persecution of the Christians.

On this day:

Born: US astronomer George Ellery Hale (1868); French statesman Robert Schuman (1886); US civil rights activist Stokely Carmichael (1941); Sri Lankan politician and prime minister Chandrika Kumaratunga (1945)

Died: English architect and inventor of the hansom cab Joseph Hansom (1882); Polish pianist, composer and patriot Ignacy Paderewski (1941); US film actress Jayne Mansfield (1967); French couturier Pierre Balmain (1982); US singer Rosemary Clooney (2002); US film and stage actress Katharine Hepburn (2003)

48 BC Julius Caesar (100 or 102–44 BC) defeated Pompey (106–48 BC) at Pharsalia in the most bloody battle of the Roman Civil War.

1613 London's Globe Theatre burned down during a performance of *Henry VIII* by William Shakespeare (1564–1616).

1855 The *Daily Telegraph* was first published in London.

1868 The Press Association news agency was founded.

1916 Irish patriot and British consular official Roger Casement (1864–1916) was found guilty of treason in a Dublin court and sentenced to death.

1960 The BBC's Television Centre opened in West London.

1974 Isabel Perón (born 1931), taking over from her husband, Juan Perón (1895–1974) because of his illness, was sworn in as the first woman president of Argentina.

1980 Vigdís Finnbogadóttir (born 1930) was elected president of Iceland, becoming Europe's first democratically elected woman Head of State.

1986 English entrepreneur Richard Branson (born 1950) broke the record for an Atlantic crossing in his powerboat *Challenger*.

1992 President Mohamed Boudiaf (1919–92) of Algeria was assassinated.

2001 Ghanaian diplomat Kofi Annan (born 1938) was elected to a second term as Secretary-General of the United Nations.

30 June

> *An act of the British parliament, dated June 30, 1837, put an end to the use of the pillory in the United Kingdom, a mode of punishment so barbarous, and at the same time so indefinite in its severity, that we can only wonder it should not have been extinguished long before.*
>
> *Chambers Book of Days* (1864).

The pillory consisted of a wooden frame mounted on a post with holes for the head and hands. Victims were sentenced to stand in the pillory for a certain number of hours, sometimes on more than one day, while being subjected to verbal and physical abuse from the general public. Some were lucky enough to have the sympathy of the crowd: when the satirist Daniel Defoe (1660–1731) was pilloried in 1703, the people threw garlands – rather than rotten eggs – and recited his poem *A Hymn to the Pillory*, a mock ode that he had written during his imprisonment.

On this day:

Born: English poet John Gay (1685); English painter Sir Stanley Spencer (1891); English political scientist and socialist Harold Laski (1893); US singer and actress Lena Horne (1917); US boxer Mike Tyson (1966)

Died: Aztec emperor Montezuma II (1520); English mathematician William Oughtred (1660); English detective-story writer Margery Allingham (1966); English writer Nancy Mitford (1973); US country music guitarist Chet Atkins (2001)

30 June

1859 French acrobat Charles Blondin (1824–97) crossed Niagara Falls on a tightrope.

1894 London's Tower Bridge was officially opened.

1934 In Germany, during what came to be known as the Night of the Long Knives, Adolf Hitler (1889–1945) ordered the summary execution of those in the Nazi Party who opposed him.

1946 The USA began conducting nuclear bomb tests in the Marshall Islands in the Pacific Ocean.

1954 A total eclipse of the sun was visible to watchers in North America, Europe and Asia.

1971 The three crew members of the Soviet space mission Soyuz 11 were found dead, following a sudden drop in cabin pressure, after appearing to land safely.

1980 The British sixpenny piece ceased to be legal tender.

1992 Northern Ireland Protestant leaders and the Irish government met in their first talks for 70 years.

1992 Former prime minister Margaret Thatcher (born 1925) took her place in the House of Lords.

1994 US skater Tonya Harding (born 1971) was stripped of her national championship title and barred for life from the US Figure Skating Association for her part in an attack on her rival Nancy Kerrigan (born 1969).

Gemstone: Ruby
Flower: Larkspur or waterlily

> *Married in July with flowers ablaze,*
> *Bittersweet memories on after days.*
>
> Traditional rhyme.

> *July is now what our old poets loved to call 'sweet summer-time, when the leaves are green and long,' for in such brief word-painting did they picture this pleasant season of the year; and, during this hot month, we sigh while perusing the ancient ballad-lore, and wish we could recall the past, were it only to enjoy a week with Robin Hood and his merry men in the free old forests ... We feel the harness chafe in which we have hitherto so willingly worked, amid the 'fever and the fret' of the busy city, and pine to get away to some place where we can hear the murmur of the sea, or what is nearest the sound – the rustle of the summer leaves.*
>
> *Chambers Book of Days* (1864).

Origins

July, the seventh month of the year and the fifth month of the Roman calendar, is named after Julius Caesar, who was born on 12 July. Its Latin name was changed from *Quinctilis* (from *quinctus*, fifth) to *Iulius* after Caesar's assassination in 44 BC.

Characteristics

The patchwork landscape of the countryside is transformed this month, as crops ripen and fields turn from green to gold. There is little if any respite between the end of haymaking and the beginning of harvest, and it was formerly considered unlucky (or simply inconvenient) to marry at this time: 'They that wive 'twixt sickle and scythe shall never thrive.'

Soft fruits, such as strawberries, raspberries and blackcurrants, become available in abundance – on garden bushes, in shops and supermarkets, and at 'pick your own' fruit farms – and amateur jam-makers often find themselves slaving over a hot preserving-pan late into the night. The first full month of summer, July also marks the start of the holiday season.

History

Anglo-Saxon names for the month include *Heymonath* or *Maedmonath*, referring respectively to haymaking and the flowering of the meadows. The modern word *July* was formerly pronounced with the stress on the first syllable, as in *duly* and *truly*. The change in pronunciation took place in the 18th century, perhaps to make the name sound less like *June*.

Weather

> *Then came hot July, boiling like to fire,*
> *That all his garments he had cast away;*
> *Upon a lion raging yet with ire*
> *He boldly rode, and made him to obey:*
> . . .
> *Behind his back a scythe, and by his side*
> *Under his belt he bore a sickle circling wide.*
>
> Edmund Spenser, *The Faerie Queene* (1609).

Although July is one of the hottest months of the year, weather lore seems to be preoccupied with rain: 'If the first of July be rainy weather, 'twill rain more or less for four weeks together.' Similar predictions are associated with 2 July in Norway and some other European countries, 4 July in Scotland, and, most famously, St Swithin's Day (15 July).

Crop circles

July is the month when circular flattened patches begin to appear in fields of standing corn. This phenomenon dates from the early 1970s, although

there are isolated earlier examples. It has been variously suggested that crop circles are formed by visiting extraterrestrials, underlying energy fields, freak weather conditions, or pranksters. Supporters of each of these theories have taken great pains to demonstrate that the others are implausible, without conclusively proving their own to be correct. The steady increase in the complexity and number of crop circles is seen by some as evidence of 'copycat' hoaxing, by others as a sign that the force responsible for their creation is developing a more sophisticated means of communication.

Non-fixed notable dates

Non-fixed notable dates in July include:

Henley Royal Regatta: Takes place in the first week of July on a stretch of the River Thames at Henley-on-Thames in Oxfordshire. The Regatta began in 1839 with a single afternoon of rowing races; it was extended to two days in 1840, three days in 1886, four days in 1906, and five days in 1986. One of the highlights of the British social calendar (as well as being a major sporting event) it has enjoyed royal patronage since 1851.

Honiton Fair: The annual fair at Honiton in Devon, dating from the 13th century, begins on the first Tuesday after 19 July and lasts for three days. The town crier officially opens the fair by parading down the High Street with a golden glove at the end of a long pole decorated with garlands of flowers and announcing, 'Oyez, Oyez, Oyez! The glove is up! The fair has begun! No man shall be arrested until the glove is taken down! God save the Queen!' After this ceremony, hot pennies are thrown to the onlookers from the windows of various pubs and scrambled for by local children. Gloves feature in other fairs, such as the Exeter Lammas Fair (see 1 August).

Tolpuddle Festival: At Tolpuddle in Dorset, a three-day festival ending on the third Sunday in July commemorates the Tolpuddle Martyrs and their contribution to trade unionism. The Tolpuddle Martyrs were a group of six workers (George and James Loveless, Thomas and John Stanfield, James Brine and James Hammett) who were punished with transportation to Australia for their activities in the Friendly Society of Agricultural Labourers, a union founded in 1833 to campaign for fair wages. The festival features music, drama, speeches by trade unionists and other political figures, and the laying of wreaths on the grave of James Hammett (the only one of the six who is buried in Tolpuddle). It culminates on Sunday afternoon with the Tolpuddle Martyrs Procession, in which thousands of people with banners parade through the streets of the village, accompanied by marching bands.

Dunmow Flitch Trials: Every four years the Essex village of Great Dunmow holds the Dunmow Flitch Trials. In this famous ceremony, which may date from as far back as the 12th century, a married couple attempts to prove to a judge and jury that in 'twelvemonth and a day' they have 'not wisht themselves unmarried again'. If their case is proved, they win a flitch (or side) of bacon, and are carried aloft through cheering crowds. In recent years a number of celebrities have appeared as prosecutor.

Domhnach Chrom Dubh: In Ireland, the last Sunday in July is Domhnach Chrom Dubh (Black Crom's Sunday), a day on which pilgrims climb hills and mountains, saying prayers along the way and attending a special mass at the summit. The festival is a christianized form of a pagan tradition, Chrom (or Crom) Dubh being an ancient Celtic god.

July

> *O Canada! our home and native land!*
> *True patriot love in all thy sons command.*
> *With glowing hearts we see thee rise,*
> *The True North strong and free!*
> *From far and wide, O Canada,*
> *We stand on guard for thee.*
> *God keep our land glorious and free!*
> *O Canada, we stand on guard for thee.*
> *O Canada, we stand on guard for thee.*
>
> Canadian national anthem.

This is **Canada Day**, formerly known as **Dominion Day**, commemorating the Canadian Confederation of 1867: the union of Ontario, Quebec, Nova Scotia and New Brunswick in the Dominion of Canada. It is celebrated throughout the country with parades, fireworks and other festivities. At Parliament Hill in Ottawa, the nation's capital city, crowds gather for a day of ceremonial and entertainment, with marching bands, Changing the Guard, aerobatics and street performers.

On this day:

Born: French novelist George Sand (1804); German-born US film director William Wyler (1902); English aviator Amy Johnson (1903); US track and field athlete Carl Lewis (1961); US actress Liv Tyler (1977)

Died: US inventor of vulcanized rubber Charles Goodyear (1860); French composer Erik Satie (1925); Argentinian soldier and statesman Juan Perón (1974); US actor Walter Matthau (2000)

1690 The Battle of the River Boyne was fought in Ireland – Protestant William of Orange (1650–1702) defeated the Jacobite Catholic forces under James II (1633–1701) supported by the French; it is celebrated on 12 July because of the change from the Julian to the Gregorian calendar.

1837 The civil registration of births, marriages and deaths was introduced in England and Wales: in 1538 the Lord Chancellor, Thomas Cromwell (c.1485–1540), had introduced a parochial system of registration based upon baptisms, marriages and burials.

1847 The first adhesive stamps in the USA went on sale: the five cents featured Benjamin Franklin (1706–90) and the ten cents depicted George Washington (1732–99).

1858 A paper by Charles Darwin (1809–82) outlining his *Theory of Evolution by Natural Selection* was presented to the British Linnaean Society, along with a similar paper by Alfred Wallace (1823–1913): neither man was present at the historic occasion.

1863 In the American Civil War the Battle of Gettysburg began as General Robert E Lee (1807–70) launched the Confederate attack of Northern troops.

1912 The first Royal Variety Command Performance took place at the Palace Theatre in London's West End.

1916 World War I – the Battle of the Somme began. A major British offensive against German troops in north-western France, it developed into the bloodiest battle in world history.

1937 The world's first telephone emergency service began in the UK.

1940 World War II – the Channel Islands were invaded by German troops.

1941 The first television commercial – a ten-second advertisement for a Bulova watch – was shown on New York station WNBT (later WNBC-TV).

1967 Regular colour television broadcasts began on BBC2.

1969 Queen Elizabeth II (born 1926) invested her son Charles (born 1948) as Prince of Wales at Caernarvon Castle.

1971 In the USA the 26th Amendment was ratified, changing the voting age from 21 to 18.

1977 Virginia Wade (born 1945) defeated Betty Stove (born 1945) to win the women's singles title at Wimbledon.

1997 Hong Kong reverted to Chinese sovereignty.

1998 David Trimble (born 1944) was elected First Minister of Northern Ireland with Seamus Mallon (born 1936) as deputy leader at the inaugural session of the Northern Irish Assembly at Stormont.

1999 The Scottish Parliament took up its full legislative powers following an official opening ceremony.

2 July

> *Once writing has become your major vice and greatest pleasure only death can stop it.*
>
> Ernest Hemingway, interview in *Paris Review* (Spring 1958).

The US writer Ernest Hemingway shot himself on 2 July 1961 at his home in Ketchum, Ohio. His wife issued a statement claiming that the death was accidental, but Hemingway had been suffering from depression, and it is generally assumed that he committed suicide – as did his father, brother, sister and granddaughter (the actress Margaux Hemingway).

Born in Chicago in 1899, Hemingway had an eventful life, working as an ambulance driver during World War I and a war correspondent in the Spanish Civil War and World War II. He was married four times, developed a reputation as a drinker and brawler, and had a passion for big-game hunting and bullfighting. His writing career began in journalism and progressed through short stories and novels to the ultimate accolade, the Nobel Prize for Literature in 1954. Among his best-known works are *A Farewell to Arms* (1929), *Death in the Afternoon* (1932), *For Whom the Bell Tolls* (1940) and *The Old Man and the Sea* (1952).

On this day:

Born: English Archbishop of Canterbury Thomas Cranmer (1489); German composer Christoph Gluck (1714); English physicist and Nobel Prize winner Sir William Bragg (1862); English bandleader and theatrical impresario Jack Hylton (1892); Mexican politician Vicente Fox Quesada (1942)

Died: English ecclesiastic and Bishop of Winchester St Swithin (862); French political philosopher, educationalist and author Jean Jacques Rousseau (1778); German physician and founder of homeopathy Samuel Hahnemann (1843); Northern Irish motorcycle racer Joey Dunlop (2000)

1266 In the Treaty of Perth the Norwegians ceded the Western Isles and the Isle of Man to the Scots.

1644 In the English Civil War, the troops led by Oliver Cromwell (1599–1658) defeated the Royalist Cavaliers of Prince Rupert (1619–82) at the Battle of Marston Moor near York.

1900 The German Zeppelin airship departed on its maiden flight from Manzell on the banks of Lake Constance.

1938 US tennis champion Helen Wills Moody (1905–98) won her eighth Wimbledon women's singles title; her record was eventually broken by Martina Navratilova (born 1956).

1964 US President Lyndon B Johnson (1908–73) signed the US Civil Rights Act, prohibiting racial discrimination.

1985 Andrei Gromyko (1909–89) became president of the USSR.

2000 Football world champions France beat Italy to win the final of Euro 2000 in Rotterdam.

2002 Millionaire adventurer Steve Fossett (born 1944) became the first person to circumnavigate the globe alone in a balloon.

3 July

On this day:

Born: Irish politician Henry Grattan (1746); Czech-born Austrian novelist Franz Kafka (1883); Czech-born British dramatist Sir Tom Stoppard (1937); New Zealand cricketer Sir Richard Hadlee (1951)

Died: French queen Marie de Médicis (1642); English guitarist with the Rolling Stones Brian Jones (1969); US singer with the Doors and poet Jim Morrison (1971); Spanish architect Enric Miralles (2000); Canadian novelist Mordecai Richler (2001)

1608 French explorer Samuel de Champlain (c.1570–1635) founded Quebec.

1863 In the American Civil War the Battle of Gettysburg ended with a Union victory.

1886 German engineer Karl Benz (1844–1929) gave a public demonstration of the first motor car, patented earlier that year. He drove around the streets of Mannheim, Germany, reaching a top speed of 10mph.

1890 Idaho became the 43rd state of the USA.

1898 Joshua Slocum (1844–c.1910) landed in his fishing boat *Spray* at Newport, Rhode Island, having completed the first solo circumnavigation of the globe.

1920 Bill Tilden (1893–1953) became the first US tennis player to win the Wimbledon men's singles title.

1928 John Logie Baird (1888–1946), Scottish television pioneer, made the world's first colour television transmission from London's Covent Garden.

1938 The London and North Eastern Railway's engine *Mallard* became the world's fastest steam locomotive with a speed of 126mph.

1940 World War II – British ships destroyed the French fleet in Oran and Mers-el-Kebir, Algeria, to prevent vessels falling into enemy hands; over 1,000 French died.

1962 French president Charles de Gaulle (1890–1970) declared Algeria as independent from France.

1987 Former German SS officer Klaus Barbie (1913–91) was sentenced to life imprisonment for crimes against humanity committed while he was in charge of the Gestapo in Lyons during World War II.

4 July

I'm a Yankee Doodle Dandy
A Yankee Doodle, do or die;
A real live nephew of my Uncle Sam's
Born on the fourth of July.

George M Cohan, 'Yankee Doodle Boy' (1904).

In the USA this is **Independence Day**, a holiday in all states and territories, commemorating the formal adoption by the Continental Congress of the Declaration of Independence on 4 July 1776. This historic document, proclaiming the secession of the 13 North American colonies from Great Britain, was largely drafted by Thomas Jefferson, who succeeded John Adams as president of the USA in 1801. (Coincidentally, both Adams and Jefferson died on Independence Day in 1826.)

> *We hold these truths to be self-evident, that all men are created equal, that they are endowed by their Creator with certain unalienable rights, that among these are Life, Liberty, and the Pursuit of Happiness. … That whenever any form of Government becomes destructive of these ends, it is the Right of the People to alter or abolish it, and to institute new Government, laying its foundation on such principles, and organizing its powers in such form, as to them shall seem most likely to effect their Safety and Happiness.*
>
> Declaration of Independence (1776).

The first official celebrations took place in Massachusetts in 1781. By the mid-1800s the tradition had become widespread and today the day is still marked by public celebrations throughout the USA. Some towns hold traditional celebrations, such as Woodstock, Vermont, where patriotic speeches (known as **Fourth of July Orations**) are given and '1890' flags are made. One of the largest 4 July parades takes place in Atlanta, while the oldest continuous celebration takes place in Bristol, Rhode Island. Established in 1785, the festivities now include a popular parade and spectacular fireworks finale.

Other activities include readings of the Declaration of Independence, as well as sporting events, concerts and more informal family festivities (notably picnics and barbecues). Eating is central to one of Coney Island's 4 July traditions. **Nathan's Famous 4th of July Hot Dog Eating Contest** has been held there every year since 1916. Contested by the winners of 19 regional qualifying contests throughout the world, plus the defending champion, competitors try to eat as many hot dogs as they can in twelve minutes. The record set in 2002 by Takeru Kobayashi of Japan was an astonishing 50½.

On this day:

Born: French balloonist and inventor of the parachute Jean Pierre Blanchard (1753); Irish doctor and philanthropist Thomas Barnardo (1845); 30th President of the USA Calvin Coolidge (1872); Russian-born US film producer Louis B Mayer (1885); US tennis player Pam Shriver (1962)

Died: Second President of the USA John Adams (1826); Third President of the USA Thomas Jefferson (1826); Polish-born French physicist and Nobel Prize winner Marie Curie (1934); French tennis player Suzanne Lenglen (1938); US singer and songwriter Barry White (2003)

1817 Construction of the Erie Canal began at Rome, New York.

1829 George Shillibeer (1797–1866) established London's first regular omnibus service; his horse-drawn coaches ran four times daily from Paddington via Regent's Park to Bank in the City carrying up to 20 passengers.

1840 The first Cunard paddle steamer *Britannia* sailed from Liverpool to Halifax, Nova Scotia, and on to Boston, taking 14 days to cross the Atlantic.

1848 The *Communist Manifesto* written by Karl Marx (1818–83) and Frederick Engels (1820–95) was published.

1904 Construction of the Panama Canal began.

1919 Jack Dempsey (1895–1983), known as 'the Manassa Mauler', defeated Jess Willard (1881–1968) to win the world heavyweight boxing title.

1946 The Philippine Islands gained independence from the USA; Manuel Roxas (1892–1948) became the first president.

1968 Alec Rose (1908–91), British yachting greengrocer, landed at Portsmouth after sailing single-handed around the world in 354 days.

1969 British tennis player Ann Jones (born 1938) defeated the US favourite Billie Jean King (born 1943), to win the Wimbledon women's singles title.

1976 One hundred hostages held by pro-Palestinian hijackers at Entebbe Airport in Uganda were rescued by Israeli commandos.

1981 Riots broke out in Toxteth, Liverpool.

1995 The then British prime minister John Major (born 1943) defeated challenger John Redwood (born 1951) to retain leadership of the Conservative Party.

1997 The US Mars Pathfinder space mission successfully landed an unmanned craft on Mars.

1998 Japan launched its first interplanetary mission when it sent the Nozomi probe to Mars.

5 July

In the Isle of Man this is **Tynwald Day**, on which a ceremonial meeting of the Manx Parliament (the Tynwald) and other public officials is held in the village of St John's, in accordance with a legal requirement established more than 1,000 years ago. (If 5 July falls on a Saturday or Sunday, Tynwald Day is usually moved to the following Monday.) The ceremony was originally held on 24 June, which is St John's Day and Midsummer's Day; the date was adjusted in 1753 to compensate for the loss of eleven days in the changeover from the 'Old Style' Julian calendar to the 'New Style' Gregorian calendar in September 1752. The Tynwald claims to be the world's oldest continuous parliament.

The assembly takes place in the open air on Tynwald Hill (a four-tiered artificial mound that is said to contain a sod of earth from each parish) in the presence of the residents of the island. Summaries of laws that have been passed in the previous year are read out, in English and Manx-Gaelic, and then signed by the Lieutenant-Governor. The island's four coroners are sworn in, and the people have the opportunity to seek justice and air their grievances, an ancient right that dates back to the days of Norse rule.

Tynwald Day is also a time for merrymaking and family gatherings at St John's. There is folk-dancing, music and other entertainment throughout the day, a traditional fair, and a firework display on Tynwald Hill in the evening.

On this day:

Born: English-born South African statesman Cecil Rhodes (1853); US public official and founder of the Davis Cup for tennis Dwight Davis (1879); French poet, playwright and film director Jean Cocteau (1889); French statesman, prime minister and president Georges Pompidou (1911); Scottish-born first cloned sheep Dolly (1996)

Died: English colonial administrator and oriental scholar Sir Stamford Raffles (1826); French chemist and pioneer of photography Nicéphore Niepce (1833); German-born US architect Walter Gropius (1969); English historical and detective novelist Georgette Heyer (1974); US baseball player Ted Williams (2002)

1791 Britain's first ambassador to the USA, George Hammond, was appointed.

1811 Venezuela declared its independence from Spain, sparking off a war between the two countries.

1841 Thomas Cook (1808–92) organized a rail excursion for 500 people, the first beginnings of his travel agency.

1946 The bikini was launched in Paris.

1948 The British National Health Service came into operation.

1965 Opera singer Maria Callas (1923–77) gave her last operatic performance, singing *Tosca* at London's Covent Garden.

1969 The Rolling Stones rock group gave a free concert to 250,000 fans in London's Hyde Park following the death of the group's guitarist Brian Jones (1944–69) a few days earlier.

1975 US tennis player Arthur Ashe (1943–93) defeated defending champion Jimmy Connors (born 1952) to become the first black man to win a Wimbledon men's singles title.

1977 Pakistan's prime minister Zulfikar Ali Bhutto (1928–79) was ousted by an army coup under General Mohammed Zia ul-Haq (1924–88).

1980 Sweden's Bjorn Borg (born 1956) won the Wimbledon men's singles tennis championship for a record fifth consecutive time.

1989 Former White House aide Oliver North (born 1943) was fined $150,000 and given a suspended prison sentence for his involvement in the Iran-Contra affair.

1991 UK branches of the Bank of Commerce and Credit International (BCCI) were closed down by the Bank of England over allegations of fraud.

6 July

Each year on this date the famous **San Fermin Festival** opens in the Spanish city of Pamplona. The festivities begin at noon, when they are started quite literally with a bang as a firework is set off over the city's central square. Running until 14 July, the festival, in honour of a saint who is neither patron saint of the city nor the region, is world famous. One of the most singular traditions associated with the festival is the **Pamplona Bull-Running**. At 8 o'clock each morning from 7 to 14 July those who are either foolhardy or brave enough to risk life and limb run approximately 800m to the bull ring while being chased by six stampeding bulls. The event lasts for two or three minutes only, but is watched by thousands. Unfortunately fatalities have been known. The festival officially ends at midnight on 14 July with the *pobre de mí* ('poor me'), when participants gather to sing of their sorrow that the fun is over. Originally celebrated in October, the date for the Pamplona festival was moved to July in 1591, to avoid bad weather.

On this day:

Born: Austrian archduke and Mexican emperor Ferdinand Maximilian (1832); Mexican artist Frida Kahlo (1907); Tibetan spiritual leader the 14th Dalai Lama (1935); 43rd President of the USA George W Bush (1946); English broadcaster, writer and environmentalist Jonathon Porritt (1950)

Died: English king Edward VI (1553); French novelist Guy de Maupassant (1893); US chemist and inventor Edward Acheson (1931); Welsh politician Aneurin Bevan (1960); German conductor Otto Klemperer (1973)

1535 Former Lord Chancellor Thomas More (1478–1535) was executed for high treason after refusing to take the Oath of Supremacy.

1685 The last battle on English soil took place at Sedgemore in Somerset when forces loyal to King James VII and II (1633–1701) defeated the rebel troops of the Duke of Monmouth (1649–85).

1854 The first official US Republican Party meeting was held in Jackson, Michigan, USA.

1885 French chemist Louis Pasteur (1822–95) used his pioneering treatment for rabies for the first time; the patient survived.

1893 The future King George V (1865–1936) married Princess Mary of Teck (1867–1953).

1907 Brooklands, the world's first purpose-built motor racing circuit, held its first official race.

1919 The first airship to cross the Atlantic, the British R34, arrived in New York City.

1928 The first all-talking feature film, *The Lights of New York*, had its première in New York City.

1950 East Germany and Poland signed a treaty recognizing the Oder-Neisse Line as the permanent border between the two countries.

1957 Paul McCartney (born 1942) was introduced to John Lennon (1940–80) and his group, the Quarrymen, at a church fête in Liverpool.

1957 Althea Gibson (1927–2003) became the first black player to win a Wimbledon singles title.

1966 Malawi, formerly Nyasaland, became a republic with Dr Hastings Banda (1898–1997) as its first president.

1967 Civil war broke out in Nigeria.

1988 A fire on the Piper Alpha off-shore North Sea oil platform killed 167 workers.

July

This was formerly St Thomas Becket's Day, commemorating the date on which the saint's relics were transferred to a new shrine at Canterbury in 1220. (The feast day of St Thomas Becket now falls on 29 December, the date of his death.) Various country fairs and other festivities were associated with the day, notably the **Bodmin Riding**, which took place on the Sunday and Monday following 7 July in the Cornish town of that name. The origin of this event (which has recently been revived in modified form) and its connection with St Thomas Becket are uncertain, but it is popularly believed to commemorate the recovery of the relics of St Petroc, which had been stolen from the priory church at Bodmin in 1177. The Riding itself is a horseback procession around the town led by a band of musicians and two riders bearing a garland of flowers and a pole decked with ribbons. In former times, this was preceded and followed by general merrymaking and sporting contests; these have been replaced in the modern revival by other entertainments.

On this day:

Born: Czechoslovakian-born Austrian composer Gustav Mahler (1860); Russian-born French painter Marc Chagall (1887); French fashion designer Pierre Cardin (1922); English drummer with the Beatles Ringo Starr (1940); English golfer Tony Jacklin (1944)

8 July

Died: English king Edward I (1307); Italian architect Giacomo da Vignola (1573); Scottish writer Sir Arthur Conan Doyle (1930); English publisher and pioneer of paperback books Sir Allen Lane (1970); Nigerian politician Moshood Abiola (1998)

1814 The novel *Waverley*, by Walter Scott (1771–1832), was published.

1898 The USA officially annexed Hawaii.

1937 Chinese and Japanese troops clashed near the Marco Polo Bridge, south-west of Beijing, an incident that was to lead to full-scale war between China and Japan.

1946 The first children's television programme, the BBC's *For the Children*, was broadcast.

1952 The US liner *United States* won the Blue Riband for the fastest Atlantic crossing on its maiden voyage.

1952 After nearly one hundred years of service the last tram ran in London.

1964 English statesman Winston Churchill (1874–1965) made his last appearance in the House of Commons.

1965 *Tomorrow's World* was first shown on the BBC.

1971 US jurist Sandra Day O'Connor (born 1930) became the first woman to be nominated as Associate Justice of the US Supreme Court.

1985 German tennis player Boris Becker (born 1967) became the youngest ever men's singles champion at Wimbledon.

2001 Racial tension led to two nights of violence in the English city of Bradford.

> *The growth of a large business is merely a survival of the fittest.*
>
> John D Rockefeller, quoted in W J Ghent, *Our Benevolent Feudalism* (1902).

The US industrialist John D Rockefeller was born in New York on this day in 1839. He was the co-founder and president of the first major US oil company, Standard Oil, which gradually gained control of the country's oil industry. He also founded a dynasty whose name became synonymous with wealth and philanthropy: the Rockefeller Institute for Medical Research was established in 1901 and the Rockefeller Foundation in 1913, 'to promote the well-being of mankind throughout the world'. At the time of his death in 1937, at the age of 97, Rockefeller had contributed more than half a billion dollars to these and other charitable causes.

On this day:

Born: French poet Jean de La Fontaine (1621); German army officer and airship pioneer Count Ferdinand von Zeppelin (1838); US politician Nelson Rockefeller (1908); US actress Angelica Huston (1951)

Died: English lyric poet and writer Percy Bysshe Shelley (1822); British actress Vivien Leigh (1967); US naval engineering officer Hyman G Rickover (1986); North Korean soldier and political leader Kim-Il Sung (1994)

1663 King Charles II (1630–85) granted a Royal Charter to the colony of Rhode Island in the American colonies.

1709 At the Battle of Poltova the Swedes were defeated in a famous Russian victory in the Great Northern War.

1777 Vermont was the first US state to abolish slavery in its state constitution.

1889 The *Wall Street Journal* was published for the first time.

1965 Great Train Robber Ronnie Biggs (born 1929) escaped from Wandsworth prison and fled to Australia then Brazil, where he stayed until his return to the UK in 2001.

2000 US tennis player Venus Williams (born 1980) won her first Wimbledon women's singles title.

9 July

On this day:

Born: US inventor of the sewing machine Elias Howe (1819); English popular romantic novelist Dame Barbara Cartland (1901); English politician Sir Edward Heath (1916); English artist David Hockney (1937); US actor Tom Hanks (1956)

Died: Roman emperor Nero (68 BC); Flemish painter Jan van Eyck (1441); Irish statesman and philosopher Edmund Burke (1797); US film actor Rod Steiger (2002)

1686 The League of Augsburg, an alliance against French territorial expansionism by the Holy Roman Emperor, Spain, Sweden and Saxony, was formed.

1810 Holland was annexed to France.

1816 The Congress of Tucuman declared Argentina's independence from Spain.

1877 The first games were played on the first day of the first ever Wimbledon Lawn Tennis Championship.

1984 A fire caused by lightning destroyed large parts of York's historic York Minster, the largest Gothic cathedral in northern Europe.

2000 US tennis player Pete Sampras (born 1971) beat Australian Pat Rafter (born 1972) to win the Wimbledon men's singles championship for a seventh time, claiming a record 13th grand slam title.

10 July

On this day:

Born: French theologian John Calvin (1509); Scottish writer and publisher of the first *Book of Days* Robert Chambers (1802); Italian artist Giorgio de Chirico (1888); German composer Carl Orff (1895); Scottish percussion player Evelyn Glennie (1965)

Died: Roman emperor Hadrian (AD 138); Spanish hero El Cid (1099); English painter and etcher George Stubbs (1806); US jazz pianist, composer and bandleader Jelly Roll Morton (1941); English jurist Lord Shawcross (2003)

1296 King of Scots John Balliol (c.1250–1313) was forced to surrender his crown by Edward I (1239–1307) of England.

1553 Jane Grey (1537–54) was proclaimed Queen of England. She was forced to abdicate nine days later, was arrested and then beheaded.

1890 Wyoming became the 44th state of the USA.

1943 World War II – the Allied invasion of Sicily began.

1962 Telstar, the first privately owned satellite, was launched – transmitting the first live pictures between the USA and Europe.

1973 The Bahamas gained independence.

1980 A large area of the Alexandra Palace in London was destroyed by fire.

1985 The Greenpeace ship *Rainbow Warrior* sank in Auckland harbour following two explosions which killed one crew member.

11 July

The British doctor and man of letters Thomas Bowdler was born on this day in 1754. In 1818, having retired from medical practice, he produced an edition of the works of Shakespeare in which 'those words and expressions ... which cannot with propriety be read aloud in a family' (ie anything remotely indecent or impious) were omitted. This, together with other similarly expurgated works, led to the coining of the term *bowdlerize*, used in a derogatory manner with reference to such unnecessary and detrimental editing of texts. He died in 1825.

On this day:

Born: Scottish king Robert the Bruce (1274); Sixth President of the USA John Quincy Adams (1767); Australian statesman and prime minister Gough Whitlam (1916); Mongolian-born US actor Yul Brynner (1920); US singer and musician Suzanne Vega (1959)

Died: US composer George Gershwin (1937); English archaeologist Sir Arthur Evans (1941); Imam of the Ismaili sect of Muslims Aga Khan III (1957); English actor, producer and director Sir Laurence Olivier (1989); English prelate and Archbishop of Canterbury Lord Robert Runcie (2000)

1804 US Vice-President Aaron Burr (1756–1836) shot and fatally wounded Alexander Hamilton (1757–1804), a former Secretary of the Treasury; Hamilton had apparently insulted Burr, and refused to make a public apology.

1848 London's original Waterloo Station opened.

1921 Mongolia declared its independence from China.

1977 The blasphemous libel trial of *Gay News* for publishing a poem about a homosexual centurion's love for Jesus ended with a fine of £1,000 for the newspaper; it was the first case of its kind for over 50 years.

1979 The USA's *Skylab* spacecraft returned to earth after orbiting for six years, breaking up on entering the earth's atmosphere and scattering over the Indian Ocean and Australia.

1986 British newspapers were banned from printing extracts from *Spycatcher*, memoirs by Peter Wright (1916–95) of his time in MI5 (counter-intelligence).

1991 The Labour MP and poll tax protestor Terry Fields (born 1937) was sentenced to 60 days in prison for non-payment of his poll tax bill.

12 July

This is **Orangemen's Day**, when Irish Protestants in Northern Ireland and elsewhere march with banners and regalia, celebrating the defeat of the former King James II of England and Ireland by his son-in-law William III, also known as William of Orange, at the Battle of the Boyne (1 July 1690, Old Style) and the Battle of Aughrim (12 July 1691, Old Style). James, a Catholic convert, had been ousted by William (who was supported by those who feared for the future of Protestantism in the British Isles) and had gone to Ireland in an attempt to reclaim the throne. As soon as it became obvious that the battle was going against him at the River Boyne, he fled to Dublin, and then to France, leaving his army to fight on until their defeat at Aughrim.

> *The anniversary of the day has ever since been held in great regard by the Protestants in Ireland. As it gave them relief from the rule of the Catholic majority, the holding of the day in affectionate remembrance was but natural and allowable. Almost down to our time, however, the celebration has been managed with such strong external demonstrations – armed musterings, bannered processions, glaring insignia, and insulting party-cries – as could not but be felt as grievous by the Catholics; and the consequence has been that the fight begun on Boyne Water in 1690, has been in some degree renewed every year since.*
>
> *Chambers Book of Days* (1864).

The **Orange Marches**, or **Orange Walks** as they are known in Scotland, held on Orangemen's Day mark the climax of the 'marching season'. The Orange Order was formed in 1795 to uphold Protestant supremacy in Ireland. It subsequently became involved in resistance to the Home Rule movement, which sought to repeal the Act of Union with Great Britain and ultimately led to the partition of Ireland in the 1920s. Since the beginning of the

'Troubles' between Protestants and Catholics in Northern Ireland in 1968, the Orange Lodge parades of 12 July have often provoked sectarian unrest, especially in sensitive or controversial parts of their traditional routes.

On this day:

Born: Roman emperor Gaius Julius Caesar (100 BC); US photographic inventor and philanthropist George Eastman (1854); US lyricist and librettist Oscar Hammerstein II (1895); US actor and comedian Bill Cosby (1937)

Died: Irish rebel Jack Cade (1450); Dutch humanist and scholar Desiderius Erasmus (1536); English car manufacturer and aviator Charles Rolls (1910); French soldier Albert Dreyfus (1935); US alto saxophonist, trumpeter and composer Benny Carter (2003)

1543 Henry VIII (1491–1547) married his sixth wife, Catherine Parr (1512–48).

1792 The Brunswick Manifesto was issued by Charles William Ferdinand, Duke of Brunswick (1735–1836), warning the Jacobins in Revolutionary France that Paris would face heavy reprisals if any harm were to befall the French King or Queen. This marked the commencement of the Wars of the Coalition.

1862 The Congressional Medal of Honor, the USA's highest military award for bravery in the face of the enemy, was formally established; the first recipients were soldiers in the American Civil War.

1975 São Tomé and Príncipe gained full independence from Portugal.

1979 Kiribati (formerly the Gilbert Islands) gained independence from the UK.

1998 Host nation France beat Brazil 3–0 to win the football World Cup.

13
July

One of the most ambitious and successful fundraising events of all time, the Live Aid concert at London's Wembley Stadium and at the JFK Stadium in Philadelphia, took place on this day in 1985. It was organized by the rock singer Bob Geldof to raise money for the starving in Africa. In 1984, Geldof had been moved by news reports about the Ethiopian famine to co-write (with Midge Ure) the song 'Do They Know It's Christmas' and to gather together some of the biggest stars of the music business to record it, under the name Band Aid. The record sold in huge numbers and raised £8m.

The Live Aid concert featured bands and singers such as Status Quo, Dire Straits, Queen, David Bowie, Paul McCartney and Elton John at Wembley, and the Beach Boys, Duran Duran, Bob Dylan and Madonna in Philadelphia. Phil Collins performed for the London audience at about 3.30pm and then flew across the Atlantic to reappear on-stage at JFK Stadium at about 1.00am (UK time). The concert began at midday in the UK and ended 16 hours later in the USA; it was watched by more than 1,500,000,000 worldwide, in the 160 countries that received the live television broadcast. Bob Geldof and others made frequent appeals, urging spectators and viewers to 'give us your money', and donations made or pledged during the course of the event amounted to £30m, three-quarters of the final total of £40m.

On this day:

Born: English alchemist, geographer and mathematician John Dee (1527); English peasant poet John Clare (1793); English social reformer, social historian and economist Sidney Webb (1859); Nigerian dramatist, poet, novelist and Nobel Prize winner Wole Soyinka (1934); US film actor Harrison Ford (1942)

Died: French revolutionary, physician and journalist Jean Paul Marat (1793); English architect Sir George Gilbert Scott (1811); US explorer and politician John C Frémont (1890); Austrian-born US composer, conductor and teacher Arnold Schoenberg (1951); Turkish-born Canadian photographer Yousuf Karsh (2002)

1837 Queen Victoria (1819–1901) became the first British monarch to live at Buckingham Palace.

1863 Riots broke out in New York City in protest against the drafting of men to fight in the American Civil War.

1930 The first matches were played in the first ever football FIFA World Cup, held in Uruguay.

1936 Spanish politician José Calvo Sotelo (1893–1936) was assassinated, triggering the military rising that led to the Spanish Civil War.

1955 Welsh murderess Ruth Ellis (1926–55) was hanged. She was the last woman to receive the death penalty in the UK.

1977 A 25-hour blackout in New York City saw fires and looting.

> *Allons, enfants de la patrie,*
> *Le jour de gloire est arrivé.*
> *(Come, children of our native land,*
> *The day of glory has arrived.)*
>
> Claude Joseph Rouget de Lisle, *La Marseillaise* (1792).

On this day in 1789, the people of Paris stormed the Bastille, the state prison, which was regarded as a symbol of the despotic rule of the Bourbon kings. The prisoners held there – just seven in number – were released and the governor was captured and killed. This historic event is generally regarded as the beginning of the French Revolution, which led to the overthrow of the monarchy and the birth of the republic. (On hearing of the attack, King Louis XVI is said to have asked the Duke of La Rochefoucauld-Liancourt, 'Is this a revolt?'; the duke allegedly replied, 'No, sir, it's a revolution'.)

The anniversary of the storming of the Bastille is commemorated with a national holiday known simply as **Le Quatorze Juillet** in France; in the UK it is called **Bastille Day**. It is marked with a military parade on the Avenue des Champs-Élysées in Paris and with local festivities such as games, dances and firework displays throughout the country.

The Bastille was built in the late 14th century as part of the fortifications against the English during the Hundred Years War. It comprised eight towers linked by walls 100ft high and was surrounded by a moat. In the early 17th century the fortress began to be used as a prison for spies, political troublemakers and similar undesirables (rather than common criminals). It was also used to store arms and ammunition, and gaining access to these supplies was the original intention of the attack on 14 July 1789. The building was subsequently demolished.

On this day:

Born: US animated cartoonist William Hanna (1910); US folk-singer, songwriter and author Woody Guthrie (1912); Swedish film and stage director and writer Ingmar Bergman (1918); English journalist and editor Lord Rees-Mogg (1928)

Died: US outlaw Billy the Kid (1881); German arms manufacturer Alfred Krupp (1887); English chemist Sir William Henry Perkin, Snr (1907); Swiss clown Grock (1959); Australian nuclear physicist Sir Mark Oliphant (2000)

1795 *La Marseillaise* – composed three years earlier by French soldier Claude Joseph Rouget de Lisle (1760–1836) – was declared the national song of France.

1865 English wood-engraver and mountaineer Edward Whymper (1840–1911) completed the first ascent of the Matterhorn.

1867 Swedish chemist Alfred Nobel (1833–96) first demonstrated dynamite at Merstham Quarry in Surrey.

1902 The Campanile di San Marco (the bell tower of St Mark's Cathedral in Venice) collapsed without warning.

1965 The USA's *Mariner IV* spacecraft made the first successful fly-by of Mars.

2002 An assassination attempt was made on the life of French president Jacques Chirac (born 1932) at the annual Bastille Day celebrations in Paris.

15 July

> *St Swithin's Day, if thou dost rain,*
> *For forty days it will remain:*
> *St Swithin's Day, if thou be fair,*
> *For forty days 'twill rain nae mair.*
>
> Traditional rhyme.

St Swithin was an English monk who became Bishop of Winchester in 852 and died ten years later. According to popular belief, at his own request he was buried in the churchyard, so that his grave would be watered by rain and trodden by the feet of passers-by. On 15 July 971 his remains were moved to a more appropriate resting-place inside the cathedral, an operation that was allegedly disrupted by heavy rain, which continued for 40 days thereafter. This story is the basis of the meteorological prediction that a wet or dry **St Swithin's Day** will be followed by 40 days of rain or fair weather, respectively – a long-range forecast that has proved far from accurate over the years.

> *The question now remains to be answered, whether the popular belief we have been considering has any foundation in fact, and here the observations at Greenwich for the 20 years preceding 1861, must be adduced to demonstrate its fallacy. From these we learn that St Swithin's Day was wet in 1841, and there were 23 rainy days up to the 24th of August ... [there follows a similar statement for each of the remaining 19 years] ... It will thus be seen, by the average of the foregoing 20 years, that the greatest number of rainy days, after St Swithin's Day, had taken place when the 15th of July was dry.*
>
> *Chambers Book of Days* (1864).

On this day:

Born: Dutch painter Rembrandt (1606); Irish novelist, playwright and philosopher Dame Iris Murdoch (1919); Argentinian soldier, statesman and president Leopoldo Galtieri (1926); English guitarist and lutenist Julian Bream (1933)

Died: Italian theologian and Doctor of the Church St Bonaventure (1274); English claimant to the throne James Scott, Duke of Monmouth (1685); Russian dramatist and short-story writer Anton Chekhov (1904); Italian fashion designer Gianni Versace (1997)

1099 The Crusaders captured Jerusalem.

1869 Margarine was patented in France by Hippolyte Mège Mouries (1817–80).

1914 World War I – the Battle of the Marne began, in which French and British troops halted German forces which had crossed the Marne and were approaching Paris.

1916 William Boeing (1881–1956) incorporated his fledgling aeroplane manufacturing business as the Pacific Aero Products Company; the name was changed to the Boeing Airplane Company the following year.

1965 The first close-up pictures of the surface of Mars were received from the US Mariner IV mission.

1966 The ban on black workers at London's Euston station was lifted.

1975 The first international space flight began as the USA's Apollo mission and the USSR's Soyuz craft were both launched; the two craft docked in space several days later.

16 July

The unleashed power of the atom has changed everything save our modes of thinking and we thus drift toward unparalleled catastrophe.

Albert Einstein, telegram, in *New York Times* (25 May 1946).

The first atomic bomb was detonated on this day in 1945, at a desert site in New Mexico near the Los Alamos laboratory where it was built. Just three weeks later, on 6 August 1945, a similar device was used with devastating effect against the Japanese at Hiroshima.

The development of the atomic bomb, known as the Manhattan Project, was led by the US nuclear physicist Robert Oppenheimer (1904–67), with a team of military and civilian scientists. Albert Einstein (1879–1955) had helped to initiate the project, having warned President Franklin D Roosevelt (1882–1945) in 1939 that such a device could be developed by the enemy. After World War II Einstein campaigned vigorously for nuclear disarmament, painfully aware of the part he had played in the atomic age. 'If only I had known,' he once remarked, 'I would have become a watchmaker.'

On this day:

Born: Italian painter Andrea del Sarto (1486); Norwegian explorer and first man to reach the South Pole Roald Amundsen (1872); Norwegian politician and first United Nations Secretary-General Trygve Lie (1896); US actress and dancer Ginger Rogers (1911); Australian lawn tennis player Margaret Court (1942)

Died: German princess and English queen Anne of Cleves (1557); German air commander and field marshal Albert Kesselring (1960); Austrian conductor Herbert von Karajan (1989); Canadian author and academic Carol Shields (2003)

1790 George Washington (1732–99) established the Dictrict of Columbia as the permanent seat of the federal government.

1935 The first US parking meters were installed in Oklahoma City.

1948 The prototype of the first turboprop aircraft, the Vickers Viscount, took its maiden flight.

1965 The Mont Blanc Tunnel opened between France and Italy.

1969 The USA's Apollo II mission was launched.

1970 A state of emergency was declared in the UK, to deal with the strikes at British ports.

1993 The UK's internal security service, MI5, held its first photocall when it launched a brochure outlining its activities.

17 July

Punch magazine was first published on this day in 1841. Founded by Mark Lemon (1809–70) and Henry Mayhew (1812–87), among others, it aimed to combine humour with political comment. Its title, subsequently associated with the famous puppet-show character, is said to have been originally inspired by a punning comment that a good satirical magazine, like good *punch*, needs Lemon.

Punch is perhaps best remembered for its cartoons and their witty captions. The phrase *curate's egg*, referring to something that is only partly good, derives from a *Punch* cartoon of 1895 in which a timid young curate is seen breakfasting with his bishop. The bishop says, 'I'm afraid you've got a bad egg, Mr Jones', to which the curate replies, 'Oh no, my Lord, I assure you! Parts of it are excellent!' The cartoon was drawn by George du Maurier (1834–96), who was on the staff of the magazine from 1864.

On this day:

Born: English hymnwriter Isaac Watts (1674); US financier John Jacob Astor (1763); Spanish sports administrator and diplomat Juan Antonio Samaranch (1920); English dancer and choreographer Wayne Sleep (1948)

Died: Scottish economist and philosopher Adam Smith (1790); French noblewoman Charlotte Corday (1793); US artist James McNeill Whistler (1903); US jazz singer Billie Holiday (1959); US newspaper proprieter Katharine Graham (2001)

1945 World War II – world leaders from the USA, USSR and the UK began the Potsdam Conference, the last of the great World War II strategic conferences.

1955 English racing driver Stirling Moss (born 1929) won his first British Grand Prix.

1955 Disneyland theme park opened in Anaheim, California.

1964 Donald Campbell (1921–67) broke the land speed record at Lake Eyre in South Australia with a speed of 403.1mph.

1975 Apollo (USA) and Soyuz (USSR) spacecraft docked in space.

1981 The Humber Bridge was officially opened by Queen Elizabeth II (born 1926).

1984 In the USA, the Minimum Legal Drinking Age law was passed, making it illegal for anyone under 21 to buy or publicly possess alcohol.

2002 In the UK, Home Secretary David Blunkett (born 1947) announced proposed law reforms, including an end to the 800-year-old 'double jeopardy' rule.

Shortly before midnight on 18 July 1969, Senator Edward Kennedy (born 1932) left a party on the island of Chappaquiddick with Mary Jo Kopechne (born 1940). Their car plunged off a narrow bridge into the water and Mary Jo was drowned. Although doubt was cast on the Senator's account of what actually happened, there was no clear evidence that he was guilty of any serious crime or impropriety. He remained in office, but his political career was irreparably damaged.

On this day:

Born: English novelist William Makepeace Thackeray (1811); South African lawyer, statesman and Nobel Prize winner Nelson Mandela (1918); US astronaut and politician John Glenn (1921); English entrepreneur and businessman Sir Richard Branson (1950)

Died: Italian painter Caravaggio (1610); Russian tsar Peter III (1762); English novelist Jane Austen (1817); Czech composer Vitezslav Novák (1949); US psychiatrist Karl Menninger (1990)

64 BC Fire broke out in Rome, destroying much of the city.

1870 The Vatican Council proclaimed the doctrine of Papal infallibility.

1872 The Ballot Act introduced voting by secret ballot in the UK.

1934 King George V (1865–1936) opened the Mersey Tunnel.

1976 Romanian gymnast Nadia Comaneci (born 1961) made Olympic history by gaining the first ever perfect score in gymnastics.

1992 John Smith (1938–94) was elected leader of the British Labour Party.

19 July

Lizzie Borden took an axe
And gave her mother forty whacks;
And when she saw what she had done
She gave her father forty-one.

Nursery rhyme.

Lizzie Borden was born on this day in 1860, in Fall River, Massachusetts. Her mother died in 1863 and her father, Andrew Borden, married Abby Gray two years later. In 1892, Andrew and Abby were brutally murdered and Lizzie (who was known to have hated her stepmother) was charged with the crime. After a two-week trial that caused a national sensation, Lizzie was acquitted – the evidence against her being largely circumstantial – but found herself ostracized by those who were convinced of her guilt. Nevertheless, she spent the remainder of her life in Fall River, moving with her sister to a grand house in a prestigious area of the town just a few weeks after the trial was over. She died there of natural causes in 1927.

On this day:

Born: US inventor of the revolver Samuel Colt (1814); French artist Edgar Degas (1834); Scottish novelist A J Cronin (1896); English artist and writer John Bratby (1928); Romanian tennis player Ilie Nastase (1946)

Died: English explorer Matthew Flinders (1814); Korean statesman and president Syngman Rhee (1965)

1333 Scotland were defeated by England in the Battle of Halidon Hill during the Scottish Wars of Independence.

1545 The *Mary Rose*, flagship of the battle fleet of King Henry VIII (1491–1547), sank off Portsmouth; the wreck was raised on 11 October 1982.

1821 The coronation of King George IV (1762–1830) took place in Westminster Abbey; he excluded his wife Caroline (1768–1821) from the ceremony.

1843 *Great Britain*, the first ocean going propeller-driven vessel, designed by Isambard Kingdom Brunel (1806–59), was launched at Bristol.

1848 US womens rights campaigner, Amelia Bloomer (1818–94), introduced 'bloomers' at a New York convention.

1870 France declared war, starting the Franco-Prussian War.

1900 The Paris Métro (underground) opened.

1903 French cyclist Maurice Garin (1871–1957) won the first Tour de France.

1941 World War II – Winston Churchill (1874–1965) inaugurated the 'V for Victory' campaign in Europe, with the BBC using the first four notes of Beethoven's Fifth Symphony (which match the morse code for the letter V) to introduce news bulletins.

1996 The centennial Olympic Games opened in Atlanta, Georgia.

1997 The IRA declared a ceasefire.

2001 English novelist and Conservative politician Jeffrey Archer (born 1940) was sentenced to four years' imprisonment on charges of perjury and perverting the course of justice.

20 July

Houston, Tranquillity Base here. The Eagle has landed.

Edwin 'Buzz' Aldrin, radio transmission
from the Moon (20 July 1969).

On 20 July 1969, the lunar module *Eagle* touched down in the Sea of Tranquillity, the first manned spacecraft to land on the surface of the Moon. Part of the Apollo 11 space mission, its crew comprised the US astronauts Neil Armstrong (born 1930) and Edwin 'Buzz' Aldrin (born 1930); their colleague Michael Collins (born 1930) remained in orbit in the command module, *Columbia*. After carrying out various checks and observations, Neil Armstrong stepped out of the spacecraft onto the surface of the Moon with the words, 'That's one small step for man, one giant leap for mankind.' (Armstrong later claimed that he said 'a man', making the necessary distinction between the individual and the human race, but tape recordings of the historic moment seem to confirm that the crucial indefinite article was omitted.)

Watched by millions of television viewers all over the world, Armstrong and Aldrin collected samples, set up experiments and perfected the art of 'walking' across the lunar landscape. They unveiled a plaque bearing the words 'Here men from the planet Earth first set foot upon the Moon, July 1969 AD. We came in peace for all mankind', planted the Stars and Stripes, and received a telephone call from President Richard Nixon (1913–94) congratulating them on their success. (It later emerged that the president had a more solemn speech prepared for broadcast to the nation in case of disaster, which was happily consigned to the archives unused.)

About 21½ hours after touchdown, Armstrong and Aldrin left the Moon in the lunar module and made a successful rendezvous with Collins in *Columbia*. On 24 July the three astronauts returned safely to earth, splashing down in the Pacific Ocean. After a further 21 days in quarantine, they were finally able to enjoy the hero's welcome they so richly deserved.

On this day:

Born: Italian poet and scholar Francesco Petrarch (1304); Brazilian aeronaut Alberto Santos-Dumont (1873); Scottish engineer and pioneer of broadcasting Lord Reith (1889); New Zealand mountaineer and explorer Sir Edmund Hillary (1919); English actress Dame Diana Rigg (1938)

Died: Mexican revolutionary Pancho Villa (1923); Italian physicist, inventor and Nobel Prize winner Guglielmo Marconi (1937); French poet and writer Paul Valéry (1945); Jordanian king Abdullah ibn Hussein (1951); US martial arts film actor Bruce Lee (1973)

1944 World War II – a failed attempt was made on the life of Adolf Hitler

(1889–1945), when a bomb was placed in a briefcase and left at a meeting.

1957 In a speech at Bedford Prime Minister Harold Macmillan (1894–1986) used the famous phrase, 'Let's be frank about it. Most of our people have never had it so good'.

1960 Sirimavo Bandaranaike (1916–2000) was elected as the world's first woman prime minister in Ceylon (now Sri Lanka).

1974 Turkey invaded Cyprus.

1976 USA's *Viking 1* spacecraft conducted operations on the surface of Mars.

1982 IRA bombs exploded in both Hyde Park and Regent's Park in London, killing a total of eleven people and injuring 50. The targets were soldiers on horseback performing ceremonial duty.

21 July

On this day:

Born: French astronomer Jean Picard (1620); US writer and Nobel Prize winner Ernest Hemingway (1899); US politician and lawyer Janet Reno (1938); English poet Wendy Cope (1945)

Died: Scottish poet and songwriter Robert Burns (1796); English historian G M Trevelyan (1962); South African black resistance leader and Nobel Prize winner Chief Albert Luthuli (1967); Scottish composer Iain Hamilton (2000)

1403 King Henry IV (1366–1413) defeated a rebel army, including nobleman Henry 'Hotspur' Percy (1364–1403), at the Battle of Shrewsbury.

1831 Leopold I (1790–1865) came to the throne as the first king of the Belgians.

1861 In the first major clash of the American Civil War, the Confederates won the first Battle of Bull Run.

1897 London's Tate Gallery was officially opened.

1944 World War II – US forces liberated Guam from the Japanese.

1960 Francis Chichester (1901–72) won the first solo transatlantic yacht race, arriving in New York in his boat *Gipsy Moth III* just 40 days after leaving Plymouth.

1994 Tony Blair (born 1953) became leader of the British Labour Party.

22 July

Feast day of **St Mary Magdalen**, patron saint of pharmacists, hairdressers, repentant sinners and prostitutes.

On this day:

Born: Castilian king Philip I (1478); Austrian botanist Gregor Mendel (1822); English clergyman and educationalist William Spooner (1844); English actor Terence Stamp (1938)

Died: US theatre manager Florenz Ziegfeld (1932); US gangster John Dillinger (1934); US poet Carl Sandburg (1967); English archaeologist Sir Mortimer Wheeler (1976)

1933 US aviator Wiley Post (1900–35) completed the first solo round-the-world flight; the journey had taken him 7 days, 18 hours and 49 minutes.

1944 The Bretton Woods Conference ended in New Hampshire, USA; this international conference led to the establishment of the International Monetary System, including the International Monetary Fund (IMF) and the World Bank (International Bank for Reconstruction and Development).

1946 The King David Hotel in Jerusalem, the headquarters of British rule in Palestine, was bombed by terrorists.

1972 The Soviet Venera 8 mission successfully landed a space probe on Venus.

1977 In China the disgraced Communist politician Deng Xiaoping (1904–97) was reinstated to the Chinese government.

1991 Prime Minister John Major (born 1943) launched his citizen's charter, designed to improve the UK's public services.

On the 23d of July 1690, died Richard Gibson, aged seventy-five; and nineteen years afterwards, his widow died at the advanced age of eighty-nine. Nature thus, by length of years, compensated this compendious couple, as Evelyn terms them, for shortness of stature – the united heights of the two amounting to no more than seven feet. Gibson was miniature-painter, in every sense of the phrase, as well as court-dwarf, to Charles I; his wife, Ann Shepherd, was court-dwarf to Queen Henrietta Maria. ... The marriage was an eminently happy one. The little couple had nine children, five of whom lived to years of maturity, and full ordinary stature.

Chambers Book of Days (1864).

On this day:

Born: US novelist Raymond Chandler (1888); English architect Lord Rogers (1933); English cricketer Graham Gooch (1953); US actor Woody Harrelson (1961)

Died: Italian composer Domenico Scarlatti (1757); US pioneer film director D W Griffith (1948); French soldier and statesman Marshal Phillippe Pétain (1951); US novelist and short-story writer Eudora Welty (2001); Australian actor Leo McKern (2002)

1903 The Ford Motor Company sold its first car (a two-cylinder Model A).

1952 A military coup in Egypt banished King Farouk I (1920–65) and initiated the 'Egyptian Revolution'.

1974 Military rule in Greece ended and democracy was restored.

1986 Prince Andrew (born 1960) became Duke of York on his marriage to Sarah Ferguson (born 1959) in Westminster Abbey, London.

2000 US golfer Tiger Woods (born 1975) won the British Open championship and became the youngest person ever to win a 'career grand slam' of all four major championships.

24 July

On this day in 1704, Gibraltar was captured from Spain by a British fleet, commanded by Sir George Rooke (1650–1709) and Sir Cloudesley Shovel (1650–1707), and British and Dutch troops. (This was the time of the War of the Spanish Succession, when the British and Dutch were fighting as allies against France and Spain.)

> *No other rock or headland in Europe, perhaps, equals Gibraltar for commanding position and importance. Situated at the mouth of the Mediterranean, where that celebrated sea is little more than twenty miles wide, the rock has a dominating influence over the maritime traffic of those waters. … It is evident either that the Spaniards did not regard the place as of sufficient importance to justify a strenuous defence, or that the defence was very ill-managed; for the attack, commenced on the 21st of July, terminated on the 24th by the surrender of the stronghold. From that day to this, Gibraltar has never for one moment been out of English hands. When it was lost, the Spaniards were mortified and alarmed at their discomfiture; and for the next nine years they made repeated attempts to recapture it, by force and stratagem.*
>
> *Chambers Book of Days* (1864).

Gibraltar was formally ceded to the British by the Treaty of Utrecht in 1713–14.

On this day:

Born: French criminal Francois Vidocq (1775); Venezuelan-born South American revolutionary leader Simón Bolívar (1783); French novelist and playwright Alexandre Dumas, known as Dumas père (1802); US aviator Amelia Earhart (1897); US baseball player Barry Bonds (1964)

Died: Eighth President of the USA Martin van Buren (1862); English swimmer Matthew Webb (1883); English physicist and Nobel Prize winner Sir James Chadwick (1974); English actor and comedian Peter Sellers (1980)

1701 French soldier and colonialist Antoine de la Mothe Cadillac (1656–1730) arrived in Detroit. The first settlement on the site was Fort Pontchartrain du Détroit.

1927 The Menin Gate was unveiled; standing at the entrance to the Belgian town of Ypres, it is a memorial to those soldiers who died in Belgium in World War I but have no known grave.

1936 In the UK the speaking clock ('TIM') was first introduced.

1969 The Apollo 11 astronauts returned safely to earth.

1987 Jeffrey Archer (born 1940) won his libel case against the *Daily Star* newspaper; he was later jailed for perjury in the case.

1998 A gunman shot dead two policemen and injured a civilian in an attack on the Capitol Building in Washington, DC.

Till St James's Day be come and gone, you may have hops or you may have none.

Traditional saying.

This is **St James's Day**, feast day of St James the Greater, patron saint of Spain, and formerly the start of the oyster season (until the calendar reform of 1752 moved that date forward eleven days to 5 August). A tradition of uncertain origin associated with St James's Day is **Ebernoe Horn Fair**, which takes place on 25 July in the Sussex village of that name. The highlight of the day is a cricket match between Ebernoe and a neighbouring village, played on the common; meanwhile a whole sheep is roasted in the open air, its horns being awarded as a prize to the highest-scoring member of the winning team.

A further tradition associated with this day is the **Knill Ceremony** in St Ives, Cornwall. In 1782 local worthy John Knill constructed a three-sided stone obelisk on a hill outside the town, which became known as Knill's Steeple. He originally intended this to be his mausoleum, but it was never used. However, he did draw up a complicated deed which gave strict instructions for an unusual ceremony to take place at the Steeple every five years on the feast of St James. The ceremony involves ten girls (who must be the daughters of fishermen, tinners or seamen), two widows, a fiddler and three trustees (the mayor, the vicar and the customs officer of the day). The girls dance around the steeple to Cornish tunes played on the fiddle, and then everyone sings the 100th Psalm. Knill attended the first ceremony himself, in 1801.

On this day:

Born: Scottish statesman and philosopher Lord Balfour (1848); US film actor Walter Brennan (1894); English X-ray crystallographer Rosalind Franklin (1920); US footballer Walter Payton (1954)

Died: English poet Samuel Taylor Coleridge (1834); Scottish industrial chemist and inventor Charles Macintosh (1843); Austrian statesman and chancellor Engelbert Dolfuss (1934); English actor and film, stage and opera director John Schlesinger (2003)

1581 The Netherlands proclaimed their independence from Spain.

1909 French aviator Louis Blériot (1872–1936) made the first aeroplane crossing of the English Channel.

1943 World War II – in Italy, a meeting of the Fascist Grand Council led to the overthrow and arrest of Benito Mussolini (1883–1945).

1959 The experimental British Hovercraft SR.N1 made its first English Channel crossing.

1978 In England, the birth of the world's first-ever test-tube baby was announced.

2000 In France, the supersonic airliner Concorde crashed shortly after take-off from Charles de Gaulle Airport, killing 113 people.

On this day:

Born: Irish dramatist, critic and Nobel Prize winner George Bernard Shaw (1856); Swiss psychiatrist Carl Jung (1875); US screenwriter, film producer and director Stanley Kubrick (1928); English singer and songwriter with the Rolling Stones Sir Mick Jagger (1943); English actress Dame Helen Mirren (1945)

Died: English courtier and poet John Wilmot, 2nd Earl of Rochester (1680); US soldier and politician Samuel Houston (1863); Argentinian popular leader and social reformer Eva Perón (1952); US public opinion pollster George Gallup (1984)

1788 New York became the eleventh state to ratify the Constitution of the USA.

1845 *Great Britain*, the first ocean going propeller-driven vessel, designed by Isambard Kingdom Brunel (1806–59), set out on its maiden voyage across the Atlantic.

1847 Established in 1822 by the American Colonization Society as a homeland for former slaves, Liberia became an independent state.

1908 In the USA the Federal Bureau of Investigation (FBI) was established, originally known as the Office of the Chief Examiner.

1956 Egyptian president Gamal Abd al-Nasser (1918–70) announced the nationalization of the Suez Canal Company.

1963 An earthquake measuring 6.9 on the Richter scale killed over 1,000 people at Skopje in Yugoslavia.

1965 The Maldives in the Indian Ocean achieved independence.

1994 Fourteen people were injured when a car bomb exploded outside the Israeli embassy in London.

> *I am a sundial, and I make a botch*
> *Of what is done much better by a watch.*
>
> Hilaire Belloc, 'On a Sundial' (1938).

The British writer Hilaire Belloc was born in France on this day in 1870. His family settled in England in 1872, but Belloc did not become a naturalized British subject until 1902. He served as MP for Salford from 1906 to 1910, first as a Liberal and then as an Independent. Belloc's writings include travel books, historical studies of figures such as Richelieu and Robespierre, and religious books, but he is best remembered for his collections of comic and nonsensical verse for children, notably *The Bad Child's Book of Beasts* (1896) and *Cautionary Tales* (1907). He died in 1953.

On this day:

Born: French writer Alexandre Dumas, known as Dumas fils (1824); English dancer and choreographer Anton Dolin (1904); English thriller writer Jack Higgins (1929); English politician Shirley Williams (1930)

Died: English chemist and natural philosopher John Dalton (1844); US writer Gertrude Stein (1946); Portuguese dictator Antonio Salazar (1970); Iranian shah Muhammad Reza Pahlavi (1980); British-born US comedian Bob Hope (2003)

1694 A Royal Charter was sealed, creating the Bank of England.

1866 A transatlantic telegraph cable was successfully completed.

1921 Canadian physiologist Frederick Banting (1891–1941) and his assistant Charles Best (1899–1978) isolated insulin.

1965 Edward Heath (born 1916) became the leader of the Conservative Party.

1996 A bomb exploded at the Centennial Olympic Park in Atlanta, Georgia, as the USA hosted the Summer Olympic Games.

2002 More than 75 people were killed in Ukraine when a jet crashed into spectators at an airshow in the town of Lviv.

On this day:

Born: English author and illustrator of books for children Beatrix Potter (1866); French-born US painter Marcel Duchamp (1887); US First Lady Jackie Kennedy Onassis (1929); West Indian cricketer Sir Garfield Sobers (1936)

Died: Italian violinist and composer Antonio Vivaldi (1741); German composer Johann Sebastian Bach (1750); French Revolutionary politician Maximilien de Robespierre (1794); English archaeologist and Egyptologist Sir Flinders Petrie (1942); US ornithologist and artist Roger Tory Peterson (1996)

1540 Henry VIII (1491–1547) married his fifth wife, Catherine Howard (c.1520–1542).

1586 Often said to be the date that Thomas Harriot (c.1560–1621) first introduced the potato to Europe.

1821 Peru declared independence from Spain.

1868 In the USA the 14th Amendment was ratified, granting citizenship to 'all persons born or naturalized in the United States'.

1914 World War I – Austria declared war on Serbia.

1933 The BBC's Sheila Barrett became the first woman radio announcer.

1959 Postcodes were introduced in the UK.

1987 Laura Davies (born 1963) became the first British golfer to win the US Women's Open.

1988 Paddy Ashdown (born 1941) became leader of the British Social and Liberal Democrat Party.

2000 The last prisoners were freed from the Maze prison in Northern Ireland.

29 July

> *The scouts' motto is founded on my initials, it is be prepared, which means, you are always to be in a state of readiness in mind and body to do your duty.*
>
> Robert Baden-Powell, *Scouting for Boys* (1908).

On 29 July 1907, Robert Baden-Powell (1857–1941) took a group of boys to Brownsea Island in Poole Harbour, on the south coast of England, for what was effectively the first Scout camp. The aim of this venture was to try out some of the ideas that were to become the basic principles and activities of the Scout movement: fostering a sense of honour, loyalty and good citizenship; achieving physical fitness through exercise; and developing practical skills such as woodcraft, tracking, observation, signalling and first aid. The boys, drawn from different social classes, were divided into four patrols, each assigned a tent for sleeping quarters. Morning prayers were followed by drills, games and instruction, interspersed with quiet rest periods, and the day ended with stories around the campfire. The experiment was deemed to be a great success, and Scouting was born.

On this day:

Born: English printer of railway guides and timetables George Bradshaw (1801); French historian and political scientist Alexis de Tocqueville (1805); Italian dictator Benito Mussolini (1883); Swedish statesman and Nobel Prize winner Dag Hammarskjöld (1905); US modern-dance choreographer Paul Taylor (1930)

Died: English philanthropist and reformer William Wilberforce (1833); Dutch Post-Impressionist painter Vincent Van Gogh (1890); British crystallographer and Nobel Prize winner Dorothy Hodgkin (1994); Polish politician Edward Gierek (2001)

1588 The Spanish Armada, a fleet of 130 Spanish ships sent by Philip II (1527–98) of Spain to invade England, was defeated.

1900 King of Italy Umberto I (1844–1900) was assassinated by an anarchist.

1948 The 14th Olympic Games opened at London's Wembley Stadium; the Games were the first to be televised by the BBC.

1949 Weather forecasts were first broadcast by BBC television.

1954 *The Lord of the Rings: The Fellowship of the Ring* by J R R Tolkien (1892–1973) was published.

1955 The first episode of *This is Your Life* was broadcast on the BBC.

1968 Pope Paul VI (1897–1978) issued an encyclical confirming a ban on the use of artificial contraception.

1976 A fire destroyed the pier in Southend on the south-eastern coast of England.

1981 The wedding of Charles, Prince of Wales (born 1948) and Lady Diana Spencer (1961–97) took place in St Paul's Cathedral.

30 July

The referee looks at his watch – any second now – and here comes Hurst ... Some people are on the pitch – they think it's all over – it is now! ... Ten seconds to go – Hurst has got a hat trick – It is all over, England are the world champions, and Bobby Moore comes up to receive the Jules Rimet trophy for England.

Kenneth Wolstenholme, commentary at the World Cup final (30 July 1966).

On this day in 1966, England's football team, captained by Bobby Moore, won the World Cup for the first time, beating West Germany by four goals to two at London's Wembley Stadium. Geoff Hurst's first goal of the match brought the half-time score to 1–1; Martin Peters scored a second goal for England, but just 15 seconds from full time Germany drew level again when Wolfgang Weber scored from a free kick. However, Geoff Hurst's two goals in extra time (one of which was dubious, but allowed when the moustachioed Russian linesman confirmed to the referee that the ball had crossed the line) secured the victory for England and made Hurst the first player to score a hat-trick in a World Cup final.

On this day:

Born: English poet and novelist Emily Brontë (1818); US car engineer and manufacturer Henry Ford (1863); English sculptor Henry Moore (1898); English electronic engineer and inventor Sir Clive Sinclair (1940); Austrian-born US film actor and politician Arnold Schwarzenegger (1947)

Died: English Quaker and founder of Pennsylvania William Penn (1718); English poet Thomas Gray (1771); German statesman Prince Otto von Bismarck (1898); US labour leader Jimmy Hoffa (1975)

1619 The first legislative assembly in America, the House of Burgesses, was held at Jamestown, Virginia.

1900 The Central Line of the London underground railway opened with a service between Shepherd's Bush and Bank.

1930 Uruguay beat Argentina 4–2 to win the first Football World Cup.

1935 The first Penguin paperbacks were published.

1963 It was reported in the Soviet press that British double-agent Kim Philby (1911–88) had been granted asylum in Moscow.

1965 Medicare was introduced in the USA, providing medical insurance for many elderly and disabled people.

1974 Following the Turkish invasion of Cyprus on 20 July, a peace agreement was signed by the foreign ministers of Greece, Turkey and the UK.

1980 Vanuatu became an independent republic within the Commonwealth.

1998 The British Court of Appeal overturned the conviction of Derek Bentley (c.1933–1953), who was hanged for murder in 1953.

31
July

> *When eastern lovers feed the funeral fire,*
> *On the same pile the faithful pair expire:*
> *Here pitying heav'n that virtue mutual found*
> *And blasted both, that it might neither wound.*
> *Hearts so sincere th'Almighty saw well pleased,*
> *Sent his own lightning, and the victims seized.*
>
> Alexander Pope, 'On Two Lovers Struck Dead by Lightning', quoted in *Chambers Book of Days* (1864).

These lines were written as an epitaph to John Hewit and Sarah Drew, young lovers who were killed by lightning on 31 July 1718 as they worked in an Oxfordshire field at harvest time. According to an account of the incident written by John Gay (1685–1732), the couple were in their mid-twenties and soon to be married – they had obtained the consent of Sarah's parents that very morning. As the storm broke, the young woman collapsed in fright on a heap of barley; her fiancé remained at her side in a vain attempt to protect her. There was a flash of lightning and an ear-splitting crash of thunder, and the other workers ran to where John and Sarah lay: the couple were found dead in each other's arms amid the smoking barley.

On this day:

Born: German chemist Friedrich Wöhler (1800); Swedish-born US inventor John Ericsson (1803); English cricketer Sir George 'Gubby' Allen (1902); US economist and Nobel Prize winner Milton Friedman (1912); Australian tennis player Evonne Goolagong Cawley (1951)

Died: Spanish soldier and founder of the Jesuits St Ignatius Loyola (1556); 17th President of the USA Andrew Johnson (1875); Hungarian composer and pianist Franz Liszt (1886); French novelist and airman Antoine de Saint-Exupéry (1944); Belgian king Baudouin I (1993)

1498 Christopher Columbus (1451–1506) first landed at Trinidad.

1635 King Charles I (1600–49) issued a proclamation allowing the general public to use the Royal Mail; it was previously only used for delivering state documents.

1910 The *Weekly Dispatch* newspaper included the headline 'Crippen's Life At Sea Described by "Wireless"', after the ship's wireless, developed by Marconi (1874–1937), was used to catch the murderer Dr Crippen (1862–1910).

1917 World War I – the Battle of Passchendaele began; it was notable for appallingly muddy conditions, minimal gains, and British casualties of at least 300,000.

1954 The first ascent of K2 in northern India was made by an Italian climbing team.

1971 Astronauts on the Apollo 15 mission became the first to use a moon buggy (Lunar Roving Vehicle) on the Moon's surface.

1998 The British government announced a ban on landmines.

Gemstone: Peridot or sardonyx
Flower: Poppy or gladiolus

> *Married in August's heat and drowse,*
> *Lover and friend in your chosen spouse.*
>
> Traditional rhyme.

> *August comes, and though the harvest-fields are nearly ripe and ready for the sickle, cheering the heart of man with the prospect of plenty that surrounds him, yet there are signs on every hand that summer is on the wane, and that the time is fast approaching when she will take her departure. ... But, far as summer has advanced, several of her beautiful flowers and curious plants may still be found in perfection in the water-courses, and beside the streams – pleasanter places to ramble along than the dusty and all but flowerless waysides in August.*
>
> *Chambers Book of Days* (1864).

Origins

August, the eighth month of the year and the sixth month of the Roman calendar, is named after the Roman Emperor Augustus (63 BC–AD 14). In 8 BC its Latin name was changed from *Sextilis* (from *sextus*, sixth) to *Augustus*, perhaps because August had been a lucky month for the Emperor, in terms of achievements and victories, or perhaps because it follows the month named after his illustrious predecessor, Julius Caesar.

Characteristics

August is a busy time for those who work in agriculture or tourism, being the beginning of the grain harvest and the height of the holiday season. For many others, it is a time of relaxation and recreation, at home or abroad.

In the mass media, August is also the height of the 'silly season', when the lack of newsworthy stories results in the printing and broadcasting of trivia – often items directly or indirectly related to the weather, such as the arrest of a nude hiker or an attempt to fry an egg on the bonnet of a car.

History

The Irish-Gaelic and Scottish-Gaelic names for the month, *Lunasa* and *Lunasdal*, refer to the festival of Lughnasadh (in honour of the pagan god Lugh) on 1 August, which became synonymous with Lammas. The Anglo-Saxons called it *Weodmonath* ('month of weeds').

Weather

The hottest days of the year often fall in the month of August. Such weather is welcomed by farmers: 'Dry August and warm doth harvest no harm.' However, it may augur a hard winter: 'If the first week of August be warm, the winter will be white and long.' An August heat wave is sometimes accompanied by drought, which is less desirable: 'August rain gives honey and wine.'

The festival season

A number of cultural festivals are held in August, notably the **Edinburgh Festival** in Scotland and the **Royal National Eisteddfod** in Wales. The Edinburgh International Festival, dating from 1947, is primarily a celebration of the performing arts, with live concerts, plays, ballets, operas and other shows. The Edinburgh Festival Fringe offers varied entertainment, and can be an opportunity for new talent, and there are also book, film and jazz festivals in the Scottish capital city during this month. The Eisteddfod is an older tradition, revived in the 19th century. It originated as a medieval gathering of bards and minstrels, attended by people from across Wales, who competed for the prize of a chair at the nobles' table. Held in the first week of August, the venue for the Eisteddfod alternates each year between North and South Wales. Celebrating Welsh arts and culture, the Gorsedd of Bards (an association of distinguished Welsh men and women, headed by an Archdruid) holds three events: a Prose Medal ceremony, a Crowning ceremony for the best free verse poet, and the central event, the Chairing ceremony for the winner of the demanding *cynghanedd* form ('strict metrical verse').

Non-fixed notable dates

Non-fixed notable dates in August include:

Summer Bank Holiday: The last Monday in August is a public holiday in most of the UK. As the final Bank Holiday weekend of the year, and often blessed with fine weather, it is marked by various outdoor festivities. The naval dockyards of Plymouth and Portsmouth are opened to the public in alternate years for **Navy Days**, with a wide variety of exhibits, attractions and displays. In London, thousands of people take to the streets in the **Notting Hill Carnival**, which features colourful processions, elaborate and extravagant costumes, and the music of steel bands. The carnival originated in the mid-1960s as a way of celebrating and maintaining the cultural traditions of the Caribbean immigrants who live in and around the area of Notting Hill.

Battle of the Flowers: Takes place in Jersey, the largest of the Channel Islands, in mid-August. The first Battle of the Flowers was held in 1902, to celebrate the coronation of King Edward VII. The highlight of the festival is a parade of colourful floats bearing magnificent floral 'sculptures' made up of thousands of fresh flower heads or paper flowers. In former times, onlookers were invited to tear up the exhibits at the end of the day and pelt one another with flowers – hence the name of the festival.

Edinburgh Military Tattoo: Dating from 1950, this display of military music and action takes place in August on the floodlit esplanade of Edinburgh Castle. It features the massed pipes and drums of military bands, as well as dancing, drills and parades, performed not only by the battalions and regiments of Scotland, but by armed forces from all over the world.

The Burry Man: Now held on a Friday near the beginning of August, the origins of the Burry Man ritual in South Queensferry, near Edinburgh, are lost in the mists of time. Each year, to continue this ancient custom, the chosen volunteer wins the honour of dressing in a flannel costume covered from head to toe in burrs from the two native burdock plants, as well as flowers and ferns, all of which he must collect himself. Whether a representation of fertility, or a scapegoat for all the town's woes (the burrs which cling to him might represent the evil he cleanses from the town), the Burry Man parades around the streets (walking with the help of two flower-bedecked staves), collecting money and whisky wherever he goes.

1 August

> *This was one of the four great pagan festivals of Britain, the others being on 1st November, 1st February, and 1st May. The festival of the Gule of August, as it was called, probably celebrated the realisation of the first-fruits of the earth, and more particularly that of the grain-harvest. When Christianity was introduced, the day continued to be observed as a festival on these grounds, and, from a loaf being the usual offering at church, the service, and consequently the day, came to be called Hlaf-mass, subsequently shortened into Lammas, just as hlaf-dig (bread-dispenser), applicable to the mistress of a house, came to be softened into the familiar and extensively used term, lady. This we would call the rational definition of the word Lammas. There is another, but in our opinion utterly inadmissible derivation, pointing to the custom of bringing a lamb on this day, as an offering to the cathedral church of York. Without doubt, this custom, which was purely local, would take its rise with reference to the term Lammas, after the true original signification of that word had been forgotten.*
>
> *Chambers Book of Days* (1864).

Lammas was also the time when hay meadows were reopened for common grazing, marked by country fairs (especially sheep fairs) and other festivities. After the 'loss' of eleven days in the calendar reform of 1752, some of these traditional events moved to 12 August, known as Old Lammas Day. One of the customs associated with Lammas fairs was that of 'handfasting', whereby a couple could embark on a trial marriage for a year, at the end of which they were free to choose whether to remain together or apart for the rest of their lives. In the city of Exeter in Devon the old **Lammas Fair** used to begin at noon on 31 July, and last into the first few days of August. Exeter still holds a Lammas Fair, although the date has now been moved to early July to allow the participation of schoolchildren and to link it with the Exeter Festival Craft Fair. The Lord Mayor reads a Lammas Fair Proclamation (based in part on the original Proclamation of Lammas Fair of 1330), and the White Glove (a large stuffed leather glove made of white leather, attached to the end of a pole and festooned with ribbons and flowers) is held aloft. Traditionally, the glove was displayed throughout the fair to signify the royal protection of the peace. The town of Ballycastle in County Antrim in Northern Ireland also holds an **Ould Lammas Fair**, in the last week of August. Held since 1606, the fair involves stalls, music and horse trading, and traditional delicacies include dulse, an edible seaweed, and yellow man, a bright yellow honeycombed toffee.

In Ireland and Scotland, 1 August was **Lughnasadh** (or **Lughnasa**), a festival in honour of Lugh, the pagan god of light and wisdom. Loaves were baked from the first corn of the harvest and either presented as offerings or eaten at the celebratory feast, which also included newly dug potatoes and fresh summer fruits. The day-long festivities featured games and sports, singing, dancing and story-telling, followed by general merrymaking around bonfires in the evening.

On this day:

Born: Roman emperor Claudius I (10 BC); US novelist, short-story writer and poet Herman Melville (1819); English composer and lyricist Lionel Bart (1930); French designer Yves Saint Laurent (1936)

Died: French king Louis VI (1137); British queen Anne (1714); Scottish scholar and missionary Robert Morrison (1834); English pianist and composer John Ogdon (1989)

1086 King William I (1027–87) received the Salisbury Oath, an oath of allegiance from all who held land in England.

1715 The first Doggett's Coat and Badge Race, the oldest rowing contest in the world, took place on the River Thames from London Bridge to Chelsea.

1715 The English Riot Act came into effect; when twelve or more people were unlawfully assembled and refused to disperse, they were, after the reading of a section of this Act by a person in authority, immediately considered to be criminals.

1740 'Rule Britannia' was first heard as part of the masque *Alfred* by Thomas Arne (1710–78) at a performance given at Cliveden House, Maidenhead in the presence of Frederick, Prince of Wales (1707–51).

1774 Joseph Priestley (1733–1804) discovered a gas which he called 'dephlogisticated air'; it later became known as oxygen. Swedish chemist Carl Wilhelm Scheele (1742–86) is also known to have independently discovered it.

1778 The first savings bank opened in Hamburg.

1793 A by-product of the French Revolution, the first metric weight, the kilogram, was introduced in France.

1798 Lord Nelson (1758–1805) destroyed the French fleet in the Battle of the Nile, cutting off supplies to the army of Napoleon I (1769–1821) in Egypt.

1831 The new London Bridge was opened; in the 1960s it was transported, stone by stone and reassembled at Lake Havasu in Arizona.

1834 Slavery was abolished throughout the British Empire.

1876 Colorado became the 38th state of the USA.

1883 Parcel post began in the UK, and letter carriers became known as 'postmen'.

1936 The eleventh Olympic Games were opened in Berlin by Adolf Hitler (1889–1945); the Olympic Flame was carried from Greece for the first time.

1939 The Glenn Miller Orchestra recorded *In The Mood*, which became its signature tune.

1944 World War II – Anne Frank (1929–45) made the final entry in her famous diary, three days before she was sent to a concentration camp.

1965 Cigarette advertising was banned from British television.

1966 Yakubu Gowon (born 1934) took power in Nigeria following a military coup.

1969 Unmanned US spacecraft *Mariner* 6 successfully took 49 far-encounter and 26 near-encounter images of Mars.

1975 The Western powers and Russia signed the Final Act of the Helsinki Agreement upholding human rights.

1981 The music-video channel MTV was launched.

2 August

William II, King of England (known as William Rufus, because of his red face) was killed by an arrow while hunting in the New Forest on this day in 1100. Born in c.1056, the son of William the Conqueror, he had succeeded to the throne in 1087 but was not well liked by his subjects, having broken his promises to relax the game laws of the forest and to relieve the burden of taxation. His death may or may not have been an accident: the fatal arrow was

shot by another member of the royal hunting party and glanced off an oak tree before hitting the King. His body was left where it lay and was later discovered by a charcoal-burner, who transported it to Winchester in a cart. The oak tree was subsequently destroyed by souvenir hunters and vandals, but a triangular pillar, known as the Rufus Stone, was erected in its place. The memorial bears the following inscription:

> *Here stood the oak tree, on which an arrow shot by Sir Walter Tyrell at a stag, glanced and struck King William the Second, surnamed Rufus, on the breast, of which he instantly died, on the second day of August, ANNO 1100. King William the Second, surnamed Rufus, being slain, as before related, was laid in a cart belonging to one Purkis, and drawn from hence, to Winchester, and buried in the Cathedral Church of that city.*

On this day:

Born: US inventor Elisha Gray (1835); English trade union leader Lord Murray (1922); English broadcaster and journalist Alan Whicker (1925); Irish actor Peter O'Toole (1932)

Died: English landscape and portrait painter Thomas Gainsborough (1788); US frontier marshall Wild Bill Hickok (1876); Scottish-born US inventor of the telephone Alexander Graham Bell (1922); French aviator Louis Blériot (1936); US writer William S Burroughs (1997)

1784 The first British mail coach service ran from Bristol, via Bath, to London.

1858 The British Parliament passed the Government of India Act, dissolving the East India Company and transferring the government of India to the Crown.

1873 The first cable car line in the world made a successful trip, driven by inventor Andrew Smith Hallidie (1836–1900), on Clay Street Hill in San Francisco.

1875 London's Belgravia Roller-Skating Rink opened.

1894 Death duties were introduced in the UK by William Harcourt (1827–1904), then Chancellor of the Exchequer.

1898 The very first disc record was recorded in UK; it featured soprano Syria Lamonte singing *Comin' Thro the Rye.*

1945 World War II – the Potsdam Conference between Allied war leaders concluded.

1973 In a tragedy in Douglas, Isle of Man, more than 50 people perished in a fire at the Summerland entertainment complex.

1990 Iraq invaded Kuwait presaging the Gulf War.

3 August

> *We are all born crazy. Some remain that way.*
>
> Samuel Beckett, *Waiting for Godot* (1955).

The English-language version of the play *Waiting for Godot by* Samuel Beckett (1906–89) was first performed on this day in 1955, at the Arts Theatre in London. (The French-language version, *En attendant Godot*, had had its première in Paris two years earlier.) The play consists largely of a dialogue between two tramps, Estragon and Vladimir; they have an appointment with the mysterious Godot, who never appears, although his arrival is announced at the end of each of the two acts. Directed by Peter Hall, the production was not an immediate success. On hearing the now-famous line 'Nothing happens, nobody comes, nobody goes, it's awful!', a member of the audience is said to have shouted, 'Hear! Hear!' However, an enthusiastic review in the *Sunday Times* helped to turn the tide of public opinion, and *Waiting for Godot* was soon recognized as a major new development in 20th-century drama, paving the way for the works of such writers as Harold Pinter (born 1930) and Joe Orton (1933–67).

On this day:

Born: English gardener and architect Sir Joseph Paxton (1801); English politician and prime minister Stanley Baldwin, 1st Earl Baldwin of Bewdley (1867); English detective-story writer Dame P D James (1920); US jazz and popular singer Tony Bennett (1926); English dramatist, actor and director Steven Berkoff (1937)

Died: English king Henry V (1422); English industrialist and inventor of mechanical spinning Sir Richard Arkwright (1792); Polish-born British novelist Joseph Conrad (1924); US satirical comedian Lenny Bruce (1966); English politician Lord Longford (2001)

1492 Christopher Colombus (1451–1506) sailed from Palos de la Frontera in Spain on his first voyage of discovery in the *Santa Maria* accompanied by the *Pinta* and the *Niña*.

1610 English navigator Henry Hudson (c.1550–1611) discovered Hudson Bay.

1778 La Scala Opera House in Milan opened with a performance of *Europa riconosciuta* by Antonio Salieri (1750–1825).

1858 English explorer John Speke (1827–64) arrived at Lake Victoria, believing it to be the source of the River Nile.

1914 World War I – Germany declared war on France.

1958 The world's first nuclear submarine, the USS *Nautilus*, became the first vessel of any description to cross the North Pole by passing under the Arctic icecap.

1960 Niger gained independence from France.

1963 The Beatles pop group played their final performance at the Cavern Club in Liverpool.

2001 A car bomb exploded near Ealing Broadway railway station in West London just after midnight, injuring eleven people.

4 August

On 4 August 1914, the UK declared war on Germany, and this date is generally regarded as the beginning of World War I. The conflict had been precipitated by the assassination of Archduke Franz Ferdinand, the heir to the throne of Austria-Hungary, by a Serbian nationalist on 28 June 1914. Austria-Hungary, supported by Germany, had declared war on Serbia, and the other countries of Europe had begun to take sides. It was the German invasion of Belgium that brought the UK into the conflict, a move that was initially greeted with enthusiasm by the British people.

> *Now in thy splendour go before us*
> *Spirit of England, ardent-eyed,*
> *Enkindle this dear earth that bore us,*
> *In the hour of peril purified.*
>
> *The cares we hugged drop out of vision,*
> *Our hearts with deeper thoughts dilate.*
> *We step from days of sour division*
> *Into the grandeur of our fate.*
>
> Laurence Binyon, 'The Fourth of August' (1914).

On this day:

Born: English lyric poet and writer Percy Bysshe Shelley (1792); US jazz trumpeter and singer Louis Armstrong (1901); English cartoonist and writer Sir Osbert Lancaster (1908); New Zealand politician and prime minister David Lange (1942); US actor Billy Bob Thornton (1955)

Died: English statesman William Cecil, 1st Baron Burghley (1598); Danish writer Hans Christian Andersen (1875); Canadian-born British newspaper and television magnate Lord Thomson (1976); US physiologist, paediatrician and Nobel Prize winner Frederick C Robbins (2003)

1853 Newspaper advertisement duty was abolished in the UK.

1954 The UK's first supersonic fighter, the English Electric Lightning P-1, made its maiden flight over Boscombe Down.

1964 The FBI found the bodies of three civil rights activists in Mississippi.

1982 Prince William of Wales (born 1982) was christened at Buckingham Palace.

1995 Croatia launched an offensive to regain Serb-held Krajina.

2000 Celebrations took place throughout the UK to celebrate the 100th birthday of HM Queen Elizabeth, the Queen Mother (1900–2002).

5 August

Greengrocers rise at dawn of sun
August the fifth – come haste away
To Billingsgate the thousands run
Tis Oyster Day! Tis Oyster Day!

William Hone, *Every-Day Book* (1829).

This is the first day of the oyster season, although those who believe that oysters should only be eaten when there is an 'R' in the month prefer to wait until 1 September. It was formerly thought that anyone who ate an oyster on 5 August would not lack money for the remainder of the year. In parts of London, children had their own way of making money around this time: they would collect the oyster shells discarded from fish shops and restaurants and build cone-shaped grottos with a lighted candle inside or on the top, begging coins from passers-by as a reward for their efforts.

On this day:

Born: English explorer and colonist Edward John Eyre (1815); French novelist Guy de Maupassant (1850); US film director John Huston (1906); US astronaut Neil Armstrong (1930)

Died: Scottish architect James Gibbs (1754); German philosopher and politician Friedrich Engels (1895); US film actress Marilyn Monroe (1962); Bulgarian statesman Todor Zhivkov (1998); English actor Sir Alec Guinness (2000)

1583 Having landed at Newfoundland, English navigator Humphrey Gilbert (1537–83) claimed it for the crown.

1858 Queen Victoria (1819–1901) and US President James Buchanan (1791–1868) exchanged greetings to inaugurate the first transatlantic telephone cable.

1891 The first traveller's cheque, issued by American Express, was cashed in a Leipzig hotel.

1914 The first electric traffic lights were installed in Cleveland, Ohio.

1960 Burkina Faso gained autonomy from France.

1962 Nelson Mandela (born 1918) was arrested near Howick, South Africa, and charged with incitement.

1963 The first signatures were added to the Nuclear Test-Ban Treaty, a treaty prohibiting the testing of nuclear weapons which was signed by more than 100 governments, although it was boycotted by two nuclear nations, France and China.

2001 Eight foreign aid workers were arrested by the Taliban regime in Afghanistan on charges of promoting Christianity.

6 August

On 6 August 1945 the USA dropped the first atom bomb on the city of Hiroshima in Japan. At 8:15am the atomic bomb (named 'Little Boy') was dropped on the city from the B-29 bomber *Enola Gay*. Approximately 150,000 people were killed or wounded as a result, and 75 per cent of the city's buildings were destroyed or severely damaged.

The day is now remembered in many parts of the world as **Hiroshima Day**, and is commemorated in a number of different ways, including peace protests, the observation of a minute's silence at the time at which the bomb fell and symbolic gestures such as the release of white doves.

On this day:

Born: English prelate and Archbishop of Canterbury Matthew Parker (1504); Irish champion of Catholic emancipation Daniel O'Connell (1775); English poet Alfred, Lord Tennyson (1809); Scottish bacteriologist and discoverer of penicillin Sir Alexander Fleming (1881); English mountaineer and photojournalist Chris Bonington (1934)

Died: English dramatist Ben Jonson (1637); Spanish painter Diego Velázquez (1660); English journalist and broadcaster Sir Robin Day (2000); US musician and self-taught harmonica virtuoso Larry Adler (2001); Brazilian novelist Jorge Amado (2001)

1825 Bolivia declared its independence from Spanish rule.

1889 The Savoy Hotel in London opened, incorporating such revolutionary features as full electric lighting.

1890 William Kemmler (1862–1890), a convicted murderer, became the first person to be executed in the electric chair when he was put to death in Auburn State Prison, New York.

1915 World War I – Allied landings at Suvla Bay on the Gallipoli Peninsula began.

1926 US swimmer Gertrude Ederle (1906–2003) became the first woman to swim the English Channel, doing so in 14 hours and 39 minutes, nearly two hours faster than the existing men's record.

1962 Jamaica gained full independence within the British Commonwealth.

1965 In the USA the Voting Rights Act of 1965 became law; it was designed to stop discrimination against minority groups at the polls.

1987 David Owen (born 1938) resigned as leader of the Social Democrat Party.

On the 7th of August 1821, expired the ill-starred Caroline of Brunswick, stricken down, as was generally alleged, by vexation at being refused admission to Westminster Abbey in the previous month of July, when she desired to participate in the coronation ceremonies of her consort George IV. The immediate cause, however, was an illness by which she was suddenly attacked at Drury Lane Theatre, and which ran its course in the space of a few days.

Chambers Book of Days (1864).

The union of the future King George IV (1762–1830) and his cousin Caroline of Brunswick (1768–1821), contracted in 1795 while George was Prince of Wales, was a loveless marriage of convenience. After the birth of their daughter, Princess Charlotte, in 1796, they lived apart for the remainder of their married life. On George's accession to the throne, Caroline was offered a large annuity in return for renouncing the title of queen. When she refused to accept the bribe, George tried to divorce her on grounds of adultery, but public sympathy was on Caroline's side and the charges against her were dropped.

After her death, Caroline's remains were transported to Brunswick (in Germany), for burial with her ancestors. She had requested that her coffin bear the inscription 'Here lies Caroline of Brunswick, the injured Queen of England', but the British authorities refused to permit this, and removed the offending plaque before the cortège left the country.

On this day:

Born: Dutch alleged spy Mata Hari (1876); British archaeologist and physical anthropologist Louis Leakey (1903); US diplomat and Nobel Prize winner Ralph Bunche (1904); Australian cricketer Gregg Chappell (1948); English actor, comedian and writer Alexei Sayle (1952)

Died: English naval commander Admiral Robert Blake (1657); French inventor of the silk loom Joseph Jacquard (1834); Russian actor, theatre director and teacher Konstantin Stanislavsky (1938); US comic actor Oliver Hardy (1957); English writer and critic Brigid Brophy (1995)

1485 Henry Tudor, later Henry VII (1457–1509), landed at Milford Haven in Wales.

1711 Queen Anne (1665–1714) attended Ascot horse race, thus giving it the title 'Royal Ascot'.

1782 George Washington (1732–99) ordered the creation of the Badge of Military Merit, later known as the Purple Heart.

1926 The first British Grand Prix was held at the Brooklands circuit in Surrey.

1958 US playwright Arthur Miller (born 1915) was cleared of contempt more than a year after he refused to name names to the House Un-American Activities Committee.

1972 Ugandan president Idi Amin (1925–2003) gave all Asians who were not Ugandan citizens 90 days to leave; eventually around 50,000 were expelled.

1976 The US space probe Viking 2 went into orbit round Mars.

1998 US embassies in Kenya and Tanzania were bombed within minutes of each other; at least 200 people were killed.

8 August

In the early hours of 8 August 1963, the Royal Mail train from Glasgow to Euston was stopped and raided in Buckinghamshire in what was to become known as the Great Train Robbery. The robbers, disguised as railway workers, used a false red signal light to bring the train to a halt, coshed the driver, 58-year-old Jack Mills, and then uncoupled the front part of the train and drove it further up the line to a bridge where their getaway truck was waiting. They made off with more than £2m, mainly in the form of used notes that were scheduled for destruction.

In their country hideout, the robbers amused themselves by playing Monopoly with real money. The fingerprints they left on the board and pieces were instrumental in tracking them down and bringing them to justice: one by one, the members of the gang were caught, tried, sentenced and jailed. Two of them, Charlie Wilson (c.1932–1990) and Ronnie Biggs (born 1929), subsequently escaped from prison; Charlie Wilson was recaptured in Canada but Ronnie Biggs made his way to Brazil and resisted all subsequent attempts to arrest or extradite him. He finally returned to the UK in 2001 for medical treatment and was promptly sent back to prison to complete his sentence.

On this day:

Born: Scots–Irish philosopher Frances Hutcheson (1694); US physicist and Nobel Prize winner Ernest Lawrence (1901); US swimming champion and actress Esther Williams (1923); US actor Dustin Hoffman (1937)

Died: English statesman and prime minister George Canning (1827); English surgeon and antiquary Sir Erasmus Wilson (1884); French painter James Joseph Jacques Tissot (1902); German naturalist and evolutionist Ernst Haeckel (1919); English aeronautical engineer and inventor Sir Frank Whittle (1996)

1576 The first stone was laid for the observatory at Uraniborg on the Danish island of Ven, built for the astronomer Tycho Brahe (1546–1601).

1588 Queen Elizabeth I (1533–1603) reviewed her troops on the shores of the English Channel at Tilbury, prior to the final naval engagement with the Spanish Armada, and gave her famous speech: 'I know I have the body of a weak and feeble woman, but I have the heart and stomach of a king, and a king of England too'.

1870 The first challenge for the America's Cup took place in Lower New York Bay.

1900 The first Davis Cup tennis competition was played in Brookline, Massachusetts. The cup was donated by Dwight Filley Davis (1879–1945).

1902 The British Academy received its Royal Charter from King Edward VII (1841–1910) on the eve of his coronation.

1940 World War II – the most intensive phase of the Battle of Britain began with daylight air raids by Germany's Luftwaffe on the UK.

1950 US swimmer Florence Chadwick (1918–95) set a (then) women's record for swimming the English Channel in 13 hours 20 minutes.

1974 US President Richard Nixon (1913–94) announced he would resign because of his implication in the 'Watergate Scandal' – he was the first president of the USA to resign from office.

1991 John McCarthy (born 1957), the UK's longest-held hostage in Lebanon, was released after more than five years in captivity.

9 August

No life, my honest scholar, no life so happy and so pleasant as the life of a well-governed angler; for when the lawyer is swallowed up with business, and the statesman is preventing or contriving plots, then we sit on cowslip-banks, hear the birds sing, and possess ourselves in as much quietness as these silver streams, which we now see glide so quietly by us.

Izaak Walton, *The Compleat Angler* (1653).

Izaak Walton was born in Stafford on this day in 1593. The son of an innkeeper, he moved to London as a young man and worked as a draper, prospering in the trade and moving in clerical and literary circles – the poet and clergyman John Donne was among his friends. Walton married twice: his first wife and their seven children died young, but a son and a daughter of his second marriage survived. He began writing in his forties and produced a number of biographies: of Donne (1640), Sir Henry Wotton (1651) and George Herbert (1670), among others. These brought him great esteem at the time, but it is for *The Compleat Angler* that he is remembered. Angling was his lifelong hobby, and this classic work went through five editions before his death in 1683, at the age of 90. Its descriptions of fish and technical advice on rods, lines and bait are interspersed with moral reflections, poems, sayings and exquisite word-pictures of idyllic country life, giving it a timeless and universal appeal and prompting Charles Lamb to write (in a letter to Samuel Taylor Coleridge in 1796), 'It would sweeten a man's temper at any time to read it'.

On this day:

Born: Russian dancer and choreographer Léonide Massine (1896); US film director Robert Aldrich (1918); English poet, librarian and jazz critic Philip Larkin (1922); Australian tennis player Rod Laver (1938)

Died: English naval officer and novelist Captain Frederick Marryat (1848); Swiss novelist, poet and Nobel Prize winner Hermann Hesse (1962); English dramatist Joe Orton (1967); Russian composer Dmitri Shostakovich (1975); US rock and country musician and singer Jerry Garcia (1995)

1842 The Webster–Ashburton Treaty between the USA and the UK, defining the boundary between the USA and Canada from Maine to the Great Lakes, was signed.

1902 The Coronation of King Edward VII (1841–1910) took place at Westminster Abbey.

1945 World War II – the second atomic bomb of the war was dropped on Nagasaki.

1946 A Royal Charter established the Arts Council of Britain.

1963 The first transmission took place of the pop record programme *Ready Steady Go*, which promised that 'the weekend starts here'.

1965 Singapore became independent from the Malaysian Federation.

1974 Gerald Ford (born 1913) was sworn in as 38th President of the USA after the resignation of Richard Nixon (1913–94) became effective.

1999 Charles Kennedy (born 1959) won the Liberal Democrat leadership race, succeeding Paddy Ashdown (born 1941).

10 August

Feast day of **St Lawrence**, patron saint of cooks (because his martyrdom involved being grilled over a slow fire – his emblem is a gridiron).

On this day:

Born: Italian statesman and prime minister Count Camillo Cavour (1810); 31st President of the USA Herbert Hoover (1874); US inventor and electronic musical instruments manufacturer Leo Fender (1909); Spanish actor Antonio Banderas (1960)

Died: German aeronautical inventor and pioneer of gliders Otto Lilienthal (1896); US physicist, rocket engineer and inventor Robert H Goddard (1945); US political leader Estes Kefauver (1963); Pakistani soldier Agha Muhammad Yahya Khan (1980); English chef and television presenter Jennifer Paterson (1999)

1500 Portuguese navigator Diego Diaz landed at Madagascar and named it St Laurent in honour of the saint's feast day.

1675 The foundation stone of the Royal Observatory at Greenwich was laid by King Charles II (1630–85).

1792 Revolutionaries imprisoned King Louis XVI of France (1754–93) and the monarchy was suspended.

1821 Missouri became the 24th state of the USA.

1842 The Mines Act came in force in the UK releasing all women and girls, as well as boys under ten, from underground employment.

1846 The Smithsonian Institute in Washington, DC, was established from funds left at the bequest of English scientist James Smithson (1765–1829).

1885 The first commercial electric street railway began operation in Baltimore, Maryland.

1889 Dan Rylands, of Hope Glass Works, Barnsley, Yorkshire, patented the screw-top bottle.

1893 German engineer Dr Rudolf Diesel (1858–1913) first tested his prototype 'diesel' engine at the Krupps works in Augsburg.

1895 Henry Wood (1869–1944) presented his first 'Promenade Concert' at the Queen's Hall in London.

1952 The European Steel and Coal Community, founded by the Treaty of Paris 1951, came into existence.

1954 Gordon Richards (1904–86), champion British jockey, retired after riding 4,870 winners.

1984 In the 3,000m final of the Los Angeles Olympics, Zola Budd (born 1966), South African athlete, accidentally tripped US champion Mary Decker (born 1958).

11 August

On this day in 1999, millions of people in Europe and Asia witnessed the last full solar eclipse of the 20th century and the second millennium. In the UK, people flocked to Cornwall, the best vantage point on the British mainland, to experience this strange phenomenon – total darkness less than an hour before midday, as the Moon completely blacked out the sun for some two minutes. While thousands stood on Cornish beaches to watch the rare treat, some 40,000 people sailed from the south coast to watch it from sea. In some areas of Britain the eclipse was, inevitably, obscured by cloud, although many people reported that wildlife, particularly birds, had been silenced by the event.

On this day:

Born: English sculptor Joseph Nollekens (1737); English children's writer Enid Blyton (1897); Pakistani soldier and politician Pervaiz Musharraf (1943); US computer pioneer and entrepreneur Steve Wozniak (1950)

Died: English autobiographer, poet and religious writer Cardinal John Newman (1890); Scottish-born US industrialist and philanthropist Andrew Carnegie (1919); US artist Jackson Pollock (1956); English actor Peter Cushing (1994)

AD 117 Hadrian (AD 76–138) became Emperor of Rome on the death of his adoptive father Trajan (c.53–117 AD).

1906 Eugene Augustin Lauste (1857–1935) applied for a patent for his pioneering process for recording sound on film.

1909 The SOS distress signal was used for the first time.

1952 Crown Prince Hussein (1935–99) succeeded his father, King Talal of Jordan (1909–72), who was deposed because of mental illness.

1960 Chad gained independence from France, becoming a republic.

1971 English prime minister Edward Heath (born 1916) captained the British yachting team to victory in the Admiral's Cup.

12 August

This is the **Glorious Twelfth**, the first day of the grouse-shooting season. The sport is concentrated in NE England and Scotland, where it makes a significant contribution to the rural economy. Like all blood sports, grouse-shooting is no stranger to controversy, but the increasing demand for the end-product seems likely to ensure its survival: within hours of the first shots being fired on the northern moors, the race is on to ship the birds to restaurants in London and elsewhere in time for lunch or dinner.

On this day:

Born: British king George IV (1762); English poet and writer Robert Southey (1774); US film producer and director Cecil B de Mille (1881); Scottish actor Fulton Mackay (1922); US tennis player Pete Sampras (1971)

Died: English poet, painter, engraver and mystic William Blake (1827); Czech composer Leos Janáček (1928); German novelist and Nobel Prize winner Thomas Mann (1955); German-born British biochemist and Nobel Prize winner Sir Ernst Chain (1979); US actor Henry Fonda (1982)

1851 US inventor and manufacturer Isaac Singer (1811–75) began production of home sewing machines.

1898 The Hawaiian Islands were formally annexed by the USA.

1944 World War II – PLUTO, the Pipe Line Under the Ocean, came into operation supplying petrol from Shanklin Chine on the Isle of Wight to Allied forces in Europe.

1960 The first communications satellite, ECHO 1, was launched by the USA.

1964 Charlie Wilson (c.1932–1990), one of the Great Train Robbers, escaped from prison.

1981 IBM's first personal computer was released.

1985 A Japan Airlines jumbo jet crashed into a mountainside killing more than 524 people.

2000 The *Kursk*, one of the Russian Navy's most sophisticated nuclear-powered submarines, sank in the Barents Sea after two explosions, killing all of its 118-strong crew.

13 August

The first complete performance of the opera cycle *Der Ring des Nibelungen* by Richard Wagner (1813–83) began on this day in 1876, at the new Festival Theatre in Bayreuth, Germany, and continued on 14, 16 and 17 August. The *Ring* cycle comprises four operas, *Das Rheingold* ('The Rhinegold'), *Die Walküre* ('The Valkyrie'), *Siegfried* and *Götterdämmerung* ('Twilight of the Gods'), traditionally performed on consecutive nights. The first two operas had already had their premières at Munich, in 1869 and 1870 respectively, but the composer had set his heart on staging the cycle in its entirety for the first time in a theatre of his own, built to visual and acoustic specifications that would do full justice to his works. To this end, he began raising funds for the theatre at Bayreuth; the foundation stone was laid in 1872, and with the aid of various loans and donations the building was finally ready for the grand opening in 1876.

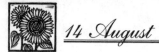

On this day:

Born: Scottish electrical engineer and television pioneer John Logie Baird (1888); English film-maker Sir Alfred Hitchcock (1899); Scottish architect Sir Basil Spence (1907); US golfer Ben Hogan (1912); Cuban leader Fidel Castro (1927)

Died: French painter Eugène Delacroix (1863); English nurse and hospital reformer Florence Nightingale (1910); French composer Jules Massenet (1912); English novelist, short-story writer and popular historian H G Wells (1946); English mountaineer Alison Hargreaves (1995)

1704 The Battle of Blenheim was fought on the Danube during the War of the Spanish Succession.

1940 World War II – German attacks on the UK during the Battle of Britain intensified, with air-raids across England, Scotland and Wales; the Nazis had intended that it would be the day of their invasion of the UK, known as 'Adler Tag' or 'Eagle Day'.

1942 The première of the Walt Disney animated film *Bambi* was held in New York City.

1961 The border between East and West Berlin was closed and the 'Berlin Wall' was begun.

1964 The last executions in the UK were carried out. Peter Allen, aged 21, was hanged in Walton, Liverpool, and Gwynne Evans, aged 24, was hanged in Strangeways, Manchester.

1991 Charles, Prince of Wales (born 1948), resigned as the patron of Scotland's National Museum, following disagreements over the design of a new building.

14 August

On this day in 1893 the driving test and driving licence were introduced in France for male citizens over the age of 21. Those who passed the test were allowed to drive within the municipal boundaries of Paris at a maximum speed of 8mph. France was a pioneer in this field; it was more than 40 years before the UK followed suit, with the introduction of voluntary testing in 1934 and compulsory testing in 1935.

On this day:

Born: German psychiatrist Richard Krafft-Ebing (1840); English novelist, playwright and Nobel Prize winner John Galsworthy (1867); English snooker player Fred Davies (1913); US cartoonist Gary Larson (1950)

Died: Irish journalist and newspaper magnate Alfred Harmsworth (1922); German playwright and poet Bertolt Brecht (1956); English novelist, playwright and critic J B Priestley (1984); Italian car manufacturer Enzo Ferrari (1988)

1816 The UK annexed the remote island of Tristan da Cunha.

1941 World War II – the Atlantic Charter was signed by Prime Minister Winston Churchill (1874–1965) and President Franklin D Roosevelt (1882–1945) on board a warship off the coast of Newfoundland; it expressed certain common principles in their national policies to be followed in the postwar period.

1945 World War II – President Harry S Truman (1884–1972) announced that hostilities between Japan and the USA had ceased.

1948 Australian cricketer Don Bradman (1908–2001) played his last Test Match at the Oval in London.

1969 British troops were sent to Northern Ireland.

1979 The disgraced former MP John Stonehouse (1925–88), who faked his own death, was released from prison.

15 August

> *The Bomb brought peace, but man alone can keep that peace.*
>
> Winston Churchill, speech in the House of Commons (16 August 1945).

In 1945 this was **VJ Day** (Victory over Japan Day), marking the surrender of Japan to the Allies and the end of World War II. Victory in Europe had already been marked by **VE Day** on 8 May, and both occasions were celebrated with great enthusiasm on the streets of the UK, the USA and other Allied nations. The Japanese entered the conflict on 7 December 1941, with the attack on Pearl Harbor in Hawaii, and their resistance continued after the fall of Berlin and the surrender of Germany in May 1945. It was the controversial deployment of the atomic bomb at Hiroshima and Nagasaki on 6 and 9 August, respectively, that finally brought the hostilities to a close.

The events of August 1945 have become associated with the Buddhist ceremony of **Toro Nagashi**, in which lanterns lit with candles in memory of the dead are set afloat. This ancient custom, unconnected in origin with World War II, is practised in Buddhist communities of Japan and elsewhere at the end of the festival of **Obon** in mid-August. The spirits of departed loved ones are said to return for the period of Obon; they are sent back to the spirit world in this sombre and moving ceremony of floating lanterns.

On this day:

Born: French emperor Napoleon I (1769); Scottish novelist and poet Sir Walter Scott (1771); Scottish Labour leader and politician Keir Hardie (1856); Anglo-Irish soldier and writer T E Lawrence, known as Lawrence of Arabia (1888); US actor Ben Affleck (1972)

Died: Scottish king Macbeth (1057); US actor, rancher and humorist Will Rogers (1935); Belgian Surrealist painter René Magritte (1967); Bangladeshi statesman Mujibur Rahman (1975); English architect Sir Hugh Casson (1999)

1843 Copenhagen's Tivoli Pleasure Gardens opened.

1867 The UK's Parliamentary Reform Act extended suffrage to landowners, householders paying rates and lodgers paying rent of £10 a year.

1914 SS *Ancon* became the first ship to sail through the Panama Canal.

1947 The separate dominions of India and Pakistan achieved independence within the Commonwealth.

1967 A law came into force banning pirate radio stations.

1969 The three-day Woodstock Festival began.

1987 Corporal punishment was abolished in British state schools.

1998 A car bomb in the town of Omagh in Northern Ireland killed 27 people.

16 August

In the city of Siena in Tuscany, Italy, this is the date of **Il Palio**, one of two horse races dating from the Middle Ages. (The other, considered of lesser importance, is run on 2 July.) The race takes place in the central, sloping, shell-shaped Piazza del Campo and is under two minutes long, but the associated festivities last all day and the event is a major tourist attraction. Ten horses, each representing a different district (*contrada*) of the city, compete for the prize of a painted silk banner (*il palio*) bearing an image of the Madonna. There are 17 *contrade* altogether, but the space is too restricted – and the race too fast and dangerous – for that number of horses, so lots are drawn to decide which *contrade* will take part.

After three days of trials, betting and speculation, the day of the race begins with a special Mass for the competitors, followed by colourful processions of residents and standard-bearers in traditional costume and the blessing of the horses at local churches. Inter-*contrada* rivalries are much in evidence throughout, and underhand activities (such as drugging the horses or kidnapping their jockeys) are not unknown. The excitement builds to fever pitch in the early evening, when the race is run, and the celebrations of the winning *contrada* continue late into the night.

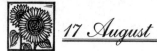

On this day:

Born: French Symbolist poet Jules Laforgue (1860); Israeli statesman and Nobel Prize winner Menachem Begin (1913); English Poet Laureate Ted Hughes (1930); Canadian film director James Cameron (1954); US pop singer and actress Madonna (1958)

Died: German chemist, physicist and inventor of the gas burner Robert Bunsen (1899); US baseball player Babe Ruth (1948); Hungarian-born US actor Bela Lugosi (1956); US popular singer Elvis Presley (1977); Ugandan soldier and politician Idi Amin (2003)

1513 The Battle of the Spurs between France and England took place at Thérouanne, so called because of the speed with which the French force retreated.

1819 The Peterloo Massacre took place in St Peter's Fields, Manchester, when the Militia charged an orderly group of people gathered to listen to speakers on Parliamentary reform.

1952 Severe floods swept through the village of Lynmouth in Devon, killing 34.

1960 Cyprus became an independent republic.

1987 Northwest Airlines flight 255 crashed on take-off in Detroit, killing 154 people; the sole survivor was a four-year-old girl.

1999 Vladimir Putin (born 1952) was granted the Duma's approval to become prime minister of Russia.

17 August

The French mathematician Pierre de Fermat was born on this day in 1601. Mathematics was his hobby rather than his profession – he was a parliamentary councillor in Toulouse – but he made major contributions to number theory and probability theory and discovered principles that anticipated the development of differential calculus. He is perhaps best-remembered for his 'last theorem', a problem that remained unsolved for nearly 400 years, despite Fermat's tantalizing marginal note, 'I have discovered a truly remarkable proof which this margin is too small to contain'. Fermat died in 1665.

On this day:

Born: US frontiersman and politician Davy Crockett (1786); Trinidadian novelist and Nobel Prize winner V S Naipaul (1932); US actor and director Robert de Niro (1943); English ice skater Robin Cousins (1957)

Died: Prussian king Frederick II, the Great (1786); German-born US architect Mies van der Rohe (1969); US lyricist Ira Gershwin (1983); German Nazi politician Rudolf Hess (1987)

1896 Bridget Driscoll became the first known car fatality when she was knocked down by Arthur Edsell who was driving at 4mph.

1960 Gabon gained full independence from France.

1978 Three US citizens became the first to cross the Atlantic in a hot-air balloon.

1988 Pakistani general and president Zia ul-Haq (1924–88) was killed when the plane he was travelling in exploded.

1998 In a televised address to the grand jury, US President Bill Clinton (born 1946) admitted he had had an 'inappropriate relationship' with Monica Lewinsky (born 1973).

1999 An earthquake measuring 6.7 on the Richter scale hit Turkey, killing over 17,000 people.

18 August

Feast day of **St Helena** (the mother of Constantine the Great), who is credited with the discovery of Christ's cross in the 4th century.

On this day:

Born: Austrian emperor and Hungarian king Franz Joseph I (1830); English cricketer Godfrey Evans (1920); French–Polish film director, scriptwriter and actor Roman Polanski (1933); US film actor and director Robert Redford (1937)

Died: Mongol warrior and ruler Genghis Khan (1227); Italian pope Paul IV (1559); French novelist Honoré de Balzac (1850); US automobile manufacturer Walter P Chrysler (1940); US psychologist B F Skinner (1990)

1587 The first child of English parents to be born in the American colonies, a girl named Virginia Dare, was born.

1920 In the USA, the 19th Amendment was ratified, extending the right to vote to women.

1932 Scottish aviator Jim Mollison (1905–59) made the first westbound transatlantic solo flight from Ireland to New Brunswick.

1941 World War II – the National Fire Service was established in the UK.

1960 In the USA the Searle Drug Company began marketing the first oral contraceptive.

1962 Ringo Starr (born 1940) joined the Beatles, replacing drummer Pete Best (born 1941).

1991 In the USSR the August Coup began, a conservative attempt to reverse the process of reform, which ended in failure.

19 August

The US comedian Groucho Marx died on this day in 1977. He was born Julius Henry Marx in New York City in 1895, the son of German immigrants. With his brothers Chico (1891–1961), Harpo (1893–1964), Zeppo (1901–79) and Gummo (1894–1977) – real names Leonard, Adolph, Herbert and Milton, respectively – he appeared on stage in vaudeville

and musical comedy before moving into films. Gummo had already left the act when the Marx Brothers first appeared on the silver screen, in *The Cocoanuts* (1929), and Zeppo stayed for just four more films: *Animal Crackers* (1930), *Monkey Business* (1931), *Horse Feathers* (1932) and *Duck Soup* (1933). Groucho, Chico and Harpo went on to make *A Night at the Opera* (1935), *A Day at the Races* (1937) and several other films before going their separate ways in 1950.

The threesome always played the same roles: Groucho the fast-talking joker with moustache and cigar, Chico the incompetent pianist with an Italian accent, and Harpo the childlike mute harpist. The best and most memorable lines from the Marx Brothers' zany comedies were delivered by Groucho; they include:

> *What's a thousand dollars? Mere chicken feed. A poultry matter. (The Cocoanuts)*
>
> *One morning I shot an elephant in my pyjamas. How he got into my pyjamas I don't know. (Animal Crackers)*
>
> *I could dance with you till the cows come home. On second thoughts I'll dance with the cows and you come home. (Duck Soup)*
>
> *There ain't no Sanity Claus. (A Night at the Opera)*
>
> *Either he's dead or my watch has stopped. (A Day at the Races)*

On this day:

Born: English poet and Poet Laureate John Dryden (1631); English astronomer and first Astronomer Royal John Flamsteed (1646); French couturier Coco Chanel (1883); 42nd President of the USA Bill Clinton (1946)

Died: Roman emperor Augustus (AD 14); Russian ballet impresario Sergei Diaghilev (1929); South African industrialist Harry Oppenheimer (2000); South African journalist and campaigner Donald Woods (2001)

1561 Mary, Queen of Scots (1542–87), returned from exile in France to assume the throne in Scotland.

1812 The USS *Constitution* frigate, known as 'Old Ironsides', commanded by Isaac Hull (1773–1843) captured the British frigate *Guerrière* during the War of 1812 between the UK and the USA.

1839 In Paris, the details of the practical photographic process developed by Louis Daguerre (1789–1851) were released.

1987 A gunman shot 14 people dead in the Berkshire town of Hungerford.

1994 US President Bill Clinton (born 1946) announced that refugees from Cuba would no longer be guaranteed residency in the USA.

2002 A Russian military transport helicopter was shot down by Chechen rebels near Grozny, killing more than 100 people.

20 August

> *Never in the field of human conflict was so much owed by so many to so few.*
>
> Winston Churchill, speech in the House of Commons (20 August 1940).

These historic words have been much quoted, both in and out of their original context. Churchill was referring to the pilots involved in the Battle of Britain – the prolonged conflict between the Royal Air Force and the German Luftwaffe in August, September and October 1940 that could have resulted in Germany's invasion of the UK.

On this day:

Born: Swedish chemist Jöns Jacob Berzelius (1779); 23rd President of the USA Benjamin Harrison (1833); French statesman and prime minister Raymond Poincaré (1860); Indian politician and prime minister Rajiv Gandhi (1944); English cricketer John Emburey (1952)

Died: English writer Emily Brontë (1818); English religious leader and founder of the Salvation Army William Booth (1912); German bacteriologist and Nobel Prize winner Paul Ehrlich (1915); Russian revolutionary Leon Trotsky (1940); English astronomer and mathematician Sir Fred Hoyle (2001)

1882 The première of the *1812 Overture*, by Pyotr Ilyich Tchaikovsky (1840–93), was held in Moscow, Russia.

1914 World War I – German troops captured Brussels.

1929 The BBC made the first transmissions using the 30-line mechanically scanned television system developed by John Logie Baird (1888–1946).

1968 Soviet troops invaded Czechoslovakia to put down the reform programme known as the Prague Spring.

1989 The Thames pleasure boat *The Marchioness* was rammed by a dredger and sank, killing 51 people.

1991 Independence was declared in Estonia.

21 August

On this day in 1879, at Knock in County Mayo, Ireland, an apparition of Mary, Joseph and St John the Evangelist was allegedly seen by 15 people – men, women and children – at the village church. They claimed to have watched the apparition for two hours, in the pouring rain, and an official inquiry ruled that their evidence was trustworthy. A shrine built at the site became a place of pilgrimage, and a number of miraculous cures are said to have occurred there. Knock International Airport opened in 1986 to cater for the pilgrims who travel there, who number one and a half million each year.

On this day:

Born: Scottish engineer and pioneer of gas lighting William Murdock (1754); British king William IV (1765); US jazz pianist, organist and bandleader Count Basie (1904); Australian film director Peter Weir (1944)

Died: English writer and traveller Lady Mary Wortley Montagu (1762); Italian car manufacturer Ettore Bugatti (1947); English composer, conductor and critic Constant Lambert (1951); US-born British sculptor Sir Jacob Epstein (1959); Philippine politician Benigno Aquino (1983)

1911 The world's most famous painting, the *Mona Lisa*, was stolen from the Louvre, Paris; the painting was not recovered for over two years.

1944 World War II – the Dumbarton Oaks Conference began in Washington, DC, at which US, British, Soviet and Chinese diplomats drafted the preliminary proposals that became the basis for the UN Charter.

1959 Hawaii became the 50th state of the USA.

1965 The first substitute allowed under new Football League rules, Keith Peacock of Charlton Athletic, ran on to the pitch at Bolton.

1983 Philippine politician Benigno Aquino (1932–83) was assassinated on his return to Manila, following exile in the USA.

1986 A massive escape of carbon dioxide gas from Lake Nyos in the Cameroon killed over 1,700 people.

22 August

> *The 22d of August 1485 was an important day for England, not merely in putting an end to the reign and the life of a usurper and murderer, whose rule was a disgrace to it, but in finally freeing it from the civil contentions comprehended under the title of the Wars of the Roses. It must, after all, be admitted that the atrocious Crookback somewhat redeemed his life by the way he ended it. It was worthy of his brave race, and of the pretensions he had set up, that he should perish in the thick of a fight which was to conclude his dynasty.*
>
> *Chambers Book of Days* (1864).

The Battle of Bosworth Field was fought on this day in 1485, between Richard III, King of England (1452–85) and the 'Crookback' of the above quote, and Henry Tudor, Earl of Richmond (1457–1509), the future King Henry VII. Shakespeare's play *Richard III* gives perhaps the best-known account of the battle (including the famous line 'A horse, a horse, my kingdom for a horse') and of the events leading up to Richard's accession to the throne in 1483, but not necessarily the most accurate: it is not known for

certain whether Richard was guilty of all the murders that have been attributed to him.

The battle marked the end of the Wars of the Roses, 30 years of civil war in England between the rival houses of York and Lancaster, both descended from King Edward III and both claiming the crown. Richard was the last Yorkist monarch; Henry was a Lancastrian. Richard's defeat at Bosworth Field was largely due to the treachery of the Stanley brothers and their followers, who switched sides at a crucial point in the battle, having secretly assured Henry of their support. Richard died on the battlefield, and Henry became the first Tudor monarch of England.

On this day:

Born: French composer Claude Debussy (1862); US wit, short-story writer and journalist Dorothy Parker (1893); French photographer and artist Henri Cartier-Bresson (1908); English snooker player Steve Davis (1957)

Died: English king Richard III (1485); French painter and engraver Jean Fragonard (1806); Irish politician and Sinn Fein leader Michael Collins (1922); Russian-born US dancer and choreographer Michel Fokine (1942); Kenyan nationalist and political leader Jomo Kenyatta (1978)

1642 King Charles I (1600–49) raised his standard in Nottingham, a clear signal of the Civil War which was to follow.

1851 The America's Cup was inaugurated by the Royal Yacht Squadron for the fastest sail around the Isle of Wight, so named because the yacht *America* was the first winner.

1864 The Geneva Convention for the Amelioration of the Condition of the Wounded in Armies in the Field was signed, leading to the formation of the International Red Cross.

1960 *Beyond the Fringe*, an influential satirical review, opened at the Edinburgh Festival.

1964 *Match of the Day* was first broadcast by the BBC.

1973 Henry Kissinger (born 1923) was named US Secretary of State.

23 August

On this day:

Born: French king Louis XVI (1754); US actor, dancer, choreographer and film director Gene Kelly (1912); Australian golfer Peter Thomson (1929); English playwright Willy Russell (1947)

Died: US lyricist and librettist Oscar Hammerstein II (1960); US biochemist and Nobel Prize winner Stanford Moore (1982); German-born US photojournalist Alfred Eisenstaedt (1995); Grenadian politician Sir Eric Gairy (1997)

1305 Scottish patriot and hero William Wallace (c.1274–1305) was hanged, drawn and quartered in London. His quarters were sent to Newcastle, Berwick, Stirling and Perth.

1628 English politician and court favourite, George Villiers, 1st Duke of Buckingham (1592–1628) was assassinated by a discontented subaltern called John Felton.

1866 The Austro-Prussian War ended with the signing of the Treaty of Prague.

1939 The German–Soviet Pact was signed, an agreement (including a Secret Protocol) which defined territorial interests in Eastern Europe (effectively partitioning the region between Germany and the USSR).

1948 The World Council of Churches was officially constituted at its first general assembly in Amsterdam.

1979 Bolshoi ballet dancer Alexander Godunov (1949–95) defected to the USA.

24 August

If St Bartholomew's Day be fair and clear, then a prosperous autumn comes that year.

Traditional saying.

This is the feast day of St Bartholomew, one of Christ's apostles, who is said to have been flayed alive and then beheaded – his emblem is a butcher's knife, and he is the patron saint of tanners and leatherworkers. An assortment of weather lore is associated with **St Bartholomew's Day**, which falls at the end of the 40-day period of rainy or fair weather following St Swithin's Day on 15 July: 'St Bartholomew's mantle wipes dry all the tears that St Swithin can cry.' It is also thought to herald the cooler weather of autumn: 'Saint Bartholomew brings the cold dew.'

St Bartholomew is also associated with the famous hospital in Smithfield, London, generally known as Barts. The hospital and a priory were founded there in 1123, by a man called Rahere who had fallen ill while on a pilgrimage to Rome and had received an inspirational vision of St Bartholomew. In 1133 Smithfield's first **St Bartholomew's Fair** took place in the grounds of the priory. Originally established for trading purposes, supplying food and drink to worshippers and pilgrims, the fair gradually developed into a boisterous carnival. It ran until 1855. St Bartholomew's Fairs were also held in other parts of the country, although most disappeared in the 1800s. Some attempts have been made recently to revive the tradition.

At West Witton in Yorkshire, a ceremony known as **Burning Bartle** takes place on or around St Bartholomew's Day. A huge straw effigy is paraded through the village, to the accompaniment of a traditional chant by the bearers and the cheers of onlookers, then set alight. The identity of Bartle (and hence the origin of the custom) is uncertain: he is variously thought to represent a local thief, a pagan god of the harvest, a giant who lived on a nearby hill, or St Bartholomew himself, patron saint of the village church.

In France in 1572, the night of 23–4 August was the beginning of the **St Bartholomew's Day Massacre**, in which thousands of Huguenots (Protestants) were butchered by Catholic mobs. The slaughter was authorized by King Charles IX, acting under the influence of his mother, Catherine de Médicis, who dominated him throughout his reign.

24 August

All the streets in Paris rang with the dreadful cry: 'Death to the Huguenot! kill every man! kill! kill!' Neither men, women, nor children were spared; some asleep, some kneeling in supplication to their savage assailants .... All that day it continued; towards evening the king sent out his trumpeter to command a cessation; but the people were not so easily controlled, and murders were committed during the two following days. ... The large cities of the provinces, Rouen, Lyon, &c., caught the infection, which the queen-mother took no steps to prevent, and France was steeped in blood and mourning.

Chambers Book of Days (1864).

On this day:

Born: French count of Anjou and founder of the Plantagenet dynasty Geoffrey IV (1113); English philanthropist and reformer William Wilberforce (1759); Argentinian writer Jorge Luis Borges (1899); Palestinian resistance leader Yasser Arafat (1929); Scottish golfer Sam Torrance (1953)

Died: Irish adventurer who stole the Crown Jewels Captain Thomas Blood (1680); English poet Thomas Chatterton (1770); Russian admiral and circumnavigator of the world Adam Krusenstern (1846); English archaeologist Dame Kathleen Kenyon (1978); English explorer Sir Wilfred Thesiger (2003)

AD 79 Mt Vesuvius erupted and buried the town of Pompeii.

1814 British troops burned the White House in Washington, DC.

1940 Australian pathologist Howard Florey (1898–1968) and his team reported their findings on penicillin in *The Lancet*.

1949 The North Atlantic Treaty came into effect, having been ratified by all the participating states.

1990 Irish hostage Brian Keenan (born 1950) was released after spending more than four years as a hostage in Lebanon.

1992 Hurricane Andrew hit southern Florida, causing widespread devastation.

25 August

On this day in 1770, the body of the poet Thomas Chatterton was found in his garret room in London. He had committed suicide by taking arsenic, at the age of 17 years and 9 months. The tragic event is depicted in a famous painting by Henry Wallis, *The Death of Chatterton* (1856), and the French writer Alfred de Vigny gave a dramatized account of the young poet's short life in his play *Chatterton* (1853).

Chatterton's main contribution to the literary canon was a series of pseudo-archaic poems that he attributed to the 15th-century monk Thomas Rowley, which were judged to have genuine merit in their own right, even after they had been exposed as forgeries. He became a hero of Romanticism: Wordsworth described him as 'The sleepless soul that perished in his pride', Keats dedicated the poem *Endymion* (1818) to his memory, and Shelley paid tribute to him in *Adonais* (1821).

On this day:

Born: Russian tsar Ivan IV, the Terrible (1530); Scottish-born US detective Allan Pinkerton (1819); US conductor, pianist and composer Leonard Bernstein (1918); Scottish film actor Sir Sean Connery (1930)

Died: Scottish philosopher and historian David Hume (1776); Scottish engineer and inventor of the modern steam engine James Watt (1819); English chemist and physicist, creator of classical field theory Michael Faraday (1867); German philosopher, scholar and writer Friedrich Nietzsche (1900); US writer Truman Capote (1984)

1825 Uruguay declared its independence from Brazil.

1875 Captain Matthew Webb (1848–83) became the first recorded person to swim the English Channel, taking just under 22 hours.

1944 World War II – Paris was liberated.

1989 The *Voyager 2* spacecraft sent back its first close-up pictures of Neptune.

1991 Belarus declared its independence from the USSR.

1997 Former East German head of state Egon Krenz (born 1937) was sentenced to six and a half years in jail for shooting people attempting to cross the Berlin Wall in the Communist era.

26 August

The French chemist Antoine Laurent Lavoisier was born in Paris on 26 August 1743. His many scientific achievements included the discovery of oxygen and the development of a systematic method of naming chemical compounds. He was also involved with the collection of taxes, which made him an object of suspicion during the French Revolution; he was arrested, tried and guillotined in 1794. The day after his death, the mathematician Joseph Lagrange remarked, 'It took only a moment to sever that head, and perhaps a hundred years will not be sufficient to produce another like it.'

On this day:

Born: English politician and first British prime minister Sir Robert Walpole (1676); French aeronautical inventor Joseph Montgolfier (1740); Scottish writer and statesman John Buchan (1875); US journalist and author Benjamin Bradlee (1921); US film actor Macaulay Culkin (1980)

Died: French king Louis Philippe (1850); US philosopher and psychologist William James (1910); US film and stage actor Lon Chaney (1930); Ethiopian emperor Haile Selassie I (1975)

1346 The English defeated the French at the Battle of Crécy; the victory was due in part to the skill of the English archers.

1789 The French Assembly adopted the *Declaration of the Rights of Man and Citizen*, proclaiming liberty of conscience, of property and of the press, and freedom from arbitrary imprisonment.

1972 The 20th Olympic Games opened in Munich.

1978 Cardinal Albini Luciano (1912–78) was elected Pope John Paul I. He died only 33 days later.

1994 A patient received the world's first battery-powered heart at Papworth Hospital in Cambridgeshire.

27 August

On this day in 1883, there occurred on the islet of Krakatoa in Indonesia a massive volcanic eruption that was heard over a radius of nearly 3,000 miles. The volcano had become active earlier in the year, but this was the climax of the eruption, one of the most devastating of all time. Ash was propelled some 50 miles into the air, causing total darkness in the surrounding region, and huge tidal waves struck the nearby islands of Java and Sumatra, killing 36,000 people in coastal towns there.

In 1968, the disaster became the subject of a feature film, memorable for the inaccuracy of its title, *Krakatoa, East of Java* – Krakatoa actually lies to the west of that island.

On this day:

Born: German philosopher Georg Hegel (1770); US painter, sculptor, photographer and film-maker Man Ray (1890); 36th President of the USA Lyndon B Johnson (1908); South African Zulu leader and politician Chief Mangosuthu Buthelezi (1928)

Died: Venetian painter Titian (1576); English originator of penny postage Sir Rowland Hill (1879); French architect Le Corbusier (1965); US photojournalist Margaret Bourke-White (1971); French political leader Pierre Poujade (2003)

1859 The first commercial oil well was drilled in West Pennsylvania by Edwin Drake (1819–80).

1928 The Kellogg–Briand Pact renouncing war was signed in Paris.

1950 The BBC transmitted its first television programme from continental Europe.

1979 English naval commander and statesman Earl Mountbatten (1900–79) was killed by an IRA bomb on his boat while he holidayed in Ireland.

1991 Moldova declared its independence from the USSR.

1995 Rugby Union became fully professional.

28 August

Feast day of **St Augustine of Hippo**, one of the greatest thinkers of the Christian Church, whose *Confessions* (AD 397) is regarded as a classic work of spiritual and philosophical literature.

On this day:

Born: German poet, dramatist and scientist Johann von Goethe (1749); Russian writer, aesthetic philosopher, moralist and mystic Count Leo Tolstoy (1828); English poet, broadcaster and writer on architecture Sir John Betjeman (1906); English electrical engineer and Nobel Prize winner Sir Godfrey Hounsfield (1919); Angolan politician, nationalist and president Jose Eduardo Dos Santos (1942)

Died: Numidian Christian St Augustine of Hippo (AD 430); English poet and essayist Leigh Hunt (1859); Czech composer Bohuslav Martinu (1959); US film director John Huston (1987)

1850 The English Channel telegraph cable was completed between Dover and Cap Gris Nez, near Calais.

1922 The world's first radio commercial was transmitted by a radio station in New York City.

1963 US clergyman, civil rights leader and Nobel Prize winner Martin Luther King, Jnr (1929–68) made his 'I have a dream' speech at the Lincoln Memorial on the March on Washington for Jobs and Freedom.

1988 Three aeroplanes collided during aerobatic manoeuvres at an airshow in Ramstein, West Germany, killing more than 70 spectators.

1994 A change in Sunday trading laws allowed shops to trade legally on Sundays for the first time

1996 The marriage of Charles, Prince of Wales (born 1948) and Diana, Princess of Wales (1961–97), ended in divorce.

29 August

On this day in 1893, the US engineer Whitcomb L Judson patented an early form of the zip, known as the 'clasp-locker' or 'hookless fastener', designed to enable boots or shoes to be fastened and unfastened with one hand. He set up a company to manufacture and market this new invention, but it was not a great success. After Judson's death, the Swedish-born engineer Gideon Sundback produced an improved version of the device, which was used on army clothing and gear during World War I, and it soon became an indispensable part of everyday life.

On this day:

Born: French painter Jean Ingres (1780); Swedish film and stage actress Ingrid Bergman (1915); English film actor, producer and director Lord Attenborough (1923); English racing driver James Hunt (1947); US pop singer Michael Jackson (1958)

Died: English authority on card games Edmond Hoyle (1769); Irish statesman Éamon de Valera (1975); Swedish film and stage actress Ingrid Bergman (1982); US actor Lee Marvin (1987); English artist and ornithologist Sir Peter Scott (1989)

1833 The Factory Act became law, making it illegal for children under nine to work in factories, and for those between nine and 13 to work for more than nine hours a day.

1842 The Treaty of Nanjing ended the first Opium War between the UK and China.

1860 Europe's first street tramway opened in Birkenhead, England.

1871 On an expedition to the North Pole, US explorer Charles Hall (1821–71) reached, via Smith's Sound, 82° 16' N, then the highest latitude attained.

1882 'The Ashes' were instituted in cricket between England and Australia after the *Sporting Times* published an obituary on English cricket concluding: 'The body will be cremated and the ashes taken to Australia'.

1895 The Northern Football Union (later called Rugby League) was founded.

1929 The German airship *Graf Zeppelin* completed its circumnavigation of the world.

1966 The Beatles played their last public concert at Candlestick Park, San Francisco.

1991 The Communist Party was suspended in the USSR.

30 August

Cleopatra, Queen of Egypt, died on this day in 30 BC. She is said to have committed suicide by allowing herself to be bitten by a snake (traditionally, an asp on her breast), a creature that had symbolic significance for the Egyptians.

> *Come, thou mortal wretch,*
> *With thy sharp teeth this knot intrinsicate*
> *Of life at once untie. Poor venomous fool,*
> *Be angry, and dispatch. … Peace, peace.*
> *Dost thou not see my baby at my breast,*
> *That sucks the nurse asleep?*
>
> William Shakespeare, *Antony and Cleopatra* (1606).

Born in 69 BC, Cleopatra was appointed joint ruler of Egypt in 51 BC with her younger brother, Ptolemy XIII, by the terms of her father's will. Ousted by Ptolemy's guardians, she was restored to the throne in 47 BC by Julius Caesar, who became her lover. After the death of Caesar, she met the Roman triumvir Mark Antony and became his mistress, bearing him three children. Their liaison caused political problems for Antony, giving his fellow-ruler Octavian (later Augustus) the opportunity to turn public opinion against him, and in 32 BC Octavian declared war on Antony and Cleopatra. Defeated at the Battle of Actium the following year, they fled to Egypt; Antony committed suicide in 30 BC after receiving a false report of Cleopatra's death, and she subsequently chose to take her own life rather than be carried off to Rome as a trophy of victory.

On this day:

Born: French painter Jacques Louis David (1748); English writer Mary Wollstonecraft Shelley (1797); New Zealand physicist and Nobel Prize winner Ernest Rutherford, 1st Baron Rutherford of Nelson (1871); French skier Jean-Claude Killy (1943)

Died: French king Louis XI (1483); Irish politician and Chartist leader Feargus O'Connor (1855); French social philosopher Georges Sorel (1922); US actor Charles Bronson (2003)

1862 Confederate General 'Stonewall' Jackson (1824–63) was victorious in defeating the Unionists at the second Battle of Bull Run in Virginia during the American Civil War.

1901 Hubert Cecil Booth (1871–1955), a British engineer, received a British patent for a vacuum cleaner.

1933 Air France was founded.

1963 The 'hot line' teletype link between the Kremlin in Moscow and the White House in Washington, DC, was inaugurated.

1976 London's Notting Hill Carnival ended with violent clashes with the police.

2001 The European Central Bank revealed the design of the new Euro banknotes in preparation for the launch of the single currency in January 2002.

31 August

Diana, Princess of Wales, died on this day in 1997, after sustaining fatal injuries in a car crash in Paris. The accident also claimed the lives of Diana's companion, Dodi Fayed, and their driver, Henri Paul; the princess's bodyguard, Trevor Rees-Jones, survived. The car was being driven at high speed, pursued by press photographers on motorcycles, when it crashed into the wall of the Pont d'Alma tunnel in the centre of the city.

On this day:

Born: Roman emperor Caligula (AD 12); Mughal emperor Jahangir (1569); English astronomer and radio astronomy pioneer Sir Bernard Lovell (1913); West Indian cricketer Clive Lloyd (1944); Northern Irish rock singer and songwriter Van Morrison (1945)

Died: English king Henry V (1422); English writer and preacher John Bunyan (1688); US film director John Ford (1973); US jazz musician and bandleader Lionel Hampton (2002)

1928 *The Threepenny Opera* by Kurt Weill (1900–50) and Bertolt Brecht (1898–1956) had its première at the Theater am Schiffbauerdamm, Berlin.

1936 The BBC's Elizabeth Cowell became the first woman television announcer.

1958 Race riots broke out in London's Notting Hill.

1959 British prime minister Harold Macmillan (1894–1986) and US President Dwight D Eisenhower (1890–1969) made an historic live broadcast from Downing Street.

1962 Trinidad and Tobago became an independent state and member of the Commonwealth.

1962 Chris Bonington (born 1934) and Ian Clough (1937–70) became the first Britons to climb the north face of the Eiger.

1980 In Poland the trade union Solidarity was formed.

Autumn

Season of mists and mellow fruitfulness,
Close bosom-friend of the maturing sun;
Conspiring with him how to load and bless
With fruit the vines that round the thatch-eaves run.

John Keats, *Lamia, Isabella, The Eve of St Agnes and Other Poems*, 'To Autumn' (1820).

O Autumn, laden with fruit, and stained
With the blood of the grape, pass not, but sit
Beneath my shady roof; where thou may'st rest,
And tune thy jolly voice to my fresh pipe,
And all the daughters of the year shall dance!
Sing now the lusty songs of fruits and flowers.

William Blake, *Poetical Sketches*, 'To Autumn' (1783).

Origins

The word *autumn* comes from the Latin *autumnus* and its use in English dates back to the 14th century. Although it is now the usual term for this season in the UK, in the USA *fall* is preferred. Both *autumn* and *fall* were used synonymously in British English at one time. The latter appears in 16th-century texts in the longer phrase 'fall of the leaf', but by the second half of the 17th century the shorter *fall* was certainly in use.

> *What crowds of patients the town doctor kills,*
> *Or how, last fall, he raised the weekly bills.*
>
> John Dryden, *Juvenal* (1693).

Interestingly, this interchangeability with the word *fall* led, by the mid-19th century, to the use of *autumn* as a slang term for execution by hanging. It came from a play on the phrase 'go off with the fall of the leaf', which also alluded to hanging, the gallows being described as the 'leafless tree'.

Season

Astronomically taken to be the period from the autumnal equinox to the winter solstice (occurring around 23 September and 22 December respectively in the northern hemisphere), autumn is the time of maturity and harvest in the temperate zones.

Harvest time

Harvest is the culmination of the farming year. In the past, the very survival of a community hung upon its success. Naturally, therefore, harvest celebrations have characterized the season of autumn throughout history. In the Middle Ages the celebration of the harvest was linked to the social hierarchy and economic realities of the emerging farming system. With many workers now directly employed by one landowning farmer, the **Harvest Supper** (or **Harvest Home** or **Mell Supper**) was ostensibly a celebration feast, given by the farmer to his workers in an expression of gratitude for their achievement in bringing in the harvest. However, in reality it was probably expected by the workers as part of the payment for their labour. As there was an immense sense of relief after the stresses of the harvest itself, Harvest Suppers were inevitably joyous celebrations, accompanied by feats of excessive drinking, games, and songs.

There were many different regional rituals to accompany the final act of finishing the grain harvest, some of them indicating that there was an element of local competition involved. It was common for the cutting of the last sheaf

to be accompanied by a triumphant shout, known as 'Crying the Neck'. This swaggering was sometimes taken a stage further by forming the last sheaf into a figure and using it to taunt neighbouring farmers who had not yet finished. In many areas the last sheaf was then paraded with a doll made from the corn, variously called a **Kern Doll**, **Kern Baby**, or **Harvest Queen**. This has been revived in recent times in the craft of making **Corn Dollies**.

The modern **Harvest Festival** or **Harvest Thanksgiving**, held on or near the **harvest moon** (the full moon in September), owes its origin to the Victorians. The celebration of harvest by bringing produce to the church and giving thanks with prayers and hymns was seen as a more appropriate Christian celebration than the drunkenness and general overindulgence associated with the original farm-based Harvest Supper.

Autumn fruit

As well as the farmed harvest of grain, and the picking of apples and grapes in orchards and vineyards, there is a natural harvest of fruit at this time of year. **Blackberries**, for one, form a plentiful (and free) tasty treat, being common in hedgerows and on almost every area of uncultivated land. However, it is considered extremely bad luck to pick them late in the season (the final date for picking is given in some areas as Michaelmas, 29 September) because by this time the Devil, or witches, will have 'damaged' them. The original (and less polite) version of how they were 'damaged' probably stemmed from the observation that the berries became watery and sour after the first frost! Conversely, experts in the making of sloe gin would not dream of picking sloes (the sour fruit of the blackthorn tree) until after they have been touched by frost, as this is reputed to improve the flavour of the resulting liqueur. In a rather ironic twist, the optimistic sight of a bountiful harvest of berries has a downside – it is commonly believed to be an indicator of a harsh winter to come.

Conkers

Not all of the fruits gathered at this time of year are taken for their nutritional value. The game of conkers probably evolved from a game called 'conquerors', which was originally played with snail shells. A variant of the game was later played with hazelnuts, on strings. By the 20th century these earlier games had almost universally been replaced by the version we now know using horse chestnuts. There are, of course, many regional variations in the rules of the game and it has also been known by different names. In some parts of the English Midlands it was known as 'oblionker' and play was accompanied by such rhymes as 'Obli, obli, onker, my nut will conquer'. The World Conker Championship is now held annually in Ashton in Northamptonshire on the second Sunday in October. Conkers have also been carried in the pocket to help prevent piles and rheumatism, and used in wardrobes to keep away moths.

Characteristics

Juxtaposed with the positive celebration, the season of autumn carries with it a negative association of decay. It marks the transition into the barren months of winter. At this time of year the landscape changes dramatically as the leaves fall from the trees, migratory birds head south, and many animals prepare for a period of reduced activity or even hibernation. Parallels are drawn with the passing of years in the human lifetime and the imminent approach of death. To move into old age is often described as entering the 'autumn of one's life'.

Food

In days gone by much of the period immediately after harvest was taken up with the work involved in preserving food so that it would last through the lean months ahead. Many of the foods that we now enjoy as treats owe their origins to the life-or-death battle to survive the winter. Jams, pickles, and smoked and salted meats and fish were all produced by processes that prevent foods from going off, allowing them to be stored for many months. The Christmas pudding is also traditionally made at this time of year, six to eight weeks before Christmas. The custom of gathering every member of the household together each to stir the mix and make a wish dates back to the mid-19th century.

Religious festivals

A number of important religious festivals occur during the autumn season:

Diwali (or **Deepavali**) is the Hindu festival of lights, and is also celebrated by Sikhs and Jains. A five-day festival that falls in the Hindu month of Kartikka (October–November), it is held in honour of Lakshmi, goddess of good fortune, and is also the Hindu new year festival.

In Britain Diwali is celebrated with fireworks, lamps, parties and traditional Indian sweets. Lights and fireworks represent the triumph of good over evil, and Hindus look back to Lord Rama returning from 14 years in exile, having defeated the demon Ravana. Sikhs celebrate the return of Guru Hargobind Ji to Amritsar, and Jains commemorate the achievement of nirvana by their leader Mahavira.

The birthday of Guru Nanak Dev, founder of Sikhism, is celebrated by Sikhs in India and elsewhere at the time of the full moon in the month

of Kartikka. It is marked by a procession in which the holy book of Sikhism, the *Adi Granth* (or *Granth Sahib*), is carried on a flower-decked float, and by activities centred on Sikh temples (*gurdwaras*), where community lunches are served to people of all faiths.

Rosh Hashanah is the Jewish festival of the New Year. Falling in the month of Tishri (September–October), it marks the creation of the world and is also considered a day of judgement. Rituals include the blowing of a *shofar*, or ram's horn, 100 times in the synagogue to remind the faithful to spend time in self-reflection, and in homes a special meal is eaten. The holy time for Jews continues for ten days after Rosh Hashanah, culminating with the **Day of Atonement** or **Yom Kippur**.

Sukkot (or **Succoth**) is the Jewish **Feast of Tabernacles** (or **Booths**), a festival of thanksgiving that lasts for seven days in the month of Tishri. During this period people eat, drink, and sleep in temporary shelters built in homes, gardens and synagogues, in memory of the makeshift living quarters of the Israelites during their wanderings in the desert after the exodus from Egypt.

September

Gemstone: Sapphire
Flower: Aster

> *Married in September's golden glow,*
> *Smooth and serene your life will go.*
>
> Traditional rhyme.

> *Beautiful are the fern and heath covered wastes in September – with their bushes bearing wild-fruits, sloe, and bullace [wild plum], and crab; and where one may lie hidden for hours, watching how beast, bird, and insect pass their time away, and what they do in these solitudes. In such spots, we have seen great gorse-bushes in bloom, high as the head of a mounted horseman; impenetrable places where the bramble and the sloe had become entangled with the furze and the branches of stunted hawthorns, that had never been able to grow clear of the wild waste of underwood.*
>
> *Chambers Book of Days* (1864).

Origins

September, the ninth month of the year, was the seventh month of the Roman calendar and its name is derived from the Latin *septem*, seven.

Characteristics

September marks the end of summer and the beginning of autumn – towards the end of the month the leaves of deciduous trees begin to change colour. The children go back to school, and life returns to humdrum normality after the disruptions and diversions of the summer holidays. For the farming community, this is the climax of the grain harvest, a time of hard work followed by the celebrations of **Harvest Home** (see Autumn).

History

The Anglo-Saxons called it *Gerstmonath* ('barley month'), with reference to the harvest of that crop, the main ingredient of their favourite alcoholic beverage. Some of the Celtic names of the month are also linked to the harvest, though less specifically: the Welsh *Medi* means 'reaping' and the Scottish-Gaelic *Sultuine* means 'plenty'.

Weather

Farmers and apple-growers hope for temperate weather in September, so that their crops will not be damaged before they are gathered in: 'September blow soft, till fruit be in loft.' Other weather lore relates to the latter part of the month, especially Michaelmas (29 September). The three days preceding the autumnal equinox (23 September) are supposed to determine the weather for the following three months, although interpretations vary: some say that calm weather during these days will continue until the end of the year, whereas others say that such weather predicts a compensatory stormy period to follow.

Hops

In Kent and other hop-growing counties, September was the month when casual workers from London and elsewhere would arrive for the hop-picking season.

> *See, from the great metropolis they rush,*
> *The industrious vulgar! They, like prudent bees*
> *In Kent's wide garden roam, expert to crop*
> *The flow'ry hop, and provident to work,*
> *Ere winter numb their sunburnt hands, and winds*
> *Engaol them, murmuring in their gloomy cells.*
>
> Christopher Smart, 'The Hop Garden' (1752).

Although the growing of hops is now in decline, it remains an important crop, and a number of customs associated with its harvest are still observed. One of these is **Hop Hoodening**, which takes place on the first Saturday in September at Canterbury Cathedral. It consists of a procession of morris dancers, led by the Hop Queen and accompanied by two Hooden Horses, followed by a service of blessing and a display of dancing.

Non-fixed notable dates

Non-fixed notable dates in September include:

Braemar Gathering: Takes place on the first Saturday of September at the village of Braemar in NE Scotland. It is a day of traditional Highland sports and games – including tossing the caber, throwing the hammer, and a hill race – as well as performances by Highland dancers and pipers. The Gathering dates from the early 18th century in its current form, but the history of Highland gatherings at Braemar goes back to the days of Malcolm III, King of Scotland in the 11th century.

Abbots Bromley Horn Dance: A traditional dance performed in and around the village of Abbots Bromley, Staffordshire, on the local 'Wakes Monday' – usually the first Monday after 4 September. There are ten dancers, six of whom carry reindeer antlers mounted on wooden heads; the other four represent a Fool, a Hobby Horse, a Bowman (or Robin Hood) and a male Maid Marian. Accompanied by two musicians, they walk around the parish, stopping at various places to perform the dance. The custom dates from the 13th century (the horns themselves have been carbon-dated to around 1066) and is of uncertain origin, possibly being connected with the preservation of hunting rights or a fertility ritual.

Widecombe Fair: The Dartmoor village of Widecombe holds its famous fair annually on the second Tuesday in September. The fair dates from the 1850s or earlier and was originally an agricultural fair where livestock was shown and auctioned. The agricultural theme is still strong today, and the fair includes show animals and a produce tent as well as Maypole dancing and a gymkhana. The fair is perhaps most famous because of the song associated with it – a folk song which can be traced back further than the fair and existed in a number of regional variations (although the story of Tom Pearce and Tom Cobley remained consistent).

Tom Pearce, Tom Pearce, lend me your grey mare,
All along, down along, out along, lee,
For I want for to go to Widecombe Fair,
With Bill Brewer, Jan Stewer, Peter Gurney,
Peter Davy, Dan'l Whiddon, Harry Hawke,
Old Uncle Tom Cobley and all,
Old Uncle Tom Cobley and all.

Last Night of the Proms: The annual season of Promenade Concerts, in London's Royal Albert Hall, comes to an end in mid-September with a night of music old and new, performed in a party atmosphere and broadcast to millions on radio and television. The first half of the concert usually includes the world première of a newly commissioned work, and the second half is largely made up of traditional British favourites: Elgar's *Pomp and Circumstance March* No. 1 ('Land of Hope and Glory'), *Fantasia on British Sea Songs* by Henry Wood and Percy Grainger, 'Rule Britannia', and 'Jerusalem'. The promenaders (mainly young enthusiasts who occupy the standing space at the front of the auditorium) are in festive mood throughout, and the whole audience joins in with the singing. A recent innovation is the simultaneous staging of outdoor concerts (**Proms in the Park**) in various cities of the UK.

Egremont Crab Fair: On the Saturday nearest to 18 September, the village of Egremont in Cumbria plays host to various games and competitions associated with its charter fair, dating from 1267. The fair is thought to take its name from the crab-apples that were formerly distributed during the course of the proceedings. The events of the day include the climbing of a greasy pole for the prize of a joint of meat nailed to the top, wrestling, racing, and scrambling for apples thrown from a moving van. The highlight and grand finale is the **gurning** championship, in which contestants put their head through a horse collar and compete to produce the most ugly or grotesque contortion of their facial features.

Oktoberfest: The Oktoberfest, Munich's biggest annual celebration, is associated throughout the world with beer drinking and Bavarian music. However, the festival has not always been centred around beer (the first beer tents arrived in 1896) and its origin lies in the public festivities which were held for the wedding of Crown Prince Ludwig of Bavaria to Princess Thérèse in October 1810; subsequently the celebrations became an annual event. In its long history the festival has been cancelled on 24 occasions (for reasons including cholera and inflation). Still called the Oktoberfest, the festival now begins in September, to take advantage of the more favourable September weather.

1 September

This is the feast day of St Giles, a 7th-century Greek hermit who lived in France. He is said to have been partly nourished by the milk of a hind that visited him daily, and to have mortified himself by refusing treatment for his lameness, for which two reasons he is regarded as the patron saint of nursing mothers and people who are lame (as well as lepers and beggars). The King of the region discovered his hermitage while hunting the hind and established a monastery there, with Giles as its abbot. (In another version of the legend, the King shot an arrow that wounded Giles in the leg as he protected the animal.) The hind is immortalized on the coat of arms of the city of Edinburgh, whose cathedral bears the saint's name.

> *Veneration for St Giles caused many churches to be dedicated to him in various countries. ... It was customary that Giles's Church should be on the outskirts of a town, on one of the great thoroughfares leading into it, in order that cripples might the more conveniently come to and cluster around it. We have a memorial of this association of facts in the interesting old church of St Giles, Cripplegate, in the eastern part of the city of London.*
>
> *Chambers Book of Days* (1864).

In Oxford, **St Giles's Fair** is held in the week following **St Giles's Day**. It developed in the 17th century from the parish wake and is largely a pleasure fair, with amusements for children and adults alike. The street of St Giles, closed to traffic for the duration, is lined with stalls, sideshows, and the mechanical attractions of the modern funfair, and local residents from all walks of life are drawn together for a few days before going their separate ways again to university, office, shop, factory and farm.

On this day:

Born: German composer Engelbert Humperdinck (1854); Irish patriot and British consular official Sir Roger Casement (1864); US boxer 'Gentleman' Jim Corbett (1866); US popular author Edgar Rice Burroughs (1875); US boxer Rocky Marciano (1923)

1 September

Died: English cleric and pope Adrian IV (1159); French navigator Jacques Cartier (1557); Dutch portrait and genre painter Frans Hals, the Elder (1666); Irish essayist, dramatist and politician Sir Richard Steele (1729); English painter Sir Terry Frost (2003)

1807 Former US Vice-President Aaron Burr (1756–1836) was acquitted of treason.

1858 The East India Company's formal control of India ended when the British crown took over its territories and duties.

1923 An earthquake in Japan left Tokyo and Yokohama in ruins, with over 140,000 people dead.

1928 Albania was formally declared a kingdom by its Constitutional Assembly, and King Zog I (1895–1961) became its first ruler.

1928 The Morris Minor car was launched by Morris Motors at Oxford.

1939 World War II – Germany invaded Poland, marking the beginning of the war.

1939 World War II – the BBC's regular television service was shut down in the middle of a Mickey Mouse cartoon amidst fears that transmissions could aid navigation for enemy bombers; the new wartime *Home Service* programme began instead on the radio.

1960 The UK government announced that betting shops, as well as other types of gambling for small sums, would be legalized in the UK.

1969 Muammar Gaddafi (born 1942) led a military coup in Libya, overthrowing King Idris and becoming the country's head of state.

1972 Bobby Fischer (born 1943) became the USA's first world chess champion when he defeated the USSR's Boris Spassky (born 1937) in Reykjavik.

2 September

> *London was only a few months freed from a desolating pestilence ... when, on the evening of the 2d of September 1666, a fire commenced by which about two-thirds of it were burned down, including the cathedral, the Royal Exchange, about a hundred parish churches, and a vast number of other public buildings. The conflagration commenced in the house of a baker named Farryner, at Pudding Lane, near the Tower, and, being favoured by a high wind, it continued for three nights and days, spreading gradually eastward, till it ended at a spot called Pye Corner, in Giltspur Street.*
>
> *Chambers Book of Days* (1864).

The **Great Fire of London** is undoubtedly the most devastating event in the history of that city. The horrific days of its duration were chronicled in vivid detail by two contemporary diarists, Samuel Pepys (1633–1703) and John Evelyn (1620–1706). The latter wrote, 'God grant my eyes may never behold the like, now seeing above 10,000 houses all in one flame; the noise and cracking and thunder of the impetuous flames, ye shrieking of women and children, the hurry of people, the fall of Towers, Houses, and Churches, was like an hideous storme, and the aire all about so hot and inflam'd that at last one was not able to approach it ... London was, but is no more!'. The death toll of the disaster was considerably lower than that of the Great Plague, which had killed more than 75,000 in the two preceding years, but probably somewhat higher than the single-figure official estimate, and many thousands were made homeless.

The reconstruction of London allowed a number of improvements to be made in the structure and layout of the city, straightening streets and replacing timber with brick, although the grand design drawn up by the architect Sir Christopher Wren (1632–1723) was not implemented. Wren was, however, responsible for the rebuilding of more than 50 churches, notably St Paul's Cathedral, and for the construction of a Monument to the Great Fire, which stands 202ft in height and the same distance from the site of the infamous bakery in Pudding Lane where it all began.

On this day:

Born: English philanthropist and reformer John Howard (1726); German physical chemist and Nobel Prize winner Wilhelm Ostwald (1853); English radio chemist and Nobel Prize winner Frederick Soddy (1877); US tennis player Jimmy Connors (1952); US actor Keanu Reeves (1964)

Died: Scottish civil engineer Thomas Telford (1834); French primitive painter Henri Rousseau (1910); French educator and reviver of the Olympic Games Baron Pierre de Coubertin (1937); South African-born British writer and philologist J R R Tolkien (1973); South African surgeon Christiaan Barnard (2001)

1898 Anglo-Egyptian troops under Lord Kitchener (1850–1916) won the Battle of Omdurman, restoring the Sudan to Egypt.

1906 Norwegian explorer Roald Amundsen (1872–1928) became the first man to negotiate Canada's Northwest Passage.

1923 The first elections were held in the newly independent Irish Free State.

1945 World War II – Japan formally surrendered to the Allies on board the US battleship *Missouri*.

1945 Vietnamese statesman Ho Chi Minh (1890–1969) and his colleagues proclaimed the Democratic Republic of Vietnam.

1958 China's first television station, Beijing Television, went into operation – it was later renamed China Central Television (CCTV).

1979 In the UK the first Ceefax-subtitled television programme was broadcast.

1985 It was announced that the wreckage of the *Titanic* had been located by an international expedition about 560 miles off the coast of Newfoundland.

3 September

> *This morning, the British ambassador in Berlin handed the German Government a final note stating that, unless we heard from them by 11 o'clock, that they were prepared at once to withdraw their troops from Poland, a state of war would exist between us. I have to tell you that no such undertaking has been received, and that consequently this country is at war with Germany.*
>
> Neville Chamberlain, radio broadcast (3 September 1939).

This announcement by Neville Chamberlain (1869–1940), prime minister of the UK, marked the beginning of World War II. Chamberlain had initially followed a policy of appeasement, recognizing Germany's claim to the Sudetenland (a region of what was then Czechoslovakia) set out in the Munich Agreement, signed in September 1938 – an event famously described by him as achieving 'peace with honour' and 'peace for our time'. In March 1939, however, Hitler's troops occupied the remainder of Czechoslovakia, and on 1 September they invaded Poland, a country that the UK and France had pledged to support. Two days later, Chamberlain's 'peace' was in tatters and his nation at war.

On this day:

Born: English engineer Matthew Boulton (1728); Australian immunologist, virologist and Nobel Prize winner Sir Macfarlane Burnet (1899); New Zealand rugby player Brian Lochore (1940); English cricketer Geoff Arnold (1944)

Died: English soldier and statesman Oliver Cromwell (1658); Russian novelist Ivan Turgenev (1883); Vietnamese statesman and president Ho Chi Minh (1969); US film critic Pauline Kael (2001)

1189 The coronation of King Richard I (1157–99), known as Richard the Lionheart, took place in Westminster Abbey, London.

1752 Britain switched from the Julian calendar to the Gregorian calendar by designating the day of 3 September as 14 September.

1783 England recognized American independence by signing the Treaty of Paris, which ended the War of Independence.

1939 World War II – two days after hostilities began in Poland, the UK and France declared war on Germany.

1943 World War II – the British Eighth Army invaded Italy; Italy signed a secret armistice with the Allies on the same day.

1954 The National Trust for Scotland purchased the remote island of Fair Isle, an important location for the observation of British bird life.

1976 The US space probe Viking 2 landed on Mars and began to send colour pictures back to earth.

1976 A riot in Hull Prison, which had lasted for nearly three days and destroyed most of the prison, ended peacefully.

1984 Typhoon Ike struck the southern Philippines, leaving thousands of people dead and over a million others homeless.

1994 China and Russia reached an agreement not to use force or target nuclear arms against one another.

1998 A Swissair plane en route to Geneva crashed into the sea off Nova Scotia, killing 229 people, including ten UN officials.

4 September

On this day in 1957, a three-year inquiry into homosexuality and prostitution, chaired by Sir John Wolfenden (1906–85), came to an end with the official publication of its report, which became known as the Wolfenden Report. It recommended the decriminalization of homosexual acts performed in private between consenting adults over the age of 21. This highly controversial proposal was rejected by the UK government, however, and it was a further ten years before it entered the statute books, with the Sexual Offences Act of 1967.

On this day:

Born: French writer and statesman René de Chateaubriand (1768); Austrian composer and organist Anton Bruckner (1824); French composer Darius Milhaud (1892); Australian swimmer Dawn Fraser (1937); US golfer Tom Watson (1949)

Died: English nobleman Robert Dudley, Earl of Leicester (1588); French statesman Robert Schuman (1963); French novelist Georges Simenon (1989); US actress Irene Dunn (1990)

1886 Apache leader Geronimo (1829–1909) surrendered for the final time to General Nelson Miles in Arizona.

1888 US inventor George Eastman (1854–1932) was granted a patent for his roll-film camera, and registered the Kodak tradename.

1948 Queen Wilhelmina of the Netherlands (1880–1962) abdicated in favour of her daughter, Juliana (born 1909).

1962 The last of Glasgow's green and yellow trams ran in the city's East End, ending a transport system that had run for 90 years.

1962 The Beatles began their first recording session with producer George Martin (born 1926) at EMI's Abbey Road studios in London.

1964 The Forth Road Bridge in Scotland was opened to traffic.

1978 Severe floods in northern India left at least two million people homeless.

1997 A series of suicide bomb attacks in central Jerusalem killed or injured nearly two hundred people.

5 September

> *I am grateful, and I'm very happy to receive it, in the name of the hungry, of the naked, of the homeless, of the crippled, of the blind, of the lepers, of all those people who feel unwanted, unloved ... people who have become a burden to the society and are shunned by everybody – in their name.*
>
> Mother Teresa, on being awarded the Nobel Peace Prize (1979).

Mother Teresa died on this day in 1997. Born Agnes Bojaxhiu in 1910, of Albanian parents, she spent her childhood in Skopje and decided at an early age to dedicate her life to Christ. In 1928 she went to India and joined an Irish order of nuns, teaching at a convent school and taking her final vows in 1937. She left her post as principal of the school in 1948 to work with the poor and sick in the slums of Calcutta. Two years later, she founded her own religious order, the Missionaries of Charity, and in 1952 she opened a House for the Dying, after finding a woman close to death who had been literally discarded by her family in a dustbin.

On this day:

Born: French king Louis XIV (1638); US Wild West outlaw Jesse James (1847); US composer John Cage (1912); German film director Werner Herzog (1942); Zanzibar-born British pop singer Freddie Mercury (1946)

Died: Flemish artist Pieter Brueghel, the Elder (1569); French philosopher and social theorist Auguste Comte (1857); English aviator Sir Douglas Bader (1982)

1174 Canterbury Cathedral caught fire after sparks from a fire in the city blew onto its roof.

1698 Russian tsar Peter the Great (1672–1725) imposed a tax on beards to encourage the westernization of fashion in his country.

1781 British and French fleets fought against one another in the Battle of Chesapeake Bay off the east coast of the USA.

1905 The Treaty of Portsmouth was signed in New Hampshire, ending the Russo-Japanese War.

1922 The first coast-to-coast flight across the USA was completed by US air force officer James Doolittle (1896–1993) in 21 hours and 19 minutes.

1951 Maureen Connolly (1934–69) – the 16-year-old known as 'Little Mo' – became the youngest-ever winner of the US tennis championship.

1959 The UK's first trunk call from a public call-box was made in Bristol by the Deputy Lord Mayor.

1963 English model and showgirl Christine Keeler (born 1942) was arrested and charged with perjury in connection with the Profumo Affair.

1972 At the Olympic Games in Munich, a hostage crisis began that eventually resulted in the deaths of eleven Israeli athletes at the hands of Palestinian guerillas.

1975 In California, US President Gerald R Ford (born 1913) survived an assassination attempt by Lynette 'Squeaky' Fromme, a disciple of Charles Manson (born 1934).

2002 Afghan president Hamid Karzai (born 1957) survived an assassination attempt by unidentified gunmen in Kandahar.

6 September

On this day:

Born: French soldier and revolutionary the Marquis de Lafayette (1757); Scottish physiologist and Nobel Prize winner John Macleod (1876); US businessman, diplomat and founder of a political dynasty Joseph Kennedy (1888); Yugoslavian king Peter II (1923)

Died: Ottoman emperor Süleyman I (1566); 25th President of the USA William McKinley (1901); US novelist, film producer and director James Clavell (1994); Hungarian-born British conductor Sir Georg Solti (1997); Japanese film director Akira Kurosawa (1998)

1552 The first circumnavigation of the world was completed by Portuguese navigator Juan Sebastian del Cano (died 1526) in Ferdinand Magellan's ship *Vittoria*, after Magellan (c.1480–1521) died in battle during the voyage.

1852 The UK's first free public lending library opened in Manchester.

1899 The first cans of evaporated milk were produced, by what would become the Carnation Milk Company, in the USA.

1940 King Carol II of Romania (1893–1953) abdicated in favour of his son Michael (born 1921).

1941 World War II – in Nazi Germany and occupied areas, it became compulsory for Jewish citizens over the age of six to wear the yellow Star of David.

1952 In the UK a jet fighter disintegrated and fell into a crowd at Farnborough Air Show, killing a total of 31 people.

1966 South African prime minister Hendrik Verwoerd (1901–66), a staunch advocate of apartheid policies, was stabbed to death by a page during a parliamentary session in Cape Town.

1968 Swaziland became an independent kingdom within the Commonwealth.

1975 Czech tennis player Martina Navratilova (born 1956) requested political asylum in the USA; she later became a US citizen.

1997 An estimated 2.2 billion people worldwide watched the televised funeral of Diana, Princess of Wales (1961–97), which was held at Westminster Abbey, London.

7
September

Several tens of thousands of men lay dead in various attitudes and uniforms on the fields and meadows … where for centuries the peasants of Borodino, Gorky, Shevardino and Semeonovsk had harvested their crops and grazed their cattle. … Over all the plain, which had been so gay and beautiful with bayonets glittering and little puffs of smoke in the morning sun, there now hung a fog of damp and smoke, and the air was foul with a strange, sour smell of saltpetre and blood. Clouds had gathered and drops of rain began to fall on the dead and wounded, on the panic-stricken and the weary, and on those who were filled with misgiving. 'Enough, enough!' the rain seemed to be saying.

Leo Tolstoy, *War and Peace* (1869), translated by Rosemary Edmonds.

The Battle of Borodino was fought on this day in 1812. (In the Russian calendar then in use, the corresponding date was 26 August.) Napoleon I's advance through Russia with his Grand Army was halted at Borodino, a village to the west of Moscow, by Russian troops commanded by Mikhail Kutuzov. After a long and bloody battle, the Russians were severely beaten (but not totally defeated) and the French considered that they had won the day: Napoleon later said of the encounter, 'The French showed themselves to be worthy victors, and the Russians can rightly call themselves invincible.'

Napoleon proceeded to Moscow but failed to force the city to surrender, and in October the French began their humiliating and disastrous retreat, an event celebrated in Tchaikovsky's *1812 Overture*, which was composed to commemorate the 70th anniversary of the Russian victory in 1882.

The Battle of Borodino itself is remembered with an annual re-enactment at the site in early September.

On this day:

Born: English queen Elizabeth I (1533); Scottish-born Australian explorer John McDouall Stuart (1815); US primitive artist Grandma Moses (1860); English poet Dame Edith Sitwell (1887); English actor and director Sir Anthony Quayle (1913)

Died: English queen Catherine Parr (1548); English architect William Butterfield (1900); English painter Holman Hunt (1910); English drummer with the Who Keith Moon (1978); Zairean soldier and politician Mobutu Sese Seko (1997)

1822 Brazil proclaimed its independence from Portugal.

1838 English lighthousekeeper's daughter Grace Darling (1815–42), with her father, rescued the nine survivors of the wrecked SS *Forfarshire* off the coast of Northumberland.

1892 US boxer 'Gentleman' Jim Corbett (1866–1933) defeated John L Sullivan (1858–1918) in the 21st round to become the world heavyweight champion.

1901 The signing of the Peace of Beijing ended China's Boxer Rebellion against foreign influence in the country.

1906 The ill-fated ocean liner *Lusitania* embarked on her record-breaking maiden voyage to New York, arriving on 13 September after averaging a speed of 23 knots.

1940 World War II – in London, two months of nightly bombings by Germany's Luftwaffe began, known as the Blitz.

1952 Egyptian prime minister Aly Maher was forced out of office by his country's army following a bloodless coup.

1977 The Panama Canal Agreement, regarding the transfer of control of the canal to Panama in the year 2000, was signed in Washington, DC.

1986 South African Anglican prelate Bishop Desmond Tutu (born 1931) was enthroned as the first black Archbishop of Cape Town in South Africa.

2000 Protestors against high fuel prices in the UK began to blockade the main UK oil refineries.

8 September

Feast day of the **Nativity of the Blessed Virgin Mary**, often celebrated with traditional festivities by churches that bear her name.

On this day:

Born: English king Richard I, the Lionheart (1157); French poet and Nobel Prize winner Frédéric Mistral (1830); English poet and novelist Siegfried Sassoon (1886); English architect Sir Denys Lasdun (1914); English dramatist, journalist and humorist Michael Frayn (1933)

Died: Oglala Sioux chief Crazy Horse (1877); German physiologist and physicist Hermann von Helmholtz (1894); German composer Richard Strauss (1949); French Fauvist artist André Derain (1954); German film director Leni Riefenstahl (2003)

1664 The American city of New Amsterdam was captured from the Dutch by the British Army and renamed New York.

1943 World War II – US general Dwight D Eisenhower (1890–1969) announced the unconditional surrender of Italy.

1952 *The Old Man and the Sea* by Ernest Hemingway (1899–1961) was published.

1967 Uganda became a republic, with Milton Obote (born 1924) as its president.

1968 British tennis player Virginia Wade (born 1945) defeated the top-seeded US player Billie Jean King (born 1943) to win the first amalgamated US Open women's singles title.

1974 US President Gerald Ford (born 1913) granted former President Richard Nixon (1913–94) a full pardon for all federal crimes he might have committed whilst in office during the Watergate scandal.

1977 Canadian Cindy Nicholas (born 1957) became the first woman to swim a two-way crossing of the English Channel, completing the feat in 19 hours and 55 minutes.

1986 Chilean dictator Augusto Pinochet (born 1915) survived an assassination attempt by rebel fighters.

9
September

On the 9th of September 1513, was fought the battle of Flodden, resulting in the defeat and death of the Scottish king, James IV, the slaughter of nearly thirty of his nobles and chiefs, and the loss of about 10,000 men. It was an overthrow which spread sorrow and dismay through Scotland, and was long remembered as one of the greatest calamities ever sustained by the nation. With all tenderness for romantic impulse and chivalric principle, a modern man, even of the Scottish nation, is forced to admit that the Flodden enterprise of James IV, was an example of gigantic folly, righteously punished.

Chambers Book of Days (1864).

The Battle of Flodden was fought in Northumberland between the Scottish troops of King James IV (1473–1513) and English forces led by Thomas Howard, Earl of Surrey (1443–1524). King Henry VIII (1491–1547) was engaged in the invasion of France at the time: it was this attack on his country's old allies that had prompted the Scottish king's action, despite his new alliance with England (through his marriage with Margaret Tudor, daughter of Henry VII, in 1503). James's army had the advantage of numbers and position on the battlefield, but the English had superior weaponry and tactics. The heavy Scottish losses struck the whole country – James had been a popular and well-respected king, and had had no difficulty in persuading a huge body of men, both Highlanders and Lowlanders from all classes of society, to follow him across the border.

Still from the sire the son shall hear
Of the stern strife, and carnage drear,
Of Flodden's fatal field,
Where shivered was fair Scotland's spear
And broken was her shield!

Sir Walter Scott, *Marmion* (1808).

On this day:

Born: French prelate and statesman Cardinal Richelieu (1585); English naval officer William Bligh (1754); Austrian theatre manager Max Reinhardt (1873); US soul singer Otis Redding (1941)

Died: English navigator Sir Humphrey Gilbert (1583); French painter and lithographer Henri de Toulouse-Lautrec (1901); Chinese Communist leader Mao Zedong (1976); US physicist Edward Teller (2003)

1087 King William I of England, known as William the Conqueror, (1027–87) died from injuries sustained in the Battle of Mantes five weeks earlier.

1850 California became the 31st state of the USA.

1948 The Democratic People's Republic of Korea (known as North Korea) was proclaimed, with Pyongyang as its capital.

1956 Elvis Presley (1935–77) made his first appearance on US television's *The Ed Sullivan Show.*

1968 The first amalgamated US Open tennis tournament was won by US amateur player Arthur Ashe (1943–93).

1997 Former South African prime minister and Nobel Prize winner F W de Klerk (born 1936) retired from Parliament.

1997 Sinn Fein formally announced a ceasefire, and took its place in multi-party talks on Northern Ireland's future.

1999 In the UK, a report published by the Police Review Commission suggested that the Northern Ireland's police force, the Royal Ulster Constabulary, should undergo widespread reform.

2001 Afghanistan's opposition leader Ahmed Shah Massood (1953–2001) was fatally wounded in a suicide bomb attack by assassins posing as journalists.

10 September

> *American Express? That'll do nicely, sir.*
>
> Advertising slogan.

The American Express credit card service came to the UK on this day in 1963. It was the first credit card available in the country that could be used in a wide range of outlets all over the world (its only significant competitor, Diner's Card, being restricted in usage), but it was soon to be followed by many more.

On this day:

Born: English physician Thomas Sydenham (1624); English architect Sir John Soane (1753); Scottish explorer Mungo Park (1771); German archaeologist Robert Koldewey (1855); US golfer Arnold Palmer (1929)

Died: Italian writer Ugo Foscolo (1827); English dog show organizer Charles Cruft (1938); Angolan nationalist and politician Agostinho Neto (1979); South African politician and president John Vorster (1983)

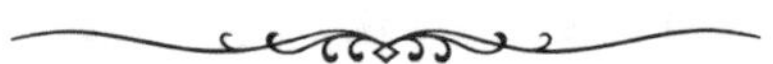

1514 Thomas Wolsey (c.1475–1530) became Archbishop of York.

1846 The sewing machine was patented by US inventor Elias Howe (1819–67) in Spencer, Massachusetts.

1897 London taxi driver George Smith drove into the frontage of a building on Bond Street, Mayfair, and became the first person in the UK to be charged with drunk-driving; he was fined £1.

1939 World War II – Canada declared war on Germany.

1945 Norwegian fascist leader Vidkun Quisling (1887–1945) was sentenced to death for treason after collaborating with the Nazis.

1977 In France, the guillotine was used as a form of capital punishment for the last time.

1988 German tennis player Steffi Graf (born 1969) won the US Open women's final, completing a grand slam.

1998 US President Bill Clinton (born 1946) met with his cabinet to apologize for the Monica Lewinsky scandal.

2000 UK forces rescued six soldiers from the Royal Irish Regiment who were being held hostage by rebels in the Sierra Leonean jungle.

2002 Switzerland joined the United Nations.

11 September

Today our fellow citizens – our way of life, our very freedom – came under attack in a series of deliberate and deadly terrorist acts. The victims were in airplanes, or in their offices: secretaries, businessmen and women, military and federal workers, mums and dads, friends and neighbours. Thousands of lives were suddenly ended by evil, despicable acts of terror.

George W Bush, television address to the nation (11 September 2001).

The events of this day in 2001 have become known by the date itself: **September 11** or **9/11** (using the US month-first convention). Terrorist attacks on the USA, by the Islamic militant group Al-Quaeda, killed around 3,000 people. Two hijacked civilian planes were flown into the twin towers of the World Trade Center in New York, which subsequently collapsed, a third aircraft struck the Pentagon in Washington, DC, and a fourth crashed in a field near Pittsburgh. The site where the World Trade Center towers had stood became known as Ground Zero, and the first official memorial service took place there on 28 October 2001. People from around the world were invited to submit plans for a memorial at Ground Zero, with 'Reflecting Absence' chosen as the winning design.

On this day:

Born: Scottish poet James Thomson (1700); English agriculturist and writer Arthur Young (1741); English novelist, poet and essayist D H Lawrence (1885); Indian land reformer Vinoba Bhave (1895); English motorcycle racer Barry Sheene (1950)

Died: English political economist David Ricardo (1823); Soviet politician Nikita Khrushchev (1971); Chilean politician Salvador Allende (1973); US actress Jessica Tandy (1994); US American football player Johnny Unitas (2002)

1297 Scottish patriot William Wallace (c.1274–1305) led his troops to victory over the English forces in the Battle of Stirling Bridge.

1649 English soldier and statesman Oliver Cromwell (1599–1658) besieged the Catholic garrison of Drogheda in Ireland, and was reported to have massacred most of the inhabitants.

1777 During the American War of Independence, the British defeated troops led by George Washington (1732–99) at the Battle of Brandywine Creek in Pennsylvania.

1855 Crimean War – the Russian stronghold Sevastopol was abandoned to the Allies after a twelve-month siege.

1895 The FA Cup was stolen from a shop window in Birmingham, where Cup winners Aston Villa had placed it on display; it was only in 1963 that an 83-year-old man admitted he had melted the trophy down to make counterfeit coins.

1951 The première of the opera *The Rake's Progress* by Igor Stravinsky (1882–1971), with a libretto partly written by W H Auden (1907–73), was held in Venice.

1978 Bulgarian dissident writer and broadcaster Georgi Markov died of blood poisoning after being stabbed four days earlier by an attacker using an umbrella tipped with ricin.

1980 The famous Marlborough Diamond was stolen by two Chicago gangsters from a London jeweller's shop.

1997 The Referendum on Devolution in Scotland was approved by an overwhelming majority, leading to the creation of a new Scottish Parliament.

12 September

On this day in 1940, the world-famous cave paintings at Lascaux, in the Dordogne region of France, were discovered by four boys in search of their dog (which had fallen down a hole). The prehistoric paintings, around 16,000 years old, chiefly depict the animals hunted at that time: bison, reindeer, bulls, bears, etc. The cave was opened to the public in 1948, but the passage of more than a million visitors during the following years took its toll on this valuable site, precipitating the growth of moss and algae and the deposition of white calcite on the walls. Since 1963 the cave has been closed to all but a privileged few who are allowed limited access for the purposes of research. A replica cave was created nearby for the benefit of disappointed tourists.

On this day:

Born: US inventor and industrialist Richard Hoe (1812); US inventor of the gatling machinegun Richard Gatling (1818); US athlete Jesse Owens (1913); English actor Sir Ian Holm (1931)

Died: Prussian field marshal Gebhard von Blücher (1819); South African black activist Steve Biko (1977); US actor Anthony Perkins (1992); US country music singer, songwriter and guitarist Johnny Cash (2003)

1440 Eton College in England received its foundation charter from King Henry VI (1421–71).

1609 English navigator Henry Hudson (c.1550–1611) first sailed into the river in North America that would later be named after him.

1878 Cleopatra's Needle, an Ancient Egyptian obelisk dating back to approximately 1500 BC, was erected on the Thames Embankment in London.

1910 Alice Stebbins Wells was appointed to the Los Angeles Police Department, becoming the world's first policewoman with arrest powers.

1936 Fred Perry (1909–95), British tennis champion, defeated J Donald Budge (1915–2000) at the US Open, becoming the first non-US player to win three US men's singles titles.

1953 Massachusetts senator John F Kennedy (1917–63) married Jacqueline Lee Bouvier (1929–94) in Rhode Island.

1959 The USSR successfully launched the Luna II rocket towards the Moon, where it landed thirty-six hours later.

1974 Military leaders in Ethiopia deposed Emperor Haile Selassie (1891–1975) in a coup.

2000 Under Dutch law, homosexual marriages were granted the same legal status as heterosexual marriages.

13
September

> *Que la mort me trouve plantant mes choux, mais nonchalant d'elle, et encore plus de mon jardin imparfait. (I would like death to come to me while I am planting cabbages, caring little for death and even less for the imperfection of my garden.)*
>
> Michel de Montaigne, *Essais* (1580),
> translated by Charles Cotton.

The French essayist Michel de Montaigne died on this day in 1592 at the Château de Montaigne, Périgord, his birthplace and home for the latter part of his life. Born in 1533, he had a somewhat experimental early education: his father hired a German tutor with no knowledge of French and ordered that the boy be addressed only in Latin by the entire household. At the age of six he was sent to the Collège de Guyenne in Bordeaux; just seven years later, he embarked on the study of law. In 1557 he was appointed to the post of *conseiller* at the *parlement* of Bordeaux, an office he held until his resignation in 1570. His father had died, and Montaigne was able to retire to the family estate, where he lived the life of a country gentleman and devoted himself to writing. His philosophical and autobiographical *Essais* (1572–80), the work for which he is best remembered, set out his thoughts on a wide range of topics – from fatherhood to suicide, from idleness to the persecution of witches – and introduced a new literary genre.

On this day:

Born: English statesman William Cecil, 1st Baron Burghley (1520); US inventor Oliver Evans (1755); German pianist and composer Clara Schumann (1819); Austrian-born US composer, conductor and teacher Arnold Schoenberg (1874); British children's author, short-story writer, playwright and versifier Roald Dahl (1916)

Died: English humanist and scholar Sir John Cheke (1557); English politician and debater Charles James Fox (1806); English artist, cartoonist and book illustrator Heath Robinson (1944); English-born US conductor Leopold Stokowski (1977); Czechoslovak-born British tennis and hockey player Jaroslav Drobny (2001)

1759 In the French and Indian War, British forces defeated the French on the Plains of Abraham near Quebec City.

1788 New York City was declared the temporary national capital of the USA.

1942 World War II – Germany began an attack on Stalingrad.

1943 General Chiang Kai-shek (1887–1975) became president of China.

1980 Hercules, a trained bear who had escaped during the filming of a television commercial on the Hebridean island of Benbecula, was recaptured after nearly four weeks and made a full recovery.

1989 In Cape Town, South Africa, a major anti-apartheid demonstration was led by Archbishop Desmond Tutu (born 1931).

1993 At the White House, Israel and the Palestine Liberation Organization signed a peace agreement relating to future Palestinian self-rule in the occupied territories.

1997 The first post-war municipal election was held in Bosnia.

1997 The funeral of Roman Catholic nun, missionary and Nobel Prize winner Mother Teresa (1910–97) was held in Calcutta.

2001 English politician Iain Duncan Smith (born 1954) was elected leader of the Conservative Party.

14 September

This is **Holy Cross Day**, also known as **Holy Rood Day**, the **Triumph of the Cross**, or the **Exaltation of the Cross**.

> *The discovery of the cross on which Christ was supposed to have suffered, by the Empress Helena (see under May 3), led to the sacred relic being raised or exalted in view of the people, in a magnificent church built by her son the Emperor Constantine, at Jerusalem; and this ceremony of the exaltation of the holy cross, which took place on the 14th September 335, was commemorated in a festival held on every recurrence of that day, by both the Greek and Latin churches.*
>
> *Chambers Book of Days* (1864).

Holy Cross Day is one of two days also known as **Devil's Nutting Day**, the other being St Matthew's Day (21 September). It was said that those who went nutting (gathering hazelnuts) on this day would meet the Devil engaged in the same task. The Devil was also said to go nutting on Sundays, and the superstition may have been an attempt to discourage young people from indulging, on a holy day, in the frivolous and amorous activities that inevitably accompanied any such foray into the woods.

> *The Devil, as some people say,*
> *A nutting goes Holy-Rood day.*
> *Let women then their children keep*
> *At home that day, better asleep*
> *They were, or cattle for to tend*
> *Than nutting go, and meet the Fiend;*
> *But if they'll not be ruled by this,*
> *Blame me not if they do amiss.*
>
> *Poor Robin's Almanack* (1693).

On this day:

Born: Italian composer Luigi Cherubini (1760); German naturalist Lord Alexander von Humboldt (1769); Czechoslovak diplomat

and politician Jan Masaryk (1886); English artist, ornithologist and conservationist Sir Peter Scott (1909); New Zealand actor Sam Neill (1947)

Died: North African Christian St Cyprian (AD 258); Italian poet and author Dante Alighieri (1321); US dancer and choreographer Isadora Duncan (1927); Czechoslovak statesman and first president of Czechoslovakia Tomáš Masaryk (1937); US film actress and princess Grace of Monaco (1982)

1741 German–English composer George Frideric Handel (1685–1759) completed his *Messiah* oratorio after more than three weeks of non-stop work.

1814 US lawyer and poet Francis Scott Key (1780–1843) wrote the words to 'The Star Spangled Banner' during an attack on Fort McHenry in Baltimore, Maryland. The song became the USA's national anthem in 1931.

1860 Niagara Falls was illuminated for the first time, using Bengal lights, in honour of the visiting Prince of Wales.

1868 The first recorded 'hole in one' was scored by Scottish golfer 'Young' Tom Morris (1851–75) during the Open Golf Championship at Prestwick, which he won.

1901 Following President William McKinley's (1843–1901) assassination, Theodore Roosevelt (1858–1919) became the 26th President of the USA.

1911 Russian premier Peter Stolypin (1862–1911) was attacked by an assassin at the Kiev Opera House, and died four days later.

1948 In New York City, a groundbreaking ceremony was held on the future site of the United Nation's international headquarters.

1974 Chia Chia and Ching Ching, a pair of giant pandas presented to Prime Minister Edward Heath (born 1916) during his visit to China, arrived in London.

1975 The painting known as 'The Night Watch' by the Dutch painter Rembrandt (1606–69) was slashed by an unemployed teacher wielding a bread knife.

2001 The names of the 19 hijackers suspected of taking part in the 11 September terrorist attacks were released by the FBI.

15 September

> *One of the 'red-letter' days in the history of railways, a day that stamped the railway-system as a triumphant success, was marked by a catastrophe which threw gloom over an event in other ways most satisfactory.*
>
> *Chambers Book of Days* (1864).

The *Rocket*, a steam locomotive produced by George Stephenson (1781–1848) and his son Robert (1803–59), together with several others built to the same design, took part in the opening ceremony of the Liverpool and Manchester railway on 15 September 1830. Among the distinguished guests invited to travel on the inaugural journey were the Duke of Wellington, Sir Robert Peel, and William Huskisson, a former government minister and MP for Liverpool. The procession was led by the *Northumbrian*, pulling a carriage in which Wellington and Peel were seated; the remaining locomotives and their carriages followed on the other line. At about 17 miles from Liverpool, the trains stopped for water and some of the passengers alighted, one of whom was Huskisson, who crossed the track to speak to the Duke of Wellington. Shortly afterwards, the *Rocket* passed at speed alongside and Huskisson, unable to escape in time, sustained serious leg injuries. The procession continued to Manchester in subdued mood, and Huskisson died later that day.

On this day:

Born: Roman emperor Trajan (AD 53); English 'Popish Plot' conspirator Titus Oates (1649); English writer Dame Agatha Christie (1890); New Zealand pioneer aviator Jean Batten (1909); British prince Harry, Prince of Wales (1984)

Died: English engineer and inventor Isambard Kingdom Brunel (1859); US inventor William Seward Burroughs (1898); Austrian composer Anton Webern (1945); Swedish king Gustav VI (1973)

1776 During the American War of Independence, British forces captured the city of New York.

1916 World War I – military tanks were used for the first time by the British Army during the Battle of the Somme.

1935 Under the Nuremberg Laws, German Jews were deprived of their citizenship and the swastika became Nazi Germany's official symbol.

1938 Adolf Hitler (1889–1945) and British prime minister Neville Chamberlain (1869–1940) met at Berchtesgaden, Germany, for peace talks.

1940 World War II – during the Battle of Britain, the RAF claimed that British forces had shot down 185 German planes on this particular day.

1964 The UK newspaper, *The Sun*, which bore the slogan 'A paper born of the age we live in', was launched as a replacement for the defunct *Daily Herald*.

1966 The UK's first Polaris missile submarine, HMS *Resolution*, was launched.

1982 Pope John Paul II (born 1920) granted Palestinian resistance leader Yasser Arafat (born 1929) a private audience at the Vatican.

1985 The European golf team led by Tony Jacklin (born 1944) won the Ryder Cup, defeating the USA for the first time since 1957.

1988 The Museum of the Moving Image opened on London's South Bank.

1994 The USA withdrew the last of its marines from Somalia, ending nearly two years of US intervention.

2000 The opening ceremony of the 27th Olympiad was held in Sydney's Stadium Australia.

16 September

On 16 September 1620 the *Mayflower* set sail from Plymouth in SW England, bound for North America. Its 102 passengers were the Pilgrim Fathers, a group of Puritans who had broken away from the Church of England and had suffered persecution under King James I. An earlier attempt to make the crossing in two ships, the *Mayflower* and the *Speedwell*, had had to be abandoned when the *Speedwell* became unseaworthy.

After a nine-week voyage the *Mayflower* arrived at Cape Cod, with an extra passenger on board – one of the women had given birth at sea, to a son she named Oceanus. The pilgrims had been granted territory in Virginia, but adverse weather and waters prevented them from reaching it, and they finally landed at Plymouth, Massachusetts, in December 1620. There they established the first settlement in what was to become known as New England.

On this day:

Born: Russian soldier Mikhail Kutuzov (1745); Alsatian sculptor and poet Hans Arp (1887); Hungarian-born British film producer Sir Alexander Korda (1893); US blues singer and guitarist B B King (1925); Scottish rugby player Andy Irvine (1951)

Died: Spanish Dominican monk and first Inquisitor-General of Spain Tomás de Torquemada (1498); French king Louis XVIII (1824); British physician and Nobel Prize winner Sir Ronald Ross (1932); English singer with T-Rex Marc Bolan (1976); Greek-born US soprano Maria Callas (1977)

1630 The village of Shawmut in Massachusetts was renamed Boston.

1810 Mexicans began a revolt against the continuation of Spanish rule.

1812 The French army led by Napoleon I (1769–1821) destroyed a large part of Moscow by fire.

1859 Scottish explorer David Livingstone (1813–73) first reached Lake Nyasa (now Lake Malawi), which forms Malawi's boundary with Tanzania and Mozambique.

1861 The Post Office Savings Bank opened in the UK.

1963 Malaysia was officially established as an independent country; on the same day, a mob burned down its British embassy.

1968 The UK introduced the world's first two-tier postal system of first and second class mail.

1987 The Montreal Protocol, an agreement outlining plans for the reduction of ozone-depleting chemicals, was signed by 25 nations.

1992 On the day that became known as 'Black Wednesday', the UK suspended its membership of the European Exchange Rate Mechanism.

17 September

> *We the People of the United States, in Order to form a more perfect Union, establish Justice, insure domestic Tranquility, provide for the common defence, promote the general Welfare, and secure the Blessings of Liberty to ourselves and our Posterity, do ordain and establish this Constitution for the United States of America.*
>
> Preamble to the US Constitution.

In the USA this is **Constitution Day**, commemorating the signing of the constitution on 17 September 1787. The document was drawn up by the Constitutional Convention, an assembly of delegates from 12 of the 13 states of the USA (all but Rhode Island) and bore 39 signatures, including that of George Washington, first president of the USA. It defined the powers of the central government and the role of the states (most of which had already framed constitutions of their own) and replaced the Articles of Confederation, adopted in 1781. Conflict arose with regard to the representation of individual states, which varied greatly in size, within the national legislature. Unsurprisingly, the larger states wanted representation in proportion to their size, while the smaller states wanted equal representation for all. A compromise was reached whereby states are represented proportionally in the lower chamber of Congress (the House of Representatives) and by two senators per state in the upper chamber (the Senate).

The constitution was adopted in 1789 and gained its first ten amendments in 1791. Since then, amendments have been added at irregular intervals; the 13th amendment (1865), for example, abolished slavery, and the 19th amendment (1920) introduced national women's suffrage.

In 1952, Constitution Day was amalgamated with I am an American Day (formerly celebrated in May, by naturalized citizens) and renamed **Citizenship Day**. It is a day devoted to study of the constitution in schools and to general discussion and recognition of the privileges and responsibilities of being a US citizen. The week commencing 17 September was designated **Constitution Week**.

On this day:

Born: English reformer John Cartwright (1740); English dancer and choreographer Sir Frederick Ashton (1904); Irish-born Israeli president Chaim Herzog (1918); US country singer and songwriter Hank Williams (1923); English racing driver Sir Stirling Moss (1929)

Died: English and Scottish king James II and VII (1701); Scottish novelist Tobias Smollett (1771); English physicist and pioneer of photography William Henry Fox Talbot (1877); Turkish statesman and prime minister Adnan Menderes (1961); US politician Spiro T Agnew (1996)

1862 At the American Civil War battle of Antietam, won by Union forces, over 23,000 men were killed, wounded or captured in a single day.

1871 The seven-mile Mont Cenis railway tunnel, linking France and Italy, was opened.

1939 World War II – the USSR invaded Poland.

1944 World War II – the British airborne invasion of Arnhem, Holland, known as 'Operation Market Garden', began.

1980 Former Nicaraguan president Anastasio Somoza Debayle (1925–80) was assassinated while in exile in Paraguay.

1988 The opening ceremony of the 24th Olympiad was held in Seoul, South Korea.

1993 The right-wing British National Party won its first council seat in an east London by-election; the seat was lost a year later in a landslide victory for the Labour Party.

1999 US President Bill Clinton (born 1946) lifted the trade, travel and banking restrictions that the USA had imposed on North Korea 50 years earlier.

2001 After a six-day shutdown following the 11 September attacks, Wall Street trading resumed in New York.

18 September

> *I never said, 'I want to be alone.' I only said, 'I want to be left alone.' There is all the difference.*
>
> Greta Garbo, quoted in John Bainbridge, *Garbo* (1955).

The film actress Greta Garbo was born Greta Lovisa Gustafsson in Stockholm, Sweden, on this day in 1905. It was the Swedish director Mauritz Stiller who changed her name and took her to Hollywood, where she starred in silent films such as *Flesh and the Devil* and *Love* (both 1927). Already renowned for her aloof beauty and great acting talent, she became equally famous for the rich, accented, low voice that was first heard in *Anna Christie* (1930). A string of successes followed in the 1930s – *Queen Christina* (1933), *Anna Karenina* (1935), *Camille* (1936), *Ninotchka* (1939) – but the poor reviews of her final film, *Two-Faced Woman* (1941), drove her into retirement and total seclusion for the remainder of her life. She died in 1990.

On this day:

Born: English writer, critic, lexicographer, and conversationalist Samuel Johnson (1709); US atomic scientist and Nobel Prize winner Edwin M McMillan (1907); English football goalkeeper Peter Shilton (1949)

Died: Swiss mathematician Leonhard Euler (1783); English essayist William Hazlitt (1830); English nuclear physicist and Nobel Prize winner Sir John Cockcroft (1967); US rock guitarist and singer Jimi Hendrix (1970); US writer Katherine Anne Porter (1980)

1759 France formally surrendered Quebec to Britain.

1793 The foundation cornerstone of the USA's Capitol Building in Washington, DC, was laid by President George Washington (1732–99).

1810 The people of Chile declared their independence from Spain.

1851 *The New York Times* was first published, with the announcement 'We publish today the first issue of the New-York Daily Times, and we intend to issue it every morning (Sundays excepted) for an indefinite number of years to come'.

1894 A production of the British musical *A Gaiety Girl* opened at Daly's Theatre in New York.

1922 Hungary joined the League of Nations.

1978 Israeli and Egyptian leaders reached a settlement at Camp David in the USA, leading to a peace treaty the following year.

1981 The French government announced that capital punishment and the use of the guillotine would be abolished.

19 September

On this day:

Born: English Quaker, chocolate manufacturer and social reformer George Cadbury (1839); English soapmaker and philanthropist William Hesketh Lever, 1st Viscount Leverhulme (1851); US jurist Lewis F Powell, Jnr (1907); English actor Jeremy Irons (1948); English model and actress Twiggy (1949)

Died: German financier Mayer Amschel Rothschild (1812); 20th President of the USA James A Garfield (1881); US inventor of the xerography process Chester Carlson (1968); Italian novelist, essayist and journalist Italo Calvino (1985); English historian Rosalind Mitchison (2002)

1356 The Battle of Poitiers was fought between England and France during the Hundred Years War; the English forces, under Edward the Black Prince (1330–76), were victorious and French king John II (1319–64) was captured.

1870 The siege of Paris began during the Franco-Prussian War.

1876 US retailer Melville Bissell of Grand Rapids, Michigan, patented the first carpet sweeper.

1893 New Zealand became the first country in the world to give women the vote in parliamentary elections.

1945 British traitor William Joyce (1906–46), known as Lord Haw-Haw, who had broadcast propaganda against the UK from Radio Hamburg during World War II, was sentenced to death at the Old Bailey in London.

1955 Argentinian president Juan Domingo Perón (1895–1974) was overthrown in a military coup.

1959 During a visit to Los Angeles, Soviet leader Nikita Khrushchev (1894–1971) became angry and upset at the news that concerns for his own security would mean he was not allowed to visit Disneyland.

2002 US President George W Bush (born 1946) requested permission from Congress to use military force as a means of overthrowing Saddam Hussein (born 1937) if certain United Nations' demands were not met.

20 September

The Italian street name Via XX Settembre, found in many towns and cities, commemorates the date in 1870 when national troops entered Rome, then under papal control, a historic event that effectively completed the unification of Italy. The power of the pope was thereafter confined to the Vatican, an independent state within the city.

On this day:

Born: English manufacturer and philanthropist Sir Titus Salt (1803); Scottish chemist and physicist Sir James Dewar (1842); English poet and novelist Stevie Smith (1902); Italian film actress Sophia Loren (1934)

Died: German folklorist Jacob Grimm (1863); German poet and novelist Theodore Fontane (1898); US lawyer and politician Fiorello La Guardia (1947); Finnish composer Jean Sibelius (1957); English theatre director Joan Littlewood (2002)

1519 Portuguese navigator Ferdinand Magellan (c.1480–1521) embarked from Seville on his round-the-world voyage. Although the voyage was successful, Magellan died en route.

1854 Seven Victoria Crosses were won at the Battle of Alma during the Crimean War.

1961 Argentinian Antonio Abertondo began the first return swim across the English Channel, setting off from England on the first crossing; he completed the trip in 43 hours and five minutes, with a four-minute break in the middle.

1967 The ocean liner the *Queen Elizabeth II*, often known as the QE2, was launched by Queen Elizabeth II (born 1926) at Clydebank, Scotland.

1973 In Houston, Texas, US tennis player Billie Jean King (born 1943) defeated a male player, Bobby Riggs (1918–95), in a $100,000 'Battle of the Sexes' tennis match.

1981 Belize, which had been known as British Honduras until 1973, became independent within the Commonwealth.

1999 International peacekeeping forces arrived in East Timor.

2000 The Whitewater inquiry, investigating charges of criminal conduct against Bill (born 1946) and Hillary Clinton (born 1947), was suspended because of insufficient evidence of any wrongdoing on their part.

21 September

> *St Matthew's Day bright and clear brings good wine in next year.*
>
> Traditional saying.

This is the feast day of Christ's Apostle Matthew, writer of the first gospel of the New Testament. Matthew collected taxes for the Romans before being called to follow Christ, and is therefore the patron saint of tax-collectors, bankers and accountants.

St Matthew's Day falls close to the autumnal equinox (23 September), which marks the end of summer and the beginning of autumn. It is time to close

the beehives for the year ('St Matthee shut up the bee') and to prepare for the darker nights ahead ('St Matthew get candlesticks new'). It is also one of two days known as Devil's Nutting Day (described at 14 September), when it is unwise to go off to the woods to gather hazelnuts.

On this day:

Born: Italian religious and political reformer Girolamo Savonarola (1452); Scottish inventor of macadamized roads John Loudon McAdam (1756); English composer Gustav Holst (1874); Ghanaian politician, prime minister and president Kwame Nkrumah (1909); US author Stephen King (1947)

Died: Roman poet Virgil (19 BC); Holy Roman emperor Charles V (1558); Scottish novelist and poet Sir Walter Scott (1832); German philosopher Arthur Schopenhauer (1860); US track and field sprinter Florence Griffith-Joyner (1998)

1745 In Scotland, Bonnie Prince Charlie's (1720–88) Jacobite Army defeated English forces at the Battle of Prestonpans.

1792 The French National Convention voted to abolish the monarchy and declare France a republic.

1809 The UK's foreign minister, George Canning (1770–1827), and the war minister, Viscount Castlereagh (1769–1822), attempted to resolve a political disagreement by duelling. Both survived, and resigned.

1931 The UK abandoned the gold standard.

1937 The novel *The Hobbit* by J R R Tolkien (1892–1973) was published.

1964 Malta became independent after 164 years of British rule.

1979 An RAF Harrier jump jet crashed into the centre of a town in Cambridgeshire, England, killing three people.

1998 Grand jury testimony by US President Bill Clinton (born 1946) about his relationship with Monica Lewinsky (born 1973) was broadcast to the US public.

1999 In Taiwan, an earthquake measuring 7.6 on the Richter scale killed over 2,000 people and injured over 8,000.

22 September

Joseph Smith (1805–44), founder of the Church of the Latter-Day Saints (the Mormons), claimed to have received a set of gold plates inscribed with the text of the Book of Mormon on 22 September 1827. He had apparently been told of the existence of these plates four years earlier, at the age of 17, by a heavenly messenger named Moroni. With divine inspiration, Smith set about translating the characters in which the text was written, and the first edition of the Book of Mormon was published at Palmyra, New York, in 1830. In the preface, a number of witnesses testify to the existence of the gold plates, which were subsequently taken away by Moroni. The book itself is an account of certain ancient ancestors of the Native Americans, to whom Christ is said to have appeared after his ascension.

On this day:

Born: English statesman and man of letters Philip Stanhope, 4th Earl of Chesterfield (1694); English suffragette Christabel Pankhurst (1880); Austrian film director and actor Erich von Stroheim (1885); English writer Fay Weldon (1931)

Died: English preacher and founder of English Unitarianism John Biddle (1662); French writer Alain-Fournier (1914); Russian-born US composer Irving Berlin (1989); US actor George C Scott (1999); Russian-born US violinist Isaac Stern (2001)

1735 Robert Walpole (1676–1745) became the first British politician to occupy 10 Downing Street.

1776 During the American War of Independence, American spy Nathan Hale (1755–76) was hanged by the British. Before dying, he reportedly stated, 'I regret that I have but one life to lose for my country'.

1862 US President Abraham Lincoln (1809–65) issued the preliminary Emancipation Proclamation, which declared that all slaves in rebel states would be free as of 1 January 1863.

1934 An explosion and fierce fire at Gresford colliery near Wrexham, North Wales, cost 265 miners their lives.

1949 The USSR exploded its first atomic bomb.

1955 Independent Television (ITV) programmes began in the London area. To meet the new competition, BBC radio 'killed off' Grace Archer, a character in its popular radio serial *The Archers,* on the same night.

1980 The conflict in the Persian Gulf erupted into a war between Iran and Iraq.

1989 The IRA bombed the Royal Marines School of Music at Deal, Kent, killing eleven bandsmen and injuring many others.

23 September

The great question that has never been answered and which I have not yet been able to answer, despite my thirty years of research into the feminine soul, is 'What does a woman want?'

Sigmund Freud, letter to Marie Bonaparte, quoted in Ernest Jones, *Sigmund Freud: Life and Work* (1955).

Sigmund Freud, the founder of psychoanalysis, died on this day in 1939. Born in 1856 of Jewish parents, he spent most of his life in Vienna, moving to London after the annexation of Austria by Nazi Germany in 1938, the year before his death. In his early medical studies he specialized in neurology, but he subsequently switched to psychopathology, anxious to investigate the possibility of treating hysteria and similar conditions with a technique of conversational 'free association', rather than hypnosis.

Freud's controversial theories were set out in a number of influential texts, notably *Die Traumdeutung* (1900, 'The Interpretation of Dreams'), which argued that dreams can be interpreted to reveal repressed sexual desires. Weekly meetings at his home with like-minded colleagues such as Alfred Adler and Carl Jung developed into the Vienna Psychoanalytical Society in 1908 and, two years later, into the International Psychoanalytical Association.

In his later career, Freud elaborated on a theoretical division of the unconscious mind in *Ego and Id* (1923) and put forward his thoughts on religion in *The Future of an Illusion* (1927). He was awarded the Goethe prize in 1930 and elected to the Royal Society in 1936. A number of his descendants have won fame in various fields: his daughter Anna (1896–1982) was a pioneer of child psychoanalysis and his grandsons include the painter Lucien Freud (born 1922) and the writer, broadcaster and caterer Sir Clement Freud (born 1924).

On this day:

Born: French physicist Armand Fizeau (1819); US entertainer Mickey Rooney (1920); US jazz saxophonist and composer John Coltrane (1926); US singer and pianist Ray Charles (1930); US rock singer and guitarist Bruce Springsteen (1949)

Died: French novelist Prosper Mérimée (1870); Chilean poet and Nobel Prize winner Pablo Neruda (1973); US theatre and film choreographer and director Bob Fosse (1987)

1779 During the American War of Independence, Scottish-born US naval commander John Paul Jones (1747–92) defeated the British ships *Serapis* and *Countess of Scarborough* in a naval battle.

1846 German astronomer Johann Gottfried Galle (1812–1910) discovered the planet Neptune.

1952 English film actor and director Charlie Chaplin (1889–1977) visited England for the first time in over 20 years.

1957 In Arkansas, a mob of white protestors forced nine black students to leave Little Rock High School.

1972 The president of the Philippines, Ferdinand Marcos (1917–89), declared martial law.

1973 Former Argentinian president Juan Perón (1895–1974) returned to office.

1974 The BBC launched Ceefax, the world's first teletext service.

1997 An outburst by the Ulster Unionist politician Ken Maginnis (born 1938) threatened to derail peace negotiations in Northern Ireland.

24 September

The George Cross was instituted by King George VI (1895–1952) on this day 1940. Its purpose was to provide a means of recognizing civilian acts of heroism that would be equivalent in status to the Victoria Cross, which is restricted to military personnel. (Members of the armed forces are also eligible to receive the George Cross, for deeds performed outside the field of battle.) The silver cross-shaped medal, inscribed 'For Gallantry', replaced the Empire Gallantry Medal, and holders of the latter were given the George Cross in exchange. The first new recipient was Thomas H Alderson, an ARP detachment leader in Bridlington, Yorkshire, who rescued a number of people trapped under the wreckage of demolished houses during the Blitz.

On this day:

Born: English writer Horace Walpole, 4th Earl of Oxford (1717); US novelist F Scott Fitzgerald (1896); Australian pathologist, developer of the antibiotic penicillin and Nobel Prize winner Lord Florey (1898); Spanish-born US geneticist and Nobel Prize winner Severo Ochoa (1905); US puppeteer and fantasy film-maker Jim Henson (1936)

Died: German alchemist and physician Paracelsus (1541); Scottish soprano Dame Isobel Baillie (1983); US children's author and illustrator Dr Seuss (1991)

1869 In the USA, there was a panic on Wall Street when unscrupulous financiers Jay Gould (1836–92) and James Fisk (1834–72) attempted to corner the gold market; thousands of people were financially ruined as a result.

1930 The première of the play *Private Lives* by Noël Coward (1899–1973) was held at the Phoenix Theatre in London.

1960 The first nuclear powered aircraft carrier, the USS *Enterprise*, was launched at Newport News, Virginia.

1976 Responding to international pressure, the government of Rhodesia announced that it would introduce black majority rule within two years.

1988 Canadian athlete Ben Johnson (born 1961) won the 100m at the Seoul

Olympics, but was later tested positive for anabolic steroids and stripped of his gold medal.

1992 The UK's Minister for Heritage, David Mellor (born 1949), resigned from the government after widespread media coverage of his affair with the actress Antonia de Sancha.

1996 All the major nuclear powers in the world signed the Comprehensive Test Ban Treaty, agreeing to end all testing and development of nuclear weapons.

2002 UK prime minister Tony Blair (born 1953) unveiled an intelligence dossier that was later alleged to have been 'sexed up' in order to emphasize the potential dangers of Iraqi weapons of mass destruction.

25 September

The Battle of Stamford Bridge took place in Yorkshire on 25 September 1066. In a day of fierce hand-to-hand fighting, King Harold II (c.1022–1066) of England and his Saxon army defeated Harald III (1015–66), King of Norway, who had designs on the English throne. Harald was supported by Harold's brother Tostig; both died on the battlefield. Harold had thus disposed of two dangerous rivals, but a third was to land on the Sussex coast just three days later. Harold and his exhausted men marched south again to meet William of Normandy (c.1028–1087) at the Battle of Hastings on 14 October.

On this day:

Born: Italian Baroque architect and sculptor Francesco Borromini (1599); US novelist and Nobel Prize winner William Faulkner (1897); English comic actor Ronnie Barker (1929); Canadian pianist and composer Glenn Gould (1932); Indian cricketer Bishen Bedi (1946)

Died: English satirist Samuel Butler (1680); Austrian violinist, conductor and composer Johann Strauss, the Elder (1849); German-born US novelist Erich Maria Remarque (1970); Palestinian-born US academic, political activist and literary critic Edward Said (2003)

1513 Spanish explorer Vasco Balboa (1475–1519) climbed a peak in Central America and sighted the Pacific Ocean, the first European to do so; he claimed the ocean for Spain.

1690 America's first newspaper, *Publick Occurrences*, was published in Boston, Massachusetts.

1818 The first blood transfusion using human blood was performed at Guys Hospital, London.

1857 During the Indian Uprising the siege of the Lucknow garrison, which had begun on 1 July 1857, was temporarily relieved as forces led by Sir Henry Havelock (1795–1857) broke through and reinforced the garrison; they in turn were then besieged by the determined rebel forces until November.

1956 The first transatlantic telephone cable system was brought into use, linking the US and UK telephone networks.

1959 Prime Minister S W R D Bandaranaike (1899–1959) of Ceylon (now Sri Lanka) was shot by a Buddhist monk; he died the next day.

1979 *Question Time* was first broadcast on BBC television.

26 September

On this day in 1973, Concorde made its first non-stop transatlantic flight with passengers, from Washington to Paris. The supersonic aircraft completed the crossing in just over three and a half hours, flying at twice the speed of sound for approximately two-thirds of that time. The final Concorde flight was made on 24 October 2003.

On this day:

Born: French painter Théodore Géricault (1791); English aeronautical engineer Sir Barnes Wallis (1887); US-born British poet, critic and dramatist and Nobel Prize winner T S Eliot (1888); English art historian and Soviet spy Anthony Blunt (1907); US tennis player Serena Williams (1981)

Died: US frontiersman Daniel Boone (1820); English antislavery campaigner Thomas Clarkson (1846); Scottish Labour leader and politician Keir Hardie (1915); US blues singer Bessie Smith (1937); English pop singer Robert Palmer (2003)

1580 In his ship the *Golden Hind*, English navigator Francis Drake (c.1540–1596) arrived back in Plymouth, England, becoming the first Englishman to circumnavigate the world; he was subsequently knighted by Queen Elizabeth I (1533–1603).

1777 British troops occupied the city of Philadelphia during the American War of Independence.

1815 The Holy Alliance treaty was signed by Russia, Prussia and Austria.

1907 The British colony of New Zealand became a self-governing Dominion.

1934 The ocean liner the *Queen Mary* was launched on Clydebank, Scotland, by King George V (1865–1936) and Queen Mary (1867–1953).

1953 Sugar rationing ended in the UK, partly because of pressure from sweet manufacturers.

1957 The première of the musical *West Side Story* was held at the Winter Garden Theater on Broadway, New York.

1968 Censorship on the British stage was abolished under the Theatres Act.

1977 English business executive Freddie Laker (born 1922) began his low-cost 'Skytrain' airline service from the UK to the USA.

1997 Two earthquakes struck Italy, killing ten people. A number of cathedrals and priceless art treasures were badly damaged.

27 September

On this day:

Born: Florentine financier, statesman and philanthropist Cosimo de' Medici (1389); American revolutionary politician Samuel Adams (1722); South African soldier, statesman and first

prime minister Louis Botha (1862); English physicist, radio astronomer and Nobel Prize winner Sir Martin Ryle (1918)

Died: English churchman and statesman William of Wykeham (1404); French priest and philanthropist St Vincent de Paul (1660); French artist Edgar Degas (1917); Afghan politician Sayid Mohammad Najibullah (1996)

1825 The UK's first public railway, the Stockton and Darlington link, was opened by railway engineer George Stephenson (1781–1848), operating the engine *Locomotion*.

1922 King Constantine I of Greece (1868–1923) abdicated in favour of his son, George II (1890–1947), following a military revolt.

1930 US golfer Bobby Jones (1902–71) won the US Amateur Championships to become golf's grand slam champion; he then retired from competitive golf at the age of 28.

1938 The ocean liner the *Queen Elizabeth* was launched on Clydebank, Scotland.

1939 The city of Warsaw surrendered to Nazi forces after a 19-day period of resistance.

1959 A typhoon killed nearly 5,000 people on the Japanese island of Honshu.

1964 The Warren Commission, led by Earl Warren (1891–1974), submitted its final report after the investigation into the assassination of US President John F Kennedy (1917–63); it was found that the killing was not part of a domestic or foreign conspiracy.

1968 The day after censorship was abolished on the British stage, the musical *Hair*, featuring 13 naked actors, opened at the Shaftesbury Theatre in London.

1996 In Kabul, Afghanistan, a group of former seminary students known as the Taliban staged a coup, successfully driving out the existing government.

1998 In Germany, 16 years of conservative government ended when Gerhard Schröder (born 1944), a Social Democrat, was elected chancellor.

28 September

Pope John Paul I died on this day in 1978, after one of the shortest papal reigns in history – he had been elected just 33 days earlier. The cause of his sudden death was apparently a heart attack, but there was no autopsy, which gave rise to various conspiracy theories. Born Albino Luciani in 1912, he was the first pope to adopt a double name, which he chose in honour of his two predecessors: Pope John XXIII, who had made him a bishop, and Pope Paul VI, who had made him a cardinal. He was succeeded by Karol Wojtyla as Pope John Paul II, the first non-Italian pope for almost half a century.

On this day:

Born: English physician Richard Bright (1789); French journalist, statesman and prime minister Georges Clemenceau (1841); German heavyweight boxer Max Schmeling (1905); French film actress Brigitte Bardot (1934)

Died: Bohemian prince-duke and patron saint St Wenceslas I (929); French novelist Émile Zola (1902); US jazz trumpeter and bandleader Miles Davis (1991); Canadian statesman Pierre Trudeau (2000); Turkish-born US stage and film director Elia Kazan (2003)

1066 William the Conqueror (1027–87) invaded England, immediately capturing the towns of Pevensey and Hastings.

1396 The Battle of the Clans, a fight to the death between the Chattan (or Mackintosh) and Mackay (or Kay) clans, took place in Perthshire, Scotland; the Chattans were victorious.

1745 The British national anthem, 'God Save the King', had its first public performance at the Theatre Royal, Drury Lane, London, in the wake of the defeat of King George II (1683–1760) by the Jacobites at Prestonpans.

1923 The *Radio Times* was first published; it cost tuppence.

1924 Two specially built US aircraft known as Douglas World Cruisers landed in Seattle, completing the first ever round-the-world flight. The journey had taken 175 days.

1972 Diplomatic relations between Japan and Communist China were re-established.

2000 Israeli opposition leader Ariel Sharon (born 1928) toured the site known as Temple Mount, sparking violent clashes between Israeli troops and Palestinian citizens.

29 September

Michaelmas chickens and parsons' daughters never come to good.

Traditional saying.

This is **Michaelmas**, the feast day of St Michael ('Michael and All Angels' in the Anglican Church; 'Michael, Gabriel, and Raphael' in the Roman Catholic Church). It is the anniversary of the dedication of a church in his honour, the Basilica of St Michael, near Rome.

Michael is regarded in the Christian world as the chief of angels, or archangel. His history is obscure. In Scripture, he is mentioned five times, and always in a warlike character; namely, thrice by Daniel as fighting for the Jewish church against Persia; once by St Jude as fighting with the devil about the body of Moses; and once by St John as fighting at the head of his angelic troops against the dragon and his host. … Sometimes Michael is represented as the sole archangel, sometimes as only the head of a fraternity of archangels, which included likewise Gabriel, Raphael, and some others. He is usually represented in coat-armour, with a glory round his head, and a dart in his hand, trampling on the fallen Lucifer.

Chambers Book of Days (1864).

Michaelmas is one of the four days on which quarterly rents are paid. The tradition of serving goose for dinner on this day may stem from the practice of giving one's landlord such a bird as a gift:

> *And when the tenants come to pay their quarter's rent,*
> *They bring some fowl at Midsummer, a dish of fish in Lent,*
> *At Christmas a capon, at Michaelmas a goose,*
> *And somewhat else at New-year's tide, for fear their lease fly loose.*
>
> George Gascoigne, *The Posies of George Gascoigne* (1575).

It was also thought that eating goose on Michaelmas Day would bring financial prosperity in the year to come. The geese were fattened for the table by allowing them to glean fallen grain on the stubble fields after the harvest.

Much of September's weather lore relates to Michaelmas: 'So many days old the moon is on Michaelmas Day, so many floods after'; 'If St Michael brings many acorns, Christmas will cover the fields with snow'. It is generally said that good weather on this day augurs a fine Christmas, but – as always – some proverbs suggest the opposite: 'A dark Michaelmas, a light Christmas'.

Contracts of employment often began and ended at Michaelmas, and a number of **hiring fairs** (also called **mop fairs** or **statute fairs**) were held at this time. Those looking for work would gather in a public place, bearing the tools of their trade or some other form of identification, and employers would pick and choose among them.

> *At one end of the street stood from two to three hundred blithe and hearty labourers waiting upon Chance .... Among these, carters and waggoners were distinguished by having a piece of whip-cord twisted round their hats; thatchers wore a fragment of woven straw; shepherds held their sheep-crooks in their hands; and thus the situation required was known to the hirers at a glance.*
>
> Thomas Hardy, *Far from the Madding Crowd* (1874).

Over the years, other attractions and festivities attached themselves to these gatherings, and some of them developed into the pleasure fairs that still take place in various parts of the UK in late September or early October. Chipping Norton in Gloucestershire holds its mop fair in September; King's Norton in Birmingham holds a mop fair on the first Monday in October and these fairs (often including a pig or ox roast) remain popular, even though their original purpose is lost. Marlborough in Wiltshire holds a 'Little Mop' fair on the Saturday before 11 October (Old Style Michaelmas) and a 'Big Mop' fair on the Saturday after; Stratford-Upon-Avon holds one of the larger mops

on or around 12 October, with a second smaller fair taking place on the Friday of the following week. In both Marlborough and Stratford-Upon-Avon, the second fair is what is known as a **runaway fair**, and comes from the tradition that those who had been hired at the first hiring fair could 'run away' if they found their master too hard and try to be hired by someone else.

On this day:

Born: Italian painter Tintoretto (1518); Spanish writer Miguel de Cervantes (1547); English admiral Lord Nelson (1758); Italian film director Michelangelo Antonioni (1912); Polish trade unionist, politician and Nobel Prize winner Lech Walesa (1943)

Died: German engineer Rudolf Diesel (1913); English-born US poet and essayist W H Auden (1973); US painter Roy Lichtenstein (1997); Vietnamese soldier and political leader Nguyen Van Thieu (2001)

1399 English king Richard II (1367–1400) resigned the Crown, and the next day was deposed by parliament in favour of the Duke of Lancaster who succeeded as King Henry IV (c.1366–1413).

1829 The Metropolitan Police Force was founded in London.

1885 The first electric street trams ran in Blackpool, England.

1938 The Munich Agreement was signed by the prime ministers of the UK and France, Neville Chamberlain (1869–1940) and Édouard Daladier (1884–1970), and the two fascist dictators of Italy and Germany, Benito Mussolini (1883–1945) and Adolf Hitler (1889–1945).

1939 World War II – the UK government carried out a Registration Day, to enumerate the population and provide information for the issuing of identity cards.

1979 Pope John Paul II (born 1920) arrived in Dublin at the start of an historic visit to Ireland.

30 September

The official opening of Pinewood Studios, near Iver Heath in Buckinghamshire, took place on this day in 1936. The site had been bought and developed, at a cost of £1m, by the building tycoon Charles Boot, in partnership with J Arthur Rank (1888–1972). Their aim was to create a British rival for Hollywood and the US cinema industry. The first film to be produced in its entirety at Pinewood was *Talk of the Devil* (1936), directed by Carol Reed (1906–76), and the first of many James Bond films to be made there was *Dr No* (1962).

On this day:

Born: German physicist Hans Geiger (1882); English film director, scriptwriter and producer Michael Powell (1905); Scottish actress Deborah Kerr (1921); Romanian-born US writer and Nobel Prize winner Elie Wiesel (1928)

Died: English evangelist and co-founder of Methodism George Whitefield (1770); English engineer and canal builder James Brindley (1772); US film actor James Dean (1955); US seismologist Charles Richter (1985)

1258 Salisbury Cathedral in Wiltshire was consecrated.

1791 The première of the opera *The Magic Flute*, by Wolfgang Amadeus Mozart (1756–91), was held in Vienna, Austria.

1863 The première of the opera *The Pearl Fishers*, by Georges Bizet (1838–75), was held in Paris.

1935 The première of the opera *Porgy and Bess*, by George Gershwin (1898–1937), was held in Boston, Massachusetts, USA.

1938 Prime Minister Neville Chamberlain (1869–1940) famously declared to crowds outside 10 Downing Street that he had secured 'peace for our time' having returned from signing the Munich Agreement.

1946 The judges in the Nuremberg trials of Nazi war criminals following World War II began reading their verdicts.

1951 The 'Festival of Britain' came to an end.

1952 The first demonstration film in Cinerama®, *This is Cinerama*, was shown in New York City.

1966 Botswana became an independent republic with Seretse Khama (1921–80) as its first president.

1967 BBC Radio 1 was launched at 7am with DJ Tony Blackburn's (born 1943) *Breakfast Show*. The first record played was 'Flowers In The Rain' by The Move.

October

Gemstone: Opal or tourmaline
Flower: Marigold

Married when leaves in October thin,
Toil and hardship for you begin.

Traditional rhyme.

The woods never look more beautiful than from the close of last month to the middle of October, for by that time it seems as if nature had exhausted all her choicest colours on the foliage. We see the rich, burnished bronze of the oak; red of many hues, up to the gaudiest scarlet; every shade of yellow, from the wan gold of the primrose to the deep orange of the tiger-lily … and all so blended and softened together in parts, that like the colours on a dove's neck, we cannot tell where one begins and the other ends.

Chambers Book of Days (1864).

Origins

October, the tenth month of the year, was the eighth month of the Roman calendar and its name is derived from the Latin *octo*, eight.

Characteristics

The season of autumn is best appreciated in October, when deciduous trees are ablaze with the rich and varied colours of their dying foliage.

Summer is still alive in the memory, and thoughts of winter are another month away. With the grain harvest safely gathered in, it is time to prepare agricultural land for next year's crops: 'In October dung your field, and your land its wealth shall yield.' Another proverb refers to the all-important production of malt for beer and whisky: 'Dry your barley in October or you'll always be sober.'

History

Anglo-Saxon names for October include *Wynmonath* ('wine month') and *Winterfyllith* (referring to a calendar in which the full moon of this month marked the beginning of winter). The Irish-Gaelic name also makes premature reference to the changing of the seasons: *Deireadh Fomhair* means 'end of autumn'.

Weather

Strong winds are sometimes welcome in October – 'A good October and a good blast to blow the hog acorns and mast' – but one can have too much of a good thing, as some residents of the UK discovered on the infamous night of 15–16 October 1987. On the other side of the Atlantic, this is the end of the hurricane season, celebrated in the Virgin Islands with a public holiday on the third Monday of October, **Hurricane Thanksgiving Day**.

A spell of unusually warm, dry, calm weather occurring in October (or early November) is generally called an **Indian summer**, a name that originated in the USA, perhaps with reference to its occurrence in regions inhabited by Native Americans. The phenomenon is also called **St Luke's (little) summer** or **St Martin's (little) summer** when it occurs around the feast days of those saints, 18 October and 11 November, respectively.

Apples

October is the main month for apple-picking and cider-making.

> *Debarred by the adverse influences of climate from the profitable cultivation of the vine, the northern nations of Europe have endeavoured to supply this deficiency by the manufacture of exhilarating liquors from fruits and grains of various kinds, more congenial to their soil and skies. Of these rivals to the grape, with the exception of John Barleycorn and his sons, there is none which may more fairly claim to contest the palm of agreeableness and popularity than the apple and her golden-haired daughter, the bright and sparkling*

> *cider, whom some ardent admirers have even exalted to a level with the regal vintage of Champagne.*
>
> *Chambers Book of Days* (1864).

Since the early 1990s, as part of a campaign to raise public awareness of the plight of the apple industry in the UK and to promote the growing and eating of traditional British varieties, 21 October has been celebrated as **Apple Day**. Events organized on or around this date include guided tours of orchards, apple tastings, and advice sessions for fruit-growers, as well as more light-hearted or trivial activities (eg a national contest to produce the longest unbroken piece of peel from a single apple).

Non-fixed notable dates

Non-fixed notable dates in October include:

Columbus Day: Observed since 1971 in the USA as a public holiday on the second Monday of October. It was formerly celebrated on 12 October, the anniversary of Christopher Columbus's discovery of the New World in 1492. The Italian explorer had set sail from Spain ten weeks earlier in his flagship the *Santa Maria*, accompanied by the *Pinta* and the *Nina*. Firmly convinced that the world was round, not flat, he had sailed west in the expectation of finding a new route to India and other parts of Asia. Landing on one of the islands of the Caribbean (probably Watling's Island in the Bahamas), he assumed that he had achieved his goal – it was he who first called the indigenous inhabitants of the Americas 'Indians'. Columbus Day is celebrated throughout the USA with parades, pageants and other festivities.

Nottingham Goose Fair: This annual fair, now held on the first Wednesday, Thursday, Friday and Saturday in October, is of uncertain origin. The most likely explanation is that geese were formerly brought in large numbers from the Fens and elsewhere to be sold at Nottingham around this time. (More fanciful derivations include the tale of a wild goose that carried off an angler – together with rod, line and fish – from the riverbank and deposited him safely in the marketplace.) It is probably associated with a former medieval charter fair held on 21 September (St Matthew's Day), which was moved to 2 October after the calendar reform of 1752. Like many other such events, it has gradually attracted all the paraphernalia of the pleasure fair, with mechanical rides, games, sideshows and other amusements.

Canadian Thanksgiving: Thanksgiving in Canada is celebrated on the second Monday in October, a date which was fixed in 1957 when the Canadian Parliament announced that each year this would be 'a day of general thanksgiving to almighty God for the bountiful harvest with which Canada has been blessed'. The day is marked by parades and family meals, similar to those associated with US Thanksgiving (see November).

Punkie Night: In the village of Hinton St George in Somerset, on the evening of the last Thursday in October, the children parade through the streets bearing 'punkies' – hollowed-out mangel-wurzels with lighted candles inside, a local variant of the turnip or pumpkin lanterns made elsewhere for Hallowe'en (31 October). Well-disposed householders are persuaded to part with money or sweets as the children sing:

It's Punkie Night tonight
It's Punkie Night tonight
Give us a candle, give us a light
It's Punkie Night tonight.

The tradition is said to commemorate the use of such makeshift lanterns by the women of the village, in the dim and distant past, to guide their drunken menfolk home from nearby Chiselborough Fair.

1 October

This is a Chinese national holiday, celebrating the founding of the People's Republic of China on 1 October 1949. The republic was created by Mao Zedong (Mao Tse-tung) (1893–1976), leader of the Chinese Communist Party, who had defeated the Guomindang (Nationalist People's Party) led by Chiang Kai-shek (1887–1975). Mao became Chairman of the People's Republic, a post he held for ten years, and Chiang Kai-shek fled to Taiwan, where he established the Republic of China.

On this day:

Born: English king Henry III (1207); French composer Paul Dukas (1865); US timber merchant and aircraft manufacturer William Boeing (1881); Austrian-born British physicist Otto Frisch (1904); English singer and actress Dame Julie Andrews (1935)

Died: French dramatist Pierre Corneille (1684); English animal painter Sir Edwin Landseer (1873); British archaeologist and physical anthropologist Louis Leakey (1972)

1843 The *News of the World* was first published.

1868 St Pancras Station in London was opened by the Midland Railway Company.

1870 The first official postcard in the UK was issued by the Post Office; it carried a prepaid halfpenny stamp

1908 Henry Ford (1863–1947), US motor manufacturer, introduced his 'Model T' Ford, the first left-hand drive model.

1918 World War I – T E Lawrence (1888–1935), known as Lawrence of Arabia, led the Arabs in occupying Damascus.

1936 General Franco (1892–1975) was declared Spain's head of state.

1938 World War II – German troops occupied the Sudetenland, a region in Czechoslovakia on the western border with Germany.

1938 *Picture Post,* a British weekly devoted to photojournalism, was launched.

1939 Winston Churchill (1874–1965) made his first wartime broadcast on the BBC.

1958 In the USA, the National Aeronautics and Space Administration (NASA) was formally established.

1960 Nigeria gained independence from the UK; it declared itself a federal republic in 1963.

1961 *Songs of Praise* was first broadcast on the BBC.

1962 Race riots broke out at Mississippi State University following the admission of a black student.

1969 The British Post Office was nationalized.

1971 Walt Disney World opened in Orlando, Florida.

1985 Serious riots erupted in Toxteth, Liverpool, eventually leading to measures of urban regeneration.

October

> *Non-violence is not a garment to be put on and off at will. Its seat is in the heart, and it must be an inseparable part of our very being.*
>
> Mahatma Gandhi, *War or Peace*, 'Young India' (1926).

Mohandas Karamchand Gandhi, known as Mahatma Gandhi, was born on this day in 1869. His birthday is celebrated in India as **Gandhi Jayanti**, a public holiday on which people pay tribute to the 'Father of the Nation', remembering Gandhi's life, work and doctrine with religious readings, prayers and songs.

Born in Porbandar, Kathiawar (in W India), Gandhi studied law in London and worked as a lawyer in South Africa for more than 20 years before returning to his native land in 1914. After World War I he became involved in India's Home Rule movement, leading a series of non-violent campaigns of civil disobedience for which he was repeatedly arrested and imprisoned. Revered by the Indian people as a moral teacher, and always ready to practise what he preached, Gandhi sought to create a more equal and less materialistic society. His diminutive dhoti-clad figure, seen on newsreels worldwide, became a symbol of the principles he held so dear.

Gandhi's negotiations with the British government eventually bore fruit: in 1947, India was granted independence from the UK. The separate state of

Pakistan was created for the Muslim minority, but the continuing strife between Hindus and Muslims caused Gandhi great distress in the last months of his life. His advocacy of religious tolerance was resented by extremists, and he was assassinated by a Hindu fanatic on 30 January 1948.

On this day:

Born: English king Richard III (1452); Scottish chemist and Nobel Prize winner Sir William Ramsay (1852); US politician, Nobel Prize winner and UN pioneer Cordell Hull (1871); Scottish chemist and Nobel Prize winner Alexander Todd (1907); English singer-songwriter and actor Sting (1951)

Died: German composer Max Bruch (1920); Scottish businessman, tea merchant and philanthropist Sir Thomas Lipton (1931); British birth-control pioneer and author Marie Stopes (1958); French-born US painter Marcel Duchamp (1968)

1187 Saladin (1138–93) captured Jerusalem from the Christians, provoking the Third Crusade.

1608 Hans Lippershey (c.1570–c.1619), Dutch optician, demonstrated the first telescope.

1870 Rome became the capital city of the newly unified Italy.

1901 *Holland 1*, the first submarine built for the British Navy, was launched at Barrow-in-Furness.

1909 The first rugby football match at Twickenham, in the UK, was played between Harlequins and Richmond.

1935 Italian forces invaded Abyssinia.

1942 The British cruiser HMS *Curacao* sank off the coast of Ireland with the loss of 338 lives after a collision with the liner *Queen Mary*.

1950 The comic strip Peanuts, created by Charles M Schulz (1922–2000), was published for the first time.

1983 Welsh politician Neil Kinnock (born 1942) was elected leader of the Labour Party.

3 October

On 3 October 1906, at the Berlin Radiotelegraphic Conference, it was decided that SOS would become the international distress signal. Popularly thought to stand for 'save our ship' or 'save our souls', the letters were chosen because they could be easily and unambiguously transmitted by Morse code (dot dot dot dash dash dash dot dot dot). SOS replaced CQD, which was a general call to all stations (CQ) followed by D for distress, and not – as was generally believed – an abbreviation for 'Come quick(ly), danger!'

On this day:

Born: Scottish physician Sir Patrick Manson (1844); French painter and lithographer Pierre Bonnard (1867); Australian cricketer Ray Lindwall (1921); US novelist, essayist and polemicist Gore Vidal (1925)

Died: Italian founder of the Franciscan Order St Francis of Assisi (1226); English soldier, colonist and leader of the Pilgrim Fathers Myles Standish (1656); English craftsman, poet and socialist William Morris (1896); English conductor Sir Malcolm Sargent (1967); English actor Roddy McDowall (1998)

1811 In the UK, the first inter-county women's cricket match took place between Hampshire and Surrey.

1888 The première of the opera *Yeomen of the Guard*, by W S Gilbert (1836–1911) and Arthur Sullivan (1842–1900), was held at the Savoy Theatre, London.

1889 US inventor J S Thurman patented his motor-driven vacuum cleaner.

1900 The première of the oratorio *Dream of Gerontius*, by Edward Elgar (1857–1934), was held in Birmingham.

1922 Rebecca Felton (1835–1930) became the first woman senator in the US Senate; she was appointed by the governor of Georgia to fill a vacancy following the death of the previous incumbent.

1929 The Kingdom of Serbs, Croats and Slovenes became officially known as the Kingdom of Yugoslavia.

1941 US research chemists, L D Goodhue and W N Sullivan patented their invention of the aerosol.

1952 UK tested its first atomic bomb on the Monte Bello Islands off NW Australia.

1952 Tea rationing, introduced in the UK during World War II, came to an end.

1981 The IRA Maze Prison hunger strikes effectively ended.

1990 East and West Germany were reunified.

1995 US American football player O J Simpson (born 1947) was found not guilty of the murders of his ex-wife and her friend.

4 October

> *Lord, make me an instrument of your peace.*
> *Where there is hatred, let me sow love;*
> *Where there is injury, pardon;*
> *Where there is doubt, faith;*
> *Where there is despair, hope;*
> *Where there is darkness, light;*
> *Where there is sadness, joy.*
>
> 'Prayer of St Francis'.

This is the feast day of **St Francis of Assisi**, founder of the Franciscan order of mendicant friars (also known as the Grey Friars, for the colour of their clothes, or the Friars Minor, for their humility), commemorating the date of his death in 1226. Francis was born in Assisi, probably in 1181, the son of a wealthy merchant, and led the extravagant life of a carefree man-about-town until his mid-twenties. His sudden decision to embrace a life of poverty and religious devotion has been variously attributed to severe illness, military experience and a visionary dream.

Others were inspired to follow Francis's example, and his brotherhood gradually grew from eleven in 1210 to several thousand in 1219. In 1224 he is said to have received the stigmata – bodily wounds resembling those suffered by Christ at his crucifixion.

4 October

One morning, when he was praying, he saw in vision a seraph with six wings, and in the midst of the wings the crucified Saviour. As the vision disappeared, and left on his mind an unutterable sense of delight and awe, he found on his hands and feet black excrescences like nails, and in his side a wound, from which blood frequently oozed, and stained his garment. These marks, in his humility, he hid with jealous care, but they became known, and by their means were wrought many miracles.

Chambers Book of Days (1864).

St Francis of Assisi is also remembered for his sympathy with the natural world – holy pictures often show him preaching to birds or surrounded by other animals. In 1980 he was proclaimed patron saint of ecologists and ecology.

On this day:

Born: French painter Jean François Millet (1814); US writer and journalist Damon Runyon (1884); US film comedian Buster Keaton (1895); South African cricketer Basil D'Oliveira (1931); US actress Susan Sarandon (1946)

Died: Spanish mystic, writer and first woman Doctor of the Church St Teresa of Ávila (1582); French sculptor Frederic Bartholdi (1904); German theoretical physicist and Nobel Prize winner Max Planck (1947); US rhythm and blues singer Janis Joplin (1970); English comic actor and writer Graham Chapman (1989)

1535 The first English translation of the whole Bible was published in Zurich by Miles Coverdale (1488–1568).

1582 Catholic countries adopted the Gregorian calendar; to catch up on 11 'lost' days this day became 15 October, 1582.

1830 In Belgium, a provisional government declared independence from the Netherlands.

1883 The Boys' Brigade was founded in Glasgow by Sir William Alexander Smith (1854–1914).

1895 The first US Open golf tournament was held at Newport, Rhode Island.

1957 The first satellite to orbit the Earth, Sputnik 1, was launched by the USSR.

1965 Pope Paul VI (1897–1978) became the first reigning pope to visit the USA when he addressed the United Nations in New York.

1966 Basutoland, a former British colony, became the independent kingdom of Lesotho.

1976 British Rail's 125mph High Speed Train (HST) service began.

2000 The last 'Mini Morris' car rolled off the production line in the UK.

5 October

Come on follow the Geordie boys,
They'll fill your heart with joy,
They're marching for their freedom now.
Come on follow the Jarrow lads,
They'll make your heart feel glad,
They're saying now, yes now is the hour.

Alan Price, 'Jarrow Song' (1974).

On 5 October 1936, 200 unemployed men set off from Jarrow, on the southern bank of the River Tyne in NE England, to walk to London. Their departure was preceded by a special service of blessing at Christ Church in the town centre, which was attended by various local dignitaries, some of whom were to accompany the marchers for much or all of their arduous journey. The aim of this protest march, also known as the Jarrow Crusade, was to draw the attention of the nation in general, and the government in particular, to the plight of Jarrow and other towns that had been hard hit by the demise of heavy industry in the depression of the 1930s. The men were bearing a petition signed by more than 11,000 inhabitants of the town, which they eventually presented to the House of Commons on 5 November. In the towns and cities all along their route, cheering crowds of well-wishers lined the streets to offer support and sustenance.

On this day:

Born: French writer Denis Diderot (1713); French pioneer of motion photography Louis Lumière (1864); US founder of

McDonald's fast-food restaurants Ray Kroc (1902); Czech dramatist and statesman Václav Havel (1936); Irish rock musician and philanthropist Bob Geldof (1954)

Died: English actor Leonard Rossiter (1984); US super-computer designer Seymour R Cray (1996); US mountaineer Alex Lowe (1999)

1762 The première of the opera *Orpheus and Eurydice*, by Christoph Gluck (1714–87), was held in Vienna, Austria.

1908 Bulgaria proclaimed its independence from the Ottoman Empire.

1910 Portugal was proclaimed a republic after the abdication of King Manuel II (1889–1932).

1925 The Locarno Conference of European nations began; treaties were signed guaranteeing the post-1919 frontiers between France, Belgium and Germany, and the demilitarization of the Rhineland.

1930 The British airship R101 crashed near Beauvais in France killing all but six of the passengers and crew.

1968 A civil rights march in Derry was broken up by police; the event is often considered to be the start of the Northern Ireland 'Troubles'.

1969 BBC screened the first episode of the *Monty Python's Flying Circus* comedy series.

1970 Anwar el-Sadat (1918–81) was named to succeed Gamal Abd al-Nasser (1918–70) as president of Egypt.

1974 In the UK, two IRA bombs in Guildford pubs killed five people and injured more than 60.

1983 Cecil Parkinson (born 1932), Secretary of State for Trade and Industry in the British government, admitted an affair with his former secretary, Sara Keays; he resigned from his post on October 14.

1999 Two trains collided at Ladbroke Grove outside London's Paddington Station, killing 31 people and injuring dozens.

2000 Protestors stormed the Yugoslav parliament and declared Vojislav Kostunica (born 1944) as president.

6 October

No man has a right to fix the boundary of the march of a nation. No man has a right to say to his country, 'Thus far thou shalt go and no further.'

Charles Stewart Parnell, speech at Cork (21 January 1885).

Charles Stewart Parnell died on this day in 1891. Born in 1846, he became President of the Irish National Land League (later revived as the National League), chairman of the Irish Parliamentary Party, and an ardent advocate of Home Rule for Ireland, and was a popular figure in Irish politics in the late 1870s and 1880s. He lost some support in 1890, when he was named as corespondent in the divorce of Captain William Henry O'Shea from his wife Katherine (who married Parnell just five months before his death), but he remained a national hero in the hearts and minds of his followers.

Parnell's life and work are remembered in Ireland on **Ivy Day**, the anniversary of his death, when allegiance to his cause is demonstrated by wearing a sprig of ivy in the buttonhole. Ivy Day was brought to the attention of the wider world as the setting of a short story by James Joyce, 'Ivy Day in the Committee Room', which ends with a poem entitled 'The Death of Parnell', composed and recited by one of the characters:

He is dead. Our Uncrowned King is dead.
O, Erin, mourn with grief and woe
For he lies dead whom the fell gang
Of modern hypocrites laid low.

He lies slain by the coward hounds
He raised to glory from the mire;
And Erin's hopes and Erin's dreams
Perish upon her monarch's pyre.

James Joyce, *Dubliners*, 'Ivy Day in the Committee Room' (1914).

On this day:

Born: English Astronomer Royal Nevil Maskelyne (1732); Swedish soprano Jenny Lind (1820); Irish physicist and Nobel Prize winner E T S Walton (1903); Norwegian anthropologist Thor Heyerdahl (1914); Swedish actress Britt Ekland (1942)

Died: German churchman St Bruno of Cologne (1101); English religious reformer and translator of the Bible William Tyndale (1536); US inventor, philanthropist and breakfast cereal pioneer W K Kellogg (1951); English actor Denholm Elliot (1992)

1889 The Moulin Rouge opened in Paris.

1890 The Mormons in Utah renounced polygamy.

1927 The première of the film *The Jazz Singer*, starring Al Jolson (1886–1950), was held; it was the first full-length film with sound – although only in the songs and some spoken dialogue.

1968 British racing drivers Jackie Stewart (born 1939), Graham Hill (1929–75) and John Surtees (born 1934) took the first three places in the US Grand Prix.

1973 Arab states launched a massive attack on Israel, starting the Yom Kippur War.

1981 Egyptian president Anwar el-Sadat (1918–81) was assassinated at a military parade.

1987 Fiji was formally declared a republic by military coup leader Sitiveni Rabuka (born 1948).

2000 Yugoslav president Slobodan Milosevic (born 1941) resigned following pressure over allegations of vote-rigging.

On this day in 1806, the British inventor Ralph Wedgwood (a relative of the

potter Josiah Wedgwood) secured a patent for a machine that made the first documented use of carbon paper, a commodity that would eventually become an indispensable part of office life. Wedgwood's 'carbonated paper' was impregnated with ink on both sides and was initially intended to produce a single copy by placing it between two sheets of paper and writing with a metal stylus on the top sheet.

On this day:

Born: Danish physicist and Nobel Prize winner Niels Bohr (1885); German Nazi leader and chief of police Heinrich Himmler (1900); South African Anglican prelate and Nobel Prize winner Desmond Tutu (1931); Russian politician and President Vladimir Putin (1952); Chinese–US cellist Yo-Yo Ma (1955)

Died: US poet and short-story writer Edgar Allan Poe (1849); US businessman and inventor of the frozen food process Clarence Birdseye (1956); Italian-born US inventor of the whirlpool bath Candido Jacuzzi (1986); US film actress Bette Davies (1989)

1571 In the Battle of Lepanto off the Greek coast, Christian allied forces, commanded by Don John of Austria (1547–78), defeated the Ottoman Turks.

1769 Captain James Cook (1728–79) reached New Zealand and landed a few days later on the North Island.

1913 Henry Ford (1863–1947) introduced the first moving assembly production line at his Michigan plant.

1919 Dutch airline KLM – the oldest existing airline in the world – was founded.

1946 *Woman's Hour* was first broadcast on BBC radio.

1949 The German Democratic Republic – East Germany – was formally established.

1959 The USSR's spacecraft Luna 3 took the first-ever pictures of the far side of the Moon.

1959 A fire on the pier at Southend, England, lead 300 people to be trapped; they were all successfully rescued.

1985 Palestinian terrorists hijacked the Italian cruise liner *Achille Lauro* with 420 passengers and crew aboard and demanded the release of Palestinian prisoners held in Israel; the crisis ended on 10 October.

1986 In the UK the newspaper *The Independent* was launched.

2001 The USA launched an air strike against the Taliban in Afghanistan.

8 October

In the evening of Sunday 8 October 1871, a fire started in a Chicago barn (possibly after a cow kicked over a lantern) and developed into one of the worst disasters in that city's history, the Great Chicago Fire.

> *During Sunday night, Monday, and Tuesday, this city has been swept by a conflagration which has no parallel in the annals of history, for the quantity of property destroyed, and the utter and almost irremediable ruin which it wrought. A fire in a barn on the West Side was the insignificant cause of a conflagration which has swept out of existence hundreds of millions of property, has reduced to poverty thousands who, the day before, were in a state of opulence, has covered the prairies, now swept by the cold southwest wind, with thousands of homeless unfortunates, which has stripped 2,600 acres of buildings, which has destroyed public improvements that it has taken years of patient labor to build up, and which has set back for years the progress of the city, diminished her population, and crushed her resources.*
>
> *Chicago Tribune* (11 October, 1871).

The devastation caused by the blaze, which killed about 300 people and left some 90,000 homeless, was exacerbated by the strength and direction of the wind and by the excessively dry summer that had gone before. The fire burned for nearly 30 hours, beyond human control, before it was finally extinguished by the welcome arrival of rain on the morning of Tuesday 10 October.

On this day:

Born: Argentinian soldier and statesman Juan Perón (1895); US politician, clergyman and black civil rights activist Jesse Jackson (1941); Argentinian-born British molecular biologist, immunologist and Nobel Prize winner César Milstein (1927); Welsh snooker player Ray Reardon (1932); US actress Sigourney Weaver (1949)

Died: English novelist Henry Fielding (1754); 14th President of the USA Franklin Pierce (1869); English statesman and prime minister Clement Attlee (1967); German statesman and Nobel Prize winner Willy Brandt (1992)

1925 Eileen Joel riding Hogier became the first woman jockey to win an 'open' race when she won the four-mile Newmarket Town Plate.

1952 Three trains collided at Harrow, London, killing 112 and injuring more than 300 people.

1965 One of London's most recognized buildings, the Post Office Tower, topped by a revolving restaurant, became operational; it was opened to the public in May of the following year.

1970 The Nobel Prize for Literature was awarded to Russian novelist Aleksandr Solzhenitsyn (born 1918).

1973 The UK's first commercial radio station, LBC (London Broadcasting Company), began transmissions.

1980 British Leyland Motor Company launched its Mini Metro.

1982 The Polish parliament dissolved Solidarity, eastern Europe's first trade union.

1990 The UK joined the ERM (Exchange Rate Mechanism).

1998 The US House of Representatives voted to authorize a committee to investigate whether sufficient grounds existed for the impeachment of President Bill Clinton (born 1946).

2001 British prime minister Tony Blair (born 1953) set up a War Cabinet to supervise the UK's participation in the US-led military action in Afghanistan.

9 October

This is the feast day of **St Denis** (or Denys or Dionysius), patron saint of France. Probably born in Rome, he was sent as a missionary to the Gauls in the mid-3rd century and became the first Bishop of Paris. He was beheaded at Montmartre (which literally means 'Hill of Martyrs') and is said to have walked from there to his burial place at Saint-Denis, carrying his severed head. Of this miraculous feat, the French noblewoman Mme du Deffand remarked, in a letter to the philosopher Jean d'Alembert (7 July 1763), '*La distance n'y fait rien; il n'y a que le premier pas qui coute* (The distance does not matter; it is only the first step that counts)'.

On this day:

Born: French composer and music critic Camille Saint-Saëns (1835); French actor, author and film producer Jacques Tati (1908); English songwriter, vocalist and rhythm guitarist with the Beatles John Lennon (1940); English athlete Steve Ovett (1955)

Died: Italian anatomist Gabriele Falloppius (1562); Yugoslavian king Alexander I (1934); Italian pope Pius XII (1958); French novelist and biographer André Maurois (1967); Austrian-born British psychoanalyst Anna Freud (1982)

28 BC The Temple of Apollo on the Palatine Hill in Rome was dedicated.

1701 Yale University was founded in New Haven, Connecticut.

1799 British frigate HMS *Lutine* sank off the Dutch coast with its cargo of gold bullion. Its salvaged bell was presented to Lloyds of London where it was rung when news of overdue ships arrived; it is still rung on ceremonial occasions.

1874 The Treaty of Bern establishing the Universal Postal Union (originally called the General Postal Union) was signed; the day is now celebrated as World Post Day.

1899 Paul Kruger (1825–1904), president of the South African Republic, issued his ultimatum to the UK which provoked the Anglo-Boer War.

1959 In British politics the Conservatives (under Harold MacMillan, 1894–1986) won a third successive term.

1962 Uganda, formerly a British protectorate, became independent.

1973 US singer Elvis Presley (1935–77) divorced his wife Priscilla Presley (born 1945).

1975 An IRA bomb blast in Piccadilly, London, killed one and injured 20.

1988 Thousands of Latvians protested for greater independence from the USSR.

1991 The first Sumo wrestling tournament to be staged outside Japan began at the Royal Albert Hall, London.

10 October

After the calendar reform of 1752, some of the activities traditionally associated with Michaelmas Day (29 September) moved forward eleven days to 10 October, which is sometimes called 'Old Michaelmas Day'. One of these is **Pack Monday Fair**, at Sherborne in Dorset, which now takes place on the first Monday after 10 October. It is allegedly so called because this was the day in 1490 on which the masons packed up their tools after completing work on the abbey. The fair was formerly heralded by the cacophonous 'music' of **Teddy Rowe's Band**, a group of young people armed with horns, bugles, whistles, tin trays, etc, who paraded through the streets of the town in the early hours of the morning.

On this day:

Born: Italian composer Giuseppe Verdi (1813); Norwegian explorer, biologist, oceanographer and Nobel Prize winner Fridtjof Nansen (1861); English motor magnate and philanthropist William Morris (1877); US jazz pianist and composer Thelonious Monk (1917); English dramatist Harold Pinter (1930)

Died: English actor Sir Ralph Richardson (1983); US film director and actor Orson Welles (1985); Mongolian-born US actor Yul Brynner (1985); Sri Lankan politician and world's first woman prime minister Sirimavo Bandaranaike (2000)

1886 The dinner jacket made its US debut, worn by tobacco tycoon Griswold Lorillard at the Tuxedo Country Club – hence the use of the term 'tuxedo' in the USA.

1903 English suffragette Emmeline Pankhurst (1857–1928) founded the Women's Social and Political Union (WSPU) to fight for women's suffrage.

1911 The Chinese Revolution which eventually overthrew the Manchu dynasty began under the leadership of Sun Yat-sen (1866–1925).

1913 The final Panama Canal breakthrough came as US President Woodrow Wilson (1856–1924) pushed a button in the White House that relayed, via telegraph, the signal to blow up the Gamboa Dyke.

1928 The Tyne Bridge – the icon of Newcastle – was opened by King George V (1865–1936), accompanied by Queen Mary (1867–1953).

1930 Transcontinental and Western Airlines (TWA) was formed by the merger of three American airlines.

1935 The première of the opera *Porgy and Bess*, by George Gershwin (1898–1937), was held in New York City.

1955 The BBC began to broadcast test television transmissions in colour.

1961 A volcanic eruption on the South Atlantic island of Tristan de Cunha caused the entire population to be evacuated to the UK; almost all returned in 1963 when the island was declared safe.

1969 It was announced that the Ulster Special Constabulary, known as the B Specials, was to be disbanded.

1970 Fiji became an independent member of the British Commonwealth.

1975 Welsh actor Richard Burton (1925–84) and US actress Elizabeth Taylor (born 1932) married for the second time in Botswana; they divorced a year later.

1980 At the Conservative Party conference British prime minister Margaret Thatcher (born 1925) made her famous speech, 'You turn if you want to. The lady's not for turning'.

2001 The Nobel Peace Prize was awarded jointly to United Nations Secretary-General Kofi Annan (born 1938) and the UN itself 'for their work for a better organized and more peaceful world'.

11 October

In ancient Rome, this was the day of the **Meditrinalia**, when the new season's wine was tasted and libations were offered to the gods. It was customary to taste the new and old wine together, apparently for healing purposes, while reciting the following lines: *Novum vetus vinum bibo, novo veteri morbo medeor*. Loosely translated, this means 'I drink old and new wine to cure old and new disease'. The name of the festival was probably derived from the Latin verb *mederi*, meaning 'to heal' (rather than from a goddess called Meditrina, as has also been suggested).

On this day:

Born: English social reformer and founder of the YMCA Sir George Williams (1821); US food manufacturer and packer H J Heinz (1844); US humanitarian Eleanor Roosevelt (1884); French novelist and Nobel Prize winner François Mauriac (1885); English footballer Sir Bobby Charlton (1937)

Died: English organist and composer Samuel Wesley (1837); English natural philosopher James Prescott Joule (1889); French artist Maurice de Vlaminck (1958); Scottish politician and First Minister Donald Dewar (2000)

1727 George II (1683–1760) was crowned in London.

1797 At the Battle of Camperdown the British virtually destroyed the Dutch fleet; when the admiral's flag was shot down, the young sailor Jack Crawford, gripping the admiral's colors in his teeth, scaled what was left and nailed the flag to the shattered top to ensure that the rest of the British fleet didn't mistake a lowered flag for surrender.

1887 Dorr Eugene Felt (1862–1930), US inventor, was granted a patent for the Comptometer – the first practical key-driven calculator.

1899 The Boer War began in South Africa between the UK and the republics of Transvaal and the Orange Free State.

1958 *Grandstand* was broadcast by the BBC for the first time.

1962 The Second Vatican Ecumenical Council opened under Pope John XXIII (1881–1963).

1967 Pop group The Move had to apologize to the British prime minister, Harold Wilson (1916–95), following a High Court ruling; the band had published a promotional postcard which featured a caricature of Wilson in the nude.

1968 NASA launched the Apollo 7 space mission.

1979 Godfrey Hounsfield (born 1919), English electrical engineer who developed the technique of computer-assisted tomography (CAT scanning), was awarded the Nobel Prize in Physiology or Medicine, together with US physicist Allan MacLeod Cormack (1924–98), who had independently developed a similar device.

1980 Cosmonauts in Salyut 6 ended a mission of 185 days in space – a record at the time.

1982 The *Mary Rose*, flagship of King Henry VIII's (1491–1547) navy, was raised from the bottom of the Solent after 437 years.

12 October

On this day:

Born: English king Edward VI (1537); Scottish statesman and first Labour prime minister Ramsay MacDonald (1866); English composer Ralph Vaughan Williams (1872); Italian tenor Luciano Pavarotti (1935); US athlete Marion Jones (1975)

Died: English Quaker prison reformer Elizabeth Fry (1845); English mechanical and structural engineer Robert Stephenson (1859); US Confederate general Robert E Lee (1870); French writer and Nobel Prize winner Anatole France (1924); Norwegian-born US ice-skater Sonja Henie (1969); English jurist and politician Lord Hailsham (2001); US jockey Willie Shoemaker (2003)

1492 Christopher Columbus (1451–1506) made first landfall in the New World, arriving at San Salvador Island in the Bahamas.

1822 Pedro I (1798–1834) was proclaimed Emperor of Brazil.

1928 The first 'iron lung' was used in the USA at Boston's Children's Hospital.

1957 The Lovell telescope – the world's first giant radio telescope – planned by Bernard Lovell (born 1913), went into operation at Jodrell Bank Experimental Station (now the Nuffield Radio Astronomy Laboratories) in Cheshire, England.

1967 *The Naked Ape* by Desmond Morris (born 1928) was published. In it, Dr Morris described human behaviour in the way that scientists describe ape behaviour.

1968 The 19th Olympic Games opened in Mexico. They were the first games to introduce sex testing for women, and the first to see an athlete disqualified for drug use (excessive alcohol).

1971 The musical *Jesus Christ Superstar* premièred on Broadway.

1973 Juan Perón (1895–1974) was inaugurated as president of Argentina for the second time; his third wife Isabelita (born 1931) became vice-president.

1978 Sid Vicious (1957–79) was arrested on suspicion of murdering his girlfriend Nancy Spungen (1958–78).

1984 In the UK, five people were killed and 34 were injured when an IRA bomb exploded at the Conservative Party conference hotel in Brighton.

2002 At least 190 people were killed in two explosions in Bali.

13 October

Sir Henry Irving, the first actor to receive a knighthood, died on this day in 1905 at his Bradford hotel during a farewell tour of the provinces. His ashes were buried in Westminster Abbey.

Born John Henry Brodribb in Somerset in 1838, Irving entered the theatre in his late teens, making his London debut in 1866. The finest Shakespearean actor of his time, he gave memorable performances both in title roles, including those of *Macbeth* (1875) and *Othello* (1876), and in character parts, such as Shylock and Malvolio. In 1878 he became actor-manager of the Lyceum Theatre, with Ellen Terry as his leading lady, playing Ophelia to his Hamlet in the opening production. Their successful partnership lasted for 25 years.

The two sons of Irving's short and unhappy marriage (1869–71) followed their father into the theatre, Henry Brodribb Irving ('H B') as an actor-manager and Laurence Sidney Brodribb Irving as a playwright. H B's son Laurence Henry Forster Irving was a stage designer and the author of a biography of his grandfather, *Henry Irving, the Actor and his World* (1951).

On this day:

Born: German politician, pathologist and founder of modern pathology Rudolf Virchow (1821); Italian-born French actor and singer Yves Montand (1921); English politician and first woman prime minister Baroness Thatcher (1925); US singer, songwriter and guitarist Paul Simon (1941)

Died: US physicist and Nobel Prize winner Walter Brattain (1987); Vietnamese politician Le Duc Tho (1990); New Zealand-born

Rhodesian politician Sir Garfield Todd (2002); Canadian physicist and Nobel Prize winner Bertram Brockhouse (2003)

1307 Philip the Fair of France (1268–1314) had all the Knights Templar arrested on charges of heresy; it was a Friday, leading some to hypothesize that this is why Friday the 13th is regarded be an unlucky day.

1399 Henry IV (c.1366–1413) was crowned the first king of the house of Lancaster.

1774 In America, a resolution of the Continental Congress marked the establishment of what is now the US Navy.

1792 The cornerstone of the White House in Washington, DC, was laid by President George Washington (1732–99).

1815 Joachim Murat (1767–1815), one of Napoleon I's (1769–1821) marshals and King of Naples, was executed trying to recapture his kingdom after the defeat at Waterloo.

1884 Greenwich was adopted as the initial meridian of longitude from which standard times throughout the world are calculated.

1894 In English football, the first Merseyside derby between Everton and Liverpool was played at Goodison Park with Everton winning 3–0.

1908 Emmeline Pankhurst (1857–1928) and her daughter Christabel (1880–1958), suffragette pioneers, were arrested for 'inciting the public to rush the House of Commons'.

1980 Adolfo Perez Esquivel (born 1931), Argentinian civil rights leader and human rights activist, won the Nobel Peace Prize.

1988 The Archbishop of Turin Cardinal Ballestrero (1913–98) announced that carbon dating tests showed that the 'Shroud of Turin', purporting to carry the imprint of Christ's face, was actually of medieval origin, dating from around 1260 to 1390.

1988 The British Government lost its battle to stop the publication of *Spycatcher*, the memoirs of former MI5 agent Peter Wright (1916–95).

1992 The British government announced plans to close one third of British deep coal mines.

2002 British runner Paula Radcliffe (born 1973) set a new women's world marathon record of 2 hours, 17 minutes and 18 seconds at the Chicago Marathon.

14 October

The Battle of Hastings was fought on this day in 1066. Sometimes called the Battle of Senlac, it took place at Senlac Hill near what is now the town of Battle in East Sussex, about eight miles from Hastings. King Harold II of England (c.1022–1066) and his Saxon army had recently returned from their victory at the Battle of Stamford Bridge in Yorkshire on 25 September; William, Duke of Normandy (c.1028–1087), had landed at Pevensey on the Sussex coast with an army of knights on 28 September to lay claim to the English throne.

> *The future Conqueror of England was the last to land, and as he placed his foot on shore, he made a false step, and fell on his face. A murmur of consternation ran through the troops at this incident as a bad omen, but with great presence of mind William sprang immediately up, and shewing his troops his hand filled with English sand, exclaimed: 'What now? What astonishes you? I have taken seisin of this land with my hands, and by the splendour of God, as far as it extends it is mine – it is yours!'*
>
> *Chambers Book of Days* (1864).

The battle was hard-fought: Harold's foot-soldiers armed with battle-axes and spears succeeded for several hours in repulsing William's cavalry, archers and crossbowmen. A change of tactics during the afternoon, however, in which William's men repeatedly feigned flight only to turn and attack their pursuers, finally broke down the English defence, and Harold himself was killed by a stray arrow that entered his left eye and penetrated his brain.

After the death of Harold and the defeat of his army, William proceeded to London, where he was crowned King William I of England on Christmas Day. During the following years he subdued rebellions in various parts of the country, and by 1072 the Norman Conquest was virtually complete.

The events leading up to the Battle of Hastings, and the battle itself, are depicted in the Bayeux Tapestry, a strip of embroidered linen that is said to have been commissioned by Odo, Bishop of Bayeux in NW France and half-brother of William the Conqueror.

On this day:

Born: Irish statesman Éamon de Valera (1882); 34th President of the USA Dwight D Eisenhower (1890); US actress Lillian Gish (1893); English actor Roger Moore (1927); English pop singer Sir Cliff Richard (1940)

Died: German soldier Erwin Rommel (1944); US film actor Errol Flynn (1959); English stage and film actress Dame Edith Evans (1976); US singer and film actor Bing Crosby (1977); US novelist Harold Robbins (1997)

1855 Meetings on the high price of food were held in London's Hyde Park on this day, and subsequent Sundays, helping to create the tradition of 'Speaker's Corner'.

1878 The first floodlit football match was played at Bramall Lane, Sheffield, UK.

1913 The UK's worst pit disaster occurred at the Universal Colliery in Glamorgan when an explosion killed 439.

1930 The Belgian National Congress announced Belgium's independence.

1939 World War II – the British battleship HMS *Royal Oak* was torpedoed in Scapa Flow, Orkney with the loss of more than 800 lives.

1947 US test pilot Chuck Yeager (born 1923) flew the Bell X-1 rocket research aircraft to a level speed of more than 670mph, thus breaking the sound barrier.

1954 Emperor of Ethiopia, Haile Selassie I (1891–1975) was received by Queen Elizabeth II (born 1926) on his tour of the UK.

1964 Martin Luther King, Jnr (1929–68), US civil rights leader, was awarded the Nobel Peace Prize.

1964 Mary Rand (born 1940) became the first British woman to win an Olympic track and field gold medal – for the long jump – at the Tokyo Olympics.

1969 The seven-sided fifty-pence coin was first issued in the UK to replace the ten-shilling note.

1994 Israeli prime minister Yitzhak Rabin (1922–95), foreign minister Shimon Peres (born 1923) and Palestine Liberation Organization chairman Yasser Arafat (born 1929) shared the Nobel Peace Prize.

15 October

On this day:

Born: Roman poet Virgil (70 BC); Italian physicist, mathematician and inventor Evangelista Torricelli (1608); English novelist Sir P G Wodehouse (1881); Canadian-born US economist J K Galbraith (1908); Northern Irish politician and Nobel Prize winner David Trimble (1944)

Died: French soldier, colonialist and founder of Detroit Antoine de la Mothe de Cadillac (1730); French Vichy politician Pierre Laval (1945); German Nazi politician Hermann Goering (1946); US composer Cole Porter (1964); German-born US biochemist and Nobel Prize winner Konrad Bloch (2000)

1581 Often considered to be the first ballet, *Le Ballet Comique de la Reine*, commissioned by Catherine de Médicis (1519–89), was performed in Paris.

1666 Samuel Pepys (1633–1703) recorded King Charles II (1630–85) wearing the first 'waistcoat'.

1815 Napoleon I (1769–1821) arrived on St Helena, where he had been exiled after the Battle of Waterloo.

1839 Queen Victoria (1819–1901) proposed to Prince Albert of Saxe-Coburg and Gotha (1819–61).

1895 The UK's first motor show was held at Tunbridge Wells, Kent.

1928 The German airship *Graf Zeppelin* completed its first transatlantic flight.

1951 The first televised party political broadcast was given by Herbert Samuel (1870–1963) on behalf of the Liberal Party.

1969 In the USA millions of peace protestors march in the Vietnam Moratorium.

1974 Iceland unilaterally extended its fishing rights from 50 to 200 miles, precipitating the third Cod War.

1990 Russian statesman Mikhail Gorbachev (born 1931) was awarded the Nobel Peace Prize.

16 October

> *Earlier on today, apparently, a woman rang the BBC and said she'd heard that there was a hurricane on the way. Well, if you're watching, don't worry – there isn't.*
>
> Michael Fish, weather forecast (15 October 1987).

Many of those residents of S England who had managed to sleep through the night awoke to a scene of devastation on 16 October 1987 – garden fences and greenhouses smashed, power lines down, uprooted trees barring roads and railways, roofs blown off, and boats aground. Very few were totally unaffected by the storms that had swept through the southern counties in the early hours of the morning, with winds reaching hurricane force in places: gusts of 94mph were recorded in London and over 100mph elsewhere. Eighteen people lost their lives in what became known as the 'Great Storm of 1987', hundreds more were injured, and some 15 million trees were destroyed, including six of the oaks for which the Kent town of Sevenoaks was famous.

In her Booker Prize-winning novel *Possession* (1990), A S Byatt (born 1936) set the dramatic climax of her story on the night of the Great Storm of 1987. Two of the characters are attempting to make off with a box they have unearthed from a grave in a Sussex churchyard when all hell breaks loose: tiles crash from the roof of the church and trees fall all around them.

> *Around his very feet the earth quaked and moved; he sat down; there was a sound of rending and great mass of grey descended before his eyes like a tumbling hill, accompanied by the sweeping sound of a whole mass of leaves and fine branches whipping the moving air. The final sound of all these – except the original rushing which persisted – was a mixture of drums, cymbals and theatrical thundersheet. His nostrils were full of wet soil and sap and gasoline fumes. A tree had fallen directly across the Mercedes.*
>
> A S Byatt, *Possession* (1990).

On this day:

Born: Irish playwright, novelist, essayist, poet and wit Oscar Wilde

(1854); Polish-born Israeli statesman and first prime minister David Ben-Gurion (1886); US playwright Eugene O'Neill (1888); Welsh snooker player Terry Griffiths (1947); US actor, screenwriter and director Tim Robbins (1958)

Died: English Protestant reformers Hugh Latimer and Nicholas Ridley (1555); French queen Marie Antoinette (1793); Pakistani politician and first prime minister Liaquat Ali Khan (1951); US soldier, politician and Nobel Prize winner George C Marshall (1959); US writer James Michener (1997)

1759 The third Eddystone Lighthouse – Smeaton's Tower – was lit for the first time.

1834 As the Houses of Parliament burned down the artist J M W Turner (1775–1851) made sketches of the blaze from a boat on the River Thames.

1846 The first use of ether as an anaesthetic was demonstrated in Massachussetts by dentist William Morton (1819–68) in an operation to remove a tumour from his patient's jaw.

1847 Charlotte Brontë's (1816–55) novel *Jane Eyre* was published under the pseudonym Currer Bell.

1859 US abolitionist John Brown (1800–59) seized the Federal arsenal at Harper's Ferry in Virginia, intending to launch a slave insurrection; he was later hanged.

1908 Samuel Franklyn Cody (1862–1913), US-born British aviator, made the first official powered flight in the UK at Laffans Plain, Farnborough.

1916 The first birth control clinic in the USA was opened in Brooklyn, New York by Margaret Sanger (1883–1966).

1922 One of the world's longest railway tunnels, the Simplon II Tunnel under the Swiss Alps, opened.

1923 British watchmaker John Harwood (1893–1965) registered the patent in Switzerland for the first self-winding wristwatch. He was awarded the patent on 1 September, 1924.

1946 Nazi war criminals of World War II, Joachim von Ribbentrop (1893–1946), Alfred Rosenberg (1893–1946) and Julius Streicher (1885–1946) were executed following the Nuremberg trials.

1958 Children's programme *Blue Peter* was broadcast by the BBC for the first time.

1964 China exploded its first nuclear bomb at a test site.

1964 Harold Wilson (1916–95), leader of the Labour Party, became British prime minister.

1967 US folk-singer Joan Baez (born 1941) was arrested at a Vietnam peace protest.

1978 Cardinals elected the first non-Italian pope for more than 400 years, Pope John Paul II (born 1920).

1995 The Skye Bridge, linking the island of Skye with mainland Scotland, was opened.

1996 The British government announced that all handguns over .22 calibre would be banned.

1998 The Nobel Peace Prize was awarded jointly to John Hume (born 1937) and David Trimble (born 1944) 'for their efforts to find a peaceful solution to the conflict in Northern Ireland'.

1998 The former dictator of Chile, General Pinochet (born 1915) was arrested during private treatment at a London hospital on a warrant from Spain requesting his extradition on murder charges: he was eventually allowed to return to Chile.

17 October

This is one of the feast days of **St Etheldreda**, better known as **St Audrey**.

> *This saint, commemorated in the Romish calendar on 23rd June, but in the English calendar on 17th October, in celebration of the translation of her relics from the common cemetery of the nuns to a splendid marble coffin within the church of Ely, was the daughter of a king of East Anglia, and earned an exalted reputation both by her piety and good works, and the maintenance of an early vow of virginity which she observed through life, though married successively to two Saxon princes. She founded the convent and church of Ely on the spot where the cathedral was erected at a subsequent period, and died in 679 as its abbess.*
>
> *Chambers Book of Days* (1864).

At **St Audrey's Fair**, formerly held on 17 October at Ely, various items of merchandise were offered for sale, including necklaces, silk ribbons and lace neckerchiefs that became known as St Audrey's laces, shortened to 'tawdry laces'. (Ironically, and perhaps appropriately, the saint was said to have blamed the jewelled and golden necklaces she had favoured in the vanity of youth for the throat tumour that finally caused her death.) It was cheap imitations of these ornaments that gave rise to the use of *tawdry* to describe anything that is showy but without quality, taste or worth.

On this day:

Born: English politician and libertine John Wilkes (1727); US strip cartoonist and co-creator of Superman Jerry Siegel (1914); US playwright Arthur Miller (1915); US film actress and dancer Rita Hayworth (1918); English tennis player, table tennis player and broadcaster Ann Jones (1938); South African golfer Ernie Els (1969)

Died: English soldier, poet and patron Sir Philip Sidney (1586); Polish composer and pianist Frédéric Chopin (1849); US feminist, reformer and writer Julia Ward Howe (1910); English actress Joan Hickson (1998)

1651 King Charles II (1630–85), defeated by Cromwell at the Battle of Worcester, escaped to the continent to begin over eight years in exile.

1777 In the Battle of Saratoga British troops surrendered to American colonists during the American War of Independence.

1860 The first professional Open golf tournament was held at Prestwick in Scotland and was won by Willie Park of Musselburgh.

1902 The first Cadillac motor car was made in Detroit.

1917 The Trans-Australian Railway running from Kalgoorlie in Western Australia to Port Augusta in South Australia was completed; it was extended to Port Pirie in 1937.

1956 The world's first full-scale nuclear power station, Calder Hall in Cumbria, England, was officially opened by Queen Elizabeth II (born 1926).

1979 Mother Teresa of Calcutta (1910–97) was awarded the Nobel Peace Prize.

1989 An earthquake measuring 6.9 on the Richter scale hit San Francisco, killing 63 and injuring thousands.

2000 Four people were killed when a train derailed at Hatfield, north of London.

October

> *On St Luke's Day the oxen have leave to play.*
>
> Traditional saying.

This is the feast day of St Luke, a doctor by profession and the writer of the third gospel of the New Testament (and probably also of the Acts of the Apostles). He is the patron saint of physicians, surgeons, artists and butchers; his symbol is a horned ox.

St Luke's Day is supposed to be a good time to choose a spouse, and various rituals are prescribed for young women who wish to dream of their future husband. It was also formerly the date of the **Charlton Horn Fair**, held in London until 1872. On sale at the fair were horns of every description, merchandise made of horn, and figures bearing horns. All the visitors to the fair wore or carried horns, and all the stalls were decorated with horns. This preoccupation with horns is of uncertain origin – they may be the horns of the cuckold (according to a popular legend concerning King John and a miller's wife) or the horns of St Luke's ox.

On this day:

Born: Italian painter Canaletto (1697); English novelist and poet Thomas Love Peacock (1785); French philosopher and Nobel Prize winner Henri Bergson (1859); Czechoslovak-born US tennis player Martina Navratilova (1956)

Died: English statesman Henry Temple, 3rd Viscount Palmerston (1865); English mathematician Charles Babbage (1871); US inventor and physicist Thomas Edison (1931); US beautician and businesswoman Elizabeth Arden (1966)

1867 The USA bought Alaska from Russia.

1910 The trial of Dr Hawley Crippen (1862–1910) for the murder of his wife began in London.

1922 The British Broadcasting Company (BBC) was established; it was dissolved in 1926 and reconstituted under Royal Charter in 1927 as the British Broadcasting Corporation.

1963 Alec Douglas-Home (1903–95) succeeded Harold Macmillan (1894–1986) as British prime minister and renounced his peerage.

1967 The USSR's spacecraft Venera-4 entered the atmosphere of Venus and transmitted data back to Earth.

1968 In the UK the Post Office began its banking service, National Giro (later Girobank).

1995 British legendary racehorse Red Rum, winner of the Aintree Grand National in 1973, 1974 and 1977, died aged 30; he is buried near the finishing post at Aintree.

19 October

On this day in 1781, the British army led by Charles Cornwallis (1738–1805) surrendered to George Washington (1732–99), Commander-in-Chief of the American forces, after a two-week siege at Yorktown in Virginia. This final defeat of the British effectively brought the American War of Independence to a close.

On this day:

Born: English writer and physician Sir Thomas Browne (1605); English poet and essayist Leigh Hunt (1784); French pioneer of motion photography Auguste Lumière (1862); Indian-born US astrophysicist and Nobel Prize winner Subrahmanyan Chandrasekhar (1910); Irish-born British actor Sir Michael Gambon (1940)

Died: Anglo-Irish satirist and clergyman Jonathan Swift (1745); US businessman and inventor of the railroad sleeping car George Pullman (1897); Italian physician and criminologist Cesare Lombroso (1909); English cellist Jacqueline du Pré (1997); Bosnia and Herzogovinian politician Alija Izetbegovic (2003)

1469 Ferdinand of Aragon (1452–1516) married Isabella of Castile (1451–1504) uniting their kingdoms to form the basis of modern Spain.

1813 Napoleon I (1769–1821) was defeated by the armies of the Fourth Coalition at the Battle of the Nations at Leipzig.

1845 The première of the opera *Tannhäuser*, by Richard Wagner (1813–83), was held in Dresden, Germany.

1967 The Tyne Tunnel under the River Tyne, connecting Jarrow in Durham to Howdon in Northumberland, was opened for vehicles.

1970 Oil was first discovered in the British sector of the North Sea by the British Petroleum Company.

1987 'Black Monday' on the Wall Street Stock Exchange as the Dow Jones Industrial Average fell by 22 per cent and wiped millions off share prices around the world.

1989 The 'Guildford Four', four people who were imprisoned for their part in IRA bombings in Guildford in 1974, had their convictions quashed.

20 October

On this day:

Born: English architect Sir Christopher Wren (1632); French poet and adventurer Arthur Rimbaud (1854); US philosopher and educationalist John Dewey (1859); English physicist and Nobel Prize winner Sir James Chadwick (1891); English actress Dame Anna Neagle (1904); US singer, songwriter and musician Tom Petty (1953)

Died: English physician and founder of the Royal College of Physicians Thomas Linacre (1524); English explorer, linguist and diplomat Sir Richard Burton (1890); US educator Anne Sullivan (1936); 31st President of the USA Herbert Hoover (1964); English aviator Sheila Scott (1988)

1714 King George I (1660–1727) was crowned at Westminster Abbey, London.

1818 The Joint Occupation Treaty between the USA and the UK established the 49th parallel as the boundary between the USA and Canada.

1822 The *New Observer*, launched in 1821, became the *Sunday Times*.

1827 During the Greek War of Independence, the Battle of Navarino ended with the British and French (with the agreement of the Russians) sinking the Turkish and Egyptian fleets.

1842 The première of the opera *Rienzi*, by Richard Wagner (1813–83), was held in Dresden, Germany.

1944 World War II – the Allies captured Aachen, the first city on German soil to be taken by them.

1952 The British declared a state of emergency in Kenya as a result of Mau Mau atrocities.

1955 *The Lord of the Rings: Return of the King*, by J R R Tolkien (1892–1973) was published.

1967 In Oakland, California, the then biggest Vietnam protest took place, as thousands joined the antiwar movement.

1968 Greek shipowner Aristotle Onassis (1906–75) married Jacqueline Kennedy (1929–94), widow of US President John F Kennedy (1917–63).

1973 Sydney Opera House was officially opened by Queen Elizabeth II (born 1926).

1973 The spiritual and temporal head of Tibet, the Dalai Lama (born 1935), made his first visit to the UK.

1994 Conservative MP Tim Smith (born 1947), resigned as Northern Ireland Minister because of allegations that he had accepted money to table parliamentary questions.

21 October

> *England expects that every man will do his duty.*
>
> Signal sent from Admiral Nelson's flagship HMS *Victory* before the Battle of Trafalgar (21 October 1805).

The Battle of Trafalgar, fought on this day in 1805, was the most significant naval engagement of the Napoleonic Wars, establishing British supremacy at sea for many years thereafter. The British fleet, led by Lord Nelson (1758–1805), attacked an allied fleet of French and Spanish ships off Cape Trafalgar (which lies east of Cádiz) with the intention of preventing them from passing through the Straits of Gibraltar into the Mediterranean. Nelson's tactics outwitted Villeneuve (1763–1806), commander of the French and Spanish fleet, and the British won the day.

Sadly, at the height of the battle, Nelson was fatally wounded by a musket shot and his illustrious career was brought to an untimely end. As he lay dying in the cockpit of the *Victory*, Captain Thomas Hardy brought him frequent reports on the progress of the battle. Finally, Nelson is said to have uttered his last request, 'Kiss me Hardy,' and then to have died with the words, 'Now I am satisfied. Thank God, I have done my duty.'

The famous 'England expects ...' signal, quoted above, was originally to have read 'Nelson confides that every man will do his duty'. 'Nelson' was changed to 'England' to make the message less personal, and 'confides' was changed to 'expects' for simple reasons of practicality and speed: 'expects' was a word in the signalling vocabulary that could be signalled with a single combination of flags, whereas 'confides' would have had to be spelt out with eight single-letter signals.

Trafalgar Square in London, dominated by Nelson's Column, commemorates the British victory at the Battle of Trafalgar, and 21 October is celebrated as **Trafalgar Day**, with parades, wreath-laying, and other ceremonies.

On this day:

Born: French poet, politician and historian Alphonse de Lamartine (1790); Swedish chemist, manufacturer, inventor of dynamite and founder of the Nobel Prizes Alfred Nobel (1833); US jazz

trumpeter, composer and bandleader Dizzy Gillespie (1917); English composer Sir Malcolm Arnold (1921); South African-born British prima ballerina Nadia Nerina (1927); English cricketer Geoffrey Boycott (1940)

Died: Italian poet Pietro Aretino (1556); English poet and politician Edmund Waller (1687); US novelist Jack Kerouac (1969); French film critic and director François Truffaut (1984)

1519 Portuguese navigator Ferdinand Magellan (c.1480–1521) entered the strait which now bears his name.

1824 Portland cement was patented by Joseph Aspdin (1779–1855) of Wakefield, Yorkshire.

1858 The première of the opera *Orpheus in the Underworld*, by Jacques Offenbach (1819–80), was held in Paris.

1958 In the UK the first two women peers – Baroness Wootton of Abinger (1897–1988) and Baroness Swanborough (1894–1971) – took their seats on the benches of the House of Lords.

1960 The UK's first nuclear-powered submarine, HMS *Dreadnought*, was launched at Barrow-in-Furness.

1966 A coal slag heap slipped and engulfed a school in Aberfan, Wales, killing 116 children and 28 adults.

1969 Willy Brandt (1913–92) was elected Chancellor of West Germany.

1984 Austrian racing driver Niki Lauda (born 1949) became the world champion for the third time.

22 October

On this day in 1797, the French aeronaut André-Jacques Garnerin (1769–1823) made the first documented human parachute descent, from a balloon 3,000ft above the Parc Monceau, Paris. He travelled safely to the ground in a basket suspended below the umbrella-shaped parachute, suffering little more than motion sickness from the violent oscillations of the contraption.

On this day:

Born: US railway magnate Collis Huntington (1821); French actress Sarah Bernhardt (1844); US biochemical geneticist and Nobel Prize winner George Beadle (1903); Rhodesian writer Doris Lessing (1919); English actor Sir Derek Jacobi (1938)

Died: Scottish geologist Sir Roderick Murchison (1871); French painter Paul Cézanne (1906); Spanish cellist, conductor and composer Pablo Casals (1973); US biochemist and Nobel Prize winner Albert Szent-Györgyi (1986); English novelist and playwright Eric Ambler (1998)

1878 In the UK, the first recorded rugby match under floodlights took place when Broughton played Swinton at Broughton's Yew Street ground in Salford, Greater Manchester.

1881 The magazine *Tit-Bits* was launched by George Newnes (1851–1910).

1883 The Metropolitan Opera House in New York opened with a performance of Gounod's (1818–93) *Faust*.

1909 Elise Deroche (1886–1919) – also known as Baroness de Laroche or Elise de Laroche – became the first woman to fly an aircraft solo at Chalons, France; she became the world's first qualified woman pilot on 8 March the following year.

1910 Dr Hawley Crippen (1862–1910) was sentenced to death at the Old Bailey for murdering his wife.

1930 A BBC Symphony Orchestra concert, conducted by Adrian Boult (1889–1983), was broadcast for the first time.

1962 The 'Cuban Missile Crisis' began as US President John F Kennedy (1917–63) ordered a naval blockade of Cuba until Soviet missiles were removed from the island.

1962 The trial of Nelson Mandela (born 1918) for treason began in South Africa.

1964 Jean-Paul Sartre (1905–80), French novelist and philosopher, declined to accept the Nobel Prize for Literature, claiming that a writer 'should refuse to allow himself to be transformed into an institution'.

1966 The notorious British double agent George Blake (born 1922) escaped from Wormwood Scrubs Prison and fled to Moscow.

1979 The exiled Shah of Iran (1919–80) was flown to New York for cancer treatment.

1983 The Campaign for Nuclear Disarmament led protests in major cities across Europe.

23 October

In Thailand this is **Chulalongkorn Day**, commemorating the death of King Chulalongkorn, also known as King Rama V, on 23 October 1910. He was born in 1853 and his 42-year reign is celebrated as a time of major reform and modernization, including the abolition of slavery, the introduction of postal and telegraph services, and the building of roads, railways, hospitals and schools. He features in Margaret Landon's novel *Anna and the King of Siam* (loosely based on fact, and subsequently adapted for stage and screen as *The King and I*) – his father King Mongkut was the King of Siam who employed Anna Leonowens as governess to Prince Chulalongkorn, heir to the throne, and his many siblings.

On this day:

Born: French publisher, lexicographer and encyclopedist Pierre Larousse (1817); English politician and first woman leader of the House of Lords Baroness Young (1926); Brazilian footballer Pelé (1940); English retail entrepreneur Dame Anita Roddick (1942)

Died: English statesman and prime minister Edward Stanley, 14th Earl of Derby (1869); English cricketer and doctor W G Grace (1915); Scottish inventor who produced commercially practical pneumatic tyres John Boyd Dunlop (1921); Lithuanian-born US actor and singer Al Jolson (1950); Chinese 'First Lady' Madame Chiang Kai-shek (2003)

1642 The Battle of Edgehill, the first major engagement of the English Civil War, took place.

1915 More than 25,000 women marched up Fifth Avenue in New York City demanding the right to vote – it was the largest parade ever organized for women's suffrage.

1922 Scottish statesman Arthur Bonar Law (1858–1923) became the UK's prime minister for the shortest term of office in the century; he retired because of ill health seven months later.

1942 World War II – the Battle of El Alamein began in North Africa; it ended in the victory of the British Eighth Army commanded by Montgomery (1887–1976) over Rommel's (1891–1944) Afrika Corps and proved to be a turning point in the war in Africa.

1956 Tens of thousands of protestors took to the streets in Hungary, demanding an end to Soviet rule – the event became known as the Hungarian Uprising.

1970 The Blue Flame, a unique engine propelled by Liquid Natural Gas driven by the USA's Gary Gabelich (1940–84), reached 622.407mph (998.341km/h) on Utah Flats, breaking the land-speed record at the time.

2001 In response to an appeal from the Republican Sinn Fein Party, the IRA announced that it had begun to decommission a proportion of its weaponry.

24 October

We the peoples of the United Nations determined to save succeeding generations from the scourge of war, which twice in our lifetime has brought untold sorrow to mankind, and to reaffirm faith in fundamental human rights, ... and to ensure, by the acceptance of principles and the institution of methods, that armed force shall not be used, save in the common interest, and to employ international machinery for the promotion of the economic and social advancement of all peoples, have resolved to combine our efforts to accomplish these aims.

Preamble to the Charter of the United Nations.

On 24 October 1945 the UN officially came into existence, after ratification of the Charter of the United Nations by a majority of its signatories, including the UK, the USA, the USSR, China and France. (The charter had been signed by delegates from the 50 member nations at San Francisco on 26 June 1945, at the end of the United Nations Conference on International

Organization.) A UN resolution of 1947 stated that 24 October would henceforth be known as **United Nations Day** 'and shall be devoted to making known to the people of the world the aims and achievements of the United Nations, and to gaining their support for the work of the United Nations'.

On this day:

Born: Dutch amateur scientist Antoni van Leeuwenhoek (1632); English retailer Sir Robert Sainsbury (1906); Italian baritone and opera producer Tito Gobbi (1913); English musician with the Rolling Stones Bill Wyman (1936)

Died: English queen Lady Jane Seymour (1537); Danish astronomer Tycho Brahe (1601); English poet, critic and poetry anthologist Francis Palgrave (1897); Norwegian prime minister and fascist leader Vidkun Quisling (1945); US scriptwriter, producer and director Gene Roddenberry (1991)

1648 The Treaty of Westphalia ended the Thirty Years War between the Holy Roman Empire and France.

1861 The first transcontinental telegram was sent from the chief justice of California to President Abraham Lincoln (1809–65) in Washington, DC.

1964 Zambia (previously Northern Rhodesia) became an independent republic within the Commonwealth.

1986 The British government broke off diplomatic links with Syria following the discovery of a bomb plot.

1992 The Toronto Blue Jays became the first baseball team from outside the USA to win the World Series, defeating the Atlanta Braves.

2003 The supersonic aeroplane Concorde made its final flight.

25 October

> *The twenty-fifth of October*
> *Cursed be the cobbler*
> *That goes to bed sober.*
>
> Traditional rhyme.

This is the feast day of **St Crispin and St Crispinian**, patron saints of shoemakers. Crispin and Crispinian were brothers of Roman birth and Christian converts. According to legend, they travelled to France and settled in Soissons, where they preached by day and earned their living by night, making shoes for the poor from leather supplied by an angel. The feast day of Crispin and Crispinian was formerly celebrated with great merrymaking by fellow members of their trade.

St Crispin's Day is chiefly remembered, however, as the date of the Battle of Agincourt, thanks to a famous speech from Shakespeare's *Henry V*.

> *This day is called the Feast of Crispian.*
> *He that outlives this day and comes safe home*
> *Will stand a-tiptoe when this day is named*
> *And rouse him at the name of Crispian*
> ...
>
> *And Crispin Crispian shall ne'er go by*
> *From this day to the ending of the world*
> *But we in it shall be rememberèd,*
>
> *We few, we happy few, we band of brothers.*
> *For he today that sheds his blood with me*
> *Shall be my brother; be he ne'er so vile,*
> *This day shall gentle his condition*
> *And gentlemen in England now abed*
> *Shall think themselves accursed they were not here,*
> *And hold their manhoods cheap whiles any speaks*
> *That fought with us upon Saint Crispin's day.*
>
> William Shakespeare, *Henry V* (1598–9).

The battle was fought on 25 October 1415 near the village of Azincourt, now in the Pas-de-Calais department of France. It was one of the most decisive victories for England in the Hundred Years War, despite the fact that King Henry's men were tired, hungry and ill after a long march from Harfleur in Normandy and greatly outnumbered by their French adversaries, commanded by Charles d'Albret, Constable of France.

> *As in the two previous great battles between the English and French [Crécy and Poitiers], the success of the former was mainly owing to their bowmen, whose arrows threw the French cavalry into confusion, and who themselves afterwards broke into the enemy's ranks, and did terrible execution with their hatchets and billhooks. The chivalry of France was fearfully thinned, upwards of 7000 knights and gentlemen, and 120 great lords perishing on the field, whilst the loss of the English did not exceed 1600 men.*
>
> *Chambers Book of Days* (1864).

On this day:

Born: English writer and politician Thomas Macaulay, 1st Baron Macaulay of Rothley (1800); Austrian violinist, conductor, and composer Johann Strauss, the Younger (1825); Spanish painter Pablo Picasso (1881); US explorer and aviator Richard Byrd (1888); US novelist and short-story writer Anne Tyler (1941)

Died: English king Stephen I (1154); English poet Geoffrey Chaucer (1400); British king George II (1760); German-born British pianist and conductor Sir Charles Hallé (1895); US film actor Vincent Price (1993); Irish actor Richard Harris (2002)

1854 'The Charge of the Light Brigade' took place at Balaclava during the Crimean War when the Light Brigade, under the command of the Earl of Cardigan (1797–1868), charged the main Russian artillery.

1900 British troops annexed the Transvaal.

1906 Lee de Forest (1873–1961), US physicist and inventor, patented his 'Audion' – the basis of recording and broadcasting amplification; he is known as the 'father of radio' in the USA.

1924 The 'Zinoviev Letter' was published in British newspapers, allegedly from Russian politician Grigori Zinoviev (1883–1936) exhorting British Communists to revolution; it is thought to have contributed to the defeat of the Labour Party in the General Election four days later but was later denounced as a forgery.

1967 In the UK an outbreak of foot-and-mouth disease, in Oswestry, Shropshire, was announced.

1971 The People's Republic of China was admitted to the United Nations.

1976 Queen Elizabeth II (born 1926) officially opened the UK's National Theatre on London's South Bank.

1978 Queen Elizabeth II (born 1926) attended a service of thanksgiving to mark the completion of Liverpool's Anglican Cathedral – the largest cathedral in the UK.

1983 US troops invaded Grenada in the West Indies.

1994 Conservative MP Neil Hamilton (born 1949) resigned as Trade and Industry Minister, over allegations of corruption in the 'cash for questions' affair.

1999 J M Coetzee (born 1940), South African novelist, made history by becoming the first author to win the Booker Prize a second time.

26 October

The gunfight at the OK Corral, the most infamous shoot-out in the history of the Wild West, took place in Tombstone, Arizona, on 26 October 1881. The Earp family (Virgil, Wyatt and Morgan) had come into conflict with the Clantons (Ike, Phineas and Billy) and the McLaurys (Tom and Frank). Virgil Earp was marshal of Tombstone; Wyatt and Morgan helped him to maintain law and order. On 25 October, Ike Clanton and Tom McLaury rode into town and got into a fight with Doc Holliday in the Alhambra Saloon. The following day, Virgil Earp arrested Ike and Tom for carrying firearms, confiscated the offending weapons, and then released them. They were joined by Billy Clanton and Frank McLaury at the OK Corral, and the Earps and Doc Holliday were faced with the difficult and dangerous task of disarming the new arrivals. Virgil asked them to hand over their guns, Billy Clanton fired at him in response, and in the ensuing battle all but Wyatt Earp were wounded (but carried on shooting, regardless). The unarmed Tom McLaury was shot dead as he ran away, Ike Clanton escaped, and Billy and Frank were killed.

The site of the gunfight is now a tourist attraction, with life-size replicas of the combatants and a daily re-enactment of the 30-second exchange of bullets that has resounded through history and captured the imagination of cowboy enthusiasts worldwide.

On this day:

Born: Italian composer Giuseppe Domenico Scarlatti (1685); French Revolutionary leader Georges Danton (1759); French statesman and president François Mitterrand (1916); US politician, lawyer and former First Lady Hillary Rodham Clinton (1947); English biographer and Poet Laureate Andrew Motion (1952)

Died: English king of Wessex Alfred, the Great (899); English painter and engraver William Hogarth (1764); Russian-born US aeronautical engineer Igor Sikorsky (1972)

1905 Norway and Sweden severed their political union.

1950 The first meeting was held in the rebuilt Chamber of the House of Commons; it had been destroyed by enemy action on 10 May 1941.

1965 The members of the pop group the Beatles received their MBEs from Queen Elizabeth II (born 1926) at Buckingham Palace.

1967 On his 48th birthday, the Shah of Iran (1919–80) crowned himself king and his wife queen in a magnificent coronation ceremony.

1981 A bomb disposal expert was killed while trying to defuse an IRA bomb in London's Oxford Street.

1986 Jeffrey Archer (born 1940) resigned as Deputy Chairman of the Conservative Party following allegations in the press regarding a prostitute.

1989 British Chancellor of the Exchequer, Nigel Lawson (born 1932), resigned and was replaced by John Major (born 1943).

2002 129 people died during a siege in a Moscow theatre when Russian troops released lethal gas into the auditorium where Chechen rebels were holding several hundred hostages.

27 October

> *My birthday began with the water-*
> *Birds and the birds of the winged trees flying my name*
> *Above the farms and the white horses*
> *And I rose*
> *In rainy autumn*
> *And walked abroad in a shower of all my days.*
>
> Dylan Thomas, 'Poem in October' (1946).

The Welsh poet Dylan Marlais Thomas was born in Swansea on this day in 1914. The son of a schoolmaster, he worked as a journalist before publishing his first book of poems in 1934. His other works include the autobiographical short-story collection *Portrait of the Artist as a Young Dog* (1940) and *Under Milk Wood*, a radio 'play for voices' first broadcast by the BBC in 1954. The latter has become a classic: in Thomas's characteristic poetic style, it paints a vivid, moving, often humorous portrait of the inhabitants of a Welsh seaside town as they go about their daily lives, introducing such characters as the fastidious Mrs Ogmore-Pritchard ('Before you let the sun in, mind it wipes its shoes'), the promiscuous Polly Garter ('Nothing grows in our garden, only washing. And babies'), blind Captain Cat, and would-be wife-murderer Mr Pugh.

Known throughout his life for his exuberant, flamboyant behaviour, Thomas died from chronic alcohol abuse in 1953, during a lecture tour of the USA.

On this day:

Born: English navigator James Cook (1728); 26th President of the USA Theodore Roosevelt (1858); English comic actor and writer John Cleese (1939); Italian actor and director Roberto Benigni (1952)

Died: Russian grand duke and grand prince of Moscow Ivan the Great (1505); US playwright Eugene O'Neill (1953); French boxer Georges Carpentier (1975); US detective-story writer Rex Stout (1975)

1553 Spanish physician and theologian who discovered the pulmonary circulation of the blood, Michael Servetus (1511–53), was burnt at the stake in Geneva for heresy.

1662 King Charles II (1630–85) sold Dunkirk to King Louis XIV (1638–1715) for 2,500,000 livres (pounds).

1936 US socialite Wallis Simpson (1896–1986) was granted a decree nisi in divorce proceedings against her second husband, leaving her free to marry King Edward VIII (1894–1972), who abdicated the throne in order to marry her.

1971 The Republic of the Congo changed its name to the Republic of Zaire; in 1997 it became the Democratic Republic of the Congo.

1978 Egyptian president Anwar el-Sadat (1918–81) and Israeli prime minister Menachem Begin (1913–92) were named as winners of the Nobel Peace Prize.

1986 The 'Big Bang' took place in the British stock exchange when new regulations took effect and the automated price quotation system was introduced.

28 October

This government, as promised, has maintained the closest surveillance of the Soviet military build-up on the island of Cuba. Within the past week, unmistakable evidence has established the fact that a series of offensive missile sites is now in preparation on that imprisoned island. The purpose of these bases can be none other than to provide a nuclear strike capability against the western hemisphere.

John F Kennedy, television address to the nation (22 October 1962).

The anxious days that followed this speech by the US President John F Kennedy (1917–63) finally came to an end on 28 October 1962, when the Soviet president Nikita Khrushchev (1894–1971) agreed to dismantle the Cuban missiles and ship them back to the USSR. In return, Kennedy promised that Cuba would not be invaded by the USA and that the naval blockade of the island would eventually be lifted.

28 October

The Cuban missile crisis of 1962 was the closest the world has ever come to all-out nuclear war: Kennedy had made clear his intention to respond in kind to any Soviet attack on the USA. The state of international tension was such that everybody – from political commentators to children in school playgrounds – was talking fearfully about the possibility of an imminent World War III.

The US naval blockade of Cuba was lifted in November 1962 and the offending Soviet missiles had been dismantled and removed by the end of December. The Cold War between the USA and the USSR, however, continued for another 27 years.

On this day:

Born: Dutch Roman Catholic theologian and founder of Jansenism Cornelius Jansen (1585); British artist Francis Bacon (1909); US virologist Jonas Salk (1914); English actress and stage director Joan Plowright (1929); US computer scientist and businessman Bill Gates (1955)

Died: Dutch humanist Rudolphus Agricola (1485); English philosopher John Locke (1704); English civil engineer John Smeaton (1792); German-born US inventor of the Linotype typesetting machine Ottmar Mergenthaler (1899); English Poet Laureate Ted Hughes (1998)

1636 Harvard University, the oldest university in the US, was founded; it was named after the English Puritan John Harvard (1607–38) who bequeathed £779 and over 300 volumes to the newly-founded college.

1831 Michael Faraday (1791–1867), English chemist and physicist, invented the first dynamo.

1886 The Statue of Liberty was dedicated by President Grover Cleveland (1837–1908) and he accepted it, on behalf of the people of the USA, as a gift from France.

1918 Czechoslovakia became independent following the collapse of the Austro-Hungarian empire.

1922 In Naples, Italian Fascists under Benito Mussolini (1883–1945) began their march on Rome.

1957 The *Today* programme, presented by Alan Skempton and Raymond Baxter, was first broadcast on the BBC.

1958 The State Opening of Parliament was televised for the first time on the BBC.

1971 The British Parliament voted in favour of joining the European Economic Community (now the EU).

29 October

What is our life? a play of passion;
Our mirth the music of division;
Our mothers' wombs the tiring-houses be
Where we are dressed for this short comedy.
Heaven the judicious sharp spectator is,
That sits and marks still who doth act amiss;

Our graves that hide us from the searching sun
Are like drawn curtains when the play is done.
Thus march we, playing, to our latest rest,
Only we die in earnest – that's no jest.

Sir Walter Raleigh, 'On the Life of Man' (1612).

The English explorer Sir Walter Raleigh was beheaded on this day in 1618. He had been accused of high treason in 1603 and condemned to death, but his sentence was commuted to life imprisonment and he was released in 1616 to make a final goldmining expedition to South America. The mission was a failure, a Spanish town was burned, and on Raleigh's return to England he was executed under the terms of his original death sentence.

Raleigh died nobly. The bishop who attended him, and the lords about him, were astonished to witness his serenity of demeanour. He spoke to the Lord Arundel to desire the king to allow no scandalous writings, defaming him, to be written after his death … and he observed calmly: 'I have a long journey to go, therefore must take leave!' He fingered the axe with a smile, and called it 'a sharp medicine,' 'a sound cure for all diseases;' and laid his head on the block with these words in conclusion: 'So the heart be right, it is no matter which way the head lies.'

Chambers Book of Days (1864).

Born in Devon in 1552, Raleigh was a courtier and favourite of Queen Elizabeth I (1533–1603), although the famous story of his laying his cloak over a puddle for her to step on is probably untrue. An ambitious adventurer, he was involved in various expeditions to the Americas in the 1580s and 1590s and is credited with the introduction of tobacco and potatoes to his native land. His last official post was as Governor of Jersey (1600–3).

On this day:

Born: Scottish writer and biographer James Boswell (1740); English cricketer Wilfred Rhodes (1877); US singer and actress Fanny Brice (1891); German Nazi politician Joseph Goebbels (1897); US actor Richard Dreyfuss (1947)

Died: English printer to the House of Commons Luke Hansard (1828); Hungarian-born US newspaper proprietor Joseph Pulitzer (1911); Swedish king Gustav V (1950)

1787 The première of the opera *Don Giovanni*, by Wolfgang Amadeus Mozart (1756–91), was held in Prague.

1863 The Geneva International Conference, convened by the International Committee of the Red Cross, ended with the adoption of ten resolutions, which provided for the establishment of the future Red Cross, and later, Red Crescent, Societies.

1888 The Convention of Constantinople declared the Suez Canal neutral and open to vessels of all nations.

1923 The Turkish Republic was proclaimed with Kemal Atatürk (1881–1938) as its first president.

1929 The New York Stock Exchange crashed – the day became known as 'Black Tuesday'.

1964 The United Republic of Tanganyika and Zanzibar was renamed the United Republic of Tanzania.

1998 The report of South Africa's Truth and Reconciliation Commission accused leading political figures of human rights violations.

30
October

A wave of mass hysteria seized thousands of radio listeners throughout the nation between 8:15 and 9:30 o'clock last night when a broadcast of a dramatization of H. G. Wells's fantasy, "The War of the Worlds," led thousands to believe that an interplanetary conflict had started with invading Martians spreading wide death and destruction in New Jersey and New York.

The broadcast, which disrupted households, interrupted religious services, created traffic jams and clogged communications systems, was made by Orson Welles, who as the radio character, "The Shadow" used to give "the creeps" to countless child listeners. This time at least a score of adults required medical treatment for shock and hysteria.

New York Times (31 October 1938).

Orson Welles's (1915–85) infamous radio adaptation of H G Wells's (1866–1946) sciencefiction novel *The War of the Worlds* (1898) was broadcast on 30 October 1938. The original story tells of a Martian invasion of Earth, and Welles scripted his play in the form of a simulated news broadcast so convincing that many terrified listeners fled their homes, firmly believing that aliens from Mars had actually landed in New Jersey, bent on destruction of the USA. A brief introduction to the programme, making its fictional nature quite clear, was missed, ignored or forgotten as people wrapped wet towels around their heads to protect themselves from poison gas, hid in cellars, and called police stations and media offices for further advice.

Nationwide panic was replaced by outrage when the country returned to reality and normality, and there were calls for government regulation of broadcasting to prevent such a thing from ever happening again. Some, however, saw the whole incident as a valuable lesson that demonstrated the power and potential danger of mass communications as a means of manipulating public opinion and behaviour.

On this day:

Born: Irish dramatist Richard Brinsley Sheridan (1751); Russian novelist Fyodor Dostoevsky (1821); US poet, translator and critic Ezra Pound (1885); German biochemist and Nobel Prize winner Gerhard Domagk (1895); Argentinian footballer Diego Maradona (1960)

Died: English clergyman and inventor of the power loom Edmund Cartwright (1823); Swiss philanthropist, Nobel Prize winner and International Red Cross founder Henri Dunant (1910); Canadian-born British prime minister Bonar Law (1923); English novelist and essayist Dame Rose Macaulay (1958)

1918 World War I – the Mudros Armistice which took the Ottomans out of World War I, was signed at Mudros, a harbour on the Aegean island of Lemnos.

1918 The Slovaks agreed to unite with Czechs under the name Czechoslovakia.

1922 Benito Mussolini (1883–1945) was asked by Victor Emmanuel III (1869–1947) to form a Fascist government.

1957 The British government announced planned reforms to the House of Lords which included the admission of women peers for the first time.

1959 Ronnie Scott's (1927–96) jazz club opened in London.

1974 Muhammad Ali (born 1942) regained the world heavyweight boxing title from George Foreman (born 1949) in the 'Rumble in the Jungle' in Kinshasa, Zaire.

1975 In Spain, the Franco era came to an end as it was announced that Prince Juan Carlos (born 1938) would take over as acting head of state because of General Franco's (1892–1975) ill health.

31 October

Hey how for Hallow E'en
A' the witches tae be seen
Some in black and some in green
Hey how for Hallow E'en.

Traditional rhyme.

This is **All-Hallows Eve**, better known as **Hallowe'en**, when witches fly abroad and ghosts, fairies, evil spirits and other supernatural beings are at their most active. The traditional beliefs and practices of Hallowe'en may be connected in origin with rituals performed during the night before Samhain, the Celtic festival celebrated in Ireland and Scotland on 1 November. They may also have been influenced by the Christian feast of All Souls on 2 November, when the dead are remembered in prayer. However, the 'diabolical' activities that became associated with Hallowe'en were shunned by the Christian Church, in which 31 October is simply the eve of All Saints' Day (All Hallows Day), a joyous and holy occasion.

The modern Hallowe'en is chiefly celebrated by children, who dress up as witches, ghosts or devils and make turnip or pumpkin lanterns by scooping out the flesh, cutting shapes in the shell to represent a face, and placing a lighted candle inside. The recent arrival in the UK of **trick or treat**, which involves going from door to door demanding sweets or money with menaces, has been widely criticized and condemned as an undesirable import from the USA, although similar practices have long been associated with various regional children's customs on this or other nights of the year. More welcome is the revival of traditional Hallowe'en games such as 'bobbing' or 'ducking' for apples: trying to eat or catch with the teeth an apple suspended on a string or floating in a bowl of water.

> *Great fun goes on in watching the attempts of the youngster in the pursuit of the swimming fruit, which wriggles from side to side of the tub, and evades all attempts to capture it; whilst the disappointed aspirant is obliged to abandon the chase in favour of another whose turn has now arrived. The apples provided with stalks are generally caught first, and then comes the tug of war to win those which possess no such appendages. Some competitors will deftly suck up the apple, if a small one, into their mouths. Others plunge manfully overhead in pursuit of a particular apple, and having forced it to the bottom of the tub, seize it firmly with their teeth, and emerge, dripping and triumphant, with their prize.*
>
> *Chambers Book of Days* (1864).

In former times, Hallowe'en was also an occasion for love divination rituals. One of these involved placing a pair of nuts in the fire or on a hot grate: if the nuts burned quietly together or exploded simultaneously, the lovers they represented would be married. Another involved going blindfold into the garden and pulling up a cabbage stalk: the length, straightness and thickness of the stalk predicted the stature and build of one's future spouse, the amount of earth adhering to its root was an indication of the fortune or dowry he or she would bring to the marriage, and the taste of the pith denoted bitterness or sweetness of temperament.

On this day:

Born: Dutch painter Jan Vermeer (1632); English poet John Keats (1795); Chinese general, politician and prime minister Chiang Kai-shek (1887); US astronaut Michael Collins (1930); New Zealand film director Peter Jackson (1961)

Died: Hungarian-born US magician and escape artist Harry Houdini (1926); US anthropologist and mythologist Joseph Campbell (1987); Italian film director Federico Fellini (1993)

1517 German religious reformer, and founder of the Reformation, Martin Luther (1483–1546) nailed his list of 95 theses on indulgences to the church door at Wittenberg.

1864 Nevada became the 36th state of the USA.

1903 Glasgow's Hampden Park football ground was opened.

1922 Benito Mussolini (1883–1945) became premier of Italy.

1952 The world's first hydrogen bomb was exploded by the USA in the Pacific Ocean.

1955 In the UK, Princess Margaret (1930–2002) announced that she would not be marrying divorcee Group Captain Peter Townsend (1914–95).

1971 An IRA bomb explosion at the top of the London Post Office Tower caused damage but no injuries; the Post Office Tower and its revolving restaurant were subsequently closed to the public.

1984 Indian politician and prime minister Indira Gandhi (1917–84) was assassinated in New Delhi by Sikh extremists who were members of her bodyguard.

1997 Mary McAleese (born 1951) was elected president of Ireland.

2000 The International Space Station received its first residents, from the USA, Russia, Europe, Canada and Japan.

November

Gemstone: Topaz
Flower: Chrysanthemum

Married in veils of November mist,
Fortune your wedding ring has kissed.

Traditional rhyme.

November is the pioneer of Winter, who comes, with his sharp winds and keen frosts, to cut down every bladed and leafy bit of green that is standing up, so as to make more room for the coming snowflakes to fall on the level waste, and form a great bed for Winter to sleep on ... But amid all these images of desolation, which strike the eye more vividly through missing the richly-coloured foliage that threw such beauty over the two preceding months, November has still its berries which the early frosts have ripened to perfection.

Chambers Book of Days (1864).

Origins

November, the eleventh month of the year, was the ninth month of the Roman calendar and its name is derived from the Latin *novem*, nine.

Characteristics

In nature, November is the time of transition into winter (although autumn does not 'officially' end until late December, in the astronomical division of the seasons). The last leaves fall from deciduous trees this month and many hibernating species commence their winter sleep. Traditionally, for people living closer to the land, it has marked a period of final preparation for the cold, dark months ahead.

History

To the Celts it was the beginning of the new year, marked by the festival of Samhain, which started as the old year ended on 31 October. *Samhain* or *Samhuin* (meaning 'end of summer') became the modern Irish-Gaelic and Scottish-Gaelic names for the month, referring also to the Christian feast of All Saints (1 November). In Scotland and Ireland, fires in houses were traditionally extinguished at the end of the old year and relit from the celebration bonfires. Vestiges of the rituals associated with this time of the year survive to the present day in some of the practices associated with Hallowe'en (31 October) and Bonfire Night (5 November).

The Anglo-Saxons named it *Blotmonath* ('blood month') or *Windmonath* ('wind month') – the former because it was the time to butcher livestock to lay down salted meat for the winter, and the latter for obvious meteorological reasons. It was at this time of year that fishing stopped and boats were tied up for the winter, as the seas became too dangerous.

Weather

Weather lore includes variations on 'if the ice in November will bear a duck then all the rest will be slush and muck' – the implication being that the severity of the months ahead could be predicted by the weather in November. A cold November means a mild, wet winter. Judging by some of the regional variations of the rhyme, this predictive power of ducks is reputed to be at its peak on Martinmas (11 November).

Whether the ducks are skating or swimming, November's weather is never thought of as kind. The English poet and humorist Thomas Hood (1799–1845) wrote these happy lines when reflecting on a foggy day in London:

> *No warmth, no cheerfulness, no healthful ease,*
> *No comfortable feel in any member –*
> *No shade, no shine, no butterflies, no bees,*
> *No fruits, no flowers, no leaves, no birds –*
> *November!*
>
> Thomas Hood, 'No' (1844).

And the poet Ted Hughes (1930–98) described November as 'The month of the drowned dog' in his poem 'November' (1960).

Skies

If you decide to venture out of doors at this time of year, and are greeted by

a cold, clear night, November offers the opportunity to see two sets of annual meteor showers – the **Taurids** (25 October–25 November) and the **Leonids** (14–20 November). The Leonids, so called because they appear to speed outwards from the constellation of Leo, put on an especially spectacular display on average three times a century, although it is only within the last few years that scientists have managed to predict with any accuracy exactly when these meteor 'storms' will occur.

Non-fixed notable dates

Non-fixed notable dates in November include:

Remembrance Sunday: Observed on the closest Sunday to 11 November (the anniversary of the signing of the armistice at the end of World War I). Originally intended to commemorate those who died during the two World Wars, it is now the day on which we remember all those who have fallen in battle. Wreaths of poppies are laid at the Cenotaph in London and other war memorials, and at church services across the country a two-minute silence at 11am is ended by the sounding of the Last Post.

Election Day (USA): The USA holds elections every two years on the first Tuesday in November. Once every four years a presidential election is held, with the congressional elections held on the same day. Midway through the presidential term there are elections for members of the House of Representatives, state governors and sometimes senators. Although elected in November, the new president is not inaugurated to the office until the following January.

Thanksgiving: Usually held on the last Thursday in November, Thanksgiving is one of the most widely celebrated US holidays. Dating from the time of the Pilgrim Fathers in the 17th century, Thanksgiving was recommended by the President each year from 1863 and fixed as a public holiday in 1941. Families gather together and traditionally a meal including roast turkey and pumpkin pie is eaten. (See October for Canadian Thanksgiving.)

Sadie Hawkins Day: On the first Saturday in November, girls and women across the USA are encouraged to take the initiative by asking out the male of their choice (typically to a high-school or college dance). This tradition, which dates from the late 1930s, derives from the 'Li'l Abner' comic strip created by Al Capp: Sadie Hawkins was a 'homely gal' who seemed destined to remain single, until her father devised an annual event in which unmarried women could literally chase and catch a husband from among the bachelors of the town.

1 November

On Champions blest, in Jesus' name,
Short be your strife, your triumph full,
Till every heart have caught your flame,
And, lighten'd of the world's misrule,
Ye soar those elder saints to meet,
Gather'd long since at Jesus' feet,
No world of passions to destroy,
Your prayers and struggles o'er, your task all praise and joy.

John Keble, *The Christian Year*, 'All Saints' Day' (1827).

This is **All Saints' Day**, also known as **All Hallows Day** or **All-Hallowmas**, when all the saints and martyrs of the Christian Church are remembered. The feast of All Saints (or All Martyrs) was formerly celebrated earlier in the year; it was moved to 1 November to commemorate the dedication of a chapel in St Peter's on this date in the 8th century. Although it is a joyous religious festival, it also marks the eve of All Souls' Day, when prayers for the dead are said.

In Ireland and Scotland, 1 November is **Samhain** or **Samhuin**, a term that originally referred to a pagan festival marking the transition between summer and winter. It began during the night of 31 October, with bonfires and superstitious rituals, and was thought to be a time when supernatural activity was at its height, giving rise to many of the customs and beliefs now associated with Hallowe'en.

On this day:

Born: Italian goldsmith, sculptor and engraver Benvenuto Cellini (1500); English statesman Spencer Perceval (1762); Irish brewer Sir Benjamin Lee Guinness (1798); English poet and critic Edmund Blunden (1896); South African golfer Gary Player (1935); US country music singer, guitarist, songwriter and actor Lyle Lovett (1957)

Died: English physician John Radcliffe (1714); English anti-Catholic

agitator Lord George Gordon (1793); Vietnamese statesman Ngo Dinh Diem (1963); US comic actor Phil Silvers (1985); US American football player Walter Payton (1999)

1512 The frescoes painted by Michelangelo (1475–1564) on the ceiling in the Sistine Chapel were first seen by the public.

1755 A series of violent earthquakes struck the Portuguese city of Lisbon, killing around 30,000 people.

1800 US President John Adams (1735–1826) moved into the White House, the first US President to live there.

1848 The first W H Smith railway bookstall opened at Euston Station.

1848 The Boston Female Medical School, the first medical school exclusively for women students, opened.

1922 The broadcasting licence fee of ten shillings was introduced in the UK.

1954 In Algeria the revolt against French rule began.

1981 Antigua and Barbuda became fully independent from the UK.

1990 Geoffrey Howe (born 1926) resigned from the British Cabinet, following disagreements over European policy.

1993 The Maastricht Treaty came into effect. It was signed by the twelve founding nations of the European Community to create the European Union.

2 November

All Souls' Day (also known as **Soulmas** or the **Commemoration of the Faithful Departed**) is said to have been instituted in the 10th century by Odilo, Abbot of Cluny (c.962–1048). It is a day on which prayers are said and masses celebrated for all those who have ever lived and died, specifically the souls of the dead in purgatory. In Roman Catholic countries, the souls of deceased relatives were thought to return to their homes at this time:

2 November

> *At Salerno, also, we are told, that a custom prevailed previous to the fifteenth century, of providing in every house on the eve of All-Souls-Day, a sumptuous entertainment for the souls in purgatory who were supposed then to revisit temporarily, and make merry in, the scene of their earthly pilgrimage. Every one quitted the habitation, and after spending the night at church, returned in the morning to find the whole feast consumed, it being deemed eminently inauspicious if a morsel of victuals remained uneaten. The thieves who made a harvest of this pious custom, assembling, then, from all parts of the country, generally took good care to avert any such evil omen from the inmates of the house by carefully carrying off whatever they were unable themselves to consume.*
>
> *Chambers Book of Days* (1864).

In parts of the UK, the custom of **souling** (practised on 30 October, 1 November or 2 November) involved visiting houses and asking for money, food or drink in exchange for a song. It was formerly thought that giving alms on All Souls' Day would ensure the release from purgatory of the souls of loved ones, so these 'soulers' were made welcome and special cakes (**soul cakes**) were baked for the occasion. The tradition declined after the Reformation but was subsequently revived in some areas. The songs sung by the visiting 'beggars' varied from place to place; the following example comes from the Welsh border country:

> *Soul! soul! for a soul cake!*
> *I pray, good missus, a soul cake!*
> *An apple or pear, a plum or a cherry,*
> *Any good thing to make us merry.*
>
> Traditional souling song.

On this day:

Born: French painter Jean Chardin (1699); Eleventh President of the USA James K Polk (1795); Italian stage and film director Luchino Visconti (1906); US film actor Burt Lancaster (1913); Canadian singer and songwriter k d lang (1961)

Died: US humorist and cartoonist James Thurber (1961); US singer Eva Cassidy (1996); English philanthropist Baroness Ryder (2000)

1785 London coachbuilder Lionel Lukin (1742–1834) patented the first 'unsinkable' lifeboat.

1889 North Dakota became the 39th state of the USA.

1889 South Dakota became the 40th state of the USA.

1903 The British newspaper the *Daily Mirror* was launched.

1924 The first crossword in a British newspaper appeared in the *Sunday Express*.

1930 Prince Ras Tafari Makonnen (1891–1975) was crowned as Haile Selassie I, Emperor of Ethiopia.

1936 The BBC's first regular high-definition television service was officially inaugurated with a transmission from Alexandra Palace, London; the programme was received by just 20,000 television-owning homes within 35 miles of the Palace and was described as 'flickering'.

1960 Penguin were found 'not guilty' of obscenity in publishing *Lady Chatterley's Lover* by D H Lawrence (1885–1930) at the end of the famous Old Bailey trial.

1976 Jimmy Carter (born 1924) was elected 39th President of the USA.

1982 Channel 4 Television was launched in the UK.

1995 The South African ex-defence minister, General Magnus Malan (born 1930), was charged with apartheid murders.

3 November

Karl Baedeker, founder of the publishing house known for its guidebooks, was born in Essen, Germany, on this day in 1801. The son of a printer and bookseller, he set up in business in 1827 to produce books containing all the information that tourists traditionally obtained from guides of the human variety. The first of these books was a guide to the city of Koblenz, where the company was situated, but coverage had extended across most of Europe by the time of the founder's death in 1859. The Baedeker became an indispensable part of every traveller's luggage, and in the early 20th century E M Forster (1879–1970) poked gentle fun at people's reliance on it:

3 November

> *The clever lady then said that she was going to spend a long morning in Santa Croce, and if Lucy would come too she would be delighted.*
>
> *'I will take you by a dear dirty back way, Miss Honeychurch, and if you bring me luck we shall have an adventure.'*
>
> *Lucy said that this was most kind, at once opened the Baedeker, to see where Santa Croce was.*
>
> *'Tut, tut! Miss Lucy! I hope we shall soon emancipate you from Baedeker. He does but touch the surface of things. As to the true Italy – he does not even dream of it. The true Italy is only to be found by patient observation.'*
>
> E M Forster, *A Room with a View* (1908).

On this day:

Born: Canadian explorer Vilhjalmur Stefánsson (1879); US photographer Walker Evans (1903); Scottish singer and actress Lulu (1948); US heavyweight boxer Larry Holmes (1949)

Died: French painter Henri Matisse (1954); Central African Republic soldier and politician Jean Bédel Bokassa (1996); Scottish singer and skiffle songwriter Lonnie Donegan (2002)

1903 Panama declared its independence from Colombia.

1957 USSR's Sputnik 2 mission put the first living creature, a dog called Laika, into space; Laika died soon after launch from overheating and stress.

1975 Queen Elizabeth II (born 1926) officially opened the UK's first pipeline to bring oil from the British North Sea.

1978 Dominica became a republic.

1986 With the Compact of Free Association between the Federated States of Micronesia and the USA, Micronesia effectively became independent.

1992 Bill Clinton (born 1946) won the election to become 42nd US President.

1997 Striking lorry drivers in France blockaded the roads.

4 November

On this day:

Born: British king William III (1650); English empiricist philosopher G E Moore (1873); Irish engineer and inventor of the Ferguson farm tractor Harry Ferguson (1884); US actress Loretta Swit (1937)

Died: German composer Felix Mendelssohn (1847); English Quaker reformer and cocoa industrialist Joseph Rowntree (1859); English poet Wilfred Owen (1918); French composer Gabriel Fauré (1924); Israeli soldier, statesman and Nobel Prize winner Yitzhak Rabin (1995); English poet and children's writer Charles Causley (2003)

1879 The first mechanical cash register was patented by James Ritter, keeper of a saloon in Dayton, Ohio.

1899 Sigmund Freud (1856–1939), the founder of psychoanalysis, published his seminal work, *The Interpretation of Dreams*; it appeared in English in 1913.

1922 The first steps leading to the tomb of Tutankhamun were discovered by English Egyptologist Howard Carter (1874–1939).

1946 The United Nations Educational, Scientific and Cultural Organization (UNESCO) was formally established.

1952 General Dwight D Eisenhower (1890–1969) won the election to become 34th US President.

1956 The USSR's troops invaded Budapest.

1979 The US embassy in Tehran, Iran, was stormed and hostages were taken; the final 52 hostages were released on 21 January 1981, 444 days later.

1980 Ronald Reagan (1911–2004) won a landslide victory in the election for 40th US President.

1987 Land's End in Cornwall was bought by millionaire property tycoon Peter de Savary (born 1944).

1995 Israeli prime minister Yitzhak Rabin (1922–95) was assassinated in Tel Aviv.

5 November

> *Remember, remember the fifth of November*
> *Gunpowder treason and plot.*
> *I see no reason why gunpowder treason*
> *Should ever be forgot.*
>
> Traditional rhyme.

On this day in 1605 the conspirator Guy Fawkes (1570–1606), or Guido Fawkes, as he also liked to be known, was arrested following the most audacious attempt at an act of political terrorism in British history. Contrary to the popular image of a Spanish Catholic mercenary, he was actually born in York of Protestant parents.

While still a boy, Fawkes was taught about King Henry VIII's (1491–1547) ruthless subjugation of the Catholics some 40 years earlier and he was appalled by the continuing persecution of his Catholic friends. At the age of 22 he fought alongside the Spanish in the Netherlands and, eleven years later in 1603, he rode to Spain in a failed attempt to persuade the King to raise an army against his Protestant homeland. On his return to England the following year, he joined a small group of conspirators, led by Robert Catesby (1573–1605), who had already been named as an accomplice in the 1603 plot against King James VI and I (1566–1625). They planned to blow up the Houses of Parliament during the state opening ceremony attended by the King. This was intended to be a prelude to a Catholic uprising.

The **Gunpowder Plot** was foiled because one of the conspirators, Francis Tresham (c.1567–1605), wrote to his brother-in-law, Lord Monteagle (1575–1622), warning him not to attend. Lord Monteagle became suspicious and informed the government. Government troops were lying in wait for the hapless conspirators when they returned to the vaults below the Houses of Parliament to light the fuse. There is some speculation that the plot was allowed (or even encouraged) to develop to this stage to ensure a spectacular public humiliation of the conspirators and an opportunity to suppress the rising Catholic dissent within the country at the time.

Although not a day remembered with fondness by Guy Fawkes during his few brutally painful remaining days, 5 November was officially declared a day of national celebration. It became combined with the fire festivals already prevalent at this time of year and survives to the present day as **Bonfire Night**,

Firework Night or **Guy Fawkes Night**. There are records of effigies being burnt on the celebration bonfires as early as the 1670s – although until the 19th century these were more likely to be of the Pope (or an unpopular political figure) than of Guy Fawkes. Indeed, the tradition of burning unpopular contemporary political figures still forms part of the mass Bonfire Night celebrations in the East Sussex town of Lewes. At the annual Sticklepath Fireshow, in the village of Sticklepath, Devon, the bonfire itself forms a stage on which a play involving Guy Fawkes as an arch-villain is enacted by ten-foot-tall puppets. The play inevitably ends with Guy Fawkes consigned to the flames.

> *In former times, in London, the burning of the effigy of Guy Fawkes on the 5th of November was a most important and portentous ceremony. The bonfire in Lincoln's Inn Fields was conducted on an especially magnificent scale. Two hundred cart-loads of fuel would sometimes be consumed in feeding this single fire, while upwards of thirty 'Guys' would be suspended on gibbets and committed to the flames. Another tremendous pile was heaped up by the butchers in Clare Market, who on the same evening paraded through the streets in great force, serenading the citizens with the famed 'marrow-bone-and-cleaver' music. The uproar throughout the town from the shouts of the mob, the ringing of the bells in the churches, and the general confusion which prevailed, can but faintly be imagined by an individual of the present day.*
>
> *Chambers Book of Days* (1864).

The modern festivities are generally now more subdued than those of the 17th and 18th centuries. The raucous, drunken celebrations involving burning tar barrels, guns and fireworks were disapproved of in 19th-century society and have mostly disappeared. Examples of tar barrel rolling can still be witnessed in Hatherleigh and Ottery St Mary in Devon, however, and elsewhere the sound, smell and light of fireworks – from humble sparklers and bangers in back gardens to spectacular, colourful displays at official events – fill the air throughout the evening of 5 November (and often for many days before and after).

On this day:

Born: English writer and royal governess in Siam Anna Leonowens (1834); French chemist and Nobel Prize winner Paul Sabatier (1854); English jockey Lester Piggott (1935); US vocalist Art Garfunkel (1941)

Died: French-born US experimental surgeon and Nobel Prize winner

Alexis Carrel (1944); Russian-born US pianist Vladimir Horowitz (1989); Dutch astronomer Jan Oort (1992); English film director and producer Roy Boulting (2001)

1688 William of Orange (1650–1702) landed at Torbay, arriving from the Continent on his way to becoming King of England.

1854 British and French troops defeated the Russians at the Battle of Inkerman during the Crimean War.

1912 The British Board of Film Censors was first established.

1914 The UK annexed Cyprus.

1940 Franklin D Roosevelt (1882–1945) was re-elected for an unprecedented third term as US President.

1968 Richard Nixon (1913–94) was elected 37th US President.

1991 Czechoslovak-born British publisher and politician Robert Maxwell (1923–91) died at sea; his body was found off the coast of Tenerife.

1996 Benazir Bhutto (born 1953) was dismissed as Pakistan's prime minister.

2000 The remains of Emperor Haile Selassie (1891–1975) were reburied at Trinity Cathedral, Addis Ababa, 25 years after his death.

6 November

Feast day of **St Leonard of Noblac**, patron saint of blacksmiths, coopers, greengrocers, prisoners of war, slaves and women in labour.

On this day:

Born: English dramatist Thomas Kyd (1558); Scottish mathematician and inventor James Gregory (1638); Belgian inventor of the saxophone Adolphe Sax (1814); Canadian educationalist regarded as the inventor of basketball James A Naismith (1861); US actress Sally Field (1946)

Died: English soldier Sir John Fastolf (1459); Russian empress Catherine II, the Great (1796); French king Charles X (1836);

Russian composer Pyotr Ilyich Tchaikovsky (1893); Russian-born British philosopher and historian of ideas Sir Isaiah Berlin (1997)

1860 Abraham Lincoln (1809–65) was elected 16th US President.

1869 Queen Victoria (1819–1901) opened Blackfriars Bridge over the Thames in London.

1928 US inventor Jacob Schick (1878–1937) patented the world's first electric razor.

1929 *The Week in Parliament* was first transmitted; it is now the world's longest-running political programme, broadcast as *The Week in Westminster*.

1962 The UN adopted a resolution condemning South Africa's apartheid policy and encouraging member states to apply economic sanctions.

1999 In a referendum, Australia rejected a proposal to become a republic.

7 November

On this day:

Born: Polish-born French physicist and Nobel Prize winner Marie Curie (1867); French writer and Nobel Prize winner Albert Camus (1913); South African politician and anti-apartheid campaigner Helen Suzman (1917); Australian soprano Dame Joan Sutherland (1926); Canadian singer and songwriter Joni Mitchell (1943)

Died: English Roman Catholic archbishop Cardinal John Heenan (1975); US boxer Gene Tunney (1978); US actor Steve McQueen (1980); Czechoslovak statesman Alexander Dubček (1992)

1631 French philosopher and scientist Pierre Gassendi (1592–1655) made the first observation of the transit of the planet Mercury.

1783 The execution of forger John Austin was the last public hanging to take place at Tyburn Tree in London.

1872 The *Mary Celeste* (later popularly known as the *Marie Celeste*) set sail from New York – it was later found drifting and mysteriously abandoned.

1885 The Canadian Pacific Railway was completed.

1917 In Russia the October Revolution began (25 October, old style). The Russian Provisional Government was overthrown by Bolshevik-led armed workers (Red Guards), soldiers and sailors.

1944 Franklin D Roosevelt (1882–1945) was re-elected US President for a record fourth term.

1974 English alleged murderer Lord Lucan (born 1934) disappeared.

1989 The Communist-dominated government of East Germany resigned.

1990 Mary Robinson (born 1944) won the election to become first woman president of the Republic of Ireland.

1998 Senator John Glenn (born 1921) returned to Earth following a nine-day space mission as the world's oldest astronaut.

2000 Hillary Rodham Clinton (born 1947) became the only First Lady of the USA ever to be elected to the Senate, as Democratic Senator for New York.

Jeanne Manon Roland de la Platière, born in 1754 and known as Madame Roland, was executed at the guillotine on this day in 1793. Her crime was membership of the moderate Girondin faction of the revolutionists, together with her husband and many of the friends who visited her Parisian salon in the early 1790s. Jean Marie Roland (1734–93), then Minister of the Interior, had spoken out against the massacres committed by the Jacobins, drawing the rage of this bloodthirsty rival faction on himself and his associates. He fled to Rouen, but Madame Roland refused to leave the house. She was arrested and spent five months in prison, where she wrote the *Mémoires* on which her literary reputation rests, before being put to death.

On the fatal day, and at the same hour and place with herself, a man was to be guillotined. To die first on such an occasion had become a sort of privilege among the wretched victims, as a means of avoiding the agony of seeing others die. Madame Roland waived this privilege in favour of her less courageous companion. The executioner had orders to guillotine her before the man; but she entreated him not to shew the impoliteness of refusing a woman's last request. As she passed to the scaffold, she gazed on a gigantic statue of Liberty erected near it, and exclaimed: 'O Liberty! how many crimes are committed in thy name!' The guillotine then took the life of one who was, perhaps, the most remarkable woman of the French revolution.

Chambers Book of Days (1864).

On this day:

Born: English car manufacturer Herbert Austin, 1st Baron Austin of Longbridge (1866); English composer Sir Arnold Bax (1883); US novelist Margaret Mitchell (1900); South African surgeon Christiaan Barnard (1922)

Died: Scottish Franciscan philosopher and theologian Duns Scotus (1308); English poet John Milton (1674); US illustrator Norman Rockwell (1978); Soviet politician Vyacheslav Molotov (1986); English social reformer and mountaineer Lord Hunt (1998)

1519 Spanish conquistador and conqueror of Mexico Hernán Cortés (1485–1547) reached the Aztec capital Tenochtitlán and took the Aztec leader Montezuma (1466–1520) hostage.

1793 The Louvre in Paris was first opened to the public.

1887 The first gramophone for playing discs (as opposed to wax cylinders) was patented in America by German-born inventor Émile Berliner (1851–1929).

1889 Montana became the 41st state of the USA.

1895 German physicist Wilhelm Röntgen (1845–1923) discovered X-rays.

1920 The first Rupert Bear cartoon appeared in the *Daily Express* newspaper.

1942 World War II – Allied troops landed in North Africa.

1967 Radio Leicester was launched, the first operational local radio station in the UK.

1987 An IRA bomb exploded at a Remembrance Day service in Enniskillen, Northern Ireland, killing eleven people.

9 November

I'm standing on top of the Berlin Wall, which for years has been the most potent symbol of the division of Europe, and there can be few better illustrations of the changes which are sweeping across this continent than the party which is taking place here on top of it tonight.

Brian Hanrahan, BBC news broadcast (9 November 1989).

The night of 9 November 1989 saw the beginning of the end of the Berlin Wall, which had divided that German city for 28 years, separating relatives and friends living on opposite sides of the border. The wall was constructed in August 1961 to stem the flow of refugees from the East escaping to the West, and during the following decades many lost their lives attempting to cross it.

The dramatic political changes that were taking place throughout Eastern Europe in the late 1980s led to mass pro-democracy demonstrations and the collapse of the Communist government in East Germany. A decision to allow free passage through the border gates in the Berlin Wall was announced during the evening of 9 November 1989: citizens promptly converged on the hated structure from both sides to join in noisy, ecstatic celebration, and it was only a matter of time before chunks of concrete were being hacked off as trophies. Less than eleven months later, on 3 October 1990, Germany was reunified as a single country.

On this day:

Born: Russian novelist Ivan Turgenev (1818); British king Edward VII (1841); English architect Sir Giles Gilbert Scott (1880); US astronomer Carl Sagan (1934)

Died: English statesman and prime minister Neville Chamberlain (1940); Welsh poet Dylan Thomas (1953); French general and

president Charles de Gaulle (1970); Scottish novelist Dorothy Dunnett (2001)

1918 World War I – Germany was declared a republic.

1938 A night of violence against German Jews began, known as Kristallnacht, ostensibly because of the murder in Paris of a German official by a Polish Jew. The result was the massive destruction of Jewish property in Germany and the deaths of 91 Jews.

1947 Telerecording was used for the first time, when the Remembrance Service from the Cenotaph in London was filmed by the BBC and recorded for retransmission that evening.

1953 Cambodia became fully independent from France.

1960 John F Kennedy (1917–63) won the US presidential election, becoming the youngest elected US President.

1965 In the USA the Great Northeast Blackout left 30 million people in an area of 800,000 square miles without power.

1979 A training tape led to a full-scale nuclear alert in the USA.

1985 Garry Kasparov (born 1963) beat Anatoly Karpov (born 1951) in Moscow to become world chess champion.

10 November

D H Lawrence's (1885–1930) novel *Lady Chatterley's Lover* was first published in its entirety in the UK on 10 November 1960, and the first run of 200,000 copies had sold out by the end of the day.

First printed in Florence in 1928, the unexpurgated version of the novel had been banned in the UK because of its sexual content (although a bowdlerized edition was passed by the British censors in 1932). It deals with the passionate, adulterous relationship of Lady Constance Chatterley and her gamekeeper Oliver Mellors and describes their erotic assignations in what was then considered highly explicit detail.

She clung to him unconscious in passion, ... and then began again the unspeakable motion that was not really motion, but pure deepening whirlpools of sensation swirling deeper and deeper through all her tissue and consciousness, till she was one perfect concentric fluid of feeling, and she lay there crying in unconscious inarticulate cries. The voice out of the uttermost night, the life! The man heard it beneath him with a kind of awe, as his life sprang out into her.

D H Lawrence, *Lady Chatterley's Lover* (1928).

In October 1960 the novel (and its publisher, Penguin Books) went on trial at the Old Bailey under the new Obscene Publications Act. A number of prominent and influential figures – ecclesiastics as well as academics – spoke in its defence, and Mervyn Griffith-Jones (1909–79), prosecuting, famously told the jury to ask themselves: 'Would you approve of your young sons and daughters (because girls can read as well as boys) reading this book? Is it a book you would have lying around in your own house? Is it a book you would even wish your wife or your servants to read?' This patronizing question did not help the prosecution's case, and Penguin ultimately won the day – a landmark victory in the fight against censorship.

On this day:

Born: German religious reformer and founder of the Reformation Martin Luther (1483); Irish playwright, novelist and poet Oliver Goldsmith (1728); German dramatist, poet and historian Friedrich Schiller (1759); US-born British sculptor Sir Jacob Epstein (1880); Welsh stage and film actor Richard Burton (1925)

Died: Turkish general and statesman Kemal Atatürk (1938); Soviet statesman and president Leonid Brezhnev (1982); US writer Ken Kesey (2001)

1775 The US Marine Corps was established by Continental Congress.

1871 British–US explorer and journalist Henry Morton Stanley (1841–1904) 'found' Scottish missionary David Livingstone (1813–73) in Ujiji on the shore of Lake Tanganyika.

1917 World War I – the Battle of Passchendaele ended, following the Canadian capture of the village.

1924 The BBC transmits the first live running commentary on an outside broadcast from the Lord Mayor's Show in London.

1928 Hirohito (1901–89) was crowned Emperor of Japan.

1969 The popular educational children's show *Sesame Street* was first broadcast in the USA.

1970 The USSR's Luna 17 space mission was launched. The unmanned spacecraft landed successfully on the Moon, and released a radio-controlled vehicle to gather data.

1983 Microsoft announced the release of its first Windows operating system.

1995 Nigerian writer and minority-rights activist Ken Saro-Wiwa (1941–95) was executed in Nigeria, despite worldwide protests.

11 November

They shall grow not old, as we that are left grow old:
Age shall not weary them, nor the years condemn.
At the going down of the sun and in the morning
We will remember them.

Laurence Binyon, 'For the Fallen' (1914).

In 1918, at the eleventh hour of the eleventh day of the eleventh month, the hostilities of World War I officially came to an end, after the signing of the armistice a few hours earlier. This historic event, and the meetings that led up to it, took place at a suitably discreet location – a railway carriage in the forest of Rethondes, near Compiègne in France.

The anniversary of this day is known in the UK and some other countries as **Armistice Day**, in Australia and Canada as **Remembrance Day**, and in the USA as **Veterans Day** (in honour of all who have served in the armed forces). From 1919 to 1939 it was a day of remembrance for those who died in World War I, marked by a two-minute silence and cessation of activity at the moment when the guns of war had been finally hushed. After the end of World War II in 1945, the main observance in the UK switched to Remembrance Sunday (see November), but in the mid 1990s the two-minute silence at 11am on 11 November was revived, to a mixed reception and with varying degrees of success.

Armistice Day is sometimes called **Poppy Day**, from the custom of wearing red paper replicas of this flower on 11 November and the preceding days. Sold to raise funds for needy or disabled ex-service personnel and their relatives, these poppies represent the flowers that grew in the battlefields of Flanders during and after World War I, their bright red colour poignantly symbolic of the blood that had been shed there. The adoption of the poppy as the emblem of remembrance was inspired by a poem written by a Canadian serviceman, John McCrae (1872–1918), three years before his own death in France:

> *In Flanders fields the poppies blow*
> *Between the crosses, row on row*
> *That mark our place; and in the sky*
> *The larks, still bravely singing, fly*
> *Scarce heard amid the guns below.*
>
> John McCrae, 'In Flanders Fields' (1915).

It is perhaps appropriate that 11 November is also **St Martin's Day**, or **Martinmas**, the feast day of St Martin of Tours, patron saint of soldiers. Born into a pagan family, Martin served in the army before his baptism in AD 354, which allegedly followed a miraculous vision of Christ he experienced after sharing his military cloak with a freezing beggar. He became Bishop of Tours around AD 371 and died on 8 November AD 397; 11 November is the date of his burial. The cloak became a sacred relic, carried into battle as a banner by various French monarchs and stored at other times in a sanctuary known as the *chapelle* or *capella* (from the Old French *chape* or Latin *capella*, cloak), from which the English word 'chapel' is derived.

In former times, St Martin's Day was marked with much festive eating and drinking, mainly because it fell at the time of the year when livestock were being slaughtered for winter food, when geese were at their fattest and when the new wine of the season was ready for tasting.

On this day:

Born: Austrian pacifist and Nobel Prize winner Alfred Fried (1864); US general George S Patton (1885); French film director René Clair (1898); Australian cricketer Rodney Marsh (1947); US actor Leonardo DiCaprio (1974)

Died: US slave insurrectionary Nat Turner (1831); Danish philosopher and theologian Søren Kierkegaard (1855); Australian bushranger and criminal Ned Kelly (1880); English explorer and scientist Sir Vivian Fuchs (1999)

1889 Washington became the 42nd state of the USA.

1920 The bodies of two unknown Word War I soldiers were buried, one in Westminster Abbey and one beneath the Arc de Triomphe in France.

1920 The Cenotaph was unveiled by King George V (1865–1936) in London's Whitehall.

1927 The BBC held its first fundraising 'Christmas Fund for Children' appeal, later to become known as 'Children in Need'.

1946 Stevenage was designated as the UK's first 'New Town'.

1953 The first edition of *Panorama* was broadcast on the BBC.

1954 *The Lord of the Rings: The Two Towers*, by J R R Tolkien (1892–1973), was published.

1965 Ian Smith (born 1919) made his Unilateral Declaration of Independence, which attempted to maintain white supremacy in Southern Rhodesia (Zimbabwe).

1975 Angola became independent from Portugal.

1987 *Irises*, a painting by Vincent Van Gogh (1853–90), sold for a record £27m.

1992 General Synod of the Church of England voted narrowly in favour of the ordination of women.

12 November

The Reverend Chad Varah was born on this day in 1911. He set up the Samaritans, a telephone service for the suicidal and despairing, at the London church of St Stephen Walbrook in 1953. The service subsequently spread throughout the UK, with thousands of trained volunteers offering a listening ear and words of comfort to distressed callers, at any time of the day or night.

On this day:

Born: Prussian soldier and military reformer Gerhard Scharnhorst (1755); US social reformer and suffragette Elizabeth Cady Stanton (1815); Russian composer and scientist Aleksandr

Borodin (1833); Chinese revolutionary politician and president Sun Yat-sen (1866); Romanian gymnast Nadia Comaneci (1961)

Died: English, Danish and Norwegian king Knut Sveinsson, also known as Canute or Cnut (1035); English novelist Elizabeth Gaskell (1865); Spanish writer, communist orator and politician Dolores Ibarruri, known as La Pasionaria (1989)

1094 King of Scots Duncan II was killed by the mormaor of the Mearns.

1660 English writer and preacher John Bunyan (1628–88) was arrested while preaching in a farmhouse and spent the next twelve years in prison in Bedford.

1859 In Paris, French acrobat Jules Leotard (1842–70) first performed a flying trapeze act without a safety net.

1920 The Treaty of Rapallo was signed, a treaty of friendship and neutrality bringing together a defeated Germany and an ostracized Russia.

1982 Polish trade unionist and founder of Solidarity, Lech Walesa (born 1943), was released following eleven months in prison.

1982 Yuri Andropov (1914–84) came to power in the USSR.

1990 Akihito (born 1933) was officially enthroned as the 125th emperor of Japan.

1997 The Brazilian Supreme Court rejected a British request for the extradition of great train robber Ronnie Biggs (born 1929).

13 November

This was formerly the date of the **Stamford Bull-Running**, a tradition that apparently originated in the early 13th century, when a runaway bull was pursued through the streets of that Lincolnshire town by local butchers and their dogs. The lord of Stamford Castle (from whose field the bull had originally escaped) joined in the chase and had such a good time that he decided to make it an annual public amusement.

The sport was latterly conducted in the following manner: About a quarter to eleven o'clock, on the festal-day, the bell of St Mary's commenced to toll as a warning for the thoroughfares to be cleared of infirm persons and children; and precisely at eleven, the bull was turned into a street, blocked up at each end by a barricade of carts and wagons. ... The bull, irritated by hats being thrown at him, and other means of annoyance, soon became ready to run; and then, the barricades being removed, the whole crowd, bull, men, boys, and dogs, rushed helter-skelter through the streets.

Chambers Book of Days (1864).

The chase continued across the river and the fields beyond, until all were exhausted. It ended with the slaughter of the bull and a beef supper.

In the 1830s, various unsuccessful attempts were made to abolish the event, on the grounds of cruelty to animals, with an ever-increasing military and police presence in the town around the time of 13 November. The townspeople ultimately decided that the money required for these security measures could be better spent, and the Stamford Bull-Running was discontinued. The famous Pamplona Bull-Running has fared better and still takes place each year as part of the San Fermin Festival (see 6 July).

On this day:

Born: English king Edward III (1312); German Catholic theologian Johann Mayer von Eck (1486); English author and adventurer Edward John Trelawny (1792); Scottish writer Robert Louis Stevenson (1850); Canadian singer and songwriter Neil Young (1945)

Died: Italian pope St Nicholas I, the Great (867); Portuguese prince Henry (1460); Italian operatic composer Gioacchino Rossini (1868); French Impressionist artist Camille Pissarro (1903); Italian actor and film director Vittorio De Sica (1974)

1887 Clashes took place between police and demonstrators in Trafalgar Square, London, at a meeting called to protest against a ban on open-air meetings and to call for the release of an Irish MP who had been supporting a rent strike. Two demonstrators were killed on what became known as Bloody Sunday.

1940 The première of the Walt Disney film *Fantasia* was held in New York City, USA.

1941 World War II – the British aircraft-carrier the *Ark Royal* was torpedoed 30 miles from Gibraltar and sank the following day.

1956 The US Supreme Court ruled that bus segregation in Montgomery and all of Alabama was illegal.

1967 Carl Burton Stokes (1927–96) became the first black elected mayor of a major city in the US when he won the mayoral election in Cleveland, Ohio.

1971 US spacecraft Mariner 9 went into orbit around Mars.

1979 After almost a year's absence because of strike action, *The Times* newspaper returned to the news-stands.

1985 A volcanic eruption in Colombia killed thousands.

2001 The Taliban regime withdrew from Kabul, Afghanistan, as US and UK coalition troops approached the city.

14 November

On this day:

Born: French Impressionist painter Claude Monet (1840); Belgian-born US chemist and inventor of Bakelite Leo Baekeland (1863); US composer Aaron Copland (1900); British prince Charles, Prince of Wales (1948); French cyclist Bernard Hinault (1954)

Died: English actress and mistress of Charles II Nell Gwyn (1687); English inventor Robert Whitehead (1905); US educationalist Booker T Washington (1915); Spanish composer Manuel de Falla (1946); US jockey Eddie Arcaro (1997)

1770 Scottish explorer James Bruce (1730–94) arrived at what was then considered to be the source of the Blue Nile.

1851 The first US edition of Herman Melville's (1819–91) *Moby-Dick* was published.

1889 US journalist Nellie Bly, pseudonym of Elizabeth Cochrane Seaman (c.1867–1922), set out around the world in an effort to beat the fictional Phileas Fogg's trip of 80 days. She returned successfully on the 73rd day.

1896 The 'Emancipation Run' from London to Brighton (later to become the London to Brighton Car Rally) took place to celebrate the increase in the British speed limit from 4 to 14mph.

1922 The BBC began its first regular radio broadcasts from Marconi's studios in London.

1940 World War II – heavy German bombing of Coventry destroyed much of the city and killed hundreds.

1952 The first British singles chart appeared in *New Musical Express* with Al Martino's 'Here In My Heart' at number one.

1973 Princess Anne (born 1950) married Captain Mark Phillips (born 1948) at Westminster Abbey.

15 November

In Brazil this is **Republic Day**, a public holiday commemorating the revolution of 1889 that replaced the empire with a republic. The deposed Emperor, Dom Pedro II (1825–91), was a popular and benevolent ruler who had achieved much for his country, but some sectors of society were not happy with his reforms and edicts, not least the military, who were instrumental in his downfall.

On this day:

Born: English statesman and orator William Pitt, the Elder, 1st Earl of Chatham (1708); German-born British astronomer Sir William Herschel (1738); German dramatist, novelist and Nobel Prize winner Gerhart Hauptmann (1862); US painter Georgia O'Keeffe (1887); Israeli pianist and conductor Daniel Barenboim (1942)

Died: German philosopher and cleric St Albertus Magnus (1280); German astronomer and founder of modern planetary astronomy Johannes Kepler (1630); Chinese dowager empress Cixi (1908); French sociologist Émile Durkheim (1917); English murderess Myra Hindley (2002)

1777 The American Continental Congress agreed the Articles of Confederation for the union of the USA.

1864 During the American Civil War, General William Sherman (1820–91) captured and burned Atlanta, at the beginning of the 'March to the Sea'.

1899 Whilst working as journalist reporting on the Boer War, Winston Churchill (1874–1965) was captured – he later escaped.

1920 The first assembly of the League of Nations was held in Geneva.

1926 The National Broadcasting Corporation (NBC) began broadcasting in the USA.

1968 BBC1 and ITV began broadcasting in colour.

1985 The Anglo-Irish agreement was signed by the British and Irish prime ministers, Margaret Thatcher (born 1925) and Garrett Fitzgerald (born 1926).

16 November

On this day:

Born: Roman Emperor Tiberius (42 BC); German composer Paul Hindemith (1895); English politician and founder of the British Fascist Party Sir Oswald Mosley (1896); Nigerian novelist, poet and essayist Chinua Achebe (1930); Scottish jockey Willie Carson (1942)

Died: English robber Jack Sheppard (1724); English printer and newspaper publisher of *The Times* John Walter (1812); Canadian politician Louis Riel (1885); US film actor Clark Gable (1960)

1849 Russian novelist Fyodor Dostoevsky (1821–81) was sentenced to death for participating in the socialist 'Petrashevsky Circle'. His sentence was later commuted to imprisonment in Siberia.

1907 Oklahoma became the 46th state of the USA.

1918 Hungary was proclaimed an independent republic.

1959 *The Sound of Music* had its Broadway première at the Lunt-Fontanne Theater.

1988 Benazir Bhutto (born 1953) was elected prime minister of Pakistan, becoming the first modern-day woman leader of a Muslim nation.

2000 President Bill Clinton (born 1946) arrived in Vietnam, the first US head of state to visit there since the end of the Vietnam War.

17 November

Elizabeth I (1533–1603), Queen of England and Ireland, came to the throne on this day in 1558, after the death of her half-sister, Queen Mary I (Mary Tudor, 1516–58). During her short reign, Mary had taken steps to 'undo' the Reformation of her father, King Henry VIII (1491–1547), and Elizabeth's first task was to repeal Mary's Catholic legislation and re-establish the Church of England on a firm footing.

In 1568, the tenth anniversary of Elizabeth's accession was marked with the ringing of bells, and 17 November subsequently became known as **Queen Elizabeth's Day**, celebrated with increasing fervour as her reign progressed. Long after her death, the observance continued as a day for Protestant rejoicing and expression of anti-Catholic feeling, with triumphal parades and processions, the preaching of sermons against papalism, and the burning of the Pope in effigy on bonfires (see 5 November).

> *It had been usual to observe the anniversary of the accession of Queen Elizabeth with rejoicings; and hence the 17th of November was popularly known as 'Queen Elizabeth's day;' but after the great fire, these rejoicings were converted into a satirical saturnalia of the most turbulent kind. The Popish Plot, the Meal-tub Plot, and the murder of*

17 November

> *Sir Edmundbury Godfrey, had excited the populace to anti-papistical demonstrations, which were fostered by many men of the higher class, who were members of political and Protestant clubs. ... They organised and paid for the great ceremonial processions and pope-burnings that characterised the years 1679–1681, and which were well calculated to keep up popular excitement, and inflame the minds of the most peaceable citizens.*
>
> *Chambers Book of Days* (1864).

On this day:

Born: German mathematician August Ferdinand Möbius (1790); English soldier Field Marshal Bernard Montgomery (1887); English comedian and actor Peter Cook (1937); US film director Martin Scorsese (1942)

Died: Scottish queen St Margaret (1093); Welsh social and educational reformer Robert Owen (1858); French sculptor Auguste Rodin (1917); French novelist Marcel Proust (1922); South African-born Israeli diplomat and politician Abba Eban (2002)

1603 Walter Raleigh (1552–1618) went on trial accused of treason against Queen Elizabeth I (1533–1603).

1800 The US Congress was scheduled to meet for the first time in Washington, DC, as opposed to Philadelphia.

1869 The Suez Canal was opened for navigation.

1973 US President Richard Nixon (1913–94) famously declared 'people have got to know whether or not their president is a crook. Well, I'm not a crook'.

1997 At Luxor in Egypt a group of foreign tourists were killed by Egyptian militants.

2003 Austrian-born US actor Arnold Schwarzenegger (born 1947) was sworn in as Governor of California.

18 November

On this day:

Born: French photographic pioneer and painter Louis Daguerre (1787); English parodist and librettist Sir W S Gilbert (1836); Polish pianist, composer, patriot and first prime minister Ignacy Jan Paderewski (1860); English novelist, painter and critic Wyndham Lewis (1882); Turkish-born British automobile designer Sir Alec Issigonis (1906); US astronaut Alan Shepard (1923)

Died: 21st President of the USA Chester A Arthur (1886); French cyclist Jacques Anquetil (1987); US film actor James Coburn (2002)

1477 English printer William Caxton (c.1422–c.1491) published his first dated book, *The dictes or sayengis of the philosophres.*

1626 St Peter's Basilica in Rome was consecrated by Pope Urban VIII (1568–1644).

1852 The State Funeral of the Duke of Wellington (1769–1852) took place.

1918 Latvia declared its independence.

1928 The première of *Steamboat Willie*, the first cartoon to feature Mickey Mouse, was held at the Colony Theater on Broadway, New York City, USA.

1963 In the USA the first touch-button phones were introduced.

1978 At Jonestown in Guyana, more than 900 members of the 'People's Temple' religious group committed suicide or were murdered.

1987 A fire broke out at London's King's Cross, killing 31 people.

1991 English religious adviser Terry Waite (born 1939), special envoy of the Archbishop of Canterbury, was released after having spent nearly five years as a hostage of an Islamic militia in Beirut.

2002 UN inspectors led by Hans Blix (born 1928) returned to Iraq to search for weapons.

19 November

> *It is ... for us to be here dedicated to the great task remaining before us, that from these honoured dead we take increased devotion to that cause for which they gave the last full measure of devotion; that we here highly resolve that the dead shall not have died in vain, that this nation, under God, shall have a new birth of freedom; and that government of the people, by the people, and for the people, shall not perish from the earth.*
>
> Abraham Lincoln, dedication address, Gettysburg National Cemetery (19 November 1863).

The Gettysburg Address was delivered by President Abraham Lincoln (1809–65) on this day in 1863, at the dedication of a cemetery on the Gettysburg battlefield in Pennsylvania. The Battle of Gettysburg, generally regarded as the most significant engagement of the American Civil War and marking a turning point in the fortunes of both sides, was fought in July 1863. The Confederates, led by General Robert E Lee (1807–70), were finally defeated by Federal troops after three days of fighting, with great losses on both sides.

On this day:

Born: English king Charles I (1600); French diplomat and entrepreneur Ferdinand de Lesseps (1805); 20th President of the USA James Garfield (1831); Cuban chess player José Raúl Capablanca (1888); US film actress Jodie Foster (1962)

Died: French painter Nicolas Poussin (1665); Irish nationalist Wolfe Tone (1798); German-born British electrical engineer Sir William Siemens (1883); US heiress Christina Onassis (1988)

1794 The Jay Treaty between the USA and Britain was signed in London; it ended British occupation of military posts in the northwestern parts of US territory and altered the terms of US commerce with Britain and its colonies.

1916 World War I – the Battle of the Somme ended.

1969 Brazilian soccer player Pelé (born 1940) scored his 1,000th career goal, playing for Santos.

1977 Egyptian president Anwar Sadat (1918–81) became the first Arab leader to visit Israel.

1990 A summit held by leaders of the Conference on Security and Cooperation in Europe opened in Paris. The treaty signed at the summit, reducing the number of weapons in Europe, effectively ended the Cold War.

2002 The stricken oil tanker *Prestige* broke in two and sank off the coast of Galica, Spain, causing a major environmental disaster in the area.

20 November

On 20 November 1947, Princess Elizabeth (born 1926), the 21-year-old elder daughter of King George VI (1895–1952), married her distant cousin Philip Mountbatten (born 1921 and created Duke of Edinburgh on the eve of the wedding), the son of Prince Andrew of Greece, at Westminster Abbey. The union of the future Queen Elizabeth II and Prince Philip was to prove one of the most durable royal marriages of the 20th century.

The 45th anniversary of their wedding was marred by a devastating fire at one of the royal residences, Windsor Castle, on 20 November 1992. The blaze raged for 15 hours, causing damage to 100 rooms. The cost of the five-year restoration project was estimated at around £40m, some of which was raised by opening Buckingham Palace to the public in 1993.

On this day:

Born: German engineer and physicist Otto von Guericke (1602); US astronomer Edwin Hubble (1889); Russian-born US dancer and teacher Alexandra Danilova (1904); South African golfer Bobby Locke (1917); South African novelist and Nobel Prize winner Nadine Gordimer (1923)

Died: Russian pianist and composer Anton Rubinstein (1894); English admiral Lord Jellicoe (1935); English physicist and

Nobel Prize winner Francis Aston (1945); Spanish general and dictator Francisco Franco (1975); Central African Republic politician and president David Dacko (2003)

1805 The première of the opera *Fidelio*, by Ludwig van Beethoven (1770–1827), was held in Vienna.

1815 The Holy Alliance was concluded between Austria, the UK, Prussia and Russia – designed to ensure the exclusion of the House of Bonaparte from power in France and to guarantee the monarchist order in Europe.

1910 The Mexican Revolution began.

1936 Spanish fascist leader José Antonio Primo de Rivera (1903–36) was shot dead in an Alicante jail.

1943 World War II – US troops began their offensive against Japan in the Central Pacific by landing on Makin, one of the Gilbert Islands.

1944 World War II – after five years of blackout, the lights of London's Piccadilly Circus and the Strand were switched on again.

1945 The Nuremberg Trials, to try Nazi war criminals, began.

2002 Professor Gunther von Hagens (born 1945) carried out the UK's first public autopsy in 170 years.

21 November

On this day:

Born: French writer and historian Voltaire (1694); Canadian ship-owner Sir Samuel Cunard (1787); US tenor saxophonist Coleman Hawkins (1904); Australian pianist Eileen Joyce (1912); English novelist and actress Dame Beryl Bainbridge (1933)

Died: English financier and philanthropist Sir Thomas Gresham (1579); German mystical writer and alchemical thinker Jakob Böhme (1624); English composer Henry Purcell (1695);

Austrian emperor and Hungarian king Franz Joseph I (1916); Pakistani theoretical physicist and Nobel Prize winner Abdus Salam (1996); Czech athlete and middle-distance runner Emil Zatopek (2000)

1783 The first untethered hot-air balloon flight was made in Paris in a Montgolfier balloon.

1789 North Carolina became the twelfth state to ratify the Constitution of the USA.

1847 Scottish obstetrician James Young Simpson (1811–70) announced his pioneering work on chloroform as an anaesthetic in the *Lancet*.

1877 Thomas Edison (1847–1931) announced his invention of a phonograph.

1953 It was announced that the 'Piltdown Man' fossils, discovered 40 years earlier and claimed to belong to our 'ancient ancestor', were fakes.

1974 IRA bombs were detonated in two Birmingham pubs, killing 19 and injuring over 180 people.

1989 The proceedings of the House of Commons were televised for the first time.

1995 A peace agreement for Bosnia-Herzegovina was reached.

2002 NATO invited Bulgaria, Estonia, Latvia, Lithuania, Romania, Slovakia and Slovenia to become members of the alliance.

President Kennedy, and Governor John Connally of Texas, were shot today from an ambush as President Kennedy's motorcade left the centre of Dallas, where the President was on a speaking tour. Mrs Kennedy (first reports say) jumped up and grabbed her husband and cried, 'Oh no,' and the motorcade sped on. From then, all was confusion.

BBC news broadcast (22 November 1963).

President John F Kennedy (1917–63) was assassinated on this day in 1963, shot in the head and throat as he drove through Dallas, Texas, in an open car. A third bullet hit Governor John B Connally, who was wounded but survived. The shots were allegedly fired from the sixth-floor window of a building overlooking the scene, and a 24-year-old man, Lee Harvey Oswald (1939–63), was arrested and charged with the offence soon afterwards. Two days later, Oswald himself was shot and killed by Jack Ruby (1911–67), a nightclub owner. This gave rise to various conspiracy theories, the most famous of which suggested that another gunman had been present on 22 November, firing at the President's car from a sloping hill now known as the 'grassy knoll'.

Kennedy was a popular leader, and his death shocked the nation and people around the world. It is said that everybody can remember exactly where they were and what they were doing when they heard about the assassination, a phenomenon that was subsequently studied by psychologists and termed 'flashbulb memory'.

On this day:

Born: English railway excursion and tourism pioneer Thomas Cook (1808); English writer George Eliot (1819); French novelist, writer, diarist and Nobel Prize winner André Gide (1869); US pioneer aviator Wiley Post (1899); US tennis player Billie Jean King (1943)

Died: US writer Jack London (1916); English astronomer Sir Arthur Eddington (1944); US vaudeville performer and film actress Mae West (1980); Australian rock singer Michael Hutchence (1997)

1718 English pirate Edward Teach (known as Blackbeard) was killed by the British navy off the coast of North Carolina.

1943 The French mandate under which Lebanon was administered ended.

1968 The Beatles' *White Album* was released.

1975 King Juan Carlos I (born 1938) succeeded General Franco (1892–1975) as Spain's Head of State.

1988 The high-tech B-2 stealth bomber was unveiled in Palmdale, California.

1990 Margaret Thatcher (born 1925) resigned as British prime minister.

23 November

This is the feast day of St Clement, patron saint of blacksmiths and hatters. St Clement was the first pope of that name, the second or third successor of St Peter in the 1st century AD, and the author of a famous letter to the church at Corinth (c.95 AD) on the subject of internal dissensions there. According to legend, he was martyred by drowning with an anchor tied around his neck.

In former times, **St Clement's Day** was celebrated by children with a custom known as **clementing**, which involved begging for money, fruit or cakes in exchange for a song. In some parts of the UK, blacksmiths celebrated their patron saint's feast day with a special meal called a **Clem Supper**, financed by money collected during a parade around the village or town with an effigy of St Clement called **Old Clem**.

On this day:

Born: Holy Roman emperor Otto I, the Great (912); English mathematician John Wallis (1616); Swedish politician and Nobel Prize winner Karl Branting (1860); Danish electrical engineer Valdemar Poulsen (1869); Australian swimmer Shane Gould (1956)

Died: English geographer, cleric and historian Richard Hakluyt (1616); Hanoverian electress and wife of English king George I Sophia Dorothea (1726); US murderer Dr Hawley Crippen (1910); English-born US actress Merle Oberon (1979); English media decency campaigner Mary Whitehouse (2001)

1499 The Flemish impostor who claimed to be Richard, Duke of York, but was in fact Perkin Warbeck (c.1474–1499), was executed in London.

1852 The first British public pillar boxes were erected in Jersey – they were originally green, rather than pillar-box red.

1858 The General Medical Council held its first meeting in London.

1936 The first issue of *Life* magazine was published.

1963 The first episode of the BBC series *Dr Who* was screened with William Hartnell (1908–75) as the doctor.

1999 The Royal Ulster Constabulary was awarded the George Cross.

2002 Ellen MacArthur (born 1977) won the monohull class of the transatlantic Route du Rhum race in her yacht *Kingfisher*, the first woman to win the race.

2002 The controversial Miss World beauty competition, due to be held in Nigeria, was cancelled following riots.

24 November

One of the most pleasing incidents in humble life, within the present century, was the heroic achievement of Grace Darling. Her very pretty name, too, had something to do with the popularity which she acquired; for, without attaching over-importance to the matter, there can be little doubt that lovable actions become more fixed in the public mind when connected with such gentle and pleasant names as Grace Darling and Florence Nightingale.

Chambers Book of Days (1864).

Grace Darling was born in Bamburgh, Northumberland, on this day in 1815. She was the daughter of the Longstone lighthousekeeper in the Farne Islands, off the NE coast of England. In September 1838, the steamer *Forfarshire* was wrecked on rocks about a mile from Longstone, but strong winds and high seas made any attempt to rescue the passengers and crew highly dangerous. Nonetheless, at Grace's insistence, the young woman and her father rowed out to the wrecked ship and brought nine survivors back to safety. News of this act of heroism spread far and wide, and Grace became an unwilling celebrity with suitors galore, but she chose to remain at the lighthouse with her parents. She died of tuberculosis in 1842.

On this day:

Born: Dutch philosopher and theologian Benedict de Spinoza (1632); Irish novelist Laurence Sterne (1713); US pianist and composer Scott Joplin (1868); Scottish comedian and actor Billy Connolly (1942)

Died: Scottish Protestant reformer, founder of the Church of Scotland John Knox (1572); English statesman and prime minister William Lamb, 2nd Viscount Melbourne (1848); Mexican painter Diego Rivera (1957); Zanzibar-born British rock star Freddie Mercury (1991); US political philosopher John Rawls (2002)

1434 The River Thames froze over, and on the same date 281 years later again froze sufficiently for a fair to be held on the ice.

1642 Dutch navigator Abel Tasman (1603–c.1659) sighted Van Dieman's Land, later renamed Tasmania after him.

1859 Charles Darwin's (1809–82) famous work *On the Origin of Species* was first published.

1947 For refusing to co-operate with the House Un-American Activities Committee, Congress cited ten Hollywood writers, directors and producers, known as the Hollywood 10, for contempt.

1962 The BBC satirical series *That Was The Week That Was* was screened for the first time.

1963 Lee Harvey Oswald (1939–63), the man accused of assassinating John F Kennedy (1917–63), was himself murdered by Jack Ruby (1911–67).

1992 The last US forces left the Philippines.

25 November

This is the feast day of St Catherine of Alexandria, patron saint of unmarried women, wheelwrights, millers, lacemakers, philosophers and librarians, who was martyred in the early 4th century AD. A Christian convert, the eloquent and intelligent young noblewoman astonished and angered the Roman Emperor Maximinus II by defeating all the arguments put forward by the body of learned philosophers he had assembled to confute her. She was sentenced to a painful death on a set of revolving spiked wheels (hence the name of the rotating firework known as a Catherine wheel), but a miraculous thunderbolt destroyed the machine, killing her would-be executioners and a number of spectators. Catherine did not escape death, however – she was taken away and beheaded.

A number of traditions have attached themselves to **St Catherine's Day** (and its eve). These include the baking and eating of **Cattern cakes** (made with a bread-like dough and flavoured with caraway seeds), rituals and prayers to summon a husband, and the game of **jumping the candlestick**, played by young lacemakers. This involved attempting to jump over a lighted candle without extinguishing it: if the flame went out, the jumper would have bad luck. The connection between lacemaking and St Catherine may derive from confusion with Queen Catherine of Aragon (1485–1536), who is said to have introduced that trade to England.

On this day:

Born: Spanish dramatist and poet Lope de Vega (1562); German engineer, car manufacturer and inventor Karl Friedrich Benz (1844); Chilean soldier and statesman General Augusto Pinochet (1915); Pakistani cricketer and politician Imran Khan (1952)

Died: English theatrical manager Dame Lilian Baylis (1937); US tap dancer and actor Bill 'Bojangles' Robinson (1949); English pianist Dame Myra Hess (1965); Burmese diplomat and United Nations Secretary-General U Thant (1974)

1952 Agatha Christie's (1890–1976) play *The Mousetrap* opened in London – it went on to become the world's longest running play.

1963 Assassinated US President John F Kennedy (1917–63) was buried at Arlington Cemetry.

1969 John Lennon (1940–80) returned his MBE as a protest against the UK's involvement in Biafra and US involvement in Vietnam.

1973 The Greek army deposed the government.

1975 Suriname achieved full independence.

1986 The Iran–Contra scandal became public in the USA.

26 November

On this day:

Born: English industrialist and inventor William George Armstrong (1810); Swiss linguist Ferdinand de Saussure (1857); Scottish catering and hotel magnate Charles Forte (1908); Romanian-born French playwright Eugène Ionesco (1912); US pop singer and film actress Tina Turner (1939)

Died: South African politician Sir Leander Jameson (1917); US soldier and first African-American general Benjamin Oliver Davis, Snr (1970); US graphic designer Paul Rand (1996); Malawian physician and politician Hastings Banda (1997)

1703 The 'Great Storm' raged across southern England, killing 8,000 people.

1789 Thanksgiving Day became the first US holiday to be proclaimed by the President.

1922 English Egyptologist Howard Carter (1874–1939) saw the first glimpses of the inside of the tomb of Tutankhamun.

1968 In the UK the race discrimination law was tightened, making it illegal to deny housing, employment or public services on the grounds of race.

1983 Gold bullion worth £26m was stolen from the Brinks Mat warehouse at Heathrow Airport – most of the gold has never been recovered.

2000 Florida's Secretary of State Katherine Harris (born 1957) formally certified George W Bush (born 1946) to be the winner of Florida's recounts in the disputed US presidential election.

27 November

The Swedish astronomer Anders Celsius was born in Uppsala on this day in 1701. Professor of astronomy at Uppsala University from 1733, he is chiefly associated in the wider world with the scale of temperature that bears his name. The original Celsius scale, first described by him in 1742, fixed the melting point of ice at 100°C and the boiling point of water at 0°C. The now-familiar inverted version, also known as the centigrade scale, was adopted a few years after his death in 1744.

On this day:

Born: Russian chemist and first president of Israel Chaim Weizmann (1874); Irish painter Sir William Orpen (1878); Japanese industrialist Konosuke Matsushita (1894); English comedian Ernie Wise (1925)

Died: Roman poet and satirist Horace (8 BC); Scottish millwright and inventor Andrew Meikle (1811); US playwright and Nobel Prize winner Eugene O'Neill (1953); English novelist and critic Sir Malcolm Bradbury (2000)

1868 Lieutenant Colonel George Armstrong Custer (1839–76) mounted a dawn attack on a peaceful Cheyenne village on Washita River, massacring over 100 people, including women and children.

1942 World War II – the French navy scuttled their fleet in order to keep it out of German hands.

1971 A robotic probe from the USSR's Mars 2 mission makes the first crash landing on Mars.

1983 A Boeing 747 jet aircraft crashed near Madrid's Barajas airport, killing 181 people.

1990 John Major (born 1943) won the Conservative leadership election and became British prime minister.

28 November

> *Whenever a man's friends begin to compliment him about looking young, he may be sure that they think he is growing old.*
>
> Washington Irving, *Tales of a Traveller*, 'To the Reader' (1824).

The US writer Washington Irving died on this day in 1859. Sometimes hailed as the father of American literature, he made his mark on the English language with his creation of Diedrich Knickerbocker, the fictitious author of *A History of New York* (1809), a burlesque work in which the Dutch settlers of that city were depicted in the baggy breeches that came to be known as *knickerbockers*.

Born in New York City in 1783, Irving trained and worked briefly as a lawyer before turning to literature. His first publication, *Salmagundi*, was a collection of satirical essays produced in collaboration with his brother William and James K Paulding between 1806 and 1808. Later works of note include *The Sketch Book* (1819–20), which includes the tales 'Rip Van Winkle' and 'The Legend of Sleepy Hollow', *Bracebridge Hall* (1822), and *Tales of a Traveller* (1824).

On this day:

Born: English poet, painter, engraver and mystic William Blake (1757); German philosopher and politician Friedrich Engels (1820); US inventor of celluloid John Wesley Hyatt (1837); French social anthropologist and philosopher Claude Lévi-Strauss (1908); Irish cyclist Stephen Roche (1959)

Died: Italian sculptor, architect and painter Gian Lorenzo Bernini (1680); Italian-born US nuclear physicist and Nobel Prize winner Enrico Fermi (1954); US novelist, short-story writer and critic Richard Wright (1960); Dutch queen Wilhelmina of Orange-Nassau (1962)

1520 Portuguese navigator Ferdinand Magellan (c.1480–1521) reached the ocean which he named the Pacific.

1660 The Royal Society was officially founded in London.

1893 Women were allowed to vote for the first time in an election in New Zealand.

1905 Sinn Fein, the Irish republican political party, was founded in Dublin by Arthur Griffith (1872–1922).

1912 Albania declared its independence after more than 400 years of Turkish suzerainty.

1919 Nancy Astor (1879–1964) won the Plymouth seat in a by-election – she became the first woman MP to sit in the House of Commons.

1943 World War II – the Tehran Conference, the first inter-allied conference of the war, began, attended by Joseph Stalin (1879–1953), Franklin D Roosevelt (1882–1945) and Winston Churchill (1874–1965).

1948 The first Polaroid cameras went on sale in the USA.

1962 The UK and France signed a draft treaty on the joint development of a supersonic airliner, later leading to the Concorde aeroplane.

1994 Convicted US serial killer Jeffrey Dahmer (1960–94) was beaten to death by a fellow prisoner.

29 November

The 29th of November 1814 forms an important date in the history of printing, and consequently in that of civilisation. It was the day on which a newspaper was for the first time printed by steam, instead of manual power. It seems appropriate that the Times, the newspaper which of all others throughout the world is now regarded as the most influential, should have been the one that inaugurated this vast improvement.

Chambers Book of Days (1864).

The steam printing-press used for this historic purpose was invented and patented by the German printer Friedrich König (1774–1833). Capable of printing 1,100 sheets an hour, the machine was installed in secrecy for fear

of sabotage from employees anxious to protect their jobs. Its means of functioning was described in detail in the leading article of *The Times* on the day it came into operation:

> *A system of machinery almost organic has been devised and arranged, which, while it relieves the human frame of its most laborious efforts in printing, far exceeds all human powers in rapidity and dispatch. That the magnitude of the invention may be justly appreciated by its effects, we shall inform the public that after the letters are placed by the compositors, and enclosed in what is called the form, little more remains for man to do, than to attend upon and watch this unconscious agent in its operations. The machine is then merely supplied with paper: itself places the form, inks it, adjusts the paper to the form newly inked, stamps the sheet, and gives it forth to the hands of the attendant, at the same time withdrawing the form for a fresh coat of ink, which itself again distributes, to meet the ensuing sheet now advancing for impression.*
>
> *The Times* (29 November 1814).

On this day:

Born: English-born American colonial clergyman and university founder John Harvard (1607); Austrian physicist Christian Doppler (1803); US choreographer and director Busby Berkeley (1895); French politician, prime minister and president Jacques Chirac (1932)

Died: English cardinal and politician Thomas Wolsey (1530); Holy Roman Empress, Austrian archduchess and Hungarian and Bohemian queen Maria Theresa (1780); US editor and politician and founder of the *New York Tribune* Horace Greeley (1872); English songwriter, vocalist and lead guitarist with the Beatles George Harrison (2001)

1929 US explorer and aviator Richard Byrd (1888–1957) became the first person to fly over the South Pole.

1934 The marriage of Prince George, the Duke of Kent (1902–42) and Princess Marina of Greece and Denmark (1906–68) was broadcast on BBC radio, the first Royal Wedding to be covered.

1942 World War II – coffee rationing was introduced in the USA.

1947 The UN voted in favour of a plan to partition Palestine.

1963 In the USA, the Warren Commission was established to investigate the assassination of President John F Kennedy (1917–63).

1975 English racing driver Graham Hill (1929–75) was killed when the plane he was piloting crashed near London.

1989 Communist rule ended in Czechoslovakia.

St Andrew the King, three weeks and three days before Christmas comes in.

Traditional saying.

This is the feast day of St Andrew, patron saint of Scotland, Patras in Greece, and Russia. A Galilean fisherman, Andrew was the first-called of Christ's disciples, the brother of Simon (who became St Peter). He is said to have been martyred by crucifixion at Patras; the tradition that his cross was X-shaped (as on the saltire, the Scottish flag) dates from the Middle Ages.

St Andrew's Day is celebrated in Scotland, and by expatriate Scots worldwide, with family gatherings and other reunions, general merrymaking and traditional festivities. The connection of St Andrew with Scotland derives from the legend that some of his relics were taken there, possibly for safekeeping, and housed in a chapel built for that purpose at a settlement on the E coast of Fife. The settlement grew into the city of St Andrews and the chapel was replaced by a cathedral. Another legend tells of a Scottish victory over the English that was attributed to the miraculous appearance of St Andrew's cross in the heavens, shining with white light against a blue sky – hence the colours of the national flag.

The commencement of the ecclesiastical year is regulated by the feast of St Andrew, the nearest Sunday to which, whether before or after, constitutes the first Sunday in Advent, or the period of four weeks which heralds the approach of Christmas. St Andrew's Day is thus sometimes the first, and sometimes the last festival in the Christian year.

Chambers Book of Days (1864).

On this day:

Born: Anglo-Irish satirist and clergyman Jonathan Swift (1667); US writer and journalist Mark Twain (1835); English statesman and Nobel Prize winner Sir Winston Churchill (1874); English film director Ridley Scott (1937); English footballer and commentator Gary Lineker (1960)

Died: English king Edmund II, Ironside (1016); Italian anatomist and microscopist Marcello Malpighi (1694); German conductor Wilhelm Furtwängler (1954); English writer Sir Compton Mackenzie (1972); English playwright Sir Terence Rattigan (1977); US swimmer Gertrude Ederle (2003)

1782 The preliminary articles of peace were agreed in Paris between Britain and the USA.

1936 Crystal Palace in London was destroyed by fire.

1939 World War II – the USSR invaded Finland.

1966 Barbados became an independent state within the Commonwealth.

1981 During the Cold War, representatives from the USSR and the USA opened talks to reduce intermediate-range nuclear weapons. The talks ended inconclusively.

1999 Major anti-globalization protests disrupted planned World Trade Organization talks in Seattle, Washington.

Winter

In the bleak mid-winter
Frosty wind made moan,
Earth stood hard as iron,
Water like a stone;
Snow had fallen, snow on snow,
Snow on snow,
In the bleak mid-winter,
Long ago.

Christina Rossetti, 'Mid-Winter' (1875).

A cold coming they had of it, at this time of the year; just, the worst time of the year, to take a journey, and specially a long journey, in. The ways deep, the weather sharp, the days short, the sun farthest off in solstitio brumali, the very dead of winter.

Lancelot Andrewes, *Of the Nativity*,
Sermon 15 (1622).

Origins

The word *winter* is of Old English origin. It is thought to be related to the word *wet*, probably with reference to its weather, as celebrated in Ezra Pound's (1885–1972) parody of the traditional song 'Sumer is icumen in':

> *Winter is icummen in,*
> *Lhude sing Goddamm,*
> *Raineth drop and staineth slop,*
> *And how the wind doth ramm!*
>
> Ezra Pound, *Lustra*, 'Ancient Music' (1916).

Season

Astronomically taken to be the period from the winter solstice to the vernal equinox (occurring around 22 December and 21 March respectively in the northern hemisphere), winter is the coldest and darkest time of the year, when nature sleeps.

Hibernation

Hibernation is the only means of survival for some animals during the winter months, when food is scarce and temperatures fall. It is a state of dormancy, or reduced metabolic activity, apparently triggered by seasonal changes and internal rhythms (not simply by the onset of cold weather). The body temperature drops to match that of the surroundings, the heart rate slows considerably and breathing becomes irregular. In the period before hibernation, the animal usually accumulates reserves of body fat to sustain it during the months of sleep. Some animals actually store food in their chosen place of hibernation, and rouse themselves from time to time during the winter to eat and drink.

Characteristics

Many human beings envy the lower animals' ability to hibernate, and would happily do likewise. Winter can be a dull and gloomy season, once the festivities of Christmas and the New Year are past and gone. In extreme cases, the lack of daylight at this time may lead to a depressive illness called seasonal affective disorder, appropriately abbreviated to SAD. However, some people welcome the long evenings of the winter months as a period of pleasurable inactivity, or for catching up with indoor tasks and leisure pursuits neglected at other times of the year.

O Winter! ruler of th'inverted year,
...
I love thee, all unlovely as thou seem'st,
And dreaded as thou art! Thou hold'st the sun
A pris'ner in the yet undawning east,
Short'ning his journey between morn and noon,
And hurrying him, impatient of his stay,
Down to the rosy west; but kindly still
Compensating his loss with added hours
Of social converse and instructive ease,
And gath'ring, at short notice, in one group
The family dispers'd, and fixing thought,
Not less dispers'd by daylight and its cares.
I crown thee king of intimate delights,
Fireside enjoyments, home-born happiness,
And all the comforts that the lowly roof
Of undisturb'd retirement, and the hours
Of long uninterrupted evening, know.

William Cowper, *The Task*, 'The Winter Evening' (1785).

Winter sports

Snow and ice provide various opportunities for outdoor recreation in winter. Some people head to the mountain slopes of Europe for skiing and snowboarding, while others opt for the home-grown pleasures of skiing in Scotland or simply tobogganing down a local hillside. It is now generally considered inadvisable to venture onto ice-covered lakes and rivers in the UK, but in the colder winters of yesteryear, the ice was often strong enough for skating and other activities, such as the Scottish game of curling. When the River Thames in London froze over (in 1716 and 1814, for example), traders were quick to take advantage of the crowds that flocked to the ice, setting up refreshment booths, sideshows, etc:

Musicians came, and dances were effected on the rough and slippery surface. What with the gay appearance of the booths, and the quantity of favourite popular amusements going on, the scene was singularly cheerful and exciting. On the ensuing day, faith in the ice having increased, there were vast multitudes upon it between the London and Blackfriars' Bridges; the tents for the sale of refreshments, and for games

> *of hazard, had largely multiplied; swings and merry-go-rounds were added to skittles; in short, there were all the appearances of a Greenwich or Bartholomew Fair exhibited on this frail surface, and Frost Fair was a term in everybody's mouth.*
>
> *Chambers Book of Days* (1864).

Wassailing

The word *wassail* comes from the Anglo-Saxon toast '*Waes hael!*', meaning 'To your health!' It was customary to drink this toast at Christmas or New Year from a bowl of spiced ale or wine, which was passed from person to person and became known as the **wassail bowl** or **wassail cup**. People from the poorer classes used to go from house to house with such a bowl, often decked with ribbons, flowers or evergreen leaves, singing songs in exchange for money. This tradition, known as **wassailing**, had much in common with carol singing, which eventually replaced it in most parts of the UK.

> *Here we come a-wassailing,*
> *Among the leaves so green,*
> *Here we come a-wandering,*
> *So fair to be seen.*
>
> Traditional song.

Wassailing is also associated with country rituals to ensure a good harvest of grain or fruit in the coming year. These formerly took place on 5 January, the eve of Twelfth Day, when farmers would gather with their friends, servants or labourers to perform the appropriate ceremony – lighting fires in a wheat field or singing in an apple orchard – before drinking a toast and returning to the house for a night of feasting and revelry. The wassailing of apple trees (which also involved sprinkling the tree with cider, putting offerings in its branches, beating its trunk and firing guns around it) is still practised in some areas, in mid-January or early February, and has been revived in others.

Chinese New Year

The Chinese calendar differs from that used in the Western world, and the first day of the Chinese year usually falls on a date in late January or February according to the Gregorian calendar. Each year is named after an animal, in a twelve-year cycle; thus 1998 to 2009 are, respectively, the Year of the Tiger, Hare (or Rabbit), Dragon, Snake, Horse, Sheep (or Ram), Monkey, Fowl (or Rooster), Dog, Pig, Rat and Ox.

The traditional celebrations of the Chinese New Year begin with family gatherings on the first day. All the food for these must be prepared in advance, as it is considered unlucky to use any sharp implement on New Year's Day itself. There follows a two-week festival of parties, parades and entertainments – notably the spectacular **lion dance** or **dragon dance**, accompanied by loud music and firecrackers to drive away evil spirits. On the 15th day, the festivities draw to a close with the **Lantern Festival**, when towns and cities are lit up with colourful paper lanterns of every shape and size, as well as fireworks and more sophisticated light displays.

Religious festivals

A number of important religious festivals (including Christmas and Shrovetide, described elsewhere) occur during the winter season:

Purim is the Jewish **Feast of Lots**, falling in the month of Adar (February–March). It commemorates the deliverance of the Jews from an intended massacre, related in the book of Esther. Masterminded by Haman, the massacre was to have taken place on the 13th day of the month, a date determined by casting lots; 14 and 15 Adar were subsequently set aside as 'days of feasting and joy, and of sending portions one to another, and gifts to the poor' (Esther 9.22).

Preceded by a day of fasting, Purim begins with the reading of a scroll (*megillah*) bearing the text of the book of Esther. There is a carnival atmosphere: some people (especially children) wear fancy dress, and the reading is followed by comic playlets known as Purim *shpiels*. In the home the revelry continues with a special meal for family and friends, which begins in the late afternoon and traditionally features much consumption of alcohol – it is said that one should drink until one can no longer distinguish between 'Cursed is Haman' and 'Blessed is Mordecai'.

Holi is the Hindu festival of colour, celebrating the end of winter and the beginning of spring. Falling in the Hindu month of Phalguna (February–March), it is also known as the festival of fire, commemorating the burning of Holika, who is said to have tried to turn her brother Prahlad away from the worship of Vishnu. Holi is a time of unrestrained revelry, when people sprinkle or smear coloured powder and water on one another as a gesture of affection or blessing. Pranks are played on all and sundry, risqué songs are sung and normal codes of behaviour are set aside for the duration.

December

Gemstone: Turquoise
Flower: Holly or narcissus

> *Married in days of December cheer,*
> *Love's star shines brighter from year to year.*
>
> Traditional rhyme.

> *Dark December has now come, and brought with him the shortest day and longest night: he turns the mist-like rain into ice with the breath of his nostrils: and with cold that pierces to the very bones, drives the shivering and houseless beggar to seek shelter in the deserted shed. ... Even the houses, with their frosted windows, have now a wintery look; and the iron knocker of the door, covered with hoary rime, seems to cut the fingers like a knife when it is touched.*
>
> *Chambers Book of Days* (1864).

Origins

December, the twelfth month of the year, was the tenth month of the Roman calendar and its name is derived from the Latin *decem*, ten.

Characteristics

Astronomically speaking, winter begins at the solstice on 22 December, although it has usually made its presence felt long before then. The trees are bare of leaves, and much of the wildlife has disappeared into hibernation or migrated to sunnier climes. In most households, the month of December is dominated by preparations for Christmas (baking the cake, buying presents, writing and sending cards, decorating the tree, etc), culminating in the festive season itself, from Christmas Eve to New Year's Day.

History

The Anglo-Saxons called the month *Wintermonath* before their conversion to

Christianity and *Helighmonath* ('holy month') afterwards. Other ancient names refer to the winter festival of Yule or to the darkness of this period (as in the modern Scottish-Gaelic name *Dubhlachd*).

Weather

> *One Christmas was so much like another … that I can never remember whether it snowed for six days and six nights when I was twelve or whether it snowed for twelve days and twelve nights when I was six.*
>
> Dylan Thomas, *A Child's Christmas in Wales* (1954).

The traditional December weather as depicted on Christmas cards, with frozen ponds and deep snow, is no longer an annual occurrence in much of the UK, to the disappointment of many children. There are still sharp frosts, however, to trim branches, grass and rooftops with white crystals that gleam in the morning sunlight. Weather lore for the month of December centres on Christmas: a white Christmas augurs well for next year's crops, especially if it falls at the time of a waxing moon. On 31 December, attention turns to the direction of the wind:

> *If New Year's Eve night the wind blow south,*
> *It betokeneth warmth and growth;*
> *If west, much milk and fish in the sea;*
> *If north, much cold and storms there will be;*
> *If east, the trees will bear much fruit;*
> *If north-east, flee it, man and brute.*
>
> Traditional rhyme.

Advent

In the Christian Church, the weeks preceding Christmas are collectively known as **Advent**, celebrating the coming of Christ. Advent begins on the fourth Sunday before Christmas Day, which is known as **Advent Sunday** and can fall on any of the last four days of November or the first three days of December.

In our increasingly secular society, this period is simply known as 'the run-up to Christmas', but excited children still use **Advent calendars** to count off the days. These typically take the form of a brightly coloured, Christmassy scene with 24 'doors', one to be opened each day from 1 December to 24 December, revealing a picture or some other treat behind the numbered flap.

Yuletide

The word **Yule**, now synonymous with Christmas, originally denoted a pagan festival celebrated around the time of the winter solstice. The traditional **Yule log**, which was once ceremoniously dragged in from the woods on Christmas Eve to provide warmth and light for the festive season, is a relic of the ancient bonfires that characterized this festival. In modern times, the Yule log itself survives only in symbolic form, as a chocolate-covered, log-shaped cake eaten instead of (or as well as) the traditional Christmas fruitcake.

Pantomime

Serious theatregoers must abandon any hope of intellectual stimulation in December: this is pantomime season, when various celebrities take to the stage in comic dramatized versions of children's fairy tales or folk tales. Perennial favourites include *Cinderella*, *Snow White and the Seven Dwarfs*, *Jack and the Beanstalk*, *Dick Whittington* and *Aladdin*. Among the cast are two stock characters – the attractive 'principal boy', played by a girl or woman, and the grotesque 'dame', played by a man – and audience participation is encouraged ('Oh no it isn't!' 'Oh yes it is!').

The modern pantomime has come a long way from its origin as an entertainment in mime, with elements introduced from the Italian *commedia dell'arte* in the early 18th century, notably the characters of Harlequin, Columbine and Pantaloon. It was condemned by various actors and writers of the 18th and 19th centuries, but survived and evolved to become one of the most popular and enduring traditions of the British theatre.

Non-fixed notable dates

Non-fixed notable dates in December include:

Hanukkah (or **Chanukah**): The Jewish Feast of Lights or Feast of Dedication, which begins on 25 Kislev (usually in December) and continues for eight days. It commemorates the re-dedication of the temple by Judas Maccabaeus in 165 BC, after his victory over the Syrians. Candles are lit on each day of the festival and placed in the branches of a special *menorah* (candelabrum).

Tin Can Band: On the first Sunday after 12 December, inhabitants of the village of Broughton in Northamptonshire gather at midnight with tins, pans, kettles, dustbin lids, metal buckets and whistles. With these they parade around the village, making as much noise as possible, apparently to drive away evil spirits (or other undesirables). The tradition originally may have formed part of local feast day celebrations on 11 or 12 December.

1 December

On this day in 1990, mainland Britain rejoined continental Europe when the final wall of rock was breached in the construction of the Channel Tunnel. French and British workers shook hands and exchanged flags through the gap, and the historic event was celebrated with champagne. The tunnel was finally completed and opened in 1994, more than 30 years after the commitment to build the cross-channel rail link was first announced – and nearly 200 years after the idea was originally proposed, by Napoleon I (1769–1821).

On this day:

Born: Swiss modeller in wax Madame Marie Tussaud (1761); English ballerina Dame Alicia Markova (1910); US screenwriter, actor and director Woody Allen (1935); US golfer Lee Trevino (1939)

Died: English king and Norman duke Henry I (1135); Italian goldsmith, bronze-caster and sculptor Lorenzo Ghiberti (1455); English Jesuit and martyr St Edmund Campion (1581); US writer James Baldwin (1987)

1640 The Revolt of Portugal began with an uprising in Lisbon; Spain and Portugal had been unified in 1580 but increasing dissatisfaction in Portugal led to its eventual independence.

1919 Nancy Astor (1879–1964) became the first woman MP to sit in the House of Commons, as Conservative MP for Plymouth; Constance, Countess Markievicz (1868–1927), had been elected the previous year as the Sinn Fein MP for the St Patrick's division of Dublin, but never took her seat.

1925 The Locarno Pact, an international agreement guaranteeing the post-1919 frontiers between France, Belgium and Germany, and the demilitarization of the Rhineland, was formally signed by Italy, the UK, France, Germany and Belgium; the Pact had been agreed at the conferences held in Locarno, Italy, in October 1925.

1941 World War II – points rationing (of tinned goods, dried fruit, cereal, etc) was introduced in the UK.

1951 The première of the opera *Billy Budd*, by Benjamin Britten (1913–76), was held in London.

1986 The Department of Trade and Industry began to investigate the affairs of Guinness, which eventually resulted in the arrest of four directors.

1989 Russian president Mikhail Gorbachev (born 1931) made a historic visit to Pope John Paul II (born 1920) in the Vatican.

1999 The Royal Opera House in Covent Garden was formally reopened by Queen Elizabeth II (born 1926) after a major refurbishment.

December

> *John Brown's body lies a-moulderin' in the grave,*
> *But his soul goes marching on.*
>
> Traditional song.

The US abolitionist John Brown was hanged on this day in 1859. Born in 1800, he married twice and fathered 20 children before becoming actively involved with the anti-slavery movement, although he had long been sympathetic to the cause. In the mid-1850s he took part in the violent conflict that was then raging in Kansas, and in 1858 he announced his intention to set up a mountain stronghold in Virginia as a refuge for runaway slaves. The following year he led a raid on the arsenal at Harpers Ferry and took a number of local citizens as hostages, but he and his surviving followers (several had been killed, including two of his sons) were finally forced to surrender. Arrested and tried for murder, insurrection and treason, he was convicted and sentenced to death.

In the Civil War that followed soon afterwards, Brown was hailed as a hero and martyr, and the song 'John Brown's Body', of uncertain authorship, became the anthem of soldiers fighting for the cause of universal freedom.

On this day:

Born: French artist Georges Seurat (1859); English cellist and conductor Sir John Barbirolli (1899); Hungarian-born US engineer and inventor Peter Goldmark (1906); Yugoslav-born US tennis player Monica Seles (1973); US pop singer and actress Britney Spears (1981)

Died: Spanish conquistador and conqueror of Mexico Hernando Cortez (1547); Flemish geographer and mapmaker Gerardus Mercator (1594); French writer the Marquis de Sade (1814); English poet, librarian and jazz critic Philip Larkin (1985)

1697 A service was held for the first time in the Quire, the first part of the rebuilt St Paul's Cathedral to be finished; the old building had been destroyed in the Great Fire of London in 1666, and the new Cathedral was designed by Christopher Wren (1632–1723).

1804 Napoleon I (1769–1821), who had assumed the title of Emperor on 18 May, was formally crowned by Pope Pius VII (1742–1823) in the cathedral of Notre-Dame, Paris.

1805 The Battle of Austerlitz took place, in which Napoleon I (1769–1821) inflicted a disastrous defeat on the Russians and Austrians.

1823 The Monroe Doctrine, a major statement of US foreign policy, was proclaimed; it announced US hostility to further European colonization or attempts to extend European influence and rejected European interference in US affairs.

1823 English physician and educationalist George Birkbeck (1776–1841) launched the London Mechanics', or Birkbeck, Institution; it was the first such institution in the UK, and developed into Birkbeck College, a constituent college of London University.

1877 The première of the opera *Samson and Delilah*, by Camille Saint-Saëns (1835–1921), was held in Weimar, Germany.

1907 The Professional Footballers' Association, the longest established professional sports union, was founded as the Players' Union at the Imperial Hotel in Manchester, England.

1942 The world's first 'atomic pile', or nuclear reactor, constructed by nuclear physicist Enrico Fermi (1901–54), began producing nuclear energy at the University of Chicago, USA.

1954 US politician Joseph McCarthy (1909–57) was formally censured by the Senate for his methods while conducting his fierce anti-Communist investigations.

1956 Cuban revolutionary Fidel Castro (born 1927) landed in Cuba with a small band of insurgents.

1971 The United Arab Emirates was formed as an independent state as six emirates left British control and combined as a new nation.

1977 The inquest into the death in custody of South African black activist Steve Biko (1946–77) absolved the South African security police of blame in a verdict which cause widespread outrage.

1988 A devastating cyclone hit Bangladesh.

1990 The first paying passenger went into space aboard a Soviet Soyuz TM11 flight.

1995 'Rogue trader' Nick Leeson (born 1967), who contributed to the fall of Barings Bank, was sentenced to six years in prison.

2001 The US energy giant Enron filed for bankruptcy with US$16 billion of debt.

3 December

The first heart transplant was performed on this day in 1967. In the early hours of the morning, at the Groote Schuur Hospital in Cape Town, South Africa, Professor Christiaan Barnard (1922–2001) replaced the heart of 53-year-old Louis Washkansky with that of 25-year-old Denise Darvall, who had been fatally injured in a road accident the day before. Washkansky, whose original heart had almost ceased to function after a series of heart attacks, survived for 18 days after the operation. He died from pneumonia, an indirect result of the drugs administered to prevent his body from rejecting the new organ, and which had lowered his resistance to infection.

On this day:

Born: Italian violin maker Niccolo Amati (1596); English reformer Octavia Hill (1838); Polish-born British novelist Joseph Conrad (1857); English cricketer Trevor Bailey (1923); French film director Jean-Luc Godard (1930); English singer Ozzy Osbourne (1948)

Died: Spanish Jesuit missionary St Francis Xavier (1552); Scottish writer Robert Louis Stevenson (1894); US founder of the Christian Science Church Mary Eddy (1910); Australian poet and author Dame Mary Gilmore (1962); US poet and novelist Gwendolyn Brooks (2000)

1660 Margaret Hughes became the first known woman to act on the English stage when she appeared as Desdemona in a production of *Othello* in London.

1800 The Battle of Hohenlinden, a confused but crucial battle in the closing stage of the French Revolutionary War, was fought near Munich between the French and Austrian forces.

1818 Illinois became the 21st state of the USA.

1917 The Quebec Bridge, the world's longest cantilever bridge, was fully opened across the St Lawrence River in Quebec, Canada.

1947 The première of the play *A Streetcar Named Desire*, by Tennessee Williams (1911–83), was held on Broadway, New York City.

1954 The première of the opera *Troilus and Cressida*, by William Walton (1902–83), was held at the Royal Opera House in Covent Garden, London.

1984 The city of Bhopal in Madhya Pradesh, India, became the scene of a major industrial disaster when poisonous isocyanate gas escaped from the Union Carbide factory, killing around 2,500 people and leaving 100,000 more homeless.

1988 Government minister Edwina Currie (born 1946) caused an outcry by stating on television that British eggs were infected with salmonella; she resigned two weeks later.

1989 The Malta Summit took place between President George Bush (born 1924) of the USA and President Mikhail Gorbachev (born 1931) of the USSR; many saw it as marking the end of the Cold War.

1992 Two IRA bombs exploded in Manchester city centre, injuring 64 people.

4 December

On this day:

Born: English nurse Edith Cavell (1865); Austrian lyric poet Rainer Maria Rilke (1875); Scottish comedian and actor Ronnie Corbett (1930); US actor Jeff Bridges (1949)

Died: Persian mathematician, astronomer and poet Omar Khayyám (1131); English theologian and mystic Nicholas Ferrar (1637); English political philosopher Thomas Hobbes (1679); Italian physiologist Luigi Galvani (1798); English scientist William Sturgeon (1850); English composer Benjamin Britten, Baron Britten of Aldeburgh (1976)

1154 Nicolas Breakspear (1100–59) became the first (and only) English pope as Adrian IV.

1791 *The Observer* newspaper was first published; it is the oldest British Sunday newspaper still published today.

1937 D C Thomson published the first issue of *The Dandy* comic.

1961 It was announced that the birth control pill would become freely available on the National Health Service in the UK.

1971 A loyalist bomb exploded in Belfast, Northern Ireland, demolishing McGurk's Bar and killing 15 people.

1991 The last and longest-held US hostage in the Lebanon, Terry Anderson (born 1947) was freed; he had been held since March 1985.

1997 The European Union voted to ban tobacco advertising.

5 December

> *Mozart appears as a being eccentrically formed to be a medium for the expression of music and no grosser purpose. In this he was strong: in everything else of body and mind, he remained a child during the thirty-six years to which his life was limited.*
>
> *Chambers Book of Days* (1864).

The Austrian composer Wolfgang Amadeus Mozart died on this day in 1791. In the last months of his comparatively short life, he was commissioned to write a Requiem by a mysterious stranger. The effort of composing the work compounded the illness from which he was already suffering – he is said to have exclaimed to his wife, foreknowingly, 'I am writing this Requiem for myself!' – and it remained unfinished at his death.

Born in 1756, Mozart was a child prodigy in music, mastering the keyboard at the age of four and composing his first pieces a year later; by 1772 he had written 25 symphonies and numerous other works. He married in 1782, and his most famous compositions date from the years that followed, notably the operas *The Marriage of Figaro* (1786), *Don Giovanni* (1787), *Così fan tutte* (1790) and *The Magic Flute* (1791). Nevertheless, the family was plagued by financial troubles, and Mozart's premature death left his widow Constanze heavily in debt. He was buried in an unmarked grave for paupers at St Mark's cemetery in Vienna.

On this day:

Born: English poet Christina Rossetti (1830); Polish soldier, statesman and president Jósef Pilsudski (1867); Austrian-born US film director Fritz Lang (1890); German theoretical physicist and Nobel Prize winner Werner Heisenberg (1901); US rock and roll singer and pianist Little Richard (1932)

Died: Scottish physicist Sir Robert Watson-Watt (1892); English sugar magnate, philanthropist and art gallery founder Sir Henry Tate (1899); German aircraft designer Claudius Dornier (1969); English cricketer Colin Cowdrey (2000); Burmese politician U Ne Win (2002)

1766 James Christie (1730–1803) held his first auction sale in London.

1839 A uniform postage rate of four pence per letter was introduced in the UK.

1872 The brig *Mary Celeste* (later popularly known as the *Marie Celeste*), carrying a cargo of alcohol, was found mysteriously abandoned off the Azores in the Atlantic Ocean.

1933 Prohibition ended in the USA with the formal ratification of the 21st Amendment to the Constitution.

1945 Flight 19, five US navy bombers and their crews mysteriously disappeared on a training flight over the area of ocean that became known as the 'Bermuda Triangle'.

1958 Queen Elizabeth II (born 1926) inaugurated Subscriber Trunk Dialling (STD) on the British telephone system by phoning Edinburgh's Lord Provost from Bristol Central Telephone Exchange.

1958 The UK's first motorway, the Preston Bypass, was opened to traffic.

1991 Administrators were brought in to investigate massive financial irregularities in the business empire of the late British publisher Robert Maxwell (1923–91).

2001 Delegates representing several Afghan factions at a conference in Bonn signed a landmark agreement creating a new transitional government for the country.

6 December

This is the feast day of St Nicholas, Bishop of Myra in Asia Minor (now Turkey) in the 4th century AD. Numerous legends tell of his piety and miracles: as a baby he is said to have refused to suck his mother's breast on Wednesdays and Fridays, which were religious fast days, and in later life he apparently restored to life the dismembered bodies of some young boys who had been murdered and pickled in a tub. For the latter deed he became patron saint of children; for saving a poor man's daughters from prostitution by giving their father three bags of gold he became patron saint of pawnbrokers (hence the three gold balls of the traditional pawnbrokers' sign).

In the Netherlands and neighbouring countries of Europe, St Nicholas is said to bring sweets and presents for well-behaved children on 6 December.

This tradition was imported to the USA by Dutch settlers, and St Nicholas evolved into Santa Claus, whose gift-giving rounds are performed later in the month. In this new incarnation he subsequently returned across the Atlantic to merge with the British Father Christmas.

It was formerly customary on **St Nicholas's Day** to elect a **boy bishop**, or *Episcopus Puerorum*, who would perform a juvenile version of the normal duties and ceremonies of this office, excluding the celebration of Mass, until Holy Innocents' Day (28 December).

> *Besides the regular buffooneries throughout England of the Boy-bishop and his companions in church, these pseudo-clergy seem to have perambulated the neighbourhood, and enlivened it with their jocularities, in return for which a contribution under the designation of the 'Bishop's subsidy,' would be demanded from passers-by and householders. Occasionally, royalty itself deigned to be amused with the burlesque ritual of the mimic prelate, and in 1299, we find Edward I, on his way to Scotland, permitting a Boy-bishop to say vespers before him in his chapel at Heton, near Newcastle-on-Tyne, on the 7th of December, the day after St Nicholas's Day.*
>
> *Chambers Book of Days* (1864).

On this day:

Born: Italian courtier and writer Count Baldassare Castiglione (1478); English colonial administrator Warren Hastings (1732); German-born British philologist and Orientalist Max Müller (1823); US pianist, composer and bandleader Dave Brubeck (1920); English animator Nick Park (1958)

Died: English novelist Anthony Trollope (1882); US statesman and president of the Confederate States Jefferson Davis (1889); US folk and blues singer and guitarist Leadbelly (1949); Austrian–Swiss theoretical physicist and Nobel Prize winner Wolfgang Pauli (1958); New Zealand yachtsman Sir Peter Blake (2001); German bass-baritone Hans Hotter (2003)

1492 Christopher Columbus (1451–1506) first sighted the Caribbean island of Hispaniola (now split between Haiti and the Dominican Republic).

1648 English parliamentarian Colonel Thomas Pride (died 1658) expelled over 100 Presbyterian Royalist members of Parliament in 'Pride's

Purge'; the House, reduced to about 80 members, later proceeded to bring King Charles I (1600–49) to justice.

1846 The première of the opera *The Damnation of Faust*, by Hector Berlioz (1803–69), was held in Paris.

1865 The 13th Amendment to the US Constitution, abolishing slavery, was ratified.

1877 Thomas Edison (1847–1931) made the first recording of the human voice, reciting 'Mary Had a Little Lamb' into a makeshift apparatus.

1917 Finland achieved independence from Russia.

1917 World War I – the French ship *Mont Blanc*, packed with ammunition, acid and the explosive TNT, and the Belgian relief ship *Imo* collided off Halifax, Nova Scotia, Canada; the *Mont Blanc* exploded, killing more than 2,000 people, injuring another 9,000 and destroying 325 acres of the city.

1921 The Irish Free State was established by the Anglo-Irish Treaty – 26 counties (excluding the six of Northern Ireland) were to become a Dominion under the British crown.

1978 Spain's new democratic constitution was approved, coming into effect later in the month.

1983 The UK's first heart and lung transplant was successfully completed.

7 December

On this day in 1941, the Japanese launched an attack on the US naval base at Pearl Harbor, Hawaii, and other military installations nearby, an event that brought the USA belatedly into World War II. Four battleships and 42 aircraft were destroyed, many others were badly damaged, and more than 2,400 members of the US armed forces lost their lives.

In his address to Congress the following day, President Franklin D Roosevelt (1882–1945) referred to 7 December as 'a date which will live in infamy'. Now known as **Pearl Harbor Day**, or **National Pearl Harbor Remembrance Day**, it is commemorated annually throughout the USA with ceremonies and activities in honour of those who died or were injured during the attack.

On this day:

Born: Italian sculptor, architect and painter Gian Lorenzo Bernini (1598); Italian composer Pietro Mascagni (1863); Portuguese statesman Mário Soares (1924); US linguist and political activist Noam Chomsky (1928)

Died: Roman orator, statesman and man of letters Cicero (43 BC); Dutch-born British painter Sir Peter Lely (1680); French courtesan and mistress of Louis XV Marie Jeanne, Comtesse du Barry (1793); Norwegian operatic soprano Kirsten Flagstad (1962); English poet, novelist, essayist and critic Robert Graves (1985)

1732 The Royal Opera House in Covent Garden, London, opened as the Theatre Royal with a performance of *The Way of the World* by William Congreve (1670–1729).

1787 Delaware became the first state to ratify the Constitution of the USA.

1815 French Marshal Michel Ney (1769–1815) was executed for high treason in Paris; a general under Napoleon I (1769–1821), he had submitted to Louis XVIII (1755–1824), but went over to his old master's side and fought for him during the Battle of Waterloo (1815), before being condemned upon Louis XVIII's second restoration.

1842 The New York Philharmonic gave its first concert.

1889 The première of the comic opera *The Gondoliers*, by W S Gilbert (1836–1911) and Arthur Sullivan (1842–1900), was held at the Savoy theatre in London.

1916 World War I – David Lloyd George (1863–1945) became British prime minister at the head of a coalition government.

1917 World War I – the Battle of Cambrai, the first in which tanks were used, came to an end.

1982 The first execution by lethal injection in the USA was that of kidnapper and murderer Charlie Brooks at Fort Worth prison in Texas.

1988 An earthquake measuring 6.9 on the Richter scale struck Armenia, killing 50,000 people.

8
December

On this day:

Born: Scottish queen Mary, Queen of Scots (1542); US inventor of the cotton gin Eli Whitney (1765); Norwegian writer, politician and Nobel Prize winner Bjørnstjerne Bjørnson (1832); German-born British painter Lucian Freud (1922); Northern Irish flautist and conductor James Galway (1939)

Died: US architect James Hoban (1831); English critic and essayist Thomas De Quincey (1859); English horticulturist and garden designer Gertrude Jekyll (1932); English revolutionary philosopher and evolutionist Herbert Spencer (1903)

1854 Pope Pius IX (1792–1878) declared the dogma of the Immaculate Conception of the Blessed Virgin Mary to be an article of faith in the Roman Catholic Church.

1864 The Clifton Suspension Bridge over the River Avon in Bristol was officially opened.

1914 World War I – the British Navy defeated the German fleet in the Battle of the Falkland Islands.

1941 World War II – the USA and the UK formally declared war on Japan following the previous day's attack on Pearl Harbor.

1980 English songwriter, vocalist and rhythm guitarist with the Beatles John Lennon was shot dead outside his New York apartment.

1987 The INF (Intermediate Nuclear Force) Treaty was signed in Washington, DC, by US President Ronald Reagan (1911–2004) and Soviet General-Secretary Mikhail Gorbachev (born 1931), involving the elimination of 1,286 missiles from Europe and Asia, and over 2,000 warheads.

1995 Forty-eight-year-old secondary school head teacher Philip Lawrence was murdered by a 15-year-old youth outside his school while protecting a pupil who was being attacked.

9 December

On this day:

Born: German physical chemist and Nobel Prize winner Fritz Haber (1868); Austrian–British soprano Dame Elisabeth Schwarzkopf (1915); US film actor Kirk Douglas (1916); English actress Dame Judi Dench (1934); Scottish footballer Billy Bremner (1942)

Died: Holy Roman emperor Sigismund (1437); Flemish painter Sir Anthony Van Dyck (1641); English inventor Joseph Bramah (1814); US diplomat and Nobel Prize winner Ralph Bunche (1971); English archaeologist Mary Leakey (1996)

1783 The first executions took place at Newgate Prison in London.

1842 The première of the opera *Russlan and Ludmilla*, by Mikhail Glinka (1804–57), was held in St Petersburg, Russia.

1868 William Ewart Gladstone (1809–98) became British prime minister for the first of four times (1868–74, 1880–5, 1886, 1892–4).

1905 The première of the opera *Salome*, by Richard Strauss (1864–1949), was held in Dresden, Germany.

1960 The first episode of *Coronation Street*, the world's longest-running television soap opera, was broadcast.

1961 Tanganyika (now part of Tanzania) became an independent state; on the same date in 1962 it became a republic, with Julius Nyerere (1922–99) as its first president.

1973 The British, Ulster and Irish governments signed the power-sharing Sunningdale Agreement, providing for representation in the Province's government of both the Catholic and Protestant populations.

1992 In the UK, the prime minister John Major (born 1943) announced that Charles, Prince of Wales (born 1948) and Diana, Princess of Wales (1961–97) were to separate.

10 December

The Swedish chemist Alfred Bernhard Nobel (1833–96), inventor of dynamite, died on this day in 1896. In accordance with his will, much of the fortune he amassed from this and other inventions was used for the endowment of five prizes to be awarded annually 'to those who, during the preceding year, shall have conferred the greatest benefit on mankind' in five fields: physics, chemistry, physiology or medicine, literature and peace. The first Nobel Prizes were awarded on 10 December 1901, the fifth anniversary of the founder's death; among the first laureates were the German physicist Wilhelm Röntgen (1845–1923), honoured for his discovery of X-rays, the French poet Sully-Prudhomme (1839–1907), and the Swiss philanthropist Jean Henri Dunant (1828–1910), who inspired the establishment of the International Red Cross and the Geneva Convention.

On this day:

Born: Belgian-born French composer César Franck (1822); US poet Emily Dickinson (1830); US librarian Melvil Dewey (1851); Northern Irish actor and director Kenneth Branagh (1960); Pakistani squash player Jahangir Khan (1963)

Died: US writer and journalist Damon Runyon (1946); US soul singer Otis Redding (1967); Swiss Protestant theologian Karl Barth (1968); Lithuanian-born US violinist Jascha Heifetz (1987)

1768 The Royal Academy of the Arts was founded.

1817 Mississippi became the 20th state of the USA.

1898 Cuba became independent from Spain at the end of the Spanish–American War.

1902 Egypt's Aswan Dam was completed.

1903 Marie Curie (1867–1934) became the first woman to win a Nobel Prize with the award for Physics, which she shared with her husband Pierre (1859–1906) and French physicist Antoine Henri Becquerel (1852–1908) for their work on radioactivity.

1910 The première of the opera *The Girl of the Golden West*, by Giacomo Puccini (1858–1924), was held in New York City, USA.

1919 Australian aviators and brothers Ross (1892–1922) and Keith Smith (1890–1955) became the first people to fly from England to Australia; they landed their Vickers Vimy biplane in Darwin after making the trip in just under 28 days.

1941 World War II – Japanese aircraft sank the British navy battleships HMS *Repulse* and HMS *Prince of Wales* off Malaya.

1948 The *Universal Declaration of Human Rights* was adopted and proclaimed by the General Assembly of the United Nations.

1983 Raúl Alfonsin (born 1927) was elected as civilian president of Argentina, following years of military rule.

11 December

On this day:

Born: Scottish physicist Sir David Brewster (1781); French composer Hector Berlioz (1803); Russian writer and Nobel Prize winner Aleksandr Solzhenitsyn (1918); Scottish ballet-dancer and choreographer Sir Kenneth MacMillan (1929)

Died: English journalist and pamphleteer Sir Roger L'Estrange (1704); German-born British chemist Ludwig Mond (1909); South African writer and feminist Olive Schreiner (1920); English actor, cartoonist and broadcaster Willie Rushton (1996)

1816 Indiana became the 19th state of the USA.

1844 The dentist Horace Wells (1815–48) underwent the first painless tooth extraction performed under anaesthesia induced by the inhalation of nitrous oxide (popularly known as 'laughing gas').

1903 The UK's first wildlife preservation society, the Society for the

Preservation of the Wild Fauna of the Empire, was founded; it still exists today under the name Fauna and Flora International.

1910 Neon lighting, developed by French chemist and physicist Georges Claude (1870–1960) was first demonstrated to the public in Paris.

1911 Marie Curie (1867–1934) gave her Nobel lecture, having been awarded her second Nobel Prize.

1936 King Edward VIII (1894–1972) abdicated the throne on account of general disapprobation of his proposed marriage to Wallis Simpson (1896–1986).

1941 World War II – Germany and Italy declared war on the USA, which in turn formally responded that a state of war existed between itself and the two.

1952 At the end of a famous case, Derek Bentley (c.1933–1953) and Christopher Craig (born c.1936) were both found guilty of murdering a policeman; Craig was sentenced to an indefinite period of detention, as he was too young to receive the death penalty, but Bentley was sentenced to be hanged.

1994 Russian troops invaded the province of Chechnya, which claimed independence.

1997 The Royal Yacht *Britannia* was decommissioned at Portsmouth Naval Base.

12 December

Il faut écrire pour soi, avant tout. C'est la seule chance de faire beau. (It is necessary to write for oneself, above all. It is the only hope of creating something beautiful.)

Gustave Flaubert, letter to Mlle Leroyer de Chantepie (11 July 1858).

The French novelist Gustave Flaubert was born in Rouen on this day in 1821, the son of a surgeon. The effects of the young Gustave's childhood proximity to his father's place of work are noticeable in some of the gruesomely realistic passages in his novels. His masterpiece is *Madame Bovary* (1857), the story of a disillusioned young woman's boredom with her life as a provincial doctor's wife and her subsequent recourse to adultery – a theme that initially caused the book to be condemned as immoral. Flaubert's other works include the novels *Salammbô* (1862) and *L'Éducation sentimentale* (1869) and the short-story collection *Trois contes* (1877). As a result of his painstaking attention to style, detail and structure, Flaubert was less prolific than some of the writers who followed in his footsteps – such as Guy de Maupassant (1850–93) and Émile Zola (1840–1902) – but he is deservedly regarded as the master of realism. He died in 1880.

On this day:

Born: English naval commander Samuel Hood, 1st Viscount Hood (1724); English physician and poet Erasmus Darwin (1731); Norwegian painter Edvard Munch (1863); US singer and film actor Frank Sinatra (1915)

Died: Spanish general Ferdinand de Toledo, Duke of Alva (1582); Scottish sailor Alexander Selkirk (1721); English poet Robert Browning (1889); US novelist Joseph Heller (1999)

1787 Pennsylvania became the second state to ratify the Constitution of the USA.

1896 Italian physicist and inventor Guglielmo Marconi (1874–1937) publicly demonstrated his radio for the first time at the Toynbee Hall, London.

1901 The first transatlantic radio signal (the Morse code for the letter S) was successfully transmitted from Poldhu, Cornwall, to St John's, Newfoundland, where Italian physicist and inventor Guglielmo Marconi (1874–1937) was waiting.

1913 The *Mona Lisa* by Leonardo da Vinci (1452–1519), which had been stolen from the Louvre in Paris in 1911, was recovered in Florence, Italy.

1915 World War I – the first all-metal aeroplane, a monoplane designed by German aircraft engineer Hugo Junkers (1859–1935), was flown for the first time.

1963 Kenya became an independent state. It became a republic, with Jomo Kenyatta (c.1889–1978) as president, exactly one year later.

1975 The so-called 'Balcombe Street siege' ended after almost a week as IRA terrorists released their hostages and gave themselves up.

1982 An estimated 30,000 women stood in a ring around the perimeter of the US Greenham Common missile base in Berkshire as a protest against nuclear weapons.

1988 Thirty-five people were killed at Clapham Junction railway station when two trains crashed and a third then collided with the wreckage.

1992 British princess Anne (born 1950) married Commander Timothy Laurence (born 1955) in Scotland.

13 December

This is the feast day of St Lucy, patron saint of blind people, who was martyred at Syracuse in the early 4th century AD. A devout Christian, she was allegedly denounced by a rejected suitor after giving away all her money to the poor.

> *A curious legend regarding St Lucy is, that on her lover complaining to her that her beautiful eyes haunted him day and night, she cut them out of her head, and sent them to him, begging him now to leave her to pursue, unmolested, her devotional aspirations. [An alternative version suggests that her eyes were torn out, rather than voluntarily removed.] It is added that Heaven, to recompense this act of abnegation, restored her eyes, rendering them more beautiful than ever. In allusion to this circumstance, St Lucy is generally represented bearing a platter, on which two eyes are laid; and her intercession is frequently implored by persons labouring under ophthalmic afflictions.*
>
> *Chambers Book of Days* (1864).

St Lucy is also regarded as the bringer of light: her name is derived from the Latin *lux*, *lucis*, light, and before the calendar reform of 1752 her feast day coincided with the winter solstice, after which the hours of daylight begin to lengthen.

In the Christian Church, the Wednesday, Friday and Saturday after **St Lucy's Day** are the first of four groups of **Ember Days** (days of fasting and prayer) in the ecclesiastical year. The others fall after the first Sunday in Lent, after Whit Sunday and after Holy Cross Day (14 September).

On this day:

Born: German poet and essayist Heinrich Heine (1797); US actor and entertainer Dick Van Dyke (1925); Canadian actor Christopher Plummer (1929); Imam of the Ismaili sect of Muslims Aga Khan IV (1937); English jockey, television commentator and author John Francome (1952)

Died: Spanish-born Jewish philosopher Moses Maimonides (1204); Florentine sculptor Donatello (1466); English writer, critic, lexicographer and conversationalist Samuel Johnson (1784); Russian-born French painter Wassily Kandinsky (1944)

1577 English navigator Francis Drake (c.1540–1596) left Plymouth in his ship the *Pelican*, which he later renamed the *Golden Hind*, at the beginning of his first circumnavigation of the world.

1642 Dutch navigator Abel Janszoon Tasman (1603–c.1659) became the first European to sight New Zealand.

1939 World War II – the Battle of the River Plate began as British and New Zealand ships engaged the German pocket battleship *Graf Spee* outside Montevideo, Uruguay.

1995 Riots broke out in the Brixton area of London after the death the previous week of a black man in police custody.

2000 US Vice-President Al Gore (born 1948) conceded the Presidency to Republican candidate George W Bush (born 1946).

2001 Twelve people were killed in a suicide attack on the Indian parliament in Delhi.

14 December

Break not, O woman's-heart, but still endure;
Break not, for thou art royal, but endure,
Remembering all the beauty of that star
Which shone so close beside thee that ye made
One light together, but has past and leaves
The crown a lonely splendour.

Alfred, Lord Tennyson, *Idylls of the King*, Dedication (1862).

Prince Albert of Saxe-Coburg-Gotha (1819–61), the beloved husband of Queen Victoria (1819–1901), died on this day in 1861, and his grief-stricken widow embarked on a lengthy period of mourning and seclusion. Unlike many royal marriages, theirs had been a true love match. Born in Germany in 1819, Albert married Victoria, his first cousin, in 1840 and soon became effectively her private secretary and personal adviser. In the years that followed, nine children were born to the happy couple; their eldest son later became King Edward VII.

Prince Albert made his mark on the nation with major contributions to the arts, sciences, culture and industry. He planned and managed the Great Exhibition of 1851, whose profits were used to purchase the sites that now house the Victoria and Albert Museum, the Royal Albert Hall and other notable buildings. He also designed Osborne House on the Isle of Wight, which became one of Victoria's favourite residences (and was the place of her death in 1901). The Albert Memorial in Kensington Gardens was erected in his memory, and Tennyson was moved to dedicate the 1862 edition of *Idylls of the King* to him, with a long poem of praise from which an excerpt is quoted above.

On 14 December 1895, the 34th anniversary of Albert's death, a great-grandson was born who was later to become King George VI (1895–1952), father of Queen Elizabeth II (born 1926).

On this day:

Born: Scottish explorer James Bruce (1730); French-born US economist Pierre-Samuel du Pont (1739); English artist and art critic Roger Fry (1866); English footballer Michael Owen (1979)

Died: English Lollard leader and knight Sir John Oldcastle (1417); First President of the USA George Washington (1799); English businessman and politician George Hudson (1871); Soviet physicist, dissident and Nobel Prize winner Andrei Sakharov (1989)

1819 Alabama became the 22nd state of the USA.

1900 German theoretical physicist Max Planck (1858–1947) publicly announced his revolutionary new quantum theory.

1911 Norwegian explorer Roald Amundsen (1872–1928) became the first person to reach the South Pole.

1911 Eleanor Davies-Colley became the first woman to become a Fellow of the Royal College of Surgeons.

1918 Women voted in a British general election for the first time; Constance, Countess Markievicz (1868–1927) became the first British woman MP when she was elected Sinn Fein MP for the St Patrick's division of Dublin, although she never took up her seat.

1922 John Reith (1889–1971) was appointed as the first general manager of the BBC.

1946 The United Nations General Assembly voted to accept $8.5m from John D Rockefeller, Jnr (1874–1960) to purchase 18 acres of land in Manhattan, New York City, USA, on which to build its permanent headquarters.

1962 The USA's Mariner II spacecraft made the first fly-by of Venus and sent back valuable new data about the planet's surface.

1995 The Dayton peace agreement to bring peace to the Balkans was signed in Paris by the leaders of Bosnia, Serbia and Croatia.

15 December

> *Tomorrow, I'll think of some other way to get him back. After all, tomorrow is another day.*
>
> Margaret Mitchell, *Gone with the Wind* (1936).

The première of *Gone with the Wind* took place on 15 December 1939 at Loew's Grand Theater in Atlanta, Georgia – the town that memorably burns to the ground in the climax of the story. An epic drama set against the backdrop of the American Civil War and its aftermath, the film was adapted by screenwriter Sidney Howard (1891–1939) from the best-selling novel of the same name by Atlanta-born novelist Margaret Mitchell (1900–49). The film starred Vivien Leigh (1913–67) as Scarlett O'Hara, the beautiful, spoilt, strong-willed heroine, and Clark Gable (1901–60) as Rhett Butler, who loves and leaves her with the immortal line, 'Frankly, my dear, I don't give a damn'. (The word 'frankly', not in the original novel, was added by Sidney Howard.)

The film went on to break records both at the box office and at the Academy Awards, where its haul of Oscars® included those for Best Picture and Best Screenplay. Vivien Leigh won the award for Best Actress, Victor Fleming (1883–1949) that for Best Director and Hattie McDaniel (1895–1952) made history as the first African-American to win an Academy Award with her Oscar® for Best Supporting Actress.

On this day:

Born: French engineer Gustave Eiffel (1832); Polish oculist, philologist and creator of Esperanto L L Zamenhof (1859); US oil executive, billionaire and art collector Jean Paul Getty (1892); Algerian politician Ahmed Ben Bella (1918); English-born US physicist and author Freeman Dyson (1923)

Died: Dakota Sioux chief Sitting Bull (1890); Danish physician, Nobel Prize winner and founder of phototherapy Niels Finsen (1904); Russian peasant, mystic and court favourite Grigori Rasputin (1916); US jazz pianist, composer and entertainer

Fats Waller (1943); US artist and film producer Walt Disney (1966)

1791 The Bill of Rights – the first ten amendments to the US Constitution, confirming the fundamental rights of US citizens – was ratified by Congress.

1840 Napoleon I's (1769–1821) remains were transferred from St Helena to Les Invalides in Paris.

1906 The Piccadilly Underground Line in London opened between Hammersmith and Finsbury Park.

1961 Nazi leader Adolf Eichmann (1906–62) was sentenced to death in Israel for crimes against humanity during World War II.

1964 The Canadian Parliament adopted a new national flag with a red maple leaf on a white background.

1965 Two US spacecraft, Gemini 6 and Gemini 7, made the first rendezvous in space.

1978 Laser videodiscs and players by Magnavision, part of Philips/MCA, went on sale in three stores in Atlanta, Georgia, USA.

1979 Canadians Chris Haney and Scott Abbott invented the game of Trivial Pursuit®.

1982 The border between Spain and Gibraltar was partially reopened; the frontier had been closed since 1969, and reopened fully to everyone in 1985.

1995 At the Madrid Summit of European Councils, EU leaders christened their planned new single currency the 'euro'.

16 December

On 16 December 1773, three shiploads of tea were dumped in the sea at Boston, Massachusetts, in an event that has become known as the Boston Tea Party. The British government had allowed the East India Company to export the tea to America without the usual taxes and tariffs, as a means of disposing

of surplus stocks at a time of financial difficulty. This was the latest in a series of acts perceived as unfair treatment of colonial merchants, and enough was enough. In a raid apparently masterminded by the revolutionist Samuel Adams (1722–1803), a group of citizens dressed as Mohawk Indians and armed with axes and hatchets boarded the vessels, hacked open the crates of tea and tipped their contents into the harbour.

The British government responded with the so-called Intolerable Acts of 1774, which closed the port of Boston and put Massachusetts under military control. It was these measures that precipitated the American Revolution, otherwise known as the American War of Independence, in 1775.

On this day:

Born: Spanish-born English queen Catherine of Aragon (1485); English novelist Jane Austen (1775); Hungarian composer Zoltán Kodály (1882); English actor, playwright and composer Sir Noël Coward (1899); English artist, illustrator and teacher Quentin Blake (1932)

Died: German folklorist and philologist Wilhem Grimm (1859); US trombonist and bandleader Glenn Miller (1944); British writer W Somerset Maugham (1965); US business executive and founder of Kentucky Fried Chicken Harland Saunders (1980)

1653 Oliver Cromwell (1599–1658) became Lord Protector of England.

1809 Napoleon I (1769–1821) divorced his wife Joséphine (1763–1814).

1850 The first immigrant ship, the *Charlotte Jane*, landed in Port Lyttelton, New Zealand.

1853 Antonio López de Santa Anna (1794–1876) became dictator of Mexico.

1925 Work began on the nine-year construction of the Mersey Tunnel.

1937 The première of *Me And My Girl* by Noel Gay (1898–1954) was held; it featured 'The Lambeth Walk'.

1944 World War II – German forces launched the 'Battle of the Bulge' by cutting off Allied troops in the Ardennes.

1949 Ahmed Sukarno (1902–70) was elected first president of Indonesia.

1954 H Tracy Hall (born 1919) produced the first synthetic industrial diamonds in the General Electric Research Laboratory in New York State.

1969 In the UK, MPs voted for the permanent abolition of the death penalty for murder.

1977 The extension of the Piccadilly Line to Heathrow Airport was opened by Queen Elizabeth II (born 1926); it was the first time ever that an underground railway was linked directly with a major international airport.

17 December

In ancient Roman times, this was the beginning of the festival of **Saturnalia**, in honour of the god of agriculture. It was originally restricted to 17 December itself, commemorating the dedication of a temple to Saturn, but eventually grew into a seven-day orgy of feasting and merrymaking, elements of which later reappeared in the Christmas, New Year and Twelfth Night celebrations of the UK.

The Saturnalia was a holiday period for all, including the slaves, who were waited on by their masters for the duration. Presents were exchanged, informal clothes worn, gambling games permitted and sexual mores relaxed. It was also customary to appoint a master of the revels, a character that later reappeared in England as the **Lord of Misrule** (and in Scotland as the **Abbot of Unreason**), who formerly presided over the Christmas celebrations, or over the entire period from All-Hallows Eve (31 October) to Candlemas (2 February).

On this day:

Born: German composer Ludwig van Beethoven (1770); English chemist and inventor of the safety lamp Sir Humphry Davy (1778); Canadian politician W L Mackenzie King (1874); US chemist and Nobel Prize winner Willard Frank Libby (1908); English actor Bernard Hill (1944)

Died: South American revolutionary leader Simón Bolívar (1830); Scottish physicist and mathematician William Thomson, 1st Baron Kelvin (1907); English physician, first woman doctor and first woman mayor Elizabeth Garrett Anderson (1917); English detective-story writer Dorothy L Sayers (1957)

1843 *A Christmas Carol* by Charles Dickens (1812–70) was published.

1903 US aviation pioneers Orville (1871–1948) and Wilbur Wright (1867–1912) became the first to fly in a heavier-than-air machine, with a flight of 37 metres at Kitty Hawk, North Carolina, USA.

1939 World War II – the German pocket battleship *Graf Spee* was scuttled outside Montevideo Harbour, Uruguay.

1968 In the UK, eleven-year-old Mary Bell was found guilty of murdering two toddlers.

1983 An IRA bomb exploded outside Harrods department store in London, killing six and injuring almost 100 people.

1986 The world's first heart, lungs and liver transplant was carried out at Papworth Hospital, Cambridge.

1989 Brazil held its first direct presidential election in 29 years; Fernando Collor de Mello (born 1950) became president.

18 December

The Italian violin-maker Antonio Stradivari (or Stradivarius) died on this day in 1737. Born c.1644, he lived and worked in Cremona, where he studied under Niccolo Amati (1596–1684) and is thought to have produced more than 1,000 violins, violas and cellos. The secret of the superior tone of Stradivari's instruments has been much debated and is variously attributed to fine design and workmanship, good choice of materials, and the composition and application of the varnish. Original Stradivarius violins remain the most sought-after in the world, changing hands for £1m or more, and have been owned and played by famous violinists such as Yehudi Menuhin (1916–99) and Itzhak Perlman (born 1945), as well as the 19th-century virtuoso and composer Niccolò Paganini (1782–1840).

On this day:

Born: Swiss artist Paul Klee (1879); US baseball player Ty Cobb (1886); US electrical engineer and inventor of FM radio Edwin H Armstrong (1890); English rock musician with the Rolling Stones Keith Richards (1943); US film-maker Steven Spielberg (1947); US actor Brad Pitt (1963)

Died: US amateur golfer Bobby Jones (1971); Ukrainian-born US geneticist and evolutionist Theodosius Dobzhansky (1975); French cellist, conductor and composer Paul Tortelier (1990); US actor and director Sam Wanamaker (1993); British singer and songwriter Kirsty MacColl (2000)

1787 New Jersey became the third state to ratify the Constitution of the USA.

1834 Robert Peel (1788–1850), English statesman, issued his 'Tamworth Manifesto' which is seen as laying down the principles on which the modern Conservative Party is based.

1912 The alleged 'Piltdown Man' skull discovered on the Sussex Downs was revealed to scientists and the public as proof of the 'Missing Link' between apes and humans; it was not proved to be a fake until the 1950s.

1916 World War I – the Battle of Verdun, the longest battle of the war, ended with massive casualties and loss of life on both sides.

1958 Niger voted to become a self-governing republic but remain within the French community.

1989 In line with European legislation, the British Labour Party changed its policy on trade union closed shops.

19 December

On this day:

Born: Anjou duke and Spanish king Philip V (1683); Polish-born US physicist and Nobel Prize winner Albert Abraham Michelson (1852); French author Jean Genet (1910); French singer Edith Piaf (1915); Kenyan palaeoanthropologist and politician Richard Leakey (1944)

Died: Danish navigator Vitus Bering (1741); English poet and novelist Emily Brontë (1848); English artist J M W Turner (1851); German psychiatrist and neuropathologist Alois

Alzheimer (1915); Italian actor Marcello Mastroianni (1996)

1783 William Pitt (1759–1806) became the youngest British prime minister at the age of 24 years and 205 days.

1863 Frederick Walton of London patented linoleum.

1890 The première of the opera *The Queen of Spades*, by Pyotr Ilyich Tchaikovsky (1840–93), was held in St Petersburg, Russia.

1932 The BBC's first Empire Service broadcast was made on short-wave radio; it was later to change its name to the BBC World Service.

1974 Nelson Aldrich Rockefeller (1908–79) was sworn in as Vice-President to US President Gerald Ford (born 1913); it was the first time in US history that neither the President nor Vice-President had been actually elected to office.

1981 The RNLI Penlee lifeboat *Solomon Brown* was lost in the night with all her crew while trying to rescue the *Union Star* off the Cornish coast.

1984 The Sino-British Declaration was signed, by which the UK agreed to return Hong Kong to China at the end of the 99-year lease that had been signed in 1898.

20 December

On this day:

Born: English dramatist John Fletcher (1579); Irish politician and essayist John Wilson Croker (1780); Scottish chemist Thomas Graham (1805); US physicist Robert J Van de Graaff (1901); English actress Jenny Agutter (1952)

Died: French surgeon and father of modern surgery Ambroise Paré (1590); US novelist and Nobel Prize winner John Steinbeck (1968); Polish-born US pianist Artur Rubinstein (1982); Spanish matador Antonio Ordóñez (1998); Senegalese statesman and poet Léopold Sédar Senghor (2001)

1860 South Carolina became the first state to secede from the Union; ten states followed and the Confederacy was formed in 1861, in the run up to the American Civil War.

1915 World War I – a major evacuation of Australian and New Zealand forces took place from Gallipoli, Turkey, after a disastrous campaign.

1928 The first Harry Ramsden's Fish and Chip restaurant was founded in Guiseley, near Leeds; it was a tiny painted hut.

1973 Spanish prime minister Luis Carrero Blanco (1903–73) was assassinated in a bomb attack in Madrid by Basque nationalists.

1989 Panamanian leader General Manuel Noriega (born 1940) was overthrown by a US invasion.

21 December

> *On St Thomas the divine kill all turkeys, geese, and swine.*
>
> Traditional saying.

This is one of the feast days of Christ's apostle Thomas, also called Didymus and popularly known as Doubting Thomas because he refused to believe that Christ had risen from the dead until he had actually seen him and touched his wounds (John 20.24–8). Details of his life thereafter are uncertain; he is thought to have gone as a missionary to Parthia and India and to have been martyred near Madras.

St Thomas's Day was formerly a time for almsgiving, and a number of charitable doles took place on this date. It was also marked by the associated custom of **thomasing** or **gooding**, in which children, widows, old women and other needy people went from house to house begging for money, winter provisions or Christmas treats, sometimes in exchange for a sprig of holly or mistletoe.

> *A liberal dole was distributed at the 'great house,' or the mansion of the principal proprietor in the parish; and at the kitchens of all the squires and farmers' houses, tankards of spiced-ale were kept for the special refection of the red-cloaked old wives who made in procession these*

foraging excursions on St Thomas's Day. It is said that the hospitality shewn on such occasions proved sometimes rather overpowering, and the recipients of this and other charitable benefactions found themselves occasionally wholly unable to find their way back to their own habitations, having been rendered, though the agency of John Barleycorn, as helpless as the 'Wee bit Wifikie' immortalised in Scottish song.

Chambers Book of Days (1864).

On this day:

Born: English engineer and inventor Sir Joseph Whitworth (1803); English statesman and novelist Benjamin Disraeli, 1st Earl of Beaconsfield (1804); Soviet revolutionary and leader Joseph Stalin (1879); Austrian statesman and United Nations Secretary-General Kurt Waldheim (1918); US actor Samuel L Jackson (1948)

Died: Italian writer Giovanni Boccaccio (1375); Scottish-born US mathematician Eric Temple Bell (1960); English cricketer Sir Jack Hobbs (1963)

1192 Richard I 'the Lion Heart'(1157–99), King of England, was taken prisoner in Vienna by Leopold, Duke of Austria (1157–94) and handed over to the Holy Roman Emperor, Henry VI (1165–97).

1620 The Pilgrim Fathers in the *Mayflower* landed in Massachusetts.

1844 The 'Rochdale Pioneers' opened their first 'Co-operative shop', paving the way for a worldwide co-operative movement.

1846 The first major operation in the UK using anaesthetic was performed by Robert Liston (1794–1847) at University College Hospital, London.

1864 In the American Civil War, Union forces under General Sherman (1820–91) took Savannah.

1913 The *New York World* carried the world's first crossword puzzle.

1937 The première of the first full-length coloured cartoon film, *Snow White and the Seven Dwarfs* by Walt Disney (1901–66), was held in Los Angeles, California, USA.

1956 The Montgomery Bus Boycott ended after 381 days when the bus company was persuaded by a 65 per cent drop in revenue, and a Supreme Court decision that declared bus segregation unconstitutional, to integrate its seating.

1958 General Charles de Gaulle (1890–1970) was elected as the first president of the Fifth Republic of France.

1968 Astronauts from the USA's Apollo 8 started to make the first manned orbits of the Moon – in all they made ten orbits between 21 and 27 December.

1988 Flight 103, a Pan Am jumbo jet, was blown up over the Scottish town of Lockerbie, killing 259 people on board and a further eleven people in the town below.

22 December

The winter solstice, when the hours of darkness are at their longest and the hours of daylight at their shortest, usually falls on this date (or on 21 December – 'St Thomas grey, St Thomas grey, the longest night and the shortest day'). It marks the end of autumn and the beginning of winter in the astronomical division of the seasons. In pagan times, the winter solstice was celebrated with bonfires, rituals to frighten away evil spirits, and other activities, some of which were subsequently absorbed into the festivities of Christmas and the New Year.

> *The seven days preceding, and the seven days following the shortest day, or the winter-solstice, were called by the ancients the Halcyon Days. This phrase, so familiar as expressive of a period of tranquillity and happiness, is derived from a fable, that during the period just indicated, while the halcyon bird or king-fisher was breeding, the sea was always calm and might be navigated in perfect security by the mariner. The name halcyon is derived from two Greek words [meaning 'the sea' and 'to conceive'] and, according to the poetic fiction, the bird was represented as hatching her eggs on a floating nest, in the midst of the waters.*
>
> *Chambers Book of Days* (1864).

On this day:

Born: French dramatist and poet Jean Racine (1639); US Unitarian minister and abolitionist Thomas Wentworth Higginson (1823); English magician John Maskelyne (1839); Italian

composer of operas Giacomo Puccini (1858); English actor Ralph Fiennes (1962)

Died: Mexican revolutionary José María Morelos (1815); US evangelist Dwight L Moody (1899); US film producer Darryl F Zanuck (1979); Irish writer, playwright and Nobel Prize winner Samuel Beckett (1989); English punk musician with the Clash Joe Strummer (2002)

1135 King Stephen of England (c.1097–1154) was crowned.

1715 James Stuart (1688–1766), the 'Old Pretender', landed at Peterhead from exile in France.

1849 Moments before his execution in Moscow, Fyodor Dostoevsky (1821–81), Russian novelist, had his sentence commuted to four years' imprisonment in Siberia.

1877 Raoul Pictet (1846–1929), Swiss physicist, produced liquid oxygen.

1894 French army officer Alfred Dreyfus (c.1859–1935) was found guilty of selling military secrets and sentenced to be transported to Devil's Island; he was later found innocent and released.

1895 Wilhelm Röntgen (1845–1923), German physicist, made the very first X-ray – of his wife's hand.

1960 The millionth Morris Minor – the first British vehicle to reach this milestone – came off the Oxford production line.

1974 The London home of the former British prime minister, Sir Edward Heath (born 1916), was bombed by the IRA.

1989 The Brandenburg Gate in Berlin was reopened, and the leaders of East and West Germany met and shook hands.

23 December

In the Cornish village of Mousehole 23 December is celebrated each year as **Tom Bawcock's Eve**. The story runs that many years ago a period of bad weather left the inhabitants of this fishing village facing starvation as the seas were too rough for the fishing boats to set sail. One local man, Tom Bawcock, braved the bad weather to go out and returned with a catch of seven types of fish that kept the villagers alive until the storm abated. The fish were cooked in a large traditional pie, known as a Stargazy Pie because the heads of the fish stick out of the crust and look upwards to the sky. To this day locals eat Stargazy Pie on Tom Bawcock's Eve, and sing a song to praise this hero's deeds.

As 'aich we'd clunk
As 'ealth was drunk
In brummers bremmen high
And when up come
Tom Bawcock's name
We praise 'un to the sky!

A Merry place you may believe,
Was Mouzel on Tom Bawcock's Eve
To be there then who wudn't wish,
To sup on seven sorts of fish.

On this day:

Born: Russian emperor Alexander I (1777); French founder of Egyptology and translator of the Rosetta Stone Jean François Champollion (1790); Scottish writer and social reformer Samuel Smiles (1812); English film magnate J Arthur Rank, 1st Baron Rank (1888); Dutch-born US aircraft engineer Anthony Fokker (1939)

Died: English economist and clergyman Thomas Malthus (1834); US feminist and social reformer Sarah Grimké (1873); Japanese soldier and prime minister Hideki Tojo (1948); English golfer Henry Cotton (1987); Danish-born US entertainer and pianist Victor Borge (2000)

1787 The *Bounty* set sail on a voyage to Tahiti to collect plants of the bread-fruit tree, captained by William Bligh (1754–c.1817).

1888 Dutch Post-Impressionist painter Vincent Van Gogh (1853–90), in remorse for having threatened Paul Gauguin (1848–1903), cut off part of his own ear with a razor.

1913 The Federal Reserve Act was signed by US President Woodrow Wilson (1856–1924), creating the Federal Reserve system of banks.

1956 The Suez Crisis ended as the British and French withdrew from Egypt.

1972 An earthquake measuring 6.5 on the Richter scale struck the Nicaraguan capital, Managua, killing an estimated 5,000–10,000 people.

1986 Soviet dissident Andrei Sakharov (1921–89) and his wife returned to Moscow after almost seven years of internal exile in the 'closed city' of Gorky (now Nizhny Novgorod).

24 December

> *'Twas the night before Christmas, when all through the house*
> *Not a creature was stirring, not even a mouse.*
>
> Clement Moore, *The Night Before Christmas* (1822).

This is **Christmas Eve**, when children hang up stockings or pillowcases in the hope that they will wake in the morning to find that Santa Claus has filled them with presents. It is also traditional to leave a snack for Santa – perhaps a mince pie and a glass of milk, or something a little stronger. In some countries, such as France and Germany, the main Christmas celebration takes place on Christmas Eve, but in the UK it is principally a time for last-minute preparations. Many churchgoers – both Protestant and Catholic – attend a midnight service at their local place of worship.

At King's College Chapel, Cambridge, the **Festival of Nine Lessons and Carols** takes place on 24 December. This is a fixed selection of Bible readings and hymns, traditionally broadcast on television and radio. The general practice of **carol-singing** is not restricted to Christmas Eve: throughout the latter half of December, groups of singers and musicians gather in public places or go from house to house, performing carols in return for money, which is often collected on behalf of a charity. Most of today's **Christmas carols** are hymns dating from no later than the 19th century, although the carol itself (as a simple song of joy or praise) is of earlier origin.

In former times, Christmas Eve was a popular date for the performance of

mumming plays: short dramas on traditional themes with various stock characters, such as Father Christmas, St George, the Doctor and the Turkish Knight. Like carol-singers, mummers performed either in public places or private homes and expected to receive some reward for the entertainment they provided.

There were also various superstitious beliefs associated with 24 December (eg that oxen knelt in their stalls at midnight), and love divination rituals were practised by young women curious to ascertain the identity of their future husbands.

We had eyes for phantoms then,
And at bridge or stile
On Christmas Eve
Clear beheld those countless ones who had crossed it
Cross again in file: –
Such has ceased longwhile!

We liked divination then,
And, as they homeward wound
On Christmas Eve,
We could read men's dreams within them spinning
Even as wheels spin round: –
Now we are blinker-bound.

Thomas Hardy, 'Yuletide in a Younger World' (1927).

On this day:

Born: English king John Lackland (1167); US frontiersman Kit Carson (1809); English poet and critic Matthew Arnold (1822); US millionaire businessman, film producer and director and aviator Howard Hughes (1905); US actress Ava Gardner (1922)

Died: Portuguese navigator Vasco da Gama (1524); French admiral and Vichy politician François Darlan (1942); US film composer and conductor Bernard Herrmann (1975); English playwright and actor John Osborne (1994)

1582 London Bridge Waterworks began piping water to private houses.

1801 Richard Trevithick (1771–1833), English engineer and inventor, made the first road test of a self-propelled steam carriage up Camborne Hill, Cornwall.

1814 The Treaty of Ghent ended the War of 1812 between the USA and Britain.

1818 The carol 'Silent Night', with music by Franz Gruber (1787–1863) and lyrics by Father Joseph Mohr (1792–1848), was performed for the first time in St Nikolas Church in Oberndorf, Bavaria.

1828 The trial of William Burke (1792–1829), the murderer known as a body-snatcher, began in Edinburgh. His co-conspirator, William Hare (1790–1860), escaped by turning king's evidence.

1871 The première of the opera *Aïda*, by Giuseppe Verdi (1813–1901), was held in Cairo, Egypt.

1904 The first revolving stage in the UK opened at the new London Coliseum.

1906 Reginald Fessenden (1866–1932) made the first radio telephone broadcast from Brant Rock, Massachusetts, to ships within a five-mile range.

1914 World War I – the first bomb to fall on the UK landed on Dover.

1933 One of the oldest Greek manuscripts of the Bible, the *Codex Sinaiticus*, purchased by the British Museum from the USSR for £100,000, arrived in London.

1943 World War II – General Dwight D Eisenhower (1890–1969) was appointed Supreme Commander of the Allied Expeditionary Forces.

1951 Libya achieved independence.

1974 English politician John Stonehouse (1925–88), who had disappeared in Miami, Florida, USA, and was thought to have been drowned, reappeared in Australia; he was later deported to the UK.

Christmas comes but once a year, but when it comes it brings good cheer.

Traditional saying.

Christmas Day is essentially a Christian festival, celebrating the **Nativity** of Jesus Christ, which was fixed as 25 December by the mid-4th century AD.

The Christmas story – of the journey of Mary and Joseph to Bethlehem, the birth of their baby in a stable, and the arrival of wise men from the East bearing gifts – is familiar to all, whether churchgoers or not, and is annually retold in school nativity plays across the country.

> *And is it true? And is it true,*
> *This most tremendous tale of all,*
> *Seen in a stained-glass window's hue,*
> *A Baby in an ox's stall?*
> *The Maker of the stars and sea*
> *Become a Child on earth for me?*
>
> John Betjeman, *A Few Late Chrysanthemums*, 'Christmas' (1954).

Christmas has absorbed many secular or pagan traditions associated with other dates, notably the ancient Roman Saturnalia (17 December), the winter solstice (22 December), and New Year, and is celebrated to a greater or lesser degree by people of all faiths.

> *To investigate the origin of many of our Christmas customs, it becomes necessary to wander far back into the regions of past time .... We have frequently, in the course of this work, had occasion to remark on the numerous traces still visible in popular customs of the old pagan rites and ceremonies. These, it is needless here to repeat, were extensively retained after the conversion of Britain to Christianity, partly because the Christian teachers found it impossible to wean their converts from their cherished superstitions and observances, and partly because they themselves, as a matter of expediency, ingrafted the rites of the Christian religion on their old heathen ceremonies, believing that thereby the cause of the Cross would be rendered more acceptable to the generality of the populace, and thus be more effectually promoted.*
>
> *Chambers Book of Days* (1864).

An example of this is the practice of decorating homes with holly, ivy and **mistletoe**, though the practice of hanging mistletoe in places where a kiss may be stolen is of more recent (probably 18th-century) origin.

The Victorians made a major contribution to the modern conception of the archetypal Christmas, reviving traditions that had fallen into decline in the early 19th century and inaugurating new ones. The German custom of having a decorated **Christmas tree** as the focal point of the festivities was not, as widely believed, introduced into the UK by Prince Albert (1819–61),

husband of Queen Victoria (1819–1901), but it was undoubtedly popularized by the royal family. **Christmas cards** and **Christmas crackers** were British inventions, of 1843 and 1884 respectively.

Christmas presents loom large in the modern festivities – as the highlight of the season for many children, and as something of a burden for those who have to choose and buy them. The custom of giving and receiving presents on Christmas Day also dates from the mid-19th century; before then, gifts had traditionally been exchanged at New Year, between adults only. Young children are led to believe that some or all of their presents are delivered by **Father Christmas**, also known as **Santa Claus**, who travels from house to house on a sleigh pulled by reindeer. The character of Father Christmas evolved from a general personification of Christmas dating back to the 15th century. The Victorians depicted him in various costumes; his now-familiar red outfit trimmed with white fur was acquired from his alter ego, Santa Claus, of US origin. Based on St Nicholas, whose feast day is celebrated on 6 December, Santa Claus was a bringer of gifts for children, and as the British Christmas became increasingly child-centred, it was inevitable that the two characters would merge into one.

Christmas has always been a convivial affair, marked by much eating, drinking and merrymaking with family, friends and neighbours (apart from a brief period in the mid-17th century, when the Puritans held sway). Traditional **Christmas fare** has altered somewhat over the years, and formerly varied according to social class, but a roast has always been the centrepiece of the feast. For feudal chieftains it was a boar's head or peacock, whereas beef and mutton were popular in the 17th, 18th and 19th centuries. The now-ubiquitous turkey was formerly enjoyed only by the wealthy – lesser mortals had to be content with a goose. Other Christmas goodies make much use of dried fruit: the steamed **plum pudding** dates from the 17th century and the rich iced **Christmas cake** was originally baked for Twelfth Night. **Mince pies**, now filled with a mixture of dried fruit, suet and spices, formerly contained shredded meat and were sometimes called Christmas pies.

> *So, now is come our joyful feast;*
> *Let every man be jolly.*
> *Each room with ivy leaves is dressed,*
> *And every post with holly.*
> ...
> *Without the door, let sorrow lie;*
> *And, if for cold, it hap to die,*
> *We'll bury it in a Christmas pie*
> *And evermore be merry.*
>
> George Wither, 'A Christmas Carol' (1622).

On this day:

Born: English scientist and mathematician Sir Isaac Newton (1642); English writer and diarist Dorothy Wordsworth (1771); French painter Maurice Utrillo (1883); German electrical engineer and Nobel Prize winner Ernst Ruska (1906); Egyptian soldier, politician and Nobel Prize winner Anwar el-Sadat (1918); Scottish singer and songwriter Annie Lennox (1954)

Died: Czech novelist and playwright Karel Čapek (1938); US comedian W C Fields (1946); English film actor and director Sir Charlie Chaplin (1977); Romanian politician and dictator Nicolae Ceauşescu (1989); US entertainer Dean Martin (1995)

800 Charlemagne (747–814) was crowned Emperor of the Romans as 'Carolus Augustus' by Pope Leo III (c.750–816) in St Peter's Church, Rome.

1066 William the Conqueror (1027–87) was crowned King William I of England in Westminster Abbey, London.

1864 The traditional Christmas Day Swim in the Serpentine lake in Hyde Park, London, was inaugurated.

1866 The first transatlantic yacht race was won by the US yacht *Henrietta* which arrived at Cowes, Isle of Wight, having crossed the ocean in just under 14 days.

1926 Emperor Hirohito (1901–89) acceded to the throne of Japan.

1932 King George V (1865–1936) made the first Royal Christmas broadcast to the Empire; the speech was written by the English writer Rudyard Kipling (1865–1936).

1941 World War II – Hong Kong surrendered to the Japanese troops.

1950 The Stone of Scone, the Scottish 'Stone of Destiny', was stolen from Westminster Abbey in London and returned to Scotland by a small group of Scottish nationalists.

1957 The Christmas Message of Queen Elizabeth II (born 1926) was televised for the first time.

1974 The city of Darwin in Northern Australia was devastated by cyclone Tracy, which struck late on 24 December and wrought great destruction throughout the early hours.

1991 Russian statesman Mikhail Gorbachev (born 1931) resigned as president of the USSR and the USSR was then formally dissolved.

26 December

> *Blessed be St Stephen, there is no fast upon his even.*
>
> Traditional saying.

This is the feast day of St Stephen, the first Christian martyr, stoned to death for preaching that the recently crucified Christ was the Messiah. It was formerly customary to bleed horses on **St Stephen's Day**, after a long fast gallop, to protect them against disease in the following year. A tradition known as **stephening** existed in the parish of Drayton Beauchamp, Buckinghamshire, where local residents would descend on the rectory and demand as much free bread, cheese and ale as they could eat and drink. Another custom associated with this day (especially in Ireland) involved hunting and catching a wren, which was then paraded around the town, sometimes in a garland of holly or gorse, by children begging for money.

In modern times, however, 26 December is chiefly celebrated as **Boxing Day**, a public holiday throughout the UK. It is generally regarded as a continuation of the Christmas festivities (or an opportunity to recover from the excesses of the day before) and has no particular traditions of widespread observance. Boxing Day takes its name from the **Christmas boxes** given to servants, apprentices and other employees, and later to tradespeople and public-service workers in the community, on this day. The boxes contained a gift, usually of money, and the term was subsequently applied to the gratuity itself.

> *This custom of Christmas-boxes, or the bestowing of certain expected gratuities at the Christmas season, was formerly, and even yet to a certain extent continues to be, a great nuisance. ... This most objectionable usage is now greatly diminished, but certainly cannot yet be said to be extinct. Christmas-boxes are still regularly expected by the postman, the lamplighter, the dustman, and generally by all those functionaries who render services to the public at large, without receiving payment therefor from any particular individual.*
>
> *Chambers Book of Days* (1864).

It was probably the worthy practice of giving money to inferiors on 26 December, rather than any desire for historical accuracy, that was in the mind of the clergyman John Mason Neale (1818–66) when he penned the words to the Christmas carol 'Good King Wenceslas':

> *Good King Wenceslas looked out,*
> *On the Feast of Stephen,*
> *When the snow lay round about,*
> *Deep and crisp and even;*
> *Brightly shone the moon that night,*
> *Though the frost was cruel,*
> *When a poor man came in sight,*
> *Gathering winter fuel.*
> *. . .*
> *Therefore, Christian men, be sure,*
> *Wealth or rank possessing,*
> *Ye who now will bless the poor,*
> *Shall yourselves find blessing.*
>
> J M Neale, 'Good King Wenceslas' (1853).

On this day:

Born: Holy Roman emperor and German king Frederick II (1194); English writer, pacifist and Nobel Prize winner Sir Norman Angell (1873); US record producer Phil Spector (1940); East Timorese politician, campaigner and Nobel Prize winner José Ramos-Horta (1949)

Died: German astronomer Simon Marius (1624); French philosopher and hedonist Claude-Adrien Helvétius (1771); French film pioneer Charles Pathé (1957); English actor Sir Nigel Hawthorne (2001); US photographer Herb Ritts (2002)

1606 Shakespeare's (1564–1616) *King Lear* was performed at the Royal Court.

1833 The première of the opera *Lucrezia Borgia*, by Gaetano Donizetti (1797–1848), was held at La Scala, Milan, Italy.

1867 The première of the opera *The Fair Maid of Perth*, by Georges Bizet (1838–75), was held at the Théâtre Lyrique, Paris.

1898 Pierre (1859–1906) and Marie Curie (1867–1934) announced their discovery of radium.

1908 Jack Johnson (1878–1946) became the first African-American boxer to win the world heavyweight title.

1941 World War II – Winston Churchill (1874–1965) became the first British prime minister to address the US Congress.

1943 World War II – the Allies sank the German battleship *Scharnhorst*.

1948 Hungarian Roman Catholic Cardinal József Mindszenty (1892–1975) was arrested and charged with treason by the Communist government in Budapest.

1985 US zoologist Dian Fossey (1932–85) was found murdered in Rwanda.

2003 A major earthquake in the Iranian city of Bam killed 41,000 people.

27 December

Dans les champs de l'observation le hasard ne favorise que les esprits préparés. (Where observation is concerned, chance favours only the prepared mind.)

Louis Pasteur, speech at the inauguration of the Faculty of Science, University of Lille (7 December 1854)

The French chemist and microbiologist Louis Pasteur was born on this day in 1822. He worked his way up the academic ladder to become Professor of Chemistry at the Sorbonne in Paris in 1867. Pasteur's many contributions to science include the introduction of pasteurization, a method chiefly used to destroy pathogenic bacteria in milk by heating it to 60°C for 30 minutes. He also developed vaccines for anthrax, rabies and other diseases. The Pasteur Institute in Paris was founded in 1888 to further his research, and he served as its director until his death in 1895.

On this day:

Born: English amateur scientist and aviation pioneer Sir George Cayley (1773); German-born US film actress and cabaret performer Marlene Dietrich (1901); French film actor Gérard Depardieu (1948)

Died: English bookseller, philanthropist and hospital founder Thomas Guy (1724); English essayist and poet Charles Lamb (1834); Canadian statesman and Nobel Prize winner Lester Pearson (1972); US actor Jason Robards (2000); English actor Alan Bates (2003)

1831 Charles Darwin (1809–82) began his scientific voyage on board HMS *Beagle*.

1904 J M Barrie's (1860–1937) play *Peter Pan* was performed for the first time in London.

1927 The première of the musical *Showboat*, by Jerome Kern (1885–1945), was held at the Ziegfeld Theater, Broadway, New York City.

1945 The International Monetary Fund was established as its Articles of Agreement came into force.

1965 The oil rig *Sea Gem* collapsed into the North Sea near the River Humber, killing 13 crew men.

2002 Eighty people were killed in a suicide bomb attack on the Russian-backed parliament in Grozny, Chechnya.

28 December

This is **Holy Innocents' Day**, also known as **Childermas**, commemorating King Herod's massacre of all the male infants in and around Bethlehem under the age of two in an attempt to kill the young Christ. Warned by an angel, Mary and Joseph had previously escaped with their child to Egypt, where they remained until Herod's death (Matthew 2.1–18).

In the days when Christmas itself was less child-centred, Childermas was a time for indulging children with treats and parties. On a more sombre note, it was also widely regarded as an unlucky day for any enterprise, from cutting one's nails or doing the housework to embarking on a fishing trip or getting married. It was particularly unlucky for the passengers and crew of the Edinburgh–Dundee train crossing the Tay Bridge at 7.15pm on 28 December 1879. Gale-force winds caused the central section of the bridge to collapse,

the train and its six carriages plunged into the icy river, and all on board lost their lives. It is unfortunate that the tragedy is known to many only through the Scottish poetaster William McGonagall's (1830–1902) most famous poem, frequently held up to ridicule as doggerel:

Beautiful Railway Bridge of the Silv'ry Tay!
Alas! I am very sorry to say
That ninety lives have been taken away
On the last Sabbath day of 1879,
Which will be remember'd for a very long time.

Willliam McGonagall, *Poetic Gems*,
'The Tay Bridge Disaster' (1890).

On this day:

Born: Scottish astronomer Thomas Henderson (1798); Scottish geologist Sir Archibald Geikie (1835); US jazz pianist and bandleader Earl Hines (1905); English actress Dame Maggie Smith (1934); English violinist Nigel Kennedy (1956)

Died: French Roman Catholic prelate and writer St Francis de Sales (1622); British queen Mary II (1694); Scottish outlaw Rob Roy (1734); French composer Maurice Ravel (1937); US film director Sam Peckinpah (1984)

1065 Westminster Abbey in London was consecrated.

1846 Iowa became the 29th state of the USA.

1895 At the Grand Café on the Boulevard des Capucines, Paris, French film pioneers Auguste (1862–1954) and Louis Lumière (1865–1948) showed the world's first motion picture, *La Sortie des ouvriers de l'usine Lumière* ('Workers Leaving the Lumière Factory') to a paying public; the event is regarded as the birth of world cinema.

1908 A massive earthquarke struck Messina, Sicily, killing an estimated 70,000–100,000 people.

1945 The US Congress officially recognized the Pledge of Allegiance and recommended that it be recited in schools across the USA.

1973 The first volume of *The Gulag Archipelago* by Russian writer Aleksandr Solzhenitsyn (born 1918) was published in Paris.

29 December

This is now the feast day of St Thomas Becket, commemorating the date in 1170 when he was murdered in Canterbury Cathedral. (**St Thomas Becket's Day** was formerly celebrated on 7 July, the date in 1220 when his relics were transferred to a new shrine at Canterbury.) The four knights who killed Becket thought they were obeying the will of King Henry II, after hearing him utter the exasperated cry, 'Will no one rid me of this turbulent priest?'

The antagonism between Henry and Becket had begun soon after the latter became Archbishop of Canterbury in 1162 and was primarily a reflection of the ongoing battle between Church and State. Becket objected to the so-called Constitutions of Clarendon, issued by Henry in 1164 in an attempt to limit ecclesiastical authority, and went into exile in France. He returned in 1170, after an agreement had apparently been reached, but the quarrels soon began afresh, culminating in the King's impetuous outburst and its tragic consequence.

Becket was canonized in 1173 and Henry did public penance at his tomb the following year. Becket's shrine at Canterbury became one of the most important destinations for medieval pilgrims, notably those of Chaucer's (c.1345–1400) *Canterbury Tales* (c.1387–1400).

> *And specially from every shires ende*
> *Of Engelond to Caunterbury they wende,*
> *The holy blisful martir for to seke*
> *That hem hath holpen whan that they were seeke.*
>
> Geoffrey Chaucer, *Canterbury Tales*, 'General Prologue' (c.1387–1400).

On this day:

Born: French courtier and mistress of king Louis XV Madame de Pompadour (1721); English statesman William Gladstone (1809); English writer, feminist and pacifist Vera Brittain (1893); German-born British physicist and spy Klaus Fuchs (1911); English actor Jude Law (1972)

Died: US pianist, arranger and bandleader Fletcher Henderson

(1952); US bandleader Paul Whiteman (1967); English statesman Harold Macmillan, 1st Earl of Stockton (1986); English comedian Bob Monkhouse (2003)

1845 Texas became the 28th state of the USA.

1860 The UK's first ironclad warship, HMS *Warrior*, was launched.

1890 In South Dakota, USA, the final defeat of the Sioux took place when US troops massacred men, women and children at the Battle of Wounded Knee.

1937 The new Irish constitution came into effect.

1940 World War II – London suffered one of its worst air-raids.

1975 The Sex Discrimination Act and the Equal Pay Act both came into force in the UK.

1984 Indian politician Rajiv Gandhi (1944–91), the eldest son of the assassinated prime minister Indira Gandhi (1917–84) became the new prime minister of India after winning a landslide election victory.

1989 Václav Havel (born 1936) was elected president of Czechoslovakia.

30 December

On this day:

Born: Indian-born English writer and Nobel Prize winner Rudyard Kipling (1865); Russian composer Dmitri Kabalevsky (1904); English film director Sir Carol Reed (1906); US rock and roll singer and guitarist Bo Diddley (1928); US golfer Tiger Woods (1975)

Died: US champion of women's rights and dress reform Amelia Bloomer (1894); French musicologist, writer and Nobel Prize winner Romain Rolland (1944); English mathematician and

Idealist philosopher Alfred Whitehead (1947); US composer Richard Rodgers (1979); English novelist Mary Wesley (2002)

1460 The Battle of Wakefield took place during the Wars of the Roses; Richard, Duke of York (1411–60) was killed.

1879 The première of *Pirates of Penzance*, by W S Gilbert (1836–1911) and Arthur Sullivan (1842–1900), was held at the Royal Bijou Theatre, Paignton, England; the US première was held in New York City the following day.

1921 The première of the opera *The Love of Three Oranges*, by Sergei Prokofiev (1891–1953), was held in Chicago, USA.

1922 The Union of Soviet Socialist Republics (USSR) was officially formed.

1947 King Michael of Romania (born 1921) was forced to abdicate.

1948 The première of the musical *Kiss Me Kate*, by Cole Porter (1891–1964), was held at the Century Theater, Broadway, New York City.

1994 A gunman murdered two people and injured several more when he opened fire at two abortion clinics in Boston, Massachusetts, USA.

31 December

Should auld acquaintance be forgot
And never brought to mind?
...
We'll tak a cup o' kindness yet
For auld lang syne

Robert Burns, 'Auld Lang Syne' (1788).

New Year's Eve is celebrated all over the world with parties and other festivities. Most people stay up till midnight to see the old year out and the new year in. In public places, such as Trafalgar Square in London, at the Tron Kirk in Edinburgh and Times Square in New York, merrymakers gather to await the stroke of twelve, which is greeted with loud cheers and the singing of 'Auld Lang Syne', and sometimes with fireworks or the ringing of bells.

In the UK, Scotland is the place to be on 31 December, when the celebrations of **Hogmanay** begin.

> *Whilst ... the inhabitants of South Britain are settling down again quietly to work after the festivities of the Christmas season, their fellow-subjects in the northern division of the island are only commencing their annual saturnalia, which, till recently, bore, in the license and boisterous merriment which used to prevail, a most unmistakable resemblance to its ancient pagan namesake. ... This exuberance of joyousness – which, it must be admitted, sometimes led to great excesses – has now much declined, but New-year's Eve and New-year's Day constitute still the great national holiday in Scotland.*
>
> *Chambers Book of Days* (1864).

The word Hogmanay is of uncertain derivation, but it is most commonly thought to be a corruption of a Norman French word or phrase used to request a New Year's gift: on 31 December children from poor households used to go begging for oatcakes or other treats with a cry of 'Hogmanay!' Another New Year's Eve tradition formerly popular in Scotland and elsewhere was **guising**, a form of mumming, in which people in masks and fancy dress went from house to house performing songs or dramas in exchange for a token reward. Guising is now usually a children's Hallowe'en custom in Scotland, but at Allendale in Northumberland the **guisers** still come out on 31 December. There, however, they have a very different role to play, bearing blazing tar barrels in procession around the town, a custom thought to date from pagan fire festivals of the ancient past.

Fire is also central to a number of Scottish celebrations on this day. In the Borders town of Biggar a huge bonfire (known as the **Ne'erday Bonfire**) is lit each year on the High Street. In Stonehaven, Aberdeenshire, the annual **Fireball Ceremony** involves a parade of local marchers who swing balls of fire (contained in wire netting) above their heads as they process to the harbour where they throw the fireballs into the sea. And at Comrie in Perthshire the **Flambeaux Procession** sees locals process around the village with fiery torches before they are ceremonially extinguished in the River Earn. Many of these fire ceremonies are thought to be linked with driving out the devil or evil spirits before the New Year begins.

New Year's Eve was also a time for divination rituals, to predict what the coming year held in store. One popular method involved opening the Bible or another book and reading a passage at random, whilst another involved looking for significant shapes in the ashes of the fire. Superstitions associated with the turn of the year include opening doors and windows to let bad luck out at the back and good luck in at the front. In modern times it is generally regarded as an opportunity to make a fresh start: **New Year's resolutions** of reformed behaviour for the coming year are made this night – and often broken soon afterwards.

> *Ring out, wild bells, to the wild sky,*
> *The flying cloud, the frosty light:*
> *The year is dying in the night;*
> *Ring out, wild bells, and let him die.*
>
> *Ring out the old, ring in the new,*
> *Ring, happy bells, across the snow:*
> *The year is going, let him go;*
> *Ring out the false, ring in the true.*
>
> Alfred, Lord Tennyson, *In Memoriam A. H. H.* (1850).

On this day:

Born: English soldier Charles Cornwallis (1738); US astronomer Robert Aitken (1864); Austrian Nazi hunter Simon Wiesenthal (1908); Welsh-born US film and stage actor Sir Anthony Hopkins (1937)

Died: English religious reformer John Wycliffe (1384); French painter Gustave Courbet (1877); English car and speedboat racer Sir Malcolm Campbell (1948)

1879 Thomas Edison (1847–1931) gave the first public demonstration of his incandescent lamp, forerunner of the electric light bulb.

1917 World War I – sugar rationing was introduced in the UK from this date.

1926 The British Broadcasting Company was dissolved; it was reconstituted the following day under Royal Charter as the British Broadcasting Corporation.

1964 Donald Campbell (1921–67) set a new world water speed record by reaching 276.33mph on Lake Dumbleyung in Western Australia.

1973 An energy crisis in the UK led to the introduction of the three-day week.

1999 Russian president Boris Yeltsin (born 1931) resigned, naming the prime minister, Vladimir Putin (born 1952), as acting president.

1999 At midnight, the Panama Canal was returned to Panama by the USA.

Index

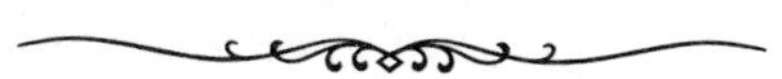

A

B

Index

C

N

O

P

Q

R

S

T

U

V

W

Y